BEGINNERS' DICTIONARY

OF

CHINESE-JAPANESE CHARACTERS

屍 四	戶 六三	虍	广 五三	鹿	廉	厂	左	产	差 九三	戉	式	气
戶 六五	戶 六五	唐	疒	麻	辰 六三	厂	仁	产		戔 九三	弐 六四	勻

LEFT   RIGHT

2	亻 九五	冫 一二	匕	力	十 二四	又 二九					乚 五五	1
3	彳 六〇	氵 一	女	弓 五七	土 三二	彡 五三	己 九〇	又 二九	匕	几 一六	卜	2
	犭 九四	忄 六一	子 三九	巾 五〇	山 三六	牙 二四	斗 九〇		力 一九	刂 二三	人 九	
	扌 六四	夕 三六	幺 五一	口 三〇	工 四八	阝 一七	干 五一		刀 一九	卩 二二	厶	
4	牛 九三	歹 七八	彡 八九	王 七二	斤 九六	止 七七	牙 九二	犭 二四	刃	卩 二二	阝 一六三	彡 五九	3
	戶 六五	方 七〇	攵 九九	爿 九八	止 七七	文 六七		双	寸 五〇	巾 五〇	夂	
	火 八六	木 七五	礻 一三	片 一	月 一三〇	文 六七		弋 五六	弋 五〇	彡 五九		
5	立 一二	禾 一二五	衤 一四五	白 一〇六	矛 二一〇	皮 一〇七		月 一三〇	戈	犬 九四	欠	4
	矢 一一	正	石 一〇九	田 一〇二	夛 五一	瓦 九八		少	斤 九六	尤	攵 九九	
	生 一〇〇	而	玄	目 一〇九	廿 九九			毛	斗 九〇	殳	支 六七	
6	缶	米 一二九	糸	虫 一二一	耳 二八	匄 一三七	臣 一三一		日 一〇〇	匕	瓦 九八	皮 一〇七	5
	缶	耒	至	舌	血 一四三	而 一二六	羊 一二三		生 一〇〇	瓜	色	羽	6
7	車 一三九	釆	貝	距 一五七	赤 一五五				艮	聿	色	多	
	豸	酉 一六四	身	言 一四九	麦 一九九				羊 一二三	式	多	谷	7
	辛 一六〇	里 一六六	角	豆	谷 一五〇				辛 一六〇	見	谷	
8	幸 三一	青 一七四	斉	舍 一三五	隹 一七二	金 一六七	食 一八四		隶 一七一	隶	頁	炎	8
9	革 一七七	音 一八〇	倉	首 一八五	香 一八六	廉 一九一			風	章	頁	飛	9
10/15	馬 一八七	骨 一八八	魚 一九五	鹵	鹿 一九八	冒 一八一	高 一八九				鬼 一九四	10
	麥 一九九	黑 二〇三	鼻 二〇九	齒	齒 二一一	齊	奐 一九五				鳥 一九六	11

| 乚 五五 | 乙 五五 | 一 一 | 口 三〇 | ！ 二二 | 十 二四 | 亅 | 人 九 | 弓 五七 | 大 三七 | 戈 九二 | 曰 七二 | 木 七五 |

尤	風	瓦	延	尾	麥	夂	曰	三	日	凡	凡	門
毛	鬼	尺	迊	走	麦	支		曰	月	戌	屍	鬥

TOP

一	二	八	ナ		ノ	匕		八	入	1/2
ト	亠	ソ	十	力	又		ト	冖	入	ム	3
工	子	䒑	土	小	夂	从	口	山	公	ㄙ	
己	亡		士	屮	夕	弋	勹	彐	岙	大	卅
止	去	父	少	业	戈	爪	勽	比	囚	朩	廿
斤	文	毌	生	少	氏	凸	日	臼	宂	水	並
矛	立	田	四	火	疋	禾	白	目	宂	夫	甘
而							自	白	聿	米	甘
画	衣	羊	巴	羽	竹	吅	血	耳		共	齒	6
雨		羑	共	非	珏	來	隹	廉	辰	齒	其	7/9
	麻	鳥	髟	鼓	黑	龍	魚	鹿	麻	鼅	興	10/16

BOTTOM

一	乙	八	力	刀	十	儿	又	口	亅	ミ	ン	1/2
土	弓	小	山	凡	子	凡	夂	大	寸	女	夕	
				卅	巾	方	攵	犬				3/4
壬	川	小	心	月	日	手	彐	水	氏	水	火	
玉	正	兩	甘	石	目	兕		矢		氷		5
立	血	示	白	同	田	母		辵				
聿	羊	糸	耳	向	回	羽	虫	米	衣	豕	舛	6
金	豆	貝	酉	言	余	見	車	足	辰	食	廉	7/15
黑	烏	馬	革	香	音	龜	風	蜀	高	齒	鹿	

BEGINNERS' DICTIONARY

OF

CHINESE-JAPANESE CHARACTERS

WITH COMMON ABBREVIATIONS, VARIANTS AND NUMEROUS COMPOUNDS

compiled by

ARTHUR ROSE-INNES

FOURTH EDITION

Dover Publications, Inc.
New York

This Dover edition, first published in 1977, is an unabridged republication of the fourth edition of the work, as published by the Meiseisha Publishing Company, Tokyo, in 1959.

International Standard Book Number: 0-486-23467-3
Library of Congress Catalog Card Number: 76-48588
Manufactured in the United States of America
Dover Publications, Inc.
180 Varick Street
New York, N.Y. 10014

INDEX

ABBREVIATION AND SIGNS

abb.	abbreviation	irreg.	irregular
adj.	adjective	lit.	literally, literary
aux. num.	auxiliary numeral	lit. st.	literary style
cal.	calendar	neg.	negative
coll.	colloquial	p. n.	proper name
epist. st.	epistolary style	prec.	preceding
foll.	following	suf.	suffix
gen.	generally		

* see at the bottom of the page; or: to insert

T—Tōyō Kanji (Tōyō Character), i.e. one of the partly simplified characters on the list officially issued since 1946 and which must be learned in the period of Japanese compulsory school education (9 years).

→ see for references; or: take into account

References to the Introduction indicate not the page, but the number of the paragraph.

A reference, f. ex. 75, 4, *after a character* means the character is to be found under Radical 75-4 strokes section.

A reference from one character to another means that one is *an alternative,* abbreviated or vulgar form of the other, respectively its Tōyō Kanji equivalent. As a rule the readings are still given under the more common form, more common at least up to 1946, without taking into account which is the more correct or the original one.

The Tōyō Kanji is preferred in printing and writing since 1946; other Kanjis are written in Kana.

The meaning of the *brackets* enclosing the last letters of a Verb, is explained in Introduction 40.

Readings *entirely in brackets* are rarely or never used except in proper names.

When a character in this Dictionary is classified under a Radical which, in *another dictionary* of characters is placed differently, the classical Radical is given in [ ] thus:

五 Go. Itsutsu five. [二]

才 See 6.2 [手]

一畫	二畫				三畫				四畫				五畫		
一 一	二 七	几 一六	卜 二五	口 三〇	子 三九	工 四八	弓 五七	心 六一	方 七〇	殳 七九	父 八八	玄 九五	广 一〇四	示 一一三
丨 二	亠 八	凵 一七	卩 二六	囗 三一	宀 四〇	己 四九	彐 五八	戈 六二	无 七一	母 八〇	爻 八九	玉 九六	癶 一〇五	内 一一四
丶 三	人 九	刀 一八	厂 二七	土 三二	寸 四一	巾 五〇	彡 五九	戶 六三	日 七二	比 八一	爿 九〇	瓜 九七	白 一〇六	禾 一一五
丿 四	儿 一〇	力 一九	厶 二八	士 三三	小 四二	干 五一	彳 六〇	手 六四	曰 七三	毛 八二	片 九一	瓦 九八	皮 一〇七	穴 一一六
乙 五	入 一一	勹 二〇	又 二九	夊 三四	尢 四三	幺 五二		支 六五	月 七四	氏 八三	牙 九二	甘 九九	皿 一〇八	立 一一七
亅 六	八 一二	匕 二一		夂 三五	尸 四四	广 五三		攴 六六	木 七五	气 八四	牛 九三	生 一〇〇	目 一〇九	
	冂 一三	匚 二二		夕 三六	屮 四五	廴 五四		文 六七	欠 七六	水 八五	犬 九四	用 一〇一	矛 一一〇	
	冖 一四	匸 二三		大 三七	山 四六	廾 五五		斗 六八	止 七七	火 八六		田 一〇二	矢 一一一	
	冫 一五	十 二四		女 三八	巛 四七	弋 五六		斤 六九	歹 七八	爪 八七		疋 一〇三	石 一一二	

RADICALS

六畫
竹 一一八　米 一一九　糸 一二〇　缶 一二一　网 一二二　羊 一二三　羽 一二四　老 一二五　而 一二六　耒 一二七　耳 一二八　聿 一二九　肉 一三〇　臣 一三一　自 一三二　至 一三三　臼 一三四　舌 一三五　舛 一三六　舟 一三七　艮 一三八　色 一三九　艸 一四〇　虍 一四一　虫 一四二　血 一四三　行 一四四　衣 一四五　襾 一四六

七畫
見 一四七　角 一四八　言 一四九　谷 一五〇　豆 一五一　豕 一五二　豸 一五三　貝 一五四　赤 一五五　走 一五六　足 一五七　身 一五八　車 一五九　辛 一六〇　辰 一六一　辵 一六二　邑 一六三　酉 一六四　釆 一六五　里 一六六

八畫
金 一六七　長 一六八　門 一六九　阜 一七〇　隶 一七一　隹 一七二　雨 一七三　青 一七四　非 一七五

九畫
面 一七六　革 一七七　韋 一七八　韭 一七九　音 一八〇　頁 一八一　風 一八二　飛 一八三　食 一八四　首 一八五　香 一八六

一〇畫
馬 一八七　骨 一八八　高 一八九　髟 一九〇　鬥 一九一　鬯 一九二　鬲 一九三　鬼 一九四

一一畫
魚 一九五　鳥 一九六　鹵 一九七　鹿 一九八　麥 一九九　麻 二〇〇

一二畫
黃 二〇一　黍 二〇二　黑 二〇三　黹 二〇四

一三畫
黽 二〇五　鼎 二〇六　鼓 二〇七　鼠 二〇八

一四畫
鼻 二〇九　齊 二一〇

一五畫
齒 二一一

一六畫
龍 二一二　龜 二一三

一七畫
龠 二一四

CHARACTERS

WHOSE RADICALS ARE DIFFICULT TO DETERMINE

2 Str.	入 11,0	川 巛 2,2	双 See	**4 Str.**	升 24,2	少 42,1
卜 25,0	匕 21,0	才 手 6,2	刃 18,1	壬 士 4,3	井 二 2,3	戶 63,0
了 6,1	七 1,1	巾 50,0	之 丶 8,2	廿 24,2	卅 24,2	尹 尸 1,3
乂 4,1	几 16,0	尸 44,0	己 49,0	廿 See / 24,1	片 91,0	弔 57,1
刀 18,0	九 5,1	夕 36,0	也 5,2	中 2,3	予 6,3	欠 76,0
力 19,0	厶 28,0	弓 57,0	凡 16,1	午 24,2	月 74,0	尺 44,1
乃 4,1	**3 Str.**	久 4,2	丸 丶 5,2	牛 93,0	内 See	爪 87,0
又 29,0	千 十 4,2	丈 1,2	小 42,0	丰 丨 24,2	內 11,2	夭 大 4,3
八 12,0	廿 24,1	叉 29,1	々 4,2	斗 68,0	丹 丶 1,3	夫 37,1

火 86,0	世 1,4	甲 田 72,1	央 37,2	戊 62,1	肉 130,0	汞 48,4
水 85,0	卅 See	申 田 72,1	本 75,1	包 20,3	舟 137,0	艮 138,0
及 29,2	世 1,4 and	丼、 2,4	未 75,1	尔 See	艸 140,0	吏 30,3
夂 20,2	卋 24,2	可 30,2	末 75,1	爾 爻 1,13	为 See	戋 See
之 丿 8,2	出 17,3	司 30,2	氷 85,1	必 61,1	爲 87,8	錢 167,8
氏 83,0	甘 99,0	矛 110,0	永 85,1	6 Str.	臾 See	曳 日 72,2
戈 62,0	目 109,0	用 101,0	疋 103,0	曲 日 72,2	臾 日 9,7	危 26,4
巴 49,1	由 田 72,1	册 冂 1,4	皮 107,0	年 千 24,4	夷 37,3	色 139,0
屯 屮 5,3	凹 17,3	弗 57,2	処 See	州 巛 2,5	米 119,0	兆 10,4
尤 尢 1,3	凸 17,3	母 80,0	處 141,5	竹 118,0	朱 75,2	旭 72,2
5 Str.	乍 4,4	瓜 97,0	史 30,2	争 See	耒 See	虫 See
生 100,0	半 24,3	失 37,2	民 83,1	爭 87,4	來 人 75,4	蟲 142,12

7 Str.	吳 30,4	門 169,0	鼡 See	臾 日 9,7	島 46,7	麥 199,0
坐 32,4	夾 37,4	肴 130,4	鼠 208,0	袁 145,4	馬 187,0	鳥 196,0
君 30,4	束 75,3	冒 See	**9 Str.**	叛 29,7	弱 57,7	爽 爻 37,8
車 159,0	求 水 6,6	冒 13,7	幽 幺 17,7	胤 肉 5,8	畝 田 8,8	匙 21,9
串 2,6	良 138,1	青 174,0	眉 109,4	勉 19,7	翅 124,4	龜 See
寿 See	我 62,3	來 人 75,4	看 109,4	飛 183,0	党 See	龜 213,0
壽 士 32,11	系 糸 4,6	果 75,4	举 See	**10 Str.**	黨 203,8	乾 乙 24,9
角 148,0	**8 Str.**	東 75,4	舉 134,11	畢 田 72,6	鬼 194,0	執 子 8,9
甫 用 24,5	些 二 1,7	承 手 6,7	韋 178,0	哥 30,7	**11 Str.**	**12 Str.**
希 50,7	并 51,5	長 168,0	革 177,0	師 巾 1,9	磊 See	棘 75,8
身 158,0	非 175,0	表 145,3	咫 口 44,6	帰 See	喬 30,9	棗 75,8
弟 弓 12,5	事 6,7	瓞 142,2	矦 111,4	歸 止 58,15	商 口 乚,9	象 152,5

喪 30,9	鼓 207,0	15 Str.	賴 154,9	19 Str.	蠶 142,18
甦 100,7	麀 198,2	輝 車 42,12	縣 糸 109,11	疆 田 57,16	25 Str.
幾 幺 62,8	黽 205,0	黎 黍 85,10	燕 86,12	攀 64,15	糶 米 124,19
黃 201,0	號 虍 30,10	養 食 123,9	17 Str.	20 Str.	釁 173,17
13 Str.	14 Str.	畿 田 62,11	營 火 30,14	耀 羽 42,17	26 Str.
譽 See	斡 斗 24,12	甌 124,9	虧 141,11	攣 112,15	釁 75,22
譽 言 134,14	孵 子 87,10	16 Str.	嬲 女 102,12	競 117,15	29 Str.
幹 干 24,11	爾 爻 1,13	翰 羽 24,14	18 Str.	22 Str.	鬱 鬯 See
肅 聿 24,11	暢 72,10	豫 152,9	歸 止 58,15	囊 口 145,18	釁 75,22
鼎 206,0	聚 1?8,8	龍 212,0	題 181,9	聽 128,16	
嗣 30,10	疑 疋 21,12	龜 213,0	叢 128,12	24 Str.	
業 75,9	兢 儿 24,12	冀 12,14	斃 66,14	顴 頁 24,22	

VARIANTS AND ABBREVIATIONS.

Every student of the characters must sometimes have felt disappointed on looking for a character in his dictionary and failing to find it, to discover afterwards— perhaps to be told by a Japanese child — that it is a well-known abbreviation of a common character.

It would seem that the remedy for this unsatisfactory state of things would be to introduce all the variants and abbreviations in the dictionary itself; but one would thus increase the volume of the book very considerably, out of all proportion to the utility of the matter added.

There are two classes of variants and abbreviations: (a) those which are isolated cases and affect only one character e. g. : 塩 for 鹽 ; the principal of these are noted in this Dictionary in their proper places, and not much notice is taken of them in this present study; (b) those which are typical of a whole series or family of characters which may be made to suffer a similar modification; e. g. : 數 is sometimes simplified to 数 ; the same element which is at the left of 數 occurs also in 樓, 屢, 窶, 縷, 鏤, 髏 and a similar simplification may be used. It was not found practical to introduce all these cases in the Dictionary, only the abbreviations of the commoner characters are noted. But those who are interested in this subject will derive some benefit from the study of the following lists, from which many abbreviations may be deduced by analogy with those given.

Naturally variants and abbreviations are more frequently met with in hand-writing than in print; but lately there has been a movement towards simplification, and abbreviations are now used in printing more than they used to be.

The abbreviations given here have been derived from various sources: we wish especially to mention, a list of abbreviations published by the MOMBUSHŌ in 1923, a list printed by the HŌCHI SHIMBUN in 1925, and Chamberlain's MOJI NO SHIRUBE.

It must be understood that this study refers only to the ordinary printed forms, *Minchō*, and to *Kaisho*, i. e. the square characters written by hand. The running hands *Gyōsho* and *Sōsho* have other innumerable forms of their own and are a study apart. But even with this limitation we are aware that the present lists are far from complete.

A. Some variations and abbreviations consist in quite insignificant changes.

(1) Adding a dot, as in:

圡 for 土 , 䂖 for 石 , 㧉 for 中 , 丈 for 丈

The above modifications are rarely used when the above characters form only part of a character, as in

地 , 砂 , 仲 , 杖

(2) Suppressing a dot, as in:

者 for 者, 辶 for 辶

(3) Prolonging a dot into a line or vice-versa; as in:

双 for 刃, 勺 for 勾, 外 for 外

(4) Prolonging lines; as in:

囬 for 回, 高 for 高

(5) Joining two squares; as in:

昌 for 品, 單 for 單

(6) Joining lines which should be separate or vice-versa:

亜 for 亞, 兹 for 兹, 研 for 研, 并 for 幷,

冊 for 册, 鶴 for 鶴, 叫 for 叫

(7) Writing — instead of a series of four dots ....
This is done only when the dots are inside an angle, as:

馬 for 馬, 鳥 for 鳥, 爲 for 爲

This is never done when the dots are not inside an
angle, as 烝, 魚, 黑

(8) Writing — across a vertical line instead of two
dots one on each side; as:

會 for 會, 黒 for 黑, 練 for 練

(9) Closing an open space or vice-versa: 卷 for 卷,
冒 for 冒

(10) Other cases: 秊 for 年, 内 for 內, 靑 for
靑, 臭 for 具, 吴 for 吳, 魚 for 魚, 温 for

溫，象 for 象，塲 for 塲，貟 for 負

B. Some variations consist in changing the relative
position of the component parts of the character. Very
often this does not mean a new character : the readings
and the meanings are identical.

鵝鵞	峯峰	勢務	蓮蓮	點點
羣群	讐讎	潤闊	蕕穢	棊棋
晢晰	鄰隣	崕崖	蒦獲	毡氈
慇慚	摹摸	畧略	荆荆	蚤蚊

Sometimes, however, the result is an entirely new character, with different readings and meanings.

忙忘	拾拿	衿衾	暉暈
愉愈	棘棗	吟含	啼啻
紋紊	腑腐	唄員	脅脇

C. Simplification is effected sometimes by omitting a
part of the character. The following are the principal
cases :

敝弊	矦候	随隨	余餘
医醫	号號	独獨	県縣
声聲	聴聽	时時	弍貳
虽雖	团團	(Used by the military)	

D. Not infrequently one Radical is used instead of
another : this happens sometimes even in printing-type, and,

of course, more often still in what is written by hand.
The explanation is usually similarity of form or similarity of meaning. It must be understood that, whatever
the original form may have been, in several of the examples given below both variants are today considered
equally correct.

Rad. 15 and Rad. 85	減 減	涼 涼	滅 滅
	況 況	決 決
Rad. 24 and Rad. 61	協 恊
Rad. 64 and Rad. 75	拄 柱	柄 抦
Rad. 94 and Rad. 153	狸 貍
Rad. 120 and Rad. 145	緼 褞	綺 袴
Rad. 19 and Rad. 66	効 效	勅 敕
Rad. 172 and Rad. 196	雁 鴈	雞 鷄	雛 鶵
Rad. 14 and Rad. 40	冤 寃	寫 寫
Rad. 118 and Rad. 140	籔 藪	莛 筳	簑 蓑
Rad. 27 and Rad. 53	厩 廐	厦 廈
Rad. 54 and Rad. 162	廻 迴	廼 迺
Rad. 169 and Rad. 191	鬪 鬭	鬧 閙	鬩 鬩

E. Certain Radicals are sometimes written in a modified
form ; and if this occurs in the part of the character
which serves to determine the Radical under which the
character is classified, the student may be entirely at a

loss to know what to do. E.g.: you may come across 齡 and if you do not know that the left part of the character is an abbreviation of 齒 (Rad. 211), you will have no idea where to look for the character. This difficulty is provided for in this Dictionary in the TABLE inside the cover, as not only the original forms but the alternative and abbreviated forms are also given.

Rad. 140 is written not only 卄 but often 艸 (the original form though not used in print) and sometimes 𢆶

Rad. 12 when at the top is written 八 and sometimes ⅄

Rad. 42 when at the top is written 小 and sometimes 𭕄

Rad.	59 is written	彡	and sometimes	夂
Rad.	90	爿		斗
Rad.	113	示		礻
Rad.	121	缶		缶
Rad.	156	走		走
Rad.	184	食		食
Rad.	189	高		高
Rad.	195	魚		臭
Rad.	198	鹿		鹿

Rad. 199	麥	麦
Rad. 210	齊	斉
Rad. 211	齒	歯

If the abbreviated form occurs in the part of the character other than that which serves to classify the character; e. g.: 済 for 濟 the difficulty is analogous to that which we find in the cases mentioned below in our groups F, G, and H.

F. When a character may be abbreviated as a whole, it generally happens that we may use the same abbreviation when the character is used as a portion of another character. E. g.: we may write 万 for 萬, likewise we may write 励 for 勵.

夾
夫 } for 夾 also used in 俠 etc.

耒
来 } for 來

参 for 參 also used in 惨 etc.

赱 „ 走 „ „ „ 起 etc.

昰 „ 是 „ „ „ 提 etc.

㝍 „ 定 „ „ „ 碇 etc.

從 „ 從 „ „ „ 縱 etc.

昰 for 足 also used in 促 etc. but not used when 足 is at the left as in 路 etc.

夬 „ 臾 also used in 諛 etc.

旧 „ 臼 „ „ „ 兒 etc. 旧 is also used as an abb. of 舊

尽 „ 盡 also used in 儘 etc.

昼 „ 書 „ „ „ 畫 but not in 畫

乗 „ 乘 „ „ „ 剩 etc.

垂 „ 垂 „ „ „ 唾 etc.

広 „ 廣 „ „ „ 擴 etc.

会 „ 會 „ „ „ 繪 etc.

竜 „ 龍 „ „ „ 瀧 etc.

争 „ 爭 „ „ „ 靜 etc.

囘 „ 回 „ „ „ 廻 etc.

万 „ 萬 „ „ „ 勵 etc.

属 „ 屬 „ „ „ 囑 etc.

寿 „ 壽 „ „ „ 鑄 etc.

賛 „ 贊 „ „ „ 讚 etc.

豊 „ 豐 „ „ „ 艷 etc.

両 „ 兩 „ „ „ 滿 etc.

㚓	for	奇	also used in	崎	etc.
区	„	區	„	„	„	鷗	etc.
発	„	發	„	„	„	廢	etc.
当	„	當	„	„	„	蟷	etc.
本	„	本	„	„	„	体	etc.
坐	„	坐	„	„	„	座	etc.
喬	„	喬	„	„	„	橋	etc.
賓	„	賓	„	„	„	濱	etc.
国 国	„	國	„	„	„	摑	etc.
気 気	„	氣	„	„	„	愾	etc.
黽 黽	„	黽	„	„	„	蠅	etc.
尓	„	爾	„	„	„	彌	etc.
単	„	單	„	„	„	戰	etc.
左	„	左	„	„	„	佐	etc.
虎	„	虎	„	„	„	號	etc.
陰	„	陰	„	„	„	蔭	etc.
覧	„	覽	„	„	„	纜	etc.

丗 for 世 also used in 葉 etc. 丗 is also used as an abb. of 卅.

並 for 並 also used in 普 etc. Conversely,

虚 „ 虛

G. When a part of a character may be abbreviated, it generally happens that that portion may suffer the same abbreviation if it enters into the composition of another character. E. g. : we may write 数 for 數 , likewise we may write 楼 for 樓 etc.

即 }
卽 } for 卽 In a similar way we may simplify 鄉 etc.

郎	„ 郞	....	朗 etc.
卆	„ 卒	....	雜 etc.
談	„ 談	....	淡 etc.
烟	„ 煙	....	湮 etc.
経	„ 經	....	輕 etc.
続	„ 續	....	讀 etc.
籤	„ 籤	....	纖 etc.
数	„ 數	....	樓 etc.
総	„ 總	....	聰 etc.
沢	„ 澤	....	驛 etc.

仏	for	佛	In a similar way we may simplify	拂	etc.
温	„	溫		饂	etc.
変	„	變		蠻	etc.
観	„	觀		勸	etc.
倹	„	儉		檢	etc.
孝 学 }	„	學		覺	etc.
猟	„	獵		蠟	etc.
営	„	營		勞	etc.
甾	„	留		溜	etc.
脳 腦 }	„	腦		惱	etc.
沢	„	澤		譯	etc.
芦	„	蘆		艫	etc.
监	„	監		賢	etc
掲	„	揭		葛	etc.
抜	„	拔		跋	etc.
残	„	殘		淺	etc.

Both 銭 and 戔 are used as abb. of 錢.

H. When three or four similar elements are found together in a character as in the following examples, it often happens that the two bottom elements may be replaced by four dots. E. g.: 疊 for 疊, 綴 for 綴 etc. The abbreviation 楽 for 樂 seems to be based on the same idea.

I. 口 and 厶 when they enter into the composition of a character are often used the one instead of the other. E. g.:

强 for 強   貟 for 員

枩 for 松   舩 for 船

夂 (three strokes) and 夊 (four strokes) are also sometimes used the one for the other. You may find 變 for 變, and 倏 for 倐. Even when not used mistakenly, it is not always easy to distinguish between them and to count the strokes correctly, unless the printing or the writing is very clear.

GEOGRAPHICAL NAMES AND OTHER TERMS
USED ON ENVELOPES.

The following list may prove useful to those who wish to address their envelopes in Japanese, in the hopes of shortening the delays of the Japanese and Chinese Post-Offices.

JAPAN(NIPPON) 日 本			Hiroshima	廣	島	
METROPOLITAN DISTRICTS			Kure		吳	
(To) 都			Miyajima	宮	島	
Tōkyō	東	京	Hyōgo	兵	庫	
(Fu) 府			Akashi	明	石	戸
Kyōto	京	都	Kōbe	神	戸	
Ōsaka	大	阪	Suma	須	磨	
PREFECTURES (Ken) 縣			Ibaraki	茨	城	川
Aichi	愛	知	Ishikawa	石	川	
Nagoya	名 古	屋	Kanazawa	金	沢	
Akita	秋	田	Iwate	岩	手	川
Aomori	青	森	Kagawa	香	川	
Chiba	千	葉	Kagoshima	鹿	兒	島 川
Ehime	愛	媛	Kanagawa	神	奈	川
Matsuyama	松	山	Kamakura	鎌	倉	下
Fukui	福	井	Miyanoshita	宮	浜	
Fukuoka	福	岡	Yokohama	横	須	賀
Hakata	博	多	Yokosuka	横	須	子
Moji	門	司	Zushi	逗	子	
Fukushima	福	島	Kōchi	高	知	本
Gifu	岐	阜	Kumamoto	熊	本	重
Gumma	群	馬	Mie	三	重	城
Ikao	伊 香	保	Miyagi	宮	城	台
			Sendai	仙	台	

Miyazaki	宮	崎	Hokkaidō	北	海	道
Nagano	長	野	Hakodate	函	館	
Karuizawa	軽 井	沢	Sapporo	札	幌	
Nagasaki	長	崎				
Sasebo	佐 世	保	CHINA (SHINA) 支那			
Unzen	雲	仙	Amoy	厦	門	
Nara	奈	良	Canton	廣	東	
Niigata	新	潟	Changchung			
Ōita	大	分	(Chōshun)	長	春	
Okayama	岡	山	Chefoo (Chiifū)	芝	罘	
Kasaoka	笠	岡	Dalny (Dairen)	大	連	
Saga	佐	賀	Hankow (Kankō)	漢	口	
Saitama	埼	玉	Harbin (Harupin)	哈 爾	賓 港	
Shiga	滋	賀	Hongkong	香	港	
Shimane	島	根	Macao	澳	門	
Shizuoka	静	岡	Manchuria (Manshū)	満	洲	
Atami	熱	海	Mukden (Hōten)	奉	天	
Tochigi	栃	木	Nanking	南	京	
Chūzenji	中 禅	寺	Peking	北	京	
Nikkō	日	光	Port Arthur			
Tokushima	徳	島	(Ryojun)	旅	順	
Tottori	鳥	取	Shanghai	上	海	
Toyama	富	山	Tientsin (Tenshin)	天	津	
Wakayama	和 歌	山	Tsingtau (Seitō)	靑	島	
Yamagata	山	形	Weiheiwei (Ikaiei)	威 海	衛	
Yamaguchi	山	口				
Shimonoseki	下	関				
Yamanashi	山	梨				

SOME OTHER USEFUL PLACE NAMES:

Akasaka	赤	坂
Asakusa	淺	草
Azabu	麻	布
Fukagawa	深	川
Hommoku	本	牧
Hongō	本	鄉
Honjo	本	所
Kanda	神	田
Koishikawa	小 石	川
Kōjimachi	麴	町
Kyōbashi	京	橋
Motomachi	元	町
Nakamura	中	村
Naniwa	難	波
Negishi	根	岸
Nihombashi	日 本	橋
Ōura	大	浦
Sannomiya	三	宮
Shiba	芝	
Shitaya	下	谷
Tsukiji	築	地
Ushigome	牛	込
Yamashita	山	下
Yamate	山	手
Yotsuya	四	谷

VARIOUS

— fuka	府	下
— gun	郡	
— shi	市	
— machi; — chō	町	
— mura	村	
Aza —	字 一	
— ku	區	
— chōme	丁	目
— banchi	番	地

Mr. —; Mrs. —
      (— sama) — 樣

Mr. — (business:
      — dono) — 殿

When addressing a Bank, Company, Store, etc.
      (— onchū) — 御 中

c/o — (— kata) — 方

Registered (Kakitome) 書留

Express delivery
      (Sokutatsu) 速 達

Contains — (— zaichū)
      — 在 中

P.O. Box 私 書 函

ELEMENTARY *KANA* SYMBOLS

(*Kata-kana* above; *Hira-gana* below).

Note that *i* and *e* are repeated in the Y column, and that *u* is repeated in the W column.

パ ば pa	バ ば ba	ダ だ da	ザ ざ za	ガ が ga	ワ わ wa	ラ ら ra	ヤ や ya	マ ま ma	ハ は ha	ナ な na	タ た ta	サ さ sa	カ か ka	ア あ a
ピ ぴ pi	ビ び bi	ヂ ぢ ji	ジ じ ji	ギ ぎ gi	ヰ ゐ (w)i	リ り ri	イ い (y)i	ミ み mi	ヒ ひ hi	ニ に ni	チ ち chi	シ し shi	キ き ki	イ い i
ブ ぶ pu	ブ ぶ bu	ヅ づ zu	ズ ず zu	グ ぐ gu	ウ う (w)u	ル る ru	ユ ゆ yu	ム む mu	フ ふ fu	ヌ ぬ nu	ツ つ tsu	ス す su	ク く ku	ウ う u
ペ べ pe	ベ べ be	デ で de	ゼ ぜ ze	ゲ げ ge	エ ゑ w)e	レ れ re	エ え (y)e	メ め me	ヘ へ he	ネ ね ne	テ て te	セ せ se	ケ け ke	エ え e
ポ ぼ po	ボ ぼ bo	ド ど do	ゾ ぞ zo	ゴ ご go	ヲ を (w)o	ロ ろ ro	ヨ よ yo	モ も mo	ホ ほ ho	ノ の no	ト と to	ソ そ so	コ こ ko	オ お o

ン (*Kata-kana*), ん (*Hira-gana*) n (end of syllable).

ALTERNATIVE FORMS OF *KANA* AND VARIOUS SIGNS USED WHEN WRITING IN *KANA*

(Kata-kana at left; Hira-gana at right).

a	ア	あ	ひ		to	ト	と を
i	イ	い	ひ		na	ナ	な あ
u	ウ	う	ち		ni	ニ	に ふ す
e	エ	え	れ		nu	ヌ	ぬ
o	オ	お	れ		ne	ネ 子	ね 比 称
ka	カ	か あ ら		no	ノ	の 比 乃 参
ki	キ	き れ 裳		ha	ハ	は そ ハ
ku	ク	く く る		hi	ヒ	ひ む 烟
ke	ケ	け ぎ る		fu	フ	ふ 区
ko	コ	こ た を		he	ヘ	へ ほ
sa	サ	さ を		ho	ホ	ほ ま 不 傳
shi	シ	し し 去	ma	マ	ま み
su	ス	す そ に	mi	ミ	み 竺
se	セ	せ を		me	メ	め も を
so	ソ	そ る 揵	mo	モ	も 屈
ta	タ	た な さ	ya	ヤ	や ゆ と
chi	チ	ち ほ		yu	ユ	ゆ ゆ
tsu	ツ	つ ほ 川	yo	ヨ	よ
te	テ	て そ				

ra	ラ	ら	ら
ri	リ	り	り
ru	ル	る	る
re	レ	れ	れ
ro	ロ	ろ	ろ
wa	ワ	わ	わ
(w)i	ヰ 井	ゐ	ゐ
(w)e	エ	ゑ	ゑ
(w)o	ヲ	を	を
n	ン	ん	
v	ヴ		
shime		ノ	
koto	コ		と

toki	斤	
tomo	厇	
yori		ら
sōrō		ん

In both *Kata-kana* and *Hira-gana*.

| serves to prolong a sound.

ヽ { is the sign of re-
ゝ { petition.

〳 shows that more
〵 than one syllable is repeated.

IRREGULAR READINGS OF THE *KANA* SYMBOLS AND OF THEIR COMBINATIONS.

Note that besides the irregular pronunciations given here the regular readings are also used according to cases. This Table applies likewise to the corresponding Hira-gana symbols. Several of the combinations are merely theoretical. The double consonants formed by ッ before a *k*, *s*, *sh*, *t*, *ts*, *ch*, *h* or *f* sound, and by ヤ and ヰ before a *k* sound are not given.

ア ウ	ō	ギ ュ	gyu	シ ヤ ウ	shō	チ ウ	chū
ア フ	ō	ギ ヨ	gyo	シ ユ	shu	チ フ	chū
イ ウ	yū	ギ ヨ ウ	gyō	シ ヨ	sho	チ ヤ	cha
イ フ	yū	ク リ	ka	シ ヨ ウ	shō	チ ヤ ウ	chō
エ ウ	yō	ク リ ウ	kō	ジ ウ	jū	チ ユ	chu
エ フ	yō	グ リ	ga	ジ フ	jū	チ ヨ	cho
オ ウ	ō	グ リ ウ	gō	ジ ヤ	ja	チ ヨ ウ	chō
オ フ	ō	ケ	ka, ko, ga	ジ ヤ ウ	jō	ヂ ウ	jū
カ ウ	kō	ケ ウ	kyō	ジ ユ	ju	ヂ フ	jū
カ フ	kō	ケ フ	kyō	ジ ヨ	jo	ヂ ヤ	ja
ガ ウ	gō	ゲ ウ	gyō	ジ ヨ ウ	jō	ヂ ヤ ウ	jō
ガ フ	gō	ゲ フ	gyō	セ ウ	shō	ヂ ユ	ju
キ ウ	kyū	コ ウ	kō	セ フ	shō	ヂ ヨ	jo
キ フ	kyū	コ フ	kō	ゼ ウ	jō	ヂ ヨ ウ	jō
キ ヤ	kya	ゴ ウ	gō	ゼ フ	jō	テ ウ	chō
キ ヤ ウ	kyō	ゴ フ	gō	ソ ウ	sō	テ フ	chō
キ ユ	kyu	サ ウ	sō	ソ フ	sō	デ ウ	jō
キ ヨ	kyo	サ フ	sō	ゾ ウ	zō	デ フ	jō
キ ヨ ウ	kyō	ザ ウ	zō	ゾ フ	zō	ト ウ	tō
ギ ウ	gyū	ザ フ	zō	タ ウ	tō	ト フ	tō
ギ フ	gyū	シ ウ	shū	タ フ	tō	ド ウ	dō
ギ ヤ	gya	シ フ	shū	ダ ウ	dō	ド フ	dō
ギ ヤ ウ	gyō	シ ヤ	sha	ダ フ	dō	ナ ウ	nō

ナ フ	nō	ヒ ユ	hyu	ヘ フ	pyō	ヤ フ	yō
ニ ウ	nyū	ヒ ヨ	hyo	ホ	o	ヨ ウ	yō
ニ フ	nyū	ヒ ヨ ウ	hyō	ホ ウ	hō, ō	ヨ フ	yō
ニ ヤ	nya	ビ ウ	byū	ホ フ	hō, ō	ラ ウ	rō
ニ ヤ ウ	nyō	ビ フ	byū	ボ ウ	bō	ラ フ	rō
ニ ユ	nyu	ビ ヤ	bya	ボ フ	bō	リ ウ	ryū
ニ ヨ	nyo	ビ ヤ ウ	byō	ポ ウ	pō	リ フ	ryū
ニ ヨ ウ	nyō	ビ ユ	byu	ポ フ	pō	リ ヤ	rya
ネ ウ	nyō	ビ ヨ	byo	マ ウ	mō	リ ヤ ウ	ryō
ネ フ	nyō	ビ ヨ ウ	byō	マ フ	mō	リ ユ	ryu
ノ ウ	nō	ビ ウ	pyū	マ ヲ	mō	リ ヨ	ryo
ノ フ	nō	ビ フ	pyū	ミ ヤ	mya	リ ヨ ウ	ryō
ハ	wa	ビ ヤ	pya	ミ ヤ ウ	myō	レ ウ	ryō
ハ ウ	hō, ō	ビ ヤ ウ	pyō	ミ ウ	myū	レ フ	ryō
ハ フ	hō	ビ ユ	pyu	ミ フ	myū	ロ ウ	rō
バ ウ	bō	ビ ヨ	pyo	ミ ユ	myu	ロ フ	rō
バ フ	bō	ビ ヨ ウ	pyō	ミ ヨ	myo	ワ ウ	ō
バ ウ	pō	フ	u, o	ミ ヨ ウ	myō	ワ フ	ō
バ フ	pō	ヘ	e	メ ウ	myō	ヱ フ	yō
ヒ	i	ヘ ウ	hyō	メ フ	myō	ヲ ウ	ō
ヒ ウ	hyū	ヘ フ	hyō	メ ヲ	myō	ヲ フ	ō
ヒ フ	hyū	ベ ウ	byō	モ ウ	mō	ン	m
ヒ ヤ	hya	ベ フ	byō	モ フ	mō		
ヒ ヤ ウ	hyō	ベ ウ	pyō	ヤ ウ	yō		

INTRODUCTION

1. The object of this work. Three elements enter into the study of the Chinese characters: (a) the character itself, i.e. the printed or written form: (b) the readings, i.e. the sounds corresponding to the character: (c) the meanings, i.e. the expression in English of the ideas contained in the character. There are, therefore three kinds of questions which may be considered: (1) given a character we may wish to know the reading and meaning: (2) given a Japanese word we may be asked to find its meaning and how it is written: (3) given an idea or an English word, we may want to discover the written character and its pronunciation. The present work is concerned exclusively with the first of these three problems. Those who wish to solve questions of the second or third class must have recourse to existing Japanese-English or English-Japanese Dictionaries.

2. Selection of characters. The present Dictionary with less than 5000 characters does not pretend to be a complete dictionary. It does not even contain all the characters which one may meet in a newspaper, as the great Tōkyō dailies stock about 7500 or 8000 different characters in the ordinary sizes. However, considerable time and care have been given to the choice of the characters and it is hoped that very few of the common ones have escaped.

3. In making this selection the sources used were: (a) *Shimbun-yō, Zasshiyō 9 pointo tekiyō mihon* a selection of 5000 characters for the use of newspapers and magazines, made by the Tōkyō Tsukiji Type Foundry. An interesting feature of this list is that each character is weighted according to its utility or to the frequency with which it is used. Thus the less important characters are marked 5 or 10 and the more common ones are marked as high as 200 and 250: (b) *Shimbun narabi ni zasshi-yō 8 pointo kana-tsuki shotai mihon* a collection of all the types in 8 point size which have *kana* alongside in the same type (e.g. 人に 人ひ). This collection consists of upwards of 6800 types corresponding to over 3500 different Chinese characters: many characters, of course, have, (as in the example above), two or more types each one with a different reading in *kana*. It stands to reason that, on the whole, only the more common characters and only the more useful readings will deserve the distinction of being made in this kind of type. (c) A list made some years ago of about 5000 characters which were all the characters known to our then assistant out of the 15000 contained in Ueda's *Daijiten*. The characters in the Dictionary we are now offering to the public have been selected by our present assistant after comparing the three above lists and we confidently trust they will prove sufficient for beginners.

4. Characteristics of this Dictionary. We beg to call attention to the following points in which the present Dictionary differs from others made for the use of foreigners. (a) The system of classification is somewhat different to the classical usage, and, when once mastered, we trust it will prove more practical. (b) A considerable number of compounds are given and we believe they will be very useful to students. (c) Though the verbs are given in their colloquial form, the brackets which enclose the last letters of the verb indicate to which conjugation the verb belongs in the literary style.

5. How to find a character. The characters are usually classified under 214 elements, called radicals. In order to find a character we must first determine to which radical it corresponds and then count the strokes in the non-radical part of the character.

6. How to determine the radical. If only one radical entered into the composition of each character, it would be a simple matter to determine which the radical is: but it frequently happens that two or more radicals are found in the same character and we may lose a lot of time, and perhaps patience, in looking in the wrong places. In order to reduce this inconvenience to a minimum we have followed a plan which, while preserving the usual classification of the characters in general, saves a lot of time when once it is understood.

As regards their general construction, characters may be divided into three great classes, and you must first of all determine to which of these classes the character in question belongs.

CLASS A comprises all those characters which have an enveloping element, i.e. one which occupies 2, 3, or the 4 sides of the character. E.g. 通 起 (left and bottom), 度 屋 (top and left), 或 氣 (top and right), 岡 區 (3 sides), 圓 (4 sides). In cases like the following 殿 歐 the enveloping element concerns only half the character, so these are not considered as belonging to **Class A**. Nearly 10% of the characters belong to this **Class A**.

CLASS B consists of those characters which have not got the enveloping element, but which are constructed from top to bottom in layers, or from left to right in strips, so that they can be divided into two or more horizontal layers or vertical strips *without cutting through any line.*

It will often be necessary to separate lines which are joined, that does not matter ; the resulting layers or strips may be very unequal, that does not matter either ; the thing is you must not cut through any line. E.g. 不 has two layers, the top one of one stroke, the bottom one of three ; 丑 has two layers, the top one of three strokes, the bottom one of one ; 乘 has two layers, the top one of one stroke, the bottom one of nine ; 京 has three layers, the top one of two strokes, the middle one of three and the bottom one also of three. But 事 although constructed in general from top to bottom, cannot be divided into layers without passing through the central vertical stroke, so this character does not belong to Class B. Note that in making the divisions, the layers need not be strictly horizontal ; they sometimes resemble geological strata : e. g. we consider that 分 can be divided into top and bottom though the bottom element 刀 intrudes somewhat into the upper. In the case of characters constructed from left to right in strips, the strips can usually be distinguished without difficulty and no special observations seem to be needed. The vast majority of characters belongs to this Class B.

CLASS C. About 3% of the characters cannot readily be reduced to the above two classes : these remnants form Class C.

Once we have determined to which of the above three classes the character in question belongs, we can proceed to find the number of the radical by means of the Table of elements to be found inside the cover at the beginning and at the end of the book.

7. In the case of characters belonging to Class A, if the envelope is given in the Table, the character will be classified by the envelope and not by the enveloped. An important observation must be made : when in doubt between two radicals, one simpler and the other more complex, always choose the more complex. E.g. 摩 is classified under radical 200 and not under radical 53 ; 唇 is classified under radical 161 and not under radical 27. A black triangle in the corner of some of the squares in the Table indicates that a similar but more complex radical exists : in these cases you must be on your guard. If the envelope is not given in the Table (e g. 甦, 匙, 虱) the character is classified by the enveloped as a whole, or by its most conspicuous component.

8. In the case of Class B, preference is always given, ceteris paribus, to the element at the top (if the character consists of horizontal layers), or to the element at the left (if the character consists of vertical strips). If, therefore, on dividing the character mentally, you find that the top layer is among the elements marked TOP in the Table, you will immediately have the number of the radical under which it is to be found, no matter what the bottom part of the character is. Thus in 分 the top part 八 is found among the elements marked TOP, and the number of the radical is 12 : the bottom part need not bother us although 刀 is also found among the elements marked BOTTOM. Or again, 巽 may be divided into three or four layers; the top layer, (i.e. the top six strokes 巳巳) is found among the elements marked TOP, so the other layers do not matter : the radical is number 49. If the top element is not found among those marked TOP, take the bottom element and look for it among the elements marked BOTTOM. E.g. 恕 the top six strokes are not to be found as a whole among the elements marked TOP, so look for the bottom four strokes among the elements marked BOTTOM: we find the radical to be number 61.

Two observations must be made. (1) In dividing the character into layers do not look for all the possible ways of doing it, but give preference to the natural line of cleavage if such a one exists. E.g. 惡 might be divided into four layers 一, the cross, 一, 心 ; but the natural way would be to take the top eight strokes as one layer and the four bottom ones as the other : as the eight top strokes 亞 do not appear as an element among those marked TOP, this character is classified by the bottom layer, viz., radical 61. (2) When two radicals might meet the case, again give preference to the more complex one : a black triangle in the corner of some of the squares in the Table will be of assistance in this matter. E.g. 齊 is classified under radical 210 not under radical 8.

In most of what we have said regarding Class B we have spoken of horizontal layers; the characters which are formed of vertical strips are treated in just the same way. As a matter of fact these latter are about double as numerous as the others, but as a rule they are much easier to classify.

9. No general rule can be given as regards the characters

classified under Class **C,** but many of the characters of this class
are noticeable in that the radical is crossed by other lines or
occupies a central position. The principal radicals in which this
may occur are given in the Table. If a character contains two or
more radicals which are crossed by other lines or occupy a central
position, it will be classified under the radical which is furthest to
the right in the Table. E.g.: in 事 radicals 1, 30, and 6 are
crossed by other lines; this character is classified under radical 6.
In 東 we find both radicals 72 and 75 in a central position; this
character is classified under radical 75. The character 來 contains
both radical 9 and radical 75; it is classified under radical 75.

10. Some characters cannot be classified by adhering strictly to
the above rules; but they offer no difficulty if common sense is
applied. E.g. 聽 belongs to Class B, it consists of two vertical
strips. Neither the left part nor the right are in the Table. It is
easy, however, to notice several radicals, and especially the radical
耳 which is not only conspicuous but is at the left and top; and
so has all the qualifications for being chosen as a radical under
which this character is to be classified.

When the student is entirely at a loss, he may consult the LIST
OF CHARACTERS WHOSE RADICALS ARE OBSCURE given
at the end of the Dictionary.

11. It must be clearly understood that the Table inside the
cover is in no sense a list of radicals. Some radicals are given 3
or 4 times some radicals do not figure even once; and besides
many of the forms given are not radicals at all. The Table merely serves to determine the number of the radical under which the
characters are found. Note for instance, that 幸 though it figures
in the part labeled LEFT is not a radical, but the characters
which have this element at the left (執 報) are to be found under
radical 32, viz. 土. Likewise 舍 is not a radical, but 舒 舖 and
館 will be found under radical 135, viz. 舌.

12. Counting the strokes. Counting the strokes of the non-
radical part of a character is an operation not easily explained in
print. It may be stated in a general way that the method is based
on the number of strokes used in writing the character with a
brush: but the subject is full of surprises and vagaries, and the
classical authors do not always seem to be consistent with themselves. The difficulty of the subject arises principally from three
causes: (1) Doubt as to whether a straight line is to be consider-

ed continuous or not; (2) Doubt as to whether an angle is continuous or not; (3) Variants.

13. The difficulty as regards a continuous straight line will be best understood by the aid of the following example. The well-known character 市 is evidently written with 5 strokes, and 姉 is classified as 5 strokes under radical 38, but 肺 is 4 strokes under radical 130; here the long straight line is continuous, in the other two cases it is not. There is a reason for this into which we need not enter here, but the mere fact of there being a reason does not make it any the less confusing for a beginner. This particular combination is always 'counted as 5 in this dictionary; but many other cases of doubt will present themselves about which it is difficult to give advice beforehand. One combination, however, deserves special notice. A horizontal line crossed by two short vertical ones ⧻ is generally counted 4; i.e. the horizontal line is supposed to be discontinuous as if written ⁺⁺; however, if the two vertical lines are joined at the bottom, as in 廿, or are standing on a straight line as in 共 then the combination ⧻ is generally counted as 3, and, with the bottom line, 4.

14. The corners that give most trouble in the counting of strokes are those formed by a downward stroke followed by one towards the right, i.e. angles pointing to S.W. or W. We give a few typical examples, but no rule seems to be of much use. In the following cases the lines forming the angle in question are continuous: 厶 (2 strokes), 比 (4, 毋 (5), 糸 (6), 臣 (6), 徑 (10), 區 (11). In these other examples the lines are discontinuous: 口 (3 strokes), 田 (5), 瓦 (5), 耳 (6), 似 (7), 馬 (10). Note in this connection that 辶 is counted as 4, and 阝 is counted as 3.

15. Another cause of uncertainty arises from the variants and abbreviations to be found not only in what is written by hand, but also in the printed type, and even in the school-books published by the Mombushō. Most of the common variants are noted in this Dictionary, but there are many others.

Some of the variants, though not very conspicuous, make a difference in the number of strokes. As an example we may call attention to the element at the top right-hand corner of the following: 格終修條 and at the bottom of 憂變. You will notice that some of these characters are written as if this element came from Rad. 34 or 35 (3 strokes) and others as if it came from Rad. 66 (4 strokes). Strictly speaking these elements are neither identical nor interchangeable; but people do not always know when the one or the other should be used, and the men who have engraved the matrices of the printing types seem, in many cases, to have known no better.

The above is sufficient to show that it is not always easy to be sure you have counted the strokes correctly. After an experience of counting the strokes of tens of thousands of characters we have reluctantly come to the conclusion that one is frequently liable to make mistakes, and that it is often necessary to allow for a possible error of 1 or 2 in the counting.

16. It is important to note, concerning the counting of the strokes, that the Tables inside the cover at the beginning and end of the book are intended only for determing the number of the radical under which a character is classified, they do not give, in some few cases, the radicals themselves; but in counting the strokes the radical itself must be taken into account. Thus, the table informs us that characters that have 耂 on the top are classified under Rad. 125. Now, if we look up Rad. 125 we shall find 老; that is why 耆 is classified under 4 strokes and not under 6 strokes. Again, we learn from the same table that characters with 夫 at the top are to be found under Rad. 37: we might therefore expect 奉 to be under 3 strokes; it is placed under 5 strokes because Rad. 37 is 大.

17. Order of Characters having the same number of strokes. If we study in any native dictionary the characters under a certain radical, which have the same number of strokes, we notice that they seem to be arranged without any definite plan. It cannot even be said that they conform to some traditional order as the dictionaries differ in this one from another. We ourselves have followed a plan which, if not helpful, will at least in no way inconvenience those who wish to ignore it. We have placed first those characters in which the radical is on the left side, or shall we say, in the West. Then proceeding clockwise come the characters in which the radical is in the N.W.: after that, the N. etc: last of all we place those in which the radical occupies a central position. Thus 堤 報 壹 are all classified under Rad. 32, 9 strokes, and they are placed in the above order.

18 Characters having the same number of strokes under the same radical, and which have the radical placed in the same position, are arranged as follows. Leaving out of account the radical and considering only the rest of the character, we have arranged them according to the order invented by Rosenbeg. It may be stated roughly thus : consider the lowest stroke of the character, or if two or morè strokes may be considered to be the lowest take the one on the right. The characters are arranged according to the direction of this stroke, in this order.

一 口 丨 丿 乀 乛 乁 乂 乚 乙 丶

Further subdivisions of the system need not detain us.

19. Readings of the Characters. As a rule the characters have two kinds of readings : those of Chinese origin and those of native origin. The reason for this is easy to understand. The characters, a Chinese invention, were introduced into Japan about 1500 years ago, and we can imagine the teacher telling his pupil that, say, the character 人 is read *nin* in Chinese and it means what you call *hito* (man).

20. Now, if this were all, things would have been relatively simple : as a matter of fact, however, many characters serve to represent a whole family of cognate ideas and in the case of a verb, for instance, the same character may, not only serve for the passive and causative conjugations (*miru* to see, *miseru* to show, i.e. to cause to see), but also for the corresponding transitive verb (*kaeru* to go back, *kaesu* to send back : *meguru, megurasu, mawaru, mawasu* to turn) : and further still, it may serve for the corresponding adjective and noun (*tanoshimu* to have pleasure in, *tanoshimasu* to please, give pleasure to, *tanoshimi* pleasure, *tanoshii* pleasant). All this seems reasonable enough, but what is less so is, that one character may represent ideas entirely unrelated to each other, (the same character 息 is read *musuko* son and *iki* breath). We have, therefore, to face the unpleasant fact that each character may have, and in fact often has, more than one Japanese reading.

21. But unfortunately we are not yet at the end of our troubles : the Chinese readings are also frequently more than one : and the explanation of this is as follows. The language spoken by the inhabitants of the various provinces of China is, even today, so diverse that people from different parts of the country cannot understand each other. Hundreds of years ago when communications were more difficult than they are today, this diversity was certainly not less; and besides, even in one same place, the pronunciation has no doubt changed in the course of centuries. Now, there have come to Japan from different parts of China and at different times, various waves of learning or intellectual invasions. Of these, two deserve special mention. The oldest that has left its mark is one from the old province of *Go* 吳 ; the other came many years afterwards from the old province of *Kan* 漢. In the present Dictionary we have distinguished the Chinese readings (*on* 音) from the Japanese readings (*kun* 訓) by printing the former in SMALL CAPITALS and the latter in *italics*, We have not attempted, however, to distinguish the *Go* and the *Kan* readings (*Go-on* 吳音 : *Kan-on* 漢音), as this is of little interest for a beginner.

22. When we talk of a Chinese reading, it must not be understood that this is the same as the reading of the Chinese today. When the scholars from *Go*, for instance, came, the Japanese tried to imitate, probably with only partial success, the sound emitted by their masters. Since then, with the passing of years and centuries, this Japanese imperfect pronunciation has certainly been slowly modified, and the people of *Go* themselves are no doubt pronouncing their language different to what their forefathers of centuries ago did. The result is that between the so-called Chinese reading of the Japanese today, and the reading of the Chinese themselves, there is often little or no similarity.

23. The student may be surprised to find that various characters have the same Japanese reading : quite a few characters, for instance, are read *yorokobu*, several are read *kewashii* etc., etc. The reason is that the meanings are not really identical : but pure Japanese is often poor in synonyms and being incapable of expressing the finer shades of meaning it is obliged to use one word to express various similar ideas. Every beginner must have been astonished when told that *aoi* meant both blue and green.

24. **Meanings of the Characters.** As we have just explained the Japanese reading, *kun*, may be considered an explanation or translation into Japanese of the Chinese reading, *on*. In order to understand the meaning of a character, all that a foreigner, an Englishman, needs, would seem to be an English translation of the *kun*. However, it occurs fairly frequently that the Chinese reading may have a meaning which is not contained in any of the Japanese readings. In a dictionary of characters written for the Japanese, this meaning is naturally explained in Japanese but it is not a reading strictly speaking. To take an obvious example, let us consider the character 里. We find in Ueda's Dictionary the following : RI : *Sato* : *San-jū-roku-chō*. Now, it is evident that the phrase *San-jū-*

roku-chō is not a reading of the character, but merely an explanation in Japanese of the Chinese reading RI, a distance of 36 *chō*,
about 2½ miles. The Japanese reading is *Sato*.

25. The opposite case, namely, when the Japanese reading has
an idea not contained in the Chinese reading, is less common and
of less practical importance. So we may take it as a general rule,
that the Chinese reading has all the meanings of all the Japanese
readings, and besides, it may have a special meaning of its own.
Therefore, if we find in this Dictionary:

市 SHI city: town. *Ichi* market.

we must interpret this as signifying that this character when
read SHI may mean city, town, or market; but when read *Ichi* it
can mean only market.

26. Regular Compounds. Compounds, which are very numerous, usually consist of two characters. A compound may be considered regular when (a) its reading is regular, and (b) its meaning
may be readily deduced from the meanings of the components. (a)
The reading of a compound is regular when both characters are
read according to the *on* or both according to the *kun*: 汽車 *kishı*
(both *on*): 花見 *hanami* (both *kun*). (b) The meanings of the two
components may be related in various ways: (1) one is a qualifier
of the other, 馬車 *basha* horse, vehicle, means a carriage, drawn
by horse-power not by men: (2) the two may form a kind of
verbal phrase, 花見 *hanami* flower, look, means the viewing of
flowers; 登山 *tozan* ascend, mountain: (3) the two may be simply
enumerative 車馬 *shaba* vehicles and horses: (4) the two may
form a kind of contrast from which results an abstract idea not
always easy to guess nor easy to express in English, 遠近 *enkin*
far, near, i.e. distance: 寒暖 *kandan* cold, heat, i.e. temperature.

27. Irregular Compounds. A compound may be irregular
because its reading is irregular, because its meaning is irregular,
or because both are irregular. 一人 the reading *hitori* is irregular
though the meaning is clear, one man. 淺黃 the reading *asagi* is
regular; but, who would guess the meaning which is light blue,
from the meanings of the components which mean shallow, yellow?
In a case like 百合 not only is the reading *yuri* entirely irregular,
but the meaning, a lily, is impossible to guess from the meanings
of the components, a hundred, to join.

28. In choosing the compounds for the **Beginners' Dictionary
of Chinese-Japanese Characters**, we have endeavoured to include

all the common compounds, especially those which are irregular.
Unfortunately it is not always easy to determine whether a compound should be considered irregular or not; for, as regards the
reading, most characters have obscure but real readings besides
the more common ones; and as regards the meaning, some things
which one man will find easy, another will not. In the abridged
edition of this Dictionary, called **Pocket Dictionary of Chinese-Japanese Characters,** the compounds have been omitted.

29. In order to economize space we have not repeated the top
character or first component of the compounds. The student must
supply this mentally: we trust he will not be inconvenienced on
this account. Example:

天 TEN. *Ame; sora* heaven; sky.
人 *Tennin* nature and man; angel.
上 *Tenjō* heaven.
下 *Tenka* the whole country; the world.

We must understand this as if written;

天 TEN. *Ame; sora* heaven; sky.
天人 *Tennin* nature and man; angel.
天上 *Tenjō* heaven.
天下 *Tenka* the whole country; the world.

30. Notice that in an ordinary Japanese text, the mere fact that
two characters follow each other is not a proof that they form a
compound. They very often are entirely independent of each
other. No rule can be given: experience alone will teach.

31. Compounds consisting of three Characters. Japanese
has a decided preference for 2-character compounds; however,
compounds of 3 characters are not rare: e.g. 人力車 *jinrikisha*
the components of which mean, man, power, carriage. Nevertheless, the tendency to form binary combinations is often very apparent even in these 3-character compounds: in 呉服屋 *gofuku-ya*
for instance, *gofuku* is a compound which means dry goods; this
as a whole enters into combination with *ya* to form a new compound which means dry-goods store. In 大賣出 *ō-uridashi* we
have *uridashi* which means a clearance sale; this, preceded by *o*
means big clearance sale.

32. Phonetic peculiarities of Compounds. We wish to call
attention to the following modifications in sound which sometimes
one component, sometimes the other, and sometimes both, experience

on entering into composition. The first three can hardly be considered irregularities; the first two especially are extremely common. (a) *Nigori:* (b) Double consonants; (c) Change of *e* or *o* into *a*: (d) *n* dropped or added; (e) Various ellipses and changes.

33. (a) Nigori. In virtue of *Nigori* it very frequently happens that the initial sound of the second component is modified as follows: *k* becomes *g; s* and *ts* become *z; sh* and *ch* become *j; t* becomes *d;* and *f* and *h* become *b* or *p.* For instance, *tama-go* from *tama, ko.* The *nigori* takes place in both the *on* and the *kun* readings.

34. (b) Double Consonants. When the last syllable of the first component is *tsu* or *chi* and the first sound of the second component is *k, s, sh, t, ts, ch, f,* or *h,* they often coalesce and form a double consonant. Thus *Tekkan* from *tetsu, kan.* When forming a double consonant *f* and *h* always take the nigori'ed form *p: N'ppon* from *nichi, hon.* Note also that double consonants are found sometimes when the first component ends in *ku* or *ki* and the second begins with a *k* sound. Thus: *gakkō* from *gaku, kō; sekken* from *sek', ken.* Double consonants are frequently met with in the *kun* and still more frequently in the *on.* Note especially the case when the first component is one of the numerals, *ichi, roku, hachi, jū, hyaku.*

35. (c) Change of *e* and *o* into *a*. When the first component ends in *e* or *o* it sometimes changes to *a:* for instance *ama-do* from *ame, to,* shira-ki* from *shiro, ki.* This change takes place only in the *kun.*

36. (d) N dropped or added. Some of the commoner cases are; *moji* for *monji; unnun* for *un-un; zennaku* for *zen-aku; ten-nō* for *ten-ō; kannon* for *kan-on; kin-nō* for *kin-ō.*

37. (e) Various ellipses and changes. Here are some examples: *keshiki (kei, shiki); Akashi (akarui-ishi); jis-s'n (jū-sen); jip-pen (jū-hen); fubuki (fuki-yuki); kawara (kawa-hara).*

38. Abbreviated Compounds. Compounds are sometimes obtained by abbreviation. Thus: 昨今 *sak-kon* recently, from 昨日 *sakujitsu* yesterday and 今日 *ko-nichi* today. 出入口 *de-iriguchi,* from 出口 *deguchi* exit and 入口 *iriguchi* entrance. These abbreviated compounds are very frequently used in the case of proper names; and be it noted, the character taken from the full name is not necessarily the first; it may be the last, it may be a middle one. They are especially common when the names of two places or countries are coupled together as in the name given to a railway, a war, a treaty, etc. 日露 *Nichi-Ro* Japanese-Russian (war); in this case the first character of each name is taken, (日本 *Nihon*, 露西亞 *Roshiya*). 京浜 *Kei-Hin* Tōkyō-Yokohama (tramway); here the bottom character of each name is taken, (東京 *Tōkyō*, 横浜 *Yokohama*). 阪神 *Han-Shin* Ōsaka-Kōbe; here the bottom character of Ōsaka and the top character of Kōbe are taken, (大阪, 神戸). The name America is abbreviated by taking the second character 米 *Bei* of the four characters with which the word is written 亞米利加. The student will notice that the reading given to a character in the abbreviated compounds is not always the same as the reading it has in the full name: the *kyō* of Tōkyō for instance, is read *kei* in the compound. The reason for this is often obscure as is also the reason for choosing that particular character to represent the place. However, it is always the same character which is used to represent the same place, and it is read in the same way: thus for *Tōkyō* you always take the bottom character 京 and you read it *kei*. But various places may be represented by the same character: thus 京 is used to represent 東京 *Tōkyō*, 京都 *Kyōto;* 京城 *Keijō* and 北京 *Pekin:* it is read *kei* in all these cases. The context must help you to guess what place it stands for.

39. Various remarks concerning compounds. (1) It sometimes happens that each one of the components of a compound means practically the same as the compound itself: e.g. 死, 亡, and 歿 each mean death: but the compounds 死亡 *Shibō* and 死歿 *Shibotsu* are also used, and they likewise means death. (2) Sometimes two characters are used where the first one by itself would seem sufficient: e.g. 息 by itself is read *musuko,* but *musuko* is also written 息子; 井 by itself is read *ido,* but *ido* is also written 井戸. (3) Sometimes the order of the characters of a compound has an influence on the meaning: 馬車 *basha* carriage, horse-drawn vehicle: 車馬 *shaba* vehicles and horses. Sometimes the meaning is the same whichever character comes first: 便利 *benri* and 利便 *riben* both mean convenience; 宛名 *atena* and 名宛 *na-ate* both mean an address. (4) Sometimes the order of the characters changes the reading without changing the meaning: 左右 is read *sayū,* but 右左 is read *migi-hidari,* they both mean the same, right and left: 東西 is read *tō-zai,* 西東 is read *nishi-higashi,* both mean east and west (5) Occasionally in a Japanese text a short Chinese phrase is introduced and it is necessary to read the characters in a different order to that in which they are

Two syllables in brackets: termination *eru*.

ta(beru)	*shimo ni-dan*	ば-*gyō*
na(deru)	" "	だ-*gyō*
u(eru)	" "	わ-*gyō*
ka(h)eru)	" "	は-*gyō*
sa(geru)	" "	が-*gyō*
u(keru)	" "	か-*gyō*
ya(meru)	" "	ま-*gyō*
ha(neru)	" "	な-*gyō*
i(reru)	" "	ら-*gyō*
yo(seru)	" "	さ-*gyō*
su(teru)	" "	た-*gyō*
ki(y)eru)	" "	や-*gyō*
ma(zeru)	" "	ざ-*gyō*

Two syllables in brackets: termination *iru*.

no(biru)	*kami* or *naka ni-dan*		ば-*gyō*
o(chiru)	"	" "	た-*gyō*
su(giru)	"	" "	が-*gyō*
shi(h)iru)	"	" "	は-*gyō*
ha(jiru)	"	" "	だ-*gyō*
i(kiru)	"	" "	か-*gyō*
shi(miru)	"	" "	ま-*gyō*
o(riru)	"	" "	ら-*gyō*
ku(y)iru)	"	" "	や-*gyō*

One syllable in brackets: preceded by hyphen.

e	before the bracket	*ke(-ru)*	*shimo ichi-dan*	
i	" " "	*mi(-ru)*	*kami*	"

The verb *uryōru* ウレフル is puzzling because of the *kana* combination レフ which is pronounced *ryō;* in *kana* it is perfectly regular, though it appears irregular when romanized. *Uryōru* is used only in the literary style: theoretically, the colloquial form would be *ure(h)eru).*

The verb エフ (pronounced *yō*) is also worthy of note. In the literary style it is conjugated regularly according to its *kana* orthography; the bases are: エフ *yō,* エヒ *ei,* エハ *ewa,* エヘ *ee.* In the colloquial, the sound only is considered; and as, in this, it is analogous to オモフ which is pronounced *omō* in the literary style written. 不可 *bekarazu*, the first character corresponds to *zu* and the second to *bekara*: 如此 *kakunogotoshi* is also read the second character, first. When compounds are read in this inverted order the fact is noted in this Dictionary. (6) Occasionally, in proper names, the particles *no* and *ga*, though not expressed between two Chinese characters, must be introduced in the reading. Thus: 井上 *I(no)ue*, 木下 *Ki(no)shita*, 霞浦 *Kasumi(ga)ura*. The *ga*, in cases like the above, when expressed, is always written ケ, thus 霞ケ浦. The *no* is especially liable to be dropped before the characters 上 and 下; but it is sometimes omitted in other cases, and very rarely in combinations which are not proper names: 箕輪下 *Mi(no)-washita*, 数子 *Ka:u(no)ko* (dried roe of herring). (7) Compound characters corresponding to proper names, whether Japanese or foreign, are generally formed, if there is any semblance of regularity, according to one of these two plans: (a) the characters correspond to the idea expressed by the name, e.g. *Nagasaki* 長崎, Mediterranean 地中 (earth, middle); or else (b) the characters attempt to reproduce the sound, e.g. *Nagoya*, 名 *na*, 古 *ko*, 屋 *ya*, Canada 加 *ka*, 奈 *na* 陀 *da*. In the case of foreign names this phonetic represent-ation is often very imperfect; but it must be remembered that oriental languages are wanting in many sounds contained in European lan-guages, and also that many of these combinations of characters were chosen in China where the readings of the characters are different to the so-called Chinese readings used by the Japanese.

40. Verbs. Verbs are always given in the colloquial form unless otherwise stated. However, those who are studying the written language will be able to deduce the conjugation to which each verb belongs in the literary style by noticing the position of the brackets which enclose the last letters of the verb.

The following examples will make this clear to those who know the grammar of the written language.

One syllable in brackets: no hyphen.

yo(bu)	*yo-dan*	ば-*gyō*
sawa(gu)	"	が-*gyō*
ka(ku)	"	か-*gyō*
yo(mu)	"	ま-*gyō*
ki(ru)	"	ら-*gyō*
ka(su)	"	さ-*gyō*
ta(tsu)	"	た-*gyō*
ka(u)	"	は-*gyō*

but *omo-u* in the colloquial, the verb *yō* is also pronounced *yo-u* in the colloquial, and conjugated throughout as if written ヨ フ.

As far as the conjugation of all other verbs in the colloquial is concerned, all *ni-dan* and *ichi-dan* verbs would be marked with a dot before the *ru*, in the system of notation adopted in our Elementary Grammar of the Japanese Spoken Language, paragraphs 28 et seqq.

41. Verbs formed by adding Suru. Many characters and compounds read according to the Chinese reading may be used as verbs by adding the irregular verb *suru*. 愛 *ai* love; 愛する *aisuru* to love. 白狀 *hakujō* confession : 白狀する *hakujō suru* to confess. This verb *suru* when used thus sometimes takes the modified form *zuru* (literary style) or *jiru* (colloquial). From 命 *mei* command, we have *meizuru* (literary), *meijiru* (colloquial) to command. *Suru* serves occasionally, but much less frequently, to form verbs from the Japanese readings.

42. Chronological Series. Two series of characters are of considerable importance in Japanese. They are often met with especially in connection with Japanese chronology.

The first series 十干 *jik-kan*, we shall call the ten Calendar Signs; it consists of the following characters; 甲 *Kinoe*, 乙 *Kinoto*, 丙 *Hinoe*, 丁 *Hinoto*, 戊 *Tsuchinoe*, 己 *Tsuchinoto*, 庚 *Kanoe*, 辛 *Kanoto*, 壬 *Mizunoe*, 癸 *Mizunoto*. The 10 Calendar Signs form 5 pairs, each pair consisting of an elder brother (*e*) and a younger brother (*to*). The 5 pairs are dedicated to the 5 elements 五行 *gogyō*, *ki* wood, *hi* fire, *tsuchi* earth, *ka*(*ne*) metal, and *mizu* water. (Compare the 5 days of the week *kayō, suiyō, mokuyō, kin-yō, doyō*).

The second series consists of twelve characters and is called 十二支 *jū-ni-shi;* it corresponds vaguely to our signs of the Zodiac. The series is as follows : 子 *Ne* rat, 丑 *Ushi* ox, 寅 *Tora* tiger, 卯 *U* hare, 辰 *Tatsu* dragon, 巳 *Mi* snake, 午 *Uma* horse, 未 *Hitsuji* sheep, 申 *Saru* monkey, 酉 *Tori* bird, 戌 *Inu* dog, 亥 *I* hog.

One sign from each series is taken in consecutive order and applied to the years and days which are considered as belonging to or consecrated to the corresponding signs. The combination of the two series forms a cycle of 60 years (or days) after which time it will be seen that the one series has been repeated exactly 6 times and the other exactly 5; and we begin all over again. The year 1924 was *kinoe ne* and 1984 will also be *kinoe ne;* between these two there will be 5 years *kinoe* and 4 years *ne;* but not the combination *kinoe ne.*

The 31st of March 1927 was *kinoe ne* as was also the 30th of May, 60 days after: and so forth.

Naturally these signs are the occasion of many superstitions, and certain signs and combinations are considered lucky or unlucky.

43. The 10 Calendar Signs are also used for enumeration or classification much as we use: first, second, third.. or A,B,C,..; the first four characters especially are frequently used in this sense. When used for enumeration the 10 Calendar signs are read as follows:

甲	*Kō,*	乙	*Otsu,*
丙	*Hei,*	丁	*Tei,*
戊	*Bo,*	己	*Ki,*
庚	*Kō,*	辛	*Shin,*
壬	*Jin,*	癸	*Ki.*

In old Japan the day was divided into 12 parts, each part being thus equal to 2 hours' duration. These parts were dedicated to the Zodiacal Signs as noted below; we likewise append the old-fashioned names for the hours.

12 midnight	子	*ne*	*kokonotsu doki*
2 a.m.	丑	*ushi*	*yatsu doki*
4 a.m.	寅	*tora*	*nanatsu doki*
6 a.m.	卯	*u*	*mutsu doki*
8 a.m.	辰	*tatsu*	*itsutsu doki*
10 a.m.	巳	*m.*	*yotsu doki*
12 midday	午	*uma*	*kokonotsu doki*
2 p.m.	未	*hitsuji*	*yatsu doki*
4 p.m.	申	*saru*	*nanatsu doki*
₆ p.m.	酉	*tori*	*mutsudoki*
8 p.m.	戌	*inu*	*itsutsu doki*
10 p.m.	亥	*i*	*yotsu doki*

Formerly also the cardinal points were designated by the Zodiacal Signs: North was 子 *ne* and working towards the right we had East 卯 *u*, South 午 *uma* and West 酉 *tori*. Each one of the 12 signs corresponded to an angle of 30 degrees.

44. Weights and Measures.

LINEAR MEASURE

1 *rin* 厘	=0.012 inch 吋	=0.303 millimetre 粍
10 *rin* =1 *bu* 分	=0.12 „	—3.03 „
10 *bu* =1 *sun* 寸	=1.2 „	=3.03 centimetres 糎
10 *sun* =1 *shaku* 尺	=0.994 foot 呎	—30.3 „
6 *shaku*=1 *ken* 間	=1.99 yard 碼	—1.82 metre 米
„ =1 *hiro* 尋	=0.994 fathom	— „ „
10 *shaku*=1 *jō* 丈	=3.31 yards	—3.03 „
60 *ken* =1 *chō* 町,丁	—119 „	—109 „
	1 sea mile 浬	—1852 „
36 *chō* —1 *ri* 里	—2.44 miles 哩	=3.93 kilometres 粁

CLOTH MEASURE

The units of Cloth Measure are $\frac{1}{4}$ longer than the corresponding units of Linear Measure.

1 *rin* 厘	=0.015 inch 吋	—0.379 millimetre 粍
10 *rin* —1 *bu* 分	—0.15 „	—3.79 „
10 *bu* =1 *sun* 寸	—1.5 „	—3.79 centimetres 糎
10 *sun* =1 *shaku* 尺	—1.243 foot 呎	=37.9 „
10 *shaku*=1 *jō* 丈	—4.14 yards 碼	—3.79 metres 米
	1 *tan* 反 (piece) about 25-30 *shaku*	
2 *tan* =1 *hiki* 匹, 疋		

N.B. The *shaku* of ordinary linear measure is sometimes called *kane-jaku* or *kane-zashi* 曲尺, that of cloth measure *kujira-jaku* or *kujira-zashi* 鯨尺.

SQUARE MEASURE (for land)

1 sq. *ken* 間—1 *tsubo* 坪	—3.95 sq. yards	=3.31 sq. metres
=1 *bu* 步	— „	„ — „ „
30 *bu* —1 *se* 畝	—119 sq. yards	=0.992 ares
10 *se* —1 *tan* 段, 反	—0.245 acres	=9,92 „
10 *tan* —1 *chō* 町	—2.45 „	=0.992 hectares
—1 *chōbu* 町步		

ACKNOWLEDGEMENTS

The compiler wishes to draw attention to the fact that, in order to meet certain criticisms, the classification of the characters under the 214 radicals has been somewhat changed in this edition.

He wishes, also, to acknowledge his indebtedness to his friend Mr. Naganuma who has collected and selected the numerous compounds which have been added, and has thoroughly revised the readings of the characters, especially in the sense of suppressing those of no practical use.—

In rearranging the present new edition we are indebted to the book Tōyō Kanji Jiten, Tokyo 1958, 5th ed., compiled by Messr. Toyama and Seki, and published by the Chūkyō Shuppan Co.

DICTIONARY

OF

CHINESE-JAPANESE CHARACTERS.

一 ——◂

T **一** ICHI one; according to context may mean a; a certain; the; beginning; after place name has sometimes force of superlative (*Tōkyō ichi*) the best, biggest, etc. in Tōkyō); the whole (*Izu ik-koku*) the whole province of Izu); each; every (*ichi-boku is-sō* every single tree and every blade of grass): ITSU one: ITSU (*ni*) verily; solely; in another way. *Hitotsu* one. (*Kazu*) (*Hajime*).

々 *Ichi-ichi* one by one

人 *Hitori; ichi-nin* one person.

入 *Hitoshio* still more; much more.

口 *Hitokuchi* one mouthful; in a word; a share; aparcel.

口話 *Hitokuchibanashi* a joke; a short tale.

寸 *Issun* one *sun: chotto* a little; just.

大事 *Ichidaiji* a uniquely great event; an emergency.

日 *Ichinichi* one day: *tsuitachi* first day of the month.

日千秋 *Ichijitsusenshū* many a weary day.

片 *Ippen* a fragment; one half; a portion of anything.

介 *Ikkai* mere.

手 *Itte* by oneself; only means; solely: *hitote* one side or party.

手販賣 *Itte-hambai* sole agency.

月 *Ichi-gatsu; ichi-getsu* January; *hitotsuki* one month.

切 *Issai; issetsu* all; without exception.

方 *Ippō* one side; on the other hand: *hitokata* (*narazu*) greatly.

天 *Itten* the whole sky; universe.

天萬乘 *Itten-banjō* lit. One heaven and ten thousand chariots; adj of high praise (peerless, divine) applied only to Emperor especially that of Japan.

1

木一草 *Ichiboku-issō* each single tree and every blade of grass.

文字 *Ichimonji* a straight line.

心 *Isshin* one's whole mind; concentrated attention.

心不亂 *Isshin furan* with concentrated attention; with all one's might.

戸 *Ikko* a house; one household.

旦 *Ittan* once.

生 *Isshō* lifetime; a whole life.

生涯 *Isshōgai* a whole life.

生懸命に *Isshōkemmei ni* with all one's might.

目 *Ichimoku; hito-me* a glance.

目散に *Ichimokusan ni* at full, top speed.

目瞭然 *Ichimokuryōzen* as clear as day.

本立 *Ippondachi* independence.

世 *Issei* lifetime; age; the world.

世紀 *Isseiki* one century.

代 *Ichidai* one generation; a life.

打 *Hitouchi* a stroke: *ichidāsu* a dozen.

失 *Isshitsu* a disadvantage; a defect.

件 *Ikken* an affair.

伍一什 *Ichigo-ichijū; Ichibushijū* the whole; the full particulars.

名 *Ichimei* another name; one person.

存 *Ichizon* the individual opinion (of a person); a single idea.

同 *Ichidō* all the persons concerned; all together.

向 *Ikkō* at all (with neg.).

先 *Hitomazu* for the present.

任 *Ichinin* rely upon; leave something with one.

行 *Ikkō* an act; a party (as of travellers): *Ichigyō* one line.

式 *Isshiki* a complete set.

次 *Ichiji* primary; first.

言 *Ichigon; ichigen* in a word.

言一行 *Ichigen ikkō* words and deeds; everything.

言半句 *Ichigon hanku* a single word.

別 *Ichibetsu* (of persons) separation; parting.

身 *Isshin* oneself; one's person.

決 *Ikketsu* to decide; settle; make a resolution.

足 *Issoku* a pair (of boots, socks, etc.): *hitoashi* a step; a second.

足飛に *Issokutobi ni* at a single bound.

見 *Ikken* a sight; a glance.

利 *Ichiri* the smallest advantage (with neg.); one advantage.

利一害 *Ichiri-ichigai* an advantage and a disadvantage.

2

系 *Ikkei* one family line.

体 *Ittai* one body; on earth; in the world.

命 *Ichimei* one's life.

門 *Ichimon* the whole family or clan.

兩日 *Ichiryō-jitsu* a day or two.

物 *Ichibutsu; ichimotsu* one thing; (with neg.) nothing.

味 *Ichimi* the same party.

定 *Ittei* certain; being fixed or settled.

念 *Ichinen* an ardent desire; concentrated thought.

周 *Isshū* one round; one revolution.

杯 *Ippai* a cup; one cup-full; the whole.

刹那 *Issetsuna* an instant; a moment.

知半解 *Itchihankai* superficial knowledge.

刻 *Ikkoku* a moment; a minute.

刻千金 *Ikkoku-senkin* a moment worth a thousand pieces of gold.

面 *Ichimen* the whole surface; all over; one side.

面識 *Ichi-menshiki* meeting once; slight acquaintance.

昨日 *Issaku-jitsu; ototoi* the day before yesterday.

昨年 *Issaku-nen; ototoshi* the year before last.

首 *Isshu* an ode.

段 *Ichidan* one step; one degree; still more; especially.

段落 *Ichidanraku* one stage; conclusion.

派 *Ippa* a faction.

括 *Ikkatsu; hitokukuri; hitokurume* bundle; sum up.

思 *Hito-omoi* one effort.

封 *Ip-pū* an enclosure, e.g. money in envelope or wrapped in paper.

座 *Ichiza* the whole assembly; all the persons present; a theatrical troupe.

個人 *Ikkojin* an individual.

時 *Ichiji* one o'clock; all at once; once; for a time; for the time being; (in poetry, also, *hitotoki*.)

時的 *Ichiji-teki* temporary; passing.

笑 *Isshō* hearty laugh; ridicule.

家 *Ikka* whole family; one's family; school (as of painting).

般 *Ippan* general; universal.

般投票 *Ippan-tōhyō* plebiscite.

致 *Itchi* union; harmony.

眠 *Hito-nemuri* sleep without interruption; a short nap.

員 *Ichiin* one member (of a family, etc.).

班 *Ippan* a part; summary; general view.

流 *Ichiryū* of the first rank; characteristic.

3

一

得一失 *Ittoku-isshitsu* an advantage and a disadvantage.

部分 *Ichibubun* a portion; a part.

部始終 *Ichibushijū* the whole; full particulars.

掃 *Issō* to disperse; drive away.

掬 *Ikkiku* one handful.

族 *Ichizoku* the whole family.

通 *Hitotōri* in a general way; one kind. *Ittsū* one document; a letter.

途 *Ichizu ni* with all one's heart.

望 *Ichibō* a look.

着 *Itchaku* the first arrival; one suit (of clothes).

番 *Ichiban* number one; often has a superlative meaning.

等 *Ittō* first class; best; most.

朝 *Itchō* suddenly; in a moment.

朝一夕 *Itchō-isseki* a brief period of time.

視同仁 *Isshidōjin* universal brotherhood.

散 *Issan ni* at the top of one's speed.

圓 *Ichien* one yen; all; the whole.

新 *Isshin* complete transformation; revolution; change.

廉 *Hitokado* special.

際 *Hitokiwa* particularly.

齊 *Issei ni* altogether; at one time.

對 *Ittsui* a pair; set.

說 *Issetsu* another opinion; some say that......

層 *Issō* still more.

緒 *Issho ni* together.

樣 *Ichiyō* same; alike; similar; similarity; one kind.

徹者 *Ittetsu-mono* a stubborn person.

概 *Ichigai ni* in general; in a careless manner; at once.

興 *Ikkyō* fun; an amusement.

頻 *Hito-shikiri* for some time; for a while.

點張 *Ittembari* caring for one thing only and not minding any other; persisting in line of action; unyielding.

瞬 *Isshun* one wink of the eye; a moment; an instant.

舉 *Ikkyo* one action, or effort; a slight act.

舉手 *Ikkyoshu* a slight act.

舉一動 *Ikkyoichidō* every action.

舉兩得 *Ikkyoryōtoku* killing two birds with one stone.

應 *Ichiō* once; anyhow.

騎打 *Ikki-uchi* a single combat.

騎當千 *Ikkitōsen* able alone to face a thousand horsemen (in fighting); very courageous.

躍 *Ichiyaku* at one bound.

覽拂 *Ichiran-barai* payable at sight.

體 *Ittai* one body; on earth; in short.

變 *Ippen* complete change.

驚 *Ikkyō* to be startled.

一二 See 7,0. T

T 丁 TEI servant; (in enumerations) fourth; D; CHO division of a ward of town; unit of length, about 120 yards. *Hinoto* the 4th calendar sign. See Introduction 42, 43, 44.

年 *Teinen* full age.

抹 *Demmaruku* Denmark.

度 *Chōdo* just; exactly.

稚 *Detchi* apprentice.

寧 *Teinei* civility; care.

T 七 SHICHI. *Nanatsu* seven.

夕 *Tanabata* festival of the Weaver, 7th day of the 7th month.

日 *Nanuka; nanoka* 7 days; the 7th day of the month.

月 *Shichigatsu* July; *nanatsu-ki* 7 months.

五三 *Shichi-go-san* the lucky numbers of three, five and seven.

里濱 *Shichiri-ga-hama* the beach from Kamakura to Enoshima; it has less than 2 *ri* according to the present value of the *ri*.

夜 *Shichiya* the 7th evening after the birth of a child.

面鳥 *Shichimenchō* a turkey.

福神 *Shichifukujin* seven deities of fortune.

轉八起 *Nanakorobi-yaoki* vicissitudes of fortune.

轉八倒 *Shichiten-battō* writhing with pain.

顚八倒 Same as above.

寶 *Shippō* cloisonné.

寶燒 *Shippōyaki* cloisonné ware.

三 SAN. *Mitsu* three.

T 々五々 *Sansan-gogo* groups of small numbers.

十三間堂 *Sanjūsangen-dō* a temple in Kyōto.

十日 *Sanjū-nichi* 30th day of the month; 30 days: *misoka* the last day of the month.

日 *Mikka* 3 days; 3rd day of the month.

日月 *Mikazuki* (not *mikka-zuki*) crescent moon.

井 *Mii* place name; *Mitsui* surname.

月 *San-gatsu* March; *mi-tsuki* 3 months.

尺 *San-jaku* 3 feet; a waistband.

毛 *Mike* having hairs of 3 colours; tortoise-shell (cat).

州 *San-shū* another name for the province of *Mikawa*.

伏 *Sampuku* the dog days.

角 *Sankaku; misumi* a triangle.

(二一)

三

河 *Mikawa* p. n. (Province in Shizuoka Prefecture).

味線 *Samisen* a three-stringed guitar.

省 *Sansei* to examine one's conscience; keep strict watch over one's conduct.

界 *Sangai* the three states of existence (Buddhism).

昧 *Sammai* to give oneself up to (luxury, etc.).

重 *Sanjū* threefold: *Mie* p. n. (Prefecture in which Ise shrine is).

面記事 *Sammenkiji* chronique scandaleuse; general news column.

軍 *Sangun* a great army.

郎 *Saburō* man's name.

流 *Sanryū* third rate.

絃 *Sangen* a musical instrument; a *samisen*.

唱 *Sanshō* three cheers.

菱 *Mitsubishi* p. n.; the Iwasaki family.

景 *Sankei* the three famous views of Japan viz. *Matsushima, Amano-Hashidate*, and *Miyajima*.

等 *Santō* third class.

種の神器 *Sanshu no jingi* the three sacred vessels or treasures supposed to have been given to the founders of the Japanese dynasty by the gods. The treasures are (1) the mirror *Yata-no-kagami;* (2) the sword *Kusanagi-no-tsurugi;* (3) the gem *Yasakani-no-magatama.*

韓 *Sankan* old name for Korea.

工 See 48,0.

下 GE; KA, in or belonging to; especially in the expressions 府下 *fuka*, 縣下 *kenka*, 都下 *toka.* *Shita; shimo; moto* below; low; inferior; preliminary: *kudasa(ru)* (irreg. in coll.) please; to give; grant: *kuda(ru); kuda(su); o(riru); oro(su)* to descend; send down: *saga(ru); sa(geru)* to hang down; hang; lower.

士 *Kashi* non-commissioned officer (army); petty officer (navy).

女 *Gejo* a female servant.

手 *Heta* not skilful; *shitade* deference; *shimote* a certain part of a theatre.

手人 *Geshu-nin* a murderer.

戸 *Geko* a temperate, abstemious person.

火 *Shitabi* the state of a conflagration on the decline; a smouldering fire.

心 *Shita-gokoro* real desire or intentions (as different to apparent).

水 *Gesui* sewer; drain.

司 *Gesu* lowness (of character).

半 *Kahan* latter half.

旬 *Gejun* term used for the last ten days of a month.

劣 *Geretsu* ignoble; depraved.

谷 *Shitaya* p. n.

車 *Gesha* alighting.

(二一)

6

（二）

男 *Genan* man servant or employee.

足 *Gesoku* foot-gear.

役 *Shitayaku* subordinate; underling.

知 *Geji* to order.

卷 *Gekan* the second (of two) or the third (of three) volume.

附 *Kafu* grant; give.

品 *Gehin* vulgar.

界 *Gekai* this earth.

拵 *Shitagoshirae* preliminary preparation.

降 *Kakō* come down; drop.

級 *Kakyū* lower grade; the lower classes; junior; inferior.

流 *Karyū* the lower waters of a river; the lower classes (of the people).

院 *Kain* the Lower House.

書 *Shitagaki* rough copy.

宿 *Geshuku* lodging.

婢 *Kahi* a female servant.

野 *Shimotsuke* p. n. (Province of Tochigi).

情 *Kajō* the condition of the people.

帶 *Shitaobi* a loin-cloth.

略 *Geryaku* the concluding part omitted.

痢 *Geri* diarrhoea.

等 *Katō* low rank or class; bad quality.

落 *Geraku* to fall; become lower (of prices).

（二）

働 *Shita-bataraki* subordinate work; a subordinate.

摺 *Shitazuri* proof.

駄 *Geta* wooden clogs.

僕 *Kaboku* a man-.servant.

層 *Kasō* lower layer; lower classes.

調 *Shitashirabe* preliminary inquiry; preparation.

賜 *Kashi* Imperial grant.

髪 *Sagegami* the hair hanging down the back.

賤 *Gesen* ; *hashita* mean.

總 *Shimōsa* p. n. (Province of Chiba).

關 *Shimonoseki* p. n.

干 T See 51,0.

万 T See 萬 140,9.

兀 KOTSU; GOTSU lofty; high; bald. 【儿】

然 *Kotsuzen* loftily.

才 T See 6,2. 【手】

与 T See 與 134,7.

丈 T JŌ measure of length equal 10 *shaku*. See Introduction 44. *Take* stature; *dake* only; as much as.

夫 *Jōbu* strong: *jōfu* a hero; man.

餘 *Jōyo* more than one *jō* in length.

7

三
T **王** See 96,0.

T **互** Go. *Tagai ni* mutually.
【二】 Do not confound with 瓦.

角 *Gokaku* equal; well matched.

惠條約 *Gokeijōyaku* reciprocal treaty.

違 *Tagaichigai ni* alternately.

選 *Gosen* election by a body of men of one or more of its members.

T **五** Go. *Itsutsu* five. 【二】

十 *Go-jū; iso* fifty.

十三次 *Go-jū-san-tsugi* the post-stations on the old Tōkaidō road from Kyōto to Edo (now Tōkyō) which numbered fifty three.

十鈴 *Isuzu* p. n.

十步百步 *Gojippo-hyappo* there is not much to choose between them.

日 *Itsuka* five days; the 5th day of the month.

月 *Go-gatsu* May: *itsu-tsuki* 5 months.

月雨 *Samidare* old fashioned name for long continued rain in early summer; the *nyūbai*.

月蠅 *Urusai* annoying.

分々々 *Gobu-gobu* evenly matched; evenness.

百 *Gohyaku* five hundred: *io* abundant.

里霧中 *Gori-muchū* dazed; in the air; at sea.

官 *Gokan* the five senses.

重塔 *Go-jū-no-tō* five-storied pagoda.

感 *Gokan* the five senses.

穀 *Gokoku* the five cereals, viz. rice (*kome*), barley and wheat (*mugi*), millet (*awa*), sorghum (*kibi*) and beans (*mame*). Beans, though not a cereal were considered to be one by the Chinese.

體 *Gotai* the five parts of the body; head and four limbs; the whole body.

开 *So wa* that. 【二】

牙 See 92,0.

天 Ten God; imperial (referring to Emperor of Japan). *Ame* heaven; sky. 【大】
T Do not confound with 夭 4,3 nor with 夫 37,1.

人 *Tennin* nature and man; angel.

上 *Tenjō* heaven.

下 *Tenka* the whole country; the world.

子 *Tenshi* Emperor (of Japan).

才 *Tensai* a genius; natural talent.

井 *Tenjō* ceiling.

文 *Temmon* the heavens; astronomy: *Tembun* name of an era.

分 *Tembun* inherent talent.

守閣 *Tenshu-kaku* a castle-tower.

(三)

地 *Tenchi* heaven and earth; the world; top and bottom.

成 *Tensei* born; gifted.

佑 *Ten-yū* the grace of Heaven.

災 *Tensai* natural calamity.

竺 *Tenjiku* India.

空 *Tenkū* the sky.

性 *Tensei* nature; natural disposition.

命 *Temmei* fate.

長節 *Tenchō-setsu* Emperor's birthday.

使 *Tenshi* angel.

皇 *Tennō* Emperor (especially the Emperor of Japan).

津 *Tenshin* Tientsin.

則 *Tensoku* natural law.

降 *Amakudari* descended from heaven; recommended by superiors.

神 *Tenjin* a Japanese god.

候 *Tenkō* weather.

氣 *Tenki* weather.

氣豫報 *Tenki-yohō* a weather forecast.

恩 *Ten-on* benevolence of the Emperor; blessings of Heaven.

眞爛漫 *Tenshin-ramman* open-hearted.

產 *Tensan* natural produce.

理 *Tenri* natural law; natural principles.

國 *Tengoku* the Kingdom of God; Heaven.

授 *Tenju* Heaven-sent; gifted by nature.

晴 *Appare* admirably.

然 *Tennen* nature.

誅 *Tenchū* killed by heaven.

稟 *Tempin; tenrin* natural disposition.

照人神 *Amaterasu-ōmikami* the chief goddess according to Japanese mythology.

資 *Tenshi* natural quality.

罰 *Tembatsu* vengeance of Heaven.

壽 *Tenju* natural span of life.

幕 *Tento; temmaku* tent.

賦 *Tempu* innate; inherent; conferred by heaven.

龍 *Tenryū* p. n.

鵝絨 *Birōdo* velvet.

職 *Tenshoku* a mission in life.

顏 *Tengan* Imperial countenance.

壤 *Tenjō* heaven and earth.

覽 *Tenran* Imperial inspection or perusal.

變 *Tempen* natural calamity.

體 *Tentai* heavenly bodies.

聽 *Tenchō* hearing of the Emperor.

不 FU; BU neg. affix; often dis-, un-, in-, etc. *Zu* verbal suffix; not; sometimes used in inverted order.

一 *Fuitsu* uneven (humble expression used at end of letter).

二 *Fuji* Mt. Fuji; unequaled

才 *Fusai* inability.

(三)

(⼀⼀)

不

仁 *Fujin* inhumanity; cruelty.

文律 *Fubunritsu* unwritten rule or law.

日 *Fujitsu* at no distant date.

毛 *Fumō* barrenness.

手際 *Futegiwa* bad workmanship.

平 *Fuhei* complaint; discontent.

可 *Fuka* wrong; unadvisable: *bekarazu* (inverted order) shall not; must not.

可抗力 *Fukakōryoku* inevitability; force majeure.

可思議 *Fukashigi* mystery.

可能 *Fukanō* impossibility.

可解 *Fukakai* mysterious.

用 *Fuyō* useless.

本意 *Fuhon-i* reluctance.

出來 *Fudeki* bad make.

正 *Fusei* unlawfulness; impropriety.

申 *Mōsazu* (inverted order) do not (used in letter writing).

仕 *Tsukamatsurazu* (inverted order) do not (used in letter writing).

在 *Fuzai* absence.

名譽 *Fumeiyo* dishonour; disgrace.

如意 *Funyoi* going contrary to one's wishes; being hard up.

如歸 *Hototogisu* the cuckoo.

吉 *Fukitsu* an ill omen.

自由 *Fujiyū* inconvenient; not free.

仲 *Funaka* bad terms.

行屆 *Fuyukitodoki* neglect.

行狀 *Fugyōjō* misconduct.

行跡 *Fugyōseki* misconduct.

行儀 *Fugyōgi* impropriety.

朽 *Fukyū* perpetual; incorruptible; enduring.

安 *Fuan* uneasiness.

向 *Fumuki* unsuitable for.

作 *Fusaku* bad harvest.

利 *Furi* disadvantage; unprofitable.

孝 *Fukō* unfilial; disobedient to parent.

肖 *Fushō* a fool; an ignorant person; I (humble).

身持 *Fumimochi* misconduct; profligacy.

快 *Fukai* indisposition; ill; sickness.

束 *Futsutsuka* ignorant; rustic.

良 *Furyō* bad; evil; wicked.

足 *Fusoku* insufficient; want; shortage.

見識 *Fukenshiki* undignified.

屆 *Futodoki* rudeness.

和 *Fuwa* discord.

始末 *Fushimatsu* irregularity; mismanagement.

幸 *Fukō* unfortunate; misfortune.

例 *Furei* indisposition.

味 *Mazui* unsavoury.

承々々 *Fushō-bushō* reluctantly.

取敢 *Toriaezu* (inverted order) at once; in haste

(三一)

(end of letter or on taking leave).

拔 *Fubatsu* indomitable.

服 *Fufuku* dissatisfaction.

況 *Fukyō* dullness; depression.

具 *Fugu* deformity.

忠 *Fuchū* disloyal; unfaithful; dishonest.

治 *Fuji* incurable.

恰好 *Bukakkō* ill-shaped.

相變 *Aikawarazu* (inverted order) as usual.

便 *Fuben* inconvenience : *fubin* pitiableness.

貞腐 *Futekusare* sulks.

思議 *Fushigi* strange; wonder.

俱戴天 *Fugutaiten* irreconcilable, deadly (enemy).

時 *Fuji* sudden; unexpected.

料見 *Furyōken* misconduct.

埒 *Furachi* impoliteness; misconduct.

倫 *Furin* immoral.

案內 *Fuannai* ignorance.

能 *Funō* incompetence; impossibility.

振 *Fushin* depression; inactivity.

參 *Fusan* not coming or going.

細工 *Busaiku* unskilful.

祥 *Fushō* ill-luck; unlucky.

斜 *Naname-narazu* (inverted order) extremely.

得止 *Yamu wo ezu* (inverted order) unavoidably.

得手 *Fuete* poor; unskilful.

得要領 *Futoku-yōryō* irrelevant.

得策 *Futokusaku* an unwise course; unadvisable.

淨 *Fujō* uncleanliness.

釣合 *Futsuriai* incongruous.

動產 *Fudōsan* immovables; real estate.

逞 *Futei* insubordinate.

通 *Futsū* suspension (of communication, of train service).

備 *Fubi* defectiveness; fault; (humble expression used at end of letter).

都合 *Futsugō* inconvenience; reprehensible.

評判 *Fuhyōban* a bad reputation.

順 *Fujun* unsettled (of the weather); unseasonable.

景氣 *Fukeiki* depression; dullness (as of trade, etc.).

惡 *Ashikarazu* (inverted order) not ill.

測 *Fusoku* unforeseen; accidental.

爲 *Futame* disadvantage.

渡 *Fuwatari* dishonour; nonpayment.

當 *Futō* injustice; unreasonable.

敬 *Fukei* disrespect; irreverence.

運 *Fu-un* misfortune.

遇 *Fugū* unfortunate; obscure.

義 *Fugi* wrong (morally); profligacy.

義理 *Fugiri* dishonesty; ingratitude.

（三）

不

意 *Fui* suddenly; unexpectedly.

經濟 *Fukeizai* bad economy.

圖 *Futo* suddenly : *hakarazu* (inverted order) unexpectedly.

精 *Bushō* laziness ; habitual dirtiness.

遜 *Fuson* haughty.

實 *Fujitsu* dishonesty ; insincerity ; unkindness.

滿 *Fuman* dissatisfaction.

審 *Fushin* doubt ; suspicion.

憫 *Fubin* pitiableness.

調 *Fuchō* break-off ; failure.

調法 *Buchōhō* awkward.

敵 *Futeki* bold.

徹底 *Futettei* unconvincing.

撓 *Futō* tenacity ; perseverance.

潔 *Fuketsu* dirty.

德 *Futoku* immoral ; wicked ; vicious ; unworthiness.

慮 *Furyo* sudden ; unexpected ; unforeseen ; eventuality.

與 *Fukyō* ill-humour ; spleen.

躾 *Bushitsuke* ill-breeding ; rudeness.

斷 *Fudan* usual ; constant ; common.

謹愼 *Fukinshin* imprudence.

覺 *Fukaku* negligence.

體裁 *Futeisai* unseemliness.

羈 *Fuki* freedom from restraint.

T **止** See 77,0.

丑 CHŪ. *Ushi* the 2nd zodiacal sign, the ox. See Introduction 42, 43.

滿 *Ushimitsu* midnight.

廿 See 廿 24,1.

丹 TAN. *Ni* red ; medicine. 【丶】

靑 *Tansei* painting.

波 *Tamba* p. n.

念 *Tannen* assiduity.

後 *Tango* p. n.

毒 *Tandoku* erysipelas.

誠 *Tansei* diligent application ; assiduity ; exertion.

尹 (IN). 【尸】

戈 See 62,0.

尤 YŪ. *Mottomo* very ; right ; however : *toga* fault ; mistake : *toga(meru)* to blame. 【尢】

（三）

四

T **玉** See 96,0.

正 SEI ; SHŌ. *Tadashi ; masa* correct ; proper ; just ; honest ; straight ; legal : *tada(su)* to correct. 【止】

T

（四）

々堂々 *Seiseidōdō* fair and honourable.

午 *Shōgo* noon.

月 *Shōgatsu* New Year ; January.

反對 *Seihantai* direct opposition.

文 *Seibun* (official) text.

札 *Shōfuda* label showing the fixed price ; a price-mark.

行 *Masatsura* p. n.

式 *Seishiki* formality.

米 *Shōmai* spot rice (commercial).

成 *Masashige* p. n.

邪 *Seija* right and wrong.

金銀行 *Shōkin-ginkō* the Specie Bank.

直 *Shōjiki* honesty.

味 *Shōmi* net weight, or amount.

門 *Seimon* front gate.

面 *Shōmen* the front.

則 *Seisoku* a regular method.

氣 *Shōki* right mind ; soberness.

副 *Seifuku* chief and vice-chief ; original and copy.

貨 *Seika* ; *shōka* specie ; coins.

統 *Seitō* a direct line ; legitimacy.

當 *Seitō* right ; legal.

道 *Seidō* justice.

義 *Seigi* righteousness.

裝 *Seisō* full uniform.

（四）

誤 *Seigo* correction.

實 *Seijitsu* sure ; certain ; positive.

確 *Seikaku* accuracy.

鵠 *Seikō* main point ; mark.

ᵀ石 See 112,0.

平 HEI ; BYŌ.; HYŌ. *Taira* level ; equal ; even ; common ; ordinary ; family name : *hiratai ; hira* flattened shape ; level : *taira(geru)* to quiet ; subdue. 【干】

→平ᴛ

々凡々 *Heihei-bombon* commonplace.

凡 *Heibon* commonplace.

日 *Heijitsu* ordinary days.

方 *Heihō* square (*heihō-ri* a square *ri*).

生 *Heizei* always ; everyday.

民 *Heimin* common people.

民的 *Heiminteki* democratic ; popular.

年 *Heinen* an ordinary, normal year (not leap year).

行 *Heikō* parallelism.

伏 *Heifuku* to prostrate oneself.

安 *Heian* peace.

地 *Heichi ; hirachi* level land.

身低頭 *Heishinteitō* low prostration ; profound humility.

均 *Heikin* average.

作 *Heisaku* average crops.

（四）

平 坦 *Heitan* level ; smooth.

和 *Heiwa* peace.

易 *Heii* easy ; simple.

定 *Heitei* to restore order.

服 *Heifuku* ordinary dress.

信 *Heishin* peaceful tidings (on envelope, to show there is no bad news in letter).

時 *Heiji* ordinary times.

氣 *Heiki* calmness.

素 *Heiso* everyday ; usually ; ordinary.

原 *Heigen* level expanse ; moor ; a plain.

家 *Heike* Taira family (p. n.) : *hiraya* one-storied house.

野 *Heiya* a plain ; moor.

常 *Heijō* always ; ordinary times.

假名 *Hiragana* cursive forms of Japanese phonetic writing.

等 *Byōdō ; heitō* equality.

然 *Heizen* calmly ; as if nothing out-of-the-way had happened.

衡 *Heikō* balance ; true proportion ; harmony.

鎮 *Heichin* to suppress ; quell ; pacify.

癒 *Heiyu* recovery.

穩 *Heion* peace.

壤 *Heijō* Phyengyang (Korea).

T 可 See 30,2.

（四）

丙 T *Hei* "third" ; "C" (in enumerations or classifications). *Hinoe* 3rd calendar sign ; see Introduction 42, 43.

瓦 See 98,0.

T 生 See 100.0.

T 丘 See 69,1. 【一】

業 See 北 T 21,3.

且 *So* ; SHO. *Katsu* again ; besides ; moreover ; *shibaraku* short time. Do not confound with 旦 72,1.

皿 See 108,0.

T 司 See 30,2.

世 T *Sei* used to express ordinal number of monarchs'; age ; times : SE. *Yo* world. →24, 3 : 24, 4

々 *Yoyo* generations.

人 *Sejin* the people of the whole world ; the public.

上 *Sejō* the world.

才 *Sesai* worldly wisdom.

事 *Seji* worldly affairs ; civility.

俗 *Sezoku* worldly ; common.

界 *Sekai* world.

柄 *Yogara* the condition of the world.

紀 *Seiki* a century.

帶 *Shotai* housekeeping ; household.

（四）

迷言 *Yomaigoto* grumbling.

情 *Sejō* worldly affairs.

智 *Sechi* worldly wisdom.

智辛 *Sechigarai* hard.

許 *Sehyō* the public sentiment; opinion; rumour.

間 *Seken* the world; things in general; the public.

渡 *Yowatari* going through the world; living.

話 *Sewa* aid; assistance.

嗣 *Yotsugi* an heir.

態 *Setai* the condition of the world or the country.

論 *Seron* public opinion.

辭 *Seji* civility; flattery.

襲 *Seishū; seshū* transmission by heredity.

卋 See preceding and 卅 24,2.

Γ 甘 See 99,0.

册 SATSU aux. num. for counting books; book; volume. 【冂】 →13, 3 T

Γ 毋 See 80,1.

五 亘 SEN to spread; to seek. 【二】 Often used instead of 亙

T 至 See 133,0.

亙 KŌ. *Wata(ru)* to cross over; pass from one to another: *amaneku* universally. 【二】 Do not confound with 亘

（五）

百 HYAKU. *Momo* hundred; a great number; all; various. 【白】
T

方 *Hyappō* every way; in all directions.

出 *Hyaku-shutsu* to arise in great numbers.

合 *Yuri* the lily.

足 *Mukade* centipede.

姓 *Hyakushō* a peasant.

官 *Hyakkan* all the Government officials.

事 *Hyakuji* various things.

計 *Hyakkei* many different plans.

科全書 *Hyakkazensho* encyclopedia.

害 *Hyakugai* harmful in many ways.

般 *Hyappan* all; every.

鬼夜行 *Hyakkiyakō* prowling of devils at night.

發百中 *Hyappatsu - hyakuchū* hitting the mark every time.

T 西 See 146,0.

T 耳 See 128,0.

而 See 126,0.

T 兩 See 兩 1,7. 【入】

再 SAI moreover. *Futatabi* again; twice. 【冂】
T

々 *Saisai* repeatedly; several times.

三 *Saisan* again and again.

生 *Saisei* revival; regeneration.

15

（五）

再

白 *Saihaku* postscript.

申 *Saishin* postscript.

犯 *Saihan* relapse.

考 *Saikō* careful thought; mature reflection.

任 *Sainin* re-appointment.

伸 *Saishin* postscript.

來 *Sairai* second coming.

來月 *Saraigetsu* the month after next.

來年 *Sarainen* the year after next.

版 *Saihan* second edition.

拜 *Saihai* bowing twice; final salutation (in letter writing).

婚 *Saikon* second marriage.

發 *Saihatsu; saihotsu* recurrence; relapse (of illness, etc.).

會 *Saikai* to meet again.

緣 *Saien* second marriage.

與 *Saikō* restoration.

選 *Saisen* re-election.

舉 *Saikyo* to make another attempt.

T 死 SHI death, idle; useless. *Shi(nuru)* (lit. st. irreg.); *shi(nu)* (coll.) to die. 【歹】

力 *Shiryoku* one's utmost strength.

亡 *Shibō* death.

水 *Shinimizu* the last drink of a person.

生 *Shisei* life and death.

目 *Shinime* the moment of death.

去 *Shikyo* death.

刑 *Shikei* death penalty.

守 *Shishu* desperate defence.

灰 *Shikai* cinders.

因 *Shi-in* cause of death.

地 *Shichi* a fatal position

別 *Shibetsu; shiniwakare* separation by death.

物 *Shibutsu* inanimate (dead) thing.

物狂 *Shinimono-gurui* desperate struggle.

殁 *Shibotsu* death.

活 *Shikatsu* life and death.

苦 *Shiku* great suffering; intense misery.

屍 *Shishi* a dead body.

病 *Shibyō* a fatal disease.

海 *Shikai* Dead Sea.

期 *Shiki   shigo* the mome of death.

罪 *Shizai* capital punishment.

傷 *Shishō* casualties.

骸 *Shigai* a corpse.

藏 *Shizō* let lie idle.

體 *Shitai* a corpse.

靈 *Shiryō* a ghost.

T 血　See 143,0.

为　See 爲 87,8. 【火】

丞　JŌ to help. *(Suke)*

16

（五）T **舟** See 137,0.

六 **巫** FU. *Miko* female fortune teller ; witch. 〔工〕

山戲 *Fuza(keru)* to romp.

亜 See **亞** 1,7. 〔二〕

T **豆** See 151,0.

吾 See 30,4.

吞 See 30,4.

T **否** See 30,4.

酉 See 164,0.

夃 See **所** 63,4.

豕 See 152,0.

艮 See T **良** 138,1.

更 T KŌ. *Fu(keru)* to grow late: *arata(meru)*; *ka(h)eru)* to reform; change: *kawa(ru)* to be changed: *sara ni* again. 〔曰〕

々 *Sarasara* the least; not at all.

迭 *Kōtetsu* change (as in official posts).

紗 *Sarasa* printed cotton.

新 *Koshin* to renovate; restore.

（六〇）

坐 See 32,4.

里 T See 166,0.

* **亞** A. *Tsu(gu)* to follow: *tsugi* next. 〔二〕 七

丁 *Aden* Aden.

弗利加 *Afurika* Africa.

米利加 *Amerika* America; U.S.A.

拉比亞 *Arabiya* Arabia.

非利加 *Afurika* Africa.

剌比亞 *Arabiya* Arabia.

流 *Aryū* bad second.

細亞 *Ajiya* Asia.

富汗斯坦 *Afuganisutan* Afghanistan.

聖 *Asei* minor sage.

鉛 *Aen* zinc.

爾然丁 *Aruzenchin* Argentine.

盂 See 108,3.

T **画** See **畫** 129,6. 〔田〕

函 See 17,6.

T **肩** See 63,4. 〔肉〕

T **雨** See 173,0.

兩 RYŌ. *Futatsu* two; both: (unit of Japanese old money; same as yen): *teru* a tael (unit of Chinese money.) 〔入〕 →1,5T

（七） 兩
三 *Ryōsan* two or three; a few.
方 *Ryōhō* both.
天秤 *Ryōtembin* alternatives.
立 *Ryōritsu* standing together; compatible with.
全 *Ryōzen* mutually advantageous.
面 *Ryōmen* both faces or surfaces.
陛下 *Ryōheika* Their Majesties.
院 *Ryōin* both Houses (of the Diet).
極 *Ryōkyoku* the two poles.
替 *Ryōgae* exchange (money).
雄 *Ryōyū* two rival great men.
輪 *Ryōrin* two wheels.
樣 *Ryōyō* two ways.
親 *Ryōshin* both parents; father and mother.
斷 *Ryōdan* cut into two.

忝 See 61,4.

些 SA. *Isasaka*; *sukoshi* a little; a trifle. 【二】
少 *Sashō* slight.
事 *Saji* trivial matter.
細 *Sasai* a trifle.

坐 See 坐 32,4.

歪 See 77,5. 八

盃 See [T]杯 75,4.

[T]面 See 176,0.

頁 See 181,0.

[T]昼 See 晝 129,5.

拳 See 擧 134,11.
*

晉 SHIN. *Susu(mu)* to advance; increase. 【日】 九
→72, 6

晋 See preceding.

哥 See 30,7.

[T]夏 See 35,7.

[T]蚕 See 蠶 142,18.

[T]師 SHI teacher; an expert; army. (*Moro*). 【巾】
匠 *Shishō* a teacher.
弟 *Shitei* a teacher and pupil.
走 *Shiwasu* the last month of the year.
事 *Shiji* to become a pupil.
表 *Shihyō* model; one who is looked up to.
恩 *Shion* kindness or favours received from a teacher
團 *Shidan* a division (military).

 * T為 →87, 8

（九〇）範 *Shihan* an instructor

範學校 *Shihan-gakkō* normal school.

十 焉 See 86,7.

十一 雁 See 63,8. 【隹】

喬 See 30,9.

颪 See 182,3.

T 惡 See 61,8.

十三 爾 JI. *Nanji* you; *shikari* thus; just so l *nomi* only. 【爻】

來 *Jirai* since then.

後 *Jigo* thenceforth.

廉 See 麗 198,8
    T

十四 T 憂 See 35,12. 【心】

十五 麗 See 麗 198,8
     T

十七 斃 See 66,14.

十八 璽 See 96,14.

二四 蠻 See 173,17.

亅

卜 See 25,0. 一

川 SEN. *Kawa* river. 〔巛〕
T

上 *Kawakami* upper part of river.

下 *Kawashimo* lower part of river.

向 *Kawamukō* across the river.

柳 *Senryū* a witty epigrammatic poem.

筋 *Kawasuji* course of a river.

端 *Kawabata* riverside.

巾 See 50,0.

丰 See 24,2. 【亅】

中 CHŪ. *Naka; uchi* in; inside; middle; centre; among; during: *ata(ru)* to hit; strike against. *Chū* as 2nd component sometimes means the whole of (*Tōkyō-jū* in all Tōkyō).

々 *Naka-naka* very; greatly; more than one would expect.

止 *Chūshi* to suspend; stop for the time being.

元 *Chūgen* the middle day of the feast of lanterns, 15th of the 7th month; sometimes means a present given at that feast.

（三）

中

心 *Chūshin* centre.

立 *Chūritsu* neutrality.

古 *Chūko* the middle ages: *chūburu* second-hand.

外 *Chūgai* Japan and foreign countries; at home and abroad.

央 *Chūō* middle; centre.

央線 *Chūōsen* railway between Tōkyō and Nagoya via centre of Japan.

世 *Chūsei* the middle ages.

年 *Chūnen* the middle stage of life.

旬 *Chūjun* the second or middle ten days of a month.

肉 *Chūniku* medium build.

佐 *Chūsa* commander (navy); lieutenant-colonel (army).

折 *Naka-ore* a soft felt hat.

形 *Chūgata* a medium size.

空 *Chūkū* the air; hollow.

味 *Nakami* contents.

毒 *Chūdoku* poisoning.

風 *Chūfū* paralysis.

流 *Chūryū* mid-stream; middle class (people).

國 *Chūgoku* name given to certain provinces in the western part of the main island, not the centre of Japan; the Middle Republic (China).

華民國 *Chūka-minkoku* Republic of China.

尉 *Chūi* lieutenant (army); sub-lieutenant (navy).

将 *Chūjō* lieutenant-general (army); vice-admiral (navy).

庸 *Chūyō* the mean; moderation.

途 *Chūto* mid-way; on the way.

途半端 *Chūto-hampa* half-way.

堅 *Chūken* the main body.

略 *Chūryaku* omitted.

等 *Chūtō* middle-rank, medium quality; second class.

間 *Chūkan* the middle; between.

絶 *Chūzetsu* to stop; interrupt; break off.

隊 *Chūtai* a company (military).

葉 *Chūyō* middle ages.

傷 *Chūshō* defamation; slander.

腹 *Chūfuku* half-way up (a hill).

樞 *Chūsū* the centre; the pivot.

興 *Chūkō* restoration.

禪寺 *Chūzenji* p. n.

斷 *Chūdan* interruption.

井 T SEI; SHŌ. *1; ido* a well: *igeta* frame of well. 【二】

上 *Inoue* p. n.

戸 *Ido* a well.

然 *Seizen* an orderly manner.

蛙 *Seia* a frog in a well; a person with narrow views.

（三）

20

四 乍 See 4,4.

T 甲 See 72,1. 【田】

T 申 See 72,1. 【田】

丼 SEI. *Domburi* bowl. 【丶】

五 T 州 SHŪ; SU. *Shima* country; province. 【巛】

T 年 See 24,4. 【干】

六 串 KAN. *Kushi* skewer: *sa(su)* to string together.

刺 *Kushizashi* thrust a spit through.

戯 *Jōdan* a joke.

八 T 飛 See 183,0.

三 肅 See 24,11. 【聿】

三 丶

四 ノ

一 乃 DAI; NAI. *Sunawachi* namely; that is to say: *nanji* you; thou.

* T 旧 →140,14

21

(一)

木 *Nogi* p. n.

公 *Daikō* I.

至 *Naishi* from.........to.

〆 *Shime* amount; total; sign used on the flap of envelopes: *shi(meru)* to sum up. Not a real character. Do not confound with kata-kana *me* メ.

ケ This is the katakana *ke* but between two *kan-ji* it is often read *ka, ko* or *ga*. Read *ka* or *ko* after numeral; *ga* in proper names.

T 久 KYŪ; KU. *Shibaraku* a long time: *hisashii* long (of time); lasting.

々 *Hisabisa* after a long time.

振 *Hisashiburi* after a long time.

遠 *Kuon; kyūen,* long lapse of time.

濶 *Kyūkatsu* long separation.

々 Sign of repetition of Chinese character.

T 千 SEN. *Chi* thousand. 【十】

木 *Chigi* cross beams on the roof of a Shintō shrine.

代八千代 *Chiyo yachiyo* for ever.

古 *Senko* all ages; eternity.

里眼 *Senrigan* clairvoyance.

秋樂 *Senshūraku* a close; an end (used especially of theatrical performances).

（二）

千

差萬別 *Sensa-bambetsu* infinite variety.

島 *Chishima* the Kuril Islands.

鳥足 *Chidori-ashi* reeling; tottering.

萬 *Semban* exceedingly; very much : *semman* ten millions.

葉 *Chiba* p. n.

載 *Senzai* a thousand years.

種萬樣 *Senshu-ban-yō* numberless; infinite variety.

慮の一失 *Senryo no isshitsu* an oversight of a wise man.

篇一律 *Sempen-ichiritsu* monotony.

變萬化 *Sempem-banka* innumerable changes.

三
及 See 29,2.

壬 JIN ; NIN. *Mizunoe* 9th calendar sign. See Introduction 42, 43. (*Mi*) ; (*Tō*). 【士】 Do not confound with 王 96,0.

ᵀ 戶 63,0.

夭 YŌ. *Wakai* young : *wakajini* an early death. 【大】 Do not confound with 天 1,3.

死 *Yōshi* early death.

折 *Yōsetsu* early death.

ᵀ 毛 See 82,0.

（三）

之 See 8,2. 【ノ】

乍 SA ; SAKU. *Nagara* (inverted order) while : *tachimachi* (*ni*) alternate; suddenly.

不及 *Oyobazu-nagara* within the limits of my ability.

少々 *Shōshō-nagara* although little (or few).

他事 *Taji-nagara* by the way; although it is none of your concern.

失禮 *Shitsurei-nagara* although it is rude.

延引 *En-in-nagara* though rather late.

併 *Shikashi-nagara* but.

恐 *Osore-nagara* with fear and trembling; I am sorry to trouble you but:

然 *Sarinagara; shikashi-nagara* but.

憚 *Habakari-nagara* though I fear that; although it may be rude.

乎 KO. *Ka; ya* an interrogative particle; *a* particle indicating rhetorical question.

禾 See 115,0.

ᵀ 乏 BŌ. *Toboshii* deficient.

為 See 爲 87,8. 【火】

ᵀ 年 See 24,4. 【干】

四

五

22

五^T舌 See 135,0.

六 呑 See 30,4.

采 See 165,0.

兎 To. *Usagi* a rabbit; hare. 【儿】 Do not confound with 兔 10,5.

に角 *Tonikaku* at all events.

角 *Tokaku* apt to.

^T系 KEI system; line; lineage; to connect; to continue. 【糸】

統 *Keitō* genealogy; lineage.

圖 *Keizu* lineage; genealogical tree.

七 垂 SUI. *Ta(reru)* to drop down; hang down: *nannan to suru* about to. 【土】 →1,9

直 *Suichoku* vertical.

直線 *Suichokusen* perpendicular.

涎 *Suisen; suien* make one's mouth water.

敎 *Suikyō* teaching and instruction.

線 *Suisen* perpendicular.

秉 HEI to take. 【禾】

公 *Heikō* impartiality.

忝 See 61,4.

虱 See 142,2. 七

重 JŪ; CHŌ. *Omoi* heavy: 八 *kasa(neru)* to pile one on another; double: *kasanete* again; repeatedly: *omo na* important; chief: *omonjiru* (irreg.) to esteem highly: *e* (a suffix) -fold; times repeated; rank; row. (*Shige*). 【里】

々 *Jūjū; kasanegasane* exceedingly; repeatedly.

大 *Jūdai* important.

心 *Jūshin* centre of gravity.

用 *Jūyō* appoint one to a position of trust.

任 *Jūnin* important task; reappointment.

臣 *Jūshin* chief retainer.

油 *Jūyu* crude petroleum.

役 *Jūyaku* director (of a company).

厚 *Jūkō* gentle and composed.

要 *Jūyō* important.

病 *Jūbyō* serious illness.

患 *Jūkan* serious illness.

荷 *Omoni* heavy burden.

圍 *Jūi* a siege.

陽 *Chōyō* 9th of September (of lunar calendar).

量 *Jūryō* weight.

傷 *Jūshō* serious wound.

罪 *Jūzai* serious crime.

複 *Chōfuku* repetition.

（八）

重

態 *Jūtai* serious condition (of a patient).

箱 *Jūbako* nest of boxes (gen. lacquer) fitting one upon another.

鎮 *Jūchin* leader; authority.

寶 *Chōhō* serviceable; convenient.

T 看 See 109,4.

T 乘 See 乘 4,9.

────────

九 垂 See T 垂 4,7. 【土】

乘 *Jō* to multiply. *No(ru)* to ride; get upon. →1,8 T

上 *Nori-a(geru)* to strand.

出 *Norida(su)* to start; set sail.

合舟 *Noriaibune* public boat.

合馬車 *Noriaibasha* omnibus.

客 *Jōkaku; jōkyaku* passenger.

降 *Jōkō; noriori* getting in and out.

氣 *Noriki* an inclination to act; have a zeal for.

員 *Jōin* crew.

除 *Jōjo* multiplication and division.

組 *Noriku(mu)* to get on board a ship; be a fellow passenger: *norikumi* crew.

船 *Jōsen* to embark.

────────

換 *Norika(h)eru)* to change (as trains): *norikae* transfer ticket.

T 蚕 See 蠶 142,18.

喬 See 30,9.

二

五

乙

T 乙 *Otsu* (in enumeration or classification) "Second" "B". *Kinoto* 2nd calendar sign. See Introduction 42, 43. (*Oto*)

女 *Otome* girl; maiden.

夜の覽 *Itsuya no ran* Imperial perusal.

種 *Otsushu* second class.

────────

九 T 九 *Ku; Kyū*. *Kokonotsu* — nine.

日 *Kokonoka* 9 days; the 9th day of the month.

月 *Ku-gatsu* September: *kokonotsuki* 9 months.

分通 *Kubudōri* almost.

仞の功 *Kyūjin no kō* many efforts.

州 *Kyūshū* p. n.

死に一生 *Kyūshi ni isshō* a narrow escape from death.

重 *Kokonoe* Imperial Palace; Japanese palace.

段 *Kudan* p. n.

24

(一)

九拜 *Kyūhai* to bow many times.

匕 See 21,0.

T 七 See 1,1.

二 T 丸 GAN. *Maru* used after ship's name; used before a verb means completely: *tama* ball: *marui* round: *maru(meru)* to make into ball shape; dupe; delude. 【丶】

々 *Marumaru* round; plump.

木 *Maruki* log.

太 *Maruta* log.

呑 *Marunomi* swallow whole.

藥 *Gan-yaku* pill.

燒 *Maruyake* total destruction by fire.

乞 KOTSU; KITSU. *Ko(u)*; to beg; request.

食 *Kojiki* a beggar.

T 己 See 49,0.

也 YA. *Nari* is; a verbal form used to complete a declaration.

三 巴 See 49,1.

T 毛 See 82,0.

屯 TON. *Tamuro* an encampment; barracks. 【屮】

在 *Tonzai* to be stationed; stay.

(三)

營 *Ton-ei* a guard-house; barracks.

T 色 See 139,0.

T 乳 NYŪ. *Chichi; chi* milk; breasts.

兄弟 *Chikyōdai* a foster-brother or sister.

母 *Uba* a wet-nurse.

呑兒 *Chinomigo* suckling.

兒 *Nyūji* infant.

房 *Chibusa* nipple.

狀 *Nyūjō* milky.

臭 *Nyūshū* half-fledged.

胤 IN lineage; to succeed. *Tane* seed. 【肉】

嗣 *Inshi* an heir; successor.

T 乾 See 24,9. 【乙】

亂 RAN; RON confusion. *Mida(reru)* to be thrown into confusion; be in disorder. →135,1T

入 *Rannyū* (of a crowd or a body of people) to enter in a disorderly manner.

心 *Ranshin* insanity.

打 *Randa* to beat or strike at random.

用 *Ran-yō* irregular use; abuse; misuse.

世 *Ransei* disturbed times; a period of civil war.

（二一）

亂

臣 *Ranshin* treacherous subject.

行 *Rangyō* turbulent or violent conduct; riotous behaviour.

足 *Midareashi* breaking step.

軍 *R a n g u n* an army in confusion.

脈 *Rammyaku* confusion; disorder.

逆 *R a n g y a k u* rebellion; treason.

麻 *Ramma* disturbed state of a country.

筆 *Rampitsu* slovenly penmanship; careless writing.

發 *Rampatsu* random shots; irregular volley.

醉 *Ransui* to be very intoxicated.

暴 *Rambō* turbulence; violent conduct.

雜 *Ranzatsu* disorder; confusion.

黽 See 205,0.

一五 **龜** See 213,0.

六

亅

一T **了** RYŌ. *Owa(ru)* ; *shima(u)* to finish; complete; to understand; clear.

見 *Ryōken* idea; intention.

承 *Ryōshō* take note of.

知 *Ryōchi* understand.

解 *Ryōkai* understanding.

簡 *Ryōken* idea; thought; intention; will.

二 **才** SAI talent; ability; wit; years of age. 【手】

力 *Sairyoku* talent; ability.

子 *Saishi* a man of talent.

色 *Saishoku* wit and beauty.

物 *Saibutsu* a clever man.

氣 *Saiki* talent; genius.

能 *Sainō* ability; talent.

智 *Saichi* sagacity.

媛 *Saien* an able woman; a sagacious girl.

筆 *Saihitsu* a clever style.

幹 *Saikan* ability.

器 *Saiki* ability; a man of talent.

學 *Saigaku* ability and learning.

藝 *Saigei* talents.

覺 *Saikaku* plan; scheme.

三 **才** See T 等 118,6.

T **予** ① YO. *Ware* I; one's self; *ata(h)eru* to give.
② →152,9 　　*

四 T **矛** See 110,0.

五 爭 See 爭 87,4.
T

六 求 Kyū. *Moto(meru)* to re-
T quest; seek; ask; ask
for; get. 【水】

刑 *Kyūkei* prosecution.

婚 *Kyūkon* wooing; courtship.

職 *Kyūshoku* seeking for employment.

七 事 JI. *Koto* thing; deed; is
T often used in the epistolary
style after the subject of a
sentence, it is then practically equivalent to *ga* or
wa and need not be translated: *tsuka(h)eru* to
serve; obey.

切 *Kotoki(reru)* to end; die.

件 *Jiken* an event; incident;
an affair.

足 *Kotota(ru)* to answer the
purpose; be enough.

物 *Jibutsu* things; affairs.

前 *Jizen* antecedent.

故 *Jiko* an incident; a hitch.

後承諾 *Jigoshōdaku* ex post
facto approval.

柄 *Kotogara* a matter; thing.

務 *Jimu* business; work.

情 *Jijō* state; circumstances.

項 *Jikō* matters; items.

業 *Jigyō* work; deed; enterprise.

實 *Jijitsu* the facts of a case;
circumstances.

態 *Jitai* situation.

績 *Jiseki* fact; deeds; ex-
ploits; achievements

體 *Jitai* situation.

變 *Jihen* disaster; emergency;
accident.

T 承 SHŌ. *Uketamawa(ru)* to
hear; acknowledge: *u(keru)*
to receive: *tsu(gu)* to succeed to. 【手】

引 *Shōin* accept; consent.

知 *Shōchi* knowledge; assent;
consent.

服 *Shōfuku* assent.

前 *Shōzen* continued.

認 *Shōnin* reconfirm.

諾 *Shōdaku* consent.

繼 *Shōkei* to succeed as heir.

二   七

T 二 NI; JI. *Futatsu* two.

十日 *Hatsuka* 20 days; the
20th day of the month.

人 *Ni-nin; futari* 2 persons.

子 *Futago* twins.

日 *Futsuka* 2 days; the 2nd
day of the month.

月 *Ni-gatsu* February: *futa-
tsuki* 2 months.

六時中 *Nirokujichū* the
whole day (not night).

白 *Nihaku* postscript.

本棒 *Nihombō* hen-pecked.

二

百十日 *Nihyakutōka* 210th day according to old calendar.

次會 *Nijikai* an after-feast.

言 *Nigon* duplicity.

伸 *Nishin* postscript.

束三文 *Nisoku-sammon* dirt cheap.

枚舌 *Nimai-jita* a double-tongue.

重 *Nijū ; futae* duplication.

重橋 *Nijūbashi* the bridge leading to the Imperial Palace in Tōkyō.

流 *Niryū* of the second order.

進も三進も *Nitchi mo satchi mo* dead-lock.

階 *Nikai* the storey above ground floor.

舞 *Ni no mai* repetition of folly.

豎 *Niju* disease.

八

亠

Always at the top: it is called *keisan-kammuri* or jocularly *nabe-buta*.

T 亡 Bō; Mō to run away; abscond. *Naki* deceased; dead: *horobo(su)* to ruin: *horo(biru)* to be destroyed: *ushina(u)* to lose.

友 *Bōyū* deceased friend.

失 *Bōshitsu* lost.

羊 *Bōyō* being perplexed.

狀 *Bōjō* rudeness.

命 *Bōmei* to run away; abscond; desert.

者 *Mōja* the dead.

絕 *Bōzetsu* to become extinct.

魂 *Bōkon* a spirit; ghost.

靈 *Bōrei* an apparition.

T 方 See 70,0.

T 文 See 67,0.

之 SHI. *Kore ; kono* this: *no* of : *yu(ku)* to go. (*Yuki*). In letter writing used in inverted order with or without the meaning of *kore , kono* : thus 依之 *kore ni yori* by this 有之 *koreari* is 無之 *korenaku* not. 〖ノ〗

T 元 GEN old name for Mongolia: GAN. *Moto ; hajime* origin ; head ; beginning ; in former times. 〖儿〗

山 *Genzan* Yuensan (Korea).

日 *Ganjitsu* New Year's Day.

手 *Motode* capital (money).

旦 *Gantan* New Year's Day.

老 *Genrō* an elder statesman.

老院 *Gen-rōin* senate.

利 *Ganri* principal and interest.

金 *Gankin ; motokin* principal (money).

來 *Ganrai* from the first.

(二) 元

首 *Genshu* a sovereign.

帥 *Gensui* Field- (or Fleet-) marshal.

祖 *Ganso* progenitor; founder; originator.

氣 *Genki* spirits; vitality; natural strength.

值 *Motone* cost price.

帳 *Motochō* ledger.

祿 *Genroku* era name, 1688-1704.

價 *Genka* cost price.

勳 *Genkun* veteran statesman.

尢 KŌ nervous; strong. *Takabu(ru); aga(ru)* to be proud; rise.

進 *Kōshin* be excited.

T 六 ROKU. *Mutsu; muttsu* six. 【八】

日 *Muika* 6 days; the 6th day of the month.

月 *Roku-gatsu* June: *mutsuki* 6 months.

法 *Roppō* six laws.

云 UN. *I(u); iwa(ku)* to say; speak. 【二】

々 *Unnun* so and so; and so forth.

(三) 三 T 主 SHU lord: SU. *Nushi; aruji* master: *omo* principal; chief. (*Kazu*). 【丶】

人 *Shujin; aruji* master; owner.

力 *Shuryoku* main forces.

上 *Shujō* the Emperor; His Majesty.

公 *Shukō* lord; master.

任 *Shunin* the person in charge.

因 *Shuin* the principal cause.

君 *Shukun* lord; master.

治醫 *Shujii* chief physician.

命 *Shumei* the command of one's lord.

府 *Shufu* the capital of a country.

事 *Shuji* manager; secretary.

客 *Shukaku* host and guest.

計 *Shukei* a pay-master.

要 *Shuyō* chief importance.

宰 *Shusai* superintendence.

家 *Shuka* the house of one's master.

格 *Shukaku* subject (of a sentence); nominative case.

席 *Shuseki* head seat.

產地 *Shusanchi* chief centre of production.

婦 *Shufu* the mistress of a house; hostess.

張 *Shuchō* insistence; claim; advocacy.

眼 *Shugan* the aim; main point.

從 *Shūjū* master and servant.

動者 *Shudōsha* prime mover.

唱 *Shushō* promote; advocate.

務 *Shumu* competent.

（三）

主

筆　*Shuhitsu* the editor of a newspaper or magazine.

腦　*Shunō* the brain (of an enterprise); the leader.

幹　*Shukan* a superintendent.

義　*Shugi* principle;—ism (e.g. *gunkoku-shugi* militarism).

催　*Shusai* under the auspices of.

意　*Shui* principal purpose; main object.

僕　*Shuboku* master and servant.

賓　*Shuhin* the guest of honour.

謀　*Shubō* chief leader; ringleader.

題　*Shudai* the main subject.

權　*Shuken* sovereignty.

觀　*Shukan* the subject; subjective.

T **立**　See 117,0.

T **市**　S H I city; town. *Ichi* market. 【巾】

井　*Shisei* streets; town.

中　*Shichū* city; streets.

內　*Shinai* in the city.

外　*Shigai* the suburbs.

民　*Shimin* citizen; townspeople.

立　*Shiritsu* municipal establishment.

役所　*Shiyakusho* municipal office.

長　*Shichō* mayor (of town).

況　*Shikyō* the condition of a market.

政　*Shisei* municipal government.

俄古　*Shikago* Chicago.

設　*Shisetsu* municipal establishment.

區　*Shiku* municipal district.

街　*Shigai* town; city; street.

場　*Shijō;* *ichiba* market place.

價　*Shika* market price.

營　*Shiei* municipal management.

T **示**　See 113,0.

T **玄**　See 95,0.

T **衣**　See 145,0.　　　四

交　Kō season. *Majiwa(ru)* to associate with: *maji(ru)* to mix: *komogomo* alternately; mutually: *kawa(ru)* to change. T

々　*Komogomo* mutually.

叉　*Kōsa* crossing each other.

友　*Kōyū* friends; companions.

互　*Kōgo* reciprocity.

付　*Kōfu* to hand over; deliver.

代　*Kōtai* alternation.

易　*Kōeki* commerce; trade.

涉　*Kōshō* negotiation.

（三）

（四）

交

情 *Kōjō* friendship.

通 *Kotsū* communication.

通機關 *Kotsūkikan* (a means of) communication.

換 *Kōkan* exchange; barter.

替 *Kōtai* take turns; alternation.

番 *Kōban* police box.

遊 *Kōyū* companionship; friend.

際 *Kōsai* social intercourse.

誼 *Kōgi* friendship; friendly relations.

戰 *Kōsen* hostilities; war.

戰國 *Kōsenkoku* belligerent power.

驩 *Kōkan* exchange of courtesies.

T **充** JŪ. *A(teru)* to apply (as money to a certain end): *mi(teru)*; *mi(chiru)* (coll.); *mita(su)* to fill; complete. 【儿】

分 *Jūbun* enough; sufficient.

全 *Jūzen* to be complete; be perfect in all its arrangements.

血 *Jūketsu* congestion (blood).

足 *Jūsoku* sufficient.

當 *Jūtō* apply (a sum) to.

塡 *Jūten* filling up.

滿 *Jūman* fulness; abundance.

實 *Jūjitsu* fulness.

（四）

亥 GAI; KAI. *I; inoshishi* the hog; the 12th zodiacal sign. See Introduction 42, 43.

亦 *Mata* also; again; moreover.

妄 MŌ; BŌ. *Midari* improper; disorderly; deceit. 【女】

言 *Bōgen* idle talk.

念 *Bōnen; mōnen* bad thoughts.

信 *Bōshin; mōshin* credulity.

評 *Bōhyō; mōhyō* gratuitous criticism.

想 *Mōsō; mōzō* bad thoughts, fancies.

說 *Bōsetsu; mōsetsu* falsehood.

論 *Bōron* silly argument.

五

T **言** See 149,0.

T **忘** BŌ; MŌ. *Wasu(reru)* ·to forget; neglect. 【心】

却 *Bōkyaku* forgetfulness.

形見 *Wasuregatami* keepsake.

物 *Wasuremono* a thing left behind.

恩 *Bō-on* ungrateful.

六

T **盲** MŌ. *Mekura; meshii* a blind person; dark; ignorant; blind. 【目】

人 *Mōjin* a blind person.

目 *Mōmoku; mekura* a blind person.

判 *Mekuraban* stamping a seal blindly.

（六〇）

盲昧 *Mōmai* unlettered; ignorant.

從 *Mōjū* blind obedience.

進 *Mōshin* to rush on recklessly.

滅法 *Mekura-meppō* blindly; at random.

T 卒 SOTSU a private (soldier): SHUTSU to die. *O(h)eru); owa(ru)* to finish; complete: *niwaka* sudden.【十】→24, 2

中 *Sotchū* apoplexy.

去 *Sokkyo* to die.

先 *Sossen* to take the lead; be a pioneer.

忽 *Sokkotsu* sudden.

倒 *Sottō* swoon.

然 *Sotsuzen* suddenly.

塔婆 *Sotoba* a long tablet planted near a grave.

業 *Sotsugyō* completing a course of study; graduation.

爾 *Sotsuji* abruptly.

T 享 KYŌ. *U(keru)* to receive.

有 *Kyōyū* to possess; enjoy.

受 *Kyōju* to receive; accept.

樂 *Kyōraku* enjoyment.

T 育 IKU. *Soda(teru); haguku(mu)* to bring up; nourish; educate.【肉】

英 *Ikuei* education.

兒 *Ikuji* bringing up of a child.

兒院 *Ikujiin* orphanage.

T 夜 YA. *Yoru; yo* night.【夕】（六〇）

叉 *Yasha* a demon.

中 *Yachū* during the night: *yonaka* the middle of the night: *yojū* all night.

分 *Yabun* night; evening.

目 *Yome* seeing at night, in the dark.

半 *Yahan; yowa* midnight.

行 *Yakō* going by night; night train.

更 *Yofuke* late hours: *yofukashi* keeping late hours.

明 *Yoake* dawn.

來 *Yarai* throughout the whole night.

長 *Yo-naga* a long night; the long hours of the night.

具 *Yagu* bedding; bedclothes.

店 *Yomise* night-fair; night stall.

逃 *Yonige* running away under cover of night.

通 *Yodōshi* all night.

陰 *Yain* under cover of night.

間 *Yakan* at night.

業 *Yagyō* night-work.

會 *Yakai* evening party.

學 *Yagaku* evening school; learning at night.

T 京 KYŌ; KEI used as abbreviation for Tōkyō, Kyōto, Peking and Keijō: capital; city. →8, 7

32

（六）京

阪 *Keihan* Kyōto-Ōsaka.

奉線 *Keihōsen* railway from Peking to Mukden.

神 *Keishin* Kyōto-Kōbe.

城 *Keijō* Seoul (Korea).

家 *Kyōke* native of Kyōto.

都 *Kyōto* p. n.

童 *Kyōwarabe* townsfolk.

*1 濱 *Keihin* Tōkyō-Yokohama.

七 T 亭 TEI. *Chin* an arbor.

々 *Teitei* towering; lofty.

主 *Teishu* husband; master.

帝 See 50,6.

彦 See foll.

彦 GEN. *Hiko* a man. 【彡】

奕 See 37,6.

表 See 145,3.

T 哀 AI. *Aware* sadness: *kanashi(mu)* to grieve. 【口】

別 *Aibetsu* sorrow of parting; sorrowful parting.

悼 *Aitō* condolence; grief; sorrow.

惜 *Aiseki* regret.

訴 *Aiso* complaint; petition.

愍 *Aibin* pity; sympathy.

（七）

憐 *Airen* pity; sympathy.

歎 *Aitan* to grieve; display sorrow.

慕 *Aibo* yearning for.

願 *Aigan* petition.

T 変 See 變 35,19. 【言】

亮 RYŌ. *Akiraka* clear; distinct; true. (*Suke*); (*Aki*).

*2 京 See ⌈ 京 8,6.

畝 BŌ; HO. *Se* measure of 八 surface, (see Introduction 44): ridge between furrows: ridge or path between fields. 【田】
→28,7

T 畜 See 102,5.

T 高 See 189,0.

旁 See 70,6.

T 衰 SUI. *Otoro(h)eru* to decline; degenerate. 【衣】

亡 *Suibō* ruin; destruction.

弱 *Suijaku* exhaustion.

退 *Suitai* decline; decay.

微 *Suibi* decline; decadence.

運 *Sui-un* declining fortune.

勢 *Suisei* declining fortune.

頽 *Suitai* decline; retrogression.

T 衷 See 145,4.

T 恋 See 戀 61,19.

---

*1 T 表 →145,3　　33　　*2 T 衷 →8,8 T : 145,4 T

九 孰 JUKU. *Izure* what; which.
【子】

T 産 See foll.

産 SAN property. *U(mu)* to give birth; produce; lay (an egg). 【生】

出 *Sanshutsu* production.

地 *Sanchi* place where a particular article is produced.

卵 *Sanran* to lay eggs; to spawn.

物 *Sambutsu* products; productions.

後 *Sango* after confinement.

科 *Sanka* obstetrics.

婆 *Samba* a midwife.

業 *Sangyō* industry; agriculture.

蓐 *Sanjoku* child-bed.

褥 *Sanjoku* child-bed.

聲 *Ubugoe* first cry of a new-born baby.

額 *Sangaku* amount produced.

率 SOTSU; RITSU rate. *Hikii-(-ru)* to lead; control. 【玄】

先 *Sossen* to take the lead; be the first.

→率 T

直 *Sotchoku* plainness.

然 *Sotsuzen* suddenly.

爾 *Sotsuji* abrupt; sudden.

牽 KEN. *Hi(ku)* to pull. 【牛】

引 *Ken-in* pull; traction; draught.

牛花 *Kengyūka;* *asagao* morning glory.

制 *Kensei* to check; restrain.

强附會 *Kenkyō-fukai* far-fetched.

商 SHŌ. *Akinai* commerce: *akina(u)* to trade. (*Aki*).
【口】 →商 T

人 *Shōnin;* *akindo;* *akiudo* merchant.

工業 *Shōkōgyō* industry and commerce.

用 *Shōyō* commercial matters; business.

店 *Shōten* a shop.

法 *Shōhō* commercial law; trade.

況 *Shōkyō* condition of trade.

品 *Shōhin* commodity; goods; merchandise.

略 *Shōryaku* commercial policy.

船 *Shōsen* merchant ship.

量 *Shōryō* consideration.

港 *Shōkō* commercial port.

會 *Shōkai* company; firm.

業 *Shōgyō* trade; commerce.

號 *Shōgō* trade name.

廛 *Shōten* a shop.

賣 *Shōbai* trade; commerce; business.

標 *Shōhyō* a trade-mark.

機 *Shōki* season for business.

戰 *Shōsen* trade war.

館 *Shōkan* a mercantile company; firm.

34

（九）

商
議 *Shōgi* negotiation; consultation.
權 *Shōken* commercial supremacy.

袞 KON. Imperial clothes. 【衣】
龍 *Konryō; Konryū* Emperor.

毫 GŌ fine hairs. *Sukoshi* a little. 【毛】
毛 *Gōmō* trifling; very slight.
末 *Gōmatsu* the least particle.
釐 *Gōri* very slight.

烹 HŌ. *Ni(-ru)* to cook; boil. 【火】

一〇 **啻** See 30,9.

T **棄** KI. *Su(teru)* to throw away; abandon. 【木】
去 *Kikyo; sutesa(ru)* to abandon; throw away.
却 *Kikyaku* rejection; dismissal.
兒 *Sutego; kiji* abandoned child.
捨 *Kisha* voluntary contribution; alms.
業 *Kigyō* to retire from business.
擲 *Kiteki* to surrender; renounce; abdicate.
權 *Kiken* renunciation of right.

T **蠻** See 蠻 142,19.

雍 YŌ. *Yawara(gu)* to be harmonious. 【隹】　一

稟 RIN; HIN. *U(keru)* to receive; to speak (polite in 1st person). 【禾】
告 *Rinkoku* notification.
性 *Rinsei* character; nature.
質 *Hinshitsu* nature; temperament.

T **裏** RI. *Ura* the back; lining; inside. 【衣】
手 *Urate* the back.
切 *Uragi(ru)* to betray.
地 *Uraji* lining.
返 *Uragaeshi* turning inside out.
店 *Uradana* house in an alley.
面 *Rimen* the back.
海 *Rikai* Caspian Sea.
書 *Uragaki* endorsement.
道 *Uramichi* back-road.

稟 See 稟 8,11. 【禾】

膏 KŌ to grow fleshy; to enrich. *Abura* grease; fat; ointment. 【肉】　一　二
血 *Kōketsu* fruit of hard labour.
肓 *Kōkō* marrow.
藥 *Kōyaku* a plaster; an ointment.

T **豪** GŌ great; powerful; to excel. 【豕】

35

（一一）

豪

壮 *Gōsō* splendour ; pomp.

放 *Gōhō* open-hearted ; Bohemian.

雨 *Gōu* heavy rain.

宕 *Gōtō* magnanimity.

勇 *Gōyū* valour ; bravery.

俠 *Gōkyō* a chivalrous person ; a gallant fellow.

家 *Gōka* wealthy family.

商 *Gōshō* a wealthy merchant.

飲 *Gōin* excessive drinking.

奢 *Gōsha* luxurious; prodigality; extravagance.

傑 *Gōketsu* a hero.

強 *Gōkyō* strong ; powerful.

農 *Gōnō* a rich farmer.

遊 *Gōyū* to spend much money in pleasures ; indulge in expensive amusements.

邁 *Gōmai* undauntedness.

膽 *Gōtan* courageous ; valiant.

一三

褒 HŌ. *Ho(meru)* to praise. 【衣】

状 *Hōjō* certificate of merit.

美 *Hōbi* reward ; a prize.

章 *Hōshō* medal for merit.

貶 *Hōhen* praise and censure.

賞 *Hōshō* prize.

一四

雍 YŌ. *Fusa(gu)* to shut up : *heda(teru)* to shut out ; separate. 【土】

閉 *Yōhei* to suppress ; hush up.

断 *Yōdan* to block up.

（一四）

一五

襄 (JŌ). 【衣】

褻 SETSU. *Kega(reru)* to be defiled. 【衣】

一六

甕 Ō ; YŌ. *Kame* a jar : *tsurube* well-bucket. 【瓦】

一七

羸 RUI to be emaciated. 【羊】

弱 *Ruijaku* weak.

瘦 *Ruisō* to become emaciated ; grow thin.

一八

贏 EI to gain ; superfluity. *Ka(tsu)* to conquer. 【貝】

利 EIRI profit ; gain.

二一

囊 See 145,18. 【口】

九

人

When at the left it takes the modified form 亻 and is then called *nim-ben*.

丅人 JIN ; NIN. *Hito*; *te* (2nd component) man ; person ; people. Do not confound with 入 11,0 nor with 八 12,0.

人

々 *Hito-bito ; nin-nin* everybody ; people.

力 *Jinryoku* human ability : *jinriki* abbreviation of *jinrikisha.*

力車 *Jinrikisha.*

工 *Jinkō* artificial.

工呼吸 *Jinkō-kokyū* artificial respiration.

山 *Hitoyama* a crowd of people.

口 *Jinkō* population.

才 *Jinsai* man of talent.

手 *Hitode* help of another person.

夫 *Nimpu ; nimbu* a coolie.

文 *Jimbun* civilization.

心 *Jinshin* public spirit.

心地 *Hitogokochi* consciousness.

生 *Jinsei* human life.

目 *Hitome* the eyes of the public.

民 *Jimmin* the mass of the people ; populace ; subjects.

世 *Jinsei* this world.

臣 *Jinshin* a subject ; retainer.

込 *Hitogomi* a crowd.

形 *Ningyō* a doll.

足 *Ninsoku* a coolie : *hito-ashi* traffic.

材 *Jinsai* man of talent.

身攻擊 *Jinshinkōgeki* personal attack.

並 *Hitonami* the generality of men.

非人 *Nimpinin* an inhuman fellow.

事 *Jinji* personal affairs : *hitogoto* other people's affairs.

事不省 *Jinji-fusei* stupor ; syncope.

物 *Jimbutsu* person ; a man of character ; personal qualities.

性 *Jinsei* human nature.

品 *Jimpin* personal character ; appearance.

相 *Ninsō* physiognomy.

面獸心 *Nimmen-jūshin* inhumanity.

柄 *Hitogara* personal character.

後 *Jingo* behind the others.

格 *Jinkaku* personality.

倫 *Jinrin* morality.

氣 *Ninki* popularity.

員 *Jin-in* number of people ; the staff ; personnel.

員點呼 *Jin-in-tenko* roll-call.

畜 *Jinchiku* men and beasts.

家 *Jinka* human dwellings.

殺 *Hitogoroshi* murder.

望 *Jimbō* popularity ; to be trusted.

情 *Ninjō* humanity ; human nature.

參 *Ninjin* carrot.

造 *Jinzō* artificial.

人

間　*Ningen* human being.

間業　*Ningen-waza* deed of human beings (not of the Divinity).

爲　*Jin-i* the work of man (not of nature).

傑　*Jinketsu* great man.

道　*Jindō* humanity ; footway.

種　*Jinshu* race (of man).

影　*Jin-ei : hitokage* man ; usually with negative, then, emphatic, not a single man.

數　*Ninzu ; hitokazu* number of persons.

質　*Hitojichi* hostage.

類　*Jinrui* the human race.

權　*Jinken* personal right.

體　*Jintai* human body.

二
T 久　See 4,2.

二
T 仁　JIN ; NIN benevolence ; compassion ; love. (*Ni*) ; (*Hito*).

人　*Jinjin* benevolent person.

川　*Jinsen* Chemulpo (Korea).

王　*Niō* two mythological (strong) kings.

君　*Jinkun* benevolent sovereign.

政　*Jinsei* benevolent government.

恩　*Jin-on* benevolent aid ; kind favour.

術　*Jinjutsu* benevolent art of healing.

惠　*Jinkei* mercy ; clemency.

愛　*Jin-ai* benevolence ; love.

義　*Jingi* sympathy ; consideration for others.

慈　*Jinji* compassion ; pity.

德　*Jintoku* humane conduct : *Nintoku* p. n.

仆　FU.　*Tao(reru)* to fall down ; lie down.

什　JŪ thing ; utensils ; ten.

麼　*Somo* how.

器　*Jūki* utensils.

寶　*Jūhō* treasure.

仍　JŌ ; SHŌ.　*Yotte* therefore : *yo(ru)* to depend upon : *sunawachi* that is to say : *nao* yet.

T 化　KA ; KE.　*Ba(keru)* to change itself into ; assume the form of ; be transformed ; to change : *baka(su)* to bewitch. 【七】

石　*Kaseki* a fossil ; petrifaction.

合　*Kagō* chemical combination.

身　*Keshin* incarnation.

粧　*Keshō* make-up ; toilet.

學　*Kagaku* chemistry.

膿　*Kanō* suppuration.

(二)

仇 KYŪ.　*Ada ; kataki* enemy.

敵 *Kyūteki* an enemy ; foe.
讎 *Kyūshū* an enemy ; foe.

T **仏** See **佛** 9,5.

今 KON ; KIN this.　*Ima* now ; the present ; more.

一度 *Ima-ichido* once more.
上陛下 *Kinjōheika* the present Emperor.
夕 *Konseki ; kon-yū* this evening.
日 *Kyō ; konnichi* to-day.
月 *Kongetsu* this month.
生 *Konjō* this life.
年 *Kotoshi ; konnen* this year.
更 *Imasara* now ; emphatic, often used to contrast the present with the past.
夜 *Kon-ya* this evening.
昔 *Konjaku* past and present (especially as comparing or contrasting the two).
昔の感 *Konjaku-no-kan* thought of the change between the past and present.
度 *Kondo* this time ; next time.
後 *Kongo* from now on.
時 *Imadoki* nowadays.
時分 *Imajibun* now ; nowadays.
宵 *Koyoi* this evening.
般 *Kompan* now.

週 *Konshū* this week.
朝 *Kesa ; konchō* this morning.
晩 *Komban* this evening.
曉 *Kongyō* early this morning.

T **介** KAI shell-fish ; to get jammed in ; be caught between.　*Tasu(keru)* to assist.　(*Suke*).

在 *Kaizai* to lie between ; stand between.
抱 *Kaihō* nursing.
意 *Kaii* concern ; to trouble about.

T **分** See 12,2.　【刀】
T **欠** See 76,0.
T **火** See 86,0.
T **内** See **內** 11,2.

T **仕** SHI.　*Tsuka(h)eru* to serve (respectfully) : *tsukamatsu-(ru)* to do (epis. st.).

入 *Shi-ire* laying in goods ; stocking.
上 *Shiage* finishing.
方 *Shikata* the way or method of doing something ; expedient ; remedy ; mending.
立 *Shitate* tailoring.
打 *Shiuchi* bearing ; behaviour.
合 *Shiawase* fortune ; luck.

39

（三二）

仕

向 *Shimuke* treatment; conduct towards another.

込 *Shikomi* education; training.

事 *Shigoto* work; task.

事師 *Shigotoshi* a workman; schemer.

返 *Shikaeshi* revenge.

拂 *Shiharai* payment.

度 *Shitaku* preparation.

送 *Shiokuri* sending money for the support of another; supply.

組 *Shikumi* contrivance; design; plan.

掛 *Shikake* contrivance, mechanism; device.

置 *Shioki* punishment.

業 *Shiwaza* act; conduct.

遂 *Shito(geru)* to accomplish; carry out.

舞 *Shimai* end; finish; termination.

樣 *Shiyō* expedient; remedy; method.

仙

SEN hermit. *Sento* cent (money).

人 *Sennin* a hermit; recluse.

骨 *Senkotsu* unworldly person.

鄉 *Senkyō* an enchanting locality.

臺 *Sendai* p. n.

境 *Senkyō* an enchanting locality.

（三三）

仔

SHI detail; to conquer; to endure. *Ko* child.

細 *Shisai* reason; account; details; particulars.

T **付**

FU to hand over; to submit to. *Tsu(ku)* to adhere to: *tsu(keru)* to attach; affix; apply: *tsuki* for; on account of.

與 *Fuyo* to grant.

仞

JIN unit for measuring height or depth (8 Chinese feet).

仗

JŌ a warrior; to depend on. *Tsue* walking-stick.

T **代**

DAI. *Kawari* substitute; in place of; representative: *kawa(ru)* to take the place of: *yo* generations; times: *shiro* price; money.

々 *Daidai*; *yoyo* generation after generation: *kawaru-gawaru* by turns; alternately.

人 *Dai-nin* a representative; deputy.

用 *Daiyō* substitution.

言 *Daigen* pleading for another.

言人 *Daigen-nin* attorney (lawyer).

金 *Daikin* price; cash.

物 *Shiromono* goods; articles; stuff; fellow.

表 *Daihyō* representation.

書 *Daisho* any document written by one person for another person; a person who writes for another.

40

（三）

理 *Dairi* substitute ; deputy ; agency.

理公使 *Dairikōshi* a Chargé d'Affaires.

理領事 *Dairiryōji* an Acting Consul.

参 *Daisan* to pay a visit to a temple or shrine on behalf of another.

筆 *Daihitsu* to write for another person.

診 *Daishin* a doctors assistant.

数 *Daisū* algebra.

價 *Daika* price ; cost.

赭 *Taisha* red ochre.

辨 *Daiben* to act as attorney for a person.

償 *Daishō* indemnification ; compensation.

議士 *Daigishi* a representative (of the people) ; a member of parliament (Diet, etc.).

T 他 TA. *Hoka; yoso* other ; another ; besides.

力 *Tariki* intercession.

人 *Tanin* other people ; another person ; stranger ; person who is not a relation.

日 *Tajitsu* some day ; hereafter.

方 *Tahō* another side.

生 *Tashō* a previous or succeeding state of existence.

（三）

言 *Tagon; tagen* to tell a thing to others; let out a secret.

念 *Tanen* minding about anything else.

所 *Yoso; tasho* another place.

界 *Takai* death.

殺 *Tasatsu* murder.

國 *Takoku* a foreign country ; another province.

意 *Tai* minding about anything else.

聞 *Tabun* publicity; reaching other's ears.

仝 See T 同 13,4. 【口】

T 令 REI; RYŌ law; rule; command. Used before relationship is an honorific.

夫人 *Reifujin* Mrs. (on envelopes, very polite).

名 *Reimei* good reputation.

旨 *Reishi* orders; commands or recommendations of Empress or an Imperial Prince.

狀 *Reijō* warrant (of arrest).

室 *Reishitsu* your wife (honorific).

息 *Reisoku* your (his) son (honorific).

嗣 *Reishi* your (his) heir.

閨 *Reikei* your wife (honorific).

孃 *Reijō* daughter (honorific).

T 以 I. *Motte* has a very vague meaning ; on ; by ; with ; on account of; etc.

(三)
以

上 *Ijō* above; more than.

Note that figures are inclusive, thus 二人以上 is more than one person, i.e. two or more persons.

下 *Ika* below this; less than; including.

内 *Inai* within.

心傳心 *Ishin-denshin* telepathy.

外 *Igai* outside of.

北 *Ihoku* north of.

西 *Isei* west of.

來 *Irai* since.

東 *Itō* east of.

南 *Inan* south of.

降 *Ikō* since; thenceforth.

前 *Izen* before; former.

後 *Igo* after this; after that; after; since.

爲 *Omoeraku* I believe; I think.

────────

四
T 任 NIN duty; responsibility. *Maka(seru)* to leave in charge of; entrust: *ta-(h)eru* to endure: *ata(ru)* to have charge of: *hoshii-mama* wilfulness; selfishness; arbitrariness.

用 *Nin-yō* appointment.

地 *Ninchi* one's post; one's place of duty.

免 *Nimmen* appointment and dismissal.

命 *Nimmei* appointment; designation.

務 *Nimmu* duty.

期 *Ninki* a term of office or service.

意 *Nin-i* voluntary.

伍 GO five; a class; to stand in a row; to mix.

長 *Gochō* a corporal.

T 仰 GYŌ; KŌ. *Ōse* command: *ao(gu)* to look up; to respect; lie on one's back: *ossharu* (coll. irreg.) to say (polite): *ō(seru)* to say (polite).

々しい *Gyōgyōshii* exaggerated; ostentatious.

山 *Gyōsan* plenty; exaggeration.

天 *Gyōten* amazement.

云 *Ossharu* (coll. irreg.) to say (polite).

向 *Aomuki* lying on the back, face upwards.

言 *Ossharu* (coll. irreg.) to say (polite).

臥 *Gyōga* lie on one's back.

慕 *Gyōbo* to long for; idolize.

伜 *Segare* son.

T 件 KEN affair; matter. *Kudan* above mentioned.

々 *Kenken* affairs; the points of a case.

T 仲 CHŪ. *Naka* middle; state of feelings between persons; relations of friendship and harmony.

(四)

(四)

人 *Chūnin* mediator; middleman: *nak do* match-maker.

介 *Chūkai* agency.

立 *Nakadachi* middleman.

好 *Nakayoshi* a bosom friend.

直 *Naka-naori* reconciliation.

秋 *Chūshū* middle of autumn.

間 *Nakama* company; companion.

裁 *Chūsai* arbitration.

買 *Nakagai* a broker.

伊 I Italy.

太利 *Itariya*; *Itarii* Italy.

豆 *Izu* p. n.

呂波 *Iroha* a,b,c.

香保 *Ikao* p. n.

勢 *Ise* p. n.

達 *Date* foppery; p. n.

豫 *Iyo* p. n.

仿 HŌ to stand still. *Samayo-(u)* to wander about. Alternative form of 彷 60,4.

T 伏 FUKU to submit. *Fu(su)*; *fu(seru)* to lie down; to be concealed.
Often becomes the first component of compound verbs meaning bowing down, thus 伏拜む *Fushiogamu* kneel down and worship.

目 *Fushime* downcast look.

在 *Fukuzai* lying concealed.

兵 *Fukuhei* troops in ambush.

(四)

屋 *Fuseya* a humble cottage.

奏 *Fukusō* a report to the Throne.

罪 *Fukuzai* submit to sentence.

線 *Fukusen* forestalling.

魔殿 *Fukumaden* enchanted palace.

T 休 KYŪ. *Yasu(mu)* to rest.

止 *Kyūshi* rest from work.

日 *Kyūjitsu* holiday.

心 *Kyūshin* be at ease.

刊 *Kyūkan* suspension of publication.

神 *Kyūshin* be at ease.

息 *Kyūsoku* rest.

塲 *Kyūjō* closing a theatre, or other building, temporarily.

會 *Kyūkai* adjournment.

業 *Kyūgyō* rest from work; closed to business.

暇 *Kyūka* holidays.

養 *Kyūyō* rest.

戰 *Kyūsen* truce.

憩 *Kyūkei* rest.

職 *Kyūshoku* temporary retirement.

T 仮 See 假 9, 9.

伎 GI; KI. *Waza* deed; skill

倆 *Giryō* ability.

43

伐 BATSU. *Ki(ru)* to cut; cut down; fell (trees): *u(tsu)* to conquer; vanquish; defeat.

採 *Bassai* cutting down; felling.

佐 See 佐 9, 5.

全 See 11, 4.

企 KI. *Kuwada(teru); takura(mu)* to plan; plot; scheme.

及 *Kikyū* attain; be equal.

畫 *Kikaku* plan; project.

業 *Kigyō* to start an undertaking of any kind; enterprise.

圖 *Kito* a plan.

合 GŌ measure of capacity: KATSU; GATSU. *A(u)* to agree with: *awa(seru)* to join; unite; add; as 2nd component means to happen (e. g. *ki-awaseru* to happen to come). See Introduction 44.【口】

札 *Aifuda* a check; tally.

本 *Gappon* copies bound together in book form.

同 *Gōdō* to combine; unite; act together.

名會社 *Gōmeigaisha* ordinary unlimited partnership.

羽 *Kappa* rain-coat.

作 *Gassaku* joint work.

金 *Gōkin* alloy.

伝 →9,11

性 *Aishō* affinity of temperaments.

併 *Gappei* amalgamation; union.

計 *Gōkei* the sum-total.

奏 *Gassō* concerted music.

格 *Gōkaku* eligibility.

致 *Gatchi* agreement.

唱 *Gasshō; kōrasu* sing together; chorus.

理 *Gōri* reasonable.

著 *Gatcho; gōcho* joint work.

掌 *Gasshō* to pray; offer up prayers.

衆國 *Gasshūkoku* the United States of America.

意 *Gōi* mutual consent.

資會社 *Gōshi-gaisha* a limited partnership.

圖 *Aizu* signal.

戰 *Kassen* battle.

點 *Gaten; gatten* understanding.

議 *Gōgi* consultation.

體 *Gattai* alliance.

会 See 會 9,11.【日】

肉 See 130,0.

但 *Tadashi* but; however; only; often need not be translated.

書 *Tadashigaki* proviso.

馬 *Tajima* p. n.

44

(五) T 佐 SA. *Tasu(keru)* to save; assist. (*Suke*). →9, 4

世保 *Sasebo* p. n.

伯 *Saeki* p. n.

官 *Sakan* a field officer; an officer below a major-general and above a captain; also naval corresponding ranks.

賀 *Saga* p. n.

幕 *Sabaku* the Shogunate party.

T 住 JŪ. *Su(mu)* to dwell; stay.

人 *Jūnin* inhabitant.

民 *Jūmin* inhabitants.

込 *Sumiko(mu)* (of employee) living in one's master's house.

宅 *Jūtaku* dwelling; residence.

居 *Jūkyo; sumai* dwelling.

所 *Jūsho* dwelling.

持 *Jūji* the superior of a temple.

家 *Sumika* dwelling.

職 *Jūshoku* the superior of a Buddhist temple.

T 位 I. *Kurai* rank; position; degree; grade; as much as; about; to lie; to be situated.

記 *Iki* diploma of court rank.

階 *Ikai* court rank.

牌 *Ihai* wooden tablets placed on the family altar, on which the posthumous name and date of death of each member of the family who has died are inscribed.

置 *Ichi* situation; position; place.

勳 *Ikun* court rank.

伽 KA; GA. *Togi* attendance; attendant.

藍 *Garan* Buddhist temple.

お伽噺 *Otogibanashi* a fairy tale.

佑 YŪ blessing. *Tasu(keru)* to help; save.

估 KO price; value.

券 *Koken* selling price; usually used figuratively meaning dignity or credit.

T 伯 HAKU a Count; chief; head; elder brother.

父 *O i* uncle (brother older than one's parent).

母 *Oba* aunt (sister older than one's parent).

州 *Hakushū* another name for the province of Hōki.

仲 *Hakuchū* nearly equal.

林 *Berurin* Berlin.

拉爾 *Burajiru* Brazil.

剌爾 *Burajiru* Brazil.

耆 *Hōki* p. n.

爵 *Hakushaku* a Count.

佃 (*Tsukuda*).

煮 *Tsukudani* food boiled in soy.

45

（五）

作 SAKU to raise (as a crop); grow: SA. *Tsuku(ru)* to make; build: *na(su)* to do; perform; rouse; set up; make prosperous; improve.

文 *Sakubun* composition.

付 *Sakuzuke* sowing or planting.

用 *Sayō* process.

男 *Sakuotoko* a farm-servant.

成 *Sakusei* drawing up; making.

例 *Sakurei* a composition; model.

物 *Sakumotsu* crops: *sakubutsu* fiction.

法 *Sahō* good manners; etiquette.

事 *Tsukurigoto* fabrication.

者 *Sakusha* a writer.

品 *Sakuhin* works; piece.

柄 *Sakugara* crop.

家 *Sakka* a writer; novelist.

爲 *Sakui* plot.

業 *Sagyō* operation; working.

意 *Sakui* fancy.

戰 *Sakusen* military operations.

興 *Sakkō* encouragement; awaking.

聲 *Tsukurigoe* a feigned voice.

伶 REI music; musician.

（五）

伴 HAN; BAN. *Tomo* a companion: *tomona(u)* to accompany; to go with. →伴 T

奏 *Bansō* accompaniment.

侶 *Hanryo* companion.

食大臣 *Banshokudaijin* nominal minister.

黨 *Hantō* a party; company; association.

T 伸 SHIN. *No(biru)*; *noba(su)* to stretch; extend; lengthen; grow.

張 *Shinchō* elongation.

縮 *Shinshuku*; *nobichijimi* expansion and contraction; elasticity.

佇 CHO. *Tatazu(mu)* to stand still.

立 *Choritsu* to stand still.

T 何 KA. *Nani*; *nan* what; any: *izure* which; either ......or; someday: *izukunzo* how; however; why.

人 *Nampito* everybody; anyone.

日 *Nannichi*; *nanka* how many days.

方 *Dochira*; *izukata* where: *donata* who.

分 *Nanibun* anyhow; at all events; by all means; please.

心 *Nanigokoro (naku)* in an unconcerned manner; without any special intention.

所 *Doko* what place; where.

卒 *Nanitozo*; *dōzo* please.

事 *Nanigoto* everything; something; anything; nothing; what.

46

（五）

物 *Nanimono* everything；
anything; nothing; what
thing; something.

故 *Naze ; nani-yue* why.

某 *Nanigashi* so and so.

時 *Nanji ; nandoki* what time :
itsu when : *itsu mo ; itsu de
mo* always.

氣 *Nanige (naku)* undesigned-
ly.

條 *Nanjō* how.

處 *Doko ; izuko* where.

程 *Nanihodo ; nambo* how
much.

等 *Nanra* what ; any.

T 伺 SHI. *Ukaga(u)* to visit;
spy ; enquire.

侯 *Shikō* waiting upon ; pay
respect to.

佛 BUTSU ; FUTSU France. *Ho-
toke* Buddha. →9, 2 T

式 *Busshiki* Buddhist rites.

陀 *Butsuda* Buddha.

門 *Butsumon* priesthood ;
Buddhism.

法 *Buppō* Buddhism.

家 *Bukka* the Buddhist
priesthood ; a Buddhist.

敎 *Bukkyō* Buddhism.

頂面 *Butchōzura* a sulky
look.

參 *Bussan* visiting a temple,
(grave).

道 *Butsudō* Buddhism.

葬 *Bussō* Buddhistic funeral.

閣 *Bukkaku* Buddhist temples.

說 *Bussetsu* the teaching of
Buddha.

語 *Futsugo* French.

像 *Butsuzō* a Buddhist image.

蘭西 *Furansu* France.

T 体 See 體 188,13.

T 低 TEI to lower ; fall below certain standard. *Hikui* low.

下 *Teika* fall ; lowering.

利 *Teiri* low interest.

能 *Teinō* feeble-mindedness.

級 *Teikyū* inferior ; low ; vulgar.

氣壓 *Teikiatsu* atmospheric
depression.

率 *Teiritsu* low rate.

減 *Teigen* to reduce ; lessen.

落 *Teiraku* fall.

廉 *Teiren* cheap.

頭 *Teitō* to bow the head.

聲 *Teisei* low voice.

T 似 JI. *Ni(-ru)* to be like ;
resemble ; imitate.

付 *Nitsu(ku)* to become ; suit.

合 *Nia(u)* to be becoming.

而非 *Ese* false.

寄 *Niyori* similar ; like.

顏 *Nigao* likeness ; portrait.

T 含 GAN ; GON. *Fuku(mu)* to
hold in the mouth ; con-
tain. 【口】

有 *Gan-yū* to contain ; hold.

味 *Gammi* to examine criti-
cally ; digest.

（五）

（五）

含
羞 *Hanika(mu)* to be shy.

蓄 *Ganchiku* inclusion; implication.

ᴛ 余 Yo. *Ware* I; my: *ama(su)* to leave over: *amari* excess; remainder; too; more than. Sometimes used for 餘 184,7.

六 ᴛ 佳 Kᴀ. *Yoi* good; beautiful.

人 *Kajin* a beautiful woman.

作 *Kasaku* fine work.

肴 *Kakō* dainties; rare dish.

美 *Kabi* fine; splendid.

境 *Kakyō* a delightful, interesting portion.

節 *Kasetsu* a festival; public anniversary.

麗 *Karei* fine; splendid.

佯 Yō. *Itsuwa(ru)* to deceive; lie.

ᴛ 併 Hᴇɪ. *Awa(seru)* to join: *shikashi* however.
→9, 8

用 *Heiyō* to use all at the same time.

合 *Heigō* to unite; combine.

有 *Heiyū* to possess jointly; hold at the same time.

吞 *Heidon* annex; conquer.

發 *Heihatsu* to supervene; break out at the same time.

ᴛ 例 Rᴇɪ precedent; custom; habit; usual. *Tameshi* an

example; instance: *tato(h eru)* to compare; illustrate.

（六）

日 *Reijitsu* the usual day.

月 *Reigetsu* every month.

外 *Reigai* an exception.

年 *Reinen* ordinary year; every year.

刻 *Reikoku* usual hour.

規 *Reiki* established rules.

祭 *Reisai* a customary festival.

會 *Reikai* a regular (ordinary) meeting.

題 *Reidai* an example.

證 *Reishō* an instance.

ᴛ 侍 Jɪ. *Habe(ru)* (lit. st. irreg.) to attend upon; serve: *samurai* a knight.

女 *Jijo* female attendant of a noble-woman.

史 *Jishi* honorific term used specially in correspondence.

從 *Jijū* a chamberlain; person attached to the suite of the Emperor.

醫 *Jii* a court physician.

侑 Yū. *Susu(meru)* to offer insistently; urge.

侈 Sʜɪ to be extravagant; selfish; arbitrary.

偽 See 僞 9,12.

ᴛ 依 I. *Yo(ru)* to depend upon: *ni yotte*; *ni yoru* according to; by.

48

怗地　*Ekoji* morose.

怗贔負　*Eko-hiiki* partiality; prejudice.

託　*Itaku* consignment; trust.

然　*Izen* as it is; same as before.

賴　*Irai* a request; to rely on.

願免官　*Igammenkan* be relieved of one's post at one's own request.

T 使　SHI. *Tsukai* messenger: *tsuka(u)* to use; employ.

用　*Shiyō* use.

用人　*Shiyō-nin* employee.

込　*Tsukaiko(mu)* to appropriate; make free with; not to live within income.

臣　*Shishin* an envoy.

役　*Shieki* employment; service; employing (as a labourer).

命　*Shimei* mission.

者　*Shisha* a messenger.

途　*Tsukai-michi; shito* use.

節　*Shisetsu* a mission; an envoy.

侘　*Wabishii* lonely.

住居　*Wabi-zumai* lonely life.

侃　KAN strong; just; right.

佩　HAI. *O(biru); ha(ku)* to gird on; wear (as sword, medal).

用　*Haiyō* the wearing of.

劍　*Haiken* wearing a sword.

T 供　KYŌ; KU. *Sona(h)eru)* to offer; supply: *tomo* an attendant; sign of the plural.

用　*Kyōyō* to use; employ; consume.

奉　*Gubu* attendance.

物　*Kumotsu* an offering.

託　*Kyōtaku* deposit.

御　*Kugo* Emperor's food.

給　*Kyōkyū* supply.

養　*Kuyō* mass for the dead.

侫　NEI. *Omone(ru)* to flatter.

人　*Neijin* a flatterer.

臣　*Neishin* crafty courtier.

辯　*Neiben* adulation.

T 金　See 167,0.

舍　See following. *T 舍→foll

舍　SHA. *Ya* house. 【舌】

兄　*Shakei* elder brother.

弟　*Shatei* younger brother.

監　*Shakan* a dormitory inspector.

T 命　MEI orders; commands; fate: MYŌ. *Inochi* life: *mikoto* prince; lord. 【口】

(六)

命

日 *Meinichi* anniversary of the dead.

中 *Meichū* hitting the mark.

令 *Meirei* order; command.

名 *Meimei* naming.

數 *Meisū* the length of life; fate.

懸 *Inochigake* perilous; at the risk of one's life.

念 See following.

T 念 NEN. *Omo(u)* to think; wish. 【心】 →61,4

入 *Nen-iri (ni)* carefully.

佛 *Nembutsu* a Buddhist invocation.

望 *Nembō* a desire; wish.

慮 *Nenryo* thought; consideration.

頭 *Nentō* mind.

忿 See 61,4.

*1

七 俚 RI common; rustic.

耳 *Riji* ears of a common man.

諺 *Rigen* a common saying.

T 信 SHIN sincerity; truth; faith; tidings. (*Nobu*).

心 *Shinjin* faith.

用 *Shin-yō* trust; confidence; credence.

*1
T 価 →9,13

玄袋 *Shingembukuro* cloth-pouch.

仰 *Sinkō* faith.

任 *Shinnin* confidence.

州 *Shinshū* another name for the province of Shinano.

念 *Shinnen* belief.

者 *Shinja* believer.

書 *Shinsho* a letter.

託 *Shintaku* trust.

徒 *Shinto* believer.

條 *Shinjō* articles of faith.

敎 *Shinkyō* religious belief.

義 *Shingi* good faith; fidelity.

號 *Shingō* signal.

實 *Shinjitsu* sincerity; faithfulness.

濃 *Shinano* p. n.

賴 *Shinrai* reliance; confidence; trust.

憑 *Shimpyō* to rely on; reliable.

(七)

T 俗 ZOKU mean; vulgar; common; rustic; custom.

人 *Zokujin* a vulgar person; common person.

化 *Zokka* vulgarization.

世 *Zokusei* this world.

受 *Zokuuke* popularity.

事 *Zokuji* common business; everyday affairs.

物 *Zokubutsu* a vulgar person.

界 *Zokkai* the world.

氣 *Zokki* vulgarity.

*2
T 侮 →9,7

50

（七）

臭 *Zokushū* low taste.

習 *Zokushū* vulgar practice; custom.

惡 *Zokuaku* vulgar.

塵 *Zokujin* the world; earthly affairs.

語 *Zokugo* colloquial language; vulgar word.

說 *Zokusetsu* a common saying; tradition.

論 *Zokuron* unenlightened opinion.

侶 Ryo. *Tomo* fellows; companions.

俥 *Kuruma* a rikisha.

俘 Fu. *Toriko* a captive.

虜 *Furyo* a prisoner of war.

佛 *Omokage* figure; face.

侮 Bu. *Anado(ru)* to despise; mock. →9,6丁 *²

辱 *Bujoku* insult.

蔑 *Bubetsu* scorn; insult; contempt.

俠 Kyō chivalrous spirit. Kyan a hussy.

客 *Kyōkaku* gallant man; chivalrous man.

氣 *Kyōki; otokogi* a manly spirit.

俣 (*Mata.*)

T 侯 Kō a marquis; a feudal lord. Do not confound with 候 9,8. →111,4

爵 *Kōshaku* a marquis.

俟 Shi. *Ma(tsu)* to wait.

T 保 Ho; Hō. *Tamo(tsu)* to preserve; protect. (*Yasu*).

全 *Hozen* preservation; integrity.

存 *Hozon; hoson* preservation; keeping safe.

守 *Hoshu* conservation.

有 *Hoyū* holding; possession.

安 *Hoan* preservation of peace.

安林 *Hoanrin* conservation of forests.

姆 *Hobo* an infant school teacher.

持 *Hoji* holding; maintenance.

留 *Horyū* reserve.

菌者 *Hokinsha* bacteria carrier.

管 *Hokan* taking charge of; custody.

障 *Hoshō* guarantee.

養 *Hoyō* recreation; preservation of health.

險 *Hoken* insurance.

證 *Hoshō* security; guarantee.

釋 *Hoshaku* bail.

護 *Hogo* protection.

T 促 Soku. *Unaga(su)* to urge; dun; press upon.

（七）

（七）

促
進 *Sokushin* quicken; urge.

T 侵 SHIN. *Oka(su)* to violate; to outstrip; disregard; slight.

入 *Shinnyū* invasion.

害 *Shingai* infringement.

略 *Shinryaku* aggression.

T 俊 SHUN to excel. (*Toshi*).

才 *Shunsai* superior intellect.

英 *Shun-ei* man of talents.

傑 *Shunketsu* a man of great talent.

T 便 BEN convenience: BIN opportunity; means; tidings. *Tayori* news.

利 *Benri* convenience.

宜 *Bengi* convenience.

所 *Benjo* privy; water-closet.

法 *Bempō* short cut.

益 *Ben-eki* convenience; advantage.

船 *Binsen* a ship leaving for one's destination.

殿 *Benden* an Imperial resting-room.

覽 *Benran* manual.

俄 GA. *Niwaka* sudden.

然 *Gazen* suddenly; in a moment.

俛 BEN. *Ta(reru); utsumu(ku)* to put one's head down;

bow; sometimes used in the sense of 勉 work hard. （七）

T 係 KEI. to be concerned in. *Kakari* person in charge of certain work: *kaka(ru)* to concern; relate to.

爭 *Keisō* dispute; strife.

累 *Keirui* dependents.

俎 SO. *Manaita* a chopping board.

T 盆 See 108,4.

食 See 184,0.

臾 YU. *Shibaraku* a short time; by all means. 【白】

T 値 CHI. *Atai; ne* value; 八 price.

引 *Nebiki* reduction of the price.

切 *Negi(ru)* to beat down the price.

打 *Neuchi* value.

段 *Nedan* price.

T 倍 BAI double; ....fold; times; to multiply: *masumasu* more and more. (*Be*).

加 *Baika* to double a number.

舊 *Baikyū* redoubled.

倨 KYO. *Ogo(ru)* to be proud.

傲 *Kyogō* arrogant; proud.

借 (八) T SHAKU. *Kari* a debt: *ka-(riru)* (coll.); *ka(ru)* (lit. st.) to borrow; rent.

入 *Kariire* borrowing.

手 *Karite* borrower.

用 *Shakuyō* borrowing.

地 *Shakuchi; karichi* leased land.

金 *Shakkin* a debt.

受 *Kariu(keru)* to borrow.

財 *Shakuzai* debt; borrowing money.

家 *Shakuya; shakka* a rented house.

款 *Shakkan* loan.

越 *Karikoshi* outstanding debt.

個 T KO individual; KA aux. num. for counting several kinds of things that have no special aux. num. Sometimes used instead of 箇 118,8 which place see for other compounds.

人 *Kojin* an individual.

性 *Kosei* individuality; personality.

數 *Kosū* number of articles.

俤 See T併 9,6.

俸 T HŌ salary; rations.

給 *Hōkyū* a salary.

倖 KŌ happiness; luck.

俳 T HAI sport; play; to wander about. (八)

人 *Haijin* a *haiku* poet.

句 *Haiku* a poem or stanza of seventeen syllables.

諧 *Haikai* a poem or stanza of seventeen syllables.

優 *Haiyū* an actor.

倒 T TŌ; DŌ. *Tao(reru)* to fall: *tao(su)* to overthrow: *saka-sama; sakasa* upside-down.

産 *Tōsan* to become bankrupt; lose one's fortune.

樣 *Sakasama* the wrong side up.

倚 I; KI. *Yo(ru)* to rely on: *mota(reru)* to lean against; lean on.

俯 FU. *Fu(su); utsumu(ku)* to look down; bow the head.

向 *Utsumu(ku)* look downwards.

仰 *Fugyō* in private and public.

瞰 *Fukan* look down.

倫 T RIN; RON rule; regulation.

理 *Rinri* morals; ethics.

敦 *Rondon* London.

倆 RYŌ skill; ability.

修 T SHŪ; SHU. *Osa(meru)* to practise. →9,9

了 *Shūryō* to complete one's study.

53

（八）

修
正 *Shūsei* amendment; modification.

行 *Shugyō* training; discipline; study.

交 *Shūkō* contracting of friendly relations.

身 *Shūshin* moral training.

理 *Shūri* repair.

業 *Shūgyō* completing one's studies.

道 *Shūdō* ascetic practices.

飾 *Shūshoku* ornamentation.

築 *Shūchiku* repair.

養 *Shūyō* culture.

學 *Shūgaku* study; learning.

繕 *Shūzen* repairing; mending.

羅の巷 *Shura-no-chimata* seat of fighting and bloodshed.

伮　See 倣 9,10.

倏 SHUKU. *Tachimachi* quickly; suddenly.

倐　See preceding.

T 候 KŌ season; sign; to enquire after. *Sōrō;* in *kana* this verb is spelled サフラフ, it is generally used in this form and pronounced *sōrō,* occasionally *soro;* in other inflexions the *ra* sound is heard, e.g. *sōraeba.* To-day this verb is used only in the epistolary style: when

（八）

used independently it means to be, but it generally occurs as a mere suffix, something like the—*masu* of the colloquial. Do not confound with 侯 9,7.

文 *Sōrō bun* epistolary style.

段 *Sōrō dan* inasmuch as; and; therefore (epist. st.).

哉 *Sōrō ya* is it? (interrogative form in epist. st.).

得共 *Sōrae domo* although (epist. st.).

處 *Sōrō tokoro* whereas (epist. st.).

間 *Sōrō aida* because (epist. st.).

補 *Kōho* candidature; a candidate.

T 俵 HYŌ. *Tawara* a straw sack; aux. num. for counting bales.

T 倣 HŌ. *Nara(u)* to imitate.

倦 KEN. *A(kiru); u(mu)* to get tired of.

怠 *Kentai* fatigue.

厭 *Ken-en* weariness; disgust.

俺 EN. *Ore* I.

俱 GU; KU. *Tomo ni* together.

樂部 *Kurabu* a club.

倭 WA; I short; low (of stature); to obey; Japan. *Shizu* mean; poor.

54

(八)
T

倉 SŌ haste. *Kura* godown; store-house.

庫 *Sŏko* hold (of vessel); store-house.

敷 *Kurashiki* money paid for the storage of goods.

拿 DA to catch hold of; seize; to capture: lead away. 【手】

捕 *Daho* capture.

T **翁** See 124,4.

衾 KIN nightclothes. *Fusuma* bedding. 【衣】
*

九 **偖** SHA. *Sate* well; so then; now.

偕 KAI. *Tomo* companion: *tomo ni* together; with.

老 *Kairō* (of married people) growing old together.

行社 *Kaikōsha* the Military Club.

樂 *Kairaku* to enjoy together.

T **偉** I to excel. *Erai* great; admirable; large.

力 *Iryoku* might; greatness.

人 *Ijin* great man.

大 *Idai* (of things and persons) huge; great.

丈夫 *Ijōfu* a great man.

功 *Ikō* great achievement.

業 *Igyō* a great undertaking; an immense work.

(九)

勳 *Ikun* great achievement.

績 *Iseki* exploit: distinguished services.

觀 *Ikan* magnificent sight.

偷 TŌ; CHŪ. *Nusu(mu)* to steal.

安 *Tōan* idleness.

T **側** SOKU. *Kawa* the side; one side: *soba; katawara; waki* beside; close by.

目 *Wakime* looking aside; another's eyes.

杖 *Sobazue* to suffer vicariously inconvenience or pain on account of another.

面 *Sokumen* a side; lateral face; flank.

T **停** TEI. *Todoma(ru)*; *todo(meru)* to stop; stay.

止 *Teishi* suspension.

年 *Teinen* age limit.

車塲 *Teishaba; teishajō* a railway station.

留塲 *Teiryūjō; teiryūba* a tram stopping-place.

會 *Teikai* suspension of a meeting.

業 *Teigyō* to stop business for a time.

電 *Teiden* stoppage of electric current.

滯 *Teitai* stagnation; accumulation.

學 *Teigaku* suspension from attendance at school.

*
T **儉** →9,13   55

停
職 *Teishoku* suspension from office.

脩 See ᵀ修 9,8.

ᵀ 偏 HEN. *Katayo(ru)* to incline; be partial: *hitoe ni* earnestly.

人 *Henjin* eccentric person.

見 *Henken* partiality; prejudice; bias.

屈 *Henkutsu* eccentricity.

重 *Henjū* preponderate.

狹 *Henkyō* narrow-minded.

愛 *Hen-ai* partiality; favouritism.

鄙 *Hempi* out-of-the-way.

頗 *Hempa* partiality.

僻 *Hempeki* eccentricity.

ᵀ 偶 GŪ even number; consort. *Tamatama* occasionally; by chance.

成 *Gūsei* accidental.

發 *Gūhatsu* an incidental occurrence.

然 *Gūzen* chance; unexpected.

感 *Gūkan* random thoughts.

像 *Gūzō* an image; idol.

數 *Gūsū* an even number.

條 JŌ item. *Suji* line: *eda* branch; *michi* road. 【木】 →35,4T

文 *Jōbun* text of regulations.

目 *Jōmoku* articles.

件 *Jōken* the points; conditions; terms.

例 *Jōrei* regulations; rules.

約 *Jōyaku* treaty.

理 *Jōri* reason; principle.

欵 *Jōkan* stipulation; article.

章 *Jōshō* provisions; articles.

項 *Jōkō* articles; stipulations.

假 KA; KE. *Kari* temporary. →9,4T

令 *Tatoi*; *tatoe* even if; although.

托 *Kataku* pretext.

初 *Karisome* provisional; temporary.

住居 *Karizumai* temporary residence.

定 *Katei* supposition; assumption.

面 *Kamen* a mask; a disguise.

借 *Kashaku* pardon; extenuation.

病 *Kebyō* feigned sickness.

設 *Kasetsu* to erect temporarily.

裝 *Kasō* disguise; fancy dress.

想 *Kasō* imaginary.

說 *Kasetsu* hypothesis.

做 SA habit; custom. *Na(su)* to perform; do; make.

ᵀ 健 KEN. *Sukoyaka* healthy; strong; brave.

在 *Kenzai* good health.

全 *Kenzen* good health

（九）忘 *Kembō* forgetfulness.

兒 *Kenji* vigorous youth.

氣 *Kenage* gallantry; bravery.

脚 *Kenkyaku* a good walker.

康 *Kenkō* health.

勝 *Kenshō* good health.

筆 *Kempitsu* ready pen.

T 偵 TEI to spy; search.

察 *Teisatsu* reconnaissance.

偲 SHI. *Shino(bu)* to think of; reflect on; yearn after.

貪 DON; TAN. *Musabo(ru)* to covet; desire. 【貝】

欲 *Don-yoku* greed.

T 貧 See 154,4.

───

（一〇）傅 FU a tutor; to assist; nurse.

T 備 BI. *Sona(h)eru* to prepare: *sonawa(ru)* to be furnished; supplied: *tsubusa ni* in detail: *sonae* stock; preparation.

中 *Bitchū* p. n.

考 *Bikō* a note.

忘 *Bibō* an aid to the memory; a reminder.

前 *Bizen* p. n.

後 *Bingo* p. n.

砲 *Bihō* a cannon provided for a definite purpose.

T 偽 →9, 12

傍 BŌ. *Soba; waki; katawara* side; beside; close by. （一〇）

系 *Bōkei* collateral family.

若無人 *Bōjakubujin* as if no one were near; shameless.

聽 *Bōchō* attendance (at a lecture).

觀 *Bōkan* looking on.

T 傑 KETSU. *Sugu(reru)* to excel.

出 *Kesshutsu* to excel; prominent.

作 *Kessaku* a masterpiece.

物 *Ketsubutsu* extraordinary character.

傚 KŌ. *Nara(u)* to model after; imitate.

傀儡 *Kairai* doll; puppet.

傘 SAN. *Kasa; karakasa* umbrella.

翕 KYŪ to meet; to gather together. 【羽】

合 *Kyūgō* to call together.

然 *Kyūzen* in unison; in chorus.

禽 KIN. *Tori* bird. 【禸】

獸 *Kinjū* birds and beasts.

───

僅 KIN. *Wazuka* a little. 二

々 *Kinkin* only; few; little; trifle.

57

(一一)

僅
少 *Kinshō* few; little; trifle.

T 催 SAI. *Movo(su)* to hold; give; become.

促 *Saisoku* urging.

眠術 *Saiminjutsu* hypnotism.

傳 DEN biography; trick (fraudulent). *Tsuta(h)eru)* to hand on; transmit: *tsutawa-(ru)* to be handed down; transmitted: *tsuta(u)* to go or pass along. →9,4*T

手 *Tsute* an intermediary.

令 *Denrei* an orderly.

言 *Dengon* a verbal message.

來 *Denrai* imported; introduced.

染 *Densen* infection.

染病 *Densembyō* infectious disease; epidemic.

書鳩 *Denshobato* a carrier-pigeon.

記 *Denki* a biography.

授 *Denju* to instruct.

票 *Dempyō* a chit.

統的 *Dentōteki* traditional.

道 *Dendō* mission work.

達 *Dentatsu* transmission.

說 *Densetsu* tradition.

播 *Dempa* propagation.

導 *Dendō* conduction; transmission.

傭 YŌ. *Yato(u)* to employ.

人 *Yonin; yatoinin* a hired labourer.

兵 *Yōhei* hired troops.

聘 *Yōhei* employment.

T 傷 SHŌ. *Kizu* a wound: *kizutsu(ku)*; *sokona(u)* to wound; hurt; injure; damage: *ita(mu)* to mourn for; condole; grieve: *ita-mashii* piteous; pitiful.

心 *Shōshin* grief.

害 *Shōgai* injury.

T 働 DŌ. *Hatara(ku)* to work; labour.

振 *Hatarakiburi* manner of working.

傲 GŌ. *Ogo(ru)* to be proud; to disdain.

岸 *Gōgan* arrogance.

然 *Gōzen* arrogantly.

慢 *Gōman* arrogance; haughtiness.

語 *Gōgo* talk boastfully.

僊 See 仙 9,3.

T 債 SAI to borrow. *Oime* a debt; loan.

主 *Saishu* creditor.

券 *Saiken* a debenture bond.

鬼 *Saiki* a creditor.

務 *Saimu* obligation; debt; liabilities.

權 *Saiken* right of claim.

(一一)

(一一)

傾 KEI. *Katamu(ku)*; *katabu(ku)* to incline to one side; to overturn; upset.

向 *Keikō* tendency; inclination; leaning.

注 *Keichū* concentration; devotion.

城 *Keisei* a harlot.

倒 *Keitō* to devote; concentrate; squander away.

斜 *Keisha* inclination.

聽 *Keichō* listen to.

會 KAI company; meeting; to assemble: E to perceive. *A(u)* to meet: *tamatama* occasionally. 【日】 →9,4 T

心 *Kaishin* satisfactory.

合 *Kaigō* meeting; assembly.

同 *Kaidō* assemblage; meeting.

式 *Eshiki* a religious festival.

見 *Kaiken* meeting; interview.

社 *Kaisha* company; office of a business company.

長 *Kaichō* president (of a society).

計 *Kaikei* account.

津 *Aizu* p. n.

則 *Kaisoku* regulations of a society.

員 *Kaiin* member (of a society).

得 *Etoku* understanding.

堂 *Kaidō* chapel; assembly-hall.

費 *Kaihi* subscription; fee.

場 *Kaijō* meeting-place.

衆 *Kaishū* congregation.

話 *Kaiwa* conversation.

戰 *Kaisen* a battle; an encounter.

議 *Kaigi* meeting; council; conference; convention.

釋 *Eshaku* salutation.

愈 See 11,11. 【心】

幹 See 24,11. 【干】

僧 SŌ a Buddhist priest. →9,11 T *

正 *Sōjō* high rank in the priesthood; bishop.

侶 *Sōryo* a priest.

院 *Sōin* a monastery.

僭 SEN to usurp; to be proud.

越 *Sen-etsu* presumptuousness.

僞 GI. *Itsuwa(ru)* to deceive: *nise* counterfeit. →9,9 * T

印 *Giin* false seal.

名 *Gimei* a false name; name assumed as a disguise.

作 *Gisaku* spurious work.

物 *Gibutsu*; *nisemono* imitation article; not genuine.

造 *Gizō* to forge; counterfeit.

善 *Gizen* hypocrisy.

筆 *Gihitsu* forged handwriting.

59　*T 僧 →9,12

（二二）

偽
證 *Gishō* perjury.

T 僕 BOKU I (used only by men, especially young). *Shimobe* servant; fellow.

T 像 ZŌ; SHŌ. *Katachi* image; form: *katado(ru)* to copy; model on.

僥 GYŌ luck; to seek; desire; deceive.

倖 *Gyōkō* good fortune.

T 僚 RYŌ a companion; colleague.

友 *Ryōyū* a colleague.

艦 *Ryōkan* a convoy; comrade vessel.

幹 See 24,12. 【斗】

—————

一三

僻 HEKI remote; be biassed. *Higa(mu)* be prejudiced.

目 *Higame* prejudice; misunderstanding.

地 *Hekichi* out-of-the-way place.

見 *Hekiken* a biased view.

陬 *Hekisū* out-of-the-way.

遠 *Hekien* remote.

說 *Hekisetsu* prejudiced opinion.

論 *Hekiron* prejudiced opinion.

儂 NŌ *Ware; washi* I.

T 儀 GI ceremony; appearance; used in epistolary style as

（二三）

about equivalent to *wa* and applied to first person, or persons related to the first person; also in epistolary style as equivalent to *koto, mono,* affair, matter. *Nori* a rule.

仗兵 *Gijōhei* guard of honour.

式 *Gishiki* ceremony.

表 *Gihyō* model.

儉 KEN. *Tsutsumayaka* economy. →9,8*T

約 *Ken-yaku* economy.

價 KA. *Atai; ne* price; value. →9,6*T

格 *Kakaku* price; market rate.

值 *Kachi* price; value.

額 *Kagaku* price.

T 億 OKU one hundred millions.

兆 *Okuchō* all the people; all citizens.

劫 *Okkū; okkō* troublesome; eternity.

—————

一四

儘 JIN. *Mama* as; as it is.

儕 SEI; SAI companion; sort; alike.

輩 *Seihai* comrade.

T 儒 JU a Confucian scholar; Confucianism.

佛 *Jubutsu* Confucianism and Buddhism.

（一四）

者 *Jusha* a Confucian scholar.

敎 *Jukyō* Confucianism.

道 *Judō* Confucianism.

儚 *Hakanai* fleeting; sad.

翰 See 24,14. 【羽】

（一五）

優 YŪ elegance; actor. *Yasashii* easy; mild; quiet : *masa(ru)* to surpass; excel; be superior.

劣 *Yūretsu* superiority or inferiority; quality.

先 *Yūsen* preference.

秀 *Yūshū* superior; excellent.

男 *Yasaotoko* a man of gentle manners; effeminate.

良 *Yūryō* excellent.

長 *Yūchō* sedate; calm; composed.

待 *Yūtai* generous treatment.

美 *Yūbi* elegance; grace.

柔不斷 *Yūjūfudan* irresolution; vacillation.

渥 *Yūaku* gracious (of Emperor).

等 *Yūtō* superior.

勝 *Yūshō* superiority; predominance.

勝劣敗 *Yūshō-reppai* survival of the fittest.

勢 *Yūsei* superior power.

遇 *Yūgū* kind treatment.

（一五）

雅 *Yūga* elegance; grace.

償 SHŌ. *Tsuguna(u)*; *tsuguno(u)* to compensate; redeem.

却 *Shōkyaku* refundment.

金 *Shōkin* indemnity.

還 *Shōkan* refundment.

（一六）

儲 CHO. *Mō(keru)* to earn; make (money); cherish.

（一九）

儺 NA; DA. *Oniyarai* driving out the devil.

（二〇）

儼 GEN polite.

然 *Genzen* solemnly; gravely.

儿 〇

先 See 93,2. 【儿】

光 See 42,3. 【儿】

兇 KYŌ evil; wild; misfortune; a ruffian.

手 *Kyōshu* an assassin.

行 *Kyōkō* violence; outrage.

徒 *Kyōto* riot.

惡 *Kyōaku* evil; wicked.

報 *Kyōhō* ill tidings.

漢 *Kyōkan* a villain.

（四）

兒器 *Kyōki* arms; weapons.

T 兆 CHŌ a billion. *Kizashi; shirushi* a sign; an omen.

候 *Chōkō* a sign; symptom; omen.

五 兌 See 12,5. 【儿】

T 児 See 兒 134,2. 【儿】

T 免 MEN to exempt; permit. *Manuka(reru)* to escape. Do not confound with 兎 4,6. →18,5

役 *Men-eki* exemption (as from military service).

狀 *Menjō* a written permit; diploma; licence.

疫 *Men-eki* immunity.

除 *Menjo* exemption; remission.

許 *Menkyo* permission; sanction.

訴 *Menso* acquittal.

稅 *Menzei* duty-free.

職 *Menshoku* (of officials) dismissal from office.

六 凭 HYŌ. *Yo(ru); mota(reru)* to depend on; lean on. 【几】

七 T 勉 See 19,7.

T 党 See 黨 202,8. 八

T 鬼 See 194,0.

兜 TŌ. *Kabuto* a helmet. 九

町 *Kabutochō* name of a street, but is used more often for the Tōkyō Stock Exchange on account of its location.

入 二

T 入 NYŪ; JU. *I(ru); i(reru); hai(ru)* to enter; put in. Do not confound with 人 9,0 or with 八 12,0.

口 *Iriguchi; irikuchi* entrance.

日 *Irihi* setting sun.

內 *Judai* entering the Palace (said of the Empress' Marriage to the Emperor).

水 *Jusui* drowning oneself.

用 *Nyūyō; iriyō* need; want.

札 *Nyūsatsu* bidding.

社 *Nyūsha* entering a company.

門 *Nyūmon* becoming a pupil; an introduction to (a study); a primer.

來 *Jurai; nyūrai; irikita(ru)* (literary style) to enter; to come (as into one's house).

金 *Nyūkin* money received.

京 *Nyūkyō* entering the capital.

念 *Nyūnen* scrupulous; painstaking.

要 *Nyūyō* to require.

院 *Nyūin* entering a hospital.

浴 *Nyūyoku* bathing.

梅 *Nyūbai* the beginning of the rainy season.

智慧 *Irejie* suggestion; instigation.

御 *Nyūgyo* retiring of the Emperor to his private apartment.

場券 *Nyūjōken* entrance ticket.

費 *Nyūhi* expenses.

超 *Nyūchō* excess of imports.

港 *Nyūkō* entering port.

齒 *Ireba* artificial tooth.

電 *Nyūden* receiving a telegram.

會 *Nyūkai* becoming a member of a society.

亂 *Irimida(reru)* to be confused or jumbled together.

獄 *Nyūgoku* imprisonment.

閣 *Nyūkaku* become a Cabinet Minister.

魂 *Jikkon* intimacy.

墨 *Irezumi* tattooing.

質 *Irejichi* to pawn.

學 *Nyūgaku* entrance into a school.

選 *Nyūsen* picked out from among others.

營 *Nyūei* entering barracks.

黨 *Nyūtō* joining a political party.

籍 *Nyūseki* becoming legally a member of a new family.

内 NAI; DAI. *Uchi* inside.　二
→9, 2T

々 *Nainai* secretly; privately; confidentially: *uchiuchi* informal; private.

大臣 *Naidaijin* Lord Chamberlain.

分 *Naibun* to keep a matter secret.

心 *Naishin* real intention; at heart; secretly; inwardly.

外 *Naigai* inside and outside; domestic and foreign; more or less.

外人 *Naigaijin* Japanese and foreigners.

用 *Naiyō* secret business; internal use.

地 *Naichi* the interior of a country; (according to context) Japan.

助 *Naijo* private aid; the wife's aid.

金 *Uchikin* money paid on account.

拂 *Uchibarai* instalment.

命 *Naimei* private order.

帑 *Naido* Emperor's privy purse.

内

治 *Naichi* home administration.

定 *Naitei* unofficial decision.

面 *Naimen* the inside surface.

科 *Naika* medicine (not surgery).

約 *Naiyaku* private agreement.

奏 *Naisō* to report informally to the Emperor.

省 *Naisei* introspection; reflection.

政 *Naisei* State affairs.

容 *Naiyō* contents; matter.

紛 *Naifun* domestic discord.

訌 *Naikō* internal disturbance.

宮 *Naikū* Shintō shrine in Ise, the most important in Japan.

借 *Uchigari* receiving part of any money before it is due.

氣 *Uchiki* a retiring disposition.

密 *Naimitsu* secret; private.

國 *Naikoku* one's own country; (according to context) Japan.

情 *Naijō* private circumstances; interior conditions.

務大臣 *Naimu-daijin* Minister for Home Affairs.

務省 *Naimushō* Home Office.

通 *Naitsū* secret communication with the enemy.

部 *Naibu* the inner part; interior.

規 *Naiki* by-law.

意 *Naii* personal opinion.

債 *Naisai* a domestic loan.

裏 *Dairi* the Imperial Palace.

亂 *Nairan* civil war.

閣 *Naikaku* Cabinet (of Ministers).

閣總理大臣 *Naikaku-sōri-daijin* Prime Minister.

聞 *Naibun* secret; private information.

幕 *Uchimaku; naimaku* private circumstances; inside facts.

實 *Naijitsu* the truth of a matter; facts of a case; in reality.

輪 *Uchiwa* internal; private; one's family.

談 *Naidan* private conversation.

憂外患 *Naiyū-gaikan* troubles at home and abroad.

辨慶 *Uchibenkei* a lion at home and a mole abroad.

緣 *Naien* a private marriage.

諾 *Naidaku* informal consent.

應 *Naiō* treason; betrayal.

濟 *Naisai* private settlement.

職 *Naishoku* extra work; work done besides one's ordinary business.

(一一)

證 *Naishō; naisho* secret; private.

譯 *Uchiwake* items of an account.

四 T 全 ZEN. *Mattō suru* to perfect; keep in perfect condition: *mattai* whole; complete: *mattaku* truly; completely.

力 *Zenryoku* all one's energy; one's best.

文 *Zembun* whole sentence.

市 *Zenshi* whole city.

身 *Zenshin* whole body.

局 *Zenkyoku* whole aspect.

快 *Zenkai* complete recovery (from illness).

治 *Zenchi; zenji* complete recovery.

般 *Zempan* the whole.

能 *Zennō* omnipotence.

院 *Zen-in* the whole House.

書 *Zensho* complete set of books.

豹 *Zempyō* general state.

國 *Zenkoku* whole country.

盛 *Zensei* great prosperity; most flourishing.

部 *Zembu* the whole; all parts.

速力 *Zensokuryoku* full speed.

然 *Zenzen* wholly; entirely.

(四)

集 *Zenshū* complete works.

智 *Zenchi* omniscience.

會 *Zenkai* whole attendance.

滅 *Zemmetsu* annihilation.

廢 *Zempai* total abolition.

篇 *Zempen* the complete work; the whole book.

燒 *Zenshō* complete destruction by fire.

額 *Zengaku* the full amount.

權 *Zenken* full power; plenipotentiary.

體 *Zentai* the whole.

T 肉 See 130,0.

愈 YU. *Iyo-iyo* more and more; still more. 【心】 一 一

八 三

T 八 HACHI. *Yatsu; ya* eight. Do not confound with 人 9,0 or with 入 11,0.

九分 *Hakkubu* almost.

日 *Yōka* 8 days; the 8th day of the month.

月 *Hachi-gatsu* August: *yatsuki* 8 months.

八方美人 *Happōbijin* everybody's friend.

百長 *Yaochō* a put-up job.

百屋 *Yaoya* a greengrocer.

坂瓊曲玉 *Yasakani-no-magatama* one of the three Imperial sacred treasures; see 三種の神器 1,2.

卦 *Hakke* prediction; fortune-telling.

重 *Yae* double (of flowers).

咫の鏡 *Yata-no-kagami* one of the three Imperial sacred treasures; see 三種の神器 1,2.

道 *Hachidō* the eight provinces of Korea.

達 *Hattatsu* leading to all directions.

幡 *Hachiman* god of valour; in life he was the Emperor Ōjin: *Yawata* p. n.

二
T 分 BUN part; share; lot; duty; as 2nd component it means ingredient (*en-bun* salt ingredients, various salts; *tetsu-bun* iron ingredients, compounds, salts); social position: BU 1/10 of *sun*, see Introduction 44; part; share; per-cent; 1/10 of any unit which has no special sub-division: FUN 1/10 of *momme*, see Introduction 44; unit of time, minute. *Wa(keru)* to divide: *waka(reru)* to separate: *waka(tsu)* to distinguish: *waka(ru)* to know; understand. 【刀】

子 *Bunshi* molecule; element.

目 *Wakeme* parting; fateful moment.

布 *Bumpu* distribution.

列式 *Bunretsushiki* defile; march past.

岐 *Bunki* diverge; branch off.

別 *Bumbetsu* distinction; discernment: *fumbetsu* discrimination.

身 *Bunshin* parturition.

店 *Bunten* branch shop.

泌 *Bumpitsu; bumpi* secretion; excretion.

析 *Bunseki* assay; test.

明 *Bummei* clear; plain.

限 *Bungen* limit; extent; one's social position.

限者 *Bugensha* a man of wealth.

科 *Bunka* branch.

界 *Bunkai* demarcation; boundary.

前 *Wakemae* share; portion.

派 *Bumpa* an offshoot; a sect.

家 *Bunke* branch family.

配 *Bumpai* distribution; allotment.

毫 *Bungō* a trifle.

娩 *Bumben* parturition.

野 *Bun-ya* sphere of influence.

量 *Bunryō* quantity.

隊 *Buntai* squad; detachment.

（二）

裂 *Bunretsu* disruption; split.

散 *Bunsan* insolvency.

解 *Bunkai* analysis.

業 *Bungyō* division of labour.

與 *Bun-yo* distribution.

際 *Bunzai* one's social standing.

圖 *Bunzu* plan of parts and details.

銅 *Fundō* scale weights.

遣 *Bunken* detaching.

擔 *Buntan* division of work; taking over a portion of any work.

離 *Bunri* separation.

類 *Bunrui* classification.

權 *Bunken* decentralization of power.

T 父 See 88,0.

T 公 KŌ: KU Prince; you (polite). *Kimi* Lord: *oyake* public.

人 *Kōjin* a public man.

文 *Kōbun* official document.

立 *Kōritsu* public.

正 *Kōsei* uprightness; notarial deed.

民 *Kōmin* citizen.

平 *Kōhei* fairness; justness.

平無私 *Kōheimushi* impartial and disinterested.

用 *Kōyō* official business; public service.

布 *Kōfu* promulgation.

示 *Kōji* official notice.

吏 *Kōri* public official.

共 *Kōkyō* public; common; mutual.

共事業 *Kōkyōjigyō* public enterprise.

共心 *Kōkyōshin* public spirit.

安 *Kōan* public peace.

式 *Kōshiki* formal; formula.

有 *Kōyū* public possession.

私 *Kōshi* public and private.

言 *Kōgen* open declaration.

沙汰 *Ōyakezata* public affairs; litigation.

判 *Kōhan* public trial.

定 *Kōtei* official.

使 *Kōshi* Minister (representing a country).

使館 *Kōshikan* a Legation.

知 *Kōchi* common knowledge.

金 *Kōkin* public money.

明 *Kōmei* fairness.

明正大 *Kōmei-seidai* justice; fairness.

表 *Kōhyō* public announcement.

益 *Kōeki* public good; public benefit.

海 *Kōkai* high seas.

孫樹 *Ichō; kōsonju* the maidenhair-tree.

設 *Kōsetsu* public.

娼 *Kōshō* licensed prostitution.

67

（二）

公

務 *Kōmu* official business.

開 *Kōkai* open ; public.

卿 *Kuge* court noble.

評 *Kōhyō* public opinion.

衆 *Kōshū* the public.

報 *Kōhō* an official report.

然 *Kōzen* openly.

園 *Kōen* public garden or park.

達 *Kindachi* the nobility.

義 *Kōgi* justice.

道 *Kōdō* justice ; public road.

債 *Kōsai* public loan.

認 *Kōnin* official recognition.

演 *Kōen* public exhibition.

賣 *Kōbai* public sale.

憤 *Kōfun* public indignation.

論 *Kōron* public opinion.

德 *Kōtoku* public morality.

選 *Kōsen* public election.

爵 *Kōshaku* Prince.

職 *Kōshoku* a public office (occupation).

證人 *Kōshō-nin* notary public.

議 *Kōgi* public opinion ; the government opinion.

四
T 羊　See 123,0.

弁　See 弁 51,5.

T 共　See 140,3.【八】

T 谷　See 150,0.

五

T 弟　TEI ; DAI ; DE.　*Otōto ; ototo* younger brother ; junior. 〔弓〕

子 *Deshi* pupil ; disciple ; apprentice.

兌　DA to pass. 【儿】

換　*Dakan* conversion.

換券　*Dakanken* a convertible note.

T 兵　HEI ; HYŌ army ; troops ; arms ; war. *Tsuwamono ; mononofu* soldier ; warrior. (*Be*).

士 *Heishi* soldier.

法 *Heihō* strategy.

役 *Heieki* military service.

卒 *Heisotsu* common soldier.

制 *Heisei* military organization.

兒帶 *Hekoobi* soft sash.

站部 *Heitambu* supply department.

庫 *Hyōgo* p. n.

氣 *Heiki* military spirit.

隊 *Heitai* soldier ; troops.

器 *Heiki* military weapons ; arms.

營 *Heiei* military camp.

糧 *Hyōrō* military provisions.

T 並　See 140,5.【一】

六

単　See 單 30,9.

(六)

券 See 18,6.

卷 See 26,6.

忩 See 61,4.

T 具 GU utensil; tool. *Sonawa-(ru)* to be supplied with: *sona(h)eru)* to provide; offer: *tsubusa* in detail.

申 *Gushin* report.

合 *Guai* condition; state.

有 *Guyū* to have; be provided with.

足 *Gusoku* armour.

眼者 *Gugansha* intellectual circles.

備 *Gubi* to be well furnished with; be completely equipped.

體的 *Gutaiteki* concrete.

其 See 99,3. 【八】

T 典 TEN ceremony; records; code; to manage. (*Suke*).

型 *Tenkei* a typical representative; ideal.

雅 *Tenga* gracefulness.

獄 *Tengoku* a prison governor.

範 *Tempan* a law; model.

據 *Tenkyo* authority.

籍 *Tenseki* books.

七 並 See **T** 並 140,5. 【一】

* 単 T→30,9

(七)

T 盆 See 108,4.

T 首 See 185,0.

酋 SHŪ. *Tsukasa; osa* a chief; leader. 【酉】

長 *Shūchō* chief of a tribe.

酋 See preced.

*

釜 See 釜 88,6. 【金】

益 EKI benefit; profit; use. *Masu* increase: *masumasu* more and more. 「皿】 →108,5T : 140,7T See 64,6.

拳

T 翁 See 124,4.

兼 KEN. *Kanete* at the same time; previously: *ka(neru)* to discharge two functions simultaneously. As 2nd component, sometimes used incorrectl for, cannot. →140,7T

用 *Ken-yō* to use in two or more ways.

有 *Ken-yū* to possess in addition to what one already has.

任 *Kennin* an additional post.

官 *Kenkan* an additional post.

帶 *Kentai* the use of one thing for two or more purposes.

備 *Kembi* be equally versed in.

業 *Kengyō* a by-occupation.

營 *Ken-ei* to carry on in addition.

(八)

(八) T
兼　See preced.

眞　See 21,8. 【日】

九
眷　See 109,6.

T
貧　See 154,4.

一〇
曾　SŌ. *Katsute* previously; ever; never. (*So*). 【日】

祖母 *Sōsobo* great-grand-mother.

祖父 *Sōsofu* great-grand-father.

孫 *Sōson* great-grandchild.

遊 *Sōyū* previously visited.

尊　SON your (honorific). *Tō-toi; tattoi* revered; esteem-ed; sublime: *tōto(bu); tatto-(bu)* to esteem; reverence: *mikoto* honorific suffix to the name of a god; also in ancient times used for ordinary mortals. (*Taka*). 【寸】 →12,10T

大 *Sondai* arrogant; haughty.

父 *Sompu* your father.

名 *Sommei* your name.

命 *Sommei* your order.

來 *Sonrai* your coming.

重 *Sonchō* esteem; respect.

敬 *Sonkei* respect.

稱 *Sonshō* a title of honour.

嚴 *Songen* dignity.

T
尊　See prec.

奠　TEN to worship. *Sada-(meru)* to decide; to place. 【大】

都 *Tento* change of the capital.

奠　See prec.

巽　See 49,9.

冀　KI. *Koinega(u)* to entreat: *koinegawaku wa* please. 　一四

望 *Kibō* desire; hope.

輿　YO. *Koshi; kago* palan-quin; vehicle. 【車】　一五

望 *Yobō* popularity; support.

論 *Yoron* public opinion.

冂　三

巾　See 50,0.　一

T
冃　See 74,0.　二

T
円　See 圓 31,10.

丹　See 1,3. 【丶】

T
内　See 內 11,2.

70

三
T 用　See 101,0.

* 叵　See ᵀ 回 31,3.

四
T 同　Dō to agree. *Onaji* same:
onajiku corresponding ; in
the same way. 【口】
→9, 3

一　*Dōitsu* the same; identical.

人　*Dōjin* comrades in a company : *dōnin* a companion ;
the same person.

士　*Dōshi* mutual relations;
among; between.

仁　*Dōjin* impartial kindness.

化　*Dōka* assimilation.

行　*Dōkō; dōgyō* going together.

伴　*Dōhan* to go in company.

志　*Dōshi* associate.

居　*Dōkyo* to live together.

性　*Dōsei* same sex.

胞　*Dōhō; dōbō* brothers; com-
patriots.

室　*Dōshitsu* same room.

前　*Dōzen* same as above;
ditto.

封　*Dōfu* enclose in same envelope.

班　*Dōhan* the same company ;
same class.

衾　*Dōkin* to sleep together.

級　*Dōkyū* same class.

宿　*Dōshuku* stay at the same
hotel.

族　*Dōzoku* a relation.

* 冊 →1, 4
T

郷　*Dōkyō* same town ; same
province.

情　*Dōjō* compassion ; sympathy.

窓　*Dōsō* a fellow-student.

然　*Dōzen* same.

等　*Dōtō* equality.

罪　*Dōzai* same crime.

盟　*Dōmei* union ; alliance.

盟罷工　*Dōmei-hikō* a strike.

道　*Dōdō* to go together.

意　*Dōi* concurrence; agreement ; consent.

感　*Dōkan* to have identical
feelings or sensibilities.

僚　*Dōryō* a colleague ; fellow
official.

樣　*Dōyō* the same ; identical.

輩　*Dōhai* a comrade; an
equal.

斷　*Dōdan* the same.

類　*Dōrui* same kind.

權　*Dōken* the same powers;
identical rights.

T 向　See 30,3.

T 肉　See 130,0.

六

囘　See foll.

罔　Mō; BŌ. *Ami* a net. 【网】

岡　KŌ. *Oka* a hill; mound.
【山】

71

（六）
T

周 SHŪ. *Mawari* circumference : *megu(ru)* to turn round ; go round : *amaneshi* (lit. st.) universal. ⎿口⏌

回 *Shūkai* circumference.

忌 *Shūki* the anniversary of a death.

知 *Shūchi* well-known.

到 *Shūtō* thorough; complete; exhaustive.

密 *Shūmitsu* thorough ; precise ; minute.

章 *Shūshō ; awa(teru)* confusion ; agitation ; turmoil.

旋 *Shūsen* good offices ; putting oneself to trouble in order to render assistance to another.

圍 *Shūi* surrounding ; circumference ; contour.

七 冒 BŌ; MŌ. *Oka(su)* to transgress ; covet.
→foll. T

頭 *Bōtō* the beginning of a composition or speech.

險 *Bōken* expose oneself to danger.

瀆 *Bōtoku* defilement.

一四

⌁→

Always at the top; it is called *Wa-kammuri.*

二 冗 JŌ. *Muda* in vain; to be superfluous ; mischief.

*T 冒 →prec

（一一）

句 *Jōku* redundant passage.

長 *Jōchō* diffuseness.

員 *Jōin* superfluous members.

費 *Jōhi* useless expenses.

漫 *Jōman* prolixity.

談 *Jōdan* joke.

T 写 See 寫 40,12. 三

罕 See 122,3. 五

T 軍 GUN. *Ikusa* army; battle. 七
【車】

人 *Gunjin* a soldier ; a sailor.

刀 *Guntō* a sabre.

令 *Gunrei* military command.

用 *Gun-yō* military use.

功 *Gunkō* military merit.

制 *Gunsei* military organization.

事 *Gunji* military affairs.

法會議 *Gumpō-kaigi* courtmartial.

律 *Gunritsu* military discipline.

神 *Gunshin ; ikusagami* God of war ; hero.

紀 *Gunki* military discipline.

氣 *Gunki* military spirit ; morale.

略 *Gunryaku* strategy ; tactics.

曹 *Gunsō* sergeant.

（七）

國主義 *Gunkoku-shugi* militarism.

港 *Gunkō* naval port.

隊 *Guntai* troops; forces.

備 *Gumbi* military preparations.

費 *Gumpi* war expenses.

勢 *Gunzei* an army; a troop.

旗 *Gunki* a standard; an ensign.

閥 *Gumbatsu* militarists.

需品 *Gunjuhin* munitions.

器 *Gunki* weapons of war.

機 *Gunki* a military secret.

營 *Gun-ei* a camp.

職 *Gunshoku* military (naval) profession.

籍 *Gunseki* military (naval) list.

艦 *Gunkan* warship.

T 冠 KAN. *Kammuri* a head covering: *kabu(ru)* to put on one's head.

絕 *Kanzetsu* surpass; unequal.

八 冤 EN a false accusation.

罪 *Enzai* condemnation for an offence of which one is innocent.

冥 MEI; MYŌ underworld; Hades; dark; dim; faint.

々 *Meimei* dark.

（八）

土 *Meido* (a Buddhist term) Hades.

加 *Myōga* divine assistance; gratitude.

府 *Meifu* the other world.

福 *Meifuku* happiness in a future existence.

護 *Meigo* divine help.

T 輝 See 42,12. 【車】 一三

冫 一五

Called *Ni-sui*.

冲 CHŪ young; to rise. 四

天 *Chūten* mid-air.

冴 *Sa(y)eru)* to be clear; bright; mellow; skilled.

次 See 76,2. →次 T

決 See T 決 85,4.

冰 See T 氷 85,1.

T 盡 See 盡 108,9.

冶 YA to forge; cast. 五

金 *Yakin* metallurgy.

T 冷 REI. *Tsumetai* cold; cool: *hi(y)eru)* to become cold:

<table>
<tr><td>

（五）冷
</td><td>

hiyayaka coldness: *hiya(su)* to cool; soak: *hiyaka(su)* to chaff; banter.
</td></tr>
</table>

々 *Hiyahiya s ru* to be in great fear.

水浴 *Reisuiyoku* cold bath.

血 *Reiketsu* cold-blooded.

却 *Reikyaku* to cool.

笑 *Reishō* a sneer.

氣 *Reik' cold.

淡 *Reitan* indifference; cold heartedness.

遇 *Reigū* cold treatment; inhospitality.

語 *Reigo* hard words; cold comfort.

酷 *Reikoku* cruelty; cold-heartedness.

嘲 *Reichō; hiyakas'i* banter.

熱 *Reinetsu* cold and heat; temperature.

靜 *Reisei* calmness.

藏 *Reizō* cold storage.

況 See ^T況 85,5.

（八）_T准 JUN.

涸 See 涸 85,8.

凋 Снō. *Shibo(mu)* to wither; to be ruined; come down socially or financially.

落 *Chōraku* decay; ruin; (of plants) to wither.

---

^T凍 Tō. *Kō(ru); kogo(y)eru* to freeze. （八〇）

死 *Tōshi* to freeze to death.

結 *Tōketsu* to freeze.

凌 RYō. *Shino(gu)* to endure; bear; face; supersede.

辱 *Ryōjoku* insult; outrage.

駕 *Ryōga* surpass; outrival.

凉 RYō. *Suzushii* cool; refreshing: *suzu(mu)* to cool oneself. →85,8T

味 *Ryōmi* coolness.

亭 *Ryōtei; azumaya* a summer-house; pavilion.

氣 *Ryōki* coolness; a cool temperature.

凄 See 凄 85,8.

減 See^T減 85,9.　　九

馮 Hyō to rely on; go ahead of; overtop; ascend. 【馬】 （一〇）

滅 See ^T滅 85,10.

凜 RIN. *Hageshii* severe; awesome; cold. （一三）

々 *Rinrin* awe-inspiring.

乎 *Rinko* with dashing spirit.

烈 *Rinretsu* severe; intense.

然 *Rinzen* imposingly.

凝 GYŌ. *Ko(ru)* to be absorbed in : *kora(su)* to concentrate one's attention : *kori* swelling.

固 *Gyōko* solidification.

視 *Gyōshi* stare ; gaze.

結 *Gyōketsu* to coagulate.

然 *Gyōzen* ; *jitto* fixedly.

集 *Gyōshū* cohesion.

議 *Gyōgi* confer ; consult.

几

六

几 KI. *Tsukue* a low table.

張面 *Kichōmen* orderly ; exact.

凡 BON common. *Oyoso* about : *subete* all ; generally ; altogether ; entirely ; without exception ; sometimes meaning is vague like the ' now ' at the beginning of an English sentence.

人 *Bonjin* an ordinary person ; an average individual.

夫 *Bompu* ; *bombu* an ordinary man ; an average individual.

百 *Bompyaku* various.

例 *Hanrei* preface.

俗 *Bonzoku* commonplace ; vulgarity.

庸 *Bon-yō* ordinary ; commonplace.

凧 *Tako* a kite.

三

凪 *Nagi* calmness ; lull.

四

夙 SHUKU. *Tsuto ni* early. 【夕】

夜 *Shukuya* day and night.

凩 *Kogarashi* wind at the beginning of winter.

鼡 See 鼠 208,0.

六

風 See 182,0.

七

梵 BON Brahma. 【木】

九

語 *Bongo* Pali ; Sanskrit.

凱 GAI to rejoice ; shout of victory.

一〇

旋 *Gaisen* triumphal return.

歌 *Gaika* songs of victory.

鳳 HŌ. *Ō.ori* the phœnix ; a fabulous bird ; often means man of high position. 【鳥】

一二

凰 *Hō-ō* a fabulous bird.

輦 *Hōren* the Imperial palanquin.

（一一一）

鳳
聲 *Hōsei* your words; regards; compliments.

七

凵

二
T 凶 *Kyō* evil; bad; unfortunate; misfortune.

兆 *Kyōchō* bad omen.

年 *Kyōnen* year of bad harvest.

作 *Kyōsaku* bad crops.

事 *Kyōji* a calamity; death.

報 *Kyōhō* bad news.

惡 *Kyōaku* villainy; savageness.

漢 *Kyōkan* a villain.

器 *Kyōki* lethal weapons.

變 *Kyōhen* disaster.

三 臼 See 134,0.

凹 Ō. *Nakabiku* concave *heko(mu)* to be indented; be humiliated.

凸 *Ōtotsu* unevenness.

凸 Totsu. *Nakadaka* convex: *deko* a projecting part.

凹 *Dekoboko* uneven; having ups and downs.

坊 *Dekobō* name given to a mischievous or stupid boy.

起 *Tokki* convexity.

（一一二）

T 出 Shutsu; sui. *De(-ru)* (coll.); *i(zuru)* (lit. st.: this verb belongs to *shimo ni-dan* 下 *gyō*) to come out; go out; come; go: *da(su)* (coll.); *ida(su)* (lit. st.) to put out; takeout; send out; indicates beginning of action.

入 *De-iri* arrivals and departures; said of one who goes to a house regularly or ordinarily, as tradesman, doctor, etc.: *shutsu-nyū* arrivals and departures.

入口 *Deiriguchi* entrance (and exit); doorway.

口 *Deguchi* exit.

水 *Shussui* flood.

火 *Shukka* outbreak of fire.

立 *Shuttatsu* departure.

世 *Shusse* rise in the world; success.

札口 *Shussatsu-guchi* booking-office.

任 *Demakase ni* at random; without due reflection.

合 *De-a(u)* to meet; encounter.

先 *Desaki* the place one has gone or is going to.

帆 *Shuppan* departure (of vessel).

身 *Shusshin* a graduate; native.

沒 *Shutsubotsu* appearing unexpectedly at irregular intervals.

廷 *Shuttei* appearance in a law-court.

76

兵 *Shuppei* the despatch of troops.

金 *Shukkin* to invest; subscribe; contribute.

征 *Shussei* departure for the front.

奔 *Shuppon* absconding; running away.

來 *Deki* result; finish: *deki-(-ru)* (coll.) to be able; be ready; be made; be done: *shuttai suru* to happen; appear; occur; be accomplished.

來上 *Deki-aga(ru)* to be accomplished; completed.

來合 *Deki-ai* ready-made.

來事 *Dekigoto* an event; accident.

來榮 *Dekibae* result.

來心 *Dekigokoro* sudden impulse; caprice.

拔 *Dashinu(ku)* to get an advantage over others; cheat.

版 *Shuppan* publishing; printing.

京 *Shukkyō* coming to the capital.

品 *Shuppin* the act of exhibiting articles; an article exhibited.

前 *Demae* sending food from a restaurant to people's houses.

迎 *Demukae* going to meet a person.

師 *Suishi* the despatch of an army.

席 *Shusseki* attendance; presence.

納 *Suitō* expenditures and receipts.

馬 *Shutsuba* taking part in a compaign (e. g. political).

家 *Shukke* a Buddhist priest.

產 *Shussan* birth.

御 *Shutsugyo* the going out of the Emperor.

動 *Shutsudō* to move; set out.

張 *Shutchō* going to any place for official duty or business purpose.

現 *Shutsugen* appearance.

棺 *Shukkan* the departure of a coffin (for grave).

訴 *Shusso* bringing a suit (at law).

發 *Shuppatsu* setting out; departure.

港 *Shukkō* departure (of vessel).

費 *Shuppi* outlay; expense.

雲 *Izumo* p. n.

會 *De-a(u); shukkai* to meet.

勤 *Shukkin* attendance at office.

資 *Shusshi* contribution; investment.

獄 *Shutsugoku* discharge from prison.

演 *Shutsuen* address; performance.

稼 *Dekasegi* being at work in another country.

頭 *Shuttō* presence; attendance.

（山）

出

藍 *Shutsuran* better than one's parent or teacher.

願 *Shutsugan* application; making a petition.

鱈目 *Detarame* speaking at random.

六 **画**

T See **畫** 129,6. 【田】

函

KAN. *Hako* a box.

館 *Hakodate* p. n.

根 *Hakone* p. n.

七 **凾**

See preced.

幽

T YŪ. *Kasuka* dim; dark; to be hidden; retired. 【幺】

玄 *Yūgen* profoundness; mystery.

谷 *Yūkoku* deep ravine.

明 *Yūmei* this and the other world.

冥 *Yūmei* the other world; Hades.

閉 *Yūhei* confinement in one's own house; imprisonment.

邃 *Yūsui* retired and quiet.

靈 *Yūrei* a ghost.

二三 **齒**

See 211,0.

八 **刀**

When at the right it generally takes the form 刂 and is then called *Rittō*.

刀

T TŌ. *Katana* sword. Do not confound with 力 19,0.

自 *Tōji* lady; mistress of a house.

圭界 *Tōkeikai* medical world.

劍 *Tōken* a sword.

一

刃

See foll. → **刃** T →foll

刄

JIN; NIN. *Yaiba* sword; weapon: *ha* blade.

物 *Hamono* an edged tool.

傷 *Ninjō* to wound with a sword.

二

T **切**

SETSU; SAI. *Ki(ru)* to cut; divide: *kire* a cloth; piece; slice: *shikiri ni* eagerly; intently: *semete* at least; at most; even.

口上 *Kiri-kōjō* a stiff, formal way of speaking.

手 *Kitte* postage stamp; ticket.

出 *Kiridashi* a knife.

羽詰 *Seppatsuma(ru)* to be driven into a corner.

地 *Kireji* stuff for clothes.

扨 *Kirinuki* a cutting; a clipping.

迫 *Seppaku* being pressed or urged.

望 *Setsubō* earnest desire

符 *Kippu* ticket.

78

齒扼腕 *Sesshi-yakuwan* gnash one's teeth and roll up one's sleeves with chagrin.

張 *Kiribari* cutting the torn paper (as from a sliding screen) and repairing by pasting new paper over.

開 *Sekkai* operation (surgical).

腹 *Seppuku* suicide by cutting open the abdomen; what foreigners often, and Japanese seldom, call *harakiri*.

瑳琢磨 *Sessa-takuma* work hard; polish.

賣 *Kiriuri* selling by pieces.

斷 *Setsudan* cutting off; amputation.

斷面 *Setsudam-men* section.

T 刈 *Ka(ru)* to cut; reap. →140,4

入 *Kariire* harvest.

刑 KEI to condemn; punishment; rule.

事 *Keiji* a criminal case; a plain-clothes policeman; police detective.

法 *Keihō* criminal law or laws; a penal code.

務所 *Keimusho* prison.

場 *Keijō* execution-ground.

期 *Keiki* term of imprisonment.

餘 *Keiyo* ex-convict.

戮 *Keiriku* capital punishment.

罰 *Keibatsu* punishment; penalty.

刎 FUN. *Ha(neru)* to cut; behead; reject.

頸の交 *Funkei-no-majiwari* close friendship.

兔 See 10,5.

判 HAN a seal; stamp; to judge; determine. *Waka(ru)* to become known. →判 T

任官 *Hannin-kan* junior official.

決 *Hanketsu* judicial decision or sentence.

別 *Hambetsu* judgement; discrimination.

明 *Hammei* become clear.

事 *Hanji* a judge.

定 *Hantei* judgement.

官 *Hankan; hangan* a judge.

取張 *Hantori-chō* receipt-book.

然 *Hanzen* clearly; distinctly.

斷 *Handan* judgement.

讀 *Handoku* deciphering.

删 SAN; SAKU. *Kezu(ru)* to scrape off; revise.

除 *Sanjo* to reduce; curtail; lessen.

T 別 BETSU different; another. *Waka(reru)* to be separated: *wa(keru)*; *waka(tsu)* to separate; distinguish.

（五）別

々 *Betsu-betsu* separate.

宅 *Bettaku* a separate house; a villa.

居 *Bekkyo* live in a separate house.

狀 *Betsujō* unusual matter.

封 *Beppū* under separate cover.

段 *Betsudan* specially.

個 *Bekko* special; another.

格 *Bekkaku* special; out of the ordinary.

記 *Bekki* a separate paragraph.

紙 *Besshi* an enclosure in a letter.

途 *Betto* special.

莊 *Bessō* a country-place; villa.

條 *Betsujō* unusual thing.

項 *Bekkō* a separate paragraph.

當 *Bettō* the High Steward; chief commissioner; a groom.

意 *Betsui* a different opinion; objection; malice.

製 *Bessei* special make.

儀 *Betsugi* another thing; special; unusual.

懇 *Bekkon* specially intimate.

嬪 *Beppin* a beauty (woman).

離 *Betsuri* parting.

辭 *Betsuji* farewell speech.

劫 Kō; Gō; KYŌ to plunder. *Obiyaka(su)* to threaten; menace. （五）

T刷 SATSU to clear away; plane; pare; strike out. *Su(ru)* to print. 六

毛 *Hake* a brush.

新 *Sasshin* reform; renovation.

T制 SEI to control; govern; rule.

止 *Seishi* restraint; check.

定 *Seitei* enactment; establishment.

服 *Seifuku* a uniform.

限 *Seigen* restriction.

度 *Seido* a system; regulation.

海權 *Seikaiken* command of the sea.

御 *Seigyo* to control; govern.

規 *Seiki* rules.

裁 *Seisai* penalty; restriction.

刹 SATSU; SETSU a Buddhist temple.

那 *Setsuna* the moment.

T刺 SHI; SEKI a visiting card. *Sa(su)* to stab; stick: *toge* thorn; splinter.

Do not confound with 剌 18,7.

身 *Sashimi* slices of raw fish.

客 *Sekkaku; shikaku* an assassin.

殺 *Shisatsu* to kill by stabbing.

（六）

載 *Shigeki* stimulus.

激 *Shigeki* stimulus.

繡 *Shishū; nuitori* embroidery.

T 刻 KOKU a period of time. *Kiza(mu)* to carve; chop fine.

々 *Kokkoku* moment by moment; every moment.

印 *Kokuin* a stamp; seal.

苦 *Kokku* to toil; labour.

限 *Kokugen* a fixed hour; time.

剌 See prec.

券 KEN ticket; note; deed; certificate. →T 券

（七）T 負 See 154,2.

T 削 SAKU; SHŌ. *Kezu(ru); so(gu)* to scrape; cut off; take away; slice.

正 *Sakusei* to revise; correct.

除 *Sakujo* erasure.

減 *Sakugen* reduction.

剃 TEI. *So(ru); su(ru)* to shave.

刀 *Kamisori* a razor.

髮 *Teihatsu* to become a Buddhist priest.

剌 RATSU pungent. Do not confound with 刺 18,6.

（八）剖 BŌ; HŌ to divide: tear asunder; dissect. →剖 T

*1
T 剣 →18,14

81

（八）

T 剤 See 劑 210,2. 【刀】

荊 See 荆 140,6.

T 剛 GŌ; KŌ hard. *Tsuyoi* strong: *kowai* valiant.

直 *Gōchoku* integrity.

勇 *Gōyū* intrepidity.

氣 *Gōki* brave; courageous; resolute.

健 *Gōken* sturdy; strong.

愎 *Gōfuku* obstinacy.

毅 *Gōki* steadfast; sturdy.

膽 *Gōtan* brave; resolute; daring.

剝 HAKU. *Ha(gu); mu(ku)* to flay; skin; peel; deprive of: *haga(su);* to strip off: *haga(reru)* to be stripped off.

落 *Hakuraku* falling off.

奪 *Hakudatsu* to seize; take by force; deprive of.
*1

（九）副 FUKU vice-(used in official titles). *So(u)* to go along with; comply with.

官 *Fukkan* secretary (army).

使 *Fukushi* an assistant ambassador or envoy.

食物 *Fukushokubutsu* side-dish.

產物 *Fukusambutsu* by-products.

署 *Fukusho* countersignature.

業 *Fukugyō* side work; subsidiary work.

剪 See 140,8. 【刀】

*2
T 剩 →18,10

一〇 劏 GAI to cut; a sickle.

切 *Gaisetsu* appropriate; pertinent.

T 創 SŌ. *Haji(meru)* to begin: *kizu* wound.

立 *Sōritsu* establishment.

作 *Sōsaku* to create; write a literary work.

造 *Sōzō* to create.

痍 *Sōi* a wound.

痕 *Sōkon* a scar.

意 *Sōi* an original thought.

業 *Sōgyō* the commencement of an enterprise or business.

T 割 KATSU. *Wa(ru)* to divide: *wari* 10%; rate per cent; share: *sa(ku)* to tear.

引 *Waribiki* discount.

合 *Wariai* proportion: *wariai ni* relatively; comparatively.

戻 *Warimodoshi* rebate.

前 *Warimae* a share.

烹 *Kappō* cookery.

當 *Wariate* assignment.

愛 *Katsuai* spare; part with.

増 *Warimashi* extra (charge).

據 *Kakkyo* to hold one's own.

讓 *Katsujō* cession.

剰 JŌ. *Ama(ru)* to exceed; be left over: *amatsusae* in addition. →18, 9 T *²

餘 *Joyo* a surplus; balance; remainder. 一〇

剽 HYŌ to cut. *Ha(gu)* to flay. 一一

輕 *Hyōkin* witty; funny; jocular.

竊 *Hyōsetsu* literary piracy.

劃 KAKU to divide. *Kiza(mu)* to mince. 一二

劉 RYŪ a broad axe; to kill. 一三

T 劇 GEKI drama. *Hageshii* violent; extreme; very.

甚 *Gekijin* intense.

烈 *Gekiretsu* violence; severity.

務 *Gekimu* press of business.

場 *Gekijō* theatre.

壇 *Gekidan* the stage.

戰 *Gekisen* a severe fight.

藥 *Gek'yaku* strong medicine

劍 See 劍 18,14.

劈 HEKI. *Tsunza(ku)* to burst; to break: *sa(ku)* to tear.

頭 *Hekitō* very beginning.

劍 KEN. *Tsurugi* sword. →18, 8 * T 一四

呑 *Ken* non dangerous.

突 *Kentsuku* scolding.

82

（一四）

術　*Kenjutsu* fencing.

幕　*Kemmaku* the countenance.

橋　*Kemburijji* Cambridge.

一九　力

T 力　RYOKU; RIKI. *Chikara* strength; power; force: *tsuto(meru)* to endeavour; exert one's powers: *tsuto-mete* to the best of one's power: *riki(mu)* to bluster; swagger; strain. Do not confound with 刀 18,0.

士　*Rikishi* wrestler.

行　*Rikkō* exertion.

持　*Chikaramochi* strong man.

量　*Rik'ryō* physical strength; capacity; talent.

說　*Rikisetsu* to give point to; emphasize.

三 T 加　KA. *Kuwa(h)eru* to add; join; increase: *kuwawa(ru)* to join; enter.

入　*Kanyū* entrance; joining.

工　*Kakō* work upon.

之　*Shika nomi narazu; kore ni kuwōru ni* (inverted order) moreover.

州　*Kashū; Kariforuniya-shū* State of California.

奈陀　*Kanada* Canada.

味　*Kami* season with; add.

（三一）

持　*Kaji* incantation.

害者　*Kagaisha* assailant.

答兒　*Kataru* catarrh.

減　*Kagen* arrangement; adjustment; state of one's health; seasoning.

賀　*Kaga* p. n.

盟　*Kamei* joining; entrance.

勢　*Kasei* to unite forces; help; auxiliary troops.

擔　*Katan* assistance; support.

護　*Kago* divine protection.

T 助　JO. *Tasu(keru); tasuka-(ru); su(keru)* to save; rescue; help; assist.

力　*Joryoku* aid; support; assistance.

手　*Joshu* an assistant.

成　*Josei* assistance.

言　*Jogen; jogon* advice; suggestion.

役　*Joyaku* an assistant official.

命　*Jomei* sparing a life.

長　*Jochō* to help; to make prosperous; improve; cultivate.

船　*Tasukebune* a life-boat.

勢　*Josei* assistance.

T 励　See 勵 19,15.

劫　See 刧 18,5.

T 労　See 勞 19,10.

83

(五)

努 T Do. *Tsuto(meru)* to endeavour; labour; exert oneself.

力 *Doryoku* utmost effort.

劾 六 GAI to investigate crime; condemn.

効 T Kō (good) result; validity; efficacy; merit; exploit; to learn. *Shirushi* result; effect. →66, 6

力 *Kōryoku* effect; validity.

用 *Kōyō* utility.

果 *Kōka* effect; result.

能 *Kōnō* effect; result.

驗 *Kōken* benefit; good results.

劲 七 KEI. *Tsuyoi* strong; hard.

勃 BOTSU to rise; suddenly.

々 *Botsu-botsu* spirited.

牙利 *Burugariya* Bulgaria.

起 *Bokki* erection.

然 *Botsuzen* suddenly; in a flare.

爾瓦利 *Burugaria* Bulgaria.

興 *Bokkō* arising suddenly.

勅 T CHOKU Imperial. *Mikoto-nori* Imperial decree. →66, 7

令 *Chokurei* an Imperial ordinance.

任官 *Chokuninkan* an official of the Imperially-appointed class.

旨 *Chokushi* Imperial wishes.

(七)

命 *Chokumei* Imperial commands.

使 *Chokushi* an Imperial messenger.

許 *Chokkyo* Imperial permission.

裁 *Chokusai* Imperial decision.

語 *Chokugo* an Imperial rescript.

諭 *Chokuyu* an Imperial mandate.

選議員 *Chokusengiin* an Imperial nominee.

勉 T BEN. *Tsuto(meru)* to do one's best; exert oneself.

強 *Benkyō* study; diligence; effort.

學 *Bengaku* (diligent) study.

勵 *Benrei* endeavour; diligence.

勇 T YŪ courage. *Isamashii* brave : *isa(mu)* to be emboldened.

名 *Yūmei* famed for courage.

壯 *Yūsō na* lively; energetic; vigorous; courageous.

往邁進 *Yūō-maishin* dash; push.

退 *Yūtai* resign with good grace.

氣 *Yūki* courage.

烈 *Yūretsu* boldness.

猛 *Yūmō* intrepidity.

健 *Yūken* good health.

敢 *Yūkan* bravery.

八 脅 KYŌ. *Obiyaka(su)* to threaten. 【肉】

迫 *Kyōhaku* threat.

威 *Kyōi* menace; threat.

喝 *Kyōkatsu* a threat; intimidation.

嚇 *Kyōkaku* threat; menace.

九 T 動 DŌ. *Ugoka(su)*; *ugo(ku)* to move: *yayamo sureba* apt; prone; liable: *dōzuru* (irreg.) be perturbed.

力 *Dōryoku* motive power.

作 *Dōsa* action.

物 *Dōbutsu* animal.

物園 *Dōbutsuen* zoological gardens.

脈 *Dōmyaku* artery.

員 *Dōin* mobilization.

産 *Dōsan* movable property.

悸 *Dōki* palpitation; beating of the heart.

詞 *Dōshi* a verb.

搖 *Dōyō* shock; unrest.

亂 *Dōran* disturbance; upheaval.

靜 *Dōsei* motion and rest; movement; condition.

機 *Dōki* a motive.

議 *Dōgi* a motion (as in parliament.)

T 勘 KAN to consider; decide.

考 *Kankō* thought; consideration.

定 *Kanjō* account.

當 *Kandō* disowning; desinheriting.

違 *Kanchigai* mistaken impression.

察加 *Kamuchakka* Kamchatka.

辨 *Kamben* forgiveness; mercy.

努 See T 務 110,6. 【力】

勞 RŌ labour; fatigue; to get tired. *Itawa(ru)* to pity; treat with consideration. →19,5T

力 *Rōryoku* toil; labour.

役 *Rōeki* labour; toil.

苦 *Rōku* labour; hardship.

働 *Rōdō* labour.

働組合 *Rōdō-kumiai* Trade Union.

資 *Rōshi* labour and capital.

農政府 *Rōnōseifu* Soviet Government.
*

勤 KIN to be diligent. *Tsuto(meru)* to work diligently; be employed. →19,10 * T

王 *Kinnō* loyalty.

勉 *Kimben* industry; diligence.

務 *Kimmu* the performance of duties; service.

惰 *Kinda* diligence and idleness.

勞 *Kinrō* service; diligence.

儉 *Kinken* strict economy.

一
(九)
→19,○

(一二) 勤

績 *Kinzoku* continuous service.

T勧 See 勸 19,18.

T勢 SEI condition: SE. *Ikioi* power; energy; strength; force.

力 *Seiryoku* energy; vitality; influence.

力範圍 *Seiryoku-han-i* sphere of influence.

力圏 *Seiryokuken* sphere of influence.

州 *Seishū* another name for the province of Ise.

望 *Seibō* fame; reputation.

*援 *Seien* help; support.

一四 勳 KUN order of merit. *Isao; isaoshi* merit. →19, 13 * T

功 *Kunkō* merit; distinguished service.

臣 *Kunshin* a meritorious subject.

記 *Kunki* a diploma (of a decoration).

章 *Kunshō* a decoration; order of merit.

一五 勵 REI. *Hagema(su)* to encourage; stimulate; urge: *hage(mu)* to strive; endeavour; work diligently. →19, 11T

行 *Reikō* strict enforcement.

一八 勸 KAN to encourage. *Susu(meru)* to recommend; persuade. →19, 5T

*T勲 →19, 14

(一八) 工場 *Kankōba* a bazaar.

告 *Kankoku* advice; counsel.

善懲惡 *Kanzen-chōaku* to encourage virtue and repress vice.

業 *Kangyō* encouragement of industry.

業債券 *Kangyōsaiken* hypothec debentures.

銀 *Kangin* abb. for the Hypothec Bank of Japan.

誘 *Kan-yū* canvassing.

勹 二〇

勺 See foll. 一

T勺 SHAKU unit of capacity, 1/10 of *gō;* see Introduction 44; to drink (wine); ladle.

勿 MOCHI; KOTSU. *Nakare* not; do not. 二

怪 *Mokke* unexpected.

論 *Mochiron* of course.

體 *Mottai* an air of importance: *mottai nai* impious; wasteful.

T匁 *Momme* unit of weight, 1/1000 *kan;* see Introduction 44.

匂 *Nioi* scent: *nio(u)* to smell; glitter.

勾 KŌ. *Maga(ru)* to be curved; bent.

（二）玉　*Magatama* a bead.

配　*Kōbai* a slope.

三　包　HŌ.　*Tsutsu(mu)* to envelop; wrap up: *tsutsumi* a packet.

→包 T

含　*Hōgan* inclusion.

括　*Hōkatsu* to be contained in; be comprised in.

容　*Hōyō* to include; capacious; tolerance.

圍　*Hōi* envelopment; siege.

裝　*Hōsō* packing.

藏　*Hōzō* contain; conceal.

T 句　KU phrase; sentence; poem; verse.【口】

切　*Kugiri* punctuation.

點　*Kuten* punctuation marks.

讀　*Kutō* punctuation.

匆　SŌ.　*Iso'gu)* to hasten.

々　*Sō-sō* excuse haste (at end of letter).

四　匈　KYŌ.

牙利　*Hangarii* Hungary.

T 旬　JUN a period of ten days.【日】

日　*Junjitsu* a period of ten days.

七　匍　HO.　*Ha(u)* to crawl.

匐　*Hofuku* creeping.

匐　FUKU.　*Ha(u)* to crawl.　九

匕

二一

匕　HI.　*Saji* a spoon.

首　*Hishu; aikuchi* a dagger.

T 切　See 18,2.　二

T 比　See 81,0.

T 北　HOKU.　*Kita* north.　三
→1,4

氷洋　*Hokuhyōyō; hoppyōyō* Arctic Ocean

米　*Hokubei* North America.

京　*Pekin* Peking.

海道　*Hokkaidō* p. n.

海　*Hokkai* the North Sea.

叟笑む　*Hokusoe(mu)* chuckle with glee.

部　*Hokubu* the northern part.

陸　*Hokuriku* p. n.

條　*Hōjō* p. n.

極　*Hokkyoku* the North Pole.

端　*Hokutan* the northern extremity.

緯　*Hokui* north latitude.

四 旨 **T** SHI. *Mune* object; aim: *umai* pleasant to the taste; skilful: *oishii* pleasant to the taste; sweet. 【日】

趣 *Shishu* import; gist.

八 眞 SHIN. *Makoto* genuine; correct; truth; reality: *ma* as top character has often an emphatic force. (*Sane*). 【日】 →24, 8*T

人間 *Maningen* an honest man.

中 *Mannaka* the middle.

心 *Magokoro* innermost feelings; sincerity.

正 *Shinsei* genuine.

田 *Sanada* braid; p. n.

甲 *Makkō* right in the face.

平 *Mappira* earnestly.

先 *Massaki* at the very first.

如 *Shinnyo* substance; entity.

更 *Manzara* not entirely.

似 *Mane* imitation; mimicry.

空 *Shinkū* a vacuum.

宗 *Shinshū* the Shin sect.

性 *Shinsei* genuine; true.

紅 *Shinku* deep red.

相 *Shinsō* the true state or condition.

面目 *Majime* soberness; sincerity.

砂 *Masago* sand.

症 *Shinshō* genuine illness.

倒 *Massakasama* head over heels.

珠 *Shinju* pearl.

理 *Shinri* truth.

情 *Shinjō* true feelings.

意 *Shin-i* real intention.

偽 *Shingi* authenticity.

劍 *Shinken* earnest; serious; a real sword.

實 *Shinjitsu* truth.

價 *Shinka* real value.

影 *Shin-ei* photograph.

摯 *Shinshi* sincerity; earnestness.

鍮 *Shinchū* brass.

髓 *Shinzui* the pith; essence.

T 能 NŌ talent; ability; name of a dance. *Ata(u)* to be able: *yoku* well. 【肉】

力 *Nōryoku* faculty; ability.

文 *Nobun* a good style.

事 *Nōji* one's sole ideal of existence.

書 *Nōgaki* drug advertisement; boast: *nōsho* fine penmanship.

率 *Nōritsu* efficiency.

動 *Nōdō* activity; Active Voice.

登 *Noto* p. n.

筆 *Nōhitsu* good penmanship.

辯 *Nōben* eloquence.

頃 KEI recently. *Koro* about: 九 *shibaraku* a certain length of time; for some time. 【頁】

（九）

匙 SHI. *Saji* spoon.

加減 *Saji-kagen* compounding of medicine ; discretion ; management.

疑 GI. *Utaga(u) ; utagu(ru)* to doubt ; suspect ; be bewildered : *utagawashii* doubtful ; suspicious.【疋】

心 *Gishin* suspicion.

似 *Giji* to be in doubt ; quasi-.

念 *Ginen* doubt ; suspicion ; uncertainty.

問 *Gimon* a question ; doubt.

懼 *Gigu* to fear ; dread ; apprehend.

惑 *Giwaku* doubt ; suspicion ; uncertainty ; perplexity.

義 *Gigi* doubt.

獄 *Gigoku* a scandal.

團 *Gidan* doubt.

☳

匚

☶

匚

二 巨 KYO. *Ōi naru* great ; large.【工】
T

人 *Kyojin* a giant.

（一一）

大 *Kyodai* huge ; gigantic.

砲 *Kyohō* a big gun.

細 *Kyosai ; kosai* details.

富 *Kyofu* big fortune.

萬 *Kyoman* myriad.

億 *Kyooku* millions.

擘 *Kyohaku* an authority ; a star ; the thumb.

額 *Kyogaku* an enormous sum.

匹 HITSU ; HIKI aux. num. for
T counting animals, also for cloth. See Introduction 44. *Tagui* sort ; kind.

夫 *Hippu* common man ; fellow of low position.

敵 *Hitteki* equality ; comparability ; a rival.

儔 *Hitchū* equal.

匸 See 區 23,9.
T

匡 KYO. *Tada(su)* to correct ;
to assist ; save.【匚】

正 *Kyōsei* to correct ; mend.

濟 *Kyōsai* relief ; reformation.

匠 SHŌ. *Takumi* an expert ;
T a master ; a carpenter.【匚】

臣 See 131,0.
T

医 See 醫 164,11.
T

匪 HI vagabond ; bad.【匚】

四

五

八

89

(八)

匪
徒 *Hito* bandit.

賊 *Hizoku* bandit.

九 **區** KU subdivision of some cities; division; district; boundary. →23, 2 T

々 *Kuku; machimachi* diverse; various.

分 *Kubun* a distinction; difference; classification.

別 *Kubetsu* difference; discrimination.

域 *Kuiki* limits; boundaries; area.

劃 *Kukaku* division; boundary.

T **匿** TOKU. *Kaku(reru)* to hide.

名 *Tokumei* to conceal one's name.

二四 **十**

T **十** JŪ (becomes JI before a double consonant. *To; to* ten.

一月 *Jū-ichi-gatsu* November.

二月 *Jū-ni-gatsu* December.

人十色 *Jūnin-toiro* each person is different to everybody else; tot capita quot sensus.

人並 *Jūnin-nami* average.

八番 *Jūhachiban; ohako* a favourite trick or performance.

日 *Tōka* 10 days; the 10th day of the month.

中八九 *Jūchūhakku* in 8 or 9 cases out of 10.

月 *Jū-gatsu* October : *to-tsuki* 10 months.

分 *Jūbun* quite; plenty; abundance : *jūbu* 10 parts : *jippun* 10 minutes.

文字 *Jūmonji* a cross; crosswise.

字 *Jūji* in the form of a cross.

字架 *Jūjika* a cross.

全 *Jūzen* perfection.

廿 *Ni-jū* twenty. 一

才 *Nijissai; hatachi* twenty years of age.

日 *Hatsuka* 20th day of the month; 20 days.

T **丈** See 1,2.

旡 See T **左** 24,3 【工】 二

T **友** YŪ. *Tomo* friend; companion. 【又】

軍 *Yūgun* comrades in arms; fellow-soldiers.

情 *Yūjō* friendship; friendliness.

愛 *Yūai* friendship.

達 *Tomodachi* friend.

（一）

誼　*Yūgi* friendship.

禪　*Yūzen* printed muslin.

T 支　See 65,0.

T 斗　See 68,0.

T 午　Go noon. *Uma* 7th zodiacal sign, the horse. See Introduction 42, 43. Do not confound with 牛 93,0.

后　*Gogo* afternoon.

前　*Gozen* forenoon.

後　*Gogo* afternoon.

砲　*Gohō*; *don* the noon-gun.

睡　*Gosui* a nap.

餐　*Gosan* luncheon.

卆　See 卒 8,6. 【十】

T 升　SHŌ unit of capacity. See Introduction 44. *Masu* verbal termination. Sometimes used in stead of 昇 72,4. (→136,1)

卅　*San-jū* thirty.

T 市　See 8,3. 【巾】

T 牛　See 93,0.

丰　BŌ appearance. 【丨】

─────

三 T 左　SA. *Hidari* left; the following (in written language). 【工】 →24,2

右　*Sayū* left and right: *sajū suru* to influence;

─── (right column) ───

三

cause (somebody) to change; command.

官　*Sakan* plasterer.

祖　*Satan* to support.

記　*Saki* undermentioned.

程　*Sahodo* so; so much; large amount.

樣　*Sayō* yes; just so.

遷　*Sasen* degradation.

翼　*Sayoku* the left wing.

T 右　YŪ; U. *Migi* right; the above (in written language). 【口】

往左往　*Uōsaō* going to the right and left; in various directions.

翼　*Uyoku* the right wing.

T 布　FU. *Nuno* cloth; linen; woven fabric: *shi(ku)* to spread; put into force. 【巾】

令　*Furei* a decree; order; proclamation.

告　*Fukoku* notification; edict; order.

哇　*Hawai* Hawaii.

施　*Fuse* alms; offering.

設　*Fusetsu* to construct; build; lay down; establish.

敎　*Fukyō* propagation of religion.

置　*Fuchi* framing; placing.

T 古　KO. *Furui* old; stale: *inishie* old times: *furu(su)* to become old. 【口】

手　*Furu-te* second-hand.

（三三）

古今 *Kokon* ancient and modern.

代 *Kodai* olden times.

色 *Koshoku* an antique look.

老 *Korō* an old man.

物 *Kobutsu* an antique; curio.

來 *Korai* from ancient times.

典 *Koten* classics.

風 *Kofū* old fashion.

倫母 *Korombo* Colombo.

狸 *Furudanuki* an old bird (stager); an old badger.

參 *Kosan* an old official employee, or servant; senior.

稀 *Koki* seventieth year of age.

道具 *Furudōgu* old furniture.

著 *Furugi* old clothes.

跡 *Koseki* old traces; old ruins; ancient vestiges.

語 *Kogo* old saying; proverb.

蹟 *Koseki* old traces; old ruins; ancient vestiges.

顔 *Furugao* familiar face.

卉 KI grass; plant.

半 HAN half. *Nakaba* midst of; middle. →半 T

々 *Hanhan* one half.

巾 *Hankechi* a handkerchief.

月 *Hangetsu* the moon when not full: *hantsuki* half a month.

分 *Hambun* the half of anything.

（三二）

日 *Hannichi* half a day.

白 *Hampaku* grey-haired.

打 *Handāsu* half dozen.

玉 *Hangyoku* a young geisha (singing girl).

可通 *Hankatsū* half learned.

死 *Hanshi* being half dead.

信半疑 *Hanshin-hangi* in doubt; indecisive.

面 *Hammen* half the face; the one side.

島 *Hantō* peninsula.

紙 *Hanshi* a common kind of paper.

球 *Hankyū* hemisphere.

途 *Hanto* half-way.

減 *Hangen* reduction by half.

期 *Hanki* a half year.

腹 *Hampuku* half-way up a mountain.

端 *Hampa* incomplete; part; fragment.

旗 *Hanki* the flag at half-mast.

熟 *Hanjuku* half ripe; half boiled.

額 *Hangaku* a half amount.

襟 *Han-eri* an ornamental neck-band.

鐘 *Hanshō* fire-bell.

纏 *Hanten* workman's coat.

世 See T 世 1,4 and 卅 24,2.

T
在 ZAI the country. *A(ru)* (irreg.) to be; be in: *ima-* 四

92

(*su*)；*owasuru* (irreg.)：*mashima*(*su*) to be；live；be present；dwell. 【土】

中　*Zaichū* being inside；contain；e. g. "(photos)" only.

世　*Zaisei*；*zaise* when living.

外　*Zaigai* stationed abroad.

宅　*Zaitaku* at home.

任中　*Zaininchū* while in office.

位　*Zaii* a reign.

所　*Zaisho* the country.

來　*Zairai* hitherto；up to now；accustomed.

京　*Zaik,ō* residence in Tōkyō.

留　*Zair,ū* resident at.

荷　*Zaika*；*arini* stock in hand.

野　*Zaiya* out of office.

野黨　*Zaiyatō* a non-government party.

鄉軍人　*Zaigō-gunjin* ex-soldiers；military men in their homes.

勤　*Zaikin* doing duty in a place；resident.

學　*Zaigaku* be attending at a school.

職　*Zaishoku* hold office.

T 存　ZON；SON to exist；know；think；believe；remain；feel；corresponds sometimes to, I hope or suppose. 【子】

亡　*Sombō* existence；fate；life and death.

分　*Zombun* without reserve.

外　*Zongai* contrary to expectation.

立　*Sonritsu* existence.

在　*Sonzai* existence.

命　*Zommei* alive.

候　*Zonjisōrō* I think (epist. st.).

廢　*Sompai* existence；maintenance or abolishment.

續　*Sonzoku* continuance.

T 有　YŪ；U. A(*ru*) (irreg.) to be；there is；have got；to have；hold；keep；possess. 【月】

力　*Yūryoku* powerful；influential.

之　*Koreari* (inverted order) to be；there is.

用　*Yūyō* useful.

史　*Yūshi* history.

合　*Ariawase*；*ariai* pot-luck；something on hand；ready-made.

名　*Yūmei* famous.

材　*Yūzai* ability；talent；clever.

志　*Yūshi* a volunteer；person interested；supporter.

形的　*Yūkeiteki,* material；concrete.

利　*Yūri* profitable.

事　*Yūji* an emergency.

效　*Yūkō* efficiency；validity.

明　*Ariake* day-break；a night light.

耶無耶　*Uyamuya* ambiguity.

（四）

有

限責任會社 *Yūgen-sekinin-kaisha* Limited Company.

毒 *Yūdoku* poisonous.

望 *Yūbō* a bright prospect.

益 *Yūeki* profitable; beneficial.

害 *Yūgai* noxiousness; injury.

頂天 *Uchōten* ecstasy; rapture.

爲 *Yūi* capable.

爲轉變 *Ui-tempen* incessant change.

無 *Umu; yūmu; arinashi* existence or non-existence.

勝 *Arigachi* common occurrence.

象無象 *Uzōmuzō* all sorts and conditions of people.

價證券 *Yūkashōken* securities.

樣 *Arisama* state; appearance.

數 *Yūsū* prominent; celebrated.

難 *Arigatai* thankful.

難迷感 *Arigata-meiwaku* misplaced kindness.

繋 *Sasuga* notwithstanding; nevertheless; as one might have expected; truly; indeed.

觸 *Arifureta* common.

權者 *Yūkensha* elector.

體 *Aritei* without concealment; the exact truth.

灰 KAI. *Hai* ashes: *aku* lye. 【火】→27, 4 T

燼 *Kaijin* ashes.

古 See ^T世 1, 4.

^T年 NEN. *Toshi; tose* year. 【干】

々 *Nen-nen* year by year; every year.

中 *Nenjū* the whole year.

上 *Toshiue* older.

內 *Nennai* within the year.

月 *Nengetsu* years and months; time.

少 *Nenshō* young.

玉 *Toshidama* a New Year's present.

忌 *Nenki* anniversaries of the death of person.

始 *Nenshi* New Year's greetings.

明 *Nen-ake* the expiration of the term of service.

來 *Nenrai* for many years past.

長 *Nenchō* a senior.

取 *Toshi-to(ru)* to get old; be old.

限 *Nengen* a period; a term of years.

度 *Nendo* the term of one year.

貢 *Nengu* annual tribute; land-tax.

俸 *Nempō* yearly salary.

寄 *Toshiyori* an old person.

頃 *Toshigoro* for years past; marriageable age.

(四)

期 *Nenki* a fixed term of years; period of service, as a servant.

賀 *Nenga* New Year's congratulations.

報 *Nempō* annual report.

號 *Nengō* the name of an era (e. g. *Taishō* is a *nengō*).

賦 *Nempu* yearly instalment.

齒 *Nenshi* age of a person.

增 *Toshima* a middle-aged woman.

輩 *Nempai* age of a person.

齡 *Nenrei* age.

鑑 *Nenkan* year-book.

五
T 克 KOKU. *Ka(tsu)* to conquer: *yoku* well; right: *yoku suru* to be able. 【儿】

己 *Kokki* self-denial.

復 *Kokufuku* restoration.

甫 FU; HO large. *Hajime* the beginning. 【用】

六
T 協 KYŌ. *Awa(seru)* to agree with; to unite・ join together; *kana(u)* to be granted; be fulfilled.

力 *Kyōryoku* co-operation.

同 *Kyōdō* uniting together.

定 *Kyōtei* agreement.

約 *Kyōyaku* agreement.

商 *Kyōshō* negotiation.

會 *Kyōkai* society; association.

(六)

調 *Kyōchō* co-ordinate; concert.

贊 *Kyōsan* approval; consent.

議 *Kyōgi* conference; discussion.

肴 See 130,4.

T 直 CHOKU; JIKI. *Tadachi ni; sugu* direct; immediately; at once: *nao* straight; honest; right: *nao(su)* to mend; correct: *ne* price; value. 【目】

下 *Chokka* right under; directly below.

立 *Chokuritsu* stand erect.

行 *Chokkō* run through.

系 *Chokkei* direct line.

言 *Chokugen* direct speech.

披 *Jikihi* "personal" (on envelopes)

段 *Nedan* price.

徑 *Chokkei* diameter.

參 *Jikisan* immediate followers.

情徑行 *Chokujōkeikō* straight forward.

接 *Chokusetsu* direct.

通 *Chokutsū* direct communication; through traffic.

話 *Jikiwa* one's personal account of an event.

線 *Chokusen* a straight line.

樣 *Sugusama* at once; immediately.

談 *Jikidan* personal consultation.

（六）

直

輸入 *Jikiyunyū; chokuyunyū* direct import.

輸出 *Jikiyushutsu; chokuyushutsu* direct export.

營 *Chokuei* direct management.

轄 *Chokkatsu* direct control.

覺 *Chokkaku* intuition.

譯 *Chokuyaku* literal translation.

阜 See 170,0.

卑 HI. *Iyashii* mean; low; base: *iyashi(meru)* to despise; detest. →卑T

下 *Hige* (of language) humble; self-depreciatory.

劣 *Hiretsu* (of person or conduct) mean; ignoble; servile.

屈 *Hikutsu* (of person or conduct) mean; ignoble; servile.

怯 *Hikyō* cowardice.

近 *Hikin* common; ordinary.

俗 *Hizoku* vulgar.

賤 *Hisen* (of person) humble position; vulgar; mean.

七T **南** NAN. *Minami* south. (*Nami*).

氷洋 *Nampyōyō; Nanhyō ō* the Antarctic Ocean.

米 *Nambei* South America.

阿 *Nan-a* South Africa.

京 *Nankin* Nanking.

洋 *Nan-yō* South Sea (Islands). （七）

極 *Nankyoku* South Pole.

舉 See 舉 134,11.

T **索** SAKU lonely. *Nawa* a rope: *moto(meru)* to search; investigate; look for. 【糸】 八

引 *Sakuin* index; concordance.

畢 See 72,6. 【田】

眞 See 眞 21,8. 【目】

髙 See 喬 30,9. 九

T **乾** KAN; KEN heaven. *Ho-(su); kawa(ku); hi(-ru)* to dry: *inui* north-west. 【乙】

田 *Kanden* dry field (not paddy).

坤 *Kenkon* heaven and earth; the world.

物 *Kambutsu* dried vegetable.

杯 *Kampai* a toast.

板 *Kampan* a dry-plate (photography).

枯 *Hikara(biru)* to dry up.

酪 *Kanraku; chiizu;* cheese.

溜 *Kanryū* dry distillation.

燥 *Kansō* to dry up.

T **博** HAKU. *Hiroi* wide; liberal; universal. 一〇

(一〇)

士 *Hakushi; hakase* a doctor; an expert.

大 *Hakudai* wide; broad; extensive.

物 *Hakubutsu* natural history.

物館 *Hakubut.ukan* museum.

奕 *Bakuchi* gambling.

徒 *Bakuto* gambler.

愛 *Hakuai* philanthropy; benevolence.

聞 *Hakubun* learned; well-informed.·

學 *Hakugaku* extensive learning.

識 *Hakushiki* learned; erudite; well-informed.

覽 *Hakuran* wide reading.

覽會 *Hakurankai* an Exhibition.

辜 KO a sin; fault. 【辛】

賁 HI ornament; great. 【貝】

臨 *Hirin* (your) presence.

二一 T 幹 KAN to manage. *Miki* trunk (of tree); stalk. 【干】

事 *Kanji* secretary (of company); manager.

部 *Kambu* leaders; managing staff.

線 *Kansen* a main line.

T 準 JUN rule. *Nazora(h)eru* to imitate; make alike. 【水】

用 *Jun-yō* application.

(一一)

許 *Junkyo* sanction; to approve.

備 *Jumbi* preparation.

據 *Junkyo* be based upon.

肅 SHUKU to be circumspect; solemn; respectful. 【聿】
*

々 *Shuku-shuku* solemnly.

然 *Shukuzen* solemn; silent.

一二 斡 ATSU to rule; administer. 【斗】

旋 *Assen* mediation.

兢 KYŌ to be afraid; tremble (with fear). 【儿】 Do not confound with 競 117,15.

々 *Kyōkyō* cautiously; tremblingly.

一四 翰 KAN a writing; epistle. 【羽】

長 *Kanchō* the chief secretary.

二二 顰 HIN; BIN. *S'ika(meru)*; *hiso(mu)* to make a wry face; grieve. 【頁】

二五

卜

卜 BOKU. *Urana(u)* to divine; tell fortunes: *uranai* fortune-telling.

者 *Bokusha* one who practises divination; a fortune-teller.

一
T 上 Jō superior; Emperor; best; high: added to nouns composed of 2 or more characters, has a meaning of 'in regard to' and may be often translated by 'in' or 'for' e. g. *shōbai-jō* in business: *kyōiku-jō ii* good for (his) education: SHŌ. *Ue* on; above; after; besides: after a noun expressing relationship it has an honorific meaning e. g. *o b a - u e sama: nobo(ru); aga(ru)* to ascend; be completed: *a(geru)* to send up; complete; give (polite in 1st person); as 2nd component of verbs it is sometimes polite in 1st person e. g. *mō shi-a(geru)* to say: *kaite-a(geru)* to write it for you: *kami* the upper part: *tatematsu(ru)* to offer to a superior. 【一】

下 *Joge* relative rank; social position; ascent or descent; superiors and inferiors: *Shōka* Emperor and subjects; the governing and the governed.

手 *Jozu* skilful: *uwate* the better hand in doing anything.

戸 *Jogo* a drunkard.

方 *Kamigata* term applied to Kyōto and neighbourhood.

古 *Joko* remote antiquity.

申 *Josh'n* report; statement.

州 *Joshū* another name for the province of *Kōzuke*.

旬 *Jōjun* the first ten days of a month.

衣 *Uwagi* a coat.

告 *Jokoku* an appeal; demand for revision.

役 *Uwayaku* a superior official.

官 *Jokan* superior officers.

卷 *Jokan* volume I.

京 *Jokyō* to proceed to the capital.

長 *Jochō* a senior.

皇 *Jokō* an abdicated Emperor.

品 *Johin* high-class; superior quality; refined; elegant.

首尾 *Joshubi* a good result.

奏 *Josō* reporting to the Throne.

述 *Jojutsu* the above-stated.

前 *Uwamae* commission.

海 *Shanhai* Shanghai.

流 *Joryū* upper part of a river; the upper class (social); high class.

氣 *Joki* to suffer from a rush of blood to the head.

席 *Joseki* seniority; a higher seat.

級 *Jokyū* a high rank.

乘 *Jōjō* very best.

部 *Jobu* the upper part.

院 *Jin* the Upper House.

梓 *Joshi* publication.

陸 *Joriku* landing; disembarkation.

野 *Kōzuke* p. n.: *Ueno* p. n.

策 *Josaku* a good plan.

（二）

塲 *Jōjō* play on the stage.

等 *Jōtō* first class; of the best quality.

達 *Jōtatsu* progress; advance.

塗 *Uwanuri* final coating of plaster.

演 *Jōen* play on the stage.

聞 *Jōbun* being heard by the Emperor; Imperial hearing.

敷 *Uwashiki* a carpet; a sheet.

機嫌 *Jōkigen* high spirits.

騰 *Jōtō* to rise; increase.

覽 *Jōran* Imperial inspection.

三 T 占 SEN. *Shi(meru)* to occupy; take possession of: *urana-(u)* to tell fortunes; to divine: *uranai* fortune-telling. (*Ura*).

有 *Sen-yū* occupancy.

領 *Senryō* taking possession of; seizure; occupancy.

六 T 卓 TAKU a desk; high; eminent; excel.【十】

上 *Taku¯o* on the table.

子 *Teiburu* a table.

出 *Takushutsu* to excel; surpass; be superior to.

見 *Takken* foresight; excellent opinion.

絕 *Takuzetsu* to excel; be superior to.

越 *Takuetsu* to excel; surpass; be superior to.

説 *Takusetsu* excellent opinion; foresight.

識 *Takushiki* distinguished knowledge; learned.

卦 KE fortune-telling; the signs of divination; to tell fortunes; to divine.

T 貞 TEI upright; chaste. (*Sada*).【貝】

女 *Teijo* a chaste woman.

淑 *Teishuku* modesty; womanliness.

節 *Teisetsu* chastity; purity.

順 *Teijun* virtuous; modest; obedient.

實 *Teijitsu* fidelity.

操 *Teisō* chastity.

T 点 See 點 203,5.

鹵 See 197,0. 九

卩 二六

卯 BŌ. *U* 4th zodiacal sign, the hare. See Introduction 42, 43.

月 *Uzuki* poetical name for 4th month (old calendar).

T 印 IN. *Shirushi* seal; stamp; mark; sign; trace; impression.

99

(四)

印

半纏 *Shirushi-banten* workman's coat with master's crest.

刷 *Insatsu* printing.

度 *Indo* India.

紙 *Inshi* revenue stamp.

税 *Inzei* stamp duties; royalties.

象 *Inshō* an impression.

綬 *Inju* official seal.

鑑 *Inkan* impression of legal seal.

T **危** KI. *Abunai*; *ayaui* dangerous: *ayabu(mu)* to distrust.

地 *Kichi* danger.

殆 *Kitai* peril.

急 *Kikyū* emergency.

害 *Kigai* danger; harm.

懼 *Kigu* fear; apprehension.

機 *Kiki* a crisis.

機一髪 *Kiki-ippatsu* critical moment; hanging on a hair.

險 *Kiken* danger.

篤 *Kitoku* dangerously ill.

難 *Kinan* danger.

五
T **卵** RAN. *Tamago* egg.

T **却** KYAKU. *Shirizo(ku)* to retreat; withdraw: *shirizo(keru)* to refuse: *kaette* on the contrary.
→150,2

々 *Nakanaka* has an emphatic or superlative force; very, etc.

下 *Kyakka* refusal; rejection.

* 說 *Sate* by the way.

卷 KAN aux. num. for books: 六 KEN. *Ma(ku)* to roll: *maki* volume: scroll.
→26,7T *

物 *Makimono* a scroll; a roll.

附 *Makitsuku* to twine round.

紙 *Makigami* rolled letter-paper.

添 *Makizoe* to be involved.

煙草 *Makitabako* a cigarette.

頭 *Kantō* beginning of a book.

即 SOKU at once. *Sunawachi* 七 that is: *tsu(ku)* to succeed to (the throne).
→26,5T *

日 *Sokujitsu* on the same day.

死 *Sokushi* instantaneous death.

位 *Sokui* accession to the throne.

決 *Sokketsu* a summary judgment.

刻 *Sokkoku* instantly.

座 *Sokuza* at once.

時 *Sokuji* in an instant.

席 *Sokuseki* extemporary; unprepared.

答 *Sokutō* a prompt answer; immediate reply.

(五)

(五)

(七)

與 *Sokkyō* improvised amusement.

斷 *Sokudan* hasty conclusion; immediate decision.
*

一〇 卿 KYŌ; KEI a lord; you.

二七 厂

Always at top and left; it is called *Gan-dare*.

二 ㄒ 戸 See 63,0.

ㄒ 斤 See 69,0.

仄 SOKU to lean to one side. *Honoka ni* faintly: *honome-ka(su)* to hint: *honome(ku)* to be hinted. 【人】

聞 *Sokubun* to know by hearsay.

爪 See 87,0.

ㄒ 反 HAN; TAN aux. num. for counting pieces of cloth; unit of land measure. See Introduction 44. *Somu(ku)* to disobey; rebel; oppose: *sora(su)* to bend; turn aside: *ka (su)*; *kae(ru)* to change; turn; go back: *kaette* on the contrary. 【又】

古 *Hogo* waste paper; invalidity.

(一一)

目 *Hammoku* hostility.

別 *Tambetsu* area of land (speaking of farms).

抗 *Hankō* resistance.

身 *Sorimi* hold one's head erect.

物 *Tammono* piece-goods.

省 *Hansei* self-examination.

映 *Han-ei* reflection.

則 *Hansoku* irregular.

射 *Hansha* reflection.

逆 *Hangyaku* rebellion; treason.

問 *Hammon* interrogation.

動 *Handō* reaction.

復 *Hampuku* repetition.

感 *Hankan* antipathy; malice.

駁 *Hambaku* refute; contradict.

旗 *Hanki* a flag of revolt.

語 *Hango* irony.

對 *Hantai* opposition; contrary.

齒 *Soppa* projecting teeth.

影 *Han-ei* a reflection.

撥 *Hampatsu* repulsion.

應 *Hannō* reaction; response.

覆 *Hampuku* changeable; repetition.

證 *Hanshō* disproof; counter-evidence.

響 *Hankyō* an echo; reflection.

ㄒ 氏 See 83,0.

* ㄒ 卷 → 26,6

(二) 厄 T　YAKU calamity; mis-fortune; dangerous.

介　Yakkai trouble.

燃　Yakunan calamity; mis-fortune.

三 石 T　See 112,0.

斥 T　SEKI to spy. *Shirizo(keru)* to drive away; expel. 【斤】

候　Sekkō a patrol.

瓜 *　See 97,0.

四 后 T　KŌ; GO. *Kisaki* Empress. 【口】. In some cases ab-breviation of 後 *Go* after, 60,6.

灰 T　See 24, 4. 【火】

五 虎 丽　See 虎 141,2.

辰　See 161,0.

七 厘 T　RIN unit of length, money and weight. See Intro-duction 44.

毛　Rimmō the smallest sum.

盾 T　JUN. *Tate* a shield. 【目】

厚 T　KŌ. *Atsui* thick; kind; cordial.

化粧　Atsugeshō thick coating of powder.

圧 T *　→27, 15

生　Kōsei promotion of people's welfare.

志　Kōshi kind thought.

恩　Kōon great favour.

情　Kōjō kindness; benevo-lence.

遇　Kōgū kind treatment.

意　Kōi kindness.

誼　Kōgi intimate friendship.

薄　Kōhaku thickness.

顔　Kōgan; atsukamashii im-pudence.

厖　Bō large.

大　Bōdai huge; colossal.

叛　See 29,7.

原 T　GEN. *Hara* moor; field; in proper names when 2nd component sometimes *wa-ra: moto* origin; source.

文　Gembun the text.

因　Gen-in the cause; reason.

告　Genkoku plaintiff; accuser.

始　Genshi beginning; com-mencement; origin; primi-tive.

則　Gensoku a natural law; principle.

書　Gensho the original work (book).

料　Genryō materials; raw materials.

案　Gen-an the original bill.

102

野 *Gen-ya* a wilderness.

理 *Genri* principles.

動 *Gendō* action (opposite of reaction).

產地 *Gensanchi* country of origin.

著 *Gencho* original work (book).

稿 *Genkō* an original draft or manuscript.

價 *Genka; motone* the original price.

簿 *Gembo* a ledger.

籍 *Genseki* permanent domicile.

九 厠 SHI. *Kawaya* a privy; W.C.

一〇 雁 GAN. *Kari* the wild goose. 【隹】

行 *Gankō* go side by side.

厨 See 廚 53,12.

厥 KETSU. *Sono; sore* that.

厦 KA. *Ie* house.

門 *Amoi* Amoy (China).

二 厩 KYŪ. *Uma-ya* a stable.

厭 EN. *Ito(u)* to dislike: *itowashii* disagreeable; hateful: *a(kiru)* (coll.): *a(ku)* (lit. st.) to be tired of; be sated. 一二

世 *Ensei* weariness of life; pessimism. *1 *2

厲 REI sharpen; severe; strict. 一三

行 *Reikō* strict enforcement.

鷹 See 雁 27,10. 【隹】

歷 REKI clear. *He(ru)* to pass; successive. 【止】 一四 →27,12T *1

々 *Rekireki* distinguished (person); distinctly.

山王 *Rekizan-ō; Arekisandā* Alexander.

山堡 *Rukusemburugu* Luxemburg.

史 *Rekishi* history.

代 *Rekidai* successive generations or dynasties.

然 *Rekizen* plainly; evidently.

曆 REKI evidently. *Koyomi* calendar; almanac. 【日】 →27,12 *2 T

壓 ATSU. *O(su)* to oppress: *osa(h)ru)* to press down; stop. 【土】 →27,3T * 一五

制 *Assei* oppression.

迫 *Appaku* pressure.

倒 *Attō* to overwhelm; overpower.

103　*1 T 歷→27,14　*2 T 曆→27,14

(一五) 壓
殺 *Assatsu* to crush to death.
搾 *Assaku* compression.
縮 *Asshuku* compression.

一七 贋 GAN. *Nise* counterfeit; spurious. 【貝】
物 *Gambutsu; nisemono* counterfeit.
造 *Ganzō* counterfeiting; forgery.

二一 饜 EN. *A(kiru)* (coll.); *a(ku)* (lit. st.) to be tired of; be sated. 【食】

二八 厶
厶 *Gozaru* (coll. irreg.) to be.

二 允 IN to grant; faithful. 【儿】
許 *Inkyo* approval; sanction; consent.

三 ᵀ台 TAI; DAI; I to rejoice. 【口】 Often used as abbreviation of 臺 32,11; which see for other compounds.
覽 *Tairan* seeing (by Royal Princes).

ᵀ弁 See 辨 160,9; also 辯 160,14. also 160,12

牟 BŌ to seize. (MU). 【牛】 四

矣 I an emphatic suffix. 【矢】 五

ᵀ参 See 參 28,9. 六
虫 See 雖 172,9.

ᵀ怠 TAI. *Okota(ru); namake(-ru)* to neglect; be idle. 【心】 七
惰 *Taida* idleness.
業 *Taigyō* go slow; loaf.
慢 *Taiman* negligence.

甿 See ᵀ畝 8,8. 【田】

參 SAN three. *Mai(ru)* to go; 九 come; visit at a shrine: *maira(seru)* to present; offer; honorific suffix. →28,6ᵀ
上 *Sanjō* visit.
內 *Sandai* going to the Imperial Palace.
加 *Sanka* participation.
列 *Sanretsu* attendance.
考 *Sankō* fund of knowledge; reference; information.
事會 *Sanjikai* a council.
拜 *Sampai* going to worship at a shrine.
政 *Sansei* participation in the government.
政權 *Sanseiken* franchise.

(九)

宮 *Sangū* going to worship at a shrine, especially the most holy of all shrines, that at Ise.

堂 *Sandō* call at your house.

着 *Sanchaku* arrival.

着拂 *Sanchakubar i* sight payment.

集 *Sanshū* assemblage.

會 *Sankai* going to a meeting.

詣 *Sankei* to worship at a shrine or temple.

與 *San-yo* participation in public affairs; counsellor.

照 *Sanshō* comparison; reference.

謀 *Sambō* the staff (military).

觀 *Sankan* visit.

二九

又

又 YŪ. *Mata* again.

聞 *Matagiki* knowing by hearsay.

一 又 SA; SIIA. *Mata* forked; crossed: *sa(su)* to pierce; stick: *komanu(ku)* to fold or cross the arms.

銃 *Sajū* stack of arms.

T 双 See 雙 29,16.【隹】　二

T 收 See 收 66,2.

及 KYŪ. *Oyo(bu)* to reach; arrive: *oyobi* and; together with: *oyobo(su)* to affect; influence: *oyoba-nai* to be unnecessary. 29,1 T *

第 *Kyūdai* passing an examination.

T 皮 See 107,0.　三

T 叔 SHUKU younger brother or sister of father or mother.　六

父 *Oji* uncle; father's or mother's younger brother.

母 *Oba* aunt; father's or mother's younger sister.

T 受 JU. *U(keru)* to receive.

太刀 *Uke 'achi* defensive position.

付 *Uketsuke* inquiry office.

取 *Uketo(ru)* to receive: *uketori* receipt.

取書 *Uketorisho* receipt.

持 *Ukemochi* charge; duty.

信 *Jushin* receipt of message.

納 *Junō* receipt; acceptance.

領 *Juryō* receiving.

驗 *Juken* take an examination.

---

*T 及 → 29,2

七
T 叙 See 敍 66,7.

叛 HAN; HON. *Somu(ku)* to rebel; disobey.

心 *Hanshin* treachery; treacherous intent.

臣 *Hanshin* a rebel; a traitor.

服 *Hampuku* revolt and submission.

逆 *Hangyaku* treason.

徒 *Hanto* rebels.

亂 *Hanran* rebellion.

旗 *Hanki* a flag of revolt.

八
T 桑 Sō. *Kuwa* mulberry. 【木】

港 *Sanfuranshisuko; Sōkō* San Francisco.

叟 Sō an old man.

一四 叡 EI intelligent; clear; wise; also means Emperor.

智 *Eichi* far-seeing; wise.

感 *Eikan* the Imperial approval.

聞 *Eibun* the hearing of His Majesty.

慮 *Eiryo* the Emperor's mind.

覽 *Eiran* the Emperor's personal inspection.

一六 雙 Sō. *Futatsu* two; a pair; both. 【隹】 →29, 2 T

子 *Futago* twins.

方 *Sōhō* both parties.

肩 *Sōken* both shoulders.

兒 *Sōji; futago* twins.

口

When at the left it is called *Kuchi-hen.*

T 口 KŌ; KU. *Kuchi* mouth; opening; entrance; hole; kind; sort.

々 *Kuchi-guchi-ni* by every mouth; said by everybody.

入屋 *Kuchiire-ya* a servant's registry office.

上 *Kōjō* a verbal message.

止 *Kuchidome* bribing to secrecy; binding to secrecy.

外 *Kōgai* mentioning to others.

舌 *Kōzetsu* talk.

汚 *Kuc igitanai* abusive; greedy.

吟 *Kuchizusa(mu)* sing to oneself.

車 *Kuchiguruma* fair speech.

吻 *Kōfun* the manner of speaking.

走 *Kuchibashi(ru)* to make a slip of the tongue.

述 *Kōjutsu* oral statement.

前 *Kuchimae* a way of speaking; tongue.

徑　*Kōkei* calibre ; bore.

笛　*Kuchibue* a whistle.

碑　*Kōhi* oral tradition.

語　*Kōgo* spoken language.

說　*Kuzetsu* a dispute : *kudo-(ku)* to entreat ; woo.

實　*Kojitsu* excuse.

論　*Kōron* dispute ; altercation ; quarrel.

調　*Kuchō* tone.

錢　*Kosen* commission ; brokerage.

頭　*Kōtō* oral.

繪　*Kuchie* a frontispiece.

一ₜ中　See 2,3.

二叩　KŌ.　*Tata(ku)* to beat; knock.

頭　*Kōtō* a bow ; salutation.

叶　KYŌ.　*Kana(u)* to suit ; agree with ; be united.

ₜ叫　KYŌ ; KYŪ.　*Sake(bu)* to cry out.

喚　*Kyōkan* a cry ; call ; shout.

聲　*Sakebigoe* ; *kyōsei* a shrill voice.

叮　TEI.　*Nengoro ni* kindly.

寧　*Teinei* polite ; courteous ; kind.

嚀　*Teinei* polite.

叺　*Kamasu* a straw bag.

叱　SHITSU.　*Shika(ru)* to scold.

咜　*Shitta* crying out in anger or contempt.

責　*Shisseki* reproof.

ₜ号　See 號 30,10.【虍】

ₜ兄　KEI ; KYŌ.　*Ani* elder brother. (E).【儿】

弟　*Kyōdai* ; *keitei* brothers ; brothers and sisters.

只　*Tada* only.

今　*Tadaima* just now ; soon.

管　*Hitasura* earnestly.

ₜ石　See 112,0.

ₜ召　SHŌ.　*Me(su)* to call ; invite ; honorific prefix.

使　*Meshitsukai* employee ; servant.

喚　*Shōkan* summons ; call.

集　*Shōshū* summon ; call together ; muster.

還　*Shōkan* to recall.

ₜ司　SHI ; SU.　*Tsukasa* a government office ; official duties ; the head official : *tsukasado(ru)* to rule ; direct.

令官　*Shireikan* the commander of an army.

〔一〕

司

令長官 *Shireichōkan* commander-in-chief.

令部 *Shireibu* headquarters.

法 *Shihō* the administration of justice.

T可 KA may. *Yoshi* good; all right: *beshi* will; shall; must.

成 *Narubeku* (inverted order) as...as; as far as possible.

否 *Kahi* good or bad; right or wrong; advantage and disadvantage.

決 *Kaketsu* to pass; adopt; agree to.

笑 *Okashii* funny; amusing.

能 *Kanō* possibility.

惜 *Atara* regrettable; pitiful.

愛 *Kawaii* lovely; charming.

憐 *Karen* pitiful; poor; tiny.

T史 SHI annals; history.

料 *Shiryō* materials for history.

家 *Shika* historian.

劇 *Shigeki* historical play.

學 *Shigaku* historiology.

三 T吐 TO. *Ha(ku)* to vomit; spit; emit from the mouth; to utter.

川 *Hakida(su)* to breathe out; exhale; emit from the mouth.

〔三〕

血 *Toketsu* vomiting of blood.

息 *Toiki* a long breath; sigh.

瀉 *Tosha* vomiting.

露 *Toro* to express; set forth.

吋 *Inchi* inch.

呼 U. *Ā* ah!

吃 KITSU. *Domo(ru)* to stammer.

水 *Kissui* draught (of ship).

驚 *Kikkyō; bikkuri*·surprise.

吊 CHŌ. *Tsuru(su); tsu(ru)* to hang: also used instead of 弔 2,3 q. v.

足 See T足 157,0.

T后 See 27,4.【口】

T舌 See 135,0.

T向 KŌ. *Mukō* yonder; over there; opposite to: *mu.!a-(u)* to face; point to; go to: *mu(ku)* to turn: *muki* suitable for.

上 *Kōjō* rise; advance.

上心 *Kōjōshin* aspiration.

々 *Mukimuki* every direction

背 *Kōhai* attitude.

後 *Kōgo* hereafter.

島 *Mukōjima* p. n.

T吏 RI official; officer.

員 *Riin* officials.

T 虫 See 蟲 142,12.

四
T 吟 GIN. *Uta(u)* to sing; hum.

哦 *Gimmi* examination.

詠 *Gin-ei* recitation.

吶 TOTSU. *Domo(ru)* to stammer.

喊 *Tokkan* war-cry; to shout.

辯 *Totsuben* slow of speech.

吩 FUN. *Iitsu(keru)* to order; command.

吻 FUN the lips.

T 吹 SUI. *Fu(ku)* to blow.

奏 *Suisō* blowing.

雪 *Fubuki* snow-storm.

聽 *Fuichō* making public; recommendation.

呎 *Fiito* foot, feet (English unit of length).

吠 HAI; BAI. *Ho(y)eru* to bark.

T 吸 KYŪ. *Su(u)* to suck; inhale; smoke.

入 *Kyūnyū* inhalation; suction.

引 *Kyū'n* absorption.

收 *Kyūshū* absorption.

水 *Kyūsui* suction of water.

吻 *Suimono* soup.

取紙 *Suitorigami* blotting-paper.

吼 KŌ. *Ho(y)eru* to roar; bark.

呈 TEI to present to a superior; show; display; exhibit.

上 *Teijō* offering.

示 *Teiji* presentation.

呂 RO; RYO the back-bone.

宋 *Ruson* Luzon.

律 *Roretsu* pronunciation; articulation.

呆 IIŌ; BŌ. *Aki(reru)* to be astonished; dumbfounded: *baka* a fool: *bo(keru)* be in dotage.

氣 *Akke* surprise; (*akke ni torareru* to be surprised).

氣無 *Akke nai* less than expected; not enough; fleeting; transient; stupid.

然 *Bōzen* absent-mindedly.

T 足 See 157,0.

T 邑 See 163,0.

吳 Go name of an old Chinese province. *Ku(reru)* to give please: *Kure* p. n.

→吳 T

々 *Kuregure* repeatedly.

服 *Gofuku* dry goods; cloth.

越 *Goetsu* hostile States.

【四】

君 KUN an honorific used like San but less polite and applied only to men, Mr. *Kimi* lord; often means the Emperor of Japan; you (used familiarly among men, especially young); polite suffix to words expressing relationship (e. g. *Ani-gimi*).

士丹丁堡 *Konsutanchinōpuru* Constantinople.

士坦丁堡 *Konsutanchinōp.ru* Constantinople.

子 *Kunshi* a true gentleman; the superior man.

子國 *Kunshikoku* the land of noble men; Japan.

主 *Kunshu* one's feudal lord; the ruler; sovereign.

臣 *Kunshin* sovereign and subjects.

命 *Kummei* an Imperial command.

臨 *Kunrin* reign; rule.

告 See 93,3. 【口】

吾 GO. *Ware* I: *waga*; *a* my.

人 *Gojin* any one; we; we and others.

妻 *Azuma*; *Agatsuma* p. n.

合 See 9,5. 【口】

吞 DON. *No(mu)* to drink; swallow.

舟の魚 *Donshū no uo* notorious man; great scoundrel.

氣 *Nonki* easy-going

否 HI bad. *Ina(mu)* to decline; refuse: *ina*; *iya*; *iie* no; not; not so.

決 *Hiketsu* rejection.

定 *Hitei* denial; negation.

認 *Hinin* denial.

局 See 44,4.

串 See 2,6.

【五】

咀 SO. *Ka(mu)* to chew.

嚼 *Soshaku* chewing.

咄 TOTSU Pshaw! *Hanashi* a story: *shika(ru)* to scold.

嗟 *Tossa* a moment; an instant.

呻 SHIN. *Ume(ku)* to moan: *una(ru)* to groan.

吟 *Shingin* to groan; pine.

呵 KA to persecute; to laugh. *Shika(ru)* to scold; blame.

々 *Kaka* an onomatopoeic expression signifying laughter, which corresponds to our Ha! ha!

責 *Ka haku* torture.

呼 KO to exhale. *Yo(bu)*; *yobawa(ru)* to call: *a* interjection.

吸 *Kokyū* respiration; breathing; knack; secret.

物 *Yobimono* the chief attraction.

鈴 *Yobirin* a call-bell.

（五）號 *Kogō* an outcry; shout.

應 *Koō* form connection with; act in concert.

呱々 *Koko* sound of a baby's cry.

T味 MI. *Aji* taste: *ajiwa(u)* to taste. As bottom character *Mi* is used to form abstract nouns from adjectives, e. g. 弱味 *Yowami* weakness.

方 *Mikata* one's own (or somebody else's own) side; party; an ally.

氣無 *Ajikinai* irksome.

噌 *Miso* a kind of sauce.

咏 See 詠 149,5.

呶々 *Dodo* talk much; talk noisily.

咆哮 HŌKŌ to roar; bellow.

呪 JU. *Majinai* a spell: *majina(u); noro(u)* to curse; charm; enchant.

詛 *Juso* imprecation; curse.

呟 *Tsubuya(ku)* to murmur.

舍 See 舍 9,6.【舌】

咎 KYŪ; KU. *Toga* a crime: *toga(meru)* to blame.

事 See 6,7.

哇 AI; A child's voice; spit out. 六

哈爾賓 *Harupin* Harbin.

咯 KAKU to spit out; emit from the mouth.

血 *Kakketsu* spit out blood.

咽 IN. *Nodo* throat: *muse(bu)* to be choked.

喉 *Inkō; nodo* throat.

哂 SHIN. *Azawara(u)* to laugh at; ridicule.

唉 *Sa(ku)* to open (as a flower); blossom. →咲 T

咬 KŌ. *Ka(mu)* to bite.

咳 GAI. *Seki* a cough.

唾 *Gaida* spittle.

嗽 *Gaisō* a cough.

哄 KŌ noisy.

笑 *Kōshō* loud laughter.

然 *Kozen* loud laughter.

T品 HIN. *Shina* thing; goods; quality; sort. Often used as bottom component, e. g.: *buppin* goods, *yaku-/in* medicines, *kahin* a choice article.

切 *Shinagire* out of stock.

目 *Himmoku* a list of articles.

行 *Hinkō* behaviour; conduct.

位 *Hin-i* dignity.

111

(六)

品

定 *Shinasadame* criticism.

性 *Hinsei* character.

物 *Shinamono* thing; article; goods.

格 *Hinkaku* quality; dignity.

評 *Himpyō* criticism.

質 *Hinshitsu* quality.

虽 See 雖 172,9.

咨 SHI. *Haka(ru)* to consult; investigate; enquire.

問 *Shimon* to question; enquire of.

韋 See 178,0.

七 **哩** *Mairu* mile (English unit of length).

哨 SHŌ scout; sentinel.

兵 *Shōhei* troops placed in ambush.

艦 *Shōkan* vessel on scouting duty.

哺 HO to suckle a child; to bring up. *Kuku(meru)* to feed.

育 *Hoiku* bring up.

乳 *Ho-nyū* lactation.

T **唆** SA. *Sosonoka(su)* to tempt; entice: *soso(ru)* excite.

唄 BAI. *Uta* a song: *uta(u)* to sing.

哭 KOKU. *Nage(ku)* to cry out.

(七)

T **員** IN personnel; official; member. *Kazu* number. In compounds generally found at bottom, e. g.: *jimuin* clerk, *kaiin* seaman, *kaishain* employees of a company.

數 *Insū* the number.

T **哲** TETSU a philosopher; wise; intelligent.

人 *Tetsujin* a philosopher; sage.

理 *Tetsuri* philosophy.

學 *Tetsugaku* philosophy.

哥 KA song: KO. *Ani* elder brother.

倫比亞 *Korombiya* Colombia.

薩克 *Kosakku* Cossacks.

唾 DA. *Tsuba; tsubaki* 八 saliva.

液 *Daeki* saliva.

棄 *Daki* to reject with disgust.

啞 A. *Oshi; oshi* dumb person.

然 *Azen* speechless (with astonishment).

T **唯** I; YUI. *Tada* only.

々 *Tada-tada* only: *ii* yes.

々諾々 *Ii-dakud ku* yes.

一 *Yuiitsu* the only; the only one.

心論 *Yuishinron* spiritualism.

今 *Tadaima* soon ; just now.

物論 *Yuibutsuron* materialism.

T 唱 SHŌ to sing. *Tona(h)eru)* to recite ; say.

道 *Shōdō* advocacy.

歌 *Shōka* a song.

啣 *Fuku(mu)* to keep in one's mouth ; to bear in mind ; to bear malice against ; to harbour.

啖 TAN. *Kura(u)* to eat.

啄 TAKU. *Tsuiba(mu)* to peck at : *tsutsu(ku)* to pick.

木鳥 *Kitsutsuki ; takubokuchō* wood-pecker.

啜 SETSU ; TETSU to weep. *Su-su(ru)* to sip.

唸 *Una(ru)* to groan.

T 啓 KEI to say. *Hira(ku)* to open ; instruct.

上 *Keijō* to inform.

發 *Keihatsu* development ; edification.

蒙 *Keimō* enlightenment ; illumination.

喬 See 喬 30,9.

（九）

喧 KEN. *Yakamashii* noisy ; troublesome ; fault-finding ; fastidious ; severe : *kamabisushii* noisy.

嘩 *Kenka* a quarrel.

傳 *Kenden* to spread ; circulate.

騷 *Kensō* noisy ; turbulent ; tumultuous.

囂 *Kengō* noisy ; turbulent ; tumultuous.

喀 KAKU to spit out ; emit from the mouth.

唧 SHOKU. *Kako(tsu)* to lament.

筒 *Pompu* a pump.

喇叭 *Rappa* a bugle ; trumpet.

喘 ZEN ; SEN cough. *Ae(gu)* to pant.

息 *Zensoku* asthma.

喃 NAN to chatter.

々 *Nannan* chatteringly.

啼 TEI. *Na(ku)* to cry ; weep.

泣 *Teikyū* to weep.

喝 KATSU to become hoarse ; to scold.

采 *Kassai* applause.

破 *Kappa* shout out.

T 喚 KAN. *Yo(bu)* to call : *wame(ku)* to scream ; shriek ; cry out.

起 *Kanki* to wake up ; rouse.

問 *Kammon* summon for examination.

喫 KITSU to eat ; chew. *No-(mu)* to drink ; smoke.

茶店 *Kissaten ; kitchaten* a tea-house. →喫 T

(九)

喫
煙 *Kitsuen* smoking.

驚 *Kikkyō; bikkuri* to be startled.

喉 KŌ. *Nodo* throat.

元 *Nodomoto* base of the throat.

喋 CHŌ noisy. *Shabe(ru)* to babble.

々 *Chōchō* chatter; talkative.

喙 KAI. *Kuchibashi* bill; beak.

喰 *Ku(u)* to eat. as a dog

違 *Kuichiga(u)* to cross; be at cross-purposes.

喊 KAN a call; war-cry.

聲 *Kansei* sound of war-cry.

喩 YU. *Tatoe* simile; metaphor.

號 See 號 30,10. 【虎】

喪 SŌ. *Ushina(u)* to lose: *mo* mourning.

中 *Mochū* in mourning.

心 *Sōshin* dispiritedness; absent-mindedness.

主 *Moshu* chief mourner.

失 *Sōshitsu* loss; forfeiture; deprivation.

服 *Mofuku* mourning dress.

單 TAN. *Hitoe; hitori* simple; single; only. →12,7 * T

(九)

一 *Tan-ichi* unity; singleness.

刀直入 *Tantōchokunyū* going full tilt.

衣 *Hitoe* clothes without lining.

行本 *Tankōbon* separate volume.

位 *Tan-i* a unit.

身 *Tanshin* a single individual; single-handed; alone.

物 *Hitoemono* clothes without lining.

純 *Tanjun* simplicity.

葉 *Tan-yō* a single leaf; monoplane.

語 *Tango* one word; a single word; vocabulary.

複 *Tampuku* the singular and plural; unity and complexity.

調 *Tanchō* monotone.

價 *Tanka* the price apiece.

獨 *Tandoku* independent; by oneself.

簡 *Tankan* simple; brief.

善 ZEN. *Yoi* good; right; virtuous.

用 *Zen-yō* to put to a good use.

行 *Zenkō* good conduct.

男善女 *Zennan-zennyo* pious men and women.

良 *Zenryō* goodness; excellence.

美 *Zembi* good (in quality) and beautiful (in appearance).

（九）

後策 *Zengosaku* remedial measures.

根 *Zenkon* charity.

惡 *Zen-aku; zennaku; yoshiashi* good and (or) bad; morality.

意 *Zen-i* good faith.

隣 *Zenrin* good neighbourhood.

戰 *Zensen* fighting hard.

啻 SHI. *Tada; tada ni* only.

T 營 See 營 30,14. 【火】

喬 KYŌ. *Takai* high.

木 *Kyōboku* high tree.

一〇

嗟 SA to grieve : *A* ah !

嘆 *Satan* to sigh.

嗜 SHI. *Tashina(mu)* to be fond of ; to like.

好 *Shikō* taste ; liking.

眠 *Shimin* lethargy ; sleep.

嗚 O ; U to grieve. *A* ah !

呼 *Ā* ah !

嗅 KYŪ. *Ka(gu)* to smell.

覺 *Kyūkaku* sense of smell.

嗄 SA. *Kara(su)* to get hoarse.

聲 *Shagaregoe* hoarse voice.

（一〇）

嗤 SHI. *Azawara(u)* to laugh at.

笑 *Shishō* to laugh at ; to scorn.

T 嗣 SHI. *Yotsugi* heir : *tsu(gu)* to inherit ; succeed.

子 *Shishi* an heir.

號 GŌ sign ; pen-name ; to name ; shout ; number (ordinal). *Sake(bu)* to shout ; roar. 【*】
→30,2 T : 30,9

令 *Gōrei* command ; order.

外 *Gōgai* (newspaper) extra.

泣 *Gōkyū* to cry bitterly ; wail loudly.

砲 *Gōhō* a signal cannon.

嗇 SHOKU to grudge ; to covet ; stingy ; stinginess.
*

一一

嘔 Ō. *Ha(ku)* to vomit.

吐 *Ōto* vomiting.

嘩 KA noisy.

T 鳴 MEI. *Na(ku)* to sing ; cry ; chirp, etc. (of birds and insects) : *na(ru)* to make a noise ; to sound : *nara(su)* to cause to sound. 【鳥】

子 *Naruko* a noise-producing scarecrow.

動 *Meidō* rumbling.

謝 *Meisha* thanks.

嗽 SŌ cough. *Kuchisusu(gu); susu(gu)* to wash one's mouth ; gargle.

嗾 SŌ. *Sosonoka(su)* to entice; incite.

嘆 See 歡 76,11. →30, 10 *T

嘖 SEKI; SAKU to cry; be noisy.

々 *Sakusaku* noisily; widely known.

二 **嘘** KYO. *Uso* a lie.

嘶 SEI. *Inana(ku)* to neigh.

噂 SON. *Uwasa* rumour.

T **嘱** See 囑 30,21.

嘲 CHŌ. *Azake(ru)* to laugh at; make a fool of.

弄 *Chōrō* ridicule.

笑 *Chōshō*; *azawarai* ridicule.

罵 *Chōba* to revile; abuse.

T **噴** FUN. *Fu(ku)* to erupt; blow out; spout out.

水 *Funsui* fountain.

火 *Funka* eruption (of fire).

火山 *Funka-zan* volcano.

火孔 *Funkakō* crater.

出 *Funshutsu* gushing forth; eruption (of anythi g); ejection; emission.

飯 *Fumpan* ridiculous.

嘸 BU. *Sazo* very; how; much; truly.

嚻 See T器 30,13.

嘶 *Hanashi* a story.

嘯 SHŌ. *Usobu(ku)* to roar; whistle.

嘴 SHI. *Kuchibashi* bill; beak.

噪 SŌ. *Sawa(gu)* to be noisy.

音 *Sōon* unmusical noise.

噸 TON ton (English unit of weight).

數 *Tonsū* tonnage.

噤 *Tsugu(mu)* to be silent.

噫 I. *A* ah! *Okubi* an eructation.

T**器** KI talent; ability. *Utsuwa* a vessel; utensil; instrument. →30, 12

用 *Kiyō* skilful; handy.

物 *Kibutsu* vessel; utensil.

具 *Kigu* tool.

財 *Kizai* furniture; utensils.

械 *Kikai* an instrument; machine; machinery.

量 *Kiryō* talent; ability; face.

嚊 *K·/ā* w fe (humble).

天下 *Kakādenka* peticoat government.

嚀 NEI polite; kind.

嚆矢 *Kōshi* the first.

（一四）嚇 KAKU; to get angry. *Odo-(su)* to threaten; to scold.

怒 *Kakudo* fury; anger.

營 EI camp; barracks. *Itona-(mu)* to carry on business. 【火】 →30, 9 T

々 *Eiei* strenuously; with earnest efforts.

口 *Eikō* Ying-kow.

利 *Eiri* profit; money-making.

所 *Eisho* barracks.

倉 *Eisō* guard-room.

造物 *Eizō-butsu* institution.

業 *Eigyō* trade; business; calling; occupation.

業税 *Eigyōzei* business tax.

養 *Eiyō* nutrition.

一五 嚙 KŌ; GŌ. *Ka(mu)* to bite; chew.

嚠 RYŪ clear (sound).

嚠 *Ryūryō* clear; melodious.

一六 嚥 EN. *No(mu)* to swallow.

下 *Enka* swallow down.

嚮 KYŌ; KŌ. *Muka(u)* to face; be opposite : *saki ni* before; the past.

日 *Kyōjitsu* the other day; formerly.

背 *Kyōhai* attitude.

導 *Kyōdō* guidance; a guide.

嚴 GEN; GON. *Kibishii* severe: *ikameshii* stern : *ogosoka* strict; solemn. →30, 14 * T 一七

父 *Gempu* strict father; your (his) father.

正 *Gensei* strictness; solemnity; dignity.

刑 *Genkei* severe punishment.

守 *Genshu* observe strictly.

命 *Gemmei* strict order.

重 *Genjū* strict; severe; rigorous.

島 *Itsukushima* island of Miyajima.

格 *Genkaku* strict.

密 *Gemmitsu* strict; severe; rigid.

寒 *Genkan* intense cold.

禁 *Genkin* strict prohibition.

肅 *Genshuku* grave; solemn; serene.

罰 *Gembatsu* severe punishment.

談 *Gendan* demanding explanation.

囃 ZŌ. *Haya(su)* to play music; beat time; banter. 一八

子 *Hayashi* an orchestra.

囁 *Sasaya(ku)* to whisper.

囀 TEN. *Saezu(ru)* to twitter; chatter.

囂 GŌ noisy.

々 *Gōgō* noisy.

*T 嚴 →30, 17

117

(一八)

嚚 然 *Gōzen* noisy; clamorous; turbulent.

(一九)

囈 *Gei. Tawakoto* silly talk; nonsense.

語 *Geigo; tawakoto* silly talk: talk in delirium.

轡 *Hi. Kutsuwa* a bit; rein; bridle.【車】

(二一)

囑 SHOKU; ZOKU to engage; entrust to; order. →30. 12T

目 *Shokumoku* pay attention.

託 *Shokutaku* a person not on the regular staff.

望 *Shokubō* to put hopes in.

(三一)

囗

It surrounds the rest of the character and is called *Kuni-gamae*.

(一)

囗 This is not a real character, but the picture of a box-like measuring instrument called, *masu:* it is sometimes used jocosely for the verbal termination *masu.*

(二)

囚 SHŪ a prisoner; convict. *Tora(h)eru)* to arrest

人 *Shūjin; meshiudo* a prisoner.

徒 *Shūto* convicts; prisoners in gaol.

(二)

T 四 SHI. *Yotsu* four.

人 *Yo-nin; yottari* 4 persons.

日 *Yokka* 4 days; the 4th day of the month.

月 *Shi-gatsu* April: *yo-tsuki* 4 months.

分五裂 *Shibun-goretsu* divided; disrupted.

方 *Shihō; yomo* the cardinal points; 4 sides; all sides.

方山 *Yomoyama* all sorts.

半分 *Shihambun* a quarter.

谷 *Yotsuya* p. n.

角四面 *Shikaku-shimen* stern; precise; staid.

角張 *Shikakuba(ru)* to be formal.

季 *Shiki* the 4 seasons.

肢 *Shishi* the limbs.

面 *Shimen* 4 sides; all sides; 4 faces.

苦八苦 *Shikuhakku* death agony.

時 *Shiji; shii i* the 4 seasons; all the year round: *yoji* 4 o'clock.

海 *Shikai* the 4 seas; the whole world; universal.

國 *Shikoku* p. n.

通八達 *Shitsū-hattatsu* leading to every direction.

散 *Shisan* dispersion.

圍 *Shii* surroundings.

隣 *Shirin* all directions.

113

三
T 回 KAI a time. *Megu(ru)*; *mawa(su)* to turn; revolve: *megura(su)* to surround: *kae(ru)* to return. →31,4

々敎 *Fuifuikyō* Mahometanism.

收 *Kaishū* withdrawal; collection.

生 *Kaisei* revival.

向 *Ekō* saying mass.

忌 *Kaiki* anniversary of a death.

附 *Kaifu* transmit.

春 *Kaishun* recovery from illness.

航 *Kaikō* bring (ship) home; cruise.

祿 *Kairoku* destruction by fire.

章 *Kaishō* a circular.

敎 *Kaikyō* Mahometanism.

答 *Kaitō* an answer; to reply.

復 *Kaifuku* to recover.

想 *Kaisō* recollection.

遊 *Kaiyū* excursion; round trip.

漕 *Kaisō* transportation.

避 *Kaihi* to avoid; shun.

轉 *Kaiten* (of machinery, etc.) revolution; turn round.

顧 *Kaiko* to look back; dwell on the past.

T 因 IN. *Moto* origin; cause: *yo(ru)* to depend on: *china(mu)* to refer to: *chinami ni* by the way; because of.

* T 団 →31,11

州 *Inshū* another name for the province of Inaba.

果 *Inga* cause (in previous existence) and effect (in present life).

習 *Inshū* an established method; traditional usage; convention.

循 *Injun* slowness; indecision; procrastination.

業 *Ingō* hard-hearted; stubborn.

幡 *Inaba* p. n.

緣 *Innen* affinity; fate; origin; cause.

襲 *Inshū* following a long-established custom; con-
* ventional.

四

国 See 國 31,8.

囬 See T 回 31,3. Hui

囲 T See 圍 31,9.

困 T KON. *Koma(ru)*: *kurushi-(mu)* to be in a quandary; be in distress.

却 *Konkyaku* trouble; distress; suffering.

苦 *Konku* hardship.

惑 *Konwaku* perplexity.

窮 *Konkyū* trouble; distress; suffering.

難 *Konnan* difficulty.

化 KA. *Otori* a decoy-bird.

図 T See 圖 31,11.

五 T 固 Ko. *Katai* hard; firm; obstinate: *kata(meru)* to make hard; harden: *kata-ma(ru)* to become hard: *moto yori* from first to last.

守 *Koshu* to guard strictly; protect carefully.

有 *Koyū* peculiar; proper.

定 *Kotei* to settle firmly; fix; determine.

持 *Koji* persist.

陋 *Korō* narrow-mindedness; bigotry.

執 *Koshitsu* adherence.

唾 *Katazu* spittle; saliva.

著 *Kochaku* adherence.

辭 *Koji* refusal.

囹 REI jail; prison.

* 圄 *Reigo* prison.

六 囷 See 國 31,8.

七 圃 Ho field; vegetable garden.

八 國 KOKU. *Kuni* country; province; state.
→31,5 T * 31,4 : 31,6

人 *Kokujin* people of a country.

土 *Kokudo* a country.

王 *Kokuō* ruler of a country; king.

文學 *Kokubungaku* Japanese literature.

母 *Kokubo* the Empress.

* T 国 →31,8

立 *Kokuritsu* national (building).

史 *Kokushi* a national history.

本 *Kokuhon* foundation of a country.

民 *Kokumin; kunitami* a nation.

交 *Kokkō* diplomatic relations.

光 *Kokkō* national glory.

防 *Kokubō* national defence.

法 *Kokuhō* national laws.

定 *Kokutei* established by the state.

事犯 *Kokujihan* political offence.

帑 *Kokudo* national funds.

是 *Kokuze* national policy.

政 *Kokusei* the government of a country; the national administration.

威 *Kokui* national power; influence of a country.

風 *Kokufū* national customs.

庫 *Kokko* national treasury.

辱 *Kokujoku* disgrace incurred by one's country; national dishonour.

家 *Kokka* country; state.

産 *Kokusan* products of a country.

情 *Kokujō* condition of a country.

務 *Kokumu* state affairs.

務大臣 *Kokumu-daijin* minister of state; ministries.

基 *Kokki* foundation of a nation.

(八〇)

許 *Kunimoto* home; one's native place.

禁 *Kokkin* prohibition by law.

勢調査 *Kokuseichōsa* census.

葬 *Kokusō* a state funeral.

賊 *Kokuzoku* traitor.

債 *Kokusai* national debt.

會 *Kokkai* national assembly; parliament; congress.

運 *Koku-un* national destinies.

亂 *Kokuran* civil war; rebellion in the country.

際 *Kokusai* international.

際聯盟 *Kokusai-remmei* League of Nations.

語 *Kokugo* language of a country.

粹 *Kokusui* national characteristics.

歌 *Kokka* the national anthem.

境 *Kokkyō*; *kunizakai* frontier.

賓 *Kokuhin* a national guest.

憲 *Kokken* national constitution.

學 *Kokugaku* Japanese literature as opposed to Chinese.

難 *Kokunan* a national trouble.

籍 *Kokuseki* nationality.

權 *Kokken* national rights.

體 *Kokutai* national qualities and constitution.

圈 KEN circle; a cell; cage; to surround. →31,9 * T

内 *Kennai* within the sphere.

圍 I. *Kako(mu)*; *megura(su)* 九 to surround: *kakoi* a fence; enclosure: *kakuma-(u)* to conceal: *kako(u)* to preserve; keep. →31,4 T

碁 *Igo* playing the game of *go*.

繞 *Ijō*: *i-nyō* to surround; encircle.

*爐裏 *Irori* hearth.

園 EN; ON. *Sono* garden; 一 park. Often used as bottom component, e. g.: *kōen* 〇 public garden, *yōchien* kindergarten, *dobutsuen* zoological gardens, *hana-zono* flower garden. *yuan*

丁 *Entei* a gardener.

生 *Sono* a garden.

遊會 *En-yūkai* garden party.

藝 *Engei* gardening; horticulture.

圓 EN unit of money. *Marui*; *madoka* round; perfect. →13,2 T *yuan*

周 *Enshū* circumference.

滑 *Enkatsu* harmony.

滿 *Emman* friendly; peaceful; harmonious.

熟 *Enjuku* maturity; ripen.

錐形 *En uikei* a cone.

圖 ZU picture; map: TO. 一 *haka(ru)* to plan: *hakari-* 一一 *goto* plan. →31,4 T

太 *Zubutoi* bold; audacious.

拔 *Zunukete* extraordinarily.

面 *Zumen* a map; a plan.

（二一）

圖
星 *Zuboshi* the bull's eye.

書 *Tosho ; zusho* books.

書館 *Toshokan* a public library.

案 *Zuan* a design.

畫 *Zuga* drawing.

解 *Zukai* an explanatory diagram.

團 DAN ; TON to assemble ; a company ; group ; round. →31,3下 *

扇 *Uchiwa* a round (non-folding) fan.

結 *Danketsu* combination ; union ; organization.

體 *Dantai* a party ; group ; body.

欒 *Danran* making a group.

三三 土

When at the left it is called *Tsuchi-hen.*

T 土 DO; TO local. *Tsuchi* earth; soil. (*Hiji*). Do not confound with 士 33,0.

人 *Dojin* a native ; savage.

工 *Dokō* an earthwork.

方 *Dokata* a navvy.

手 *Dote* a bank ; mound.

木 *D boku* civil engineering.

木技師 *Doboku-gishi* civil engineer.

左衛門 *Dozaemon* a drowned person.

民 *Domin* the natives.

用 *Doyō* the dog-days.

地 *Tochi* land ; soil.

耳古 *Toruko* Turkey.

耳其 *Toruko* Turkey.

佐 *Tosa* p. n.

足 *Dosoku* muddy feet.

產 *Miyage* present ; souvenir ; gift.

匪 *Dohi* rebellious natives.

瓶 *Dobin* tea-pot.

著 *Dochaku* native.

間 *Doma* an unfloored part ; earthen floor ; the pit (theatre).

葬 *Dosō* interment.

臺 *Dodai* a foundation.

曜 *Doyō* Saturday.

藏 *Dozō* godown ; storehouse.

壤 *Dojō* the soil.

T 去 KYO; KO. *Sa(ru)* to leave; to go; the last; the one before the present: (*Saru ichi-nichi* means the first day of this month: *s ru san-jū-ichi-nichi* the 31st of last month; *saru jū-ni-nichi* would mean the 12th of this month if w^ are speaking after the 12th, or the 12th of last month if we are speaking on or before the 12th.) 【厶】

年 *Kyo-nen* last year.

就 *Kyoshū* course of action.

三 地 CHI; JI earth; land; local-
T ity; place.

中海 *Chichū-kai* Mediter-
ranean Sea.

方 *Chihō* region; district;
locality.

主 *Jinushi* a landlord; land
owner.

平線 *Chiheisen* the horizon.

位 *Chii* situation; position.

形 *Chikei* the shape or contour
of a piece of ground.

所 *Jisho* land; plot of land.

味 *Chimi* (degree of) fertility
of soil: *jimi* quietness.

步 *Chiho* ground; standing.

面 *Jimen* land; ground; surface of the ground.

租 *Chiso* land-tax.

紙 *Jigami* a kind of thick
paper used in certain in-
dustries.

域 *Chiiki* region; boundary.

理 *Chiri* geography.

帶 *Chitai* a zone.

球 *Chikyū* the earth; terrestrial globe.

處 *Jisho* a locality; piece of
ground; lot of land.

勢 *Chisei* topography.

雷火 *Jiraika* a mine (military).

圖 *Chizu* map.

團駄 *Jidanda* stamping the
feet.

獄 *Jigoku* Buddhist hell.

盤 *Jiban* ground; footing.

震 *Jishin* earthquake.

質 *Jishitsu* quality: *chishitsu*
geology.

圭 KEI jewel; edge.

角 *Keikaku* angles; asperity;
roughness.

T 吉 KITSU; KICHI. *Yoshi* good;
lucky. 【口】

凶 *Kikkyō* good and bad
fortune; lucky and un-
lucky; fortune.

兆 *Kitchō* lucky sign.

例 *Kichirei* time-honoured
custom.

報 *Kippō* joyful news.

T 寺 JI. *Tera* Buddhist temple.
【寸】

院 *Ji-in* Buddhist temple;
church.

走 See T 走 156,0.

T 至 See 133,0.

址 SHI. *Ato* vestige; relic. 四

T 坊 BŌ boy; town; room;
Buddhist temple.

主 *Bōzu* Buddhist priest.

間 *Bōkan* in the market.

T 均 KIN. *Hitoshii* level;
equality.

一 *Kin-itsu* uniformity.

等 *Kintō* equal; identical;
level.

（四）

均
霑 *Kinten* to share in.

衡 *Kinkō* equal; identical; level.

T 坂 HAN. *Saka* an incline; inclined road.

道 *Sakamichi* inclined road.

T 坑 KŌ. *Ana* hole; tunnel; pit.

夫 *Kōfu* miner.

道 *Kōdō* underground passage; gallery.

T 声 See 聲 128,11.

T 走 See 156,0.

T 壱 See 壹 32,9. 【士】

T 赤 See 155,0.

T 志 SHI. *Kokorozashi* intention; purpose; ambition: *kokoroza(su)* to aim at; design; intend: *shiringu* shilling. 【心】

士 *Shishi* man of high purpose.

氣 *Shiki* spirit·; morale.

望 *Shibō* desire.

望者 *Shibōsha* aspirant; applicant.

操 *Shisō* will; purpose; principle; constancy.

願 *Shigan* desire; application; volunteering.

願者 *Shigansha* a volunteer; a candidate.

*T 売 →32, 12

（四）

坐 ZA. *Suwa(ru)* to sit; squat: *sozoro ni* unaccountably.

洲 *Zasu; z·shū* to be stranded.

食 *Zashoku* eating without working.

席 *Zaseki* a seat.

視 *Zashi(suru)* to be a looker-on.

* 礁 *Zashō* stranding.

坦 TAN. *Tairaka* level; 五 plane; wide.

々 *Tantan* (of roads) level; even; (of persons) guileless; simple.

路 *Tanro* smooth·road.

道 *Tandō* smooth road.

懷 *Tankai* open-heartedness.

坩 KAN pot.

堝 *Rutsubo* a crucible.

坤 KON earth. *Hitsuji-saru* the south-west.

T 坪 *Tsubo* a land measure. See Introduction 44.

坡 HA a dike; dam.

T 幸 KŌ. *Saiwai; sachi* happiness; blessing; luck: *miyuki* going out (of Emperor). (*Yuki*). 【干】

甚 *Kōjin* to be glad.

福 *Kōfuku* happiness.

運 *Kōun* good fortune; favourable issue.

（五）

運兒 *Kōun-ji* child of fortune; a fortunate man.

坐 See 坐 32,4.

六 垣 EN. *Kaki* fence; wall.

根 *Kakine* fence; hedge.

間見 *Kaimami(-ru)* to peep.

垤 TETSU an ant-hill.

垢 KŌ; KU. *Aka* dirt; filth.

型 KEI. *Kata* type: *ikata* mould. [T]

錄 *Katarogu* catalogue.

七 埋 MAI. *Uzu(meru)*; *u(meru)*; *uzumo(reru)* to cover over; fill up; be buried. [T]

木 *Umoregi* fossil wood; living in obscurity.

立地 *Umetatechi* reclaimed land.

沒 *Maibotsu* to be buried.

葬 *Maisō* burial.

藏 *Maizō* hidden; buried.

埒 RACHI an enclosure; low fence.

埃 AI. *Hokori* rubbish; dust.

及 *Ejiputo* Egypt.

城 JŌ. *Shiro* castle. (*Ki*). [T]

下 *Jōka* a castle town.

趾 *Jōshi* site of a fort.

盍 See 108,5.

袁 (EN). 【衣】

埴 SHOKU. *Hani* clay.

堆 TAI. *Uzutakai* piled up in heaps.

積 *Taiseki* accumulation.

堀 KUTSU. *Hori* canal; moat: *ho(ru)* to dig; carve. [T]

出物 *Horidashimono* a lucky find.

建小屋 *Hottategoya* shanty.

割 *Horiwari* canal.

培 BAI. *Tsuchika(u)* to tend the roots of a plant; to manure. [T]

養 *Baiyō* to grow; cultivate.

埠 FU-wharf.

頭 *Futō; hatoba* wharf.

埼 KI. *Sak* the edge of a bank.

玉 *Saitama* p. n.

域 IKI limit; boundary; place within the boundary; country. [T]

執 SHITSU; SHŪ. *To(ru)* to take; manage; transact: *tora(h)eru* to take hold of. [T]

心 *Shūshin* devotion; attachment.

行 *Shikkō* execution; performance.

事 *Shitsuji* a steward.

（七）

八

（八〇）

執

拗 *Shūyō*; *shitsuyō*; *shitsukoi* pertinacious.

念深 *Shūnen-bukai* unforgiving; pertinacious.

務 *Shitsumu* business; work.

着 *Shūjaku*; *shūchaku* excessive fondness; attachment.

筆 *Shippitsu* write for (a magazine or newspaper).

達吏 *Shittatsuri* a bailiff.

T 堂 DŌ a public hall; temple; chamber; mansion.

々 *Dōdō* splendid; majestic; imposing; conspicuous; solemn.

島 *Dōjima*; *Dō-ga-shima* p. n.

望 BŌ; MŌ. *Nozomi* hope; ambition: *nozo(mu)* to look (used when speaking of great distance); hope; de-ire; wish; expect. (*Mochi*).【月】 →望 T

外 *Bōgai* unlooked-for; unexpected.

遠鏡 *Bōenkyō* a telescope.

T 堅 KEN. *Katai* firm; hard; strong; strict.

牢 *Kenrō* strongly built; solid; strong.

忍 *Kennin* perseverance.

固 *Kengo* strong; solid; firm; (morally or physically) steady.

氣 *Katagi* honest; respectable.

實 *Kenjitsu* steadfast.

埋 EN sink; bury; perish.

滅 *Emmetsu* destroy; disappear.

堪 KAN; TAN. *Ta(h)eru*; to endure; be able: *tamaranai* cannot endure.

忍 *Kannin* patience; forbearance.

能 *Tannō* skill.

堰 EN. *Seki*; *i* a dam.

止 *Seki-to(meru)* to dam up; check.

堵 To a fence; wall.

列 *Toretsu* to draw up in a line.

堺 KAI. *Sakai* boundary; frontier; also p. n.

塀 HEI a wall; fence.

T 場 JŌ. *Ba* circumstance; place. →32, 11

外 *Ba-hazure* being out of place.

末 *Basue* the outskirts.

合 *Baai* case; circumstances.

所 *Basho* place; space.

所柄 *Bashogara* the character of a place.

面 *Bamen* scene.

席 *Baseki* a seat.

處 *Basho* place; space.

T 堤 TEI. *Tsutsumi* a dike; bank.

九

126

防 *Teibō* a dike; bank.

T 報 HŌ news; report. *Muku-(y)iru* to pay back; recompense.

告 *Hōkoku* report; communication.

知 *Hōchi* information.

恩 *Hōon* requital of favour.

國 *Hōkoku* patriotism.

復 *Hōfuku* revenge.

酬 *Hoshū* remuneration.

道 *Hodō* to communicate; announce; report.

壺 KO. *Tsubo* jar; pot. 【士】

壹 ICHI; ITSU one. 【士】
→32,4T

T 喜 KI. *Yorokobi* joy: *yoroko-(bu)* to rejoice: *yorokobashii* joyful. 【口】

怒 *Kido* joy and anger; feeling.

怒哀樂 *Kido-airaku* one's feelings (lit.: joy, anger, grief, pleasure).

悅 *Kietsu* joy; gladness.

望峰 *Kibōhō* Cape of Good Hope.

捨 *Kisha* alms; voluntary contribution.

壽 *Kju* seventy-seventh birthday (special feast).

劇 *Kigeki* a comedy.

堯 GYŌ high; far; also p. n.

堡 HŌ. *Toride* small castle; embankment.

壘 *Hōrui* fortifications.

T 喪 See 30,9.
*

塩 See 鹽 108,19. 【鹵】 一〇

T 塔 TŌ tower; pagoda.

坿 JI. *Negura* roost.

塙 (*Hanawa*).

塚 CHŌ. *Tsuka* mound; grave.

塊 KAI. *Tsuchikure* clod of earth: *katamari* lump.

狀 *Kaijō* massive.

塡 TEN to bury; fill up; insert; go in; fit.

充 *Tenjū* to fill up; plug.

補 *Tempo* to make good; supplement.

T 塑 SO earthen figure.

像 *Sozō* plaster image.

聖 SEI; SHŌ holy; imperial; sacred. *Hijiri* a sage; learned man. 【耳】

人 *Seijin* a sage. →T 聖

上 *Seijō* His Majesty.

世 *Seisei* illustrious time.

代 *Seidai* a glorious reign.

(一〇)

聖

旨　*Seishi* Imperial idea, wish, command, will.

地　*Seichi* the Holy Land; Palestine.

勅　*Seichoku* Imperial command.

書　*Seisho* the Bible.

徒　*Seito* a saint.

恩　*Seion* Imperial favours.

訓　*Seikun* teaching of sages.

路易　*Sentorui* Saint Louis.

意　*Seii* Imperial will.

壽　*Seiju* the age of an Emperor.

德　*Seitoku* Imperial virtue or benevolence.

慮　*Seiryo* Imperial idea, wish.

賢　*Seiken* a man of wisdom; sage.

T **塗**　TO. *Nu(ru)* to paint; varnish; lacquer; plaster: *mami(reru)* to be smeared with; bedaubed: *mabu(su)* to smear.

物　*Nurimono* lacquered ware.

二 **塀**　See 塀 32,9.

塲　See ᵀ場 32,9.

境　KYŌ condition : KEI. *Sakai* border line; boundary; limit; region. →境ᵀ

内　*Keidai* precinct of a shrine or temple.

地　*Kyōchi* circumstances.

(一一)

界　*Kyōkai* boundary; frontier.

涯　*Kyōgai* condition.

域　*Kyōiki* a boundary; border land.

遇　*Kyōgū* conditions; circumstances; surroundings.

臺　DAI a stand : TAI. *Utena* calyx ; sepals.【壹】→28, 3 T

北　*Taihoku* p. n.

所　*Daidokoro* kitchen.

南　*Tainan* p. n.

紙　*Daishi* pasteboard.

詞　*Serifu* pieces of dramatic compositions spoken by actors on the stage.

閣　*Daikaku* the Cabinet.

灣　*Taiwan* Formosa.

嘉　KA good; happy. *Yomisuru* (irreg.) to regard as good; esteem. (*Yoshi*).【口】

辰　*Kashin* an auspicious occasion.

納　*Kanō* sanction.

例　*Karei* an auspicious custom.

壽　JU. *Kotobuki* long life; old age; long continued: *kotoho(gu)* to congratulate; celebrate.【士】→41, 4 T

司　*Sushi* a certain kind of Japanese food.

命　*Jumyō* life; period of existence.

塹　ZAN. *Hori* a moat; ditch.

濠　*Zangō* a trench.

塾　JUKU a private school; boarding-school.

生 *Jukusei* a pupil.

舍 *Jukusha* class-room of a private school.

増 Zō. *Ma(su)* to add; increase. →32,11 * T

大 *Zō-dai* increase.

加 *Zōka* increase.

収 *Zōshū* an additional income.

長 *Zōchō* to become puffed up, self-conceited.

設 *Zōsetsu* increasing number or size of anything.

減 *Zōgen* increase and decrease; change.

殖 *Zōshoku* increase; multiplication.

進 *Zōshin* to promote; increase.

補 *Zoho* supplement.

税 *Zōzei* an increased tax.

資 *Zoshi* increase of capital.

築 *Zōchiku* the extension of a building.

額 *Zōgaku* increase.

墳 FUN tomb; mound.

墓 *Fumbo* a tomb; grave.

賣 BAI. *U(ru)* to sell. 【貝】 →32,4 T *

卜 *Baiboku* fortune-telling.

子 *Uriko* a shop-boy.

口 *Urekuchi* market for commodities.

方 *Urikata* a seller.

手 *Urite* a seller.

切 *Urikire* being sold out.

出 *Uridashi* a sale : *urida(su)* to begin to sell; to make a sale.

行 *Ureyuki* sale.

言葉 *Urikotoba* offensive speech.

却 *Baikyaku* a disposal by sale.

名 *Baimei* striving for publicity.

物 *Urimono* an article for sale.

拂 *Urihara(u)* to get rid of by selling.

約 *Baiyaku* contract for sale.

捌 *Urisabaki* sale.

家 *Uriie* house for sale.

國奴 *Baikokudo* a traitor (to his country).

高 *Uredaka* amount of sale.

渡證 *Uriwatashishō* bill of sale.

買 *Baibai* sale; bargain; trade.

藥 *Baiyaku* patent medicine,

墮 DA. *Oto(su)*; *o(chiru)* to throw down; fall down; deteriorate. →32,9 T *

胎 *Datai* abortion.

落 *Daraku* degeneration; corruption.

墜 TSUI. *O(chiru)* to fall down.

死 *Tsuishi* to fall to death.

落 *Tsuiraku* to fall down.

---

* 増 →32,12
T

三三
T 壇 DAN platform; an altar.

墻 SHŌ. *Kaki* fence; wall.

壁 *Shōheki* fence; barrier.

墺 Ō used for its sound.

地利 *Ōsutoriya* Austria.

T 壁 HEKI. *Kabe* wall.

土 *Kabetsuchi* wall plaster.

畫 *Hekiga* wall picture.

T 墾 KON to prepare new ground for cultivation; to till.
*1 *2

一四 壕 GŌ. *Hori* moat; ditch; trench.

一六 壜 TAN; DON. *Bin* a bottle.

甕 See 212,3. 【土】

壞 KAI. *Kowa(reru)*; *kowa(su)* to break down. Do not confound with the following. →32, 13 * 1T

亂 *Kairan* corruption.

一七 壤 JŌ. *Tsuchi* the earth; fertile ground; fertile. Do not confound with the preceding. →31, 13 * 2T

三三 士

T 士 SHI man. *Samurai* military man; warrior; officer. Do not confound with 士 32,0.

女 *Shijo* men and women.

官 *Shikan* a regimental officer.

卒 *Shisotsu* the rank and file.

氣 *Shiki* chivalry; military spirit.

族 *Shizoku* man of samurai rank.

道 *Shidō* knighthood.

三四 夂

三五 夂

二

T 処 See 處 141,5.

T 冬 TŌ. *Fuyu* winter. 【冫】

至 *Tōji* winter solstice.

枯 *Fuyugare* withering in winter.

眠 *Tōmin* hibernation.

T 各 KAKU. *Ono-ono* each; 三 every. 【口】

自 *Kakuji* each individual; severally.

地 *Kakuchi* each district.

位 *Kakui* term used in addressing several people collectively; gentlemen ! you.

般 *Kakuhan* various kinds; all sorts.

員 *Kakuin* term used in addressing several persons collectively; gentlemen ! you.

個 *Kakko* individual.

國 *Kakkoku* every country.

論 *Kakuron* special treatise.

四 _T 条 See 條 9,9. 【木】

_T 麦 See 麥 199,0.

六 _T 変 See 變 35,19. 【言】

七 夏 KA; GE. *Natsu* summer.

至 *Geshi* the summer solstice.

休 *Natsuyasumi* summer holidays.

季 *Kaki* summer.

期 *Kaki* summer.

一 愛 AI love. *Me(deru)* to love;
〇 appreciate: *itsukushi(mu)*
_T to love: *airashii* lovable:
medetai congratulatory.
【心】

他心 *Aitashin* altruism.

耳蘭 *Airurando* Ireland.

知 *Aichi* p. n.

玩 *Aigan* fondness for.

惜 *Aiseki* unwilling to part; regret.

情 *Aijō* love; affection.

欲 *Aiyoku* affection; liking.

國 *Aikoku* love of one's country; patriotism.

着 *Aichaku; aijaku* love; attachment.

媛 *Ehime* p. n.

想 *Aisō* sociability; courtesy; amiableness.

敬 *Aikyō* amiability: *aikei* to respect.

憎 *Aizō* likes and dislikes.

撫 *Aibu* caress.

嬌 *Aikyō* attractiveness.

慕 *Aibo* love; yearn for.

蘭 *Airurando* Ireland.

顧 *Aiko* patronage; favour.

讀 *Aidoku* to read and greatly appreciate.

---

^T憂 YŪ. *Uree* grief: *uryōru*
(ウレフル, lit. st.: see Introduction 40) to grieve;
feel sorry for; be anxious:
ui sad: *usa* gloom. 【心】

目 *Ukime* distress.

色 *Yūshoku* worried look.

身 *Ukimi* a life of misery.

身を窶す *Ukimi wo yatsusu* devote oneself.

苦 *Yūku* anguish; agony.

一
二

131

（一二）

憂
國 *Yūkoku* anxiety on behalf of one's country.

愁
慮 *Yūshū* melancholy; grief.

慮 *Yūryo* anxiety.

欝 *Yūutsu* melancholy.

一九

變 HEN emergency. *Kawa-(ru); ka(h)eru)* to be different; change.【言】→8,7T : 35,6T

人 *Henjin* an eccentric person; crank.

化 *Henka* change.

心 *Henshin* change of mind.

死 *Henshi* violent death.

色 *Henshoku* change of colour.

名 *Hemmei* a false name.

災 *Hensai* a calamity; disaster.

形 *Henkei* transformation.

更 *Henkō* change; alteration; revision.

事 *Henji* mishap; accident.

則 *Hensoku* irregularity; anomaly.

挺 *Henteko* queer; quaint.

通 *Hentsū* adaptability.

動 *Hendō* fluctuation.

換 *Henkan* change.

節 *Hensetsu* backsliding.

說 *Hensetsu* change one's opinion.

態 *Hentai* abnormal.

遷 *Hensen* change; alteration.

調 *Henchō* abnormality.

壓 *Hen-atsu* transformation (electricity).

（一九）

蠻 See 173,17.

二二三

夕 三六

T 夕 SEKI. *Yū; yūbe* evening.

日 *Yūhi* the setting sun.

方 *Yūgata; yūkata* evening; towards evening.

立 *Yūdachi* summer shower.

刊 *Yūkan* evening paper.

刻 *Yūkoku* the evening.

陽 *Sekiyō* the setting sun.

景 *Yūkei* evening.

燒 *Yūyke* the evening glow.

暮 *Yūure* evening twilight; dusk.

顏 *Yūgao* gourd; calabash.

T 外 GAI foreign : GE. *Soto; hoka* else; other; besides; outside; beyond : *hazu(su); hazu(reru)* to unfasten. 二

人 *Gaijin* foreigners.

出 *Gaishutsu* going out.

交 *Gaikō* diplomacy.

交官 *Gaikōkan* diplomat.

交家 *Gaikōka* diplomat; sociable person.

臣 *Gaishin* a foreign subject.

形 *Gaikei* appearance; form.

見 *Gaiken* outward appearance.

泊 *Gaihaku* stopping out.

相 *Gaishō* Foreign Minister.

客 *Gaikyaku* a foreign visitor.

科 *Geka* surgery.

界 *Gaikai* outside; objective world; foreign countries.

套 *Gaitō* an overcoat.

面 *Gaimen*: *gemen* outside; outwards; appearance.

宮 *Gekū* shrine in Ise, the second in importance in Japan.

國 *Gaikoku* a foreign country.

側 *Sotogawa* the outside.

務大臣 *Gaimu-daijin* Minister of Foreign Affairs.

務省 *Gaimu-shō* Foreign Office.

寇 *Gaikō* a foreign invasion.

患 *Gaikan* trouble with a foreign country.

間 *Ga'kan* outside.

遊 *Gaiyū* a foreign tour.

電 *Gaiden* foreign telegrams.

債 *Gaisai* foreign loan.

資 *Gaishi* foreign capital.

聞 *Gaibun* reputation.

賓 *Gaihin* a foreign guest.

箱 *Sotobako* packing case.

貌 *Gaibō* appearance; face.

題 *Gedai* the title of a play.

觀 *Gaikan* outside view; external appearance.

舛 See 136,0.

^T名 MEI aux. num. for counting persons: MYŌ. *Na* name; fame; celebrated; excellent; splendid. 【口】

人 *Meijin* an expert.

工 *Meikō* a skilful or celebrated workman.

士 *Meishi* a man of distinction.

手 *Meishu* person celebrated for his skill.

目 *Meimoku*; *myōmoku* name; appellation.

古屋 *Nagoya* p. n.

代 *Nadai* famous: *myōdai* agency; representative.

字 *Myōji* family name.

君 *Meikun* an enlightened ruler.

言 *Meigen* a wise saying.

折 *Naore* disgrace.

利 *Meiri*; *myōri* fame and profit.

狀 *Meijō* describe.

門 *Meimon* noble descent; good family.

物 *Meibutsu* the product for which a place is celebrated.

物男 *Meibutsu-otoko* a man whose name is in everybody's mouth.

刺 *Meishi* visiting card.

名

指 *Nazashi* calling by name.

前 *Namae* a name.

高 *Nadakai* famous.

馬 *Meiba* splendid or famous horse.

乘 *Nano(ru)* to tell one's name; to give oneself a name.

家 *Meika* a famous or noble family.

流 *Meiryū* celebrated man.

案 *Meian* a bright idea.

望 *Meibō* reputation.

產 *Meisan* a noted product.

筆 *Meihitsu* famous and excellent handwriting.

勝 *Meishō* celebrated places.

殘 *Nagori* relics; vestiges; ruins; farewell; parting.

義 *Meigi* name.

稱 *Meishō* name; title.

實 *Meijitsu* the name and the reality.

論 *Meiron* an excellent opinion.

聲 *Meisei* reputation; honour; good name.

簿 *Meibo* name list.

譽 *Meiyo* fame; honour.

T 多 TA. *Ōi* numerous; many; much.

々 *Tata* a great deal of.

大 *Tadai* a great deal.

少 *Tashō* more or less; some.

分 *Tabun* probably; perhaps; possibly.

忙 *Tabō* busy.

岐 *Taki* digress (from the subject).

事 *Taji* eventful.

病 *Tabyō* sickly.

恨 *Takon* great discontent.

能 *Tanō* many accomplishments.

情 *Tajō* amorousness; sensibility.

量 *Taryō* plenty; much.

勢 *Tazei* a large number.

端 *Tatan* eventful.

寡 *Taka* quantity.

數 *Tasū* great many; large number.

慾 *Tayoku* covetousness.

額 *Tagaku* a great sum.

額納稅議員 *Tagakunōzeigiin* a representative of the highest tax-payers.

藝 *Tagei* having many accomplishments.

辯 *T. ben* talkative.

夛 See preceding.

麥 See 199,0. 八

麗 See 鹿 198,2. 二

夥 KA. *Obitadashii* many; numerous; very.

三七 (一一〇)

多 *Kata* great number; large quantity.

一五 斃 See 66,14.

三七

大

T 大 DAI (sometimes used as abb. for *d i-gaku*); TAI. *O; ōkii; ōi* big; great.

人 *Otona* adult: *taijin* a great man.

人物 *Daijimbutsu* a great man.

入 *Ōiri* a large, full house (theatre).

々的 *Daidaiteki* great.

工 *Daiku* carpenter.

口 *Ōguchi* large amounts.

丈夫 *Daijōbu* all right; requiring no anxiety; safely: *daijōfu* heroic man.

小 *Daishō* big and little; size; the two swords.

凡 *Ōyoso* roughly.

日本 *Dai-Nippon* Japan.

方 *Ōkata* generally; for the most part; almost.

切 *Taisetsu* importance; value: *ōgiri* the after-piece.

分 *Daibun; daibu* many; much; a great deal: *Ōita* p. n.

水 *Ōmizu* flood.

不列顛 *Daiburiten* Great Britain.

目 *Ōme* overlook.

正 *Taishō* Era name; 1912-1926.

仕掛 *Ōjikake* a large scale.

立物 *Ōdatemono* a leading figure.

出來 *Ōdeki* a great success.

半 *Taihan* great part; the majority.

本 *Taihon* great foundation.

本營 *Daihon-ei* Imperial headquarters.

全 *aizen* complete work.

任 *Tainin* important charge; a great office.

臣 *Daijin; ōomi* Minister of State.

名 *Daimyō* feudal lord.

西洋 *Taiseiyō* Atlantic Ocean.

早計 *Daisōkei* precipitancy.

同小異 *Daidō-shōi* to be much alike.

成 *Taisei* complete success; completion.

地 *Daichi* ground; earth.

別 *Taibetsu* general classification.

佐 *Taisa* colonel (army); captain (navy).

豆 *Daizu* soy-bean.

君 *Ō-gimi* Emperor; sovereign; the great lord.

言 *Taigen* big talk; bragging.

作 *Taisaku* great work.

135

大

局　*Taikyoku* general situation.

佛　*Daibutsu* large image of Buddha.

阪　*Ōsaka* p. n.

役　*Taiyaku* important office: *taieki* great war.

兵　*Taihei* big army.

志　*Taishi* great ambition.

金　*Taikin* large sum of money.

空　*Ōzora* the sky.

和　*Yamato* province in central Japan; Japan.

和魂　*Yamato-damashii* the Japanese spirit; patriotism.

命　*Taimei* an Imperial command.

事　*Daiji* matter of importance; serious affair; important; serious: *daiji ni* carefully, like something one holds in great esteem.

叔父　*Ō-oji* great-uncle.

叔母　*Ō-oba* great-aunt.

枚　*Taimai* much; large sum (of money).

使　*Taishi* ambassador.

抵　*Taitei* generally.

屋　*Oya* a landlord; owner of a house.

昔　*Ō-mukashi* very many years ago.

洋　*Taiyō* the ocean.

洋洲　*Taiyōshū* Oceania.

軍　*Taigun* great army; large force.

柄　*Ōgara* large-build; large body.

約　*Taiyaku* the gist of a matter; main points of a case.

勇　*Taiyū* great valour:

政　*Taisei* government of the country.

便　*Daiben* faeces.

風呂敷　*Ōburoshiki* a large wrapper; gross exaggeration.

悟　*Taigo* perception of truth.

悟徹底　*Taigo-tettei* perception of absolute truth.

害　*Taigai* great injury; serious damage.

酒家　*Taishuka* a heavy drinker.

家　*Taika* a distinguished scholar: *taike* a wealthy house: *ōya* owner of a house.

根　*Daikon* radish.

逆　*Daigyaku* high treason.

砲　*Taihō* cannon.

氣　*Taiki* the atmosphere.

息　*Taisoku* deep sigh.

要　*Taiyō* summary.

陸　*Tairiku* continent.

略　*Tairyaku* summary; epitome; roughly.

御心　*Ō-mikokoro* the heart of the Emperor.

御言　*Ō-mikoto* Imperial word.

部　*Daibu* much; great many; greater part; for the most part; copious.

尉 *Taii* captain (army); lieutenant (navy).

將 *Taishō* general (army); admiral (navy); head; master.

掃除 *Ō-sōji* general cleaning.

晦日 *Ōmisoka: ōtsumogori* the last day of the year.

赦 *Taisha* amnesty.

麥 *Ōmugi* barley.

連 *Dairen* Dalny.

祭日 *Taisaijitsu* the principal national holidays.

患 *Taikan* calamity; serious disaster; serious illness.

隊 *Daitai* battalion.

袈裟 *Ōgesa* exaggeration.

厦高樓 *Taika-kōrō* large and imposing buildings.

統領 *Daitōryō* President of a Republic.

黑 *Daikoku* the god of wealth; name given to certain cap worn by infants and very old men.

黑柱 *Daikoku-bashira* principal pillar.

詰 *Ōzume* the end.

勢 *Taisei* the general trend: *taizei; ōzei* a large number of people.

業 *Taigyō* a great enterprise; eminent deed; great work.

義 *Taigi* great moral obligation; righteousness.

禁 *Taikin* the laws of the state.

意 *Taii* the general idea; gist; outline.

慈大悲 *Daijidaihi* great mercy and compassion.

蠱 *Daijin* a rich man.

層 *Taisō* very.

審院 *Daishin-in* the supreme court.

廟 *Taibyō* the great shrine of Ise.

儀 *Taigi* fatigue; weariness.

學 *Daigaku* university.

概 *Taigai* generally.

舉 *Taikyo* in full force.

總統 *Daisōtō* President (of China).

禮服 *Taireifuku* full dress.

膽 *Daitan* courageous; impudent.

藏大臣 *Ōkura-daijin* the Minister of Finance.

藏省 *Ōkurashō* the Finance Department.

願 *Daigan* an earnest request; supplication.

權 *Taiken* Imperial prerogative.

變 *Taihen* remarkable; serious; terrible.

體 *Daitai* essential points.

太 **TAI: TA.** *Futoi* thick; large: *futo(ru)* to grow fat: *hanahada* very. (Ō). 一

刀 *Tachi* sword.

子 *Taishi* Crown Prince.

古 *Taiko* remote antiquity.

平 *Taihei* peace.

（一）

太

平洋 *Taiheiyō* Pacific Ocean.

平樂 *Taiheiraku* boasting; nonsense.

后 *Taikō* the Empress Dowager.

西洋 *Taiseiyō* Atlantic Ocean.

沽 *Tāku* Taku.

物 *Futomono* dry-goods.

陽 *Taiyō* the sun.

鼓 *Taiko* drum.

腹 *Fut-bara* bold; audacious.

T **犬** See 94,0.

T **夫** FU a male; man. *Otto*; *se* husbaud: *sore* that. (*O*). Do not confound with 天 1,3.

人 *Fujin* a wife; lady; M s.

子 *Fūshi* title given to learned men; Confucius.

妻 *Fisai* Mr and Mrs.

婦 *Fūfu* married couple.

二 **本** See T **本** 75,1.

T **矢** See 111,0.

T **失** SHITSU to make a mistake. *Ushina(u)* to lose: *u(seru)* to disappear. Do not confound with 矢 111,0.

火 *Shikka* an accidental fire.

名 *Shitsumei* anonymous.

言 *Shitsugen* slip of the tongue

（二）

明 *Shitsumei* loss of eyesight.

念 *Shitsunen* forgetting.

笑 *Shisshō* to burst into laughter.

望 *Shitsubō* disappointment.

敗 *Shippai; shikujiru* failure.

脚 *Shikkyaku* misstep.

策 *Shissaku* failure; mistake.

敬 *Shikkei* disrespectful; I beg your parcon; good-bye.

業 *Shitsugyō* unemployment; discontent.

意 *Shitsui* disappointment; discontent.

態 *Shittai* fault; blunder.

墜 *Shittsui* loss; waste.

踪 *Shissō* disappearance; abscondence.

錯 *Shissaku* error.

禮 *Shitsurei* discourtesy; rudeness.

職 *Shisshoku* unemployment.

戀 *Shitsuren* disappointed love; broken heart.

體 *Shittai* ignominy.

T **央** Ō. *Naka; nakaba* centre; middle.

三

夫 and **夹** See **夾** 37,4.

夷 I. *Ebis; emishi* barbarian.

狄 *Iteki* savages; barbarians.

四

夾 KYŌ. *Hasa(mu); sashihasa-(mu)* to hold between two things.

擊 *Kyōgeki* attack on both flanks.

五 **奔**
T
HON. *Hashi(ru)* to run; to gush forth.

走 *Honsō* to run about; be busily engaged.

命 *Hommei* execute order; to chase.

馬 *Homba* running horse.

流 *Honryū* rapids.

逸 *Hon-itsu* boldness; to run away; escape.

騰 *Hontō* going up (of prices).

T **奇**
KI odd number. *Kushi* (lit; st.) strange; wonderful.

人 *Kijin* an eccentric man.

々怪々 *Kiki-kaikai* most strange.

才 *Kisai* genius; talent.

功 *Kikō* a signal success.

妙 *Kimyō* wonderful.

怪 *Kikai* strange.

拔 *Kibatsu* out of the common; eccentric.

特 *Kitoku; kidoku* admirable; praiseworthy.

術 *Kijutsu* magic; jugglery.

異 *Kii* strange; unusual.

貨 *Kika* good opportunity.

勝 *Kishō* wonderful view.

遇 *Kigū* to meet in an unexpected manner.

想 *Kisō* a phantastic idea.

禍 *Kika* an accident.

聞 *Kibun* strange news.

談 *Kidan* a strange story.

緣 *Kien* unexpected connection; strange relation.

數 *Kisū* odd (as opposed to even) number.

謀 *Kibō* ingenious stratagem.

蹟 *Kiseki* miracle.

麗 *Kirei* clean; pretty.

體 *Kitai* strange.

襲 *Kishū* a sudden attack.

觀 *Kikan* wonder; singular spectacle.

奈
NA; NAI. *Ikani; nanzo* how; what; why.

何 *Ikan* how.

良 *Nara* p. n.

落 *Naraku* hell.

T **奉**
HŌ; BU to serve; follow. *Tatematsu(ru)* to present; sometimes merely a polite suffix (read in inverted order), e. g. 奉存 *Zonjitatematsuru* to think; know. Sometimes used as abb. of 奉天 Mukden.

天 *Hōten* Mukden.

公 *Hōkō* domestic or public service; apprenticeship; duty.

仕 *Hōshi* to perform one's duties; serve as an official.

存候 *Zonjitatematsurisōrō* I think (epist. style).

呈 *Hōtei* presentation.

答 *Hōtō* answer the Emperor.

賀候 *Gashitatematsurisōrō* I congratulate you.

（五）奉

納 *Hōnō* offer to the gods; dedicate.

迎 *Hōgei* going out to receive the Emperor.

送 *Hōsō* see off (the Emperor).

戴 *Hōtai* receive; have as head or president.

祝 *Hōshuku* celebrate.

謝候 *Shashitatematsurisōrō* thank you; obliged to you.

願上候 *Negaiagetatematsurisōrō* I beg you; please.

還 *Hōkan* return (to the Emperor).

職 *Hōshoku* being in office.

六 春 T SHUN. *Haru* spring (season); amorous.〔日〕

分 *Shumbun* spring equinox.

日 *Kasuga* p. n.: *shunjitsu* warm spring day.

色 *Shunshoku* spring scenery.

季 *Shunki* spring season.

雨 *Harusame; shun-u* spring rain.

秋 *Shunjū* spring and autumn; year; age.

情 *Shunjō* sexual desire.

暖 *Shundan* warmth on a spring day; spring.

奏 T Sō to report to the Throne; to say (of Emperor); accomplish. *Kana(deru)* to play (a musical instrument).

上 *Sōjō* reporting to the Emperor.

（六）任 *Sōnin* the rank of government officials who are appointed by the Cabinet and reported to the Emperor.

効 *Sōkō* success.

聞 *Sōmon* reporting to the Emperor.

請 *Sōsei* petitioning the Emperor.

樂 *Sōgaku* music.

哭 See 30,7.

契 KEI. *Chigi(ru)* to make an agreement or alliance with; a check. 契 T →

約 *Keiyaku* contract.

奕 EKI; YAKU large; great; bright; gamble.

拳 See 舉 134,11.

---

*套 Tō long; over-coat. 七

泰 SHIN name of an old dynasty in China. (*Hata*).〔禾〕

泰 T TAI calm; peaceful; easy; large; great; wide. (*Yasu*).〔水〕

山 *Taizan* p. n.; safety; steadiness.

斗 *Taito* an authority; a leading light.

平 *Taihei* peace.

西 *Taisei* the Western countries.

然 *Taizen* composedly.

奚 See 87,6.〔大〕

八 **舂** SHŌ. *Usutsu(ku)* to pound (in a mortar). 【白】

爽 SŌ. *Sawayaka* clear; pure; fluent. 【爻】

快 *Sōkai* refreshing.

然 *Sōzen* cool.

九 **奢** SHA. *Ogo(ru)* to be extravagant; profuse.

侈 *Shashi* luxury; extravagance.

奠 See **奠** 12,10. 【大】

喫 See 30,9‡

*1

一〇 **奥** Ō. *Oku* the innermost part; inside; depth; wife. →37,9 *¹T

方 *Okugata* the wife of a noble-man.

印 *Okuin* official seal.

羽 *Ōu* p. n.

床 *Okuyukashii* refined.

書 *Okugaki* endorsement.

義 *Okugi; ō-gi* the mysteries or recondite principles of any science or art.

様 *Okusama* wife (polite).
*₂

二一 **奪** DATSU. *Uba(u)* to rob; seize; take by force.
T

取 *Datsshu* take; capture.

略 *Datsuryaku* robbery.

掠 *Datsuryaku* to seize by force; capture.

還 *Dakkan* take back; occupy again.

奨 SHŌ. *Susu(meru)* to exhort; encourage. →37,10 T *²

勵 *Shōrei* encouragement.

奬 See **斃** 66,14.　二二

T
奮 FUN. *Furu(u)* to be stirred up; be excited.　一三

起 *Funki* to brace up.

發 *Fumpatsu* zealous effort; to exert oneself.

然 *Funzen* energetically.

戰 *Funsen* to fight with energy.

勵 *Funrei* to put forth all one's endeavour.

鬭 *Funtō* to struggle hard; exert oneself to the utmost.

激 *Fungeki* excitement.

蠢 See 142,15.　一八

女　三八

When at the left it is called *Onna-hen.*

女 JO; JŌ; NYŌ; NYO. *Onna; onago; me* woman; female: *musume* girl; daughter: *meawa(seru)* to marry.

々 *Memeshii* womanish; effeminate.

女

々敷 *Memeshii* womanish; effeminate.

工 *Jokō* female labourer.

子 *Joshi; onago* woman.

丈夫 *Jojōfu* a brave woman; heroine.

王 *Joō; nyoō* queen; princess.

中 *Jochū* a maid-servant.

天下 *Onna-denka* petticoat government

史 *Joshi* polite term used when referring to a learned lady.

色 *Joshoku* lust.

官 *Jokan* a maid of honour.

房 *Nyōbō; nyobo* wife.

波 *Menami* receding wave.

郎 *Jorō; joro* a prostitute.

流 *Joryū* the female sex; women.

将 *Okami: joshō* a landlady (of hotels, etc.)

婿 *Josei* a son-in-law.

優 *Joyū* an actress.

難 *Jonan* suffering caused by woman.

二 **奴** DO; NU. *Yakko* a servant; slave: *yatsu* fellow (rude): *yatsugare* I (humble).

隷 *Dorei* a slave.

三 **如** JO; NYO. *Gotoshi* (sometimes inverted order) like: *shi(ku)* to excel.
T

上 *Jojō; joshō* above-stated.

才 *Josai nai* smart; clever; tactful.

月 *Kisaragi* poetical name for 2nd month (old calendar).

此 *Kaku no gotoshi* (inverted order) like this.

何 *Ikan; ikani* how; what; in what manner: *ikaga* how: *ikanaru* whatever: *ikanimo* indeed; verily.

何程 *Ikahodo* how much.

來 *Nyorai* Buddha.

是 *Kaku no gotoshi* (inverted order) like this.

案 *An no gotoshi* (inverted order) as I (we) expected.

斯 *Kaku no gotoshi* (inverted order) like this.

露 *Joro* watering-pot.

奸 KAN wicked; to falsify.

臣 *Kanshin* a treacherous subject.

物 *Kambutsu* a crafty fellow.

佞 *Kanrei* depraved.

計 *Kankei* a sinister design.

商 *Kanshō* dishonest merchant.

智 *Kanchi* cunning.

T **好** KŌ. *Kono(mu); su(ku)* to like: *konomi* liking; fondness: *konomashii* desirable: *yoi* good: *yoshimi* friendship.

一對 *Kōittsui* a good pair.

（三）

人物 *Kōjimbutsu* a good natured man.

々 *Sukizuki* according to taste.

色 *Kōshoku* lewd; lascivious.

奇心 *Kōkishin* curiosity.

事家 *Kōzuka* a collector; antiquarian; dilettante.

物 *Kōbutsu* (of eatables only) a thing one is fond of.

果 *Kōka* a good result.

況 *Kōkyō* prosperous condition.

都合 *Kōtsugō* convenient; opportune.

評 *Kōhyō* favourable criticism.

惡 *Kōo* likes and dislikes.

感 *Kōkan* good will.

意 *Kōi* good will.

機 *Kōki* good opportunity.

戰的 *Kōsenteki* bellicose.

T 妃 HI. *Kisaki* princess (wife of a prince).

四 T 妊 NIN. *Hara(mu)*; *migomo(ru)* to be pregnant.
→38, 6

娠 *Ninshin* conception; pregnant.

婦 *Nimpu* pregnant woman.

妍 KEN bewitching; beautiful.

T 妙 MYŌ. *Tae* excellence; beauty; out of the common; admirable; wonderful; young.

手 *Myōshu* skilful person.

用 *Myōyō* secret; wise use.

技 *Myōgi* a wonderful feat.

味 *Myōmi* charms; beauty.

法 *Myōhō* wonderful law; Buddhism.

案 *Myōan* a bright idea; excellent device.

趣 *Myōshu* beauties; wonders.

諦 *Myōtei* secret principle.

藥 *Myōyaku* a specific (remedy).

齡 *Myōrei* young; youthful.

T 妨 BŌ. *Samata(geru)* to hinder; injure; object.

止 *Bōshi* prevention.

害 *Bōgai* disturbance; obstruction.

姉 See T 姉 38,5.

妖 YŌ suspicious; bewitching.

婦 *Yofu* a wicked woman.

術 *Yōjutsu* magic.

妓 GI a singing girl; prostitute.

樓 *Girō* brothel.

T 姓 SEI; SHŌ surname; family name. *Kabane* a family.

名 *Seimei* full name.

姐 *Ane*; *neisan* elder sister; now used when referring to maid-servants in an inn, etc.

御 *Anego* boss's wife.

（五）

妬 To. *Neta(mu)*; *sone(mu)* to envy; be jealous of: *netamashii* enviable; envious.

姑 Ko. *Shūtome* mother-in-law: *shibaraku* short time.

息 *Kosoku* temporizing.

T **始** Shi. *Haji(meru)*; *hajima-(ru)* to begin: *hajimete* at first; for the first time: *moto* origin: *hajime* beginning.

末 *Shimatsu* circumstances; management; procedure; thrift.

終 *Shijū* from beginning to end; always.

T **姉** Shi. *Ane* elder sister. →38,4

妹 *Shimai* sisters.

T **妹** Mai. *Imōto*; *imoto* younger sister: *imo* familiar way of calling a woman; my dear.

背 *Imose* husband and wife.

T **妻** Sai. *T.uma* wife.

女 *Saijo* a wife.

子 *Saishi*; *tsumako* wife and children.

君 *Saikun* other person's wife (honorific).

帶 *Saitai* taking a wife.

六 **姪** Tetsu. *Mei* niece.

妊 See T **妊** 38,4.

T **姬** Ki. *Hime* princess; daughter of a nobleman.

（六）

百合 *Himeyuri* red-star lily.

T **姻** In to marry (a husband); relatives.

戚 *Inseki* a relative by marriage.

姨 I. *Oba* aunt; sister-in-law.

姥 Bo. *Baba* an old woman: *uba* a wet-nurse.

姦 Kan adultery; to transgress. *Kashimashii* boisterous: *yokoshima* unrighteousness.

佞 *Kannei* wicked and servile.

淫 *Kan-in* adultery; rape.

通 *Kantsū* adultery.

雄 *Kan-yū* great villain.

賊 *Kanzoku* a traitor; a knave.

T **姿** Shi. *Sugata* figure; shape; form; appearance; manner.

勢 *Shisei* posture.

態 *Shitai* style; pose.

娛 Go. *Tanoshi(mu)* to rejoice.

樂 *Goraku* pleasure; joy. →娛 T

七

T **娠** Shin to conceive; be pregnant.

T **娘** Rō; Jō. *Musume* daughter; girl; female.

娩 Ben to bear a child.

娑 Sha; Sa to dance.

婆 *Shaba* this world.

144

八 **婬** See **淫** 85,8.

娼 SHŌ a harlot.

妓 *Shōgi* a prostitute.

婦 *Shōfu* a harlot.

T **婚** KON marriage.

姻 *Kon-in* marriage.

約 *Kon-yaku* promise of marriage.

嫁 *Konka* marriage.

儀 *Kongi* marriage ceremony.

禮 *Konrei* marriage ceremony; matrimony.

婢 HI. *Hashitame* maidservant.

僕 *Hiboku* servants.

T **婦** FU woman; wife.

人 *Fujin* woman.

女子 *Fujoshi* a woman.

婉 EN graceful.

曲 *Enkyoku* in a roundabout manner; indirectly.

麗 *Enrei* beautiful; lovely.

娶 SHU. *Meto(ru)*; *meawa(seru)* to marry (a wife).

T **婆** BA. *Baba* an old woman.

九 T**婿** SEI. *Muko* a bridegroom; a son-in-law.

媚 BI. *Kobi* flattery; coquetry: *ko(biru)* to flatter.

T **媒** BAI. *Nakōdo; nakadachi* a go-between. 九

介 *Baikai* mediation.

妁 *Baishaku* go-between for marriages.

媛 EN. *Hime* a lady; beautiful woman.

媼 Ō; ON. *Baba* an old woman. 一〇

嫦 KŌ intimacy; friendship.

和 *Kōwa* peace; reconciliation.

曳 *Aibiki* secret meeting of lovers.

嫉 SHITSU hate. *Sone(mu)* to be jealous.

妬 *Shitto* jealousy.

視 *Shisshi* regarding with jealousy.

嫌 KEN. *Kira(u)*; *iyaga(ru)* to hate; detest; dislike: *iya* hateful; disgusting.

忌 *Kenki* to feel aversion; antipathy.

味 *Iyami* cutting remark.

氣 *Iyaki* repugnance.

惡 *Ken-o* hatred.

疑 *Kengi* suspicion; distrust.

厭 *Ken-en* disgust.

T**嫁** KA. *Yome* daughter-in-law: *totsu(gu)* to marry into the husband's family.

入 *Yomeiri* marriage.

嫂 SŌ. *Aniyome* wife of one's elder brother: *ane* sister-in-law.

145

二 嫡 CHAKU; TEKI heir.

嫡 T

子 *Chakushi* eldest son.

男 *Chakunan* eldest son.

流 *Chakuryū* direct line of descent.

孫 *Chakuson* eldest grandson.

嫣 EN beautiful; smile.

然 *Enzen; nikkori* smilingly.

嫩 DON. *Wakai* young; delicate; tender.

芽 *Donga* a scion.

三 嬉 KI. *Ureshii* happy: *tanoshi(mu)* to be happy.

嬌 KYŌ. *Namamekashii* charming.

態 *Kyōtai* fascinating ways; coquetry.

艶 *Kyōen* beautiful; lovely.

*

四 嬶 *Kakā* wife (not polite). 〈鼻〉

嬰兒 *Eiji* new-born infant.

嬲 See 102,12. 【女】

七 嬢 JŌ Miss; a girl; female. →38,13T *

三九 子

T 子 SHI viscount: SU. *Ko* child; son: *ne* 1st zodiacal sign, the rat; north. See

* 嬢 T →38,17

Introduction 42, 43. As bottom component it may mean simply person, as in *danshi* man, *joshi* woman, *saishi* person of ability; after a woman's name, e. g. *Hana-ko*, it means practically nothing.

女 *Shijo* children.

守 *Komori* child's nurse.

弟 *Shitei* a pupil.

供 *Kodomo* child.

孫 *Shison* children and grandchildren; posterity; descendants.

息 *Shisoku* a son.

煩惱 *Kobonnō* excessively concerned for one's children.

爵 *Shishaku* viscount.

T 孔 KŌ; KU. *Ana* aperture; 一 hole.

子 *Kōshi* Confucius.

雀 *Kujaku* peacock.

孕 YŌ. *Hara(mu)* to be pregnant. 二

孜 SHI to strive; be diligent. 四

々 *Shishi* diligently.

T 孤 KO alone. *Minashigo* an 五 orphan.

立 *Koritsu* isolation; helpless.

兒 *Koji; minashigo* an orphan.

獨 *Kodoku* loneliness; solitary person.

146

（五）孟 Mō great; beginning.

子 *Mōshi* Mencius.

買 *Bombei* Bombay.

T 学 See 學 39,13.

六 孩 GAI a child; **infant.**

兒 *Gaiji* a young child.

七 T 孫 SON. *Mago* grandchild.

々 *Sonzon* descendants; posterity.

八 孰 See 8,9. 【子】

二 孵 See 87,10. 【子】

一三 學 GAKU learning. *Mana*(b) to learn; study. →39,5T

力 *Gakuryoku* literary attainments.

士 *Gakushi* university degree; Bachelor.

生 *Gakusei* a student.

究 *Gakkyū* a bookworm; pedagogue.

位 *Gakui* a degree (university).

制 *Gakusei* educational system.

者 *Gakusha* learned person.

科 *Gakka* book-learning; **theory.**

（一三）派 *Gakuha* a school (as of painting, philosophy).

界 *Gakkai* learned circles.

校 *Gakkō* school.

徒 *Gakuto* a student; a disciple.

理 *Gakuri* theory; principles; scientific principles.

習 *Gakushū* learning.

術 *Gakujutsu* sciences and arts.

問 *Gakumon* learning.

期 *Gakki* a school term.

殖 *Gakushoku* scholarship.

業 *Gakugyō* learning; education.

資 *Gakushi* educational expenses.

說 *Gakusetsu* theory.

歷 *Gakureki* course of studies pursued.

識 *Gakushiki* scholarship.

藝 *Gakugei* science and art.

齡 *Gakurei* school age.

一四 孺 JU an infant; little; young; to follow.

子 *Jushi* a youngster.

四〇

凵

Always at the top and is called *U-kammuri.*

二 ᴛ **穴** See 116,0.

三 ᴛ **字** Jɪ character ; written symbol ; letter ; figure . *Aza* hamlet : *azana* common name. 【子】

引 *Jibiki* dictionary.

句 *Jiku* words and phrases.

典 *Jiten* dictionary.

書 *Jisho* dictionary.

ᴛ **守** SHU ; su. *Mamo(ru)* to guard ; defend : *mori* keeper : *kami* a feudal lord

成 *Shusei* preservation.

備 *Shubi* defence.

勢 *Shusei* defence.

衛 *Shuei* a guard ; watch.

錢奴 *Shusendo* a miser.

護 *Shugo* guard ; protection.

ᴛ **宇** U the world ; house ; vast ; sky.

内 *Udai* the empire ; world.

宙 *Uchū* the universe.

ᴛ **写** See **寫** 40,12.

宅 TAKU house. (*Yake*).

地 *Takuchi* building lot, as opposed to agricultural land.

ᴛ **安** AN. *Yasui ; yasuraka* easy in mind ; peace ; tranquil ; cheap : *yasunjiru* (irreg) to set at ease : *izukunzo* however ; what. (*A*).

土府 *Antowāpu* Antwerp.

心 *Anshin* freedom from anxiety or care.

心立命 *Anshin-ritsumei* quieting the heart and standing obedient to Heaven's decrees.

平 *Ampin* Anping.

全 *Anzen* safety.

危 *Anki* welfare ; fate.

否 *Ampi* security or the reverse ; welfare.

佚 *An-itsu* living in idleness.

奉線 *Amfōsen* railway from Antung to Mukden.

房 *Awa* p. n.

東縣 *Antōken* Antung.

定 *Antei* stableness ; equilibrium.

物 *Yasumono* cheap article.

南 *Annan* Annam.

政 *Ansei* era name 1854-1860.

眠 *Ammin* sound sleep.

産 *Anzan* an easy delivery in childbirth.

堵 *Ando* tranquility ; security.

着 *Anchaku* safe arrival.

閑 *Ankan* leisure.

逸 *An-itsu* living in idleness.

寧 *Annei* public peace.

樂 *Anraku* comfort.

靜 *Anse* freedom from pain.

穩 *An-on ; annon* peace ; ease.

藝 *Aki* p. n.

四 牢 Rō prison; cage; hard; strong. 【牛】

獄 Rōgoku prison.

屋 Rōya prison.

宋 Sō p. n.

宂 See T 定 40,5.

T 完 KAN. *Mattai* complete; perfect; whole.

了 *Kanryō* to finish; complete.

全 *Kanzen* perfection.

成 *Kansei* completion; perfection.

結 *Kanketsu* to bring to a conclusion; settle.

備 *Kambi* being fully equipped or provided.

濟 *Kansai* full payment.

膚 *Kampu* a whole skin.

璧 *Kampeki* perfection.

宍 (*Shishi*); (*Shin*).

宏 KŌ. *Hiroi* wide; great; large.

大 *Kōdai* vast; wide; extensive.

壯 *Kōsō* magnificent; vast.

遠 *Kōen* profound.

五 空 See 116,3.

宝 See 寶 40,17. → 宝 T

T 宜 GI. *Yoroshii* good; right; *ube*; *mube* proper; fair; natural.

宕 TŌ; DŌ a cave. (*Tago*); (*Tagi*).

T 官 KAN office (function); public; thing pertaining to government; official; governor. Often used as bottom component; e. g.: *gaikōkan* diplomat, *bukan* military (naval) officer.

公吏 *Kankōri* government and public officials.

立 *Kanritsu* established by the government.

吏 *Kanri* government official.

位 *Kan-i* official rank.

房 *Kambō* secretariate.

命 *Kammei* official orders.

舍 *Kansha* official residence.

邸 *Kantei* official residence.

制 *Kansei* government organization.

省 *Kanshō* government office.

途 *Kanto* government service.

衙 *Kanga* a government office.

報 *Kampō* official gazette.

僚政治 *Kanryō-seiji* bureaucracy.

憲 *Kanken* authorities; officials.

營 *Kan-ei* government management.

職 *Kanshoku* government post.

權 *Kanken* official authority.

廳 *Kanchō* government office.

宙 CHŪ the universe; eternity.

返 *Chūgaeri* looping the loop.

149

（五）

ᵀ 実 See 實 40,11.

ᵀ 定 TEI; JŌ. *Sadama(ru)* to be fixed; decided; steady: *sada(meru)* to fix; decide: *sadame* rule: *sadameshi*; *sadamete* surely; no doubt. →40,4

住 *Teijū* settling down.

見 *Teiken* definite view.

命 *Jomyō* destiny; doom.

刻 *Teikoku* the appointed time.

限 *Teigen* limit.

員 *Teiin* full personnel.

理 *Teiri* axiom; principle.

連 *Joren* regular patrons.

期 *Teiki* regular; fixed.

評 *Teihyō* settled opinion.

款 *Teikan* the articles of association.

義 *Teigi* definition.

說 *Teisetsu* fixed opinions; established proposition; maxim.

論 *Teiron* established view; fixed opinions.

價 *Teika* fixed price.

宛 EN. *Ate* addressed to: *zutsu* each: *adakamo*; *sanagara* as if.

名 *Atena* an address.

嵌 *Atehama(ru)* to apply; fit.

然 *Enzen*; *sanagara* as it were; just like.

ᵀ 宗 SHŪ a sect: SŌ the origin; head; to honour; reverent. (*Mune*).

旨 *Shūshi* religion.

派 *Shūha* religious sect.

敎 *Shūkyō* religion.

ᵀ 宣 SEN. *No(beru)*; *notama(u)*; *no(ru)* to proclaim; Imperial edict. 六

布 *Sempu* propagation.

言 *Sengen* declaration; proclamation.

告 *Senkoku* sentence.

敎師 *Senkyōshi* missionary.

揚 *Sen-yō* enhancement.

誓 *Sensei* oath.

戰 *Sensen* declaration of war; manifesto.

ᵀ 室 SHITSU. *Heya* room; wife: *muro* cave; store-room. Generally used as bottom component; e. g.: *kyoshitsu* sitting-room, *kyōshitsu* school-room.

蘭 *Muroran* p. n.

ᵀ 客 KYAKU; KAKU previous. *Marōdo* visitor; guest; customer.

月 *Kakugetsu* last month.

死 *Kakushi* die abroad.

車 *Kyakusha*; *kakusha* a passenger car.

氣 *Kakki* ardour of youth.

遊 *Kakuyū* touring; travelling about.

臘 *Kakurō* last December.

觀 *Kakkan* objectivity.

（五）

（六）宥 YU to pardon. *Nada(meru)* to mitigate; appease.

免 *Yūmen* pardon.

恕 *Yūjo* to pardon; forgive.

七 害 GAI harm; calamity. *Sokona(u)* to damage; harm; injure.

毒 *Gaidoku* harm; bad influence.

惡 *Gaiaku* harm; injury.

T 宮 KYŪ; GŪ; KU. *Miya* shintō shrine; Imperial Palace; prince.

人 *Miyabito* courtiers.

下 *Miyanoshita* p. n.

女 *Kyūjo* a female attendant or official employed in the Imperial Palace.

中 *Kyūchū* Emperor's court.

內大臣 *Kunaidaijin* the Minister of the Imperial Household.

內省 *Kunaishō* the Imperial Household Department.

庭 *Kyūtei* Imperial Palace.

室 *Kyūshitsu* Imperial Palace.

城 *Kyūjō* Imperial Palace: *Miyagi* p. n.

家 *Miyake* a Prince of the Blood.

崎 *Miyazaki* p. n.

殿 *Kyūden* Imperial Palace.

T 容 YŌ. *Katachi* form; appearance: *i(reru)* to put into; admit: *yuru(su)* to pardon.

色 *Yoshoku* face; countenance.

（七）易 *Yōi, tayasui* easy.

姿 *Yōshi* face and figure.

赦 *Yōsha* pardon; indulgence.

喙 *Yōkai* interference.

量 *Yōryō* capacity.

認 *Yōnin* admit; allow.

貌 *Yōbō* looks; appearance.

儀 *Yōgi* deportment; carriage.

器 *Yōki* receptacle; vessel.

積 *Yōseki* volume; capacity.

體 *Yōdai* condition of a patient.

宰 SAI a chief; an official; to rule.

相 *Saishō* the Premier.

T 宵 SHŌ. *Yoi* evening; night.

T 案 AN a proposal; plan; bill (in the Diet) proposed but not yet passed; desk; idea; thought. *Anzuru* (irreg.) to be concerned; think out. 【木】

山子 *Kakashi* scarecrow.

內 *Annai* invitation; guide; guidance.

外 *Angai* unexpected; very.

T 家 KA; KE family; person; household; party; followers. *Ie; ya; uchi* house. As bottom component, it may mean person and is read *ka*, e. g.: *ongakuka* musician, *bijutsuka* artist; or it may mean house and is read *ya*, e. g.: *nikaiya* two-storied house, *kash'ya* house to let.

151

(七) 家

內 *Kanai* family; wife; in the house.

主 *Yanushi; ienushi* the owner of a house.

名 *Kamei* the good name of the family.

作 *Kasaku* house; building.

系 *Kakei* family descent; genealogy.

具 *Kagu* furniture.

門 *Kamon* one's family.

事 *Kaji* domestic matters.

來 *Kerai* retainer.

屋 *Kaoku* house; habitation.

計 *Kakei* pecuniary resources of a family.

柄 *Iegara* standing of a family.

長 *Kachō* head of a family.

政 *Kasei* housekeeping.

風 *Kafū* family custom.

畜 *Kachiku* domestic animals.

財 *Kazai* family property or effects.

庭 *Katei* home; family.

族 *Kazoku* members of a family.

傳 *Kaden* thing handed down in a family.

業 *Kagyō* occupation.

賃 *Yachin* house-rent.

運 *Kaun* the fortune of a family.

僕 *Kaboku* (domestic) servant.

督 *Katoku* inheritance; headship of a family.

鴨 *Ahiru* duck.

寶 *Kahō* an heirloom; an ancestral treasure.

宸 SHIN Imperial.

筆 *Shimpitsu* the Emperor's autograph.

襟 *Shinkin* Emperor's mind.

翰 *Shinkan* Emperor's letter.

T宴 EN. *Utage* feast; banquet.

會 *Enkai* feast; banquet.

T密 MITSU close; dense. *Hisoka* secret. 八

行 *Mikkō* secret going; secret patrol.

交 *Mikkō* close friendship.

告 *Mikkoku* secret information.

約 *Mitsuyaku* secret understanding.

封 *Mippū* tightly sealed.

航 *Mikkō* secret passage.

通 *Mittsū* to have illicit connection with.

接 *Missetsu* closeness; contiguity; proximity.

閉 *Mippei* to cover tightly.

集 *Misshū* mass; swarm.

着 *Mitchaku* adhesion.

會 *Mikkai* a secret meeting (of lovers).

152

著 *Mitchaku* adhere closely.

談 *Mitsudan* secret conversation.

輸入 *Mitsuyunyū* smuggling.

T 宿 SHUKU posting-station. *Yado* inn ; lodging-house ; dwelling place ; husband : *yado(ru)* to stop ; lodge.

世 *Sukuse* one's previous state of existence.

志 *Shukushi* cherished intention.

泊 *Shukuhaku* lodging ; putting up.

所 *Shukusho* dwelling place ; address.

命 *Shukumei* fate preordained from a former life.

直 *Shukuchoku* keeping nightwatch.

帳 *Yadochō* hotel-register.

屋 *Yadoya* hotel ; inn.

怨 *Shukuen* long-harboured resentment.

望 *Shukubō* cherished desire.

痾 *Shukua* chronic disease.

縁 *Shukuen* a relation existing from a previous life.

營 *Shukuei* quarters ; encampment.

題 *Shukudai* a subject. for home task.

願 *Shukugan* cherished wish.

T 寄 KI to lodge ; rely on. *Yo-(seru)* to cause to draw near ; collect : *yo(ru)* to assemble ; call in upon.

々 *Yoriyori* at times.

生 *Kisei* parasitism ; fungoid growth of any kind.

合 *Yori-ai* meeting ; assembly.

附 *Kifu* contribution.

來 *Yosekuru* to come together.

食 *Kishoku* depending on another for support.

留 *Kiryū* temporary residence.

席 *Yose* a story-teller's hall.

書 *Kisho* a contribution (of writing).

宿 *Kishuku* lodging.

進 *Kishin* a contribution.

港 *Kikō* touch at a port.

寓 *Kigū* lodging.

稿 *Kikō* a contribution (of an article to a newspaper).

贈 *Kisō* a contribution (of things).

邊 *Yorube* person on whom one depends (friend, etc.).

T 寂 SEKI ; JAKU. *Sabishii* lonely ; quiet ; calm.

寞 *Sekibaku* loneliness.

寥 *Sekiryō* loneliness.

寇 KŌ. *Ada* enemy : *ada suru* to invade ; rob.

宽 See 冤 14,8.

寅 IN. *Tora* the 3rd zodiacal sign, the tiger. See Introduction 42, 43.

九 富 FU; FŪ prosperity. *Tomi*
T wealth: *to(mu)* to be rich;
become rich.

士山 *Fujisan* Mount Fuji.

山 *Toyama*; *Tomiyama* p. n.

國強兵 *Fukoku-kyōhei* en-
riching a country and
strengthening its army.

貴 *Fūki* wealth and rank.

強 *Fukyō* wealth and power.

裕 *Fuyū* wealth; affluence.

源 *Fugen* source of wealth.

豪 *Fūgō* a wealthy person.

寓 GŪ a lodging-place; to
lodge; temporary.

言 *Gūgen* an allegory.

居 *Gūkyo* a temporary abode.

意 *Gūi* a hidden meaning.

話 *Gūwa* a parable.

寐 BI. *Ne(-ru)* to s'eep; to
rest.

寔 SHOKU. *Makoto ni* in fact;
verily.

寒 KAN. *Samui*; *samusa* cold.
T

心 *Kanshin* shuddering.

冷 *Kanrei* cold.

村 *Kanson* a poor village.

流 *Kanryū* a cold current.

晒 *Kanzarashi* exposure to
cold weather.

氣 *Kanki* the cold; a chill:
samuke a chill.

帶 *Kantai* frigid zone.

暑 *Kansho* temperature.

暖 *Kandan* temperature.

膽 *Kantan* to be horrified.

塞 SOKU; SAI. *Fusa(gu)* to stop 一
up; cover: *toride* a fortress. 〇
【土】

爾維 *Serubiya* Servia.

寤 Go to awake. 一一

寧 NEI easy. *Nengoro* kind-
T ness: *mushiro* rather.

搴 KEN to lift; to pluck out.
【手】

寥 RYŌ lonely; quiet.

々 *Ryōryō* lonely; few; little.

然 *Ryōzen* lonely.

寡 KA alone; widow. *Suku-
nai* few.

婦 *Kafu*; *yamome* a widow.

聞 *Kabun* limited information.

慾 *Kayoku* content with little.

默 *Kamoku* taciturnity.

寞 BAKU; MAKU lonely; quiet.

寢 SHIN. *Ne(-ru)*; *inuru* (lit.
st.) to sleep: *neka(su)* to
put to sleep; lay down:
yasu(mu) to rest.
→40, 10 * T

耳に水 *Nemimi ni mizu* a
surprise.

坊 *Nebō* late riser.

卷 *Nemaki* a night-gown.

食 *Shinshoku* food and sleep.

室 *Shinshitsu* bed-room.

臺 *Shindai; nedai* bed; bedstead.

覺 *Nezame* peace of mind.

賓【貝】→賓 T

HIN. *Marōdo* a guest.

客 *Hinkyaku* a guest.

賓 See prec.

實 JITSU truth; true; real; sincere; healthy; faithful; honest. *Mi* fruit: *mino-(ru)* to bear fruit; ripen. (*Sane*). →40, 5′1

用 *Jitsuyō* practical use.

在 *Jitsuzai* reality; being; existence.

行 *Jikkō* carrying into practice.

地 *Jitchi* practice.

見 *Jikken* to see for oneself; actual-observation.

例 *Jitsurei* a practical example.

物 *Jitsubutsu* the thing itself.

物大 *Jitsubutsudai* full scale; equal in size to the thing itself.

効 *Jikkō* practical results.

況 *Jikkyō* real condition.

直 *Jitchoku* faithful.

施 *Jisshi* enforcement.

家 *Jikka* the house in which one was born.

現 *Jitsugen* realization.

情 *Jitsujō* true circumstances.

務 *Jitsumu* practical business.

費 *Jippi* actual expenses.

感 *Jikkan* actual sensation.

業 *Jitsugyō* business.

際 *Jissai* truth; reality: *jissai ni* really; truly.

踐 *Jissen* practice.

質 *Jisshitsu* substance.

錄 *Jitsuroku* authentic records.

權 *Jikken* real power.

驗 *Jikken* experiment.

察 T SATSU to conjecture; to examine; to reflect.

知 *Satchi* to know; guess.

蜜 MITSU honey. 【虫】

月 *Mitsutsuki* honeymoon.

柑 *Mikan* the mandarin orange.

蜂 *Mitsubachi* bee.
*

審 T SHIN after 一(or 二) means first (or second) instance in courts of justice. *Tsumabiraka* clear; plain: *tsumabiraka ni suru* to decide; investigate; to judge. 一二

判 *Shimpan; shimban* judgement; umpireship.

查 *Shinsa* examination.

理 *Shinri* examination.

問 *Shimmon* trial.

議 *Shingi* consideration.

（二三）

寫 SHA. *Utsu(su)* to copy; draw : *utsu(ru)* to be reflected; copied.
→40, 3 T

生 *Shasei* drawing from nature ; sketching.

字 *Shaji* copying.

眞 *Shashin* photograph.

實 *Shajitsu* realism.

寬 KAN. *Yuruyaka* liberal; wide ; not strict; merciful; easy ; gentle ; to pardon : *kutsuro(gu)* to put oneself at ease. (*Hiroshi*).
→40, 11, * T

大 *Kandai* magnanimous ; lenient.

容 *Kan-yō* gentleness; magnanimity; forbearance; pardon.

恕 *Kanjo* to forgive; condone.

嚴 *Kangen* leniency and severity.

T 寮 RYŌ house ; an official.

舍 *Ryōsha.* dormitory.

一三 T 憲 KEN. *Nori* law ; constitution. 【心】

兵 *Kempei* a gendarme.

法 *Kempō* constitution ; constitutional law.

政 *Kensei* constitutional government.

政會 *Kenseikai* a certain political party.

一四 蹇 KEN. *Ashinae* lame ; cripple. 【足】

（二四）

賽 SAI presenting thank-offering at a temple. 【貝】

錢 *Saisen* an offertory; offering money.

一六 寵 CHŌ to love ; to show mercy.

臣 *Chōshin* a·favourite subject.

兒 *Chōji* a pet ; a favourite.

恩 *Chōon* great favours.

愛 *Chōai* favour ; ardent love.

寶 See foll.

一七 寶 HŌ. *Takara* treasure ; wealth.
→40, 5 T

石 *Hōseki* a precious stone.

玉 *Hōgyoku* a jewel ; a gem.

物 *Hōmotsu* a treasury.

典 *Hōten* a·treasury.

庫 *Hōko* a treasure-house.

器 *Hōki* treasure.

寸

四一

T 寸 SUN measure of length. See Introduction 44.

分 *Sumbun* the least.

志 *Sunshi* small present.

法 *Sumpō* measure ; size.

時 *Sunji* moment ; instant.

陰 *Sun-in* moment.

暇 *Sunka* moment's leisure.

斷 *Sundan* to cut to pieces.

鐵 *Sun'etsu* a weapon; an epigram.

四T寿 *1 See 壽 32,11. 【士】

六T封 FŪ seal; closing; wrap up: HŌ to appoint; a fief. *Pondo* pound (weight).

入 *Fūnyū* enclosure.

土 *Hōdo* a fief.

印 *Fūn* a stamped seal.

度 *Pondo* pound (weight).

建 *Hōken* feudal system.

書 *Fūsho* a sealed letter or document of any kind.

筒 *Fūtō* an envelope.

* 鎖 *Fūsa* blockade.

八T尉 I; JŌ a rank; compny officer.

官 *Ikan* a company officer.

專 SEN. *Moppara* chiefly; entirely; specially.
→41,6T*2

一 *Sen-itsu* specially; exclusively; with heart and soul.

心 *Senshin* concentration of mind.

用 *Sen-yō* exclusive, private use.

任 *Sennin* special duty; full service.

有 *Sen-yū* exclusive possession; monopoly.

攻 *Senkō* exclusive, special study.

制 *Sensei* absolutism; despotism.

門 *Semmon* a speciality.

政 *Sensei* despotic government; despotism.

科 *Senka* a special course.

修 *Senshū* exclusive, special study.

務 *Semmu* special duty; managing director.

業 *Sengyō* special, principal occupation; speciality.

意 *Sen-i* the whole mind.

賣 *Sembai* monopoly.

賣特許 *Sembaitokkyo* patent.

橫 *Sen-ō* arbitrariness.

斷 *Sendan* arbitrary action.

權 *Senken* an exclusive right.

屬 *Senzoku* belonging exclusively to.

T尊 See 奪 12,10. 【寸】 　九

對 TAI; TSUI a pair. *Kota-(h)eru)* to answer; meet; to face; confront; be opposite to; to be side, by side. →67,3T : 41,4*T 　一一

內 *Tainai* domestic.

比 *Taihi* to compare; contrast.

〔一一〕 對

立 *Tairitsu* standing face to face.

外政策 *Taigai-seisaku* foreign policy.

決 *Taiketsu* confrontation.

坐 *Taiza* sitting opposite.

抗 *Taikō* opposition.

面 *Taimen* interview; meeting face to face.

崎 *Taiji* confront each other.

持 *Taiji* rivalry.

校試合 *Taikō-shiai* an intercollegiate match.

陣 *Taijin* confronting armies.

馬 *Tsushima* p. n.

等 *Taitō* equality; on equal footing.

象 *Taishō* object.

策 *Taisaku* a counter-move.

話 *Taiwa* dialogue.

照 *Taishō* comparison.

談 *Taidan* discussion; conversation.

顏 *Taigan* to meet face to face.

T 奪 See 37,11.

一三 T 導 Dō. *Michibi(ku)* to lead.

火線 *Dōkasen* train of powder.

四二 小

T 小 SHŌ; KO. *Chiisai; o* small; little; young.

刀 *Ko-gatana* penknife.

人 *Shōnin* boys and girls. *shōjin* bad man; mean fellow.

口 *Koguchi* small amounts; a cut end.

川 *Ogawa* a brook; a stream.

火 *Boya* small fire.

心 *Shōshin* prudent.

切手 *Kogitte* a cheque.

生 *Shōsei* I (humble).

石川 *Koishikawa* p. n.

田原 *Odawara* p. n.

田原評定 *Odawara-hyōjō* an indecisive conference.

包 *Kozutsumi* parcel for the post.

冊子 *Shōsasshi* a pamphlet.

成 *Shōsei* small success.

豆 *Azuki* small red beans.

言 *Kogoto* scolding.

作 *Kosaku* tenancy.

判形 *Kobangata* oval (shape); shape of Japanese old gold coin.

町 *Komachi* pretty woman; a Venus; a beauty.

雨 *Kosame* drizzling rain.

波 *Sazanami* wavelet.

股 *Komata* short steps.

使 *Kozukai* a servant; petty cash.

兒 *Shōni* baby.

姑 *Kojūtome* the husband's sister.

品文 *Shōhimbun* a short piece; sketch (literature).

柄 *Kogara* small stature; small-build; small pattern (cloth).

便 *Shōben* urine.

降 *Koburi* light rain.

屋 *Koya* a cottage; a hut.

高 *Kodakai* rather high.

袖 *Kosode* a wadded silk garment.

笠原 *Ogasawara* p. n.

麥 *Komugi* wheat.

康 *Shōkō* a respite; a lull.

間物 *Komamono* toilet articles; fancy goods.

間使 *Komazukai* a lady's maid.

爲替 *Kogawase* money-order.

隊 *Shōtai* section (military).

路 *Kōji* a narrow street; lane.

暗 *Ogurai* a little dark; dim.

舅 *Kojūto* the husband's brother.

勢 *Kozei* a small force; small number of persons.

銃 *Shōjū* a rifle; a musket.

僧 *Kozō* a young Buddhist student for priesthood; shop-boy; apprentice.

遣 *Kozukai* pocket-money.

說 *Shōsetsu* novel; story.

賣 *Kouri* retail.

賣人 *Kouri-nin* a retailer.

學校 *Shōgakkō* an elementary school.

憩 *Shōkei* to rest for a short time.

膽 *Shōtan* cowardice.

躍 *Ko-odori* to leap for joy.

T 少 SHŌ young. *Sukunai*; 一 *sukoshi* few; little.

々 *Shōshō* a little.

女 *Shōjo* little girl.

年 *Shōnen* lad; youth; young boy.

佐 *Shōsa* major (army); lieutenant-commander (navy).

壯 *Shōsō* youth.

食 *Shōshoku* low diet.

尉 *Shōi* sub-lieutenant (army); second sub-lieutenant (navy).

將 *Shōshō* major-general (army); rear-admiral (navy).

量 *Shōryō* a small quantity.

數 *Shōsū* a small number.

額 *Shōgaku* a small sum.

尒 See 爾 1,13.【爻】 二

T 当 See 當 102,8. 三

T 劣 RETSU. *Oto(ru)* to be inferior to.【力】

情 *Retsujō* low passions; sexual feelings.

（三）

劣
等 *Rettō* inferiority; lower kind.

尖 SEN. *Toga(ru)* to be pointed: *saki* the extremity; point: *togara(seru)* to sharpen.

端 *Sentan* edge.

T 光 KŌ. *Hikari* light; radiance; brilliancy: *hika(ru)* to shine; flash. (*Mitsu*); (*Ter*). 【儿】

明 *Kōmyō* light; glory; splendour.

來 *Kōrai* your coming (polite).

陰 *Kōin* time.

彩 *Kōsai* brilliant; lustre.

景 *Kōkei* scene; aspect; state.

榮 *Kōei* honour; glory.

輝 *Kōki* brilliancy; bright rays.

線 *Kōsen* a ray of light.

澤 *Kōtaku* gloss; lustre.

臨 *Kōrin* your attendance (polite).

T 糸 See 絲 120,6.

四 肖 SHŌ. *Ni(-ru)* to be alike: *katado(ru)* to resemble; make like. 【肉】 →肖 T

像 *Shōzō* a portrait.

五 尚 SHŌ. *Tatto'bu)* to honour; respect; reverence; esteem: *nao* still; more; yet. (*Hisa*). →尚 T

T *学 →39,13

（五）

又 *Naomata* moreover.

々 *Nao-nao* further; still more; postscript.

更 *Naosara* still more.

武 *Shōbu* militarism.

毟 *Mushi(ru)* to pluck (feathers, hair, weeds, etc.). 【毛】
*

六 省 SHŌ a government department: SEI to look. *Habu(k'u)* to save; exclude: *kaerimi* (-*ru*) to reflect on; look back; consider. Often used as bottom component. e.g.: *Gaimushō* the Foreign Office, *Rikugunshō* the War Office. 【目】

令 *Shōrei* a departmental ordinance.

約 *Shōyaku* abridgment.

略 *Shōryaku* abbreviation.

察 *Seisatsu* perception; consideration.

県 See 縣 109,11.
*1

七 T 党 See 黨 202,8.
*2

八 T 堂 See 32,8.

雀 JAKU. *Suzume* sparrow. 【隹】

躍 *Jakuyaku* leaping with joy.

T 常 See 50,8.

九 T 掌 See 64,8.

160 *1 T 単 →30,9 *2 挙 T →134,11

一〇 嘗 See 嘗 72,10. 【口】

T 當 See 102,8.

尠 SEN. *Sukunai, sukoshi* few.

少 *Senshō* scarce; few.

二 嘗 See 72,10. 【口】

裳 See 145,8.

二 輝 KI. *Kagaya(ku); te(ru)* to shine; to shine upon. 【車】

T 賞 See 154,8.

三 縣 See 109,11. 【糸】

一七 耀 YŌ. *Kagaya(ku)* to shine. 【羽】

黨 See 203,8.

四三 **尢**

一 尤 See 1,3. 【尢】

四 尨 BŌ large. *Mukuinu* a shaggy dog.

大 *Bōdai* bulky; big.

九 T 就 SHŪ; JU. *Tsu(ku)* to take up (work or occupation):

＊T 營 → 80,14

---

tsuite regarding: *na(ru)* to become: *na su)* to do.

中 *Nakanzuku* above all others; especially.

任 *Shūnin* assumption of office.

床 *Shūshō* go to bed.

眠 *Shūmin* go to bed.

業 *Shūgyō* adoption of a profession; commencement of work.

寢 *Shūshin* go to bed.

學 *Shūgaku* entering a school; school attendance.

縛 *Shūbaku* be arrested.

職 *Shūshoku* commencing one's duties; entering into office.

四四 **尸**

Always at the top and left: it is called *Shikabane*.

尸 SHI. *Shikabane* corpse.

T 尺 SHAKU; SEKI measure of length: see Introduction 44. *Monosashi* foot-rule.

八 *Shakuhachi* a kind of flute.

〆 *Shakujime* unit of cubic measure for timber; 1 *shaku*×1 *shaku*×2 *ken* (i.e. 12 cubic *shaku*).

度 *Shakudo* a measure; gauge.

二T 民　ee 83,1.

T 尼　NI; JI. *Ama* a Buddhist nun.

僧　*Nisō* a Buddhist nun.

尻　KŌ. *Shiri* the buttocks; bottom.

目　*Shirime* a side glance.

込　*Shirigomi* receding; shrinking back.

押　*Shirioshi* a backer; instigation.

馬　*Shiriuma* to follow another.

餅　*Shirimochi* falling on one's seat.

三T 尽　See 盡 108,9.

四T 局　KYOKU room; office (government); to bend; be bent. *Tsubone* a court lady; court lady's apartment. Generally used as bottom component, e.g.: *yūbin-kyoku* post-office, *suidō-kyoku* office of the waterworks.

外　*Kyokugai* being outside of any circle or party.

面　*Kyokumen* the situation.

部　*Kyokubu* the part affected; part; section; private parts.

T 尿　NYŌ. *Ibari* urine.

屁　HI. *He* wind from the bowels.

理窟　*Herikutsu* a cavil; sophism; quibble.

T 尾　BI aux. num. for counting fishes; the end. O; *shippo* tail.

州　*Bishū* another name for the province of *Owari*.

行　*Bikō* to go after; follow; detectives on the watch.

張　*Owari* p. n.

道　*Onomichi* p. n.

籠　*Birō* indecency.

屆　*Todoke* written document 五 presented to person in authority: *todo(keru)* to send forward; deliver; report; inform: *todo(ku)* to arrive; reach. →44,5 * T

人　*Todokenin* person who presents written document.

出　*Todokeide* inform authorities.

先　*Todokesaki* addressee; person who is to receive.

T 屈　KUTSU to bend. *Kaga(mu)* to bend the body down; be humble.

曲　*Kukkyoku* to bend; be crooked.

折　*Kussetsu* refraction; inflexion.

伸　*Kusshin* elasticity.

服　*Kuppuku* submission.

指　*Kusshi* leading; distinguished.

辱　*Kutsujoku* humiliation.

託　*Kuttaku* care; trouble; vexation.

竟　*Kukkyō* strong; powerful.

162

従 *Kutsujū* to submit; yield.

強 *Kukkyō* strong; powerful.

T 居 KYO abode; residence: KO. *O(ru)* (irreg. in lit. st.); *i(-ru)* to be; be present; to dwell.

合 *I-awa seru)* to happen to be there.

住 *Kyojū* residence.

所 *Kyosho; idokoro* an abode; a dwelling place.

食 *Igui* live in idleness.

室 *Kyoshitsu* sitting-room.

酒屋 *Izakaya* drinking-house.

候 *Isōrō* a hanger-on; dependent.

留 *Kyoryū* residence.

留地 *Kyoryūchi* a (foreign) settlement.

間 *I-ma* sitting-room.

睡 *Inemuri* a doze; a nap.

六 咫 SHI short distance; close to. (*Ta*). 【口】

尺 *Shiseki* a very short distance.

T 屋 OKU. *Ya* house; shop; this character is often added to the name of a shop or inn; also to many articles of commerce, and will then signify the kind of shop or the person dealing in that article.

外 *Okugai* outdoor.

根 *Yane* roof.

號 *Yagō* firm-name.

*T 届 →44,5

163

（六）

敷 *Yashiki* plot of ground with house.

屏 See 屏 44,8.

屎 SHI. *Kuso* dung; filth; excretion.

屍 SHI. *Shikabane; kabane* a corpse.

骸 *Shigai* a corpse.

體 *Shitai* a corpse.

T 晝 See 畫 129,5.

屑 SETSU. *Kuzu* rubbish; scraps: *isagiyoshi* pure; valiant; brave. 七

T 展 TEN. *Hira(ku)* to open; roll over; exhibit: *no(biru)* to spread out.

望 *Tembō* a view; prospect.

開 *Tenkai* development; deployment.

覽會 *Tenrankai* an exhibition.

墓 *Tembo* visiting a grave.

屓 KI. *Hiiki* favourite.

屏 HEI; BYŌ a wall; fence; to cover. 八

居 *Heikyo* retirement; confinement.

風 *Byōbu* folding-screen.

息 *Heisoku* shrink; dwindle.

屠 TO. *Hofu(ru)*; to slaughter; kill. 九

（九）

屠

所 *Tosho* a slaughter-house.

殺 *Tosatsu* to kill; slaughter.

蘇 *Toso* a kind of spiced sake.

T 属 See 屬 44,18.

二 屢 RU. *Shiba-shiba* often.

* 々 *Shiba-shiba* often.

三 層 Sō stratum; floor; storey; to pile up. →44,11 * T

倍 *Sōbai* a number of times; times as much.

T 履 RI. *Ha(ku)* to put on (as boots, trousers): *fu(mu)* to tread on: *kutsu* boots.

行 *Rikō* performance; fulfilment.

物 *Hakimono* footgear; clogs.

歷 *Rireki* personal history.

一 屬 ZOKU; SHOKU family; an inferior; genus. *Tsu(ku)* to belong. →44,9 T

八

官 *Zokkan* a petty official.

國 *Zokkoku* a subject state.

僚 *Zokuryō* subordinates.

四五

少

艸 See 140,0.

* 層 →44,12
T

山

四六

When at the left it is called *Yama-hen.*

T 山 SAN; SEN. *Yama* a mountain; hill; mine.

々 *Yamayama* want very much; a great deal.

口 *Yamaguchi* p. n.

手 *Yama(no)te* a hilly district; the bluff.

分 *Yamawake* an equal division (as of profit).

水 *Sansui* landscape representing mountains and water.

羊 *Yagi* a goat.

形 *Yamagata* p. n.

車 *Dashi* a festival car.

林 *Sanrin* a forest.

門 *Sammon* the front gate of a Buddhist temple.

東省 *Santōshō* province of Shantung.

師 *Yamashi* a speculator; adventurer.

脈 *Sammyaku* chain or range of mountains.

城 *Yamashiro* p. n.

氣 *Yamagi* speculative disposition.

高 *Yamataka* hard bowler hat.

崩 *Yamakuzure* a slide; a landslip.

紫水明 *Sanshisuimei* beautiful scenery.

164

（五）

鳥 *Yamadori* copper pheasant.

梨 *Yamanashi* p. n.

陰道 *San-indō* p. n.

陽道 *San-yōdō* p. n.

腹 *Sampuku* the side of a mountain; half-way up a mountain; a hillside.

賊 *Sanzoku* a bandit; brigand; highwayman.

積 *Sanseki* to accumulate in large quantities.

嶽 *Sangaku* mountains.

三 屹 KITSU lofty; pointed. *S bada(tsu)* to tower up.

立 *Kitsuritsu* to tower high.

度 *Kitto* surely; certainly.

T 出 See 17,3.

四 T 岐 KI; GI. *Eda* branch: *mata* forks in road; forked branch: *waka rer i*) to branch off; fork; diverge.

阜 *Gifu* p. n.

道 *Kidō* cross road; a fork in a road.

路 *Kiro; wakaremichi* a fork in a road.

五 岬 KŌ. *Misaki; saki* a cape.

T 岩 GAN. *Iwa* rock; rocky cliff. Often used as substitute for 巖 46,20.

手 *Iwate* p. n.

T 岸 GAN. *Kishi* shore; bank; cliff.

邊 *Kishibe* bank.

T 岳 GAKU. *Take* lofty peak. →46,14

父 *Gakufu* father-in-law.

T 峠 *Tōge* mountain pass; ascent; climax.

崎 JI. *Sobada(tsu)* to tower aloft.

T 炭 TAN carbon. *Sumi* charcoal. 【火】

坑 *Tankō* a coal mine.

團 *Tadon* a charcoal ball.

酸 *Tansan* carbonic acid.

礦 *Tankō* a coal mine.

T 幽 See 17,7. 【幺】

*

七 T 峰 HŌ; FU; BU. *Mine* mountain peak; summit.

峽 KYŌ. *Hazama* mountain pass; gorge; chasm; strait. →46,6 T *

谷 *Kyokoku* a gorge.

峻 SHUN high; strict. *Kewashii* steep.

拒 *Shunkyo* to rebuff.

阪 *Shunhan* a steep path.

烈 *Shunretsu* keenness; sharpness.

險(峻) *Shunken* precipitous; steep.

嚴 *Shungen* strictness; sternness.

豈 KI. *Ani* how? (emphatic); an introductory exclamation. 【豆】

165　　* T 峽→46,7

七 峯 See 峰 46,7.
（

T 島 TŌ. *Shima* island.
→46, 11
根 *Shimane* p. n.
嶼 *Tōsho* an island.

八 崎 KI. *Saki* cape; promontory.

嵋 See foll.

崖 GAI. *Gake* precipice; cliff.

崔 鬼 *Saigai* high; loftily.

T 崩 HŌ to die (Emperor, etc.). *Kuzu(reru* to crumble to pieces: *kuzu(su)* to break down; destroy; demolish.
御 *Hōgyo* death of an Emperor; demise.
落 *Hōraku* fall; drop.
潰 *Hōkai* a collapse; a fall.

崑 崙 *Konron* a mountain range in China.

T 崇 SHŪ; SŪ; SŌ high. *Aga-(meru)* to honour; adore. Do not confound with 崇 113,5.
拜 *Sūhai; shūhai* worship.
高 *Sūkō* lofty; sublime.
敬 *Sūkei* reverence; veneration.

九 嵌 KAN. *Ha(meru)* to fit. into.

嵐 RAN. *Arashi* storm.

嵯 峨 *Saga* cliffy; rugged; p.n. 一〇

嵩 SŪ. *Kasa* bulk; volume: *kasa(mu)* to grow bulky; swell; high: *kōjiru* grow worse.

歳 See 歲 77,9.

嶋 See T 島 46,7. 一一

嶄 Z'N. *Takai* high; conspicuous.
然 *Zanzen* prominently.

嶮 See 險 170,13. 一三

嶼 SHO. *Shima* an island.

嶽 GAKU. *Take* a lofty peak. 一四
→46, 5T
嶺 REI. *Mine* a mountain peak.

巍 GI high; lofty. 一八
々 *Gigi* high.
然 *Gizen* loftily; sublimely; conspicuously.

巓 TFN. *Itadaki* the top of a mountain. 一九
巒 RAN mountain peak.

巖 GAN; GEN rocky cliff. 二〇
Iwa; iwao rock.

四七

《《

四七 **災** SAI. *Wazawai* calamity; T misfortune. 【火】

厄 *Saiyaku* calamity.

害 *Saigai* calamity.

禍 *Sa:ka* misfortune; calamity.

難 *Sainan* misfortune.

八 **巢** SŌ. *Su* nest; (bee's) comb; (spider's) web; den; etc. →75, 7T :

窟 *Sōkutsu* a den.

四八

工 *gong*

T **工** KŌ; KU work; craft; art; workman. *Takumi* skill.

女 *Kojo* a factory girl.

夫 *Kofu* a navvy: *kufu* plan; scheme; devic·.

合 *Guai* condition; style.

作 *Kosaku* work; engineering work.

兵 *Kohei* engineers; sappers.

事 *Koji* building or engineering works.

面 *Kumen* pecuniary means.

場 *Kojō; koba* factory; works.

程 *Kotei* the amount of work.

業 *Kogyō* manufacturing industry.

廠 *Kōshō* a naval or military work shop; arsenal.

藝 *Kōgei* artistic industry.

T **巧** KŌ. *Takumi* skill: *umai* 二 skilful.

拙 *Kōsetsu* skill.

妙 *Kōmyō* skill.

者 *Kōsha* clever; ingenious

T **功** KŌ; KU efficiency; merit; meritorious deed; achievement. 【力】

用 *Kōyō* function; use; utility.

名 *Kōmyō* glorious deed.

利主義 *Kōrishugi* utilitarianism.

勞 *Kōrō* service; exploit.

能 *Kōnō* use; effect.

業 *Kōgyō* glorious action, deed.

罪 *Kozai* merits and demerits.

德 *Kudoku* virtuous deeds.

績 *Koseki* great achievements.

T **攻** KŌ to study. *Se(meru)* to 四 attack; strike. 【攴】

入 *Seme-i(ru)* to invade; make an inroad.

立 *Seme-ta(teru)* to attack (fiercely).

守 *Kōshu* offence and defence.

勢 *Kōsei* the offensive.

擊 *Kōgeki* an attack.

汞 KŌ quick-silver; mercury. 【水】

167

七 貢 *Kō*; KU. *Mitsugi* tribute;
T tax. 【貝】

獻 *Kōken* contribution; services.

九 項 *Kō* a clause; paragraph.
T *Unaji* the nape of the
neck. 【頁】

目 *Kōmoku* items.

四九

已

T 己 KO personal : KI. *Onore;*
ono (usually followed by が)
own; self : *tsuchinoto* 6th
calendar sign. See Intro-
duction 42, 43.

已 I. *Sude ni* already : *ya-*
(mu) to end; stop : *nomi*
only.

巳 SHI. *Mi* 6th zodiacal sign,
the snake. See Introduc-
tion 42, 43.

一 巴 HA. *Tomoe* comma-shaped
figure.

里 *Parii* Paris.

奈馬 *Panama* Panama.

爾幹 *Barukan* Balkan.

二 包 See 20,3.

四 改 KAI. *Arata(meru)* to
T change; alter; reform; improve; revise. 【攴】

心 *Kaishin* conversion; reform.

札 *Kaisatsu* ticket examination.

正 *Kaisei* improvement;
amendment.

名 *Kaimei* change of name.

良 *Kairyō* improvement.

宗 *Kaishū* conversion;
change one's religion.

革 *Kaikaku* alteration; reform.

修 *Kaishū* re-adjustment.

悛 *Kaishun* repentance.

造 *Kaizō* reconstruction; re-
organization.

善 *Kaizen* improvement.

新 *Kaishin* innovation; reform.

築 *Kaichiku* rebuilding.

選 *Kaisen* re-election.

T 忌 KI. *Imi* mourning : *i(mu)*
to dislike; hate. 【心】

々 *Imaimashii* disgusting; disagreeable; unlucky.

日 *Kinichi* anniversary of
death.

中 *Kichū* mourning.

憚 *Kitan* fear; reservedness;
timidity.

諱 *Kiki* displeasure.

避 *Kihi* refusal; evasion.

巷 See 140,6. 【巳】

卷 See 26,6.

九 巽 SON. *Tatsumi* the south-east.

五〇 巾

When at the left it is called *Haba-hen*.

巾 KIN a scarf; towel. *Haba* width: *kire* a piece of cloth.

著 *Kinchaku* a purse.

三 T 帆 HAN. *Ho* a sail.

前船 *Homaesen* a sailing vessel.

掛船 *Hokakebune* a sailing ship.

船 *Hansen; hobune* a sailing vessel.

四 T 希 KI. *Mare* rare: *koinega-(u)* to request; desire earnestly.

代 *Kidai* rare.

有 *Keu* unusual; rare; uncommon.

望 *Kibō* hope; wish; desire.

望者 *Kibōsha* applicant.

臘 *Girisha* Greece.

五 帖 JŌ a measure for paper: CHŌ book (such as copy-book; account-book) that extends and folds up like an accordion; placard; poster; written notes; a document.

峡 CHITSU a case for a book. (五)

T 帥 SUI a chief. *Hik'-i(-ru)* to lead. 六

帝 TEI; TAI. *Mikado* emperor; sovereign: used as abbreviation for *Teikoku*.

大 *Teidai* abb. of 帝國大學 Imperial University.

位 *Teii* the Throne.

政 *Teisei* Imperial rule.

室 *Teishitsu* Emperor's house; belonging to the Imperial family.

展 *Teiten* Government art exhibition.

國 *Teikoku* an empire.

都 *Teito* the Imperial capital.

劇 *Teigeki* abb. of 帝國劇場 Imperial theatre.

T 師 See 1,9.【巾】 七

T 帶 See 帶 50,8.

帷 I. *Tobari* a curtain: *kata-bira* a summer garment. 八

子 *Ka'abira* a summer garment.

幄 *Iaku* headquarters.

T 帳 CHŌ an account-book; note-book. *Tobari* a curtain.

尻 *Chōjiri* balance of account.

面 *Chōmen* an account-book; note-book.

消 *Chōkeshi* squaring an account.

169 →帝 T

（八）

帳場 *Chōba* a counter; office.

簿 *Chōbo* an account-book.

T 常 JŌ usual; ordinary. *Tsune ni* always: *tokoshie; toko* for ever; eternally.

人 *Jōjin* an ordinary man.

用 *Jōyō* common use.

例 *Jōrei* usual procedure.

食 *Jōshoku* staple food.

軌 *Jōki* normal course of events.

套 *Jōtō* commonplace; conventional.

時 *Jōji* ordinary time.

陸 *Hitachi* p. n.

務 *Jōmu* routine work; a managing director.

設 *Jōsetsu* standing; permanent.

習 *Jōshū* habitual.

備 *Jōbi* to make preparations; standing.

置 *Jōchi* standing; permanent.

道 *Jōdō* the eternal reason.

態 *Jōtai* usual aspect; normal condition.

盤 *Tokiwa* everlasting; evergreen.

識 *Jōshiki* common sense.

帶 TAI zone. *Obi* belt: *o(biru)* to wear. →50,7T

封 *Obifū* a wrapper.

劍 *Taiken* a sword at one's side.

幄 AKU a curtain. 九

舍 *Akusha* a pavilion.

T 帽 BŌ hat; cap. →帽

子 *Bōshi* hat; cap.

T 幅 FUKU hanging picture; aux. num. for counting hanging pictures. *Haba* width; breadth.

員 *Fukuin* width

幀 TŌ a mounted picture.

幇 HŌ. *Tasu(keru)* to assist.

助 *Hōjo* aid; help.

幌 KŌ. *Horo* a hood (as of a carriage); awning. 一〇

幔 MAN a curtain; an awning. 一一

幕 *Mammaku* a curtain; tent.

幡 HAN; MAN. *Hata* a flag; b·nn·r. 一二

幟 SHI. *Nobori* banner; flag.

幣 HEI money; note; wealth. *Nusa; shide; mitegura* a religious symbol. →幣 T

干 五一

T 干 KAN to meddle with; to take part in; shield: to violate. *Hi(-ru); ho(su)* to dry.

戈 *Kanka* war.

物 *Hoshimono* clothes for drying : *himono* dried fish.

城 *Kanjō* a defender.

涉 *Kanshō* interference; intervention.

潮 *Kanchō ; hishio* ebb-tide.

二 T 刊 KAN to publish.【刀】

行 *Kankō* publication.

五 盂 See 108,3.

弁 HEI. *Narabi ni* and: *nara-(beru)* to arrange in a row: *awa(seru)* to join : *a(u)* to meet.

〇 T 幹 See 24,11.【干】

五二 幺

一 T 幻 GEN to deceive. *Maboroshi* an optical illusion ; magic ; vision.

惑 *Genwaku* to deceive ; delude.

滅 *Gemmetsu* disillusionment.

想 *Gensō* vision ; phantasm ; fantasy.

影 *Gen-ei* a vision ; an illusion.

覺 *Genkaku* hallucination.

T 幼 YŌ. *Osana : itokenai* 二 young.

少 Y *shō* infancy ; young.

心 *Osanagokoro* a child's mind. *young at heart*

兒 *Yoji ; osa ago* an infant ; a baby.

時 *Yoji* childhood.

稚 *Yōchi* infancy ; childhood. *Kindergarden*

蟲 *Yōchū* larva.

广　五三

Always at the top and left, it is called *Ma-dare.*

T 広 See 廣 53,12.　二
*

庄 SHŌ village.　三

T 序 JO order ; arrangement : 四 the preface ; to state. *Tsui-de* opportunity.

文 *Jobun* preface.

幕 *Jomaku* the prelude.

論 *Joron* an introduction.

T 床 SHŌ. *Toko* bed: *yuka* floor.

上 *Tokoage* recovery from illness.

屋 *Tokoya* barber's shop.

間 *Tokonoma* alcove.

（四）

庇 HI. *Hisashi* the eaves; small projecting roof: *kage* a shelter: *kaba(u)* to cover; to shelter.

護 *Higo* concealment; shelter; protection.

髮 *Hisashigami* hair brought forward over the forehead.

*

五 店 TEN. *Mise; tana* shop; store. Often used as bottom component, e.g.: *honten* head office, *shoten* shop, *yohinten* foreign-goods shop, *yo-mise* night-stall.

T

子 *Tanako* a tenant.

員 *Ten-in* a shop-assistant; clerk.

舗 *Tempo* a shop; store.

頭 *Tentō* shop-front.

T 府 FU government; urban prefecture.

下 *Fuka* suburban district of a *fu*.

立 *Furitsu* prefectural.

縣知事 *Fuken-chiji* the governors of all the prefectures (urban and suburban).

廳 *Fuchō* an urban prefectural office.

庚 KŌ. *Kanoe* the 7th calendar sign. See Introduction 42, 43.

T 底 TEI to reach. *Soko* bottom.

止 *Teishi* to stop; cease.

意 *Sokoi* underlying motive.

意地 *Sokoiji* spite; malice.

庖 HŌ kitchen.

刀 *Hōchō* kitchen knife.

厨 *Hōchū* kitchen.

T 度 DO rule; degree: TAKU. 六 *Tabi* a time; repetition; to follow; imitate: *tai* verbal suffix for the desiderative: *haka(ru)* to surmise; conjecture; measure: *wata(su)* to hand over.

々 *Tabi-tabi* repeatedly; often.

外 *Dogai* want of consideration.

胸 *Dokyō* spirit; courage; boldness.

量 *Doryō* magnanimity; capacity (of mind).

量衡 *Doryōkō* weights and measures.

數 *Dosū* the number of degrees, times.

廂 See 鹿 198,0.

T 座 ZA seat; assembly. *Suwa-* 七 *(ru)* to sit down.

上の空論 *Zajō no kūron* idle talk while sitting down, i. e. very idle talk.

右 *Zayū; zau* the right side of one's seat; constant.

長 *Zachō* chairman.

席 *Zaseki* room; space; seat.

蒲團 *Zabuton* a cushion for sitting on.

談 *Zadan* table-talk.

敷 *Zashiki* room; parlour; apartment.

（五）

172 *T 応 →53, 14

(七)

頭 *Zagashira* the head of a party of play-actors.

與 *Zakyō* an amusement; an entertainment given at a party.

唐 TŌ. *Kara; morokoshi* China. 【口】

金 *Karakane* bronze.

物屋 *Tōbutsuya* foreign-goods store.

突 *Tototsu* abrupt; sudden.

草 *Karakusa* a vine pattern.

紙 *Karakami* (opaque) sliding screens or doors: *tōshi* Chinese paper.

庫 KO. *Kura* store-house; godown. Often used as bottom component, e.g.: *sōko* store-house, *kinko* a safe. *garage*

T **席** SEKI place; seat. 【巾】

上 *Sekijō* in the room; at the meeting.

末に列 *Sekimatsu ni ressuru* to be present at a meeting (humble).

次 *Seki i* the order of seats.

卷 *Sekiken; sekken* to overwhelm.

料 *Sekiryō* the charge for a seat.

順 *Sekijun* the order of seats.

T **庭** TEL *Niwa* a garden; courtyard. (*Ba*).

上 *Teijō ri* in a garden or yard.

球 *Teikyū* lawn-tennis.

園 *Teien* garden.

八

T **庸** YŌ ordinary.

人 *Yōjin* a man of ordinary abilities; common people.

才 *Yōsai* mediocre ability.

麻 See 200,0.

T **康** KŌ to enjoy. *Yasui* easy; peaceful.

安 *Kōan* peacefulness.

鹿 See 198,0.

庵 AN. *Iori; io* a hermitage; a cottage.

庶 SHO the people; concubine's child; all; numerous. *Koinega(u)* to request. →庶T

子 *Shoshi* illegitimate child.

民 *Shomin* the people; masses.

務 *Shomu* general affairs.

廂 SHŌ; SŌ. *Hisashi* the eaves. **九**

T **廢** See 廢 53,12.

T **廊** RŌ corridor; passage; gallery. **一〇**

下 *Rōka* corridor; passage; gallery.

厨 See 廚 53,12.

廉 REN pure; disinterested; honest. *Yasui* cheap: *kado* item; point; reason. →廉T

恥 *Renchi* purity; integrity.

(一○)

廉
賣 *Rembai* bargain sale.
價 *Renka* cheap.
潔 *Renketsu* probity.

一
一 廓 KAKU large. *Kuruwa* enclosure; prostitute quarters.

清 *Kakusei* purification.

T 腐 FU. *Kusa(ru)* to rot; decay. 【肉】

心 *Fushin* to tax one's ingenuity.

敗 *Fuhai* putrefaction; to corrupt.

蝕 *Fushoku* corrosion; rot.

爛 *Furan* rotten; corrupt.

厫 See 厫 27,11.

二
三 廛 TEN market; shop; warehouse.

廚 CHŪ. *Kuriya* kitchen.

廟 BYŌ government office; tomb; an ancestral temple.

堂 *Byōdō* the government; cabinet.

議 *Byōgi* a cabinet council.

廢 HAI. *Suta(ru)* to cease; be useless; be thrown away; abolished. →53,9 T

止 *Haishi* to abolish; do away with.

刊 *Haikan* the stopping of publication.

(一一)

合 *Haigō* rearrangement.

物利用 *Haibutsuriyō* utilisation of waste products.

娼 *Haishō* abolishment of public prostitution.

棄 *Haiki* abolition; repeal.

業 *Haigyō* to cease business.

嫡 *Haichaku* disinheritance.

頹 *Haitai* corruption.

廠 SHŌ a shed; building.

T 慶 KEI congratulation; happiness; to rejoice. 【心】

大 *Keidai* abb. of Keiō University.

弔 *Keichō* congratulation and condolence.

事 *Keiji* a happy event; wedding.

賀 *Keiga* congratulation; celebration.

福 *Keifuku* happiness; good fortune.

應 *Keiō* era name, 1865-1868.

廣 KŌ. *Hiroi* broad; large; wide. →53,2 T

々 *Hirobiro* extensive; spacious.

大 *Kōdai* big; magnificent.

小路 *Hirokōji* main street; wide road.

告 *Kōkoku* advertisement.

長舌 *Kōchōzetsu* long-winded; loquacious.

東 *Kanton* Canton.

174

（二三）

狭 *Kōkyō* extent; size.

島 *Hiroshima* p. n.

袤 *Kō'ō* extent; expansion.

塲 *Hiroba* open space.

間 *Hiroma* a hall.

義 *Kōgi* a wide sense.

漠 *Kōbaku* wide; spacious.

三三 廩 RIN warehouse.

一四 膺 Yō to hold in the arms close to one's breast; to receive; to strike; the breast. 【肉】

懲 *Yōchō* chastisement.

應 Ō to consent; apply; accept; accordingly. *Kota-(h)eru); ira(h)eru)* (lit. st.) to respond to; answer; correspond to. 【心】

＊

分 *Ōbun* according to one's ability.

用 *Ōyō* practical application.

待 *Ōtai* an interview; audience.

急手當 *Ōkyū-teate* first-aid.

接 *Ōsetsu* interview; reception.

報 *Ōhō* compensation; retribution.

答 *Ōtō* reply.

募 *Ōbo* subscription; application.

援 *Ōen* aid; support.

酬 *Ōshū* retribution; a reply.

對 *Ōtai* to interview; receive.
→53,4＊T

（一四）

諾 *Ōdaku* assent; approval; permission.

戰 *Ōsen* to respond to an attack; accept battle.

一七 廳 See 廳 53,22.

二一 鷹 YŌ. *Taka* hawk; falcon. 【鳥】

二二 廳 CHŌ government office. →53,2＊T

五四 夂

四 廷 T TEI a court; Imperial court.

五 延 EN. *Noba(su); no(biru)* to postpone; extend; prolong: *hi(ku)* to pull. →延 T

引 *En-in; ennin* delay.

長 *Enchō* extension.

取引 *Nobetorihiki* a transaction in futures.

期 *Enki* to be postponed.

著 *Enchaku* delayed arrival.

滯 *Entai* delay; tardiness.

燒 *Enshō* being burnt down by a fire spreading.

六 廻 KAI. *Mawa(ru); mawa-(su); megu(ru)* to turn round; revolve: *megura-(su)* to surround. →162,6
（=2)

(六)

廻狀 *Kaijō* a circular.

送 *Kaisō* forwarding; transporting.

路 *Mawarimichi* a round-about way.

漕 *Kaisō* transport by sea.

禮 *Kairei* a round of visits.

轉 *Kaiten* revolution; rotation.

覽 *Kairan* a round of visits; circulation.

廼 DAI. *No* of: *sunawachi* therefore.

×T 建 KEN; KON. *Ta(teru)* to build; establish.

立 *Konryū* to build (a temple, etc.)

坪 *Tatetsubo* the area in *tsubo* occupied by a building.

物 *Tatemono* a building.

具 *Tategu* fittings; fixtures.

國 *Kenkoku* the foundation or beginning of a state.

設 *Kensetsu* to establish; found.

造 *Kenzō* construction.

碑式 *Kempi-shiki* the ceremony of erecting a monumental stone.

築 *Kenchiku* construction; building.

議 *Kengi* a proposal.

五五 廾

弄 RŌ. *Moteaso(bu)* to play with: *iji(ru)* to touch. 四

弊 HEI poor; mean; bad; bad habit; to break; to be tired out; to fall; die; humble term meaning my or our, as 弊屋 *Heioku* my house; my family. 一二

衣 *Heii* threadbare clothes.

店 *Heiten* my humble shop.

風 *Heifū* corrupt manners; evil custom.

害 *Heigai* evil practice; evils.

習 *Heishū* corrupt practices; bad custom.

*¹ 履 *Heiri* rejected shoes.

弋 五六

弎 See 貳 56,9. 【貝】 二

T 式 SHIKI ceremony; form; model; to model after. Often used as bottom component, e.g.: *gishiki* ceremony, *sōshiki* funeral, *kyūshiki* old-style. 三

日 *Shikijitsu* day of celebration.

部官 *Shikibukan* Master of Ceremonies.

辭 *Shikiji* congratulatory address.
*²

T 武 BU; MU military; fierce; strong. (*Take*). 【止】 五

176 *¹T 弊 → T*² 弎 →56,9 wu

（五）

力 *Buryoku* military power.

士 *Bushi ; mononofu* knight; warrior.

士道 *Bushidō* chivalry.

功 *Bukō* distinguished military services.

名 *Bumei* military fame.

州 *Bushū* another name for the province of *Musashi*.

門 *Bumon* the military class or caste ; military family.

官 *Bukan* an officer.

勇 *Buyū* courage ; bravery.

骨 *Bukotsu* bluntness ; coarseness.

備 *Bubi* military preparations.

裝 *Busō* armaments for war.

器 *Buki* weapon.

藏 *Musashi* p. n.

斷 *Budan* militarism.

藝 *Bugei* military arts.

九 弒 SHI. *Shiisuru* (irreg.) to kill ; kill a superior.

逆 *Shiigyaku* murder of one's lord or parent.

貳 NI ; JI two. 【貝】
→56, 3 T *2

二 鳶 *Tobi* kite (bird). 【鳥】

色 *Tobi-iro* brown.

五七 弓

When at the left it is called *Yumi-hen.*

T 弓 KYŪ. *Yumi* bow.

張 *Yumihari* a kind of paper lantern.

張月 *Yumiharizuki* crescent moon.

T 引 IN. *Hi(ku)* to pull ; draw ; — quote ; subtract.

力 *Inryoku* gravitation ; attraction.

上 *Hiki-a(geru)* to pull up. *on doors*

止 *Hikito(meru)* to detain ; keep back.

立 *Hik'ta(tsu)* to look well ; improve : *hikitate* favour.

用 *In-yō* to quote ; cite.

出 *Hikidashi* drawer (as of desk) : *hikida(su)* to take out.

札 *Hiki-fuda* trade circular.

合 *Hikia(u)* to be profitable : *hikiai* being involved in another's affairs.

込 *Hikko(mu)* to retire ; get in.

込思案 *Hikkomi-jian* seeking seclusion ; retiring.

見 *Inken* an audience ; interview.

牽 *Insotsu* to lead.

取 *Hiki-to(ru)* to bring to one's house.

受 *Hiki-u(keru)* to engage ; receive ; be responsible.

返 *Hiki-kae(su)* to come or go back.

177

（一）引

例 *Inrei* an instance.

致 *Inchi* taking into custody.

起 *Hikioko(su)* to cause; lead to.

退 *Intai* retirement.

張 *Hipparu* pull; draw.

張凧 *Hipparidako* be sought by many people.

換 *Hikikae* exchange.

渡 *Hiki-wata(su)* to deliver; hand over.

越 *Hikkoshi* removal (of one's dwelling).

摺 *Hikizu(ru)* to drag.

導 *Indō* guiding the soul of the dead to the other world.

證 *Inshō* a quotation.

T 弔 CHŌ. *Tomura(u)* to lament for; condole with.

文 *Chōbun* a funeral address.

客 *Chōkaku* a visitor who comes to express condolence.

砲 *Chōhō* guns of condolence.

問 *Chōmon* condolence.

電 *Chōden* a telegram of condolence.

悼 *Chōtō* sorrow; grief; offer condolences on the death of a person.

意 *Chōi* sorrow; condolence; mourning.

辭 *Chōji* condolence; a funeral oration.

弘 KŌ; GU. *Hiroi* great; large: *hiroma(ru); hiro-(meru)* to expand: *hiroga-(ru)* to spread. 二

法 *Kōbō* p. n., famous scholar and calligraphist.

弗 FUTSU. *Doru* a dollar.

弛 CHI; SHI. *Yuru'meru); taru(mu); tayu(mu)* to loosen; unfasten; relax: *yuru(mu)* to become loose. 三

緩 *Shikan; chikan* lax; careless; slack; loose.

夷 See 37,3.

T 弟 See 12,5. 【弓】 四

T 弧 KO bow; arch. 五

T 弦 GEN. *Tsuru* bowstring.

月 *Gengetsu* the crescent moon.

弩 DO. *Ishiyumi* a large bow.

級艦 *Dokyūkan* a Dreadnought.

弱 JAKU young; less than. *Yowai* weak: *yowa(ru)* to become weak. →弱 T 七

年 *Jakunen* youth.

味 *Yowami* a weak point.

者 *Jakusha* the weak.

點 *Jakuten* weak point.

蟲 *Yowamushi* a weak person.

入 張 CHŌ. *Ha(ru)* to paste on
T (paper or cloth); to cover
(with paper, etc.); to
spread.

本人 *Chōhonnin* ring'eader.

合 *Hariai* emulation.

番 *Hariban* watch; guard.

ᴦ 強 KYŌ; GŌ. *Tsuyoi* strong;
violent; to endeavour:
shi(h)iru) to force: *anagachi*
necessarily. →57, 9

大 *Kyōdai* great and powerful; influential.

壯 *Kyōsō* robust; strong;
powerful.

制 *Kyōsei* to compel; force.

迫 *Kyōhaku* to use force;
employ pressure; compel.

姦 *Gōkan* rape; violation.

弱 *Kyōjaku* strength.

健 *Kyōken* robustness.

堅 *Kyōken* strong.

情 *Gōjō* obstinacy.

欲 *Gōyoku* covetousness;
greed.

盜 *Gōtō* robber; burglar.

硬 *Kyōkō* obstinate; stubborn.

意見 *Kowa-iken* severe ad-
monition.

奪 *Gōdatsu* to rob with
vio'ence; seize.

暴 *Kyōbō* violence.

慾 *Gōyoku* avarice; rapacity.

震 *Kyōshin* a severe shock
of earthquake.

請 *Kyō ei; yusu(ru); neda(ru)*
to extort.

襲 *Kyōshū* an assault.

弼 HITSU to help; assist.　九
(*Suke*).

粥 *Kayu* rice gruel. 【米】

強 See 強 57, 8.
T

發 See 發 105, 7.
*

彈 DAN bullet; to investigate.　一
Haji(ku) to repel; fillip:　二
hi(ku) to play (as string
musical instrument). →57, 9 * T

力 *Danryoku* elasticity.

丸 *Dangan; tama* bullet;
shot.

劾 *Dangai* impeachment.

藥 *Dan-yaku* ammunition.

彊 KYŌ. *Tsuyoi* strong.　一
Often used mistakenly for　三
疆 57, 16.

彌 BI; MI to spread out;　一
everywhere; to mend. *Ya;*　四
iya; yo-yo still more.

生 *Yayoi* poetical name for
3rd month (old calendar).

次馬 *Yajiuma* a busybody;
meddler.

縫 *Bihō* patch; remedy.

疆 KYŌ boundary; limit;　一
partition. 【田】 Often used　六
mistakenly for 彊 57, 13.

彎 WAN to bend; to draw.　一
九

曲 *Wankyoku* bending; flex-
ure.

五八

彐

三　彡　See ᵀ多 36,3.

七ᵀ　帰　See 歸 58,15.　【止】

八　彗　SUI. *Hōki-boshi* comet.

星　*Suisei* a comet.

九ᵀ　尋　JIN ordinary. *Tazu(neru)* to enquire; seek; search: *hiro* a fathom: *tsuide* then; secondly; subsequently: *tsu(gu)* succeed to; follow. 【寸】

常　*Jinjō* ordinary; common.

常小學　*Jinjō-shōgaku* primary school.

問　*Jimmon* to ask; enquire.

一〇　彙　I to classify; collect; sort; kind.

一五　歸　KI end. *Kae(ru)* to return; to go. 【止】 →58,7ᵀ

一　*Kiitsu* unification.

化　*K ka* naturalization.

宅　*Kitaku* return home.

依　*Kie* conversion; believe in.

服　*Kifuku* surrender.

京　*Kikyō* return to the capital.

省　*Kisei* return to one's native place; return home.

航　*Kikō* return voyage.

（一五）

國　*Kikoku* return to one's country.

鄉　*Kikyō* return home.

途　*Kito* the way home.

參　*Kisan* return to one's late employer.

着　*Kichaku* arriving or returning home.

朝　*Kichō* return to Japan.

還　*Kikan* return.

一八

蠡　REI a gourd. 【虫】

五九

彡

四ᵀ　形　KEI; GYŌ. *Katachi; kata; nari* shape; size; figure; appearance: *katado(ru)* to model after. doll

而上　*Keijijō* abstract.

而下　*Keijika* concrete.

式　*Keishiki* forms.

見　*Katami* souvenir; keepsake.

狀　*Keijō* shape; form.

容　*Keiyō* form; modification.

跡　*Keiseki* traces; evidence.

勢　*Keisei* aspect; appearance; condition.

體　*Keitai* shape; form; size.

八ᵀ　彫　CHŌ. *Ho(ru)* to carve; engrave; sculpture

180

（八） 刻 *Chōkoku* carving; sculpture.

物 *Horimono* carving.

彩 SAI. *Irodo(ru)* to colour; paint: *aya* figure; design.

色 *Saishiki* colour. →彩 T

票 *Saihyō* a lottery ticket.

九 須 SU; SHU. *Subekaraku* by all means; ought; must; proper: *beki* ought; must: *shibaraku* short time; instant: *ma(tsu)* to wait: *mochi(h)iru* to use. 【頁】

知 *Suchi* necessary to be known.

臾 *Suyu shibaraku* a while.

磨 *Suma* p. n.

彭 BŌ; HŌ the sound of a drum; vigorous. *Fukura-(mu)* to swell.

一一 彰 SHŌ clear. *Arawa(su)* to manifest. →彰 T

十二 T 影 EI. *Kage* shadow; reflection; figure; form. *Kage* is often used to emphasize a negative sentence; e. g., *kage mo miemasen* one does not see him at all (not even his shadow).

口 *Kageguchi* backbite.

法師 *Kagebōshi* shadow.

武者 *Kagemusha* a dummy general; person behind the scenes.

辨慶 *Kagebenkei* a sham Hercules.

響 *Eikyō* influence.

彳 六〇

Always at the left and is called *Gyōnim-ben.*

T 行 See 144,0. 三

彷 HŌ to be alike. *Samayo(u)* to wander. 四

徨 *Hōkō* wandering: *samayo(u)* to wander.

彿 *Hōfutsu* resembling closely.

髣 *Hōfutsu* resembling closely.

T 役 YAKU government service; office: EKI war; duty; employment; to serve; to employ.

人 *Yakunin* government employee; official.

目 *Yakume* duty; official duty; business.

所 *Yakusho* public office.

者 *Yakusha* player; actor.

柄 *Yakugara* the nature of one's office; quality of one's business.

員 *Yakuin* an official.

割 *Yakuwari* the allotment of parts.

塲 *Yakuba* public office.

T 径 See 徑 60,7. 五

T 往 Ō ancient times. *Yu(ku);* *i(nuru)* (lit. st., irreg.) to go; leave: *saki ni* formerly.

々 *Ōō* often; sometimes.

（五）

往

日 *Ōjitsu* past days.

生 *Ōjō* rebirth in paradise; death.

年 *Ōnen* many years ago.

事 *Ōji* past events; the past.

來 *Ōrai* going and coming; traffic; highway.

昔 *Ōseki* old times.

時 *Ōji* old times.

訪 *Ōhō* to visit.

復 *Ōfuku* going and returning.

還 *Ōkan* going and returning; a highway.

T **征** SEI. *U(tsu)* to reduce to submission; subjugate.

伐 *Seibatsu* expedition; subjugation.

服 *Seifuku* to chastise and subjugate.

討 *Seitō* chastisement; expedition.

略 *Seiryaku* conquest.

誅 *Seichū* to attack and exterminate.

T **彼** HI. *Kare; are* he; she; it: *kano; ano* that.

方 *Kanata: anata* that place; that side; there.

此 *Hishi; kare-kore* this and that.

我 *Higa* self and others; this and that.

岸 *Higan* spring and autumn equinoxes; yonder shore; object; goal.

南 *Penan* Penang.

（五）

是 *Kare-kore* this and that.

得具羅土 *Petorogurādo* Petrograd.

得堡 *Peteruburugu* Petersburg.

處 *Kashiko* there; yonder.

程 *Are hodo* such; that much.

徊 KAI to wander; to stop still. 六

T **律** RITSU rhythm: RICHI law; to enquire into.

呂 *Ritsuryo* (of music) harmony.

義 *Richigi* upright; honest.

衍 EN to expand; to spread. 【行】

義 *Engi* a commentary.

T **待** TAI to treat; entertain. *Ma(tsu)* to wait.

合 *Machiai* assignation house.

合室 *Machiaishitsu* waiting-room.

伏 *Machibuse* lying in ambush.

佗 *Machiwa(biru)* to wait anxiously.

命 *Taimei* waiting orders.

草臥 *Mac'ikutabi(reru)* to grow tired with waiting.

焦 *Machikoga(reru)* to wait anxiously.

遇 *Taigū; ashirai* treatment.

構 *Machikama(h)eru* to be ready for.

遠 *Machidōi* waiting impatiently.

(〇) 徒 See T 徒 60,7.

従 See 從 60,8.

T 後 KŌ; GO. *Nochi; a'o* after; future; next: *ushiro; shirie* behind; back; rear: *oku-(reru)* to be late.

人 *Kōjin* posterity; future generations.

日 *Gojitsu* in the future.

手 *Ushirode* having the hands behind the back: *gote* being forestalled.

天的 *Kōtenteki* a posteriori.

世 *Kōsei* future generations.

半 *Kōhan* the latter half.

片付 *Atokatazuke* rearrangement of things after an incident.

任 *Kōnin* (of officials only) successor; succeeding to a post.

向 *Ushiromuki* turning the back.

光 *Gokō* halo.

先 *Atosaki* first and last; before and behind; topsyturvy; order.

尾 *Kōbi* the rear.

見 *Kōken* guardianship.

押 *Ato-oshi* backer; pushman behind a cart.

事 *Kōji* future affairs, especially what may happen after one's death.

廻 *Atomawashi* postponement.

妻 *Gosai* second wife.

始末 *Atoshimatsu* settlement of an affair; putting in order.

指 *Ushiroyubi* pointing the finger at any one behind his back; to point the finger of scorn.

刻 *Gokoku* later on.

便 *Kōbin* later mail; future opportunity.

釜 *Atogama* the successor.

悔 *Kōkai* repentance; regret.

家 *Goke* a widow.

祭 *Ato no matsuri* an action taken too late.

程 *Nochihodo* afterwards.

援 *Kōen* to assist; support.

備 *Kōbi* the second reserve.

裔 *Kōei* descendant; offspring.

楯 *Ushirodate* backing; protection.

學 *Kōgaku* future benefit.

難 *Kōnan* future trouble.

繼 *Kōkei* succeeding.

顧 *Kōko* providence for the future.

径 KEI diameter. *Komichi* bypath: *wata(ru)* to pass through; pass along; cross. →60,5 T

路 *Keiro* a path; lane; process.

T 徒 To companions; followers. *Kachi* on foot: *itazura ni* in vain: *t da; ada* for nothing; useless. →60,6

183

(七) 徒

手 *Toshu* empty hand.

步 *Toho; kachi* going on foot.

弟 *Totei* an apprentice.

食 *Toshoku* live in idleness.

跣 *Hadashi; tosen* bare feet.

勞 *Torō* vain effort.

費 *Tohi* to waste; useless expenditure.

然 *Tozen; tsurezure* tedium; ennui.

黨 *Totō* a league; party; band.

T 徐 Jo. *Omomuro ni* leisurely; gently; quietly.

々 *Jojo; soro-soro* slowly.

* 行 *Jokō* to go slowly.

八 御 GO; GYO to drive (horses).
T On; o; mi an honorific prefix.

一報 *Go-ippō* kindly favour me with a reply.

中 *Onchū* to whomsoever it may concern; a vague expression used after name of company, (public offices, banks, etc.) on envelope when not addressing any particular individual.

父樣 *Otōsama* father.

尤 *Gomottomo* reasonable; allowable.

世辭 *Oseji* a compliment; flattery.

目玉 *Omedama* a scolding.

用 *Goyō* (your) business.

母樣 *Okāsama* mother.

*從 →60,8
T

八〇

代 *Miyo* Imperial reign; period.

宇 *Gyou* Imperial reign.

伽噺 *Otogibanashi* nursery tale.

所 *Gosho* the Imperial Palace (old style).

法度 *Gohatto* law; prohibition.

苦勞 *Gokurō* a conventional expression used for thanking inferiors for their work or trouble, also when asking a service.

座 *Gozaru* (coll., irreg.); *owasuru* (lit. st., irreg.) to be

座候 *Goza sōrō* to be (more polite than simple *sōrō*).

料 *Goryō* Imperial property; Imperial use.

眞影 *Goshin-ei* an Imperial portrait.

稜威 *Miizu* the virtue of His Majesty the Emperor.

馳走 *Gochisō* entertainment.

製 *Gyosei* poem composed by Emperor.

殿 *Goten* the palace.

膳 *Gozen* rice; food; meal.

幣擔 *Goheikatsugi* a superstitious person.

蔭 *Okage* favour.

璽 *Gyoji* the Imperial seal.

覽 *Goran* to look (polite).

靈屋 *Otamaya* an ancestral shrine.

徘徊 *Haikai* wandering about.

術 JUTSU art; artifice. *Sube* means; device; trick. Frequently used as bottom component, e.g.: *bijutsu* fine arts, *sanjutsu* arithmetic. 【行】 →術 T

中 *Jutchū* snare; trap.

科 *Jukka* drill; practice; manual training.

策 *Jussaku* plan; device; stratagem.

語 *Jutsugo* a technical term.

衒 GEN to sell one's self. *Tera(u)* to boast of. 【行】

氣 *Genki* vanity.

學的 *Gengakuteki* pedantic.

T 得 TOKU gain; profit. *Uru* (lit. st., irreg.); *eru* to get; acquire; be able.

々 *Tokutoku* proudly.

手 *Ete* skill; speciality.

手勝手 *Etekatte* self-will.

心 *Tokushin* consent; understanding.

失 *Tokushitsu* advantage and disadvantage.

票 *Tokuhyō* number of votes obtained.

策 *Tokusaku* the best policy.

意 *Tokui* exaltation; pride; speciality; customer.

點 *Tokuten* a score.

徙 SHI. *Utsu(su); utsu(ru)* to remove; to change.

從 JŪ; SHŌ. *Shitaga(u)* to obey; accompany; follow: *yori* from.

→60,7 * T   →60,6

185

兄 *Itoko* cousin (male).

兄弟 *Itoko* cousin (male).

事 *Jūji* to be engaged in; pursue.

前 *Jūzen* former; previous; hitherto.

姉 *Itoko* cousin (female).

姉妹 *Itoko* cousin (female).

妹 *Itoko* cousin (female).

弟 *Itoko; jūtei* cousin (male).

來 *Jūrai* hitherto.

者 *Jūsha* an attendant; follower.

軍 *Jūgun* being attached to an army; take part in a campaign.

容 *Shōyō* with composure; composedly.

順 *Jūjun* obedience.

僕 *Jūboku* a servant; attendant.

T 循 JUN. *Megu(ru)* to revolve; 九 circulate: *shitaga(u)* to follow; obey.

環 *Junkan* circulation.

T 街 GAI; KAI cross-road; street; town. 【行】

上 *Gaijō* in the street.

路 *Gairo* road (in a town)

道 *Kaidō* highway.

頭 *Gaitō* road (in a town).

徧 HEN to revolve. *Amaneku* the whole; everywhere.

歷 *Henreki* to travel about.

(九) 復 FUKU to return; repeat. *Futatabi; mata* again.

T

仇 *Fukkyū* revenge.

古 *Fukko* restoration.

命 *Fukumei* a report (of a mission).

活 *Fukkatsu* revival; resurrection.

習 *Fukushū* review (of lessons).

與 *Fukkō* revival; renewal; recovery.

歸 *Fukki* to be restored.

舊 *Fukkyū* to revert to a former condition; recovery.

權 *Fukken* rehabilitation.

讐 *Fukushū* revenge.

一〇 衙 GA a government office. 【行】

T 微 BI; MI small; humble; mean. *Kasuka* dim.

々 *Bibi* mean; insignificant.

力 *Biryoku* little influence or strength.

行 *Bikō* to go in disguise; travel incognito.

妙 *Bimyō* delicate; profound.

風 *Bifū* a breeze.

弱 *Bijaku* weak; impotent; insignificant.

衷 *Bichū* one's true heart.

笑 *Bishō* a smile.

恙 *Biyō* slight indisposition.

細 *Bisai* minute; detailed.

意 *Bii* a humble opinion.

傷 *Bishō* a slight wound.

塵 *Mijin* an atom.

(一〇)

衝 SHŌ responsible position. *Tsu(ku)* to strike against. 【行】

T

心 *Shōshin* paralysis of the heart.

突 *Shōtotsu* collision; to strike against.

動 *Shōdō* impulse.

一二

T 衛 See 衞 60,13. 【行】

徵 CHŌ sign; symptom; clear. *Me(su)* to call; summon; levy. →60,11 *1 T

收 *Chōshū* to collect; levy.

兵 *Chōhei* conscription.

候 *Chōkō* symptom.

發 *Chōhatsu* requisition, forage.

稅 *Chōzei* tax-collection.

T 徹 TETSU clear. *Tō(ru)* to penetrate; pervade: *tō(su)* to pass through.

夜 *Tetsuya* sitting up all night.

底 *Tettei* thoroughness; completeness.

宵 *Tesshō* all night.

頭徹尾 *Tettō-tetsubi* from head to foot; from beginning to end

德 TOKU virtue; benevolence. *Nori* moral standard. --60.11 *2 T

化 *Tokka* influence of virtue.

（一二）

用 *Tokuyō* economical; serviceable.

行 *Tokkō* virtuous conduct; morality.

利 *Tokuri; tokkuri* a bottle.

育 *Tokuiku* moral education.

性 *Tokusei* morality.

島 *Tokushima* p. n.

望 *Tokubō* inspiring reverence.

義 *Tokugi* morality.

一三 衞 EI : E to protect; defend. 【行】 →61, 12T

生 *Eisei* hygiene; sanitation.

兵 *Eihei* sentinel.

戍 *Eiju* a garrison.

T 衡 KŌ level. *Hakari* scales; balance: *haka(ru)* to weigh. 【行】

一四 徽 KI a badge; good; beautiful.

章 *Kishō* badge.

二〇 黴 BAI; BI minute. *Kabi* mildew: *kabi(-ru)* to get mouldy. 【黑】

毒 *Baidoku* syphilis.

菌 *Baikin* bacillus.

二二 衢 KU crossroads; street. 【行】

六一 心

When at the left it takes the modified form 忄 and is called *Risshim-ben.*

T 心 SHIN core; wick; centre. *Kokoro* the heart, especially as the centre of sensations and emotions; mind.

中 *Shinchū* one's true motive : *shinjū* a lovers' suicide ; double suicide.

立 *Kokorodate* temper.

外 *Shingai* sorry; vexatious.

付 *Kokorozuke* a tip; small present.

地 *Kokochi* feeling; sensation.

安 *Kokoroyasui* familiar; feeling easy; on friendly terms.

血 *Shinketsu* heart's blood; great endeavour.

身 *Shinshin* mind and body.

底 *Shintei* the bottom of one's heart; will ; intention.

事 *Shinji* what is in one's mind; feelings.

服 *Shimpuku* to submit heartily.

持 *Koko omochi* feeling; sensation.

配 *Shimpai* anxiety; uneasiness.

理 *Shinri* mental phenomena.

組 *Kokorogumi* design; intention.

掛 *Kokoroa(keru)* to keep in mind: *kokorogake* aim; purpose.

心

許 *Kokoromoto nai* feeling unsafe or uneasy: *kokoro-bakari* slight; trifling.

得 *Kokoroe* rules of conduct; knowledge; preparedness: *kokoroeru* to understand.

情 *Shinjō* feeling.

棒 *Shimbō* axle; shaft.

痛 *Shintsū* mental suffering.

勞 *Shinrō* anxiety; trouble of mind.

象 *Shinshō* image (mental).

眼 *Shingan* mental view; perception.

殘 *Kokoronokori* regret.

當 *Kokoroatari* a clue.

盡 *Kokorozukushi* great kindness.

算 *Shinsan; tsumori* intention.

構 *Kokorogamae* planning; thinking over.

醉 *Shinsui* to be charmed; to adore blindly.

頭 *Shintō* the heart; mind.

機 *Shinki* the mind; mental attitude.

膽 *Shintan* the mind.

願 *Shingan* the heart's desire; earnest prayer.

懸 *Kokorogake* intention; attention.

臟 *Shinzō* heart (the organ itself).

靈 *Shinrei* spirit.

ᵀ必 HITSU. *Kanarazu* certainly; without fail.

死 *Hisshi* desperation.

定 *Hitsujō* certainly; surely.

要 *Hitsuyō* necessity; need.

須 *Hissū* indispensable.

然 *Hitsuzen* necessarily; inevitably.

携 *Hikkei* a manual; indispensable.

ᵀ忙 Bō. *Isogashii* busy.

殺 *Bōsatsu* to be extremely busy.

忖 SON to think; suppose. *Haka(ru)* to estimate.

度 *Sontaku* to conjecture; surmise.

忍 NIN. *Shino(bu)* to endure; bear with patience.　→忍ᵀ

耐 *Nintai* patience; endurance.

辱 *Ninniku* forbearance; stoicism.

ᵀ忌 See 49,4. 【心】

忸怩 *Jikuji* ashamed.

忰 See 倅 9,4.

ᵀ快 KAI. *Kokoroyoi* comfortable; happy; agreeable.

刀 *Kaitō* a sharp blade.

方 *Kaihō* convalescence; recovery.

事 *Kaiji* a pleasant matter.

哉 *Kaisai* shou jtof oy.

（四）

活 *Kaikatsu* lively; cheerful.

晴 *Kaisei* fine weather.

復 *Kaifuku* recovery.

樂 *Kairaku* pleasure; joy; delight.

諾 *Kaidaku* ready consent.

談 *Kaidan* an animate talk.

癒 *Kaiyu* restoration to health.

T 忠 CHŪ faithful; loyal; sincerity; honesty. (*Tada*).

士 *Chūshi* loyal subject.

臣 *Chūshin* loyal subject.

君 *Chūkun* loyalty.

告 *Chūkoku* advice.

孝 *Chūkō* loyalty to the Emperor and filial piety.

良 *Chūryō* loyalty.

言 *Chūgen* advice; counsel.

勇 *Chūyū* loyalty and bravery.

烈 *Chūretsu* ardent loyalty.

誠 *Chūsei* loyalty; devotion.

節 *Chūsetsu* loyalty; fidelity.

義 *Chūgi* loyalty; fidelity.

勤 *Chūkin* loyal service.

實 *Chūjitsu* honesty; fidelity.

念 See 念 T 9,6. 【心】

T 念 See 9,6. 【心】

忿 FUN. *Ika(ru)* to be angry; resent.

忽 KOTSU. *Tachimachi* at once; in a moment; suddenly:

yurugase ni suru to slight; neglect; make light of. （四）

焉 *Kotsuen* suddenly.

然 *Kotsuzen* suddenly.

諸 *Kossho* neglect; negligence.

忝 TEN. *Katajikenai* thankful; much obliged.

T 怪 KAI; KE ghost. *Ayashii* strange; wonderful: *ayashi-(mu)* to wonder; doubt. 五

力 *Kairyoku; kairiki* Herculean strength.

我 *Kega* hurt; accident.

物 *Kaibutsu* a ghost; apparition.

訝 *Kaiga; kegen* doubt; suspicion.

疑 *Kaigi* doubt; suspicion.

談 *Kaidan* ghost stories.

T 性 SEI; SHŌ sex; gender. *Saga* nature; natural disposition.

行 *Seikō* character and conduct.

向 *Seikō* disposition; nature.

分 *Shōbun* natural disposition.

急 *Seikyū; sekkachi* quick temper.

格 *Seikaku* character; personality.

情 *Seijō* mind; a person's disposition.

根 *Shōne* natural disposition.

惡 *Shōwaru* evil disposition.

慾 *Seiyoku* sexual desire.

性 *Seishitsu* nature; disposition.

癖 *Seiheki* bias; mental tendency.

懲 *Shōkori* repentance.

怙 KO. *Tano(mu)* to rely on; request.

恃 *Koji* to rely on.

怜 REI. *Satoi* intelligent.

悧 *Reiri* cleverness.

T **怖** FU. *Oso(reru); o(jiru)* to fear; dread: *osoroshii; kowai* frightful.

々 *Kowagowa* timidly.

氣 *Ojike* fear; dread.

快 Ō feel dissatisfied; unpleasant.

怺 *Kora(h)eru)* to endure; bear.

怯 KYŌ weak. *Hiru(mu)* to fear; dread; be timid.

儒 *Kyōda* cowardice; timidity.

T **急** KYŪ danger; emergency; alarm; sudden; quick. *Iso-(gu); se(ku)* to hurry; be urgent.

用 *Kyūyō* urgent business.

行列車 *Kyūkō-ressha* express train.

込 *Sekiko(mu)* to be excited.

所 *Kyūsho* a vital part.

性 *Kyūsei* acute.

派 *Kyūha* despatch

迫 *Kyūhaku* urgent.

病 *Kyūhyō* a sudden illness.

流 *Kyūryū* rapid current.

務 *Kyūmu* urgent need.

處 *Kyūsho* a vital part.

速 *Kyūsoku* quick; rapid; prompt.

塲 *Kyūba* an emergency.

報 *Kyūhō* urgent message.

進 *Kyūshin* radical; rapid.

須 *Kyūsu* small teapot.

電 *Kyūden* urgent telegram.

激 *Kyūgeki* impetuous; enthusiastic.

遽 *Kyūkyo* in haste; in a hurry.

轉 *Kyūten* a sudden change.

變 *Kyūhen* a sudden change.

忽 SŌ. *Iso(gu)* to hasten; hurry; be busy; hurried: *niwaka* sudden.

々 *Sōsō* in haste.

卒 *Sōsotsu* hasty.

T **怒** DO; NU. *Ika(ru); oko(ru)* to get angry.

氣 *Doki* anger; wrath.

鳴 *Dona(ru)* to shout at.

濤 *Dotō* raging billows; roaring waves.

號 *Dogō* roar; howl.

怨 EN; ON. *Ura(mu)* to resent; hate.

府 *Empu* object of hatred.

念 *Onnen* hatred; enmity.

恨 *Enkon* enmity; animosity.

(五)

望 *Embō* looking with chagrin.

靈 *Onryō* vindictive ghost of a deceased enemy.

*

六 恒 Γ See foll.

恆 KŌ everywhere.　*Tsune* eternal; constant.

久 *Kōkyū* permanency.

心 *Kōshin* constancy; steadiness.

例 *Kōrei* an established custom.

河 *Ganga* Ganges.

產 *Kōsan* real property.

恤 JUTSU to relieve.　*Aware-(mu)* to show kindness.

兵 *Juppei* relief of soldiers.

Γ 悩 See 悩 61,9.

恰 KŌ. *Atakamo* just as; as if.

好 *Kakkō* shape; style; suitable; fit; reasonable.

恬 TEN quiet; peaceful.

恃 JI; SHI. *Tano(mu)* to rely on; request.

恟々 *Kyōkyō* frightened; alarmed.

協 See T 協 24,6.

恢 KAI to enlarge; large; great.

復 *Kaifuku* restoration; recovery.

(六)

T 恨 KON.　*Ura(mu)* to resent; hate.

事 *Konji* matter for regret.

恍 KŌ. *Ho(reru)* to be absorbed in something : *tobo-ke(-ru)* to be in ecstasy; be absent-minded : pretend ignorance.

惚 *Kōkotsu* rapture.

恁 JIN; NIN to think.　*Kaku* thus : *kono* this.

恕 JO to excuse; bear patiently; to sympathize with; pity.

T 恩 ON kindness; favour; benefaction.

人 *Onjin* benefactor.

金 *Onkin* money benevolently lent or given; pension.

返 *Ongaeshi* requital of a favour; returning a kindness.

典 *Onten* grace; special favour.

威 *On-i* kindness and dignity.

師 *Onshi* kind teacher.

赦 *Onsha* amnesty; forgiveness.

給 *Onkyū* pension.

惠 *Onkei* favour; benevolence.

愛 *On-ai* kindness and affection.

義 *Ongi* favour.

賜 *Onshi* a gracious present of the Emperor, etc.

賞 *Onshō* reward.

澤 *Ontaku* favour.

恩
顧 *Onko* special favours.

恣 SHI. *Hoshiimama* as one pleases; one's own way.

T 恐 KYŌ. *Oso(reru)* to fear: *osoroshii* frightful: *osoraku* perhaps.

入 *Osorei(ru)* to be abashed; acknowledge one's guilt; be troubled; be sorry to trouble; be obliged to someone.

怖 *Kyōfu* fear; awe.

悦 *Kyōetsu* joy.

惶 *Kyōkō* fear and trembling.

喝 *Kyōkatsu* threat; intimidation.

慌 *Kyōkō* panic; crisis.

察 *Kyōsatsu* to sympathize respectfully with; humbly conjecture.

縮 *Kyōshuku* to be much obliged; be very sorry; be ashamed.

嚇 *Kyōkaku* intimidation; threat.

懼 *Kyōku* fear; dread.

T 恋 See 戀 61,19.

T 恭 See 140,7. 【心】

*

七 悟 GO. *Sato(ru)* to perceive;
T know; understand.

道 *Godō* philosophy.

悋 RIN to grudge; parsimonious.

* 惠 T → 61,8

氣 *Rinki* jealousy.

悍 KAN fierce; violent.

婦 *Kampu* an amazon; shrew.

悖 HAI irrational. *Moto(ru)* to oppose; rebel.

理 *Hairi* irrationality.

德 *Haitoku* evil conduct; perversity.

悄 SHŌ. *Uryōru* (ウレフル, lit. st.: see Introduction 40) to grieve: *sugo-sugo* sadly.

々 *Sugo-sugo* despondently; dejectedly.

然 *Shōzen* dispiritedly; with a heavy heart.

悔 KAI; KE. *Ku(y)iru)* to repent; regret: *kuya(mu)* to condole. → 61,5T *

恨 *Kaikon* remorse; repentance.

悟 *Kaigo* repentance.

悛 SHUN to stop. *Arata-(meru)* to amend.

悦 ETSU. *Yoroko(bu)* to rejoice; take pleasure in; enjoy.

樂 *Etsuraku* amusement; enjoyment.

T 患 KAN disease. *Uryōru* (ウレフル, lit. st.: see Introduction 40) be anxious about: *wazura(u)* to be ill.

者 *Kanja* a sick person; a patient.

部 *Kambu* affected part.

悠 YŪ long time; leisurely; far; to grieve.

（七）

々 *Yūyū* calmly; slowly; eternally; vastly.

* 然 *Yūzen* leisurely; calmly.

（八）

惟 I. *Omommi*(-*ru*); *omo*(*u*) to reflect; think: *kore* this: *tada* only.

T 惜 SEKI; SHAKU. *Oshii* regretted; deplorable: *oshi*(*mu*) to regret; begrudge; lament.

別 *Sekibetsu* sorrow of parting.

T 悼 TŌ. *Ita*(*mu*) to lament; be pained; to sympathize with: *itamashii* lamentable.

惇 TON to exert oneself: JUN kind; truth.

情 JŌ feeling; condition; aspect; taste (artistic). *Nasake* sympathy. →情 T

人 *Jōjin* a lover; sweetheart.

夫 *Jōfu; iro* a lover; paramour.

火 *Jōka* fire of passion.

死 *Jōshi* suicide of two lovers.

交 *Jōkō* intimacy.

事 *Jōji* a love affair.

狀 *Jōjō* circumstances.

味 *Jōmi* fascination.

況 *Jōkyō* condition; state of things.

深 *Nasake-bukai* compassionate; benevolent.

婦 *Jōfu; iro* a mistress; paramour.

報 *Jōhō* a report; information.

* 惡 →61,8

勢 *Jōsei* state; condition; circumstance.

愛 *Jōai* love; affection.

態 *Jōtai* state; condition; situation.

熱 *Jōnetsu* passion.

趣 *Jōshu* mood; effect; sentiment.

誼 *Jōgi* friendly sentiments.

緒 *Jōcho; jōsho* emotion.

實 *Jōjitsu* private considerations; real facts of a matter.

慾 *Jōyoku* lust; sexual desire.

操 *Jōsō* sentiment.

T 惨 See 慘 61,11.

悵 CHŌ to lament; to despair; to grieve.

然 *Chōzen* sadly; despairingly.

懼 GU. *Oso*(*reru*) to fear; feel awe.

惚 KOTSU indistinct. *Ho*(*reru*) to fall in love: *noroke*(-*ru*) to brag of one's amours: *boke*(-*ru*) to be absent-minded: *uttori suru* to be in ecstasy.

氣 *Noroke* a love affair.

悽 SEI to feel sorry; to grieve.

愴 *Seisō* distressing; deplorable.

惨 *Seisan* distressing; deplorable.

惡 AKU; O. *Warui; ashii* bad: *nikui* hateful; (as 2nd component) difficult. (e.g.

→61,7 *

193

（八〇）**惡**

shi-nikui difficult to do): *n'ku(mu)* to hate.

口 *Akkō; warukuchi* abuse; insult.

化 *Akka* deterioration.

者 *Warumono* bad fellow.

事 *Akuji* evil act; evil custom.

相 *Akusō* a bad face; evil-looking.

疫 *Akueki* epidemic.

風 *Akufū* evil customs; vice.

氣 *Warugi* malice.

習 *Akushū* a bad habit.

筆 *Akuhitsu* bad writing.

寒 *Okan* a chill.

評 *Akuhyō* unfavourable criticism; bad reputation.

意 *Akui* malice.

漢 *Akkan* a villain.

辣 *Akuratsu* unscrupulous.

樣 *Ashi-ama ni* (speak, treat) ill, badly.

弊 *Akuhei* an abuse; evil practice.

戲 *Akugi; itazura* mischief.

黨 *Akutō* blackguard; ruffian.

魔 *Akuma* the devil.

惣 Sō. *Subete* all.

T **惑** WAKU. *Mado(u)* to err; be beguiled: *madoi* doubt; delusion; superstition: *madowa(su)* to lead astray. →62,8

溺 *Wakudeki suru* to be addicted to.

亂 *Wakuran* confusion; perplexity.

惠 KEI; E clever. *Megumi* blessing: *megu(mu)* to give alms; bestow; favour. →61,6T *

投 *Keitō* to give.

與 *Keiyo* to give.

撫 *Keibu* cherish; love.

澤 *Keitaku* favour; mercy.

贈 *Keisō* to give.

惶 KŌ to be excited; to fear. 九

惱 NŌ. *Naya(mu)* to be distressed; afflicted: *nayama-(su)* to worry; persecute; annoy. →61,6T

殺 *Nōsatsu* to fascinate; charm; captivate.

惻 SOKU to be sad; be distressed; to sympathize with.

愍 *Sokubin* to feel sympathy for.

隱 *Sokuin* sympathy; compassion.

T 惰 DA to be idle, remiss; irksome.

力 *Daryoku* inertia.

性 *Dasei* inertia.

弱 *Dajaku* lazy; idle; good-for-nothing.

氣 *Daki* indolence.

愕 GAKU to be frightened; to be confused.

（九）

然 *Gakuzen; hatto* amazedly; aghast; in a sudden surprise.

愎 FUKU to oppose; be obstinate.

愉 YU to be glad; happy; comfortable. →愉 T

快 *Yukai* pleasure.

悦 *Yuetsu* pleasure; delight.

T 想 SŌ. *Omo(u)* to think; imagine.

起 *Sōki* to recollect; recall.

像 *Sōzō* imagination.

愆 KEN. *Toga; ayamachi* fault; mistake.

T 愚 GU sometimes used as prefix in depreciatory sense to indicate 1st person, 愚妻 *gusai* my wife. *Oroka* foolish.

劣 *Guretsu* foolish.

考 *Gukō* I think; my opinion.

見 *Guken* my humble opinion.

弄 *Gurō* to make a fool of.

物 *Gubutsu* a blockhead.

直 *Guchoku* simplicity and honesty.

妻 *Gusai* my wife.

昧 *Gumai* stupidity.

鈍 *Gudon* foolish; dull-witted.

痴 *Guchi* idle complaint.

圖々々 *Gu u-guzu* hesitation.

蒙 *Gumō* stupid; foolish.

T 愁 SHŪ. *Uryōru* (ウレフル, lit. st.: see Introduction 4') to grieve; sorrow.

心 *Shūshin* sad heart.

眉 *Shūbi* contracted brows; anxious look.

訴 *Shūso* appeal; complaint.

傷 *Shūshō* grief.

歎 *Shūtan* grief; sorrow.

愍 BIN; MIN. *Aware(mu)* to pity; grieve.

惻 *Binsoku* to commiserate.

然 *Binzen* pitiful; wretched; miserable.

T 感 KAN feeling; admiration; motion; to be sensitive to. →62, 9

化 *Kanka* influence; reform.

心 *Kanshin* admiration; praise.

付 *Kanzuku* to get scent of.

泣 *Kankyū* to be moved to tears.

服 *Kampuku* admiration; wonder.

佩 *Kampai* being deeply impressed with kindness.

冒 *Kambō; kaze* a cold.

染 *Kansen* to infect; permeate.

情 *Kanjō* feeling; sentiment.

動 *Kandō* to be moved; affected.

喜 *Kanki* to be pleased; be delighted.

想 *Kansō* thoughts; impressions.

銘 *Kammei* a feeling of gratitude.

賞 *Kanshō* admire and praise.

歎 *Kantan* to admire deeply.

（九）

感

慨 *Kangai* to be affected.

奮 *Kampun* deep emotion.

激 *Kangeki* deep emotion.

興 *Kankyō* interest.

謝 *Kansha* gratitude.

應 *Kannō* answer; response; induction.

觸 *Kanshoku* sensation; touch; feelings.

覺 *Kankaku* feeling; sensation.

T 慈 See 140,10. 【心】

愈 See 11,11. 【心】

一〇 慄 RITSU. *Onono(ku)*; *wana-na(ku)*; *furu(h)eru* (coll.); *furu(u)* (lit. st.) to tremble with fear: *osore* fear.

然 *Ritsuzen* horror-stricken.

慊 KEN to suspect; doubt; regret. *Akitaranai* dissatisfied.

焉 *Ken-en* dissatisfaction.

愧 KI. *Ha(jiru)* to be ashamed.

T 慌 KŌ. *Awatadashii* flurried; agitated: *awa(teru)* to be agitated; confused.

慨 GAI. *Ika(ru)* to be angry: *nage(ku)* to grieve.

慎 SHIN. *Tsutsushi(mu)* to be respectful: *tsutsumashii* circumspect. →慎 T

重 *Shinchō* respectful; careful.

*1 慈 →61,9 T

196

愬 See T 訴 149,5.

憑 YŌ to advise; encourage.

憫 IN kindly; politely; to pity; to regret; lament.

慇 *Ingin* politely; with courtesy.

T 態 TAI form; appearance; manner; condition. *Shina* gesture: *wazato*; *wazawaza* specially; purposely.

々 *Wazawaza* specially; purposely.

*2 度 *Taido* attitude; manner.

慳 KEN to begrudge; be stingy.

貪 *Kendon* covetousness; harshness.

慚 ZAN. *Ha(jiru)* to be ashamed: *haji* shame.

死 *Zanshi* to die of shame.

愧 *Zanki* shame; remorse.

慘 SAN; ZAN to torture; cruel; miserable; wretched; to feel pain or sorrow. *Mijime* misery. →61, 8 T

事 *Sanji* tragedy; tragical accident.

狀 *Sanjō* pitiful condition; wretched state.

況 *Sankyō* disastrous condition.

害 *Sangai* disastrous damage.

殺 *Zansatsu* slaughter.

禍 *Sanka* calamity.

一一

*2 T 慨 →61,11

（一一）

酷 *Zankoku* cruelty.

劇 *Sangeki* a tragedy; catastrophe.

憺 *Santan* pitiful; miserable.

慟 Dō. *Nage(ku)* to cry; lament; grieve

哭 *Dōkoku* wail.

慷 Kō to grieve over public affairs.

慨悲憤 *Kōgai-hifun* patriotic indignation.

T 慢 MAN to neglect. *Anado(ru)* to despise : *o₀o(ru)* to be proud.

心 *Manshin* arrogance; swagger.

性 *Mansei* (of disease) chronic.

慥 *Tashika ni* certainly.

慨 GAI. *Nage(ku)* to be grieved and indignant. →61,10 *² T

然 *Gaizen* indignantly.

嘆 *Gaitan* deploring; lamentation.

T 慣 KAN. *Na(reru)* to be accustomed to : *narawashi* custom.

々 *Nare-nareshiku* familiarly.

手段 *Kanshudan* usual method.

用 *Kan-yō* practice; common use.

例 *Kanrei; shikitari* usage; custom; practice.

習 *Kanshū* custom.

（一一）

慓悍 *Hyōkan* impetuous; fearless; savage.

慧 KEI; E. *Satoi; sakashii* intelligent.

敏 *Keibin* clever; smart.

眼 *Keigan* quick eyes.

憩 See ᵀ憩 61,12.

慙 See 慚 61,11.

T 慰 I. *Nagusa(meru)* to console; amuse; divert.

安 *Ian* to pacify; appease; consolation.

問 *Imon* to enquire after a person's health or welfare.

勞 *Irō* to express acknowledgement, for obligations conferred.

撫 *Ibu* soothe; pacify.

藉 *Isha* consolation.

慾 YOKU passion; lust; greed; to covet; to desire.

目 *Yokume* partial eyes.

求 *Yokkyū* desire; will.

望 *Yokubō* want; desire; wish

情 *Yokujō* desire; lust; passions.

張 *Yokubari* avarice.

慫 SHŌ to persuade; advs

慂 *Shōyō* encouragement; advice.

慼 See 戚 62,11.

一
二

憧　DŌ; SHŌ. *Akoga(reru)* to be absorbed in; be infatuated with.

憬　*Shōkei; dōkei* infatuation; longing.

憎　ZŌ; SŌ. *Niku(mu)* to hate: *nikui; nikurashii* hateful. →61,11 T *

惡　*Zōo* hatred; detestation.

憐　REN. *Aware(mu)* to pity.

愍　*Remmin* compassion; pity.

憫　*Rembin* compassion; pity.

憚　TAN. *Habaka(ru)* to fear; be shy of.

憫　BIN; MIN anxiety; concern. *Aware(mu)* to pity; grieve.

笑　*Binshō* a smile of pity.

然　*Binzen* pitiableness.

察　*Binsatsu* sympathize; feel sorry.

T 憤　FUN. *Ikidō(ru)* to be indignant; be angry.

死　*Funshi* die of indignation.

怒　*Fundo* indignation; wrath; passion.

然　*Funzen* indignantly.

慨　*Fungai* indignation.

激　*Fungeki* to become excited; become angry.

憮　BU disappointment.

然　*Buzen* disappointedly.

憔　SHŌ to get thin; emaciated.

悴　*Shōsui* emaciated.

T 憩　KEI. *Iko(u)* to rest. →61,11

憊　HAI. *Tsuka(reru)* to bo weary.

憑　HYŌ evidence; to apply; to rely on. *Tsu(ku)* to be possessed; obsessed.

據　*Hyōkyo* proof.

憺　TAN calm; quiet.

懌　EKI to rejoice.

懈　KAI; KE. *Oko'a(ru)* to be lazy.

怠　*K'etai; kaitai* laziness; idleness; negligence.

懊　Ō to be in distress.

惱　*Ōnō* anguish; mental agony.

憶　OKU. *Omo(u)* to think; remember. Sometimes used mistakenly for 臆 130,13.

出　*Omoidasu* to remember. T →憶

T 憾　KAN. *Ura(mu)* to regret.

T 懇　KON. *Nengoro* courteous; true.

々　*Kon-kon* earnestly; repeatedly.

切　*Konsetsu* kindness.

命　*Kommei* kind request; order.

（一一一）

一
三

198

（一三）

望 *Kombō* earnest desire.

情 *Konjō* kind thought.

意 *Kon-i* intimacy; friendship.

請 *Konsei* to beg earnestly; entreat.

談 *Kondan* consultation.

親 *Konshin* friendship.

篤 *Kontoku* cordiality; kindness.

願 *Kongan* to beg earnestly; entreat.

*

一四 懦 DA weak; cowardly.

夫 *Dafu* an idle fellow; coward.

弱 *Dajaku* indolent; effeminate.

懣 MAN to be troubled; be in anguish.

一五 T 懲 CHŌ *Ko(riru)* to be warned or taught by some experience: *kora(su)* to punish; convict.

役 *Chōeki* penal servitude.

戒 *Chōkai* reprimand; lesson.

惡 *Chōaku* to censure wrong-doing; reprove evil conduct.

罰 *Chōbatsu* discipline; punishment.

一六 懷 KAI to keep in mind *Omo(u)* to recollect; think: *ida(ku)* to harbour; cherish: *futokoro* breast;

*懐

→61,16　　→61,13 * T

---

bosom; purse: *natsukashii* yearning for; longing for: *natsu(ku)* to become familiar; attached to; fond of. 一六

中 *Kaichū* a pocket.

手 *Futokorode* hands in one's pockets; doing nothing.

古 *Kaiko* recall the past.

妊 *Kainin* pregnancy; gestation.

柔 *Kaijū* pacification.

胎 *Kaitai* pregnancy; conception.

疑 *Kaigi* doubt; scepticism.

舊 *Kaikyū* to dwell on the past; think over past events.

懶 RAN to be indolent. *Mono-ui* disinclined to act. 一六

惰 *Randa* idleness.

T 懸 KEN. *Kaka(ru)* to hang; depend on; concern; be anxious; cost: *ka(keru)* to hang.

念 *Kenen* anxiety; fear.

命 *Kemmei* eagerly.

案 *Ken-an* a pending question.

隔 *Kenkaku* a great difference.

想 *Kesō* to fall in love with.

賞 *Kenshō* a prize contest; offering a prize.

懺 ZAN; SAN to confess; repent. 一七

(一七) 懺
悔 *Zange* penitence.

一八 懼 KU to threaten. *Oso(reru)* to fear; to tremble.

一九 戀 REN. *Koi* love: *ko(u)* to love. →8,8T : 61,6T

々 *Ren-ren* ardently attached.

人 *Koibito* a lover.

女房 *Koinyobo* a wife whom one has married for love.

着 *Renchaku* to love; be ardently attached to.

愛 *Ren-ai* love.

路 *Koiji* love; a lover's way.

歌 *Koika* a love-song.

敵 *Koigataki* a rival in love.

慕 *Rembo* to love; yearn for.

六二 戈

戈 KA war. *Hoko* a kind of spear.

一 戊 BO. *Tsuchinoe* the 5th calendar sign. See Introduction 42, 43.

二 戌 JUTSU. *Inu* the 11th zodiacal sign, the dog. See Introduction 42, 43.

戍 JU. *Mamo(ru)* to guard.

戎 JŪ. *Ebisu* barbarian.

夷 *Jūi* barbarian.

衣 *Jūi* military costume; uniform.

器 *Jūki* military weapons; arms.

* 戔 See 錢 167,8.

三 成 SEI; JŌ to finish. *Na(ru)* to become; come into effect: *na(su)* to do; perform. (*Shige*). →62,2 * T

人 *Seijin* an adult.

分 *Seibun* composition; ingredient.

立 *Seiritsu* to come into force; come into existence; establish.

功 *Seikō* success.

年 *Seinen* majority; adult.

行 *Nariyuki* result; end; fate.

否 *Seihi* success or failure.

金 *Narikin* parvenu.

果 *Seika* result; issue; end; fate.

長 *Seichō* growth.

案 *Seian* a design; a scheme.

規 *Seiki* regulation.

敗 *Seihai* success and failure.

程 *Naruhodo* I see (exclamation).

就 *Jōju* to be finished; be completed.

200 *T 成 →62,3

（三）

業 *Seigyō* the completion of work or studies.

算 *Seisan* a plan; promising plan.

熟 *Seijuku* ripeness; mature.

績 *Seiseki* result; issue.

T 戒 KAI commandment. *Imashi(meru)* to admonish; caution; punish.

名 *Kaimyō* a posthumous name.

嚴令 *Kaigenrei* martial law.

T 我 GA. *Ware* I; my; we; our: before the postposition *ga* this character is read *wa* and it means my, mine, self-will.

々 *Ware-ware* we.

田引水 *Gaden-insui* to seek one's own advantage and ignore others.

先 *Ware saki ni* I first; each one struggling to be first.

流 *Garyū* one's own style, method.

等 *Warera* we.

勝 *Waregachi ni* I first; each one struggling to be first.

意 *Gai* selfishness; self-will.

慢 *Gaman* patience; forbearance.

蜚 *Wagahai* we; I.

儘 *Wagamama* wilfulness.

四 或 WAKU. *Aru* a certain; some: *aruiwa* or; perhaps.

咸 KAN everywhere. *Mina* all. 【口】 五

T 威 I dignity; authority; stern; majestic; fierce. *Odok i(su)* to threaten. 【女】

力 *Iryoku* power; authority; influence.

耳斯 *Ueirusu* Wales.

光 *Ikō* majesty; power; influence.

風 *Ifū* an imposing air.

信 *Ishin* credit; dignity.

海衞 *Ikaiei* Weihai-wei (Chinese port).

張 *Iba(ru)* to be proud; haughty.

勢 *Isei* power; influence; might.

德 *Itoku* benevolent virtue; majesty.

儀 *Igi* dignity.

嚇 *Ikaku* menace.

壓 *Iatsu* coercion.

嚴 *Igen* dignity; grandeur.

哉 SAI. *Kana* an interjection: *ya* an interrogative. 【口】

T 栽 SAI to plant. 【木】 六

培 *Saibai* cultivation.

戚 SEKI relatives; kinsmen. 七

戟 GEKI a double-headed lance; arms; to pierce; sting; prick. 八

201

（八）

戰 See 戰 62,12.

T 裁 SAI to discriminate. *Ta-(tsu)* to cut (especially clothes). 【衣】

可 *Saika* Imperial assent; sanction.

判 *Saiban* judgment.

判官 *Saibankan* judge.

判所 *Saibansho* law-court; court of justice.

決 *Saiketsu* decision; verdict.

決書 *Saiketsusho* a written verdict.

許 *Saikyo* Imperial approval.

縫 *Saihō* sewing; needle-work.

斷 *Saidan* decision.

惑 See ᵀ惑 61,8.

T 幾 KI. *Iku* how many; many; few: *hotondo* almost; nearly: *chikai* near: *koi-nega(u)* to request; hope; wish. 【幺】

人 *Ikunin; ikutari* how many persons.

日 *Iku-nichi; ikka* how many days; what day of the month.

分 *Ikubun* some; a part.

多 *Ikuta* many; numerous; various.

何 *Ikubaku* how many: *kika* geometry.

度 *Iku-do; iku-tabi* how often: *iku-do mo; iku-tabi mo*

*T 戰 →62, 12

202

very often; any number of （八） times.

等 *Ikura* how much: *ikura ka* a little.

程 *Ikuhodo mo naku* soon.

盞 SEN; SAN a wine-cup. 【皿】 九

感 See ᵀ感 61,9.

歳 See 歳 77,9.

T 載 SAI year. *No(seru)* to load; place on record: *no(ru)* to get on to. 【車】

積 *Saiseki* lading.

* 截 SETSU; SAI. *Ki(ru)* to cut; — to cut off. ○

斷 *Setsudan* amputation; cutting off.

慼 SEKI to grieve. 【心】 二

T 戲 See 戲 62,13.

戮 RIKU to kill; to expose (a corpse).

畿 KI limit; boundary; threshold. 【田】

内 *Kinai* the five provinces around Kyōto.

戲 See 戲 62,13. 三

戰 SEN. *Tataka(u)* to fight: *ikusa* war; battle: *onono-* →62,9 T *

(一二)

(*ku*) to tremble with fear.
soyo(*gu*) to flutter in the wind.

々競々 *Sensen-kyōkyō* trembling with fear.

士 *Senshi* combatant.

友 *Sen-yū* comrade-in-arms.

功 *Senkō* military merit.

死 *Senshi* death in battle.

地 *Senchi* battle-field.

利品 *Senrihin* spoils of battle.

局 *Senkyoku* the situation of a war.

役 *Sen-eki* war.

殁 *Sembotsu* die in batt e.

爭 *Sensō* war.

況 *Senkyō* the progress of a battle.

後 *Sengo* after-war.

略 *Senryaku* strategy.

國 *Sengoku* a country disturbed by civil war.

國爭奪 *Sengoku-sōdatsu* taking and losing territory by the different parties in a country at civil war.

捷 *Senshō* victory.

術 *Senjutsu* tactics.

備 *Sembi* war preparations.

勝 *Senshō* victory.

塲 *Senjō* battle-field.

報 *Sempō* war intelligence; report of the situation of a war.

慄 *Senritsu* trembling with fear.

亂 *Senran* wars; disturbances.

端 *Sentan* hostilities.

機 *Senki* time for battle; opportunity for a battle.

線 *Sensen* line of battle.

蹟 *Senseki* an old battle-field.

艦 *Senkan* battle-ship.

鬪 *Sentō* battle; campaign.

(一二)

戲 GI; GE. *Tawamu*(*reru*) to play: *tawa*(*keru*) to play the fool.

作 *Gesaku* composition or novel written for amusement. →62, 11 T : 62, 12

曲 *Gikyoku* drama.

樂 *Gigaku* vulgar music.

談 *Jōdan* joke.

一三

戴 TAI; DAI to sustain. *Itada*(*ku*) to put on the head; receive respectfully.

戶

六三

Always at the top and left, and is called *To-gashira*.

戶 KO aux. num. for counting houses; family. *To* door: *he* house.

→ **戶** T

口 *Kokō* number of houses.

外 *Kogai* open air.

主 *Koshu* the head of a family.

每 *Kogoto* every house.

（四）

戸

棚　*Todana* cupboard.

緔　*Tojimari* locking a door.

* 籍　*Koseki* registration; census.

四　所　SHO; SO. *Tokoro; toko*
place; thing (abstract).
Often used as bottom com-
ponent, e.g.: *jimusho* one's
place of business, *kinjo*
neighbourhood, *yakusho*
→所 T public office. →1, 6

々　*Tokoro-dokoro; sho-sho*
here and there.

用　*Shoyō* business; engagement.

以　*Yuen* reason; cause.

在　*Shozai* whereabouts.

在無　*Shozainai* tedious;
wearisome.

在地　*Shozaichi* seat; the
place where a building is.

行　*Shogyō* conduct; action.

存　*Shozon* opinion; one's
idea; view.

有　*Shoyū* possession.

作　*Shosa* conduct; behaviour.

見　*Shoken* one's view.

定　*Shotei* fixed; determined.

信　*Shoshin* belief; opinion.

持　*Shoji* possession.

持品　*Shojihin* thing in one's
possession.

望　*Shomō* hope; desire.

勞　*Shorō* illness; fatigue.

帶　*Shotai* property; housekeeping.

* T 戻 →63,4

得　*Shotoku* income.

爲　*Shoi* conduct; doings; an
act.

期　*Shoki* expectation.

詮　*Shosen* by any means:
after all; in the end.

業　*Shogyō* action; conduct.

感　*Shokan* impression.

管　*Shokan* jurisdiction.

謂　*Iwayuru* (inverted order)
the so-called.

轄　*Shokatsu* jurisdiction.

藏　*Shozō* to treasure up.

屬　*Shozoku* belonging to.

T 肩
【肉】　KEN. *Kata* shoulder.

身　*Katami* one's condition.

書　*Katagaki* the rank or title
of a person.

掛　*Katakake* a shawl.

章　*Kenshō* a shoulder-strap;
an epaulet.

揚　*Kataage* a tuck at the
shoulder.

房　BŌ room; house. *Fusa*
tassel.　→房 T

州　*Bōshū* another name for
the province of *Awa*.

總　*Bōsō* provinces of *Awa*,
Kazusa and *Shimōsa*.

戻　REI. *Modo(ru); modo(su)*
to return: *moto(ru)* to
oppose.　→63, 3 T *

扁　HEN low. *Hiratai* flat.

五

（五）平 *Hempei* flatness.

六 扇 SEN. *Ōgi* fan (folding): *ao(gu)* to fan. → 扇 T

子 *Sensu* fan (folding).

形 *Senkei*; *ōgigata* fan-shaped.

風機 *Sempūki* an electric fan.

七 屇 KO to follow.

從 *Kojū* attendant on a noble.

八 雇 T KO. *Yato(u)* to hire; employ. 【傭】

入 *Yatoiire* employment.

人 *Yatoinin* an employee.

傭 *Koyō* employment.

扉 HI. *Tobira* leaf (of a gate); title-page (of a book).

六四 手

When at the left it takes the modified form 扌 and is called *Te-hen.*

T 手 SHU. *Te* hand; arm; handle; side; person; party; group. As second component, the person who performs an action, e.g. 買手 *kaite* buyer, 砲手 *hōshu* gunner.

入 *Teire* care; attendance; repair.

下 *Teshita* the persons under one's direction.

巾 *Hankechi* a handkerchief.

水 *Chōzu* washing (oneself).

引 *Tebiki* guidance; introduction; a guide.

切 *Tegire* severing of relations.

分 *Tewake* division of work; forming into parties.

心 *Tegokoro* discretion; consideration; allowance.

加減 *Tekagen* discretion; allowance.

古擦 *Tekozu(ru)* to be embarrassed.

本 *Tehon* example; model.

早 *Tebayai* quick (of motion made by hand).

向 *Temukai* resistance; opposition: *tamuke* an offering; tribute (before an idol or at a grave).

込 *Tegome* doing or taking by force.

先 *Tesaki* the hand; an agent.

交 *Shukō* to hand over; deliver.

形 *Tegata* a bill; note; draft.

助 *Tedasuke* help; aid.

金 *Tekin* earnest-money.

附金 *Tetsukekin* earnest-money.

放 *Tebana(su)* to let go: leave unlooked after.

近 *Tejika* close by; near at hand.

手
並　*Tenami* skill.

始　*Tehajime* the outset.

首　*Tekubi* wrist.

前　*Temae* front; I; you (to one's inferiors).

前勝手　*Temae-gatte* selfishness; waywardness.

厚　*Teatsui* hospitable; careful.

持不沙汰　*Temochi-busata* feeling awkward.

拭　*Tenugui* towel.

柄　*Tegara* exploit.

段　*Shudan* means; way.

書　*Shusho* autograph.

袋　*Tebukuro* gloves.

紙　*Tegami* letter.

記　*Shuki* note-book; memorandum.

配　*Tekubari* arrangement; preparation.

術　*Shujutsu; shijutsu* surgical operation.

探　*Tesaguri* groping.

帳　*Techō* a note-book.

脱　*Tenukari* omission; slip.

眞似　*Temane* gesture.

頃　*Tegoro* of convenient size; handy.

短　*Temijika* brief; concise.

落　*Teochi* omission; slip.

筈　*Tehazu* order; arrangement.

間　*Tema* time spent in doing work; work.

腕　*Shuwan* ability.

順　*Tejun* the order; method of doing or proceeding.

當　*Teate* management; thing needed; treatment; allowance: *teatari* thing within one's reach.

傳　*Tetsudai* help; aid.

隙　*Tesuki* leisure; spare time.

輕　*Tegaru* easy; simple.

酷　*Tehidoi* severe; violent.

管　*Tekuda* to trick; deceive.

蔓　*Tezuru* means; medium.

違　*Techigai* mistake; blunder.

際　*Tegiwa* skill; workmanship.

練　*Shuren* skill acquired by practice.

數　*Tesū; tekazu* work; time spent in doing work; trouble.

數料　*Tesūryō* commission.

應　*Tegotae* rebound; response; reaction; resistance.

續　*Tetsuzuki* procedure.

打 [T] DA; CHŌ. *U(tsu); bu(tsu)* [二] to strike; beat: *u(tsu)* send (a telegraphic message): as top character often not translated, e.g. *uchi-suzu* to pass through, *uchi-sorou* to be complete: *dāsu* dozen.

出　*Uchida(su)* to discharge (a gun): *uchidashi* closing time.

合　*Uchiawase* previous arrangements.

明 *Uchia(keru)* to reveal; confess; disclose.

消 *Uchike(su)* to deny.

笑 *Uchiwara(u)* to laugh.

乘 *Uchino(ru)* to jump or vault on to.

破 *Uchiyabu(ru)* to defeat.

連 *Uchitsu(reru)* to take along with.

捨 *Uchisu(teru)* to leave; to neglect.

撲傷 *Dabokushō* bruise; contusion.

解 *Uchito(keru)* to be frank.

電 *Daden* to telegraph.

算 *Dasan* calculation; reckoning.

擊 *Dageki* a blow.

擲 *Chōchaku* to strike.

*1

三 扛 Kō. *A(geru)* to raise.

扣 Kō to knock. *Hika(h)eru* to put down; make a note of; refrain; withdraw. Sometimes used as abb. of 控 64,8.

扞 KAN to go against.

格 *Kankaku* discord; difference.

扨 *Sate* (continuative particle) well; now.

又 *Sate mata* again.

托 TAKU to entrust to; commit to the care of. Sometimes used for 託 149,3.

邦 See 163,4.

扛 See 枉 75,4.

折 SETSU. *O(ru)*; *o(reru)* to break; bend; fold: *ori* occasion.

々 *Ori-ori* sometimes; occasionally.

目 *Orime* a crease; manners.

合 *Oriai* the terms; mutual relation; compromise.

角 *Sekkaku* with much trouble.

返 *Orikaeshi* by return (of post).

柄 *Orikara* just at that time.

衷 *Setchū* compromise; the middle course.

節 *Orifushi* sometimes.

衝 *Sesshō* diplomatic negotiation.

檻 *Sekkan* chastisement.

抑 YOKU. *Osa(h)eru* to restrain; stop; govern: *somosomo* an introductory word, now; well.

々 *Somo-somo* now; well.

制 *Yokusei* to control; govern; restrain.

留 *Yokuryū* detention.

揚 *Yokuyō* intonation; modulation.

壓 *Yokuatsu* repression; restraint.

抒 JO. *No(beru)* to relate.

*1 T 払→64,5

207

*2 T 扱→64,4

抒
情詩 *Jojōshi* lyric.

T抄 SHŌ to jot down; to copy; to take; extract. *Suku(u)* to scoop up.

出 *Shōshutsu* to extract.

本 *Shōhon* an extract.

記 *Shōki* to copy; extract.

錄 *Shōroku* to copy; extract.

譯 *Shōyaku* summarized translation.

扮 FUN to adorn; assume a part; dress up; grasp.

裝 *Funsō* to dress up; disguise; play the part of.

扚 See **T拘** 64,5.

T択 See **擇** 64,13.

抓 SŌ. *Tsuma(mu)* to pick up with the fingers.

T扶 FU to protect. *Tasu(keru)* to assist; help.

助 *Fujo* aid; assistance.

植 *Fushoku* implantation.

養 *Fuyō* maintenance; support.

T技 GI expertness. *Waza* art; skill.

手 *Gishu* inferior technical official; assistant-engineer.

巧 *Gikō* technics; art.

倆 *Giryō* ability.

師 *Gishi* official charged with technical affairs; engineer.

能 *Ginō* ability.

術 *Gijutsu* handicraft.

藝 *Gigei* arts; mechanical arts; manual work; handicraft.

T投 TŌ to send (as letter); put up at an inn. *Na-(geru); hō(ru)* to throw.

下 *Tōka* throw; drop.

手 *Tōshu* a pitcher (baseball).

合 *Tōgō* agreement.

込 *Nageko(mu)* to throw into.

身 *Tōshin; minage* (inv. order) drowning oneself.

函 *Tōkan* to post (a letter).

書 *Tōsho* a contribution.

宿 *Tōshuku* to lodge; put up at.

票 *Tōhyō* to vote; ballot.

棄 *Nagesu(teru); tōki suru* to throw away; cast away.

資 *Tōshi* investment.

獄 *Tōgoku* to put in prison.

稿 *Tōkō* contribution to a magazine.

賣 *Nageuri* selling at a loss.

機 *Tōki* speculation; venture.

錨 *Tōbyō* cast anchor.

藥 *Tōyaku* medical prescription.

扱 *Atsuka(u)* to manage; handle; transact; treat: *shigo(ku)* to draw through the hand. →64,3 * ¹T

208

（四）

T 批 HI criticism; to strike; to push; to show.

判 *Hihan* criticism.

准 *Hijun* ratification.

評 *Hihyō* criticism.

難 *Hinan* criticism; censure.

扼 YAKU to crush; defeat; to catch hold of.

腕 *Yakuwan* roll up the sleeves.

把 HA. *To(ru)* to take in the hand; to grasp: *ha*; *wa* bundle; bunch.

手 *Totte*; *handoru* a handle.

持 *Haji suru* to take hold of; grasp.

T 抗 KŌ to resist; to confront; to revolt; to raise.

爭 *Kōsō* to resist; to argue.

論 *Kōron* an argument; dispute.

戰 *Kōsen* to accept a challenge.

辯 *Kōben* dispute; protest.

議 *Kōgi* a protest.

抔 HŌ to scoop up. *Nado* such as; etc.

*1 扵 See 於 70,4. *2

五 T 担 TAN to lift; raise; to drive away. *Pikoru* picul. See Introduction 44. Sometimes used as abb. of 擔 64,1?.

任 *Tannin* in charge of.

*1 T 拔 →64,5　　*2 T 拜 →64,5

（五）

拉 RATSU to seize.

丁 *Raten* Latin.

甸 *Raten* Latin.

致 *Ratchi* to arrest.

T 拒 KYO. *Koba(mu)*; *fuse(gu)* to ward off; reject.

止 *Kyoshi* to ward off; repel.

否 *Kyohi* refusal.

絕 *Kyozetsu* refusal; protest.

T 拙 SETSU I; my; ignorant. *Tsutanai*; *mazui* unskilful.

劣 *Setsuretsu* clumsy; unskilful.

者 *Sessha* I; my.

速 *Sessoku* unskilful but quick.

策 *Sessaku* poor plan.

T 拓 TAKU. *Hira(ku)* to clear; open; break up.

殖 *Takushoku* colonization.

T 招 SHŌ. *Mane(ku)* to bring upon oneself; invite.

待 *Shōdai* invitation.

魂祭 *Shōkonsai* a memorial service for those who died in battle.

聘 *Shōhei* engagement

T 拍 HAKU; HYŌ (musical) time. *U(tsu)* to beat; strike: *kashiwa* clapping.

子 *Hyōshi* (musical) time; chance.

手 *Hakushu* clapping hands.

拍

手喝采 *Hakushukassai* applause.

車 *Hakusha* spur.

T抽 CHŪ. *Hi(ku)* to pull; draw: *nu(ku)* to extract: *nukin(deru)* to excel.

斗 *Hikidashi* a drawer.

出 *Hikida(su); chūshutsu suru* to draw; pull out: *hikidashi* a drawer.

象 *Chūshō* abstraction.

籤 *Chūsen* a lottery.

拆 SEKI; TAKU. *Hira(ku)* to open.

T押 Ō. *O(su)* to push: *osa-(h)eru)* to catch hold of; take possession of. Often not translated, but has a meaning of doing things by force.

入 *Oshiire* a closet: *oshiiru* to break into.

立 *Oshita(teru)* hoist; set up.

收 *Ōshū* confiscation.

寄 *Oshiyo(seru)* to march against; press.

問答 *Oshi-mondō* repeated questions and answers.

領 *Ōryō* usurpation.

賣 *Oshiuri* pressing a person to buy.

抦 See T柄 75,5.

T拘 KŌ to seize; arrest. *Kakawa(ru)* to concern. →64,4

引 *Kōin* to arrest; take into custody.

束 *Kōsoku* to bind; restrain; confine.

泥 *Kōdei* to adhere to; cling to (the letter, formality, etc.).

留 *Kōryū* detention; confinement.

禁 *Kōkin* confinement (by force).

拂 FUTSU. *Hara(u)* to pay; clear away. →64,2T * 1

下 *Haraisage* sale of government property.

込 *Haraikomi* payment.

底 *Futtei* scarcity; deficiency.

戻 *Haraimodoshi* repayment.

渡 *Haraiwatashi* payment.

曉 *Futsugyō; fuggyō* the dawn.

拗 YŌ; Ō. *Neji(ru)* to twist: *neji(keru)* to be perverse, crooked: *sune(-ru)* to sulk; be cynical.

拐 KAI to deceive. *Kadowaka-(su)* to abduct.

帶 *Kaitai* to abscond with.

拇 BO. *Oya-yubi* the thumb.

指 *Boshi* thumb.

抹 MATSU; BATSU to strike; rub; to erase; to anoint.

殺 *Massatsu* (of writing) to erase; obliterate.

拔 BATSU to supersede. *Nu-(ku)* to pull out. →64,4 * 1T

目 *Nukeme* careless mistake; fault.

差 *Nukisashi* taking out and putting in.

萃 *Bassui* extract; selection.

群 *Batsugun* pre-eminent; surpassing.

劍 *Bakken* to draw a sword.

錨 *Bats byō* weighing anchor.

擢 *Batteki* to single out; select.

披 HI. *Hira(ku)* to open.

見 *Hiken* to open and read (correspondence).

露 *Hirō* announcement.

瀝 *Hireki* to express.

拠 See 據 64,13.

抵 TEI to reach. *Ata(ru)* to strike against; resist.

抗 *Teikō* resistance.

當 *Teitō; kata* security; mortgage.

觸 *Teishoku* conflict.

抱 HŌ. *Ida(ku); da(ku); kaka(h)eru* to embrace; clasp; hold in the arms; engage; have in the mind.

→抱

負 *Hōfu* aspiration; ambition.

腹絕倒 *Hōfukuzettō* convulsed with laughter.

懷 *Hōkai* have; hold.

拋 HŌ. *Nageu(tsu); na(geru)* to give up; discard; throw away.

棄 *Hōki* to abandon; throw away.

擲 *Hōteki* to abandon; throw away.

拜 HAI. *Oga(mu)* to worship; pray; pay respects.
→64,4 * ²T

見 *Haiken* to look; see (polite in first person).

命 *Haimei* to be appointed to office.

承 *Haishō* to take note of (what you say in your letter), (polite).

受 *Haiju* to receive (polite).

具 *Haigu* polite way of ending letter; yours respectfully.

金 *Haikin* the worship of money.

眉 *Haibi* seeing or meeting with.

啓 *Haikei* a polite way of beginning a letter (lit. I adoringly inform you); Dear Sir (Madam).

借 *Haishaku* borrowing (from the second person).

復 *Haifuku* a polite way of beginning a letter in reply; with thanks for your letter.

殿 *Haiden* hall for worship in front of a shrine.

察 *Haisatsu* to conjecture (polite).

誦 *Haishō* read with respect.

領 *Hairyō* receive (from a superior).

謁 *Haietsu* an audience.

趨 *Haisū* pay a visit to.

拜
顏　*Haigan* having the honour of seeing a person.

讀　*Haidoku* to read (polite).

聽　*Haichō* listen to.

觀　*Haikan* having the honour of seeing.

六　掛　KEI. *Ka(keru)* to hang.

冠　*Keikan* resignation.

T 拾　JŪ ten: SHŪ. *Hiro(u)* to pick up.

得　*Shūtoku* to pick up; find.

拮　KITSU to work.

据　*Kikkyo* to labour diligently.

抗　*Kikkō* rivalry.

T 括　KATSU. *Kuku(ru)* to bind; tie.

弧　*Kakko* parenthesis; brackets.

搭　KAKU to strike; to fight.

鬪　*Kakutō* hand-to-hand fighting.

T 指　SHI. *Yubi* finger: *sa(su)* to point at.

名　*Shimei* nomination.

呼　*Shiko* to point at.

定　*Shitei* to designate.

南　*Shinan* instruction; teaching.

* T 拡 →64, 15

紋　*Shimon* finger-print.

針　*Shishin* an index; a guide.

揮　*Shiki* command; order.

圖　*Sashizu* directions; commands.

摘　*Shiteki* pointing out.

嗾　*Shisō* to entice; incite.

彈　*Shidan* to fillip; disdain.

導　*Shidō* guidance; leading.

環　*Yubiwa* a ring.

拵　*Ko(hira(h)eru)* to make.

T 持　JI. *Mo(tsu)* to have; hold; keep; take in the hands.

久　*Jikyū* to hold out; endure.

分　*Mochibun* share.

主　*Mochinushi* owner; proprietor.

出　*Mochi-da(su)* to carry away.

行　*Mochi-yu(ku)* to take; carry.

合　*Mochi-awase* things on hand; ready money: *mochiai* mutual help; keeping prices steady.

前　*Mochimae* nature; quality; share.

病　*Jibyō* chronic disease.

參　*Jisan* to carry; take with one.

論　*Jiron* a cherished opinion.

藥　*Jiyaku* one's usual medicine.

續　*Jizoku* to maintain; endure; hold out; keep up.

（六）

T 拷 GŌ to torture : KŌ. *U(tsu)* to beat : *tada(su)* to investigate.

問 *Gōmon* to torture.

拭 SHIKI ; SHOKU. *Nugu(u)* ; *fu(ku)* to wipe.

T 挑 CHŌ. *Ido(mu)* to challenge; defy.

發 *Chōhatsu* provocation.

戰 *Chōsen* challenge; defiance.

拱 KYŌ. *Komanu(ku)* to fold the arms.

手 *Kyōshu* folded arms.

按 AN to consider; to restrain; to investigate; to massage.

摩 *Amma* shampoo; massage.

拳 KEN ; GEN to strike. *Kobushi* the fist.

々 *Kenken* carefully; respectfully.

固 *Genko* fist.

骨 *Genkotsu* fist; fisticuffs.

銃 *Pisutoru; kenjū* pistol; revolver.

鬭 *Kentō* boxing.

七 捏 See 捏 64 9.

挫 ZA. *Kuji(ku)* to sprain; destroy : *o(ru)* to break.

折 *Zasetsu* breakdown.

傷 *Zashō* contusion.

（七）

挿 See 插 64,9.

捌 HATSU ; HACHI to divide; to sell. *Saba(ku)* to unravel; decide: *ha(keru)* to flow; be in demand.

捐 EN to throw away; give up.

金 *Enkin* contribution (money).

T 捕 HO. *Tora(h)eru)* ; *to(ru)* to catch ; seize ; arrest.

捉 *Hosoku* seizure.

虜 *Horyo* prisoner of war; captive.

縛 *Hobaku* arrest; apprehension.

獲 *Hokaku* capture; seizure.

捗 CHOKU. *Hakado(ru)* to progress: *haka* progress.

取 *Hakado(ru)* to progress.

挾 KYŌ. *Hasa(mu)* : *sashihasa(mu)* to hold between two objects.

擊 *Kyōgeki; hasamiuchi* a double attack.

挨拶 *Aisatsu* salutation; greeting.

挾車 *Sakusha* a kind of wheelbarrow.

T 振 SHIN. *Fu(ru)* to shake : *furu(u)* to become active; shake: *furi* appearance.

方 *Furikata* plan for future.

向 *Furimu(ku)* to turn; turn one's face.

213

（七）

振

起 *Shinki* to stimulate; encourage.

動 *Shindō* shaking; vibration.

舞 *Furumai* behaviour.

與 *Shinkō* rouse; encourage; promote.

捉 SOKU. *Tora(h)eru*); *tsukamae(-ru)* to arrest; seize and bind.

挺 CHŌ aux. num. for guns, etc.: TEI. *Nu(ku)* to pull out: *nukin(deru)* to supersede: *teko* a lever.

子 *Teko* a lever.

身 *Teishin* to go ahead of others.

挽 BAN. *Hi(ku)* to pull; lead.

* 回 *Bankai* recovery; revival.

八
T 控 KŌ appeal. *Hika(h)eru*) to restrain; withdraw; jot down.

目 *Hikaeme* moderation.

除 *Kōjo* deduction.

訴 *Kōso* appeal (court of justice .

T 推 SUI; TAI. *O(su)* to push; press; guess; infer; recommend.

考 *Suikō* inference.

知 *Suichi* inference.

定 *Suitei* inference.

理 *Suiri* reasoning; inference.

參 *Suisan* to call; pay a visit.

* T 搜 →64, 10

移 *Suii* transition.

量 *Suiryō* to guess; surmise.

測 *Suisoku* conjecture.

進 *Suishin* push; propulsion.

敲 *Suikō* polish (of composition).

獎 *Suishō* recommendation.

察 *Suisatsu* to conjecture; surmise.

論 *Suiron* reasoning; ratiocination.

薦 *Suisen* recommendation; nomination.

舉 *Suikyo* recommendation.

T 掘 KUTSU. *Ho(ru)* to dig.

出物 *Horidashimono* a find; a catch.

拔 *Horinuki* an artesian well.

割 *Horiwari* canal.

T 据 KYO to rely on. *Su(eru)* to place.

置 *Sueo(ku)* to leave intact.

捨 SHA. *Su(teru)* to throw away. →捨 T

值 *Sutene* a sacrifice price.

鉢 *Sutebachi* self-abandonment.

臺詞 *Sutezerifu* parting remark.

獎 *Suishō* recommendation; promotion.

賣 *Suteuri* selling at a sacrifice.

（八）

214

（八）

措 SEKI; SO to throw away. O(ku) to put; confer.

置 Sochi management.

辭 Soji wording.

掛 Kaka(ru); ka(keru) to hang; cost; spend: kakari one who is in charge of certain work; one's duty; one's allotted work.

引 Kakehiki bargaining; transaction; tactics.

合 Kakariai implication: kakeai conference; negotiation.

金 Kakekin instalment; money due for goods sold on credit: kakegane a ring and staple.

持 Kakemochi have business in two or more places.

值 Kakene overcharge; price asked over the true one.

替 Kakegae substitute; spare thing.

賣 Kakeuri sale on credit.

聲 Kakegoe call; shout of encouragement.

掉 TŌ; CHŌ. Furu(u) to shake (as a tail); flap.

尾 Tōbi last; end.

捧 HŌ. Sasa(geru) to present to a superior; offer.

呈 Hōtei presentation.

腹絶倒 Hōfukuzettō be convulsed with laughter.

讀 Hōdoku read respectfully.

（八）

排 HAI to cause to retire; reject; to place in a row; to open; anti-.

日 Hainichi anti-Japanism.

水 Haisui draining.

斥 Haiseki to expel; exclude.

外 Haigai anti-foreign.

他 Haita exclusion.

出 Haishutsu exhaustion; transpiration.

列 Hairetsu disposition.

泄 Haisetsu purging.

除 Haijo exclusion.

貨 Haika boycott.

掃 SŌ. Ha(ku); hara(u) to sweep; clean; dust.

除 Sōji cleaning; sweeping.

溜 Hakidame a rubbish heap.

蕩 Sōtō to sweep away.

掏 TŌ. Su(ru) to steal.

摸 Suri a pickpocket.

掬 KIKU. Suku(u); musu(bu) to scoop up: ku(mu) to scoop up; sympathize.

捩 REI. Neji(ru); moji(ru); yo(ru) to wrench.

採 SAI. To(ru) to take; choose.　→採 T

用 Saiyō adoption.

光 Saikō illumination; lighting.

否 Saihi adoption or rejection.

決 Saiketsu decision; to decide by vote.

215

（八）

探掘 *Saikutsu* mining.

集 *Saishū* to collect; pick up; choose.

點 *Saiten* marking; giving marks.

鑛 *Saikō* mining.

T 探 TAN. *Sagu(ru)* to grope: *saga(su)* to search for; investigate.

求 *Tankyū* to seek; search for.

究 *Tankyū* to search for; investigate.

知 *Tanchi* to detect; find out by inquiry.

查 *Tansa* secret inquiry; investigation.

索 *Tansaku* to search.

海燈 *Tankaitō* a search-light.

訪 *Tambō* private enquiry.

偵 *Tantei* secret enquiry; detective; spy.

聞 *Tambun* ascertain.

險 *Tanken* expedition; exploration.

檢 *Tanken* expedition; exploration.

掟 JŌ. *Okite* law; rule.

捷 SHŌ near. *Ka(tsu)* to conquer: *hayai* quick; fast.

徑 *Shōkei* a short cut.

報 *Shohō* news of a victory.

路 *Shōro* a short cut.

（八）

T 授 JU. *Sazu(keru)* to give; grant; impart; bestow.

業 *Jugyō* lessons; teaching.

與 *Juyo* to give; hand over.

掖 EKI to ho'd under the arm; to assist. *Waki* the side.

捲 KEN. *Maku(ru)*; *ma(ku)* to roll up.

掩 EN. *Ō(u)* to cover; shade.

蔽 *Empei* to cover; conceal; envelop.

護 *Engo* to cover; protect.

掠 RYAKU. *Kasu(meru)* to take; rob.

奪 *Ryakudatsu* to take by force; rob; plunder.

捺 NATSU. *O(su)* to press; print.

印 *Natsuin* a seal affixed to a document.

捻 NEN; JŌ. *Hine(ru)* to twist; pinch.

出 *Nenshutsu* think out; squeeze out.

T 接 SETSU to be in contact with; associate with. *Tsu(gu)* to join; continue.

目 *Tsugime* a joint; seam.

合 *Setsugō* union; connection.

伴 *Seppan* reception; entertaining.

吻 *Seppun* a kiss.

近 *Sekkin* approach; drawing near; contiguity.

216

待 *Settai* reception; entertaining.

戰 *Sessen* hand-to-hand fight.

觸 *Sesshoku* contact; junction.

續 *Setsuzoku* joining; connection.

T 掌 SHŌ controller. *Tanagokoro* palm of the hand: *tsukasado(ru)* to control.

中 *Shōchū* within one's grasp.

握 *Shōaku* grasping.

掣 SEI to pull back; to stop.

木 肘 *Seichū* restraint.

九 揑 NETSU; DETSU to falsify. *Kone(-ru); detchi(-ru)* (coll.) to knead.

造 *Netsuzō* to forge; invent; fabricate.

T 握 AKU. *Nigi(ru)* to grasp.

手 *Akushu* handshake.

潰 *Nigiritsubu(su)* to crush in the hand; abandon consideration of (plan, etc.).

插 SŌ. *Sa(su)* to clasp: *sashihasa(mu)* to insert.

入 *Sō-nyū* insertion.

繪 *Sashie* illustration (in a book).

T 描 BYŌ. *Ega(ku)* to draw; describe; copy.

寫 *Byōsha* to draw; describe.

揶 YA. *Karaka(u)* to mock; tease; banter.

揄 *Yayu* to banter; tease.

T 揮 KI to scatter. *Furu(u)* to shake; wield; sway.

毫 *Kigō* writing; drawing.

發 *Kihatsu* evaporate.

發油 *Kihatsuyu* gasoline.

揖 SHŪ; YŪ folding the arms; salutation.

揃 *Soro(u)* to be equal; matched; complete: *sorotte* all together; without exception: *soro(h)eru* to put in order.

揣 SHI; SUI. *Haka(ru)* to conjecture.

摩 *Shima* to conjecture; guess.

揭 KEI. *Kaka(geru)* to put up; hoist. →64,8 T *

示 *Keiji* a notice; placard.

載 *Keisai* to insert; publish.

T 揚 YŌ to praise. *A(geru)*; *aga(ru)* to hoist; raise; rise.

々 *Yōyō* loftily; in a vainglorious manner.

句 *Ageku* after; upon; at the end.

子江 *Yōsukō* Yangtze River.

言 *Yōgen* to shout out; proclaim.

T 換 KAN. *Ka(h)eru* to exchange; change; as 2nd component it generally means the repetition of an action with a certain change.

217 * 揭→64,9

（九）

換
言 *Kangen sureba* in other words.

氣 *Kanki* ventilation.

骨奪胎 *Kankotsudattai* adaptation.

算 *Kansan* conversion.

揆 KI category; principle; to plot.

揉 JŪ. *Mo(mu)* to rub; crumple; massage.

消 *Momike(su)* hush up.

T 提 TEI; DAI. *Sa(geru)*; *hissa-(geru)* to carry in the hand.

出 *Teishutsu* presentation; introduction.

灯 *Chōchin* paper lantern.

供 *Teikyō* to offer; tender.

唱 *Teishō* introduction; advocacy.

案 *Teian* proposal.

携 *Teikei* concert; coalition.

督 *Teitoku* a commandant.

議 *Teigi* proposal.

援 EN. *Tasuke* aid; help: *tasu(keru)* to assist; help.

助 *Enjo* assistance; aid. 援 T

兵 *Empei* reinforcements; relieving force.

軍 *Engun* reinforcements; relieving force.

* 護 *Engo* backing; protection.

一〇

搖 YŌ. *Yu(ru)*; *yuru(gu)*; *yurame(ku)*; *yusu(ru)* to shake to and fro.
→64,9 * T

籃 *Yōran* a cradle.

搭 TŌ to strike. *No(seru)* to load.

乘 *Tōjō* to embark.

載 *Tōsai* to load; embark.

T 搾 SAKU. *Shibo(ru)* to squeeze; to milk.

取 *Sakushu* extraction.

搏 HAKU to seize; arrest. *U(tsu)* to strike.

搗 TŌ. *Tsu(ku)*; *ka(teru)* to pound.

T 携 KEI. *Tazusa(h)eru)* to carry in the hand; carry.

帶 *Keitai* to carry with one.

搦 JAKU. *Kara(meru)* to bind; arrest.

手 *Karamete* back-gate.

搜 SŌ. *Saga(su)* to search; investigate; enquire after; to seek; wish for.
→64,7 * T

出 *Sagashida(su)* to find out.

査 *Sōsa* enquiry; search.

索 *Sōsaku* search.

T 搬 HAN to transport.

入 *Han-nyū* to carry in.

T 損 SON loss; harm. *Soķona(u)* to damage; to break. As 2nd component, to fail; mistake; e.g., *shisokona(u)* to fail to do.

失 *Sonshitsu* loss; harm.

所 *Sonsho* an injured part.

（一〇）

（一〇）

盆 *Son-eki* profit and loss.

害 *Songai* damage.

料 *Sonryō* price paid for anything hired; hire.

得 *Sontoku* loss and gain.

耗 *Sommō* loss; damage.

傷 *Sonshō* damage.

搔 SŌ. *Ka(ku)* to scratch.

T 摄 See 攝 64,18.

二 **摧** SAI. *Kuda(ku)* to break; crush.

摺 SHŌ. *Su(ru)* to rub; print: *hida* a pleat.

摑 KAKU. *Tsuka(mu)* to grasp; seize.

合 *Tsukamiai* grapple; fight.

搏 DAN; TAN to roll into a ball; to grasp.

摘 TEKI. *Tsu(mu)* to pick off: *tsuma(mu)* to pinch; pick; pick up. →摘 T

出 *Tekishutsu* to quote; expose; extract.

要 *Tekiyō* summary; abstract.

記 *Tekki* summary; abstract.

發 *Tekihatsu* to disclose; make public.

摸 MO; BO to search for; to copy; to model. This character is sometimes used for 模 75,11 which place see for other compounds. →140, 11

* T 擊 →64, 13

索 *Mosaku* to grope for.

摯 SHI. *To(ru)* to take; to carry to the utmost.
*

撞 DŌ; SHU; TŌ. *Tsu(ku)* to strike.

着 *Dōchaku* contradiction; conflict.

播 HAN; IIA. *Ma(ku)* to spread; sow.

州 *Banshū* another name for the province of *Harima*.

種 *Hanshu* sowing.

磨 *Harima* p. n.

擒 KIN. *Toriko* a captive: *tora(h)eru)* to capture; take prisoner.

T **撲** BOKU. *U(tsu)* to strike; beat.

殺 *Bokusatsu* beating to death.

滅 *Bokumetsu* to destroy; exterminate.

T **撮** SATSU. *To(ru)* to take (a photograph).

影 *Satsuei* photographing.

撥 HATSU to shoot; discharge. *Ha(neru)* to jump; spatter: *bachi* a plectrum.

撒 SAN; SATSU. *Ma(ku)* to scatter; sprinkle.

水 *Sansui* to water (street); to sprinkle.

布 *Sampu* sprinkle; scatter.

T **撤** TETSU to take away; to reject; to exclude; remove.

（一一）

一二

（一二）

撤
去 *Tekkyo* withdrawal.

囘 *Tekkai* withdrawal.

兵 *Teppei* withdrawal of troops.

退 *Tettai* withdrawal.

廢 *Teppai* withdraw; abolish.

撓 Dō; NYŌ. *Tawa(mu); tayu(mu); shina(u)* to bend; to relax.

撰 SEN; SAN. *Era(bu)* to compose; write. Sometimes used instead of 選 162,13 which place see for compounds.

撫 BU to tranquilize; comfort; pity. *Na(deru)* to stroke.

育 *Buiku* to bring up; nurse.

恤 *Bujutsu* to aid; relieve.

撚 NEN. *Yo(ru)* to twist.

一三 擅 SEN. *Hoshiimama ni suru* to act arbitrarily.

T 擁 YŌ to embrace; hold; protect.

護 *Yogo* assistance; protection.

T 擔 TAN. *Nina(u)* to carry on the shoulders; be responsible: *katsu(gu); kata(geru)* to carry on the shoulders.

任 *Tannin* taking charge of.

保 *Tampo* security; guarantee.

架 *Tanka* a stretcher; litter.

當 *Tantō* to take charge of.

（一三）

擂 *Su(ru)* to grind.

擇 TAKU. *Era(bu) yo(ru)* to choose. →64,4T

T 操 SŌ to take. *Misao* chastity; virtue: *ayatsu(ru)* to manipulate; manoeuvre; manage.

行 *Sōkō* behaviour.

典 *Sōten* drill regulations.

舩者 *Sōkosha* a man of letters.

練 *Sōren* drill; practice.

縱 *Sōjū* to manage; manoeuvre.

據 KYO; KO. *Yo(ru)* to rely on: *yotte* on account of: *yondokoro nai* unavoidable. →64,5T

無 *Yondokoro-nai* unavoidable

撻 TATSU. *U(tsu)* to strike: *muchiu(tsu)* to whip; chastise.

撿 KEN to inspect; to bind; to check; to consider. Sometimes used for 檢 75,13 which place see for compounds.

撼 KAN. *Ugoka(su)* to move.

擘 HAKU; HEKI the thumb. *Tsunza('u)* to burst; break; tear apart.

擊 GEKI. *U(tsu)* to beat; strike. →64,11T *

沈 *Gekichin* sending to the bottom; sinking by an attack.

破 *Gekiha; uchiya'u(ru)* to blow up; crush; defeat.

退 *Gekitai* to repulse; repel.

劒 *Gekken* fencing.

一四 撞 TAI. *Mota(geru)* to lift up.

頭 *Taitō* raise the head.

擢 TEKI; TAKU. *Nukin(deru)* to excel: *nu(ku)* to select; pull out.

擠 SEI to overthrow; to entrap.

擱 KAKU cease. *O(ku)* to put.

坐 *Kakuza* run aground.

筆 *Kakuhitsu* leave off writing.

T 擬 GI to compare; estimate. *Nazora(h)eru)* to imitate; model after: *magai* an imitation.

人 *Gijin* to personify.

似 *Giji* false; spurious.

擯 HIN. *Shirizo(keru)* to reject; cause to retire.

斥 *Hinseki* to reject; refuse.

T 擦 SATSU. *Kosu(ru); sasu(ru); su(ru)* to rub; stroke.

擎 RAN to pick up with the fingers; **to take.**

一五 擲 TEKI; CHAKU; JAKU. *Nageu(tsu)* to throw; throw away: *nagu(ru)* to thump; thrash.

擾 JŌ vexatious; to be confused; disturbed.

亂 *Jōran* disturbance; disorder.

擴 KAKU. *Hiro(geru)*: *hiro(meru)* to spread out; widen; extend. →64,5 T

大 *Kakudai* to spread out; widen.

張 *Kakuchō* stretching; enlargement.

攀 HAN. *Yo(jiru)* to climb.

攘 JŌ. *Shirizo(ku)* to reject; expel: *hara(u)* to brush off; drive away. 一七

夷 *Jōi* exclusion of foreigners.

攝 SETSU to help; act for temporarily; pay heed to. 一八 *To(ru)* to take. →64,10 T

生 *Sessei* hygiene.

取 *Sesshu* to take.

津 *Settsu* p. n.

政 *Sesshō* Regent.

理 *Setsuri* to superintend; control; law.

攫 KAKU. *Tsuka(mu)* to grasp; to seize: *sara(u)* to kidnap; carry off. 二〇

浚 *Kassarai* a robber.

攪 KAKU; KŌ. *Kaki-mawa(su); mid (su)* to stir; stir into confusion.

拌 *Kakuhan* stir; beat.

亂 *Kakuran* to disturb; throw into confusion.

(二〇)

攬
擾　*Kakujō* to disturb; throw into confusion.

二一　攬　RAN to take up in the fingers; hold.

六五　支

T支　SHI branch; to branch off. *Sasa(h)eru)* to support; hold: *tsɪka(h)eru)* to be obstructed.

出　*Shishutsu* expenditure.

那　*Shɪna* China.

店　*Shiten* a branch (shop, office).

持　*Shiji* to maintain; preserve intact.

拂　*Shiharai* payment.

度　*Shitaku* preparation.

柱　*Shichū* a support.

配　*Shihai* government; management.

配人　*Shihainin* manager.

流　*Shiryū* branch stream.

部　*Shibu* branch; department (as of an office).

給　*Shikyū* provision; supply.

障　*Shishō* obstruction; hitch.

隊　*Shitai* a detachment (of troops).

線　*Shisen* branch line.

辨　*Shiben* to pay out.

離滅裂　*Shiri-metsuretsu* incoherence.

翅【羽】　SHI. *Tsubasa; hane* wings.　六

T敍　See 66,7.　七

攲　KI. *Sobada(teru)* to turn; to listen.　八

T鼓　See 207,0.　九

六六　支

Generally at the right in the modified form 攵

收　SHŪ to take; receive; seize. *Osa(meru)* to reap; obtain; pay in (as taxes). →29,2T　二

入　*Shūnyū* income; receipts.

支　*Shūshi* receipts and disbursements.

容　*Shūyō* to take in.

拾　*Shūshū* to adjust; arrange.

益　*Shūeki* profit; earnings.

納　*Shūnō* receipt; a harvest.

得　*Shūtoku* acquisition.

賄　*Shūwai* corrupt practices.

監　*Shūkan* put in jail.

縮　*Shūshuku* contraction.

穫　*Shūkaku* harvest; crop.

五 政　SEI; SHŌ. *Matsurigoto*
T　government; administra-
tion; politics. (*Masa*).

友會　*Seiyūkai* a certain political party.

見　*Seiken* political view.

爭　*Seisō* party politics.

治　*Seiji* politics; government.

府　*Seifu* government.

況　*Seikyō* political outlook.

界　*Seikai* the political world.

略　*Seiryaku* policy.

務　*Seimu* administration;
government affairs.

策　*Seisaku* policy.

綱　*Seikō* a policy; a platform.

論　*Seiron* political arguments;
politics.

談　*Seidan* political talk; dis-
cussions on politics.

敵　*Seiteki* political opponent.

黨　*Seitō* a political party.

權　*Seiken* political power.

體　*Seitai* the form of government.

變　*Seihen* a political change.

T 故　KO old; deceased; late.
Yue reason; because: *moto*
origin; cause: *kotosara* on
purpose.

人　*Kojin* a deceased person.

里　*Furusato* native place.

事　*Koji* old tradition; origin.

國　*Kokoku* native land.

鄉　*Kokyō* one's native place.

意　*Koi* intention; purpose.

障　*Koshō* defect; difficulty;
objection.

效　See 効 19,6.
T

*
T
教　KYŌ. *Oshie; nori* precept
instruction; doctrine: *oshi-
(h)eru)* to teach.

化　*Kyōka* enlightenment;
culture.

示　*Kyōshi* instructions; guidance.

育　*Kyōiku* education.

官　*Kyōkan* an instructor.

科書　*Kyōkasho* a text-book.

書　*Kyōsho* a message.

訓　*Kyōkun* moral teaching;
instruction; advice.

師　*Kyōshi* a teacher.

唆　*Kyōsa* to incite; instigate.

員　*Kyōin* a teacher.

理　*Kyōri* religious doctrine.

授　*Kyōju* teaching; instruction; a professor.

塲　*Kyōjō* school-room.

會　*Kyōkai* a church; religious
association.

養　*Kyōyō* education; culture.

練　*Kyōren* drill; training.

導　*Kyōdō* moral instruction.

鞭　*Kyōben* teaching.

職　*Kyōshoku* a teacher's position.

（七）敏 BIN. *Satoi* clever; quick. (*Toshi*). →66,6T *

活 *Binkatsu* alertness.

捷 *Binshō*; *hashikoi* sharp; smart; shrewd.

速 *Binsoku* swift.

腕 *Binwan* ability; able.

敕 See 勅 19,7.

T 救 KYŪ. *Suku(u)* to rescue; save; assist.

世軍 *Kyūseigun* the Salvation Army.

助 *Kyūjo* relief; succour.

恤 *Kyūjutsu* relief.

急 *Kyūkyū* temporary; first aid.

済 *Kyūsai* to help; save; relieve.

護 *Kyūgo* relief; protection.

敍 JO to confer rank upon; to enumerate; order; by the way; preface; prologue; introduction. *No-(beru)* to relate. →29,7

任 *Jonin* appointment.

述 *Jojutsu* to state in writing; relate; tell.

景 *Jokei* description of scenery.

勳 *Jokun* decoration.

敘 See preced.

（八）敢 KAN to be bold; adventurous. *Aete* daringly; boldly; positively: *aenai* pitiful.

行 *Kankō* to dare to do.

然 *Kanzen* daringly; fearlessly.

爲 *Kan-i* daring.

敦 TON. *Atsui* honest; kind.

厚 *Tonkō* honest; sincere.

圉 *Ikimaku* to be enraged.

賀 *Tsuruga* p. n.

T 散 SAN medicinal powder. *Chi(ru)* to be scattered; to fall (as of leaves): *chiri-(su)*; *chiraka(su)*; *chiraka-(ru)* to scatter; throw about.

々 *Sanzan ni* seriously; severely; in a great degree: *chirijiri* disperse.

文 *Sambun* prose.

布 *Sampu* to scatter.

在 *Sanzai* to lie scattered about.

步 *Sampo* a walk.

兵 *Sampei* skirmisher.

見 *Sanken* found here and there.

財 *Sanzai* squander; be put to expense.

開 *Sankai* extension; skirmishing; deployment.

策 *Sansaku* a walk.

會 *Sankai* adjournment.

亂 *Sanran* dispersion.

漫 *Samman* diffuseness.

髪 *Sampatsu* have one's hair cut.

敝 See 弊 55,12.

鼓 See 207,0.

T 敬 KEI ; KYŌ. *Uyama(u)* to respect ; honour ; to stand in awe of. (*Nori*) ; (*Yoshi*).

白 *Keihaku* polite way of ending letter ; yours respectfully.

具 *Keigu* polite way of ending letter ; yours respectfully.

服 *Keifuku* admire.

神 *Keishin* piety ; reverence.

虔 *Keiken* piety ; devotion.

愛 *Keiai* veneration ; respect and affection.

意 *Keii* respect.

遠 *Keien* keep at a respectful distance.

稱 *Keishō* terms of respect.

語 *Keigo* an honorific expression.

慕 *Keibo* respect and affection.

禮 *Keirei* salutation.

T 数 See 數 66,11.

敵 TEKI to confront. *Kataki* enemy. →敵 T

本主義 *Tekihonshugi* a make-believe.

討 *Katakiuchi* revenge.

情 *Tekijō* the condition of the enemy.

視 *Teki hi* hostility.

意 *Tekii* hostility.

愾心 *Tekigaishin* hostile feeling.

對 *Tekitai* to resist ; oppose.

T 敷 FU. *Shi(ku)* to spread ; to lay ; to put under.

地 *Shikichi* piece of land laid out for some particular purpose ; a site.

金 *Shikikin* money given to a landlord as security for the regular payment of rent.

物 *Shikimono* carpet ; mat.

居 *Shikii* the threshold.

衍 *Fuen* expatiate ; enlarge.

島 *Shikishima* another name for Japan.

設 *Fusetsu* construction.

數 SŪ a small number ; five or six ; several : (when 2nd component, number, e.g. 日數 *nissū* the number of days, but 數日 *sūjitsu* five or six days) : SU. *Kazu* number ; *kazo(h)eru* to count : *shiba-shiba* often. →66,9T

々 *Kazu-kazu* in great numbers.

子 *Kazu-no-ko* dried roe of herring.

名 *Sūmei* several persons.

字 *Sūji* numerals.

（二一）数

多 *Amata; sūta* many.

年 *Sūnen* several years.

行 *Sūgyō* several lines (writing); *sūkō* several streaks (rows).

奇 *Sūki* unhappiness.

度 *Sūdo* several times; frequently.

倍 *Sūbai* several times more.

寄 *Suki* artistic taste.

量 *Sūryō* quantity.

學 *Sūgaku* mathematics.

一三 斂　REN. *Osa(meru)* to collect; gather in.

一四 斃　HEI. *Tao(reru)* to fall; die. →94, 12(=11)

一九 變　See 35,19. 【言】

六七　文

T 文 BUN; MON farthing; old perforated coin of very small value. *Fumi* letter; literary composition: *aya* pattern; figure of speech.

才 *Bunsai* literary ability.

士 *Bunshi* a man of letters.

久 *Bunkyū* era name, 1861-64; name of a coin.

化 *Bunka* culture; era name, 1804-17.

句 *Monku* wording; a phrase; complaint.

名 *Bummei* literary fame.

字 *Monji; moji* character; letter.

言 *Mongon* the contents of a letter.

盲 *Mommō* uneducated; ignorant.

官 *Bunkan* a civil official; the civil service.

明 *Bummei* civilization.

房具 *Bumbōgu* stationery.

武 *Bumbu* civil and military affairs; the pen and sword.

物 *Bumbutsu* culture; learning.

法 *Bumpō* grammar.

相 *Bunshō* the Minister of Education.

書 *Bunsho* document; correspondence.

弱 *Bunjaku* effeminacy arising from exclusive devotion to artistic pursuits.

案 *Bun-an* a rough sketch; a draft.

庫 *Bunko* a box; library.

敎 *Bunkyō* education.

部大臣 *Mombu-daijin* the Minister of Education.

部省 *Mombushō* the Department of Education.

章 *Bunshō* sentence; composition.

通 *Buntsū* communication by letter.

雅 *Bunga* elegance.

筆 *Bumpitsu* literary pursuits; literary composition.

豪 *Bungō* a great writer.

壇 *Bundan* the literary world.

學 *Bungaku* literature ; letters.

學士 *Bungakushi* Master of Arts.

學博士 *Bungakuhakase; bungakuhakushi* Doctor of Literature.

藝 *Bungei* learning and accomplishments; literature and art.

獻 *Bunken* literature.

三 T 対 See 對 41,11.

吝 RIN to grudge. *Kechi* stinginess: *shiwai; yabusaka* miserly. 【口】

嗇 *Rinshoku* stinginess.

孝 See 學 39,13.

四 T 斉 See 齊 210,0.

五 彥 See 8,7. 【彡】

六 紊 BUN; BIN. *Mida(su); mida(reru)* to confuse; be disordered. 【糸】

亂 *Bunran; binran* disorder.

擾 *Bunjō; binjō* confusion; disorder. (六〇)

蚕 See 蚊 142,4.

產 See 8,9. 【生】 七

斎 T See 齋 210,3.

竟 See 覺 147,13.

齋 See 齋 210,7. 二

斗 六八

斗 T To unit of capacity; see Introduction 44. *Bakari* about; only.

斜 T SHA. *Naname; hasu* inclined; slanting; oblique. 七

面 *Shamen* a slope.

視 *Shashi* squint eyes.

線 *Shasen* slanting line.

斟 SHIN to scoop up; select. 九 *Haka(ru)* to estimate.

酌 *Shinshaku* taking into consideration; consideration of circumstances.

斡 See 24,12. 【斗】 一〇

六九 　斤

T 斤 KIN Japanese pound (weight). *Ono; masakari* axe.

量 *Kinryō* weight.

一 T 丘 KYŪ; KU. *Oka* mound.
【一】

陵 *Kyūryō* a hill.

T 斥 See 27,3. 【斤】

三 T 兵 See 12,5.

四 欣 KIN. *Yoroko(bu)* to rejoice.
【欠】

然 *Kinzen* gladly.

慕 *Kimbo* to admire; respect.

T 岳 See 46,5.

七 T 断 See 斷 69,14.

八 斯 SHI. *Kore; kono* this: *kaku* thus; so: *kakaru* such as.

道 *Shidō* the profession; one's speciality.

樣 *Kayō na* such.

九 T 新 SHIN. *Atarashii; ara; nii* new; recent; fresh: *arata ni* newly; afresh.

入 *Shinnyū* new-comer.

手 *Arate* fresh forces; reserves.

古 *Shinko* new and old.

刊 *Shinkan* new publication.

任 *Shinnin* new appointment.

西蘭 *Nyūjiirando* New Zealand.

年 *Shinnen* New Year.

式 *Shinshiki* new style.

奇 *Shinki* novelty.

來 *Shinrai* new-comer.

春 *Shinshun* early spring; new year.

柄 *Shingara* new pattern.

約全書 *Shin-yaku-zensho* the New Testament.

版 *Shimpan* new edition.

郎 *Shinrō* bridegroom.

派 *Shimpa* new school (system).

陳代謝 *Shinchin-taisha* renewal.

参 *Shin-zan* new-comer.

案 *Shin-an* new idea.

設 *Shinsetsu* new establishment.

教 *Shinkyō* Protestantism.

規 *Shinki* new.

婚旅行 *Shinkon-ryokō* honeymoon.

着 *Shinchaku* newly-arrived (goods).

進 *Shinshin* rising.

嘉坡 *Shingapōru* Singapore.

228

（九）

聞 *Shimbun* newspaper.

聞記者 *Shimbun-kisha* journalist.

調 *Shinchō* newly-made.

潟 *Niigata* p. n.

綠 *Shinryoku* fresh verdure.

曆 *Shinreki* new calendar.

橋 *Shimbashi* p. n.

築 *Shinchiku* new building.

選 *Shinsen* new selection; newly-elected.

機軸 *Shinkijiku* new device.

鮮 *Shinsen* new; fresh.

（一四）

斷 DAN to become extinct; cease; break; to decide. *Ta(tsu)* to cut off: *kotowa(ru)* to warn; give notice of; refuse; decline. →69,7T

乎 *Danko* decisive; strict.

片 *Dampen* fragment.

行 *Dankō* carrying out.

決 *Danketsu* to decide; determine.

言 *Dangen* assertion.

定 *Dantei* to decide; determine.

念 *Dannen* to give up a desire; cease to think of.

食 *Danjiki* fasting.

案 *Dan-an* a decision.

崖 *Dangai* precipice.

絕 *Danzetsu* to cut off; intercept; extinction.

然 *Danzen* positively.

腸 *Danchō* heart-rending.

續 *Danzoku* to cease and again continue.

方

（一四）

方 Hō region; to place in a row; to compare; used when giving the dimensions of a square, as 方 四町 *hōshichō* which means a square each side of which is 4 chō long *Kata* side; direction; after a verb, way of doing a thing; person; in or belonging to the house of; related in some way to; a rough indication of time, about, near, as *yoake-gata* at day-break; sign of the plural: *ata(ru)* to correspond: *masa ni* just; exactly; nearly.

々 *Hōbō* everywhere: *katagata* you (plural).

寸 *Hōsun* a mind.

正 *Hōsei* right; correct.

向 *Hōkō* direction; bearings.

式 *Hōshiki* a form; a method; formula; formalities.

里 *Hōri* square *ri.*

言 *Hōgen* dialect.

角 *Hōgaku* direction; quarter.

法 *Hōhō* method; way.

面 *Hōmen* region; direction.

便 *Hōben* expedient.

方
針 *Hōshin* course; aim; policy.

四 放 Hō arbitrariness; wilful-
T ness; as one pleases. *Hana(tsu)* to let go; set free; banish. 【攴】

火 *Hōka* incendiarism.

任 *Hōnin* non-interference.

任主義 *Hōnin-shugi* the laissez-faire principle.

免 *Hōmen* release; acquittal.

言 *Hōgen* random speech.

念 *Hōnen* to feel easy; be at ease.

將 *Hōratsu* profligacy.

恣 *Hōshi* indulgence; licence.

浪 *Hōrō* wander about.

逐 *Hōchiku* expulsion.

資 *Hōshi* investment.

置 *Hōchi* to neglect; leave alone.

棄 *Hōki* abandonment.

課 *Hōka* after school.

蕩 *Hōtō* dissipated; abandoned; dissolute.

擲 *Hōteki* abandonment.

縱 *Hōjū* indulgence; licence.

還 *Hōkan* to release; set free.

題 *Hōdai* at pleasure.

於 O; A. *Oite ; okeru* in; on; at; to.

五 施 SHI practice : SE. *Hodoko-*
T *(su)* to give alms; bestow.

行 *Shikō* to put in force; carry out.

政 *Shisei,* government; administration.

設 *Shisetsu* institution; equipment.

與 *Seyo* charity.

療 *Seryō* gratuitous treatment.

T 旅 RYO. *Tabi* travel; journey.

立 *Tabidachi* start on a journey.

先 *Tabisaki* staying place on one's journey.

行 *Ryokō* travelling.

行記 *Ryokōki* diary of a travel.

券 *Ryoken* a passport.

客 *Ryokaku* passenger; traveller.

宿 *Ryoshuku* an inn.

商人 *Tabi-akindo* travelling merchant.

程 *Ryotei* the distance travelled.

順 *Ryojun* Port Arthur.

路 *Tabiji* journey.

裝 *Ryosō* travelling suit.

費 *Ryohi* travelling expenses.

團 *Ryodan* brigade (military).

館 *Ryokan* inn; hotel.

籠 *Hatago* an inn.

旁 Bō; Hō. *Katawara; soba* side; beside : *katagata* at the same time; while.

七 旌 SEI flag.

旗 *Seiki* flag; standard.

斾 HAI. *Hata* a silken flag.

T 族 ZOKU. *Yakara* family; household; relations; persons; sort; kind.

籍 *Zokuseki* social status and domicile.

T 旋 SEN. *Megu(ru)* to revolve; to return.

回 *Senkai* turn.

風 *Sempū; tsumujikaze* whirlwind.

轉 *Senten* rotation.

九 旒 RYŪ the folds of a flag.

〇T 旗 KI. *Hata* flag.

色 *Hatairo* the tide of war.

亭 *Kitei* a public house; a restaurant.

揚 *Hataage* the levy of troops.

幟 *Kishi* a flag; attitude.

艦 *Kikan* flag-ship.

一四 旛 HAN flag; to wave.

七一 无

*既 →foll = 71,7

既 KI to finish. *Sude ni* already. →71,6 T　七

成 *Kisei* already completed; existing.

決 *Kiketsu* decided.

知 *Kichi* already known.

定 *Kitei* already decided.

往 *Kiō* the past.

記 *Kiki* already stated.

婚 *Kikon* married.

遂 *Kisui* consummated.

蠶 See 142,18.　二〇

日　七二

When at the left it is called *Nichi-hen* or *Hi-hen*.

T 日 NICHI abbreviation of *Nippon* Japan : JITSU. *Hi* sun; day : *ka* day, after simple numbers 2 to 9. (*Kusa*). Do not confound with 曰 73,0.

々 *Hibi; nichi-nichi* day by day.

一日 *Hi-ichi-nichi* day by day.

月 *Jitsugetsu* days and months; time; sun and moon.

中 *Nitchū* midday; daytime.

支 *Nisshi* Japan and China.

出 *Hi-no-de; nisshutsu* sunrise.

日

刊 *Nikkan* daily publication.

用 *Nichiyō* everyday use.

用品 *Nichiyōhin* articles of daily use.

本 *Nihon; Nippon; Hinomoto* (poetical) Japan.

本晴 *Nippombare* ideal weather.

米 *Nichibei* Japan and America.

伊 *Nichii* Japan and Italy.

向 *Hinata* sunshine: *Hyūga* p. n.

光 *Nikkō* sun's rays; sunlight; also p. n.

佛 *Nich'futsu; Niffutsu* Japan and France.

步 *Hibu* daily interest.

沒 *Nichibotsu* sunset.

延 *Hinobe* postponement

和 *Hiyori* weather.

附 *Hizuke* date.

取 *Hidori* date.

夜 *Nichiya* day and night.

英 *Nichiei* Japan and England.

限 *Nichigen* fixed day; date.

記 *Nikki* diary.

掛 *Higake* daily payment.

常 *Nichijō* everyday; ordinary; always.

參 *Nissan* daily visit to a temple or shrine.

頃 *Higoro* for a long time; of late; about that time.

程 *Nittei* the order of the day; program.

給 *Nikkyū* daily wages.

割 *Hiwari* daily rate.

進 *Nisshin* to progress day by day.

進月步 *Nisshin-geppo* rapid progress.

貸 *Higashi* lending by the day.

當 *Hiatari* exposure to the sun: *nittō* daily allowance.

嗣 *Hitsugi* the Imperial succession.

傭 *Hiyō* daily employment.

傭取 *Hiyōtori* to labour by the day; day-labourer.

傭稼 *Hiyōkasegi* working for daily wages.

誌 *Nisshi* diary.

陰 *Hikage* the shade.

增 *Himashi ni* daily.

暮 *Higure* sunset.

課 *Nikka* daily lesson, task.

輪 *Nichirin* the sun.

蝕 *Nisshoku* eclipse of the sun.

獨 *Nichidoku* Japan and Germany.

曜 *Nichiyō* Sunday.

露 *Nichiro* Japan and Russia.

旦 TAN. *Ashita* morning; early in the morning. Do not confound with 且 1,4.

夕 *Tanseki* morning and evening.

（一）

那 *Danna* master; protector; husband.

旧 See 舊 140,14.

T 白 See 106,0.

T 甲 KŌ "first" "A" (in enumeration or classification); shell: KAN. *Yoroi* armour: *kabuto* a helmet: *kinoe* 1st calendar sign. See Introduction 42, 43. 【田】

乙 *Kō-otsu* superiority or inferiority.

州 *Kōshū* another name for the province of Kai.

板 *Kampan* deck.

冑 *Katchū* helmet and armour

斐 *Kai* effect; also p. n.

斐々々 *Kaigaishii* gallant; brisk; faithful.

鐵艦 *Kōtetsukan* ironclad ship.

T 由 YŪ; YU reason. *Yo(ru)* to depend on: *yotte* accordingly; according to; on account of: *yoshi* (epist. st.) I have heard that......; they say that...; to the effect that...... 【田】

來 *Yurai* origin; cause; history.

緒 *Yuisho* lineage; history.

T 申 SHIN. *Mō(su)* (honorific verbal prefix, humble verb) to say: *saru* the 9th zodiacal sign, the monkey. See Introduction 42, 43. 【田】

上 *Mōshia(geru)* (polite; used in 1st person) to say; tell; do.

（二）

分 *Mōshibun* criticism; things that can be said against a defect; one's say.

付 *Mōshitsuke* order; command.

込 *Mōshikomi* application.

立 *Mōshitate* statement.

合 *Mōshiawa(seru)* to make a mutual agreement.

告 *Shinkoku* declaration; report.

渡 *Mōshiwata(su)* to give an order; tell; deliver judgment.

越 *Mōshiko(su)* to send a letter; give notice; order (as goods).

請 *Shinsei* application; request.

譯 *Mōshiwake* excuse; pretext; apology.

T 早 SŌ abb. of Waseda SA. *Hayai* quick; early; fast: *haya* already.

々 *Sōsō* quickly; (at end of letter) excuse haste: *hayabaya* early.

大 *Sōdai* Waseda University.

世 *Sōsei* early decease.

合點 *Hayagatten* hasty conclusion.

呑込 *Hayanomikomi* hasty conclusion.

足 *Hayaashi* quick steps.

春 *Sōshun* early spring.

計 *Sōkei* over-hastiness.

急 *Sakkyū; sōkyū* hasty; hurried.

早
速 *Sassoku* at once.

婚 *Sōkon* early marriage.

朝 *Sochō* early morning.

晩 *Sōban* sooner or later.

業 *Hayawaza* skilful motion.

熟 *Sōjuku* early maturity.

稲 *Wase* early rice.

稲田 *Waseda* p. n.

慶 *Sōkei* Waseda and Keiō.

旭 KYOKU. *Asahi* the rising sun.

日 *Kyoku-jitsu* the rising sun.

旗 *Kyokki* the national flag of Japan.

T 曲 KYOKU a tune; wicked. *Maga(ru)*; *kaga(mu)* to bend; be crooked: *kane* foot-rule; one of the two kinds of feet; see Introduction 44: *kuma* corner. 【日】

尺 *Kanejaku* the Japanese foot of linear measure; see Introduction 44.

折 *Kyokusetsu* winding; crooked; complication.

直 *Kyokuchoku* right and wrong; justice.

者 *Kusemono* ruffian; villain.

事 *Kyokuji* offence; evil act.

線 *Kyokusen* curved line.

解 *Kyokkai* wrong interpretation.

曳 See 臾 9,7. 【曰】

曳 EI. *Hi(ku)* to pull; drag. 【日】

船 *Eisen*; *hikifune* tow-boat.

旱 KAN. *Hideri* drought. 三

魃 *Kampatsu* drought.

T 車 See 159,0.

旺 Ō. *Sakan* vigorous. 四

盛 *Ōsei* flourishing condition; vigorous.

T 明 MEI abb. of *Meiji*: MYŌ next: MIN name of Chinese dynasty. *Akarui* bright; clear; well-versed in: *akiraka na* clear; distinct; obvious: *a(keru)*; *a(ku)* to open; dawn: *akari* light; brightness: *aka(su)* to publish; make known.

大 日 *Meidai* Meiji University.

日 *Myōnichi*; *ashita* tomorrow: *akuruhi* next day.

文 *Meibun* an expressed provision.

月 *Meigetsu* bright (full) moon.

方 *Akegata* daybreak.

示 *Meiji* clear statement.

石 *Akashi* p. n.

白 *Meihaku* distinct; clear; plain.

年 *Myōnen*; *akurutoshi* next year.

快 *Meikai* clear.

言 *Meigen* announcement.

治 *Meiji* era name, 1868-1912.

盲 *Akimekura* an ignoramus.

(四)

後日 *Myōgonichi; asatte* the day after to-morrow.

星 *Myōjō* Venus; a shining star:

敏 *Meibin* brightness.

細 *Masai* particulars.

巣狙 *Akisu-nerai* sneak-thief.

媚 *Meibi* picturesque.

間 *Akima* vacant room.

答 *Meitō* a definite answer.

晩 *Myōban* to-morrow evening (night).

渡 *Akewata(su)* to vacate; hand over.

朝 *Myōchō; myōasa* to-morrow morning.

晰 *Meiseki* clear; distinct.

滅 *Meimetsu* to appear and disappear.

暮 *Akekure* morning and evening; day and night.

確 *Meikaku* clearness; accuracy.

瞭 *Meiryō* clear; distinct.

昌 SHŌ. *Sakan* prosperous: *akiraka* bright; clear. (*Masa*).

昂 KŌ. *Aga(ru)* to rise; ascend: *takabu(ru)* to be proud.

進 *Kōshin* rise; excitement.

然 *Kōzen* proudly.

騰 *Kōtō* sudden rise.

T昇 SHŌ. *Nobo(ru)* to rise; ascend.

天 *Shōten* ascension.

降 *Shōkō* ascent and descent.

級 *Shōkyū* promotion (in office).

給 *Shōkyū* increase of salary.

進 *Shōshin* promotion (to a higher grade).

T易 I; EKI divination. *Yasui* easy: *ka(h)eru* to change; exchange; trade: *kawa(ru)* to change.

々 *Ii* very easy.

者 *Ekisha* a diviner; a fortune-teller

昊 KŌ the summer sky.

天 *Kōten* great heavens; vast sky.

是 See T是 72,5.

昆 KON the same; afterwards; elder brother.

蟲 *Konchū* an insect.

電 See 電 205,0.

T昭 SHŌ to shine. *Akiraka* Ii clear; bright; manifest. (*Aki*).

代 *Shōdai* glorious reign.

乎 *Shōko* bright; plain.

和 *Shōwa* era name, 1926—

覽 *Shōran* witnessing (by Heaven).

T昨 SAKU last; the one before the present one; yesterday.

日 *Sakujitsu; kinō* yesterday.

今 *Sakkon* nowadays; of late.

（五）

昨

年 *Sakunen* last year.

夜 *Sakuya; yūbe* last night; last evening.

朝 *Sakuchō* yesterday morning.

晩 *Sakuban* yesterday evening; last night.

T 映 EI. *Ha(y)eru)* to shine on : *utsu(ru); utsu(su)* to reflect.

畫 *Eiga* motion picture.

昧 MAI to obscure ; deceive. *Kurai* dark ; darkness.

爽 *Maisō* daybreak.

昵 JITSU to be intimate ; to come near.

近 *Jikkin* to be intimate ; to be friendly.

懇 *Jikkon* to be intimate ; to be friendly.

T 星 SEI. *Hoshi* star.

霜 *Seisō* years.

冒 See 13,7.

T 是 ZE just ; right ; good. *Kore ; kono* this. →72,4

迄 *Kore made* hitherto.

非 *Zehi* without fail ; positively ; right and wrong.

認 *Zenin* approval.

黽 See 黽 205,0.

六 晒 SAI. *Sara(su)* to expose to the sun ; bleach : *sarashi* white shirting.

（六）

T 時 JI o'clock ; hour. *Toki* time ; opportunity ; occasion.

々 *Toki-doki; jiji* now and then ; from time to time ; sometimes.

下 *Jika* at present.

日 *Jijitsu* hour and day ; time ; date.

分 *Jibun* time ; season.

世 *Jisei* the times.

代 *Jidai* the time ; period.

代後 *Jidai-okure* old-fashioned ; out-of-date.

代精神 *Jidaiseishin* spirit of the age.

代錯誤 *Jidaisakugo* anachronism.

局 *Jikyoku* the situation.

刻 *Jikoku* time.

事 *Jiji* current events.

雨 *Shigure* drizzle.

計 *Tokei* clock ; watch.

候 *Jikō* climate ; season.

評 *Jihyō* criticism of current events.

間 *Jikan* hour ; time.

間表 *Jikanhyō* time-table.

期 *Jiki* period ; term ; date.

節 *Jisetsu* season ; time.

勢 *Jisei* the times ; age ; condition of the times.

價 *Jika* current price.

機 *Jiki* opportunity.

晉 See 晉 1,9. 【日】

(六)

畢 HITSU. *Owa(ru) ; o(h)eru)* to end : *tsuini* at last. 【田】

生 *Hissei* the whole life.

竟 *Hikkyō* after all.

七 **晣** SETSU clear. Often used mistakenly for 晰 72,8.

晦 KAI. *Misoka ; tsugomori* the last day of the month : *kurai* dark : *kurama(su)* to obscure ; deceive.

日 *Misoka* the last day of the month.

冥 *Kaimei* darkness ; dark.

澁 *Kaijū* unintelligible.

ᵀ**晩** BAN evening ; night. *Osoi* late.

年 *Bannen* last years.

香坡 *Bankūbā* Vancouver.

秋 *Banshū* late autumn.

婚 *Bankon* to marry late.

飯 *Bammeshi* the evening meal.

學 *Bangaku* study late in life.

餐 *Bansan* the evening meal.

餐會 *Bansankai* dinner party.

匙 See 21,9.

晨 SHIN early. *Ashita* morning.

曼 MAN wide ; long ; to extend. 【日】

曹 SŌ a chief. 【日】

長 *Sōchō* sergeant-major.

(七)

達 *Sōda* soda.

晢 See 晰 72,7.

亀 See 龜 213,0.

晰 SEKI. *Akiraka* clear. 八

晴 SEI. *Ha(reru) ; hara(su)* to be clear ; to clear up. Do not confound with 暒 109,8. → 晴 ᵀ

々 *Harebare(suru) ; seisei(suru)* feel refreshed.

天 *Seiten* fine weather.

雨 *Seiu* the condition of the weather ; rain or shine.

朗 *Seirō* clear ; fine.

着 *Haregi* holiday attire ; going-out dress.

ᵀ**量** RYŌ quantity ; volume. *Haka(ru)* to measure ; weigh ; estimate. 【里】

見 *Ryōken* a thought.

ᵀ**晶** SHŌ crystal ; bright. (*Aki*).

鼎 See 鼎 206,0.

ᵀ**最** SAI. *Mottomo* most ; very ; forms a superlative. 【日】

上 *Saijō* best : *Mogami* p. n.

中 *Saichū* the very midst ; in the course of : *monaka* a kind of cake.

早 *Mohaya* already ; no longer.

初 *Saisho* the first ; the beginning.

（八）

最近 *Saikin* latest; nearest; of late.

前 *Sa'zen* before; previously.

後 *Sa'go* the last; the end.

高 *Saikō* maximum; supremacy.

寄 *Moyori* the neighbourhood.

期 *Saigo* the last; death.

善 *S izen* best.

愛 *Saiai* most dear; darling.

T 景 KEI view; scenery; appearance. (*Kage*)

色 *Keshiki; keishoku* view; scenery.

況 *Keikyō* a condition.

物 *Keibutsu* a prize; reward.

品 *Keihin* premium.

氣 *Keiki* condition of a thing, especially trade.

T 普 FU ordinary. *Amaneku* universal; all; everywhere. →72,9

及 *Fukyū* spreading; diffusion.

佛 *Fufutsu* Prussia and France.

通 *Futsū* usual; ordinary.

通選舉 *Futsū-senkyo* universal suffrage.

遍 *Fuhen* universality.

魯西 *Purosha* Prussia.

請 *Fushin* construction; repairs.

選 *Fusen* abb. of *futsū-senkyo,* universal suffrage.

智 CHI wisdom; intelligence; wise; clever. (*Tomo*).

力 *Chiryoku* intellect.

利 *Chirii* Chile.

性 *Chisei* intellect.

能 *Chinō* intellect; ability.

惠 *Chie* wisdom.

慧 *Chie* wisdom.

德 *Chitoku* learning and morality.

謀 *Chibō* wise counsel; wisdom.

識 *Chishiki* knowledge.

囊 *Chinō* wisdom; wise man.

曾 See 12,10. 【日】

T 替 TAI. *Kawa(ru); ka(h)eru*) to change; substitute. As 2nd component; to do, (write, dress, etc.) over again in order to correct or change. 【日】

*1 玉 *Kaedama* a substitute. *2

暗 AN hinting. *Kurai* dark: 九 *yami* darkness. →暗 T

中 *Anchū* in the dark.

示 *Anji* hint; suggestion.

合 *Angō* an accidental agreement.

君 *Ankun* an incapable ruler.

殺 *Ansatsu* assassination.

記 *Anki* learning by heart.

淚 *Anrui* silent tears.

黑 *Ankoku* darkness; gloom.

雲 *An-un* dark clouds.

238 *¹T 曉 →72,12 *²T 暑 →72,9

愚　*Angu* stupidity.

號　*Angō* cipher; code.

誦　*Anshō* recitation.

算　*Anzan* mental calculation.

澹　*Antan* darkness; gloom.

礁　*Anshō* a hidden rock.

鬪　*Antō* internal discord; feud.

闇　*Kurayami* the dark.

暉　KI to shine; light.

暖　DAN. *Atatakai* warm: *atatama(ru)* to become warm: *atata(meru)* to warm. →暖T

爐　*Danro* stove; fireplace.

T 暇　KA. *Itoma*; *hima* freedom from occupation; dismissal; discharge; leisure.

乞　*Itomagoi* leave-taking.

暑　SHO. *Atsui* hot (weather). →72, 8 T *²

氣　*Shoki* the heat.

熱　*Shonetsu* hot climate.

暈　UN. *Kasa* the halo of the moon or sun: *memai* dizziness: *boka(su)* to gradate.

普　See T 普 72, 8.

會　See 9, 11. 【日】

一〇 瞑　MEI; MYŌ dark; faint; night.

暢　CHŌ to stretch; to calm down.

嘗　SHO. *Katsute* previously; ever: *na(meru)* to lick. 【口】 →99, 8

一 一 T 暴　BŌ; BAKU to expose. *Arai* violent: *a(reru)* to be stormy; to be vio'e t: *abare(-ru)* to be disorderly; rowdy.

力　*Bōryoku* violence; force.

行　*Bōkō* violent conduct; outrageous behaviour.

利　*Bōri* excessive profit.

言　*Bōgen* violent language.

君　*Bōkun* tyrant.

戾　*Bōri* violent; unreasonable.

虎憑河の勇　*Bōkohyōga no yū* reckless; fire-eating.

威　*Bōi* tyranny.

食　*Bōshoku* gluttony.

風　*Bōfū* storm; gale.

風雨　*Bōfūu* violent storm with wind and rain.

虐　*Bōgyaku* tyranny.

徒　*Bōto* rioters.

動　*Bōdō* disturbance; rebellion.

飲　*Bōin* heavy drinking.

落　*Bōraku* a sudden fall; slump.

論　*Bōron* groundless argument.

漢　*Bōkan* bully.

舉　*Bōkyo* irrational conduct.

露　*Bakuro* exposure; disclosure.

騰　*Bōto* sudden rise.

（二一）T 暫 ZAN. *Shibaraku; shibashi* a short time; some time.

時 *Zanji* a short while.

朁 See 稽 115,10.

（二二）曉 GYŌ to perceive; know. *Aka'suki* the dawn. →72,8T *[1]

天 *Gyōten* the dawn.

星 *Gyōsei* morning star.

通 *Gyōtsū* to be well acquainted with.

嘹 RYŌ. *Akiraka* clear.

T 曇 DON. *Kumo(ru)* to be cloudy.

天 *Donten* overcast; cloudy.

（二三）曖 AI dark; to shade as with a screen from the sun.

昧 *Aimai* ambiguous.

曦 GI; KI sunlight.

（二四）曜 YŌ termination for days of the week; light; to shine. →曜T

日 *Yōbi* day (of the week).

曙 SHO. *Akebono* the dawn.

光 *Shokō* the dawn; daybreak; hope.

曚 MŌ; BŌ dark; dim.

昧 *Mōmai* ignorant.

（二四）T 題 See 181,9.

曝 BAKU to expose. *Sara(su)* to expose (to the sun).

露 *Bakuro* exposure; disclosure.

曠 KŌ clear; wide; long time; empty.

日彌久 *Kōjitsubikyū* procrastination.

世 *Kōsei* rare; uncommon.

職 *Kōshoku* neglect of public duties.

（二六）馨 See 186,11.

（二七）曩 NŌ. *Saki ni* previously; ancient times.

日 *Nōjitsu* the other day.

（二八）響 See 180,13.

（三〇）蠺 See 142,18.

（七三）日

Iwaku; i(u); notama(u) to say; speak. Do not confound with 日 72,0.

七四　月

T 月	GETSU; GATSU.　*Tsuki* moon; month.
日	*Tsukihi* days and months; time; lapse of time: *gappi* the date.
旦	*Gettan* criticism of persons.
刊	*Gekkan* monthly publication.
光	*Gekkō* moonlight.
並	*Tsukinami* commonplace.
步	*Geppo* advance month by month.
夜	*Tsukiyo* moonlight night.
桂樹	*Gekkeiju* laurel.
報	*Geppō* monthly report.
給	*Gekkyū* monthly salary.
經	*Gekkei* menses.
賦	*Geppu* monthly instalment.
蝕	*Gesshoku* eclipse of the moon.
極	*Tsukigime* by the month.
謝	*Gessha* monthly fee.
曜	*Getsuyō* Monday.

七五　木

When at the left it is called *Ki-hen*.

Γ 木	MOKU; BOKU.　*Ki; ko* tree; wood.

戶	*Kido* gateway; entrance.
立	*Kodachi* grove; cluster of trees.
材	*Mokuzai* wood; timber.
版	*Mokuhan* printing from wooden blocks; wood-cut.
枯	*Kogarashi* autumn and winter wind.
炭	*Mokutan* charcoal.
造	*Mokuzō* made of wood.
綿	*Momen* cotton (cloth).
鐸	*Bokutaku* leader; guide.
曜	*Mokuyō* Thursday.

T 札	SATSU paper-money.　*Fuda* ― label; ticket; charm.
幌	*Sapporo* p. n.
T 本	HON book; main; real; this; the present; I; aux. num. for counting long cylindrical things.　*Moto* origin; foot; bottom. →37, 2
人	*Honnin* the man in question; the man himself; the principal.
山	*Honzan* main temple.
土	*Hondo* mainland.
日	*Honjitsu* this day.
月	*Hongetsu* this month.
文	*Hommon; hombun* the text; the text in question.
分	*Hombun* duty; part.
心	*Honshin* true disposition; real character.
末	*Hommatsu* beginning and end; the whole course.

本旨 *Honshi* fundamental principle ; main object.

式 *Honshiki* regular way ; formality.

宅 *Hontaku* principal residence.

州 *Honshū* main island of Japan.

旨 *Honshi* main purport.

邦 *Hompō* this country.

位 *Hon-i* standard ; basis ; unit.

志 *Honshi* purpose ; object.

性 *Honsei* true character.

店 *Honten* head office ; this shop.

音 *Honne* real intention.

所 *Honjo* p. n.

來 *Honrai* originally.

妻 *Honsai* legal wife.

官 *Honkan* principal duty ; I.

科 *Honka* principal course ; this course.

家 *Honke* main family.

氣 *Honki* seriousness.

能 *Honnō* instinct.

望 *Hommō* true desire ; cherished desire.

國 *Hongoku* one's own country.

部 *Hombu* headquarters.

塲 *Homba* principal place of production.

尊 *Honzon* main Buddha ; principal figure.

復 *Hompuku* to recover from sickness.

當 *Hontō* truth.

鄉 *Hongō* p. n.

源 *Hongen* origin ; source.

意 *Hon-i* one's original idea ; intention.

領 *Honryō* characteristic feature.

箱 *Hombako* book-case.

質 *Honshitsu* essence.

職 *Honshoku* principal business ; I (official).

籍 *Honseki* registered domicile.

懷 *Honkai* satisfaction ; one's original intention ; cherished desire.

T 未 Mɪ ; Bɪ. *Mada ; imada* not yet : *h'tsuji* 8th zodiacal sign, the sheep. See Introduction 42, 43. Do not confound with 末 the following character.

了 *Miryō* not finished.

丁年 *Miteinen* minority (age).

亡人 *Mibōjin ; bibōjin* a widow

成年者 *Miseinen-sha* not of age ; a minor.

決 *Miketsu* undecided ; unconvicted.

定 *Mitei* undecided.

知 *Michi* hitherto unknown ; unfamiliar.

明 *Mimei* early dawn ; before sunrise.

來 *Mirai* future.

（一）

納 *Minō* unpaid.

婚 *Mikon* unmarried.

然 *Mizen* beforehand.

曾有 *Misō*; *mizou* unparalleled; unprecedented.

開 *Mikai* unenlightened; uncivilized.

遂 *Misui* attempted.

詳 *Mishō* unknown.

發 *Mihatsu* not yet occurring; before it occurs.

聞 *Mimon* hitherto unheard of; new.

滿 *Miman* under; below; less than.

棟 *M ren* the uselessness of crying or worrying over what can not be mended; regret.

製品 *Miseihin* an unmanufactured article.

熟 *Mijuku* unripe; unexperienced; immature.

T 末 MATSU; BATSU. *Sue* end; extremity; future; descendant. Do not confound with 未 the preceding character.

々 *Suezue* the future; the lower classes.

子 *Basshi* youngest child.

世 *Masse* future ages; corrupt generation.

代 *Matsudai* future generations; ages to come.

始終 *Sue-shijū* for ever; to the end.

（二）

席 *Basseki*; *masseki* the lowest seat.

流 *Batsuryū* descendants.

孫 *Basson* descendants.

梢 *Masshō* small or tapering end of anything.

期 *Matsugo* the hour of death.

路 *Matsuro* the last part of one's life.

節 *Massetsu* trifles.

輩 *Mappai* an inferior.

T 朴 BOKU simple; plain; docility. 二

T 朽 KYŪ. *Ku(chiru)* to decay.

T 机 KI. *Tsukue* desk; table.

下 *Kika* expression used in epistolary style after name of addressee.

上 *Kijō* academical.

朶 DA branch; to hang.

雲 *Daun* your letter.

T 米 See 119,0.

T 朱 SHU. *Ake* vermilion; red.

耒 See 來 75,4.【人】

杜 TO; ZU to shut off. *Mori* 三 a wood near a shrine: *yamanashi* a kind of pear.

若 *Kakitsubata* a kind of iris.

翁 *Taō* Tolstoi.

（三）

杜
絶 *Tozetsu; toda(y)eru)* to stop; cease.

漏 *Zurō* slovenly.

撰 *Zusan* careless; imperfect.

鵑 *Token; hototogisu* cuckoo.

鵑花 *Satsuki* a kind of azalea.

杣 *Soma* woodcutter; mountain planted with timber.

杆 KAN. *Teko* lever.

T **村** SON. *Mura* village. Do not confound with following. →163,4

民 *Sommin* a villager.

役場 *Murayakuba* village office.

雨 *Murasame* shower.

長 *Sonchō* mayor of a village.

落 *Sonraku* hamlet; village.

T **材** ZAI material; timber; ability. Do not confound with preceding.

木 *Zaimoku* wood; timber.

料 *Zairyō* materials.

幹 *Zaikan* talent.

T **杉** SAN. *Sugi* cryptomeria.

並木 *Suginamiki* rows of cryptomeria trees on roadside.

杓 SHAKU. *Hishaku* a dipper: *e* handle.

子 *Shakushi* wooden ladle.

（三）

子定規 *Shakushi-jōgi* by hard and fast rules; red tape.

杖 JŌ to strike. *Tsue* cane; walking-stick.

杞 KI name of ancient province in China. *Kuko* Duke of Argyll's tea-tree.

憂 *Kiyū* needless anxiety.

杢 (*Moku*) often used jocosely.

杏 KYŌ. *Anzu* an apricot.

林 *Kyōrin* physicians.

李 RI. *Sumomo* plum.

T **束** SOKU. *Taba* bundle; sheaf: *tsuka* hand-breadth; something short: *tsuka-(neru)* to make a bundle; to tie; bind.

縛 *Sokubaku* restriction.

T **来** See **來** 75,4. 【人】

（四）

枉 Ō. *Ma(geru)* to bend; condescend.

駕 *Ōga* your coming.

T **析** SEKI to tear; to divide; analyse.

枠 *Waku* reel; spool; spindle.

杵 SHO. *Kine; ki* mallet; pestle.

枡 *Masu* box-like instrument (various sizes) for measuring things in bulk; theatre box.

目 *Masume* measurement.

244

(四)

枥 See 栃 75,5.

T 林 RIN. *Hayashi* forest.

立 *Rinritsu* bristle.

業 *Ringyō* forestry.

檎 *Ringo* an apple.

T 板 HAN printing-block. *Ita* board.

挾 *Itabasami* dilemma.

間 *Itanoma* board flooring.

間稼 *Itanoma-kasegi* bath-house thief.

T 枝 SHI extremity; end. *Eda* branch. *(E)*

葉 *Shiyō* branches and leaves; unnecessary particulars.

T 枚 MAI; BAI aux. num. for counting flat things; piece of anything flat; to number.

擧 *Maikyo* to count; number; enumerate.

杭 KŌ. *Kui* stake; pile.

枕 CHIN. *Makura* pillow.

木 *Makuragi* a sleeper.

許 *Makuramoto* bedside.

頭 *Chintō* bedside.

邊 *Makurabe* bedside.

T 杯 HAI. *Sakazuki* wine-cup; glass. →1,8 : 108,4

T 松 SHŌ. *Matsu* pine-tree. →75,5

明 *Taimatsu* a (pine) torch.

風 *Matsukaze* wind that blows through a pine wood; a kind of cake.

脂 *Matsuyani* turpentine.

魚 *Katsuo* bonito.

露 *Shōro* kind of mushroom.

籟 *Shōrai* sound of wind that blows through pine-tree wood.

杳 YŌ wide; far. *Kurai* dim; dark. Often mis-takenly used for 杏 75,3.

T 果 KA. *Kudamono* fruit: *hate* the end; consequence; limit: *hata(su)* to carry out; discharge (one's duty); accomplish: *ha(teru)* to come to an end: *hatashite* as expected; really.

物 *Kudamono* fruit.

然 *Kazen* sure enough; just.

報 *Kahō* retribution.

敢 *Hakanai* fleeting; transient.

實 *Kajitsu* fruit.

斷 *Kadan* bold decision.

T 東 TŌ. *Higashi* east. (*Azuma*)

奔西走 *Tōhonsaisō* busy one-self about.

亞 *Tōa* Eastern Asia.

京 *Tōkyō* p. n.; also *Tonkin* Tongking.

洋 *Tōyō* the East.

屋 *Azumaya* an arbour.

風 *Kochi; tōfū* the east wind.

245

（四）

東

宮 *Tōgū* the Crown Prince.

海道 *Tōkaidō* p. n.

雲 *Shinonome* day-break.

漸 *Tōzen* proceeding eastward.

來

→75,3
T

RAI since; next; the one after the present one. *Kuru* (irreg.); *kita(ru)* (lit. st.) to come; arrive: *kita-(su)* to result in; bring about: as 2nd component it often means coming or proceeding from, e.g. *ginrai* from the first, *Rōmarai* from Rome; as 2nd component may mean coming into being or into existence, e. g. *futte kuru* to start raining. Often used before character of place-names, meaning "come to" thus 來阪 means come to *Ōsaka* and 來神 come to *Kōbe*. 【人】→75,2

月 *Raigetsu* next month.

方 *Koshikata* the days gone by.

年 *Rainen* next year.

世 *Raise* the future life.

春 *Raishun* next spring.

信 *Raishin* news or letter received.

客 *Raihyaku* a guest; visitor.

訪 *Raihō* visit.

着 *Raichaku* arrival.

朝 *Raichō* arrival in Japan.

週 *Raishū* next week.

電 *Raiden* telegram from.

遊 *Raiyū* a visit.

會 *Raikai* attending a meeting.

意 *Raii* the object of a visit or letter.

賓 *Raihin* a guest; visitor.

駕 *Raiga* to come (epist. st.)

歷 *Raireki* antecedents; history.

臨 *Rairin* coming (honorific).

觀 *Raikan* coming to see.

*

（四）

T**柱** CHŪ to support. *Hashira* pillar; post: *ji* bridge (of Japanese harp). 五

石 *Chūseki* foundation-stone; pillar.

柾 *Masa; masame* straight grain of wood.

柩 KYŪ. *Hitsugi* coffin.

柑 KAN citrus family; orange.

子 *Kōji* citrus family.

柘榴 *Zakuro* the pomegranate tree.

T**枯** KO. *Ka(reru)* to wither, be dried.

朽 *Kokyū* to decay; wither and die.

渴 *Kokatsu* to be parched, dry.

死 *Koshi* die; wither.

骨 *Kokotsu* deceased person.

枌 See T**松** 75,4.

246 *T枢→75,11

HAKU. *Kashiwa* oak.

（五）

T 相 **Sō** to assist; help; to observe; appearance; countenance: SHŌ. Minister; Premier. *Ai* together; mutual; as top component the meaning is often very vague.【日】

互 *Sōgo*; *aitagai* mutual.

手 *Aite* the other party; companion.

反 *Aihan suru* to be mutually opposed.

州 *Sōshū* another name for the province of Sagami.

同 *Aionaji* like each other; the same.

次 *Aitsu(gu)* to follow one after the other.

好 *Sōgō* feature; countenance.

伴 *Shōban* partake in (an entertainment).

見 *Aimi(-ru)* to meet.

似 *Aini(-ru)* to be like each other.

成 *Aina(ru)* to become; meaning often very vague.

並 *Ainara(bu)* to stand side by side; to be in a row.

和 *Aiwa(su)* to join; be at peace.

待 *Aima(tsu)* to co-operate.

持 *Aimochi* interdependence.

思 *Sōshi* mutual love.

殺 *Sōsai* counteraction.

通 *Aitsūzuru* (irreg.) to correspond with each other; supplement mutually.

等 *Aihitoshii* equal.

開 *Aihira(ku)* to hold; give (as a banquet).

塲 *Sōba* price; market-price; speculation.

集 *Aiatsuma(ru)* to assemble together.

異 *Aikotona(ru)* to differ.

當 *Sōtō* suitable; proper: *aiata(ru)* to fall on.

愛 *Sōai* mutual love.

達 *Aitassuru* (irreg.) to reach.

對 *Sōtai* relatively.

槌を打つ *Aizuchi wo utsu* to chime in with apt remarks.

違 *Sōi* difference.

模 *Sagami* p. n.

撲 *Sumō* wrestling.

談 *Sōdan* consultation.

營 *Aiitona(mu)* to perform.

應 *Sōō* suitable; fitness :*aiōjiru* (irreg.) to respond to each other.

識 *Sōshiki*; *aishi(ru)* to be mutually acquainted.

續 *Sōzoku* inheritance.

T 柳 **RYŪ.** *Yanagi* willow.

行李 *Yanagigōri* clothes basket.

眉 *Ryūbi* beautiful eyebrows.

栁 See prec.

柿 **SHI.** *Kaki* persimmon.

（五）T 柄 HEI. *E*; *tsuka* handle: *gara* appearance; pattern. (*Kara*). →64,5

杓 *Hishaku* dipper.

栅 SAKU. *Sh'garami* stockade; pallisade.

栃 *Tochi* a kind of horse-chestnut.

木 *Tochigi* p. n.

柿 See 柿 75,5.

T 查 SA to examine; inquire into; investigate.

定 *Satei* assessment; revision.

問 *Samon* investigation.

證 *Sashō* inspection.

T 架 KA to build (bridge, etc.); construct; erect; hang up; a shelf.

空 *Kakū*; *gakū* fancy; imagination.

設 *Kasetsu* to erect; construct.

橋 *Kakyō* bridge-building.

T 棠 See 榮 75,10.

T 染 SEN to penetrate; infect. *So(meru)*; *soma(ru)* to dye; *shi,mu)*; *shimi(-ru)* to smart.

々 *Shimijimi* heartily; fully.

物 *Somemono* dyed goods.

料 *Senryō* dyestuff.

織 *Senshoku* dying and weaving.

桓 KAN used for its sound.　六

桂 KEI. *Katsura* cinnamon-tree.

冠 *Keikan* laurel crown.

庵 *Keian* servants' agency.

栓 SEN cork; stopper; wooden peg.

框 KYŌ. *Kamachi* window or door frame: *waku* frame.

T 格 KAKU rank; right; station: KŌ to investigate; rule. *Ita(ru)* to reach.

子 *Kōshi* lattice work.

外 *Kakugai* exceptional.

式 *Kakushiki* rank; status.

安 *Kakuyasu* cheap; a bargain.

好 *Kakkō* shape; appearance; suitableness.

言 *Kakugen* maxim.

別 *Kakubetsu* exceptional; special.

段 *Kakudan* exceptional; special.

納庫 *Kakunōko* an aeroshed.

鬪 *Kakutō* a struggle.

栖 SEI. *Su(mu)* to dwell. (*Su*).

桝 See 枡 75,4.

桁 KŌ fetters. *Keta* cross-beams.

桐 DŌ; TŌ. *Kiri* the Paulownia Imperialis.

（六）

株 SHU. *Kabu* the stump of a tree or plant; stubble; aux. num. for counting bushes or vegetables; shares; stock.

主 *Kabunushi* shareholder.

式 *Kabushiki* stock; shares.

式會社 *Kabushiki-kaisha* joint-stock company.

券 *Kabuken* share-certificate.

金 *Kabukin* money for shares.

根 KON origin. *Ne* root; *nezasu* to originate.

元 *Kongen* the root.

本 *Kompon* basis.

治 *Konji* radical cure.

性 *Konjō* nature; disposition.

底 *Kontei* bottom; foundation.

柢 *Kontei* bottom; foundation.

氣 *Konki* natural vigour.

絕 *Konzetsu* eradication.

據 *Konkyo* basis; ground; foundation.

據地 *Konkyochi* the base of operations.

校 KŌ place of learning; to compare; to correct; revise; to consider; to investigate.

→校 T

友 *Kōyū* school friend.

正 *Kōsei* to read proofs.

舍 *Kōsha* school house.

長 *Kōchō* head-master; director.

訂 *Kōtei* revision.

*1 桜→75,17 T

（六）

風 *Kōfū* discipline of a school.

閲 *Kōetsu* revision.

桃 TŌ. *Momo* peach.

色 *Momo-iro* pink (colour).

核 KAKU; KAI. *Sane* kernel; stone; nucleus.

心 *Kakushin* nucleus.

栞 KAN. *Shiori* book-mark; clue; trail-marker.

桑 See 2),8. 【木】

柴 SAI. *Shiba* brushwood; firewood.

*1 *

梱 KON threshold. *Kori* bale; 七 pack.

梓 SHI. *Azusa* catalpa.

弓 *Azusayumi* a bow made of catalpa.

梢 SHŌ. *Kozue* twig; tip of a tree.

桶 YŌ; TŌ. *Oke* pail; bucket.

屋 *Okeya* cooper.

梯 TEI. *Hashigo* ladder; stairway.

子 *Hashigo* ladder.

子段 *Hashigodan* staircase.

形 *Teikei* echelon.

梅 BAI. *Ume* plum. →*3 梅 T

249 *2 栈→75,8 T

梅

干 *Umeboshi* pickled plums.

雨 *Baiu* the rain (of the rainy season): *tsuyu* the rainy season.

毒 *Baidoku* syphilis.

梗 Kō; KYō for the most part.

概 *Kōgai* outline; summary.

梃 TEI a cane. *Teko* a lever.

子 *Teko* a lever.

T 械 KAI instrument; machine; contrivance. *Kase* fetters.

梶 *Kaji* shaft.

棒 *Kajibō* shaft (of vehicle).

梳 So. *Kushikezu(ru)* to comb.

梵 See 16,9. 【木】

梨 RI. *Nashi* pear.

梁 RYō bridge. *Hari* heavy beams in a roof: *vana* weir: *utsubari* rafters.

梟 KYō. *Fukurō; fukuro* an owl.

雄 *Kyōyū* chief of scoundrels.

T 巢 See 巢 47,8.

八 T 植 SHOKU to colonize. *U(eru)* to plant; set up type.

木 *Ueki* plant.

付 *Ue-tsuke* planting.

込 *Uekomi* to plant densely.

民 *Shokumin* colonists; colonization.

民地 *Shokuminchi* colony.

物 *Shokubutsu* a plant.

林 *Shokurin* to plant forests.

椎 TSUI to strike; mallet. *Shii* kind of oak.

T 棺 KAN. *Hitsugi* coffin.

棹 Tō. *Sao* pole; oar: *saosa(su)* to row; punt.

T 棒 Bō rod; pole; bar. *Tsue* stick.

椅子 *Isu* chair.

棚 Hō. *Tana* shelf.

棉 MEN. *Wata* cotton.

花 *Menka* raw cotton.

棟 Tō. *Mune* ridge of a roof.

梁 *Tōryō* master-carpenter; leader.

棧 SAN suspension bridge; jetty; shelf; gallery.
→ 75,6 T * ²

敷 *Sajiki* gallery in a theatre.

橋 *Sambashi* pier; jetty.

棍棒 *Kombō* club; cudgel.

椀 WAN bowl; wooden-cup.

(T) 棋 KI Japanese chess.
→99,7

棕櫚 *Shuro* palm-tree.

棲 SEI. *Su(mu)* to reside: *sumika* dwelling.

息 *Seisoku* to live; inhabit.

(T) 森 SHIN stern; severe. *Mori* forest; wood.

林 *Shinrin* woods; forests.

閑 *Sh'nkan* silent.

嚴 *Shingen* solemnity.

羅萬象 *Shinrabanshō* creation; everything.

渠 KYO dock; canal; ditch. *Kare* he. 【水】

棘 KYOKU. *Ibara* thorns; brambles.

＊ 棗 *Natsume* the jujube (tree).

九(T) 極 KYOKU pole (of the earth): GOKU. *Kiwamete* very: *kiwa(meru)* to go to extremes; investigate thoroughly: *kiwama(ru)* to be carried to the extreme: *ki(meru); kima(ru)* to settle: *kiwami; kiwa* height; utmost; climax; extremity: *kimari* rule.

力 *Kyokuryoku* strenuously.

刑 *Kyokukei* capital punishment.

言 *Kyokugen* speak in unsparing terms.

限 *Kyokugen* a limit.

＊(T) 檢 →75,13

東 *Kyokutō* The Far East.

度 *Kyokudo* the extreme.

秘 *Gokuhi* strictly confidential.

致 *Kyokuchi* climax.

貧 *Kyokuhin* extreme poverty.

惡 *Gokuaku* devilish.

意 *Gokui* the essential principle; chief point.

端 *Kyokutan* extremity.

論 *Kyokuron* extreme argument.

樂 *Gokuraku* the paradise of the Buddhists.

椿 CHIN. *Tsubaki* the camellia.

事 *Chinji* terrible accident.

楮 CHO. *Kōzo* the paper mulberry.

楷 KAI square character; model; correct.

書 *Kaisho* the square style of writing Chinese characters.

梯 *Kaitei* step; guide; primer.

楢 YŪ. *Nara* oak.

椰子 *Yashi* coco-nut-tree.

楫 SHŪ; SHŌ oar. *Kaji* rudder.

楕 See 橢 75,12.

楠 NAN. *Kusu: kusunoki* camphor-tree.

楊 YŌ. *Kawayanagi* willow.

〔九〕楊

枝　*Yōji* tooth-brush; tooth-pick.

楔　SETSU. *Kusabi* a wedge; a chock.

椽　TFN; EN verandah. *Taruki* rafter: *jō* official rank.

椴松　*Todo-matsu* a kind f pine-tree.

楓　FŪ. *Kaede* maple.

樹　*Fūju* maple-tree.

T 楼　See 樓 75,11.

T 楽　See 樂 75,11.

T 業　G.Ō; GŌ destiny; karma. *Waza* deed; work: *nari-wai* occupation; calling; business: *sud ni* already.

務　*Gyōmu* business.

腹　*Gōhara* feeling resentment; vexation.

〔一〇〕槍

槍　SŌ. *Yari* lance.

榕樹　*Yōju* tree with aerial roots; banyan-tree.

榊　*Sakaki* cleyera japonica (used in religious ceremonies).

T 構　KŌ to construct. *Kamac* external appearance; attitude; preparation: *kama-(h)eru* to put oneself in a posture: *kama(u)* o matter; concern.

内　*Kōnai* the premises.

外　*Kōgai* outside the compound.

成　*Kōsei* construction.

造　*Kōzō* construction; structure.

想　*Kōsō* design.

榜　BŌ; IIŌ placard; sign; to designate; profess; to row.

榛　SHIN. *Han; hannoki; hashibami* hazel.

T 樣　See 樣 75,11.

榎　KA. *Enoki; e* Chinese tree-lotus.

槌　TS I to strike. *Tsuchi* mallet.

槙　TEN; SHIN. *Maki* a kind of fir-tree.

榮　EI. *Saka(y)eru; ha(y)eru* to prosper; be luxuriant: *hae* splendour; luxuriance. →75,5 T

光　*Eikō* sun-glow; glory.

名　*Eimei* a fair name; reputation.

枯　*Eiko* success and failure; rise and fall; ups and downs.

辱　*Eijoku* honour and disgrace.

華　*Eiga* extravagance; luxury.

達　*Eitatsu* success in life; prosperity; advancement.

轉　*Eiten* promotion in rank; to change to a better position.

* 譽　*Eiyo* honour; fame.

樫　*Kashi* oak.

（一一）

枢 SŪ important; essential. *Taboso* hinge; pivot.
→ 75, 4 * T

相 *Sūshō* chairman of the Privy Council.

府 *Sūfu* Privy Council.

要 *Sūyō* importance.

密院 *Sūmitsuin* the Privy Council.

機 *Sūki* important affairs of state.

T 権 See 權 75, 18.

槽 SŌ. *Oke* tub; vat.

樟 SHŌ. *Kusu* camphor-tree; camphor.

腦 *Shōnō* camphor.

樺 KA. *Kaba* birch; brown colour.

太 *Karafuto* Saghalien.

色 *Kabairo* brown.

T 模 MO; BO pattern; to model after; copy.

型 *Mokei* model.

做 *Mohō* to imitate.

造 *Mozō* to manufacture in imitation of.

糊 *Moko* darkness; dimness.

寫 *Mosha* copy; sketch.

樣 *Moyō* pattern; design; state; condition; circumstances; appearance.

範 *Mohan* model; pattern.

擬 *Mogi* imitation.

（一一）

樣 YŌ. *Sama* manner; way; kind; form; appearance; state; condition; circumstances; an honorific term, Mr., Mrs., etc.: *san* Mr., Mrs., etc. → 75, 10 T

々 *Sama-zama* various.

子 *Yōsu* manner; appearance; state.

式 *Yōshiki* mode; type.

樅 SHŌ. *Momi* the fir-tree.

樋 TŌ. *Hi*; *toi* water-pipe; spout; gutter.

槻 KI. *Tsuki* a kind of tree.

概 GAI. *Ōmune* generally; for the most part.
→ 75, 10 * T

言 *Gaigen* speaking generally.

況 *Gaikyō* a summary; general condition.

念 *Gainen* conception; general idea.

要 *Gaiyō* an outline.

括 *Gaikatsu* to summarise.

略 *Gairyaku* summary.

算 *Gaisan* a rough estimate.

論 *Gairon* a general remark.

觀 *Gaikan* a general view.

T 標 HYŌ mark; sign; object; target; to designate.

本 *Hyōhon* a specimen.

札 *Hyōsatsu* a door-plate.

的 *Hyōteki* mark; target.

高 *Hyōkō* altitude.

準 *Hyōjun* standard.

（二一）

標

榜 *Hyōbō* a platform (claim).

語 *Hyōgo* a motto.

題 *Hyōdai* title ; heading.

樓 Rō large house of several stories ; tower. →75,9T

閣 *Rōkaku* a tower or high building.

樂 RAKU ; GAKU music. *Tanoshimi* pleasure ; happiness ; comfort : *tanoshi(mu)* to enjoy : *tanoshii* pleasant. →75,9T

天 *Rakuten* optimism.

屋 *Gakuya* behind the scenes ; the internal condition.

書 *Rakugaki* scribbling ; scrawling.

隊 *Gakutai* musical band.

園 *Rakuen* Paradise.

器 *Gakki* musical instrument.

譜 *Gakufu* musical notes.

観 *Rakkan* optimism.

三 橙 TŌ. *Daidai* bitter orange.

T 樹 JU to plant. *Ki* tree : *ta(teru)* to erect ; establish.

木 *Jumoku* trees.

立 *Juritsu* to stand in a row ; to plant ; set up.

樽 SON. *Taru* cask ; barrel.

橢 圓 *Daen* an ellipse.

T 橋 KYŌ. *Hashi* bridge.

*T 横 →75,12

畔 *Kyōhan* near a bridge.

橘 KITSU. *Tachibana* trees of the citrus variety.

T 機 KI machinery ; important. *Hata* weaving-loom : *ori ; shio* opportunity : *hazumi* chance ; impetus.

先 *Kisen* forestalment.

宜 *Kigi* an opportunity.

密 *Kimitsu* secrecy ; a secret.

能 *Kinō* function ; power.

略 *Kiryaku* resources ; tact.

敏 *Kibin* smartness ; sharpness.

械 *Kikai* machine.

智 *Kichi* acumen ; wit.

軸 *Kijiku* axle ; plan ; device.

會 *Kikai* opportunity ; chance.

嫌 *Kigen* condition of a person's health or feelings.

運 *Kiun* turn of fortune.

微 *Kibi* inner working.

關 *Kikan* engine ; organ ; apparatus ; steam-engine.

關車 *Kikansha* locomotive (engine).

橇 *Sori* sledge.

横 Ō arbitrariness ; self-will. *Yoko* across ; sideways : *yokotawa(ru) ; yokota(h)eru)* to be placed across ; lie down : *yokogi(ru)* to cross. →75,11*

合 *Yokoai* the flank ; side ; outside.

（二一）

254

行 *Ōkō* to walk sideways; swagger; strut about.

向 *Yokomuki* turning sideways.

死 *Ōshi* violent death.

町 *Yokochō* by-street.

取 *Yokodori* seizing; usurpation.

臥 *Ōga* lying down.

柄 *Ōhei* arrogance.

着 *Ōchaku* impudent; cunning.

道 *Yokomichi* side-way; byway.

須賀 *Yokosuka* p. n.

領 *Ōryō* seizing; usurpation.

槍 *Yokoyari* interposition.

暴 *Ōbō* oppression; tyranny.

濱 *Yokohama* p. n.

顔 *Yokogao* side-face.

斷 *Ōdan* intersection.

樵 SHŌ. *Kikori* wood-cutter.

夫 *Shōfu* wood-cutter.

橿 KYŌ. *Kashi; kashiwa* oak.

檀 DAN sandal-wood tree.

檜 KAI. *Hinoki; hi* a kind of cypress highly esteemed.

舞臺 *Hinokibutai* stage-board of *hinoki;* a first-class theatre.

檣 SHŌ. *Hobashira; masuto* mast.

檄 GEKI summons; announcement.

文 *Gekibun* a declaration; a manifesto.

檢 KEN. *Arata(meru)* to examine; investigate.
→75, 8 T *
分 *Kembun* inspection.

束 *Kensoku* restraint; restriction; check.

事 *Kenji* the public prosecutor attached to a court of justice.

定 *Kentei* official approval.

査 *Kensa* inspection; examination.

疫 *Ken-eki* quarantine; medical inspection.

視 *Kenshi* inspection.

閲 *Ken-etsu* inspection; parade; censorship.

擧 *Kenkyo* custody; prosecution; arrest.

檻 KAN. *Ori* a cage; prison.

櫃 KI. *Hitsu* a box; tub.

櫂 TŌ; TEKI. *Kai* an oar.

櫓 RO an oar. *Yagura* a watch-tower.

櫛 SHITSU. *Kushi* a comb: *kushikezu(ru)* to comb.

比 *Shippi* (of houses) to extend in a row.

風沐雨 *Shippū-mokuu* be exposed to hardships.

（一五）

攀　See 6ㅏ,15.

一七　欄　RAN column (of a news-paper). *Tesuri* hand-rail.
→75, 16 * T

干　*Kankan* hand-rail.

外　*Rangai* the margin of a book or newspaper.

間　*Ramma* open ornamental work over the sliding doors.

櫻　Ō. *Sakura* cherry-tree.
→75, 6 T * 1

色　*Sakura-iro* light rose colour.

一八　權　KEN; GON power; right; authority; influence; weight.　→75, 11 T

力　*Kenryoku* power; autho-rity.

化　*Gonge* incarnation.

利　*Kenri* right; authority; power.

臣　*Kenshin* influential retain-er.

門　*Kemmon* influential person.

限　*Kengen* the limit or ex-tent of powers or of rights.

威　*Ken-i* power; authority.

能　*Kennō* power; authority; right.

幕　*Kemmaku* the countenance; threatening look.

謀　*Kembō* a craft; an intrigue.

衡　*Kenkō* balance.

欅　KYO. *Keaki* a kind of the zelkowa tree.

*T 欄 →75, 17

變　RAN round.　一九

欝　UTSU to be luxuriant; gloomy; dull. *Fusa(gu)* to be melancholy.　二二

々　*Utsu-utsu* dejected; melan-choly.

陶　*Uttōshii* dejected; melan-choly; gloomy.

憤　*Uppun* resentment.

積　*Usseki* accumulation; stag-nation.

鬱　See prec. 【鬯】　二五

欠　七六

76

T 欠　KETSU; KEN. *Akubi* yawn: *ka'ku*) to be deficient; lack; absent. Sometimes used as abb. of 缺 121,4.

伸　*Akubi* yawn.

次　JI; SHI. *Tsugi* next; vice-: *tsu(gu)* to be next; succe-ed: *tsuide* opportunity; occasion; next; secondly.　二
→15, 4 T = → 次 T

回　*Jikai* the next time.

男　*Jinan* the second son.

序　*Jijo* order; system.

官　*Jikan* vice-minister.

長　*Jichō* vice-director.

郎　*Jirō* man's name.

席　*Jiseki* the second seat or place; being next in posi-tion or rank.

第 *Shidai* order; case; reason: *shidai ni* gradually.

号 *Jigō* next issue.

七 欷 KI. *Susurina(ku)* to weep; sob; lament.

欶 See ᵀ款 76,8.

八 欹 KI. *Sobada(teru)* to listen attentively.

ᵀ欺 GI. *Azamu(ku)*; *dama(su)*; *damaka(su)* to deceive; cheat.

罔 *Gibō* deceit; fraud.

扁 *Gihen* deception; fraud.

惑 *Giwaku* deception.

ᵀ欸 KAN article; to rejoice; to enjoy; to write down; good will. →76,7

待 *Kantai* courteous treatment.

九 歇 KETSU to be exhausted. *Ya(mu)* to stop; rest.

一 歌 KA. *Uta* song; poem (Japanese style): *uta(u)* to ᴼᵀ sing.

人 *Kajin* a poet.

集 *Kashū* collection of poems.

舞伎 *Kabuki* theatre.

劇 *Kageki; opera* an opera.

二 欧 Ō Europe. →76,4 * ᵀ

文 *Ōbun* European writing.

ᵀ欧 →76,11

化 *Ōka* Europeanizing.

米 *Ōbei* Europe and America.

亜 *Ōa* Europe and Asia.

洲 *Ōshū* Europe.

羅巴 *Yoroppa* Europe.

ᵀ歓 See 歡 76,18.

歎 TAN to admire. *Nage(ku)* to grieve; mourn; sigh. →30,10 ᵀ *

美 *Tambi* to praise warmly; admire.

息 *Tansoku* sigh.

稱 *Tanshō* admire.

賞 *Tanshō* admiration.

聲 *Tansei* cries of grief; groans.

願 *Tangan* entreaty.

歔欷 *Kyoki suru* to sob.

歟 YO. *Ka; ya* an interrogative particle.

歡 KAN joy; delight. *Yoroko(bu)* to rejoice. →76,11 ᵀ

心 *Kanshin* goodwill.

呼 *Kanko* cheers; jubilation.

迎 *Kangei* warm welcome.

待 *Kantai* welcome.

喜 *Kanki* joy.

樂 *Kanraku* pleasure; enjoyment; amusement.

聲 *Kansei* shout of joy.

七

止

止 SHI. *To(meru)*; *todo-(meru)*; *ya(meru)*; *yo(su)*; *ya(mu)*; *toma(ru)*; *todoma-(ru)* to stop; leave off; discontinue; remain: *tome* forbidden.

宿 *Shishuku* lodging.

二 **此** SHI. *Kono*; *kore* this: *kaku* thus; so: *koko* here.

方 *Konata*; *kochira*; *kotchi* this side; my side; this place; here.

後 *K'nogo*; *kononochi* hereafter.

頃 *Konogoro* recently.

處 *Koko* here; this place.

通 *Kono-tōri* as you see; in this manner.

間 *Konaida*; *kono-aida* the other day.

邊 *Kono-hen*; *kokora* hereabouts.

三 **步** HO; BU; FU proportion; per cent; infantry; unit of square measure. See Introduction 44 *Aru(ku)*; *ayu-(mu)* to walk: *ashi* a step. →77,4 *[1]*T

合 *Buai* percentage; commission.

調 *Hochō* pace; step.

行 *Hokō* walk.

兵 *Hohei* infantry.

哨 *Hoshō* a sentry.

肯 KŌ. *Gaenzuru* (irreg.); *ubena(u)*; *ukega(u)* to affirm; consent; assent. 【肉】

定 *Kōtei* affirmation.

諾 *Kōdaku* assent; consent. *[1]*

歪 WAI. *Yuga(mu)* to be bent; crooked. 五

歯 See 歯 211,0. 八

歳 SAI. *Toshi*; *tose* (2nd component) year; age. →46,10 : 62,9 九

入 *Sainyū* annual revenue.

月 *Saigetsu* time; passing of time.

出 *Saishutsu* annual expenditure.

末 *Saimatsu* the close of the year.

費 *Saihi* annual expense; annual allowance.

暮 *Seibo* the end of the year; the year-end present. *[2]*

雌 SHI. *Me*; *mesu* female. 一 【佳】 〇

伏 *Shifuku* live in retirement.

雄 *Shiyū* male and female; victory or defeat.

歯 See 211,0. 二

整 SEI. *Totono(h)eru*; *totono(u)* to put in order; to be ready. 【攴】 一二

258 *[1]*T 步→77,3 　*[2]*→歳 T

二 列 *Seiretsu* to be in a row.

理 *Seiri* adjusting; regulating.

然 *Seizen* in a regular manner.

備 *Seibi* preparation; arrangement.

頓 *Seiton* order; adjustment; regulation.

一四 歸 See 58,15. 【止】

七八 歹

二T 列 RETSU row; rank; order; to be arranged in a row. 【刀】

車 *Ressha* train.

後 *Retsugo* the rear of the rank.

座 *Retsuza* the whole assemblage.

席 *Resseki* attendance.

島 *Rettō* a chain of islands.

國 *Rekkoku* the Powers.

強 *Rekkyō* the Great Powers.

傳 *Retsuden* biographies.

擧 *Rekkyo* enumeration.

四 殀 YŌ to die young.

折 *Yōsetsu* to die young.

歿 BOTSU to die.

後 *Botsugo* after death.

殆 TAI perilous. *Hotondo* 五 almost; nearly.

殃 Ō. *Wazawai* calamity; misfortune.

T殉 JUN. *Shitaga(u)* to follow 六 (even unto death); die for another.

死 *Junshi* to kill oneself on the death of one's lord with the idea of following him into the next world.

職 *Junshoku* to die at one's post.

難 *Junnan* martyrdom; massacre.

敎 *Junkyō* martyrdom.

T殊 SHU to excel. *Koto* different; special.

外 *Koto no hoka* unusually; exceedingly.

更 *Kotosara* especially.

勝 *Shushō* laudable.

遇 *Shugū* warm reception.

勳 *Shukun* special merit.

T殘 See 殘 78,8.

T殖 SHOKU. *Fu(y)eru); fuya-(su)* to increase; enlarge. 八

民地 *Shokuminchi* colony.

財 *Shokuzai* to accumulate wealth; amass riches.

產 *Shokusan* industry.

殘 ZAN to injure; destroy. *Noko(ru); noko(su)* to be left over. →78,6 T

八〇

残 Zanson survive ; remain.

存 Zanson survive ; remain.

金 Zankin balance; remainder.

忍 Zanrin cruelty ; brutality.

念 Zannen regret ; disappointment.

虐 Zangyaku cruelty ; brutality.

高 Zandaka ; nokoridaka the balance.

務 Zammu work left over.

暑 Zansho hot days in latter part of summer.

酷 Zankoku cruelty ; brutality.

餘 Zan-yo remnant.

額 Zangaku a balance.

一〇 殞 IN ; UN. O(chiru) to fall ; to die.

七九 殳

Always at the right and is called Ru-mata.

五 *1 段 DAN degree ; step ; grade ; platform ; matter ; affair ; section ; chapter : TAN unit of land mesure. See Introduction 44.

Dan-dan little by little ; gradually.

取 Dandori programme.

階 Dankai step ; ranks.

落 Danraku paragraph ; full stop ; conclusion. *2

*1 T 殷 →79,11

T 殺 →79,7 260

殷 IN prosperous.

六

々 In-in rumbling ; rolling.

富 Impu prosperity ; rich.

賑 Inshin prosperity.

殺 SATSU ; SETSU. Koro(su) to kill : so (gu) to cut ; slice off ; diminish.

人 Satsujin homicide.

生 Sesshō killing animals.

伐 Satsubatsu slaughter ; barbarity.

到 Sattō rush in ; come down upon.

風景 Sappūkei disenchanting.

害 Satsugai setsugai murder

氣 Sakki murderous spirit ; ferocity.

倒 Sattō rush in ; flood.

傷 Sasshō killing and wounding.

意 Satsui murderous intent.

戮 Satsuriku massacre
*2

殻 KAKU ; KCKU. Kara the shell ; skin. →79,7 T *3 八

毀 KI to slander. Kobo(tsu, kowa(su) to break ; damage. 九

損 Kison injury ; damage.

殿 DEN ; TEN temple ; palace. Dono Mr.; Mrs.; etc.: tono lord : shingari the last of a row.

下 Denka Imperial Highness.

方 Tonogata gentlemen (polite).

*3 T 殻 →79,8

（九）堂 *Dendō* palace.

様 *Tonosama* lord.

*1

一 殴 Ō. *Nagu(ru)* to strike; assault; beat. →79, 4 T * 2

合 *Naguriai* exchange of blows.

打 *Ōda* assault.

穀 KOKU cereals; grain.【禾】→79, 10 T * 1; 79, 12

物 *Kokumotsu* cereals; grain.

類 *Kokurui* cereals; grain.

毅 KI. *Takeshii* strong; firm; stern.

然 *Kizen* bravely.

三 穀 【米】See 穀 79, 11 【禾】

一三 轂 KOKU. *Koshiki* the hub of a wheel.【車】

八〇 母

80

一 母 T BO; MO. *Haha* mother.

子 *Boshi; oyako* mother and child.

君 *Hahagimi* mother (honorific).

音 *Boin* vowel.

衣 *Horo* a rikisha hood.

屋 *Omoya* a main house.

校 *Bokō* alma mater.

國 *Bokoku* mother-country.

堂 *Bodō* mother (honorific).

親 *Hahaoya* mother.

艦 *Bokan* mother-ship.

*2

每 MAI. *Goto ni* every time; 三 every; each; often used as 2nd component, e. g. 戸每 *kogoto* every house: *tsune ni* always. →80, 2 * 2 T

々 *Mai-mai* frequently.

日 *Mainichi* every day.

度 *Maido* each time; frequently.

*3

毒 DOKU poison; to harm. 五. →80, 4 * 3 T

々 *Dokudokushii* fiendish; sarcastic; dark; disagreeable (colour.

及 *Dokujin* weapon.

手 *Dokushu* an evil design.

牙 *Dokuga* poisonous fang.

瓦斯 *Dokugasu* poisonous gas.

味 *Dokumi* testing to prove whether a thing is poisonous or not.

害 *Dokugai* to kill by poisoning.

殺 *Dokusatsu* to kill by poisoning.

婦 *Dokufu* a wicked woman.

筆 *Dokuhitsu* venomous comments.

藥 *Dokuyaku* a poison.

*1 T 穀 →79, 11　261　* 2 T 每 →80, 3　* 3 T 毒 →80, 5

七 貫 T KAN unit of weight; see Introduction 44. *Tsuranu(ku)*; *nu(ku)* to run through; pierce through; connect. (*Tsura*). 【貝】

目 *Kamme* weight; used also instead of simple *kan* as unit of weight; see Introduction 44.

流 *Kanryū* to flow through.

通 *Kantsū* to pass through.

徹 *Kantetsu* (of ideas etc.) to penetrate; permeate; carrying out; accomplishment.

八一

比 *81*

比 T HI sort; kind; to be in a row. *Kura(beru)* to compare: *tatoe* example : *koro*; *koro-oi* about the time.

肩 *Hiken* stand abreast.

例 *Hirei* proportion.

律賓 *Hirippin*; *Fuirippin* the Philippines.

率 *Hiritsu* ratio; percentage.

喩 *Hiyu* comparison; allegory; parable.

較 *Hikaku* comparison.

隣 *Hirin* neighbouring place.

類 *Hirui* an equal; match.

五 皆 T KAI together. *Mina* all. 【白】

目 *Kaimoku* entirely; not the least.

無 *Kaimu* nothing; entirely.

樣 *Mina-sama* everybody.

濟 *Kaisai* full payment.

琵 See 96,8.

毛

毛 T MŌ a monetary unit; $\frac{1}{100}$ part of *sen*; unit of weight; see Introduction 44. *Ke* hair; wool; fur; feathers; harvest (e. g. *hanke* half the usual harvest).

布 *Mōfu* blanket; woollen cloth.

皮 *Kegawa* fur.

筆 *Mōhitsu* writing-brush.

絲 *Ke-ito* woollen yarn.

髮 *Mōhatsu* hair (of the head).

頭 *Mōtō* the least.

氈 *Mōsen* carpet.

織物 *Keorimono* woollen cloth.

毬 KYŪ. *Mari* ball: *iga* 七 chestnut burr.

氈 SEN carpet; woollen rug. 一三

八三　氏

氏 SHI. *Uji* family; household; Mr.; surname.

子 *Ujiko* people of the parish.

名 *Shimei* full name.

神 *Ujigami* tutelary deity.

一ᵀ民 MIN. *Tami* the people; subjects. Used also as bottom component, e.g.: *heimin* the common people, *kokumin* the nation, *himmin* the poor.

心 *Minshin* the feelings of the people; popular opinion or sentiment.

本主義 *Mimpon-shugi* democracy.

主主義 *Minshu-shugi* democracy.

法 *Mimpō* civil law.

有 *Min-yū* the people's possession.

事 *Minji* a civil case.

政 *Minsei* democracy.

族 *Minzoku* a nation; a people; race.

家 *Minka* people's houses.

情 *Minjō* condition of the people.

間 *Minkan* among the common people (i. e. the non-officials).

衆 *Minshū* the nation at large; the public.

福 *Mimpuku* happiness of the people.

謠 *Min-yō* folk-song.

權 *Minken* popular rights.

昏 KON evening; dark; dusk. 【日】

迷 *Kommei* to be embarrassed; be perplexed.

倒 *Kontō* swoon.

睡 *Konsui* coma; stupor.

亂 *Konran* derangement.

八四　气

气 See 84, 6

氣 KI; KE spirit; heart; vapour; mood; nature; breath. →84, 2 T *

力 *Kiryoku* energy; mental vigour.

丈 *Kijō* firm; resolute; healthy.

分 *Kibun* feeling; mood; state of health.

立 *Kidate* disposition.

色 *Keshiki* sign; appearance: *kishoku* humour; mood.

附 *Kizuku* to notice: *kitsuke* stimulant; c/o.

味 *Kimi* feeling; sensation.

取 *Kidoru* to affect.

拔 *Kinuke* dispiritedness.

（六）

氣

受 *Kiuke* popularity.

長 *Kinaga* slow; patient.

品 *Kihin* dignity.

苦勞 *Kiguro* worry; anxiety.

前 *Kimae* disposition; liberality.

持 *Kimochi* feeling; mood.

毒 *Kinodoku* sorrow; sympathy.

後 *Kiokure* faint-heartedness.

風 *Kifu* character; disposition.

高 *Kedakai* noble; dignified.

骨 *Kikotsu* spirit; mettle: *kibone* care; mental strain.

候 *Kiko* climate; weather.

脈 *Kimyaku* vein; connection.

流 *Kiryu* air current.

兼 *Kigane suru* to be afraid of giving trouble.

振 *Keburi* looks; appearance.

根 *Kikon* aerial root.

配 *Kehai* appearance; air; tone (market.

張 *Kibaru* to exert oneself; be liberal.

短 *Kimijika* short-tempered.

焰 *Kien* big words; big talk.

晴 *Kibarashi* diversion.

違 *Kichigai* insanity.

落 *Kiochi* dejection.

象 *Kisho* atmospheric phenomena; spi it; disposition.

象臺 *Kishodai* meteorological observatory.

（六）

絕 *Kizetsu* fainting.

溫 *Kion* temperature.

運 *Kiun* movement.

障 *Kiza na* disagreeable; affected.

遣 *Kizukai* fear; anxiety.

樂 *Kiraku* freedom from care.

概 *Kigai* firmness of purpose.

質 *Kishitsu; katagi* disposition; character.

儘 *Kimama* selfishness; self-willed.

隨 *Kizui* wilfulness; self-willed.

壓 *Kiatsu* atmospheric pressure.

體 *Kitai* gas; vapour.

轉 *Kiten* quick wit.

懸 *Kigakari* anxiety.

八五

水

shui water 3 left

When at the left takes the modified form 氵 and is called *San-zui.*

T 水 SUI. *Mizu; mina* water. (*Mi*).

上 *Suijo* on the water: *minakami* the upper stream.

引 *Mizuhiki* paper cord (usually red and white) for tying up presents.

牛 *Suigyu* buffalo.

分 *Suibun* moisture.

夫 *Suifu* sailor.

田 *Suiden; mizuta* paddy-field.

平 *Suihei* level.

平線 *Suiheisen* the horizon.

死者 *Suishisha* person drowned.

先人 *Mizusakinin* pilot.

交社 *Suikōsha* the Naval Club.

利 *Suiri* irrigation.

兵 *Suihei* (naval) sailor; marine.

泳 *Suiei* swimming.

泡 *Suihō* foam; fruitless.

車 *Suisha; mizuguruma* a water-mill.

害 *Suigai* damages by flood.

烟 *Suien; mizukemuri* spray.

臭 *Mizukusai* watery; cold-hearted.

産 *Suisan* sea product.

掛論 *Mizukakeron* fruitless argument.

族館 *Suizokukan* aquarium.

魚の交 *Suigyo no majiwari* close intimacy.

晶 *Suishō* rock-crystal.

無月 *Minazuki* poetical name for 6th month (old cal.).

運 *Suiun* transportation by water.

路 *Suiro* waterway.

雷 *Suirai* torpedo.

雷艇 *Suiraitei* torpedo-boat.

葬 *Suisō* burial at sea.

道 *Suidō* waterworks; water-pipe.

銀 *Suigin* mercury.

源地 *Suigenchi* the source of water.

蒸氣 *Suijōki* aqueous vapour.

練 *Suiren* practice in swimming.

曜 *Suiyō* Wednesday.

難 *Suinan* an accident by water.

T 氷 HYŌ. *Kōri* ice; icicle. — (*Hi*).

山 *Hyōzan* iceberg.

河 *Hyōga* glacier.

州 *Aisurando* Iceland.

柱 *Tsurara* icicle.

結 *Hyōketsu* freezing.

解 *Hyōkai* melting; dissolution; disappearance (as of doubts).

點 *Hyōten* the freezing point.

T 永 Eᵢ. *Nagai* long; a long time: *tokoshie* everlasting.

久 *Eikyū* perpetual; eternal.

劫 *Eigō* eternity.

別 *Eibetsu* to part for ever.

住 *Eijū* permanent residence.

持 *Nagamochi* enduring.

眠 *Eimin* death.

遠 *Eien* eternity.

續 *Eizoku* to last long; continue.

265

二
T 汁 JŪ. *Shiru; tsuyu* soup; juice; gravy.

氣 *Shiruke* juice; fluid; watery matter.

粉 *Shiruko* red-bean soup.

汀 TEI. *Migiwa* beach; sandy spit; strand.

渚 *Teisho* beach; strand.

氾 HAN to spread; to overflow; everywhere.

濫 *Hanran* overflowing.

三 T 江 KŌ. *E* river; creek; cove.

戸 *Edo* old name for Tōkyō.

州 *Gōshū* another name for the province of *Omi*.

島 *E-no-shima; Ejima* p. n.

湖 *Kōko* world; public.

T 汗 KAN. *A·e* sweat; perspiration. Do not confound with following.

牛充棟 *Kangyūjūtō* full of books.

顔 *Kangan* to feel ashamed

汙 See foll.; do not confound with prec.

T 汚 O; U puddle; filth. *Kega-(reru); ke·a(su); yogo(reru); yogo(·u)* to be dirty; polluted; defiled: *kegarawashi·; kitanai* dirty: *shimi* stain.

名 *Omei* bad name.

辱 *Ojoku* disgrace.

損 *Oson* stained and broken.

點 *Oten* a blot; stain.

汐 SEKI. *Shio* the tide; evening tide.

干狩 *Shiohigari* shell-fish gathering at low tide.

T 池 CHI. *Ike* pond.

上 *Chijō* on the pond. *Ikegami* p. n.

汎 HAN wide; to float; to drift about; pan-.

太平洋 *Han taiheiyō* Pan-Pacific.

說 *Hansetsu* a general remark.

論 *Hanron* a general remark.

汝 JO. *Nanji; nare; na; imashi* you.

等 *Nanjira* you.

汪 Ō an expanse of water; deep; wide; large.

洋 *Ōyō* expanse.

T 沖 CHŪ. *Oki* offing.

繩 *Okinawa* p. n.

沙 SA; SHA. *Suna; isago; mas·go* sand.

市 *Shiyatoru* Seattle; *Sashi* Shashih (China).

汰 *Sata* order; instruction; notice; news.

漠 *Sabaku* desert.

(三)

四

266

（四）

翁 *Saō* Shakespeare.

T沢 See 澤 85,13.

汰 TA ; TAI. *Yona(geru)* to select ; separate good from bad grains ; cleanse.

沃 YOKU to be fertile ; to pour.

土 *Yokudo* fertile soil.

野 *Yokuya* fertile plain.

T決 KETSU to distinguish. *Ki(meru)* to decide ; determine : *kesshite* never.

心 *Kesshin* resolution ; determination.

行 *Kekkō* to execute ; carry out.

死 *Kesshi* courting or braving certain death.

定 *Kettei* decision ; determination.

勝 *Kesshō* decision of a contest.

着 *Ketchaku* settlement ; conclusion ; decision.

然 *Ketsuzen* in a determined manner.

意 *Ketsui* will ; purpose.

算 *Kessan* settling or balancing accounts.

戰 *Kessen* decisive battle.

濟 *Kessai* settle accounts.

斷 *Ketsudan* decision.

鬪 *Kettō* duel.

議 *Ketsugi* resolution ; decision.

沐 MOKU to wash ; bathe ; to moisten.

雨 *Mokuu* exposed to rain.

浴 *Mokuyoku* to bathe.

沒 BOTSU ; MOTSU to disappear ; be hidden ; confiscated ; to sink ; to drown ; to be lost ; die.
→ 没 T

收 *Bosshū* confiscation ; forfeiture.

交涉 *Botsukōshō ; bokkōshō* have no connection.

却 *Bokkyaku* destruction.

常識 *Botsujōshiki* lack of common sense.

落 *Botsuraku* ruin ; failure.

頭 *Bottō* be absorbed in.

汲 KYŪ. *Ku(mu)* to draw water : *su(u)* to suck ; sip.

々 *Kyū-kyū* industrious ; untiring.

泛 HON ; HAN wide. *Uka(bu)* to float.

T汽 KI steam.

笛 *Kiteki* a steam-whistle.

車 *Kisha* train (steam).

船 *Kisen* steamship.

罐 *Kikan* steam boiler.

T沈 CHIN. *Shizu(mu) ; shizu(meru)* to sink ; be immersed.

吟 *Chingin* to ponder.

沒 *Chimbotsu* sinking.

思 *Chinshi* deep thought.

（四）沈

勇 *Chi..-yū* cool courage.

淪 *Chinrin* to fall into decay; be ruined.

痛 *Chintsū* grave; sad.

着 *Chinchaku* calmness; composure; self-possession.

溺 *Chindeki* being drowned; indulge in.

滯 *Chintai* to be dull; stationary.

靜 *Chinsei* stillness; silence.

默 *Chimmoku* silence.

沁 SHIN. *Shimi(-ru)*; *shi(mu)* to soak in; penetrate.

々 *Shim'jimi* heartily; really.

沓 TŌ to transgress; to pile up. *Kutsu* shoes.

五 注 CHŪ to concentrate. *Soso-* T *(gu)* to flow into; pour water into, on; give heed to.

入 *Chūryū* pouring; infusion.

文 *Chūmon* order; request.

目 *Chūmoku* attention.

射 *Chūsha* injection.

視 *Chūshi* attention.

意 *Chūi* attention; to pay attention.

泣 KYŪ. *Na(ku)* to cry; T weep.

虫 *Nakimushi* a blubberer.

言 *Nakigoto* a complaint.

（五）

寢入 *Nakineiri* to cry oneself to sleep; reluctant submission.

沮 SO; SHO to defeat. *Haba-(mu)* (lit. st.) to check

止 *Soshi* to check.

喪 *Sosō* discouragement.

泄 SETSU to exude; to discharge.

沾 TEN; SEN. *Uruo(u)* to be moist; to wet.

沽 KO to buy; to sell; trade; price; value.

券 *Koken* dignity; worth.

T 沼 SHŌ. *Num:* marsh.

沿 EN. *So(u)* to go alongside of. →沿 T

岸 *Engan* coast.

革 *Enkaku* history.

道 *Endō* route.

T 治 JI; CHI. *Osa(meru)*; *osama-(ru)* to govern; tranquilize; pacify: *nao(su)* to cure: *nao(ru)* to get well. *(Haru)*

世 *Chisei* the reign of a sovereign; tranquil times.

外法權 *Chigai-hōken* extraterritoriality.

安 *Chi-an* tranquility; peace.

績 *Chiseki* result of good administration.

療 *Chiryō* medical treatment.

T 泊 HAKU. *Toma(ru)* to lodge; stop: *to(meru)* to give a night's lodging.

（五）

客 *Tomarikyaku* guest in a hotel.

泪 See 涙 85,8.

T 油 YŪ; YU. *Abura* oil.

然 *Yūzen* thickly; copiously.

煙 *Yuen* lamp-soot.

蟲 *Abura-mushi* cockroach.

斷 *Yudan* negligence.

繪 *Aburae* oil-painting.

泝 So. *Sakanobo(ru)* to go up; trace back.

T 河 KA. *Kawa* (big) river.

口 *Kakō; kawaguchi* the mouth of a river.

內 *Kawachi* p n.

床 *Kashō* river-bed.

原 *Kawara* river-beach.

畔 *Kahan* bank of a river.

豚 *Fugu* globe-fish.

童 *Kappa* river goblin.

沛然 *Haizen* abundant; heavy (of rain).

T 沸 FUTSU. *Wa(ku); waka(su)* to boil.

騰 *Futtō* boiling; effervescence.

沫 MATSU foam; bubble. *Shibuki* spray.

T 泳 EI. *Oyo(gu)* to swim.

（五）

波 HA. *Nami* wave.

止場 *Hatoba* wharf.

及 *Hakyū* to spread; extend; influence.

打際 *Nami-uchi-giwa* beach washed by the waves.

浪 *Harō* waves.

紋 *Hamon* ripples.

動 *Hadō* waves; undulatory motion.

斯 *Perusha* Persia.

濤 *Hatō* waves.

瀾 *Haran* waves; disturbance.

羅的海 *Baruchikkukai* Baltic Sea.

蘭 *Pōrando* Poland.

T 泥 DEI. *Doro* mud: *nazu(mu)* to adhere (as to an opinion).

土 *Deido* mud.

除 *Doroyoke* mud-guard.

棒 *Dorobō* thief.

醉 *Deisui* being dead drunk.

濘 *Deinei; nukarumi* mud-

泡 HŌ. *Awa; abuku* foam; bubble.

沫 *Hōmatsu* bubble.

錢 *Abukuzeni* unearned money.

T 況 KYŌ state; condition. *Mashite* still more: *iwan-ya* it goes without saying.

T 泌 HITSU; HI to secrete; exude. *Shi(mu); shimi(·ru)* to smart; penetrate.

（五）T **法** HŌ to follow the example of. *Nori* rule; way; law; doctrine: *furan* franc (French money).

人 *Hōjin* legal person.

文 *Hōbun* text of the law.

王 *Hōō* Pope.

外 *Hōgai* exorbitance.

令 *Hōrei* laws and ordinances.

廷 *Hōtei* court of justice.

定 *Hōtei* legal.

事 *Hōji* Buddhist memorial service.

制 *Hōsei* legislation.

典 *Hōten* a code.

相 *Hōshō* the Minister of Justice.

度 *Hatto* a law; rule; prohibition.

律 *Hōritsu* law.

要 *Hōyō* Buddhist memorial service.

則 *Hōsoku* law; rule.

師 *Hōshi; hosshi* Buddhist priest.

案 *Hōan* a bill.

規 *Hōki* laws and regulations.

學博士 *Hōgakuhakase* Doctor of Laws.

會 *Hōe* a Buddhist religious service.

網 *Hōmō* the meshes of the law.

螺 *Hora* an exaggeration.

洽 KŌ; GŌ. *Amaneku* universally. 六

T **活** KATSU. *I(kiru)* to be active; alive; movable: *ika(su)* to keep alive: *i(keru)* to arrange flowers in a vase.

々 *Iki-iki* fresh; lively.

用 *Katsuyō* to apply; utilize; inflect.

字 *Katsuji* movable type.

版 *Kappan* printing by means of movable type.

計 *Kakkei; kurashi* livelihood.

氣 *Kakki* vigour; energy.

眼 *Katsugan* quick perception.

動 *Katsudō* activity.

動寫眞 *Katsudō-shashin* cinematograph.

路 *Katsuro* a means of escape.

潑 *Kappatsu* briskness.

劇 *Katsugeki* a scene.

辯 *Katsuben* moving picture demonstrator.

躍 *Katsuyaku* activity.

洛 RAKU the capital, especially *Kyōto*, the old capital.

中 *Rakuchū* inside the capital.

外 *Rakugai* suburbs of the capital.

陽 *Rakuyō* old capital of China; poetical name for Kyōto.

洒 SHA; SAI; SEI. *Soso(gu)* to sprinkle: *ara(u); susu(gu)* to wash; rinse.

脱　*Shadatsu* nonchalance.

落　*Share* witticism: *sharaku* open-hearted.

T 洋　YŌ wide; extensive; foreign. *Nada* ocean.

々　*Yoyō* wide; extensive.

刀　*Naifu* knife.

行　*Yokō* travelling abroad.

杖　*Sutekki* walking-stick.

服　*Yōfuku* foreign dress.

風　*Yōfū* Western style; foreign style.

食　*Yōshoku* foreign food.

裝　*Yosō* foreign binding of books; foreign dress.

T 津　SHIN. *Tsu* inlet; harbour; cove; ferry.

々　*Shinshin* overflowingly.

々浦々　*Tsuzu-uraura* everywhere.

波　*Tsunami* a tidal wave.

洲　SHŪ; SU strand; continent. *Shima* island; country.

洞　DŌ; TO deep; to penetrate. *Hora; uro* cave; cavity: *utsuro* emptiness; cavity.

見　*Dōken* insight.

穴　*Dōketsu* cave; grotto.

窟　*Dōkutsu* cave; cavern; grotto.

察　*Dōsatsu* discernment.

洵　JUN; SHUN alike; equal. *Makoto* truth.

洟　I. *Namida* a tear: *hanashiru* nasal mucus.

派　HA stream; sect; school; party; to part; divide. →派

手　*Hade* bright; gay; showy.

出　*Hashutsu* sending out.

遣　*Haken* to despatch; send.

T 浅　See 淺 85,8.

洩　EI. *Mo(ru); mo(reru); mora(su)* to leak; let leak; reveal; omit.

T 洗　SEN. *Ara(u)* to wash.

粉　*Araiko* washing-powder.

濯　*Sentaku* washing of clothes.

禮　*Senrei* baptism.

T 洪　KŌ flood; vast.

水　*Kōzui* flood.

牙利　*Hangarii* Hungary.

恩　*Kōon* great benevolence.

業　*Kōgyō* great enterprise; glorious achievement.

*1　　　　　*2

浬　RI. *Notto; mairu* knot; maritime mile.

浩　KŌ vigorous; abundance. *Hiroi* wide; vast.

然　*Kōzen* expansive; free; unrestrained.

T 浴　YOKU. *Yuami* hot bath: *(biru)* to bathe; pour water on one's body.

衣　*Yukata* bath-robe.

客　*Yokkaku* visitor at a hot spring.

浴塲 *Yokujō* bath-house.

T 酒 SHU. *Sake*; *miki* rice-wine; alcoholic drink. 【酉】

色 *Shushoku* sensual pleasures; dissipation.

肴 *Shukō* wine and food.

保 *Shuho* sutler; camp-hawker.

氣 *Shuki* taste or smell of *sake*; influence of wine.

宴 *Shuen* feast.

飲 *Sakenomi* a drinker.

塲 *Sakaba*; *bā* bar.

豪 *Shugō* a heavy drinker.

精 *Shusei*; *arukōru* alcohol.

槽 *Sakabune* large vat used in making *sake*.

T 浮 FU fickle. *U(ku)*; *uka(bu)*; *uka(mu)* to float: *uki* buoy.

立 *Ukitatsu* to be lighthearted; brighten up.

世 *Ukiyo* the world.

世繪 *Ukiyoe* a genre-picture.

名 *Ukina* infamous name; reputation for amours.

沈 *Fuchin*; *uki-shizumi* floating and sinking; successes and reverses.

氣 *Uwaki* fickleness.

浪 *Furō* wandering.

雲 *Fuun*; *ukigumo* floating cloud.

遊 *Fuyū* waft; float.

華 *Fuka* fickle; light.

標 *Fuhyō* buoy.

說 *Fusetsu* rumour.

薄 *Fuhaku* frivolous; fickle.

消 SHŌ to be digested. *Ki-(y)eru)*; *ke(su)* to become extinguished; disappear; erase. →消 T

化 *Shōka* digestion.

失 *Shōshitsu* disappearance

印 *Keshiin* cancelling stamp.

光 *Shōkō* spending time.

却 *Shōkyaku* repayment.

防 *Shōbō* the prevention and extinction of fires.

長 *Shōchō* prosperity and decay.

毒 *Shōdoku* disinfection.

耗 *Shōmō* consumption; exhaustion.

息 *Shōsoku* communication; news; movement.

極 *Shōkyoku* negative pole.

極的 *Shōkyokuteki* negative.

費 *Shōhi* consumption; spending.

散 *Shōsan* scatter.

滅 *Shōmetsu* extinction.

涌 YŌ. *Waku* to bubble up.

T 浦 HO. *Ura* beach; sea-coast; bay.

風 *Urakaze* beach wind.

港 *Hokō* Vladivostok.

潮斯德 *Urajiosutokku* Vladivostok.

涉 SHŌ. *Wata(ru)* to cross over; ford; be acquainted with.

獵 *Shōryō* read or consult many books.

涕 TEI. *Namida* tears: *na-(ku)* to weep.

泣 *Teikyū* weeping.

海 KAI. *Umi* sea. (*Mi*).
→ 85, 6 T *

上 *Kaijō* maritime.

上保險 *Kaijō-hoken* marine insurance.

牙 *Heigu* the Hague.

水浴 *Kaisuiyoku* sea-bathing.

內 *Kaidai* the whole country.

外 *Kaigai* foreign countries.

老 *Ebi* shrimp; prawn.

老茶 *Ebicha* maroon; reddish brown.

防艦 *Kaibōkan* ship for coast defence.

里 *Kairi* a nautical mile.

拔 *Kaibatsu* above the sea-level.

岸 *Kaigan* seashore.

事 *Kaiji* maritime affairs.

底 *Kaitei* sea-bottom.

底電線 *Kaitei-densen* cable (submarine).

相 *Kaishō* Minister of the Navy.

容 *Kaiyō* pardon.

苔 *Nori* an edible seaweed.

軍 *Kaigun* Navy.

軍大臣 *Kaigun-daijin* Minister of the Navy.

軍省 *Kaigun-shō* the Naval Department.

峽 *Kaikyō* straits.

流 *Kairyū* oceanic current.

員 *Kaiin* a seaman.

草 *Kaisō* seaweed.

產 *Kaisan* marine products.

港 *Kaikō* seaport.

運 *Kaiun* marine transportation.

賊 *Kaizoku* piracy; a pirate.

綿 *Kaimen* sponge.

嘯 *Kaishō; tsunami* tidal wave.

濱 *Kaihin* seashore.

T浪 RŌ disorder; recklessly wastefully. *Nami* wave.

人 *Rōnin* a vagabond; a wanderer; a detached *samurai*.

花 *Naniwa* old name of Ōsaka: *Namibana* p. n.

費 *Rōhi* waste.

漫的 *Rōmanteki* romantic.

浸 SHIN to penetrate. *Hita-(su); hita(ru)* to soak; sink; be immersed; to wet. →浸 T

水 *Shinsui* inundation.

透 *Shintō* permeation.

潤 *Shinju* to permeate.

蝕 *Shinshoku* erosion.

禮 *Shinrei* baptism.

浚 SHUN. Sara(u) to dredge; clean out: sara(h)eru) to exercise.

渫 Shunsetsu dredging.

T 流 RYŪ sort; school (as of painting); style; type; after 一, 二, etc. may also mean rank, e.g. ichi-ryū one style; first rank: RU. Nagare stream: naga(su) to throw or abandon in the water: naga(reru) to flow.

布 Rufu overspread; circulate.

用 Ryūyō diversion; appropriation.

出 Ryūshutsu flowing out; issue.

石 Sasuga as one might have expected; nevertheless; however.

失 Ryūshitsu to be washed away.

行 Ryūkō; hayari mode; fashion.

行病 Ryūkōbyō an epidemic.

言 Ryūgen; rugen a rumour.

派 Ryūha school; branch; sect.

動 Ryūdō flowing.

動物 Ryūdōbutsu liquid.

通 Ryūtsū ventilation; circulation.

浪 Rurō wandering about.

域 Ryūiki (level land in) the vicinity of a river.

感 Ryūkan influenza.

會 Ryūkai adjournment of a meeting.

暢 Ryūchō fluency.

儀 Ryūgi style; school; way.

T 浜 See 濱 85,14.
*

T 涯 GAI margin; bank. Hate, 八 kugiri bounda y.

淫 IN to play; sport lewdly. Midara obscene: midari ni at random; immodestly.

奔 Impon lewdness.

逸 In-itsu debauchery.

涵 KAN to soak; to wet.

養 Kan-yō fostering.

涸 KO. Ka(reru) to dry.

渇 Kokatsu dry up (well, rivers, etc.).

淵 See 淵 85,9.

淳 JUN gentle; virtuous. Atsui kind.

朴 Jumboku simple; plain.

樸 Jumboku simple; plain.

淨 JŌ pure; clear; to purify. →85,6 T *1 Kiyoi

土 Jōdo Paradise of the Buddhists.

書 Joshō fair copy.

財 Jozai donation.

璃瑠 Joruri a kind of Japanese singing.

八七 T 済 See 濟 85,14.

淆 KŌ to mix; to jumble together; mix up; to make muddy; to be turbid; be impure.

清 SEI; SHŌ; SHIN old name for China. *Kiyoi* pure; clear; serene.

→清 T

水 *Shimizu; seisui* clear water: *Kiyomizu* p. n.

書 *Seisho* a fair copy.

貧 *Seihin* honourable poverty.

淨 *Seijō; shōjō* pure.

爽 *Seisō* clear and refreshing.

涼 *Seiryō* cool.

廉 *Seiren* incorruptible.

楚 *Seiso* neatness.

算 *Seisan* liquidation.

適 *Seiteki* good health.

潔 *Seiketsu* cleanliness.

聽 *Seichō* hearing.

淪 RIN to sink.

落 *Rinraku* degeneration; ruin.

淘 TŌ selection; to wash (grain, for food). *Yona-(geru)* to separate the good from the bad (grains).

汰 *Tōta* selection.

涙 RUI. *Namida; nanda* tears. →85,7 * T

金 *Namidakin* consolation money.

痕 *Ruikon* a tear-stain.

淋 RIN lonely; to pour; to drip. 八〇

病 *Rimbyō* gonorrhoea.

漓 *Rinri* dripping down.

Γ 深 SHIN. *Fukai* deep; (as 2nd component referring to moral qualities) great: *mi* deep.

山 *Shinzan* depths or lonely parts of mountains.

川 *Fukagawa* p. n.

手 *Fukade* severe wound.

切 *Shinsetsu* kind.

交 *Shinkō* close friendship.

更 *Shinkō* the dead of night.

夜 *Shin-ya* the dead of night.

長 *Shinchō* deep; profound.

紅 *Shinku* crimson.

刻 *Shinkoku* deep; profound.

淺 *Shinsen* depth.

遠 *Shin-en* deep; profound.

慮 *Shinryo* thoughtfulness.

謝 *Shinsha* thousand pardons.

T 淡 TAN. *Awai, usui* of delicate (little) flavour; tasteless; flat; thin.

白 *Tampaku* simple; plain.

路 *Awaji* p. n.

淀 TEN. *Yodo* eddy; sluggish place in a stream; stagnant shallow water: *yodo-(mu)* to be stagnant; falter.

T 淑 SHUKU. *Shioyaka* virtuous; gentle; pure. (*Yoshi*).

女 *Shukujo* a lady.

淑

徳　*Shukutoku* chastity.

T 液　EKI juice ; liquid.

體　*Ekitai* liquid.

涎　EN ; ZEN.　*Yodare* saliva.

淺　SEN thin.　*Asai* shallow.
→85,6 T

兒　*Senken* shallow view.

草　*Asakusa* p. n.

黃　*Asagi* light blue.

葱　*Asagi* light blue.

慮　*Senryo* shallow-minded.

學　*Sengaku* superficial learning.

薄　*Sempaku* shallowness.

瀨　*Asase* shallow shoal.

T 混　KON to be turbid ; impure.
Maji(ru) ; *ma(zeru)* to be mixed.

入　*Konnyū* to be mixed.

合　*Kongō* mixture.

同　*Kondō* to mix with ; confound with.

成　*Konsei* mixture ; composition.

沌　*Konton* chaotic ; obscure.

淆　*Konkō* mixture.

亂　*Konran* confusion ; disorder.

濁　*Kondaku* turbid ; discoloured.

凝土　*Konkuriito* concrete.

*[1] T 渋 →85,12

戰　*Konsen* confused battle.

雜　*Konzatsu* confusion ; disorder.

淹　EN a long time ; to stop ; stay.

T 涼　See 涼 15,8.

T 添　TEN.　*So(h)eru)* to accompany ; add : *so(u)* to go with ; go in the company of ; accord with ; comply.

加　*Tenka* adding.

附　*Tempu* annexing.

削　*Tensaku* correction.

書　*Tensho* a letter of introduction or recommendation.

凄　SEI cold.　*Sugoi* uncanny ; dreadful ; gloomy ; lonesome : *susamajii* frightful ; terrible ; tremendous.

慘　*Seisan* distressing ; grievous.

*　　　　*[2]　　　　*[3]

湮　IN ; EN to fall down ; to sink ; to be closed up ; to close.

滅　*Immetsu* destruction ; extinction.

渥　AKU benevolent ; to receive benefactions.

T 湿　See 濕 85,14.

T 温　See 溫 85,10.

湛　TAN to sink ; be quiet.
Tata(h)eru) to fill to the brim.

*[2] T 渓 →85.10　*[3] T 渇 →85,9

276

（八）　（九）

（九）

渚 SHO. *Nagisa* beach; strand.

湘 SHŌ used for its sound.

南 *Shōnan* coast of Sagami province.

淵 EN. *Fuchi* deep pool; abyss.

渾 KON large; all; quite; to be turbid.

一 *Kon-itsu* consolidation.

沌 *Konton* chaotic.

身 *Konshin* the whole body.

然 *Konzen* harmoniously.

T 測 SOKU. *Haka(ru)* to measure; survey.

定 *Sokutei* measurement.

候所 *Sokkōjo* meteorological station.

量 *Sokuryō* mensuration; survey.

淳 TEI beach. *Todoma(ru)*; *todo(meru)* to stop.

游 YŪ to float. *Oyo(gu)* to swim: *aso(bu)* to play.

泳 *Yūei* swimming.

T 湖 KO. *Mizu-umi: umi* lake.

水 *Kosui* lake.

沼 *Koshō* lake and marshes.

畔 *Kohan* border of a lake.

湍 TAN. *Hayase* a rapid: *tagi(ru)* to seethe; boil.

T 渦 KA. *Uzumaki; uzu* whirlpool; eddy: *uzuma(ku)* to whirl around.

中 *Kachū* a vortex.

T 満 See 満 85,11.

渺 BYŌ far; wide; boundless.

茫 *Byōbō* vast; boundless.

渇 KATSU. *Kawa(ku)* to be dry, thirsty. →85,8 * ³T

仰 *Katsugō; katsugyō* admiration.

望 *Katsubō* eager desire.

T 湯 TŌ hot spring. *Yu* hot bath; hot water.

呑 *Yunomi* tea-cup.

治 *Tōji* medical treatment at hot spring.

氣 *Yuge* steam.

殿 *Yudono* a bath-room.

湾 See 灣 85,22. →灣 T

渤 海灣 *Bokkaiwan* Gulf of Pechili.

湧 YŪ; YŌ. *Wa(ku)* to boil: bubble or gush forth.

湊 SŌ to assemble. *Minato* harbour.

合 *Sōgō* come together.

渫 SETSU. *Sara(u)* to dredge; clean out.

T 渡 TO. *Wata(ru)* to cross over: *wata(su)* take across (a ferry): deliver: *watashi* ferry; ford.

（九）

277

渡
世　*Tosei* living; occupation.

米　*Tobei* going to America.

來　*Torai* to come from a foreign country.

英　*Toei* going to England.

航　*Tokō* a voyage.

船　*Tosen; watashi-bune* ferry-boat.

欧　*Toō* going to Europe.

T 減　GEN. *He(ru); hera(su); hike(-ru); hi(ku)* to diminish; decrease; subtract.

少　*Genshō* decrease.

收　*Genshū* decreased yield.

退　*Gentai* to fall off; decrease.

員　*Gen-in* reduction of the personnel.

額　*Gengaku* reduction; discount.

港　KŌ. *Minato* harbour.

口　*Kōkō* entrance of harbour.

內　*Kōnai* inside of a harbour.

外　*Kōgai* outside a port.

灣　*Kōwan* a harbour.

→港 T

T 滋　See 滋 85,10.

○ 溫　ON; UN calm; moderate. *Atatakai; nukui* warm; hot: *atatama(ru); atata-(meru)* to warm.
→85,9 T

良　*Onryō* meek; amiable.

和　*Onwa* mild.

厚　*Onkō* affable; gentle.

泉　*Onsen* hot spring: *Unzen* p. n.

度　*Ondo* temperature.

室　*Onshitsu* a hothouse.

情　*Onjō* kindliness.

帶　*Ontai* temperate zone.

雅　*Onga* grace; gentleness.

順　*Onjun* amiable; unassuming; gentle.

暖　*Ondan* warmth.

顏　*Ongan* serene countenance.

溢　ITSU. *Afu(reru); kobo(reru); kobo(su)* to overflow.

溘　KŌ suddenly.

焉　*Kōen* suddenly.

滔　TŌ to overflow; to spread; grow in power.

々　*Tōtō* in a large stream; rapidly; fluently.

滄　SŌ the sea; blue; green; cold; chilly.

溟　*Sōmei* ocean.

溶　YŌ. *To(keru); toka(su); toroka(su)* to melt; dissolve.
→溶 T

液　*Yōeki* a solution.

解　*Yōkai* melting.

溜　RYŪ. *Tama(ru); ta(meru)* to collect; accumulate.

息　*Tameiki* a sigh.

飲　*Ryūin* indigestion; exhilaration.

278

(一〇)

溷濁 *Kondaku* muddle; impurity.

滓 SHI. *Kasu; ori* dregs; sediment.

溯 So. *Sakanobo(ru)* to ascend a stream; trace back; retrace.

T **滑** KATSU; KOTSU. *Nameraka* slippery; smooth: *sube(ru)* to slide: *numeri* slime; slipperiness.

走 *Kassō* gliding; taxying.

脱 *Katsudatsu* free; fluent.

稽 *Kokkei* joke; humour.

T **滯** See **滯** 85,11.

漓 RI to drip.

溝 KŌ. *Mizo* ditch; drain.

渠 *Kōkyo* canal; drain.

滂 HŌ; BŌ to flow in a large stream.

沱 *Bōda* to fall in big drops (tears).

湃 *Hōhai* surging (waves).

溺 DEKI. *Obo(reru)* to be drowned; doat on.

死 *Dekishi; oborejini* drowning.

惑 *Dekiwaku* be given to.

溪 KEI rivulet. *Tani* valley. →85,8 T *²

谷 *Keikoku* den; valley; stream.

(一〇)

流 *Keiryū* mountain stream.

T **滅** METSU to be extinguished. *Horobo(su)* destroy: *horo(biru)* to be destroyed.

亡 *Metsubō* ruin; destruction.

多 *Metta* reckless; rarely.

却 *Mekkyaku* extinction.

法 *Meppō* exorbitant.

茶々々 *Mechamecha* spoil; in disorder.

裂 *Metsuretsu* breaking asunder.

溉 See **汽** 85,4.

T **滝** See **瀧** 85,16.

T **源** GEN. *Minamoto; moto* origin; source.

平 *Gempei* the two rival clans of *Genji* and *Heike*, 2th century; the two sides in a game or competition.

泉 *Gensen* the source.

滋 JI tasty: SHI to receive benefactions; be rich. *Shige(ru)* to be luxuriant: *shigeki* (lit. st.) dense; flourishing. →85,9 T

味 *Jimi* delicacies; dainties.

賀 *Shiga* p. n.

養 *Jiyō* nourishment.

黎 REI dark. *Akebono* dawn. 【禾】

* 明 *Reimei* daybreak; dawn.

灘 See **灌** 85,18.

二

* T **漢** →85,11

漕　Sō.　*Ko(gu)* to row.

扷　*Kogi-nu(keru)* to row faster than another and thus get away from him.

T 漸　ZEN to advance. *Yōyaku, yōyō* at length; at last; by degrees.

次　*Zenji* by degrees.

進　*Zenshin* gradual advance.

滴　TEKI. *Shitata(ru); tara-(su); ta(reru)* to drip: *shizuku* a drop. →滴 T

下　*Tekika* to drop.

露　*Tekiro* a drop.

滯　TAI. *Todokō(ru)* to be obstructed; to stop; stay. →85, 10 T

在　*Taizai* stay.

京　*Taikyō* staying in the capital.

納　*Tainō* non-payment of taxes, etc.

貨　*Taika* congestion of goods.

T 漏　RŌ. *Mo(ru)* to leak: *mora(su)* to let leak; reveal; omit.

洩　*Rōei* leakage.

電　*Rōden* leakage of electricity.

滿　MAN (when counting years) complete, *man roku-jissai* sixty complete years old; abb. of Manchuria. *Mita-(su)* to fill up; satisfy: *mi(teru); mi(chiru)* (coll.) to be full; be whole; be complete. →85, 9 T

了　*Manryō* expiration.

干　*Mankan* high and low tide.

々　*Mamman* full of.

月　*Mangetsu* full moon.

目　*Mammoku* the whole view.

作　*Mansaku* good crop.

足　*Manzoku* contentment; satisfaction; gratification.

面　*Mammen* the whole face.

洲　*Manshū* Manchuria

座　*Manza* the whole company.

員　*Man-in* full house; full up.

堂　*Mandō* all the audience.

腔　*Mankō* hearty; whole-hearted.

開　*Mankai* full bloom.

期　*Manki* maturity.

場　*Manjō* the whole assembly.

腹　*Mampuku* (of eating) to be satisfied.

載　*Mansai* fully loaded.

潮　*Manchō* high-tide.

點　*Manten* full marks.

鐵　*Mantetsu* abb. of South Manchurian Railroad Co.

滲　SHIN. *Shi(mu); shimi(-ru); niji(mu)* to penetrate; smart; spread.

漱　Sō. *Susu(gu)* to rinse; wash the mouth.

漠　BAKU obscure; a desert; wide.

然　*Bakuzen* vague.

漢 KAN an ancient Chinese kingdom; China; a man. →85, 10 * T

口 *Kankō* Hankow.

文 *Kambun* Chinese classics; a Chinese composition.

字 *Kanji* Chinese characters.

堡 *Hamburgu* Hamburg.

語 *Kango* a Chinese word.

學 *Kangaku* Chinese literature.

籍 *Kanseki* a Chinese book.

滌 TEKI; JŌ. *Susu(gu* to wash; rinse.

T 漆 SHITSU. *Urushi* lacquer.

器 *Shikki* lacquered-ware.

漲 CHŌ. *Minagi(ru)* to overflow; swell up.

滚々 *Konkon* to rush down; to gush up.

r 漫 MAN wide. *Habiko(ru)* to spread: *sozoro ni* without deliberate intention: *midari* self-wilfulness; arbitrariness.

步 *Mampo* strolling.

畫 *Manga* sketches; caricature.

然 *Manzen* heedlessly; thoughtlessly.

遊 *Man-yū* to travel for pleasure.

漣 REN. *Sazanami* wavelets.

漉 ROKU. *Ko(su)* to filter: *su(ku)* to make (paper).

漑 GAI. *Soso(gu)* to irrigate.

漬 SHI. *Tsu(keru)* to pickle: *hita(su)*; *tsuka(ru)* to soak.

物 *Tsukemono* pickles.

T 演 EN to amplify. *No(beru)* to speak; lecture; explain.

奏 *Ensō* musical performance.

習 *Enshū* exercises; manoeuvres.

說 *Enzetsu* a speech.

劇 *Engeki* (theatrical) play.

壇 *Endan* rostrum; platform.

藝 *Engei* performance.

繹 *En-eki* deductive.

T 漂 HYŌ. *Tadayo(u)* to drift: *sasura'u* to wander about: *sara(su)* to bleach.

泊 *Hyōhaku* wandering.

流 *Hyōryū* drifting about (as of ships).

着 *Hyōchaku* to reach land after drifting about at sea.

T 漁 GYO; RYŌ. *Isari* fishing: *sunado(ru)* to fish: *asa(ru)* to fish for; search for

夫 *Gyofu*; *ryōshi* fisherman.

夫の利 *Gyofu-no-ri* fishing in troubled water.

火 *Gyoka*; *isaribi* fire lighted on fishing boats to attract fish.

業 *Gyogyō* fishing.

澁 JŪ to suffer: SHŪ. *Shibu* the juice of an unripe persimmon: *shibui* astringent: *shibu(ru)* to be hesitating; unwilling. →85, 8 T * [1]

（一二）

澁
々　*Shibu-shibu* reluctantly.

面　*Jūmen* wry face.

滯　*Shūtai; jūtai* delay; procrastination.

T 澄　CHŌ; TŌ. *Su(mu)* to be
clear.

T 潛　See foll.

潛　SEN secretly. *Kugu(ru);
mogu(ru)* to dive; sub-
merge; creep in; pass
under: *hiso(mu)* to hide.

水艇　*Sensuitei* submersible
ship; submarine.

伏　*Sempuku* concealment.

航　*Senkō* submarine voyage.

勢力　*Senseiryoku* latent force.

潭　TAN pool; abyss; deep.

潺　SEN the sound of flowing
water.

々　*Sen-sen* the sound of flowing water.

湲　*Senkan* the sound of flowing water.

T 潤　JUN. *Uruo(u)* to be moist;
be rich; receive benefac-
tions: *uruo(su)* to moisten;
give benefactions: *uruoi*
lustre.

色　*Junshoku* to colour; to
embellish.

筆料　*Jumpitsuryō* fee for
writing or painting.

澤　*Juntaku* gloss; profit;
abundance.

潮　CHŌ. *Shio* tide: *ushio* the
water of the ocean. 潮 T

時　*Shiodoki* time for high
tide; right time.

流　*Chōryū* tidal current; pre-
vailing tendencies.

澎　HŌ; BŌ sound of waves.

湖島　*Bōkotō* Pescadore Is-
lands; Ponghou.

湃　*Hōhai* surging.

潟　SEKI. *Kata* a dry beach.

潑　HATSU. *Ha(neru)* to leap.

刺　*Hatsuratsu* vivid; active.

澆　GYŌ; KYŌ perfidious; thin;
to pour.
季　*Gyōki* degeneration.

潰　KAI. *Tsubu (reru), tsui-
(yjeru); tsubu(su)* to break;
crumble.

走　*Kaisō* a rout; disorderly
flight.

亂　*Kairan* disorderly flight.

潰　FUN. *Fu(ku)* to gush
forth.

T 潔　KETSU. *Isagiyoi* clean;
pure; manful; brave.

白　*Keppaku* pure; undefiled;
honest.

癖　*Keppeki* marked habit of
cleanliness.

澪　REI. *Mio* water-way.

（一二）

一三

（一三）

澤 TAKU abundance; benefaction. *Sawa* marsh; *tsuya* lustre; gloss. →85,4 T

山 *Takusan* much.

庵 *Takuan* pickled radish.

T 濁 DAKU; JOKU. *Nigo(ru)* to be muddy: *nigo(su)* to make muddy; make ambiguous.

音 *Daku-on* the *nigori*'ed form of syllable.

流 *Dakuryū* muddy stream.

浪 *Dakurō* muddy waves.

澳 Ū used for its sound.

太利 *Ōsutoriya* Austria.

地利 *Ōsutoriya* Austria.

門 *Makao* Macao.

漆 See 漆 85,11.

T 濃 NŌ. *Koi; komayaka* thick; deep; strong; minute. (*No*).

州 *Nōshū* another name for the province of *Mino*.

厚 *Nōkō* thickness.

淡 *Nōtan* shade; light and shade.

艶 *Nōen* beautiful; coquettish.

霧 *Nōmu* dense fog.

澱 DEN. *Yodo(mu)* to settle; be stagnant; falter: *ori* sediment.

粉 *Dempun* starch.

T 激 GEKI. *Hageshii* to be excited; fierce; sudden.

昂 *Gekikō* to be angry; be excited.

甚 *Gekijin* severe.

怒 *Gekido* indignation; rage.

烈 *Gekiretsu* excitable; passionate; violent.

論 *Gekiron* animated discussion.

震 *Gekishin* severe shock (of earthquake).

賞 *Gekishō* praise highly.

増 *Gekizō* sudden increase.

戰 *Gekisen* severe fight.

勵 *Gekirei* to encourage; stimulate.

變 *Gekihen* violent change.

濫 RAN to overflow; spread over. *Midari* reckless; unlawful.

一四

用 *Ran-yō* abuse; misappropriation.

伐 *Rambatsu* indiscriminate felling (of trees).

造 *Ranzō* over-production.

設 *Ransetsu* excessive building.

發 *Rampatsu* excessive or indiscriminate issue.

費 *Rampi* prodigality; waste.

觴 *Ranshō; ranchō* commencement; beginning.

濯 TAKU. *Susu(gu)* to rinse; wash.

濟 SAI; SEI to assist; save. *Su(mu); suma(su)* to finish: *sumanai* regrettable; unpardonable: *na(su)* to pay back; settle.
→85,8 T

283

（一四）

濟
々 *Seisei* full of.

世 *Saisei* salvation.

世會 *Saiseikai* Imperial Charity Association.

民 *Saimin* saving of people.

度 *Saido* salvation.

灣 NEI; DE mud. *Nuka(ru)* to be muddy. *Nukarumi* muddy place (on a road)

濤 TŌ. *Nami* great waves; billows.

潤 See 闊 169,9.

濡 JU. *Nu(reru)*; *nura(su)* to be wet; soak.

手 *Nurete* wet hand.

衣 *Nureginu* false charge.

鼠 *Nurenezumi* drowned rat; drenched to the skin.

鴻 KŌ large; great. *Ōtori* a large wild goose. 【鳥】

毛 *Komō* a bird's feather; very light matter; matter of no importance or value.

恩 *Kōon* great benevolence.

業 *Kōgyō* great achievement.

濛 MŌ dark; obscure; misty; foggy.

濠 GŌ. *Hori* moat.

太刺利亞 *Ōsutorariya* Australia.

洲 *Gōshū* Australia.

濱 See foll.

濱 HIN. *Hama* beach; seacoast; abbreviation of Yokohama. →85,7 T

風 *Hamakaze* land-wind.

邊 *Hamabe* shore; beach.

濕 SHITSU. *Shime(ru)*; *shito-(ru)* to be moist; wet. →85. 9 T

氣 *Shikki* dampness; moisture.

潤 *Shitsujun* damp; moist

瀉 SHA to v mit; to flow into. *Kuda(su)* to have the bowels loose.

瀑 BAKU. *Taki* wa erfall.

布 *Bakufu* waterfall.

濺 SEN. *Soso(gu)* to pour; to sprinkle.

瀆 TOKU. *Kega(su)*; *kega-(reru)* to defile.

職 *Tokushoku* official corruption.

濾 RO. *Ko(su)* to filter.

過 *Roka* to filter.

瀝 RFKI to dredge; clean out; to drip; to pour out.

瀧 RŌ. *Taki* waterfall. →85,10 T

口 *Takiguchi* ledge from which waterfall falls.

瀨 RAI. *Se* shallows; shoal; rapids. →瀬 T

（一四）

（一五）

（一六）

（一六）
瀬　*Seto* strait; porcelain; also p. n.

瀬内海　*Seto-naikai* the Inland Sea.

瀬物　*Setomono* porcelain.

瀕　HIN shore; brink; near.

死　*Hinshi* serious; dying.

一七
瀟　SHŌ pure; clean.

洒　*Shōsha* frank; clean.

瀾　RAN to drip; great waves.

瀰　BI to diffuse; spread; overflow; permeate.

漫　*Biman* to overflow; spread.

一八
灌　KAN to wash. *Soso*(*gu*) to irrigate.

木　*Kamboku* a shrub.

腸　*Kanchō* enema.

漑　*Kangai* irrigation.

一九
灘　TAN; DAN. *Nada* a sea; normally rough part of the sea.

二二
灣　WAN gulf; bay. →85,9 T

曲　*Wankyoku* curve.

八六　火

When at the left it is called *Hi-hen*. When at the bottom it

generally take the modified form ,,, and is then called *Renga* or *Rekka*.

T. 火　KA. *Hi* fire; flame.

山　*Kazan* volcano.

夫　*Kafu* fireman.

吹竹　*Hifuki-　be* bamboo tube used for blowing the fire.

災　*Kasai* a fire; conflagration.

事　*Kaji* a fire; conflagration.

急　*Kakyū* urgency.

消壺　*Hikeshi-tsubo* a pot with lid into which live charcoal is put to extinguish it.

焔　*Kaen* flame.

番　*Hi-no-ban* fire watchman.

葬　*Kasō* cremation.

蓋　*Hibuta* apron (of a gun).

傷　*Yakedo* scald; burn.

鉢　*Hibachi* brazier.

曜　*Kayō* Tuesday.

薬　*Kayaku* gunpowder.

二
灯　TEI; CHŌ; CHIN. *Hi*; *tomoshibi* a light.

三
灼　SHAKU to heat; red-hot.

熱　*Shakunetsu* to heat; to make red-hot.

灸　KYŪ. *Yaito* moxa; punishment.

四
炉　See 爐 86,16.

→炉 T

（四）
炊 T SUI. *Kashi(gu)* ; *ta(ku)* to cook rice ; cook.

夫 *Suifu* a cook.

事 *Suiji* cooking.

炎 T EN inflammation ; hot ; to burn. *Honō* flame.

上 *Enjō* burn up.

天 *Enten* hot weather ; under scorching sun.

症 *Enshō* inflammation.

暑 *Ensho* scorching heat.

炙 SHA. *Abu(ru)* to broil ; roast.

五 **炬** KYO ; KO. *Taimatsu* torch.

火 *Kyoka* ; *taimatsu* torch.

燵 *Kotatsu* a charcoal foot-warmer.

畑 T *Hatake* ; *hata* field ; dry field. 【田】

炯 KEI clear ; bright.

々 *Kei-kei* fiery ; glittering.

眼 *Keigan* glittering eyes ; clear-sightedness.

炳 HEI ; HYŌ. *Akiraka* bright.

乎 *Heiko* very clear.

炮 HŌ. *Abu(ru)* ; *ya(ku)* to roast.

点 T See **點** 203,5.

烟 See T **煙** 86,9. 六

烝 JŌ. *Mu(su)* to steam.

> fire radical

烈 RETSU. *Hageshii* ardent ; violent.

士 *Resshi* a loyal, upright, devoted person.

火 *Rekka* blazing fire.

風 *Reppū* violent wind.

婦 *Reppu* heroine ; brave woman.

烏 U ; O ; E. *Karasu* crow : *izukunzo* why ; how.

合 *Ugō* confused crowd.

有 *Uyū* being burnt down.

兎匆々 *Uto sōsō* time flies.

帽子 *Eboshi* old-fashioned head-gear.

賊 *Ika* cuttle-fish.

馬 T See 187,0. horse radical

焗 KEI bright. 七

々 *Keikei* glittering ; penetrating.

眼 *Keigan* keen-sighted ; shrewd.

魚 T See 195,0. yu fish

焉 EN. *Izukunzo* how ; why.

鳥 T See 196,0.

286

八 焰 EN. *Honō; homura* flame.

々 *En-en* blazing.

焙 HŌ; HAI; BAI. *Abu(ru)* to toast; roast; warm.

焚 FUN; HON. *Ta(ku)* to burn; kindle.

黑 See 203,0.

T 無 MU negative prefix: BU. *Nai* not.

二 *Muni* incomparable; peerless.

二無三 *Muni-musan* desperately.

人 *Bunin* want of persons.

上 *Mujō* most excellent; best.

口 *Mukuchi* taciturnity.

下 *Muge ni* extremely; very.

干渉 *Mukanshō* non-intervention.

分別 *Mufumbetsu* indiscretion.

之 *Kore naku* (inverted order) there is not; have not.

比 *Muhi* unrivalled.

心 *Mushin* innocent; artless; to ask; beg.

用 *Muyō* unnecessary; unavailable; forbidden.

用心 *Buyōjin* imprudent.

名 *Mumei* unknown.

沙汰 *Busata* neglecting to write or visit.

地 *Muji* plainness.

私 *Mushi* unselfish; disinterested.

邪氣 *Mujaki* innocence.

作法 *Busahō* bad manners.

味乾燥 *Mumikansō* uninteresting; dry.

事 *Buji* safety.

味 *Mumi* tasteless; insipid.

念 *Munen* regret.

花果 *Ichijiku* fig.

法 *Muhō* lawless; violent.

神經 *Mushinkei* insensibility.

垢 *Muku* pure; spotless.

音 *Buin* neglecting to write.

限 *Mugen* unlimited.

政府主義 *Museifu-shugi* anarchism.

差別 *Musabetsu* without discrimination.

益 *Mueki* uselessness.

根 *Mukon* without foundation; groundless.

効 *Mukō* nullity.

料 *Muryō* free of charge.

能 *Munō* incompetency.

茶 *Mucha* confused; absurd.

骨 *Bukotsu* bluntness.

理 *Muri* unreasonable.

宿 *Mushuku; mujuku* homeless.

情 *Mujō* heartless; cruel.

造作 *Muzōsa* easiness; carelessness.

責任 *Musekinin* irresponsibility.

（八）

無

視 *Mushi* to disregard.

筆 *Muhitsu* illiteracy.

智 *Muchi* illiterate; coarse.

聊 *Buryō* loneliness; ennui.

辜 *Mi.kō* innocent.

爲 *Mui; bui* doing nothing.

愛想 *Buaisō* inhospitality; unsociability.

意識 *Muishiki* unconsciousness.

道 *Budō* wickedness.

頓着 *Mutonjaku* unconcern; indifference.

意味 *Muimi* meaningless.

慈悲 *Mujihi* merciless.

勢 *Bu.ei* few persons.

盡藏 *Mujinzō* inexhaustible supply.

馱 *Muda* futile; unavailing.

遠慮 *Buenryo* unreserved; inconsiderate.

論 *Muron* beyond argument: of course.

窮 *Mukyū* inexhaustible; boundless.

數 *Musū* innumerable.

慮 *Muryo* the enormous number of.

敵 *Muteki* matchless.

實 *Mujitsu* untruth; falsity.

謀 *Mubō* rash; absurd.

賴 *Burai* villainy; mischief.

賴漢 *Buraikan* rogue.

學 *Mugaku* ignorance; illiteracy.

線電信 *Musen-denshin* wireless telegraphy.

闇 *Muyami* rashly; exclusively.

償 *Mushō* for nothing.

禮 *Burei* rude.

斷 *Mudan* without notice; without permission.

雙 *Musō; busō* unparalleled; peerless.

難 *Bunan* safe.

鐵砲 *Muteppō* rash.

體 *Mutai* compulsory; rude; insolent.

T 然 ZEN; NEN. *Shikari* yes: *shikashi; shikaru ni* but; however: *shikaru* (irreg.) to be so: *shikashite* and; it being so: *shika; sō* so: *saru* a certain; some; so; such.

迄 *Samade* so far.

諾 *Zendaku* promise.

*

T 煙 EN. *Kemuri; kemu* smoke: *kemu(ru)* to smoke: *kemui; kemutai* smoky: *kemutaga-(ru)* to be in awe (of somebody). →86,6

火 *Hanabi* fireworks.

雨 *En-u* fine, drizzling rain.

突 *Entotsu* chimney.

草 *Tabako* tobacco.

管 *Kiseru* a tobacco-pipe.

煌 *Kō* to shine forth; bright.

（八）

九

238   *T 燒 = 86, 12

(九)

々 *Kōkō; kira-kira* glittering.

煥 KAN light; to shine.

煤 BAI. *Susu* soot.

煉 REN. *Ne(ru)* to forge; temper.

瓦 *Renga* brick.

煩 HAN. *Wazurawa(su)* to vex; trouble: *wazura(u)* to be ill: *urusai* troublesome.

忙 *Hambō* busy.

勞 *Hanrō* trouble.

務 *Hammu* burdensome work.

惱 *Bonnō* worldly passions.

悶 *Hammon* annoyance; vexation.

雜 *Hanzatsu* complication.

T 照 SHŌ. *Tera(su)* to shine; illuminate; compare: *te(ru)* to shine. (*Aki*); (*Akira*).

會 *Shōkai* inquiry by letter.

臨 *Shōrin* to shine upon; look down upon.

準 *Shōjun* aim.

應 *Shōō* correspond.

覽 *Shōran* swear; appeal to Heaven as witness.

煮 See 125,8. 【火】

煎 See 140,10. 【火】
　　　　　　　　　　*

(一〇)燄 See 焰 86,8.

*T 勳 →19,13 * T

(一〇)

熔 YŌ. *Toka(su)* to melt (of minerals).

岩 *Yōgan* lava.

煽 SEN. *Ao(ru)*; *oda(teru)* to flap; stir up; incite.

動 *Sendō* instigation.

熄 SOKU. *Ya(mu)* to cease; die out; go out.

熊 YŪ; YU. *Kuma* bear.

手 *Kumade* rake.

本 *Kumamoto* p. n.

熙 KI; I light; to glitter; shine; to harmonize; wide. (*Hiroshi*).

熨 I. *Hinoshi* a flat-iron: —*noshi* label attached to —gifts: *no(su)* to smooth out; straighten out.

斗 *Noshi* a label; a flat-iron.

熱 See foll.

T 熱 NETSU fever. *Atsui* hot: *hote(ru)* to feel hot.

中 *Netchū* to be zealous.

心 *Nesshin* eagerness; zeal; diligence.

血 *Nekketsu* intense feeling.

狂 *Nekkyō* excitement.

烈 *Netsuretsu* intense; fervent.

海 *Atami* p. n.

氣 *Nekki* heat.

望 *Netsubō* ardent wish.

289

熱

帯　*Nettai* torrid zone.

情　*Netsujō* fervour.

涙　*Netsurui* burning tears.

湯　*Nettō* boiling water; hot water.

誠　*Nessei* earnestness.

辯　*Netsuben* fervent speech.

T 熟　JUKU. *U(mu)* to ripen; mature : *izure* which; anyhow : *tsukuzuku; tsuratsura* thoroughly; quite; carefully.

々　*Tsura-tsura; tsuku-zuku* carefully; thoroughly.

字　*Jukuji* Chinese compound word.

考　*Jukkō* mature reflection.

知　*Jukuchi* to have full knowledge; be acquainted with.

視　*Jukushi* gaze.

睡　*Jukusui* sound sleep.

達　*Jukutatsu suru* to become versed in.

語　*Jukugo* Chinese compound word or phrase.

練　*Jukuren* skill; experience.

慮　*Jukuryo* careful consideration.

議　*Jukugi* mature deliberations.

讀　*Jukudoku* careful reading.

T 燈　TŌ lamp. *Tomoshibi; akashi* light : *tomo(su)* to light.

火　*Tōka* lamp-light.

二二　

臺　*Tōdai* lighthouse.

籠　*Tōrō* stone or metal lantern.

燐　RIN phosphorus.

寸　*Matchi* match (for fire).

燗　KAN making *sake* warm.

熾　SHI to burn. *Sakan* flourishing.

烈　*Shiretsu* intense.

燒　SHŌ. *Ya(ku)* to burn; bake. →86,8 T *

打　*Yakiuchi* attacking and burning.

失　*Shōshitsu* burnt down.

芋　*Yakiimo* baked sweet potato.

死　*Shōshi; yakejini* burnt to death.

却　*Shōkyaku* burn.

物　*Yakimono* earthenware.

棄　*Yakisute; shōki* to burn up; destroy by fire.

跡　*Yakeato* ruins after a fire.

餅　*Yakimochi* jealousy.

T 燃　NEN. *Mo(y)eru); moya(su); mo(su)* to burn.

料　*Nenryō* fuel.

燒　*Nenshō* combustion.

燄　EN to burn. *Honō; homura* flame.

勳　See 勳 19,14.

（二二）燕 EN. *Tsubame; tsubakuro* a swallow.

尾服 *Embifuku* a swallow-tail coat.

雀 *Enjaku* common people.

麥 *Karasumugi; embaku* oats.

（一三）燭 SHOKU; SOKU candle; to illuminate. *Tomoshibi* light.

光 *Shokkō* candle-power.

T 燥 SŌ. *Hasha(gu)* to get dry; be in high spirits.

燦 SAN bright.

然 *Sanzen* glittering; brilliant.

爛 *Sanran* glittering; brilliant.

燵 TATSU. *Kotatsu* a charcoal foot-warmer.

燧 SUI a beacon. *Hiuchi* fire produced by a flint and steel.

營 See 30,14. 【火】

黗 See 點 203,5.

（一四）燼 JIN a charred piece of wood; extinguished fire-brand.

燻 KUN. *Ibu(su); ibu(ru); kusubu(ru); kusu(beru)* to emit smoke and not flame (imperfect combustion).

（一五）T 爆 BAKU explosion; to burst.

沈 *Bakuchin* to explode and sink.

破 *Bakuha* to explode; blow up.

裂 *Bakuretsu* explosion.

發 *Bakuhatsu* explosion; eruption.

彈 *Bakudan* bomb.

（一六）爐 RO furnace; hearth; fire-place. →86,4T

黨 See 203,8.

（一七）爛 RAN bright. *Tada(reru)* to be inflamed.

漫 *Ramman* splendid; in full bloom.

熟 *Ranjuku* full maturity.

87

八七

爪

爪 SŌ. *Tsume* nail; hoof; claw. Do not confound with 瓜 97,0.

牙 *Sōga* claws and teeth; chief protection or help.

先上 *Tsumasaki-agari* gentle slope.

彈 *Tsumahajiki* fillip.

（三）安 DA gentle; quiet; smooth. 【女】 →妥T

協 *Dakyō* conference; compromise.

(三) 安當 *Datō* proper; reasonable.

四 爭 Sō. *Araso(u)* to contend; struggle; quarrel: *isakai* quarrel: *ikadeka* how. →6,5 T

議 *Sōgi* dispute.

奪 *Sōdatsu* to take by force.

論 *Sōron* dispute; quarrel.

鬪 *Sōtō* fight.

釆 SAI. *To(ru)* to take; to choose. Do not confound with 采 165,0. (*Une*) 【釆】

配 *Saihai* a dusting-brush; command.

T受 See 29,6.

五 爰 EN. *Koko ni* here; therefore; thereupon.

六 奚 KEI. *Nanzo; izukunzo* how; why. 【大】

八 舜 See 136,6.

爲 I. *Na(su); suru* (irreg.) to do; work: *na(ru)* to become: *tame ni* for the sake of; for; by; to: *shi(muru)* (inverted order) serves for forming causative in lit. st. →1,8 T

人 *Hitotonari* character.

政者 *Iseisha* statesman.

替 *Kawase* (inverted order) money order; draft; bill of exchange.

T愛 See 35,10. 【心】 九

孵 FU. *Kae(ru); kae(su)* to hatch. 【子】 一〇

化 *Fuka* hatching.

爵 SHAKU peerage; court rank. 一四

位 *Shakui* peerage; court rank.

爨 See 173,17. 二一

父 八八

T父 FU. *Chichi; tete; toto* father!

子 *Fushi; oyako* father and child

兄 *Fukei* father and brother; guardians.

母 *Fubo; chichihaha* parents.

祖 *Fuso* ancestors.

斧 FU to cut. *Ono* an axe. 四 【斤】

釜 FU. *Kama* boiler; cauldron. 六 【金】

山 *Fusan* p. n.

爺 YA. *Jii; jiji; oyaji* an old man; father. 九

爻 八九

爼 See **爼** 9,7.

In Tōyō Kanjis always : 爿

爿 九〇

三 **壯** Sō magnificent. *Sakan* strong; vigorous. 【士】

丁 *Sōtei* full-grown man.

士 *Sōshi* bravo; political bully.

大 *Sōdai* grand; magnificent.

年 *Sōnen* an adult.

快 *Sōkai* magnificent and interesting.

烈 *Sōretsu* heroic.

時 *Sōji* prime of life.

健 *Sōken* health.

語 *Sōgo* big words.

擧 *Sōkyo* daring enterprise.

麗 *Sōrei* magnificent.

観 *Sōkan* grand sight.

四 **狀** Jō letter; form; appearance; state; condition; circumstance. 【犬】

袋 *Jōbukuro* envelope.

況 *Jōkyō* condition; state.

態 *Jōtai* condition; state.

牀 SHŌ. *Toko* bed; *yuka* floor. (四)

將 SHŌ a general; officer. 七 *Hata* moreover: *masa ni* nearly; almost; about; be going to. 【寸】→將 T

又 *Hatamata* or again; moreover.

士 *Shōshi* officers and men.

卒 *Shōsotsu* officers and men.

來 *Shōrai* the future.

軍 *Shōgun* a general; the Shōgun.

帥 *Shōsui* a general; commander.

校 *Shōkō* officer.

棋 *Shōgi* chess.

牆 See 墙 32,13. 一三

片 九一

T**片** HEN. *Kata* side; one side; one of a couple: *kire* piece; fragment: *hira* petal: *pensu* penny; pence.

方 *Katahō; katappo* one side; one of a couple.

手落 *Katateochi* partiality.

田舎 *Kata-inaka* remote country place.

293

片
言 *Hengen* the slightest word or hint : *katakoto* imperfect language or pronunciation.

面 *Katamen* one side.

思 *Kata-omoi* unreturned love.

時 *Kata'ok:* ; *henji* a moment.

腕 *Kataude* one arm ; right-hand man ; indispensable.

腹 *Katahara* the side (of one's body).

腹痛い *Katahara-itai* ridiculous ; laughable.

意地 *Kataiji* stubbornness.

影 *Hen-ei* shadow : more emphatic than simple 影 59,12 which see.

道 *Katamichi* one way.

親 *Kata-oya* a parent.

四 ᴛ版 HAN printing-block ; board ; plate ; edition.

下 *Hanshita* picture or writing (reversed) pasted on to bottom of wooden block to guide the engraver.

木 *Hangi* wooden block for printing.

圖 *Hanto* territory.

權 *Hanken* copyright.

八 牌 HAI playing card ; shield ; medal ; ticket ; sign.

九 牒 CHŌ record ; despatch ; copy ; tablet.

92

牙　九二

牙 GA. *Kiba* canine tooth ; tusk.

ᴛ邪 JA. *Yokoshima* wicked ; 三 evil ; wrong : *ka ; ya* an interrogative particle. 【邑】

心 *Jashin* a malicious intention.

見 *Jaken* ill-natured ; cruel.

念 *Janen* wicked thoughts.

法 *Jahō* black arts.

推 *Jasui* unjust suspicion.

智 *Jachi* perverted talent.

道 *Jadō* evil courses.

慳 *Jaken* ill nature.

魔 *Jama* hindrance ; trouble.

雅 See 172,5.　八

鴉 See 196,5.　二

93
nian

牛　九三

When at the left it is slightly modified and is called *Ushi-hen*.

ᴛ牛 GYŪ. *Ushi* cow ; ox ; bull. Do not confound with 午 24,2.

noon
meridian

294

(handwritten annotations at top: "hand 牛", "animal 牛")

肉	*Gyūniku* beef.
耳	*Gyūji* leadership.
込	*Ushigome* p. n.
津	*Okkusuhōdo* Oxford.
莊	*Nyūchan* Newchwang.
乳	*Gyūnyū* milk (cow's).
酪	*Gyūraku* butter.

一 T 生　See 100,0. *growth*

二 牝　HIN. *Me; mesu* the female of birds and animals.

T 先　SEN last (the one before the present one). *Saki* before; previous; recent; in front; tip; extremity; destination; terminal point of motion as *okurisaki* addressee; the other party or person: *sakinzuru* (irreg.) to forestall; go first: *mazu* in the first place; well then. 【儿】

々月	*Sensengetsu* the month before last.
入主	*Sennyūshu* preconception.
日	*Senjitsu* the other day.
月	*Sengetsu* last month.
方	*Sempō* the other party or person.
天的	*Sententeki* intuitive.
立	*Sakida(tsu)* to go before: *sakidachi* antecedence; precedence; a guide.
生	*Sensei* teacher; master; doctor.

年	*Sennen* former years; past years; some years ago.
代	*Sendai* the predecessor (in the family line).
以	*Mazu-motte* anyhow; for the present.
決	*Senketsu* previous decision.
見	*Senken* foresight.
非	*Sempi* past error.
例	*Senrei* precedent.
刻	*Senkoku* a little while ago; some time ago.
取特權	*Senshu-tokken* preferential right.
夜	*Sen-ya* the other night.
妻	*Sensai* former wife.
帝	*Sentei* the late Emperor.
約	*Sen-yaku* previous engagement.
便	*Sembin* previous mail.
祖	*Senzo* ancestor.
般	*Sempan* some time ago.
登	*Sentō* the head (of a column).
頃	*Sakigoro* some time ago.
程	*Sakihodo* a little while ago.
着	*Senchaku* first arrival.
發	*Sempatsu* to start in advance.
進	*Senshin* seniority.
週	*Senshū* last week.
達	*Sendatte* lately.
鋒	*Sempō* vanguard.
輩	*Sempai* senior.

先
導 *Sendō* guidance.

頭 *Sentō* the first; foremost.

覺者 *Senkakusha* elders; pioneer (intellectual).

驅 *Senku* outrider.

三 牡 Bo. *Osu; o* male of birds and animals.

丹 *Botan* tree-peony.

蠣 *Kaki* oyster.

告 KOKU. *Tsu(geru); mō(su)* to tell; inform. 【口】告 → 告 T

口 *Tsugeguchi* tale-bearing.

白 *Kokuhaku* confession.

示 *Kokuji* a notice.

別 *Koku'etsu* farewell.

訴 *Kokuso* complaint (judicial).

發 *Kokuhatsu* prosecution; charge.

四 T 物 BUTSU; MOTSU. *Mono* thing; matter; article. Frequently used as bottom component, e. g.: *d butsu* animal, *shimmotsu* a present, *kimono* clothes.

心 *Monogok ro* intelligence; take notice.

件 *Bukken* thing.

色 *Busshoku* to search for.

好 *Monogonomi* fastidiousness: *monozuki* curiosity; inquisitiveness.

事 *Monogoto* thing.

dongxi

品 *Buppin* goods.

忘 *Monowasure* forgetful.

音 *Mono-oto* sound; noise.

故 *Bukko* to die.

思 *Mono-omoi* anxiety; meditation.

笑 *Mono-warai* laughing-stock.

理學 *Butsurigaku* physics.

產 *Bussan* productions.

眞似 *Mono-mane* mimicry.

置 *Mono-oki* store-room; godown.

語 *Monogatari* tale; talking; conversation.

資 *Busshi* material; resources.

質 *Busshitsu* substance.

價 *Bukka* prices of commodities.

覺 *Mono-oboe* memory.

議 *Butsugi* public discussion.

騷 *Bussō* danger.

T 牧 BOKU; MOKU to feed; rear; breed. *Maki* field in which animals are kept.

師 *Bokushi* a pastor.

塲 *Bokujō* a pasture.

畜 *Bokuchiku* breeding and rearing of animals.

T 牲 SEI. *Ikenie* an animal sacrifice. 五

牴 TEI to meet; to strike against. *Fu(reru)* to touch.

觸 *Teishoku* to conflict with; run counter to.

六 **特** TOKU special; alone. *Toku ni* specially; only.
T

旨 *Tokushi* special grace.

有 *Tokuyū* peculiar; proper; special; characteristic.

有性 *Tokuyūsei* peculiarity.

色 *Tokushoku* speciality.

志 *Tokushi* charitable spirit; special intention.

別 *Tokubetsu* special.

効 *Tokkō* special efficacy.

使 *Tokushi* express messenger; special envoy.

長 *Tokuchō* a strong point; special talent.

命 *Tokumei* special appointment.

性 *Tokusei* special quality.

定 *Tokutei* specific.

典 *Tokuten* special favour.

待 *Tokutai* special treatment.

派 *Tokuha* despatch specially.

約 *Tokuyaku* special contract.

殊 *Tokushu* special; particular; extraordinary.

産 *Tokusan* special products.

許 *Tokkyo* special permission; licence; patent.

務 *Tokumu* special duty.

赦 *Tokusha* amnesty.

筆 *Tokuhitsu* to write in large characters; memorable.

電 *Tokuden* special telegram.

徵 *Tokuchō* characteristic.

製 *Tokusei* specially made.

質 *Tokushitsu* special quality.

選 *Tokusen* special choice.

權 *Tokken* exclusive right.

犇 HON to run. *Hishime(ku)* to clamour; make a disturbance: *hishi to* tightly. 八

犒 *Negira(u)* to entertain hospitably (especially in return for services rendered). 一〇

T**犠** See **犧** 93,16. 一三

犢 TOKU. *Koushi* calf. 一五

犧 GI. *Ikenie* animal sacrifice. →93,13 T 一六
牲 *Gisei* sacrifice; victim.

犬 gou 九四

When at the left it takes a special form and is called *Kemono-hen.*

T**犬** KEN. *Inu* dog.

馬の勞 *Kemba no rō* small service; do one's best.

猿 *Ken-en* dog and monkey; persons on bad terms.

二 犯 T HAN. *Oka(su)* to commit; perpetrate; offend; transgress.

人 *Hannin* criminal.

罪 *Hanzai* crime.

四 狂 T KYŌ. *Kuru(u)* to be mad; disordered: *kichigai* lunatic; madman.

人 *Kyōjin* madman.

犬 *Kyōken* mad dog.

句 *Kyōku* comic poem.

言 *Kyōgen* theatrical play; a play; a trick.

奔 *Kyōhon* busy oneself about.

氣 *Kyōki* insanity.

喜 *Kyōki* wild joy; rapture.

亂 *Kyōran* insanity; fury.

暴 *Kyōbō* violent.

狃 JŪ to study. *Na(reru)* to be accustomed to.

五 狙 SO. *Nera(u)* to aim at.

擊 *Sogeki* shooting.

狎 KŌ to draw near; to despise. *Na(reru)* to be accustomed to.

狗 KU; KŌ. *Inu* dog; pup.

狐 KO. *Kitsune* fox.

疑 *Kogi* to doubt; hesitate.

狩 SHU; SHŪ. *Kari* hunting: 六 *ka(ru)* to hunt.

人 *Karyūdo* hunter.

獵 *Shuryō* hunting.

狡 KŌ a pup. *Zurui; kosui* cunning; sly; underhand.

猾 *Kōkatsu* cunning.

独 T See 獨 94,13.

哭 See 30,7. *

狸 RI. *Tanuki* a badger. 七

爺 *Tanukijijii* foxy old man.

寢 *Tanukineiri* feigned sleep.

狹 KYŌ. *Semai* limited; narrow: *seba(meru)* to make narrow. →94,6 T *

量 *Kyōryō* narrow-minded.

義 *Kyōgi* narrow sense.

窄 *Kyōsaku* constriction.

隘 *Kyōai* narrowness.

狼 RŌ to be flurried. *Ōkami* wolf.

狽 *Rōbai* consternation.

藉 *Rōzeki* disorder.

狽 BAI wolf; to be flurried.

猛 T MŌ fierce; violent; strong; 八 angry.

火 *Mōka* big, violent fire.

雨 *Mōu* heavy rain.

298 * T 狹 →94,7

省 *Mōsei*; *mōshō* deep reflection; severe self-criticism.

威 *Mōi* ferocity.

烈 *Mōretsu* violence; fierceness.

獸 *Mōjū* beast of prey.

猖 SHŌ to be crazy; insane; severe; violence.

獗 *Shōketsu* violence; rage.

猜 SAI to doubt. *Sone(mu)*; *neta(mu)* to envy.

忌 *Saiki* jealousy.

疑 *Saigi* suspicion.

T 猟 See 獵 94,15.

九 猩々 *Shōjō* orang-outang.

猪 CHO. *Inoshishi*; *i* wild boar.

猫 BYŌ; MYŌ. *Neko* cat.　*mao*

撫聲 *Nekonadegoe* insinuating voice.

猶 YŪ to hesitate. *Nao* still more; again: *gotoshi* like.

太 *Yudaya* Judaea. →猶 T

更 *Naosara* still more.

豫 *Yūyo* delay; respite.

猥 WAI obscene. *Midari ni* at random; unreasonably.

褻 *Waisetsu* obscenity.

猨 EN long-armed monkey; monkey.

T 献 KEN; KON to offer; present to a superior. *Sa(su)* to pass (wine-cup). Sometimes used as abb. of 獻. 94,16. →94,16

立 *Kondate* order of dishes.

猾 KATSU cunning.

獅 SHI. *Shishi* lion.

子 *Shishi* lion.

猿 EN. *Saru*; *mashira* monkey.

轡 *Sarugutsuwa* gag.

T 獄 GOKU. *Hitoya* prison.

囚 *Gokushū* prisoners.

屋 *Gokuya* a prison-house.

窓 *Gokusō* prison.

裡 *Gokuri* in a prison.

獎 See 37,11.

獗 KETSU to be crazy; to be virulent.

獎 See 斃 66,14.

獪 KAI cunning; to be disordered.

獨 DOKU Germany (abb. for Doitsu). *Hitori* alone; by oneself. → 94,6 T

木舟 *Utsubobune*; *marukibune* canoe.

（一三）
獨

立 *Dokuritsu* independence.

立獨行 *Dokuritsu-dokkō* self-reliance.

占 *Dokusen* monopoly; occupying alone.

言 *Hitorigoto* soliloquy.

身者 *Dokushinsha; dokushin-mono* bachelor; person who leads a single life.

步 *Doppo* walk alone; no rival.

唱 *Dokushō* vocal solo.

特 *Dokutoku* speciality.

習 *Doku hū* self-study.

裁 *Dokusai* autocracy.

創 *Dokusō* originality.

逸 *Doitsu* Germany.

語 *Dokugo* soliloquy; German.

舞台 *Hitoributai* sole master of the stage.

樂 *Koma* a top.

斷 *Dokudan* self-decision.

（一四）
獰猛 *Dōmō* ferocity.

T 獲 KAKU. *Uru* (lit. st.; irreg.) to get: *to(ru)* to take; to catch; seize. →140,13

物 *Emono* a catch; spoils; prize.

得 *Kakutoku* to get; acquire.

（一五）
獵

人 *Karyūdo* hunter.

RYŌ. *Ka(ru)* to hunt: *kari* hunting. →94,8 T

犬 *Ryōken* hunting dog.

師 *Ryōshi* hunter.

獸 JŪ. *Kemono; kedamono* quadruped; beast; animal. →94,12 T *

皮 *Jūhi* hide; skin; pelt.

行 *Jūkō* immoral conduct.

慾 *Jūyoku* animal desires.

醫 *Jūi* veterinary surgeon.

獻 KEN; KON to offer or present to a superior; to pass a wine-cup. →94,9 T

上 *Kenjō* to offer or present to a superior.

立 *Kondate* bill of fare; order of dishes.

身 *Kenshin* self-sacrifice.

金 *Kenkin* contribution.

納 *Kennō* to offer; present (as to the Emperor)

獲 KAKU. *Tsuka(mu)* to grip: *sara(u)* to carry away; kidnap.

（九五）
hai? 95

玄 GEN great grand-child; black; dark.

人 *Kuroto* an expert; adept.

米 *Gemmai* unpolished rice.

妙 *Gemmyō* mystical; wondrous.

關 *Genkan* porch; entrance-hall.

五 茲 SHI. *Koko ni* here.
畜 →140,6
See 102,5.

九六

玉 *jade*

When at the left it is called *Tama-hen,* the dot is omitted.

T 玉 GYOKU Imperial; geisha. *Tama* precious stone; gem: *tama(u)* to deign.

水 *Tamamizu* drops of rain falling from the eaves.

石 *Gyokuseki* precious and common stones; good and bad.

步 *Gyokuho* footsteps of a high personage.

突 *Tamatsuki* billiards.

座 *Gyokuza* the Imperial Throne.

章 *Gyokushō; tamazusa* (honorific) your letter.

碎 *Gyokusai* to die game; die in honour.

蜀黍 *Tōmorokoshi* maize.

樓 *Gyokurō* magnificent mansion.

顏 *Gyokugan* the Imperial countenance.

露 *Gyokuro* dew; name of good tea.

體 *Gyokutai* the person of an Emperor.

T 王 Ō monarch; ruler; King. *wang* Do not confound with 壬 32,1.

女 *Ōjo* princess.

位 *Ōi* the throne.

事 *Ōji* affairs of the Emperor.

冠 *Ōkan* a crown.

侯 *Ōkō* Kings and lords.

室 *Ōshitsu* the Royal Family.

者 *Ōsha* Lord; King.

政 *Ōsei* the Imperial administration.

國 *Ōkoku* a kingdom. *wang guo*

道 *Ōdō* rule of right; royal road.

玖 KYŪ; KU used for its 三 sound.

馬 *Kyūba* Cuba.

弄 See 55,4.

玩 GAN toy. *Moteaso(bu)* to 四 play with.

弄 *Ganrō* to make a plaything of.

具 *Gangu* a toy.

味 *Gammi* to taste; appreciate.

珈琲 *Kōhii* coffee. 五

301

（五）**玲** 瓏 *Reirō* clear and bright.

珂 KA used for its sound.

珊 SAN. *Sango* coral: *sanchi* centimetre.

米突 *Sanchi-mētoru* centimetre.

瑚 *Sango* coral.

T **珍** CHIN precious treasure. *Mezurashii* rare; strange; curious.

什 *Chinjū* rare piece; precious things.

事 *Chinji* dreadful event; curious event.

奇 *Chinki* curious; strange

味 *Chimmi* delicacy; rare dish.

重 *Chinchō* to set a high value; prize.

客 *Chinkyaku* a rare guest.

聞 *Chimbun* curious news.

談 *Chindan* an interesting story.

藏 *Chinzō* to cherish; treasure.

玻 璃 *Hari* crystal; glass.

六 T **班** HAN squad (military); rank; order; to stand in a row; to distinguish.

T **珠** SHU. *Tama* pearl; gem.

盤 *Soroban* abacus.

T **理** RI principle; to manage. 七 *Kotowari* reason; right: *wake*; *suji* reason; meaning: *kime* texture.

不盡 *Rifujin* contrary to right.

由 *Riyū* reason; cause; motive.

性 *Risei* reason (as opposed to feelings).

科 *Rika* scientific subjects.

事 *Riji* director; manager.

非 *Rihi* right and wrong.

法 *Rihō* natural law.

財 *Rizai* finance.

智 *Richi* reason (as opposed to feelings).

窟 *Rikutsu* reason; theory.

詰 *Rizume* act of convincing by reason.

解 *Rikai* understanding.

想 *Risō* ideal.

論 *Riron* theory.

髮 *Rihatsu* barber.

T **球** KYŪ sphere; terrestrial globe. *Tama* ball; globe.

T **現** GEN now; present. *Arawa(su)* to show; express: represent; describe: *arawa(reru)* to show oneself; make an appearance: *arawa* frank; apparent; open: *utsutsu* reality; absence of mind.

今 *Genkon* present time.

世 *Gensei* this world.

出 *Genshutsu* appearance.

（七）

代 Gendai the present age.

行 Genkō in operation; existing.

在 Genzai present time; true; real.

存 Genson existing; living.

役 Gen-eki active service.

金 Genkin cash; immediate payment.

物 Gembutsu the actual thing; stocks.

狀 Genjō present (actual) condition.

狀維持 Genjō-iji status quo.

品 Gempin the actual thing.

場 Genjō; gemba the actual place.

象 Genshō phenomenon.

然 Genzen plainly; clearly.

價 Genka present price.

實 Genjitsu the actuality.

琉 RYŪ; RU kind of precious stone.

球 Ryūkyū Loochoo Islands.

望 See 32,8.【月】→聖 T

（八）

斑 HAN. Madara; buchi striped; spotted: fu spots; stripes.【文】

紋 Hammon speckles.

點 Hanten spots.

琢 TAKU. Miga(ku) to polish: era(bu) to choose.

磨 Takuma to polish.

（八）

琥珀 Kohaku amber.

T**琴** KIN. Koto Japanese harp.

瑟相和 Kinshitsu aiwasu to live in conjugal harmony.

琵琶 Biwa Japanese guitar; also p. n.

瑞 ZUI happy; lucky; joy: SUI abb. for Switzerland. Shirushi favourable sign: mizu fresh; beautiful.

西 Suisu; Su'ttsuru Switzerland.

兆 Zuichō a good omen.

典 Suēden Sweden.

祥 Zuishō a good omen.

雲 Zuiun clouds of good omen.

穗の國 Mizuho-no-kuni land of fresh and beautiful ears of rice and corn; Japan.

寶章 Zuihōshō the Order of the Sacred Treasure.

瑕 KA. Kizu flaw; fault.

疵 Kashi defect; flaw.

瑾 Kakin fault; flaw.

瑟 SHITSU a musical instrument (stringed).

聖 See 32,10.【耳】→T望

瑳 SA to polish.

九

一〇

303

（一〇）瑠璃 *Ruri* lapis lazuli.

瑣 SA trifling; small.

々 *Sasa* trivial; light.

末 *Samatsu* trivial; small.

事 *Saji* trifle.

細 *Sasai* trivial; small.

瑩 EI clear; bright.

三 T 環 KAN. *Wa* ring: *megu(ru)* to revolve; go round: *megura(su)* to surround: *tamaki* hand-covering when using bow and arrow.

狀 *Kanjō; wanar* ring-shaped.

海 *Kankai* surrounded by the sea.

視 *Kanshi* concentrated attention.

境 *Kankyō* environment; surroundings.

璧 HEKI. *Tama* precious stone.

一四 璽 JI a sign; the Imperial seal. *Tama* a precious stone.

一五 瓊 KEI. N. *tama* precious stone.

一六 瓏 RŌ used for its sound.

九七 瓜

瓜 KA. *Uri* melon and suchlike fruit. Do not confound with 爪 87,0.

實顔 *Urizanegao* oval-shaped face.

哇 *Jawa* Java.

二 瓢 HYŌ. *Hisago* gourd.

簞 *Hyōtan; hisago* gourd.

九八 瓦

瓦 GA. *Kawara* tile: *guramu* gramme.

全 *Gazen* live in obscurity.

斯 *Gasu* gas.

解 *Gaka.* breakdown; collapse.

三 瓩 *Kiro-guramu* kilogramme.

四 瓰 *Deshi-guramu* decigramme.

瓱 *Mri-guramu* milligramme.

六 瓶 HEI; BIN bottle. *Kame* jar; vase: *tsurube* well-bucket.

八 瓶 See preced.

九 甅 *Senchi-guramu* centigramme.

二 甌 Ō. *Kame* a jar.

九九 甘

T 甘 KAN. *Amai* sweet: *umai* of agreeable taste; pleasant to the senses; good; skilful; successful: *amanjiru* (irreg.) to be contented.

言 *Kangen* sweet words; flattery.

受 *Kanju* suffer; tolerate.

蔗 *Kansho* sugar-cane.

藷 *Kansho* sweet potato.

露 *Kanro* sweet dew; nectar.

三 邯 KAN used for its sound. 【邑】

鄲の枕 *Kantan no makura* evanescence of life.

鄲の夢 *Kantan no yume* evanescence of life.

其 *Sono; sore* that; his; her: *so* that. 【八】

上 *Sonoue* moreover.

々 *Sorezore* respectively.

内 *Sonouchi* some day; in a few days

方 *Sonohō* that direction; that one; you: *sotchi* there.

他 *Sonota* other.

外 *Sonohoka* besides.

迄 *Soremade* till then.

物 *Sonomono* the very thing.

故 *Soreyue* therefore.

後 *Sonogo* afterwards.

時 *Sonotoki* at that time; then.

處 *Soko* there.

頃 *Sonokoro* those times.

程 *Sahod* so much.

筋 *Sonosuji* the authorities; official.

節 *Sonosetsu* on that occasion.

儘 *Sonomama* as it is.

邊 *Sonohen* somewhere about there.

癖 *Sonokuse* nevertheless.

甚 JIN. *Hanahada; itaku* 四 very; extremely.

大 *Jindai* great.

T 某 BŌ. *Soregashi: nanigashi* I; a certain person; Mr. So-and-so. 【木】

氏 *Bōshi* a certain person; Mr. So-and so.

T 基 KI. *Motoi; moto* origin; 六 basis; foundation: *motozu-(ku)* to be due to; be founded on; originate in: *kiro* kilo, prefix to metric measures. 【土】

（六）基

本金 *Kihonkin* a foundation fund.

米突 *Kirométoru* kilometre.

因 *Kiin* cause; origin.

金 *Kikin* a fund.

隆 *Kiirun* Keelung.

督 *Kirisuto*; *Kurisuto* Christ.

準 *Kijun* standard.

調 *Kichō* key-note.

點 *Kiten* cardinal points.

礎 *Kiso* foundation; basis.

七 碁　See ^T棋 75,8.

八 ^T碁　^{Go} Japanese draughts.
【石】

嘗　See 嘗 72,10. 【口】

一〇〇　生

^T生　SEI; SHŌ. *Iki* life: *i(kiru)* to live: *u(mu)* to give birth to; bear; produce: *uma-(reru)* to be born: *umi no* true (father, etc.): *ha(h)-eru)* to sprout out; grow: *i(keru)* to keep alive: *ubu* inexperience; simplicity: *nama* raw (*nama-nie* half-cooked): *ki* not manufactured: original condition: *o(h)iru)* to grow. (*Fu*).

shojiru bring about

中 *Namanaka* little; imperfectly.

立 *Oitachi* growth; career.

半可 *Namahanka* incomplete.

付 *Umaretsuki* natural disposition.

母 *Seibo* the real mother.

存 *Seison* living; existence.

存競爭 *Seison-kyōsō* struggle for existence.

死 *Seishi* life and death.

地 *Seichi* birth-place.

先 *Oisaki* future; prospect.

別 *Seibetsu*; *ikiwakare* life-long parting.

附 *Umaretsuki* natural disposition.

命 *Seimei* life.

物 *Seibutsu* living things.

育 *Seiiku* grow.

長 *Seichō* grow.

來 *Seirai* inborn; by nature.

埋 *Ikiume* bury alive.

活 *Seikatsu* life; livelihood.

計 *Seikei* means of living; livelihood.

前 *Seizen* lifetime.

家 *Seika* the house where one was born; birth-place.

徒 *Seito* student of a school.

氣 *Seiki* vitality.

捕 *Ikedoru* capture alive.

殺 *Namagoroshi* to half kill: *seisatsu* life and death.

殺與奪 *Seisatsuyodatsu* life and death.

涯 *Shōgai* one's whole life.

產 *Seisan* production.

國 *Shōkoku* the native country.

絲 *Kiito* raw silk.

硬 *Seikō* crudeness.

殖 *Seishoku* reproduction; generation.

滅 *Shōmetsu* appearance and disappearance; life and death.

意氣 *Namaiki* forward; impertinent; conceited.

粹 *Kissui no* pure.

憎 *Ainiku* unluckily.

類 *Shōrui* living things.

還 *Seikan* return alive.

七 甥 SEI. *Oi* nephew.

甦 So. *Yomigae(ru)* to return to life; revive.

生 *Sosei* to revive.

一〇一 用

T 用 YŌ business; occupation; used for; as bottom component is equivalent sometimes to -able, e. g. *shokuyō* eatable. *Mochi(h)iru)* to use.

水 *Yōsui* irrigation; rainwater.

心 *Yōjin* caution.

立 *Yoda(teru)* to lend.

件 *Yōken* business; a matter.

向 *Yomuki* affairs; business.

地 *Yōchi* land for use.

兵 *Yōhei* commanding of troops; fighting.

材 *Yōzai* material used.

事 *Yōji* business; something which one has to do.

法 *Yōhō* directions for use.

命 *Yōmei* command; order.

度 *Yōdo* expenses; outlay.

紙 *Yōshi* a blank form.

務 *Yōmu* business; important affair.

捨 *Yōsha* indulgence; forbearance; pardon.

途 *Yōto* use; utility.

達 *Yōtashi* business; anything to be done; a purveyor.

意 *Yōi* preparation; provision.

語 *Yōgo* terminology; language used.

談 *Yōdan* business talk.

濟 *Yōzumi* finishing of business.

T 田 DEN field; land. *Ta* paddy-field; rice-field.

夫 *Dempu* a peasant; a rustic.

田

地 *Denji* rice-field.

舎 *Inaka* the country.

圃 *Tambo* rice-field.

畑 *Tahata; dempata* fields; farm.

野 *Den-ya* fields.

植 *Taue* transplanting rice.

園 *Den-en* fields and garden.

二 ᵀ町 CHŌ unit of length and of surface; see Introduction 44. *Machi* town; street; ward.

人 *Chōnin* townsman; merchant.

立 *Chōritsu* supported by a town.

歩 *Chōbu* unit of square measure; see Introduction 44.

家 *Chōka* tradesman's house.

ᵀ男 DAN Baron : NAN. *Otoko; o* man (male).

工 *Dankō* male hand; workman.

子 *Danshi* man; male.

女 *Danjo; nannyo* man and woman.

女同權 *Danjo-dōken* equality of sexes.

生 *Dansei* male student.

兒 *Danji* a boy; a man.

性 *Dansei* the male.

振 *Otokoburi* personal appearance.

（二）

骨女卑 *Danson-johi* superiority of the male sex; the subjection of woman.

勝 *Otokomasari* equal to men; not inferior to men; masculine.

爵 *Danshaku* Baron.

畄 Seeᵀ留 102,5.　三

ᵀ界 KAI. *Sakai* border; frontier; boundary.　四

隈 *Kaiwai* neighbourhood.

ᵀ胃 I stomach. 【肉】

ᵀ果 See 75,4.

畏 I. *Oso(reru)* to fear: *kashiko(mu)* to regard with awe: *kashikoma(ru)* to obey with respect; assent: *kashikoi* august; reverend.

友 *Iyū* respected friend.

多 *Osoreōi* overwhelming; gracious; august.

怖 *Ifu* fear; awe.

敬 *Ikei* reverence.

縮 *Ishuku suru; ijike(-ru)* to shrink (with fear).

懼 *Iku* fear; awe.

毘 BI kind; to help. 【比】

ᵀ思 SHI. *Omo(u); obo(su)* to think; reflect. 【心】

切 *Omoikiri* resignation.

308

（四）

立 *Omoita(tsu)* to intend; resolve.

出 *Omoide* recollections.

召 *Oboshimeshi* opinion; desire; choice.

付 *Omoitsuki* plan; device.

考 *Shikō* speculation; thinking.

附 *Omoitsuki* a plan; idea.

直 *Omoinao(su)* to reconsider.

案 *Shian* thought; pondering over.

索 *Shisaku* contemplation; thinking.

惟 *Shii* think; consider.

殘 *Omoinoko(su)* to regret to leave.

惑 *Omowaku* thought; intention.

當 *Omoi-ata(ru)* to occur to one's mind.

想 *Shisō* thought.

想家 *Shisōka* thinker.

違 *Omoichigai* misunderstanding.

遺 *Omoiyari* sympathy.

慕 *Shibo* to have an affection for; long for.

慮 *Shiryo* consideration; discretion.

潮 *Shichō* stream of thought; current idea.

五
T 畝 See 8,8. 【田】

畔 HAN to oppose. *Aze; kuro* a path between fields: *ho-*
→畔 T

（五）

tori boundary; bank (as of a pond).

T 留 RYŪ; RU. *Todoma(ru)·toma(ru)* to stop; remain: *todo(meru); to(meru)* to stop: *rūburi* (Russian) rouble: *rūpii* (Indian) rupee. →102, 3

任 *Ryūnin* remaining in office.

守 *Rusu* absence; not at home.

別 *Ryūbetsu* parting.

置 *Ryūchi; tome-oki* detention.

學 *Ryūgaku* studying abroad.

意 *Ryūi* attention.

畜 CHIKU domestic animals. *Ka(u)* to rear (domestic animals). →畜 T

生 *Chikushō* a beast.

產 *Chikusan* live-stock.

類 *Chikurui* animals; beasts.

（六）

畦 KEI. *Aze* ridge between fields.

T 略 RYAKU to contract; make smaller; to conquer; take by force; govern; plan; scheme. *Hobo* nearly; roughly; almost; for the most part. →foll. sign

式 *Ryakushiki* informality.

字 *Ryakuji* an abbreviated character.

言 *Ryakugen* abbreviated expression.

服 *Ryakufuku* undress; ordinary clothes.

述 *Ryakujutsu* to state briefly.

略

記 *Ryakki* a rough sketch.

裝 *Ryakusō* ordinary clothes.

儀 *Ryakugi* informality.

奪 *Ryakudatsu* plunder; pill-age.

圖 *Ryakuzu* a sketch.

稱 *Ryakushō* abbreviation.

歷 *Ryakureki* a brief history.

畧 See prec.

畢 See 72,6. 【田】

T 異 I. *Koto* different; foreign: *kotonaru* (irreg.); *taga(u)* differ: *ayashii* strange; rare.

人 *Ijin* foreigner.

才 *Isai* rare talent.

口同音 *Ikudōon* different mouths same voice; different mouths uttering the same idea; unanimity.

分子 *Ibunshi* foreign element.

存 *Izon* objection.

同 *Idō* difference.

狀 *Ijō* change (for the worse); an unusual occurrence.

性 *Isei* the other sex.

常 *Ijō* change; singularity.

彩 *Isai* conspicuous.

動 *Idō* change.

境 *Ikyō* a foreign land.

說 *Isetsu* different opinion.

端 *Itan* heresy; heterodoxy.

樣 *Iyō* strange; queer.

論 *Iron* objection; dispute.

數 *Isū* an exception.

議 *Igi* objection; protest.

變 *Ihen* an accident; a catastrophe.

T 累 RUI to tie up. *Kasa(neru)*; *kasana(ru)* to pile up: *wazurawa(su)* to cause trouble: *shikiri ni* intently; continually. 【糸】

々 *Ruirui* in heaps.

代 *Ruidai* successive generations.

年 *Ruinen* successive years.

卵 *Ruiran* a pile of eggs; hazardous.

計 *Ruikei* the total sum.

進 *Ruishin* successive promotion.

積 *Ruiseki* accumulation.

∗

崎 KI strange; cripple.

八

形 *Kikei* deformity.

畷 TETSU; TEI. *Nawate* a road through rice-fields.

當 Tō this; that. *A(teru)*; *ata(ru)* to strike against: *ate* reliance; object; expectation; hope: *masa ni* justly; duly; now. →41,3 T

人 *Tōnin* the person in question.

日 *Tōjitsu* that day; the day in question.

（八）

今 *Tōkon* the present times; nowadays.

分 *Tōbun* for the present; for the time being; for a while.

方 *Tōhō* this side; this place; we.

世 *Tōsei* the present time.

年 *Tōnen* this year.

地 *Tōchi* this place; this district.

初 *Tōsho* at first; at the very beginning.

局者 *Tōkyokusha* the authorities.

直 *Tōchoku* to do night duty.

事者 *Tōjisha* the parties; person concerned.

前 *Atarimae* proper; usual.

面 *Tōmen* the present.

座 *Tōza* the time being; current account.

座預金 *Tōza-yokin* current account.

時 *Tōji* at that time; at this time; present time.

番 *Tōban* being on duty.

然 *Tōzen* natural; proper; right.

意即妙 *Tōisokumyō* good for the occasion; improvised.

惑 *Tōwaku* trouble; perplexity.

該 *Tōgai* proper; concerned.

節 *Tōsetsu* now; at the present time; nowadays.

選 *Tōsen* being elected.

一一

鴫 *Shigi* snipe. 【鳥】

疊 See 疊 102,17.

奮 See 37,13.

一二

嬲 JŌ. *Nabu(ru)* to make sport of; to play. 【女】

一三

壘 RUI fortress. *Kasana(ru)* to be piled up. 【土】 →102,7 T *

一七

疊 JŌ aux. num. for counting mats; to repeat; to pile up. *Tatami* thick straw mat: *tata(mu)* to fold. →102,9 T *

疋

疋 HIKI aux. num. for counting animals and pieces of cloth: SHO. *Ashi* foot.

六

蛋白 *Tampaku* albumen. 【虫】

七

疎 See foll.

疏 So to pass through. *Utoi; orosoka* negligent: *utonzuru* (irreg.) to keep at arm's length: *mabara* sparse; scanty. →157,7

外 *Sogai* estrangement.

食 *Soshi; soshoku* coarse food.

通 *Sotsū* drainage; understanding.

* T 疊 →102,17

（七）疏
隔　*Sokaku* alienation.
漏　*Soro* careless.
遠　*Soen* estrangement; remissness.

八　楚　So old name for part of China; a thorn. 【木】
夕　*Soso* slender; graceful.

九 ᴛ疑　See 21,12. 【疋】

一〇四　疒

Always on top and left, and is called *Yamai-dare*.

三　疝　Sᴇɴ pain in the loins or abdomen.
氣　*Senki* colic.
痛　*Sentsū* colic.
疚　Kʏᴜ̄. *Yamashii* to have a guilty conscience : *ya(mu)* to be ill.

四 ᴛ疫　Eᴋɪ; ʏᴀᴋᴜ epidemic.
病　*Ekibyō; yakubyō* epidemic; plague.
疕　Hɪ skin-disease.

五 ᴛ症　Sʜō symptoms; nature of a disease. *Yamai* illness.

（五）
狀　*Shōjō* symptoms.

疽　So. *Kasa* a sore; ulcer.
疳　Kᴀɴ children's diseases.

ᴛ病　Bʏō; ʜᴇɪ. *Yamai; itazuki* illness; disease : *ya(mu)* to be ill.
人　*Byōnin* sick person.
中　*Byōchū* being ill; while one is ill.
死　*Byōshi* death from sickness; natural death.
身　*Byōshin* weak constitution.
床　*Byōshō* a sick bed.
的　*Byōteki* morbid.
狀　*Byōjō* conditions.
臥　*Byōga* being ill abed.
毒　*Byōdoku* the virus.
症　*Byōshō* symptoms (of a disease).
氣　*Byōki* illness.
原　*Byōgen* cause of disease.
院　*Byōin* hospital.
勢　*Byōsei* condition of a patient.
褥　*Byōjoku* sick-bed.
軀　*Byōku* a sick body.
魔　*Byōma* illness.

疹　Sʜɪɴ eruptions. *Hashika* measles.

ᴛ疾　Sʜɪᴛsᴜ. *Yamai* disease; illness : *hayai* quick; fast : *toku* early; quickly.
走　*Shissō* running fast.

312

（五）
呼 *Shikko* calling out loudly.

風 *Shippū ; hayate* gale.

病 *Shippei* disease ; sickness.

驅 *Shikku* gallop ; furious driving.

T 疲 HI. *Tsuka(reru)* to be tired ; be exhausted.

勞 *Hirō* to be tired.

弊 *Hihei* to exhaust ; impoverish.

疱 HŌ. *Mogasa* smallpox.

瘡 *Hōsō* smallpox.

疼 TŌ to pain. *Uzu(ku)* to ache ; throb ; to be sore, painful.

痛 *Totsū* pain ; ache.

六 痒 YŌ ; SHŌ to scratch. *Kayui ; kaii* itching.

痔 JI piles.

疾 *Jishitsu* piles.

痍 I. *Kizu* wound.

痕 KON. *Ato* remains ; scar.

跡 *Konseki* trace ; mark.

疵 SHI. *Kizu* wound.

七 痙 KEI. *Hikitsu(ru)* to have the cramp.

攣 *Keiren* convulsions.

（七）
T 痘 TŌ smallpox.

T 痢 RI to purge ; diarrhoea.

T 痛 Tsū. *Ita(mu)* to hurt : *itai* painful : *itamashii ; itawashii* pitiful : *itaku* very ; extremely.

手 *Itade* severe wound ; heavy blow.

切 *Tsūsetsu* urgently ; keenly.

心 *Tsūshin* anxious about.

快 *Tsūkai* great pleasure.

苦 *Tsūku* acute pain.

恨 *Tsūkon* great sorrow.

痒 *Tsūyō* pain and itch ; interest ; concern.

惜 *Tsūseki* deep regret.

棒 *Tsūbō* severe attack.

飲 *Tsūin* carouse.

罵 *Tsūba* condemnation.

歎 *Tsūtan* deep lamentation.

痣 *Aza* a birth-mark.

八
T 痴 CHI foolish.

人 *Chijin* simpleton.

情 *Chijō* blind passion.

鈍 *Chidon* dull-witted ; slow.

話 *Chiwa* lover's talk.

話狂 *Chiwagurui* billing and cooing.

漢 *Chikan* fool.

痼 KO chronic disease ; persistent complaint.

疾 *Koshitsu* chronic disease.

（八）

痺 HI palsy. *Shibi(reru)* to be numb.

瘁 SUI to be sick; to be tired, fatigued.

痾 A chronic or serious disease.

痰 TAN phlegm; mucus.

唾 *Tantsuba* spittle.

痲 RIN gonorrhoea. Often used mistakenly for following.

痳 MA to be paralysed. Often used mistakenly for preceding.

痺 *Mahi* paralysis.

醉 *Masui* anaesthesia.

痿 I cripple. *Na(y)eru)* to weaken: *shibi(reru* to be numb.

（九）

瘍 YŌ a carbuncle; anthrax.

瘋 FŪ headache.

癲 *Fūten* idiot.

（一〇）

瘡 SŌ. *Kasa* eruption: *kizu* wound: *dekimono* boil.

毒 *Sōdoku* syphilis.

痕 *Sōkon* a scar.

痍 *Sōi* a wound.

瘤 *Kobu* protuberance; swelling; wen; lump.

瘠 SEKI. *Ya(seru)* to be emaciated.

我慢 *Yasegaman* endurance beyond one's strength.

（一〇）

瘦 SŌ; SHŪ. *Ya(seru)* to be emaciated, thin.

軀 *Sōku* slender body.

（一一）

癌 GAN cancer.

癇 KAN peevishness; irritability; epilepsy.

積 *Kanshaku* irritability.

癖 *Kampeki* irritability.

癪 *Kanshaku* a quick temper.

癆 RŌ consumption.

癈 HAI chronic disease; cripple; invalid.

兵 *Haihei* crippled soldier.

疾 *Haishitsu* chronic disease.

療 RYŌ. *Iya(su)* to heal; to restore.

法 *Ryōhō* method of treatment.

治 *Ryōji* medical treatment.

養 *Ryōyō* recuperation.

（一二）

癖 HEKI. *Kuse* habit.

癒 YU. *I(y)eru)* ; *nao(ru)* ; *iya(su)* to recover; get well; heal; cure.

癪 SHAKU. *Sashikomi* internal spasms; hysteria. （一六）

癩 RAI leprosy.

癲癇 *Tenkan* epilepsy. （一九）

一〇五

火

四 **癸** KI. *Mizunoto* the last of the 10 calendar signs. See Introduction 42, 43.

T **発** See **發** 105,7.

五 T **祭** See 113,6.

七 T **登** TŌ; TO. *Nobo'ru*) to ascend; rise.

山 *Tozan* mountaineering.

用 *Tōyō* appointment; promotion.

記 *Tōki* registration.

塲 *Tōjō* entrance (to the stage).

載 *Tōsai* to record; note down.

樓 *Tōrō* go to a house of ill-fame.

壇 *Tōdan* go on the platform.

錄 *Tōroku* registration.

簿 *Tōbo* registration; entry.

廳 *Tōchō* take up a post in a government office.

發 HATSU aux. num. for counting discharges of guns; to rouse; to start; from; coming or proceeding from: HOTSU to emit; open; discharge. *Aba(ku)* to disclose. →57, 9 : 105, 4 T

心 *Hosshin* religious awakening.

句 *Hokku* 17-syllable short poem.

布 *Happu* promulgation.

刊 *Hakkan* publication.

生 *Hassei* growth; outbreak.

行 *Hakkō* issuing; publication.

狂 *Hakkyō* to become mad.

言 *Hatsugen* speech; utterance.

作 *Hossa* paroxysm.

足 *Hassoku* departure; start.

見 *Hakken* discovery.

兌 *Hatsuda* publication.

明 *Hatsumei* invention.

育 *Hatsuiku* growth.

表 *Happyō* announcement; publication.

信 *Hasshin* despatch of a message.

音 *Hatsuon* pronunciation.

射 *Hassha* firing; discharging (a gun).

案 *Hatsu-an* proposal.

送 *Hassō* to send.

起 *Hokki* proposal.

起人 *Hokkinin* promoter.

堀 *Hakkutsu* to dig out.

動 *Hatsudō* motion; manifestation.

動機 *Hatsudōki* motor.

展 *Hatten* expansion; development.

着 *Hatchaku* arrival and departure of trains, etc.

315

（七）發

揮 *Hakki* to make clear; make manifest.

揚 *Hatsuyō* exaltation.

會式 *Hakkaishiki* the opening ceremony.

達 *Hattatu* development.

端 *Hottan* beginning; the origin.

憤 *Happun* be stimulated.

賣 *Hatsubai* to sell.

頭人 *Hottōnin* originator.

議 *Hatsugi, hotsugi* proposal.

覺 *Hakkaku* detection; disclosure.

露 *Hatsuro* exhibition.

一〇六

白

T白 HAKU; BYAKU clear: evident. *Shiroi* white; pure: *shira(mu)* to grow light: *mō(su)* to say; state.

人 *Hakujin* white man; European.

日 *Hakujitsu* daylight.

木 *Shiraki; shiroki* plain wood not lacquered nor varnished.

米 *Hakumai* hulled rice.

耳義 *Berugii; Berujūmu* Belgium.

兵戰 *Hakuheisen* a close combat.

衣 *Byakui* white dress.

金 *Hakkin* platinum.

狀 *Hakujō* confession.

眉 *Hakubi* the best.

面 *Shirafu* soberness.

粉 *Oshiroi* face paint.

晝 *Hakuchū* broad daylight.

國 *Hakkoku* Belgium.

晳人種 *Hakuseki-jinshu* the white race.

痴 *Hakuchi* fool.

墨 *Hakuboku* chalk.

銅 *Hakudō* nickel.

樺 *Shirakaba* the birch.

髮 *Shiraga; hakuhatsu* white hair.

蓮 *Byakuren* white lotus.

熱 *Hakunetsu* incandescence; fervour.

三 T的 TEKI like; similar. *Mato* target; object; aim. A suffix which forms adjectives from nouns, e. g.: *keizai* economy, *keizaiteki* economical.

中 *Tekichū* hitting the mark.

確 *Tekikaku* reliable; trustworthy.

帛 HAKU. *Kinu* silk cloth.【巾】

四 皈 KI. *Kae(ru)* to return.

T皇 KŌ; Ō. *Sumeragi; sumera* Emperor; Sovereign; Imperial.

(四)

子 *Ōji* Prince (Emperor's son only).

大神宮 *Kōtaijingū* the two shrines in Ise.

女 *Ōjo* Princess (Emperor's daughter only).

太子殿下 *Kōtaishi-denka* H. I. H. the Crown Prince.

位 *Kōi* throne.

后 *Kōgō* Empress.

居 *Kōkyo* Imperial palace.

室 *Kōshitsu* Imperial house or family.

帝 *Kōtei* Emperor.

威 *Kōi* power of the Emperor.

祖 *Kōso* the Founder of the Empire.

孫 *Kōson* Imperial grandchild.

恩 *Kōon* Imperial favour.

基 *Kōki* foundation of the Imperial family.

族 *Kōzoku* the Imperial family.

國 *Kōkoku; mikuni* Emperor's country; Empire; Japan.

都 *Kōto* Imperial capital.

統 *Kōtō* Imperial line.

運 *Kōun* Imperial prosperity.

謨 *Kōbo* Imperial administrative policy.

T 泉 SFN. *Izumi* spring (of water). 【水】

水 *Sensui* spring; pond.

州 *Senshū* another name for the province of Izumi.

317

(四)

T 皆 See 81,5. 【白】

畠 *Hatake; hata* field; vegetable garden. 【田】　五

皎 *Kō* brightness of the moon; white; bright.　六

々 *Kōkō* brilliantly white.

皐月 *Satsuki* poetic name for the 5th month (old calendar).

皓 *Kō* white; clear; to be bright.　七

皚 GAI whiteness (of frost or snow).　一〇

々 *Gaigai* whiteness (of snow).

魄 HAKU. *Tamashii; tama* soul; spirit. 【鬼】

皮　一〇七

When at the left it is called *Kawa-hen*.

T 皮 HI. *Kawa* skin; leather; fur; bark.

肉 *Hiniku* malice; irony.

相 *Hisō* outward look; shallowness; superficiality

膚 *Hifu* skin.

頗 HA to be prejudiced; incline to one side. *Sukoburu* very; greatly. 【頁】　九

（九〇）鼓 See T 鼓 207,0.

一〇 皺 SHŪ; SŪ. Shiwa wrinkles; folds.

一〇八 皿

皿 BEI. Sara plate; dish; saucer.

一 T 血 See 143,0.

三 盂蘭盆 Urabon Buddhist festival of the dead.

四 T 盆 BON a tray; Buddhist festival of the dead.

栽 Bonsai a potted plant; dwarf tree.

景 Bonkei miniature garden.

暮 Bonkure June and December.

盈 EI. Mi(chiru) to be full; be completed.

盃 See T 杯 75,4.

五 監 See T 監 108,9.

T 益 See 益 12,8. 【皿】

盍 KŌ; CŌ. Nanzo why.

*¹ T 盗 →108,7　　*² T 盛 →108,7　　318

七

盗 TŌ. Nusu(mu) to steal. →108,6 *¹ T

人 Nusubito; nusutto thief.

用 Tōyō to steal.

賊 Tōzoku thief.

難 Tōnan robbery.

盛 SEI. Sakan prosperous; flourishing: sakari time of highest vigour; prime of life; full bloom (of flowers): mo(ru) to fill up; heap up. →108,6 *² T

上 Moria(geru) to heap up; pile up.

大 Seidai prosperity; success.

況 Seikyō prosperous condition.

夏 Seika mid-summer.

衰 Seisui rise and fall; flourish and decay; prosperity and adversity; ups and downs; well-being.

場 Sakariba fashionable quarter.

會 Seikai a successful meeting.

運 Seiun prosperity.

裝 Seisō full dress.

擧 Seikyo a great deed; excellent enterprise.

入

塩 See 鹽 108,19. 【鹵】

T 盟 MEI compact; alliance. Chika(u) to take an oath.

主 Meishu chief of confederate states.

約 Meiyaku covenant; confederacy.

九
T 監 KAN; KEN to take warning; govern; look at; oversee; inspect; examine. →108, 5

守 *Kanshu* custody; charge; a keeper.

査 *Kansa* inspection; auditor.

査役 *Kansayaku* auditor.

視 *Kanshi* custody; superintendence.

修 *Kanshū* supervision.

督 *Kantoku* superintendence.

禁 *Kankin* to imprison.

獄 *Kangoku* prison; gaol.

盡 J.N. *Tsu(kiru)* to be exhausted; finish: *tsuku(su)* to use up; exhaust; used often as suffix, e. g. *shi-tsu-kusu* to do everything possible: *kotogotoku* all. →44, 3 T : 15, 4 T

力 *Jinryoku* effort; exertion.

忠 *Jinchū* loyalty.

瘁 *Jinsui* to devote oneself entirely to.

一 T
〇 盤 BAN block; dish; basin; stand: HAN to wind round.

谷 *Bankokku* Bangkok.

一 一 匜 KAN to wash. *Tarai* hand-basin; wash-tub.

二 三 盪 TŌ large; to move; to stir; to wash. *Toroka(su)* to melt; fascinate.

一 四 壏 See foll.

鹽 EN. *Shio* salt 【鹵】 →32, 10 T. 108, 14

引 *Shiobiki* salted fish.

梅 *Ambai* the seasoning or taste of food as the result of artificial preparation.

一九

目

一〇九

When at the left it is called *Me-hen.*

T 目 MOKU to look; see: BOKU. *Me* eye; mesh (as of a net); used as a particle serves to convert cardinal into ordinal numbers.

上 *Me-ue* superiors.

下 *Me-shita* inferiors: *mokka* the present moment.

方 *Mekata* weight.

立 *Me-da(tsu)* to be conspicuous.

出度 *Medetai* auspicious; congratulatory.

安 *Meyasu* standard; aim.

次 *Mokuji* the contents.

附 *Metsuki* expression of eyes

明 *Meaki* one who can see; literate person.

的 *Mokuteki* object; aim.

拔 *Menuki* important.

星 *Meboshi* aim: *meboshii* costly; valuable.

前 *Mokuzen* before one's face; immediately; present.

目
姿　*Mokusō* following with the eyes.

配　*Mekubari* overseeing: *me-kubase* winking.

盛　*Memori* graduation; scale.

深　*Mabuka ni* deeply shading the eyes.

通　*Me-dōri* interview.

障　*Mezawari* an eye-sore; obstruction to the view.

睫　*Mokushō* close at hand.

藥　*Megusuri* eye-lotion.

當　*eate* an aim; purpose.

算　*Mokusan* to calculate roughly.

標　*Mokuhyō* mark; goal; objective.

論見　*Mokuromi* intention; scheme.

論見書　*Mokuromi-sho* prospectus.

擊　*Mokugeki* being an eye-witness.

錄　*Mokuroku* catalogue.

禮　*Mokurei* to salute with the eye.

覺　*Me-za(meru)* to open the eyes; awake.

一 T 自　See 132,0.

二 T 助　See 19,5.

T 見　See 147,0.

T 貝　See 154,0.　(二)

T 具　See 12,6.　三

T 県　See 縣 109,11.【糸】　四

眉　BI; MI. *Mayu*; *mayuge* eyebrows.

目　*Bimoku*; *mime* face.

宇　*Biu* eyebrow.

間　*Miken* middle of forehead.

T 看　KAN. *Mi(-ru)* to look at; watch: *mi-mamo(ru)* to watch; look after.

守　*Kanshu* to guard; look after; warder; jailer.

取　*Kanshu* observe; see.

板　*Kamban* sign-board.

病　*Kambyō* attending or nursing a sick person.

客　*Kankaku* spectator; visitor.

過　*Kanka* overlook; pass unnoticed.

破　*Kampa* to detect; perceive.

視　*Kanshi* to watch; observe.

護　*Kango* nursing a patient.

昧　MAI; BAI. *Kurai* dark; indistinct.　五

T 眠　MIN. *Nemu(ru)* to sleep.

眩　GEN faint. *Kura(mu*; *kura-me(ku)* to be dizzy: *kura-ma(su)* to obscure; dazzle: *mabayui*; *mabushii* dazzling: *mado(u)* to be bewildered.

（五）惑　Genwaku dazzle; confusion.
暈　Memai; gen-un giddiness.

六　眸　Bō the pupil of the eye.

T眼　GAN; GEN. Me eye: manako eye; eyeball.
力　Ganriki sight; power of judgment.
下　Ganka under one's eyes.
孔　Gankō orbit of the eye.
中　Ganchū principal consideration.
目　Gammoku gist; point.
光　Gankō sharp-sighted; penetration.
界　Gankai range of vision.
前　Ganzen: mano-atari before one's eyes; immediately; present.
鏡　Megane spectacles.
識　Ganshiki discrimination.

眺　CHŌ. Naga(meru) to see; view; gaze at
望　Chōbō view; appearance.

眷　KEN to consider; regard affectionately; kind.
族　Kenzoku a family.
顧　Kenko patronage.

八　睦　BOKU. Mutsumajii friendly; amicable: mutsu(bu) to be friendly; intimate with; harmonize.
月　Mutsuki poetical name for January.

T睡　SUI. Nemu(ru) to sleep; be drowsy. （八）
眠　Suimin sleep.
氣　Nemuke sleepiness.
魔　Suima sleepiness.

睚　KI; SUI. Miha(ru) to open one's eyes wide.

睥　HEI looking askance; scornful look. Nira(mu) to glare at.

睨　Heigei to glare at.

睛　SEI the pupil of the eye. Do not confound with 晴 42,8.

睫　SHŌ. Matsuge eyelashes.

睨　GEI. Nira(mu); ne(meru) to glare at; look askance.

鼎　See 206,0.

T督　TOKU to urge; to look; oversee; lead; command; control.
軍　Tokugun Chinese local military commander; to command a troop.
促　Tokusoku to press; urge; importune.
勵　Tokurei to encourage; stimulate; urge.

睹　TO. Mi(-ru) to see.　九

瞑　MEI to close the eyes; die. Nemu(ru) to sleep: kurai dark.　一〇

瞑

目 *Meimoku* to close the eyes; die.

想 *Meisō* meditation.

瞋

SHIN. *Ikari* anger: *ika-(ru)* to be angry: *ikara(su)* to make angry.

恚 *Shin-i* anger.

瞠

若 *Dōjaku* blank amazement.

瞞

MAN. *Dama(su)* to deceive: *suka(su)* to coax: *kurama-(su)* to obscure; impose upon.

着 *Manchaku* deception.

縣

KEN. *Agata* prefecture; district.【糸】109, 4 T : 42, 6 T

下 *Kenka* under the jurisdiction of a prefecture.

立 *Kenritsu* supported by prefecture.

令 *Kenrei* old name for governor.

知事 *Kenchiji* governor.

會 *Kenkai* prefectural congress.

廳 *Kenchō* prefectural office.

一二 瞳

DŌ. *Hitomi* the pupil of the eye.

孔 *Dōkō* the pupil of the eye.

T 瞬

SHUN a short time. *Maba-ki* wink: *matata(ku)*; *majiro(gu)* to wink; twinkle.

時 *Shunji* moment.

間 *Shunkan* moment.

瞰

KAN to look down; command a view. *Mi(-ru)* to see.

下 *Kanka* look down.

瞭

RYŌ. *Akiraka* clear; plain; distinct.

然 *Ryōzen* clear; plain; distinct.

瞥

BETSU to glance at.

見 *Bekken* to take a momentary glance.

瞻

SEN to look up to with desire. *Mi(-ru)* to see.

仰 *Sengyō* to look up to.

望 *Sembō* to look from afar.

瞹昧

Aimai obscurity; ambiguity.

瞼

KEN. *Mabuta* eyelids; the edge of the eyelids.→130, 13

瞽

See 207, 5.【目】

朦

MŌ. *Kurai* dark.

昧 *Mōmai* ignorant.

矚

SHOKU; ZOKU to see; to stare at; look intently.

目 *Shokumoku* pay close attention.

一三

一四

二一

二〇 矛

二一 矢

When at the left it is ca led *Hoko-hen.*

T 矛 MU; BŌ. *Hoko* spear.

盾 *Mujun* contradiction.

四 矜 KIN to be reverent. *Hoko-(ru)* to be proud: *aware-(mu)* to pity.

T 柔 JŪ; NYŪ weak; gentle. *Yawarakai; shinayaka* soft; tender: *yawara(geru)* to soften. 【木】

和 *Nyūwa* gentleness.

弱 *Jūjaku* weakness.

術 *Jūjutsu* a certain kind of Japanese wrestling.

道 *Jūdō* a certain kind of Japanese wrestling.

順 *Jūjun* obedient.

軟 *Jūnan* soft flexible.

六 務 T MU. *Tsutome* duty; task; service; business: *tsuto-(meru)* to perform one's duty; to labour. 【力】 →19, 9

九 預 T See 181,4.

二 豫 T See 152,9.

矢 SHI. *Ya* arrow; dart. Do not confound with 失 37,2.

立 *Yatate* portable inkstand with a brush.

先 *Yasaki* arrow-point; the moment.

釜 しい *Yakamashii* noisy; strict; fault-finding.

張 *Yahari; yappari* too; also; still; after all.

鱈 *Yatara ni* indiscriminately; recklessly.

T 知 CHI. *Shi(ru)* to know; 三 perceive. (*Tomo*); (*Kazu*); (*Chika*).

人 *Chijin* an acquaintance.

己 *Chiki* acquaintance; friend.

名 *Chimei* well-known.

合 *Shiriai* persons mutually acquainted.

行 *Chigyō* feudal benefice.

事 *Chiji* governor of prefecture.

命 *Chimei* fifty years old.

悉 *Chishitsu* know well.

遇 *Chigū* friendship.

邊 *Shirube* an acquaintance.

識 *Chishiki* knowledge; learning.

覺 *Chikaku* feeling; sensibility.

四 矧 SHIN. *Ha(gu)* to make arrows : *iwan-ya* still more (less) ; how much more (less).

俟 See T 侯 9,7.

五 矩 KU carpenter's square ; foot-rule. *Nori* rule.

形 *Kukei* square.

七 T短 TAN shortcoming. *Mijikai* short.

刀 *Tantō* short sword.

才 *Tansai* little talent.

日月 *Tanjitsugetsu* short while.

見 *Tanken* short-sighted view.

兵急 *Tampeikyū* headlong.

所 *Tansho* shortcoming ; failing ; defect.

命 *Tammei* short life.

徑 *Tankei* breadth ; short diameter.

氣 *Tanki* quick temper.

期 *Tanki* a short term.

艇 *Tantei ; bōto* boat.

歌 *Tanka* short poem of 31 syllables.

銃 *Pis toru* pistol.

篇 *Tampen* short piece (story).

慮 *Tanryo* quick temper.

縮 *Tanshuku* shortening.

八 雉 *Kiji* pheasant. 【隹】

矮 WAI low of stature ; short. (八〇)

小 *Waishō* small.

T疑 See 21,12. 【疋】 九

T矯 KYŌ. *Ta(meru)* to straighten ; to rectify. 一二

正 *Kyōsei* to rectify.

風 *Kyōfū* reform of manners.

石 一三

When at the left it is called *Ishi-hen*.

T石 SEKI ; SHAKU. *Ishi* stone : *iwa* rock : *koku* unit of capacity ; see Introduction 44.

川 *Ishikawa* p. n.

灰 *Sekkai ; ishibai* lime.

見 *Iwami* p. n.

材 *Sekizai* building stone.

油 *Sekiyu* petroleum.

炭 *Sekitan* coal.

炭酸 *Sekitansan* carbonic acid.

炭層 *Sekitansō* seam of coal.

垣 *Ishigaki* stone wall.

室 *Ishimuro* stone cave ; stone house.

碑 *Sekihi* a tombstone.

塔 *Sekitō* a tombstone.

積 *Kokuzumi* unit for measuring size of boats.

鹼 *Sekken* soap.

四 研 S H A K U.　*Ki(ru)* to cut.
【斤】

T 研 See 研 112,6.

T 砂 SA; SHA.　*Suna* sand : *isago* pebbles.

丘 *Sakyū* a sand-hill.

利 *Jari; zari* gravel.

金 *Sakin; shakin* gold dust.

烟 *Sunaken.uri* cloud of dust.

糖 *Satō* sugar.

塵 *Sajin* dust.

礫 *Shareki; sareki* pebbles; gravel.

鐵 *Satetsu* iron sand.

砌 SEI; SAI.　*Migiri* time; period; opportunity: *ishidatami* stone pavement.

五 T 破 HA to break; to damage; destroy.　*Yabu(ru); yabu(ku)* to tear; squander : *yare* broken; torn.

片 *Hahen* fragment.

天荒 *Hatenkō* record breaking.

瓜 *Haka* 16 years old (girl).

目 *Yabureme* rent; tear.

竹 *Hachiku* irresistible.

戒 *Hakai* breaking of Buddhist laws.

門 *Hamon* excommunication.

風 *Hafu* gable.

約 *Hayaku* breaking of contract.

格 *Hakaku* an exception; unprecedented.

產 *Hasan* failure; bankruptcy.

裂 *Haretsu* explosion; bursting.

棄 *Haki* revocation; break.

碎 *Hasai* crushing.

廉恥 *Harenchi* infamy.

毀 *Haki* destruction; breaking.

滅 *Hametsu* destruction.

損 *Hason* injury; damage.

獄 *Hagoku* prison-breaking.

綻 *H a t a n* breach; ruin; failure.

談 *Hadan* breaking off; rejection.

顏 *Hagan* a broad smile.

壞 *Hakai* demolition; destruction.

鏡 *Hakyō* divorce.

砥 SHI.　*To* whetstone.

礪 *Shirei* polish.

砲 HŌ.　*Tsutsu* gun; cannon.
→砲 T

火 *Hōka* gun-fire.

手 *Hōshu* a gunner.

兵 *Hōhei* artillery.

身 *Hōshin* gun-barrel.

烟 *Hōen* smoke from guns.

* T 砕 →112,8

325

（五）
砲

塔 *Hōtō* a turret of a battle-ship.

臺 *Hōdai* fort.

彈 *Hōdan* shell; projectile.

聲 *Hōsei* report of a cannon.

擊 *Hōgeki* bombardment.

艦 *Hōkan* gun-boat.

六　研　KEN to study. *Miga(ku)* to polish: *to(gu)* to sharpen. →112, 4 T

究 *Kenkyū* study; investigation.

磨 *Kemma* to polish up; elaborate.

鑽 *Kensan* studying.

砦　SAI. *Toride* stronghold.

七　硝　SHŌ saltpetre. →硝 T

子 *Garasu* glass.

石 *Shōseki* saltpetre.

烟 *Shōen* powder smoke.

「硬　KŌ strong. *Katai; kowai* hard.

化 *Kōka* hardening.

派 *Kō a* stalwart party.

骨 *Kōkotsu* inflexibility.

硯　KEN. *Suzuri* an ink-stone.

北 *Kenhoku* complimentary word used in letter-writing after the name of the addressee.

（七）
T硫　RYŪ sulphur.

黄 *Iō* sulphur.

酸 *Ryūsan* sulphuric acid.

碓　TAI. *Usu* mortar for 八 pounding rice in.

氷 *Usui* p. n.

碑　HI. *Ishi-bumi* monument: *tateishi* stone tablet. →碑 T

碎　SAI. *Kuda(ku)* to break to pieces. →112, 4 T *

身 *Saishin* to work hard.

碍　GAI; GE obstruction. *Sawa-(ru); samata(garu)* to be obstructed; impede; stop.

硼酸 *Hōsan* boracic acid.

碌　ROKU stony appearance.

々 *Roku-roku* fully; sufficiently; idly.

碇　TEI. *Ikari* anchor.

泊 *Teihaku* anchoring.

碗　WAN rice-bowl; tea-cup.

碩　SEKI great; eminent.　九

學 *Sekigaku* man of great learning.

T磁　JI earthenware; magnet. →112, 10

石 *Jishaku* loadstone; magnet.

（九）器 *Jiki* porcelain.

碧 HEKI. *Aoi* green; blue.

玉 *Hekigyoku* jasper.

空 *Hekikū* blue sky.

眼 *Hekigan* blue eye; European.

一〇 磋 SA. *Miga(ku)* to polish.

T確 KAKU firm; tight; hard; solid. *Tashika* sure; certain: *tashika(meru)* to make certain: *shika to* certainly; definitely.

乎 *Kakko* firm; steadfast.

立 *Kakuritsu* establishment.

固 *Kakko* firm; steadfast.

定 *Kakutei* to settle; fix; decide.

信 *Kakushin* firm belief; faith.

執 *Kakushitsu* discord.

然 *Kakuzen* decided; positive.

答 *Kakutō* a definite answer.

報 *Kakuhō* a definite report.

認 *Kakunin* confirmation.

實 *Kakujitsu* sure; certain; reliable.

證 *Kakushō* certain proof.

磅 HŌ spread. *Pondo* pound (sterling or weight).

磚 *Hōhaku* filled with; overwhelm.

碼 ME agate. *Yādo: yāru* yard.

（一〇）礫 TAKU. *Haritsuke* crucifiction.

刑 *Takukei* crucifiction.

磁 See ᵀ磁 112,9.

磊 RAI to excel.

落 *Rairaku* openness.

磐 BAN; HAN. *Iwa* rock.

手 *Iwate* p. n.

石 *Banjaku* rock.

磧 *Kawara* sandy or pebbly shore; river beach. 一一

磯 KI. *Iso* sea-shore; beach. 一二

T礁 SHŌ hidden or sunken rock.

磕 *Hata to* sound of clapping; sound of something falling. 一三

T礎 SO. *Ishizue* foundation; stone pedestal.

礒 GI rock; beach.

礙 See 碍 112,8. 一四

礪 REI to whet; to polish; a whetstone. 一五

礫 REKI. *Tsubute: ko-ishi* small stone; pebble.

327

（一五）

礦 See 鑛 167,15.

礬 BAN alum.

in Tōyō Kanjis always : ⺬

一三二

示

When at the left it is called *Shimesu-hen*. *Shimesu-hen* is usually written ⺬ with the brush.

T示 SHI; JI. *Shime(su)* to show; publish; inform; instruct.

威 *Jii ; shii* showing of power or influence; demonstration.

談 *Jidan* private settlement.

一 T礼 See 禮 113,13.

三 T社 SHA company; association. *Yashiro* Shintō shrine.

交 *Shakō* social intercourse.

長 *Shachō* the president of a company.

員 *Shain* member of a company.

會 *Shakai* society; the world.

會主義 *Shakai-shugi* socialism.

債 *Shasai* debenture.

團 *Shadan* corporation; association.

（三）

團法人 *Shadan-hōjin* juridical association.

殿 *Shaden* shrine; building.

說 *Shasetsu* editorial.

祀 SHI. *Matsu(ru)* to hold a religious celebration; deify.

T祉 SHI; CHI happiness; blessing. （四）

T祈 KI. *Ino(ru)* to pray.

念 *Kinen* prayer.

禱 *Kitō* prayer.

願 *Kigan* prayer; vow.

誓 *Kisei* a vow.

祇 GI god-protector of a country; god; peaceful. Do not confound with 祗 113,5.

園 *Gion* p. n.

T祖 So ancestor; grandfather; 五 origin; beginning.

父 *Sofu; jiji; jii* grandfather.

母 *Sobo; baba* grandmother.

先 *Sosen* ancestor.

宗 *Sosō* ancestor.

國 *Sokoku* fatherland.

述 *Sojutsu* explain; follow.

祐 YŪ happiness. *Tasu(keru)* to help. *(Suke)*

助 *Yūjo* grace; help.

祚 So rank; happiness.

神 SHIN; JIN. *Kami : kan* god (in a pagan sense); also God; sacred; divine; inspired. (*Kō*).

々 *Kōgōshii* sublime.

戸 *Kōbe* p. n. *Kambe* p. n.

主 *Kannushi* Shintō priest

田 *Kanda* p. n.

代 *Kamiyo; jindai* era of the gods; time when the gods still inhabited this earth.

去 *Kansaru* to die (of the Emperor).

出鬼沒 *Shinshutsu-kibotsu* sudden appearance and disappearance.

色 *Shinshoku* looks.

妙 *Shimmyō* praiseworthy; admirable.

官 *Shinkan* Shintō priest.

社 *Jinja* Shintō shrine.

武天皇 *Jimmu-tennō* 1st Emperor of Japan.

事 *Shinji* Shintō festival.

奈川 *Kanagawa* p. n.

勅 *Shinchoku* divine decree.

苑 *Shin-en* garden round a shrine.

祇 *Jingi* the deities of heaven and earth.

宮 *Jingū; shingū* Shintō shrine.

氣 *Shinki* spirit; vigour.

祕 *Shimpi* mystery.

速 *Shinsoku* rapidity.

童 *Shindō* an infant prodigy; a precocious child.

聖 *Shinsei* holiness.

經 *Shinkei* a nerve.

話 *Shinwa* myth; mythology.

嘗祭 *Kanname-sai* Harvest festival, Oct. 17th.

樂 *Kagura* sacred dance, accompanied with music.

器 *Jingi* sacred vessels; see 三種の神器 1,2.

劒 *Shinken* sacred sword.

橋 *Mihashi shinkyō* sacred bridge.

體 *Shintai* symbol of the divinity.

髓 *Shinzui* essence.

靈 *Shinrei* spirit of the gods.

祠 SHI to deify. *Hokora* shrine.

祓 FUTSU. *Hara(u)* to pray (Shintō worship).

祗 SHI to reverence. Do not confound with 祇 113,4.

候 *Shikō* visit.

祝 SHUKU; SHŪ. *Iwa(u); kotoo(gu)* to celebrate; congratulate : *nori* prayer (Shintō): *no(ru)* to pray; celebrate.

日 *Shukujitsu* feast-day; holiday.

文 *Shukubun* congratulatory address.

言 *Shūgen* marriage ceremony.

杯 *Shukuhai* toast; wassail cup.

典 *Shukuten* celebration.

（五）祝

砲 *Shukuhō* salute of guns.

宴 *Shukuen* feast in celebration of an event.

捷 *Shukushō* celebration of a victory.

詞 *Norito* Shintō prayers.

賀 *Shukuga* congratulation.

電 *Shukuden* congratulatory telegram.

意 *Shukui* congratulation.

誓 *Kisei* a vow.

福 *Shukufuku* blessing.

儀 *Shūgi* congratulation; a present.

辭 *Shukuji* congratulatory address.

禱 *Shukutō* benediction.

祕 See ^T秘 115,5.

崇 SUI. *Tatari* a curse: *wazawai* calamity: *tata(ru)* to incur a curse. Do not confound with 崇 46,8.

六
T祥 SHŌ congratulatory; happiness; omen.

T祭 SAI. *Matsuri* festival: *matsu(ru)* to perform religious rite concerning a deceased person.

日 *Saijitsu* national holiday; religious feast-day.

祀 *Saishi* religious celebration.

典 *Saiten* festival.

粢料 *Saishiryō* a grant of money towards the funeral service. （六）

壇 *Saidan* altar.

禮 *Sairei* festival.

T視 SHI to inspect. *Mi(-ru)* to see; look at; to watch; guard. 【見】 七

力 *Shiryoku* sight; visual power.

界 *Shikai* field of vision.

察 *Shisatsu* inspection.

線 *Shisen* line of vision.

學 *Shigaku* school inspector.

覺 *Shikaku* vision; sense of sight.

聽 *Shichō* attention.

祿 ROKU salary; ration; happiness. 八

T禁 KIN (sometimes inverted order) to forbid; stop; prohibition; aversion; repugnance; charm; spell.

止 *Kinshi* prohibition; interdiction.

中 *Kinchū* within the Imperial palace; the Imperial palace.

足 *Kinsoku* confinement.

物 *Kimmotsu* injurious thing; things prohibited.

制 *Kinsei* prohibition; interdiction.

煙 *Kin-en* no smoking.

酒 *Kinshu* abstention from drink.

一二
三

(八〇)

通行 *Tsūkō wo kinzu* (inv. order) no thoroughfare.

喫煙 *Kitsu-en wo kinzu* (inv. order) no smoking.

漁 *Kinryō* prohibition of fishing.

慾 *Kin-yoku* mortification; continence.

錮 *Kinko* imprisonment.

九
T **福** FUKU. *Saiwai* blessing; happiness; fortunate.

井 *Fukui* p. n.

引 *Fukubiki* lottery.

祉 *Fukushi* welfare.

利 *Fukuri* advantages; welfare.

岡 *Fukuoka* p. n.

音 *Fukuin* the (Christian) gospel.

島 *Fukushima* p. n

壽草 *Fukujusō* a certain plant, adonis amuraisis.

T **禍** KA to injure; harm; demolish. *Wazawai* misfortune; misery.

根 *Kakon* source of trouble.

禎 TEI happiness; good; just.
*

一
一 **禦** GYO. *Fuse(gu)* to defend; protect; ward off; stop; refuse.

三 **禧** KI happiness; joy.

*禅 T→113, 12　　　331

(一一)

禪 ZEN a Buddhist sect; state of absolute calmness and abstraction from this world. →113, 9 T *

尼 *Zenni* widow of a nobleman, who has become a Buddhist nun.

宗 *Zenshū* the Zen sect.

味 *Zemmi* mysticism.

學 *Zengaku* literature of the Zen sect.

一
三 **禮** REI; RAI thanks; acknowledgment; politeness; ceremony; to respect. →113, 1 T

式 *Reishiki* etiquette; manners.

狀 *Reijō* letter of thanks.

服 *Reifuku* dress-suit; ceremonial dress.

法 *Reihō* etiquette; courtesy.

拜 *Reihai; raihai* worship.

砲 *Reihō* salute (gun).

遇 *Reigū* respectful treatment; courteous reception.

節 *Reisetsu* etiquette.

儀 *Reigi* the rules of politeness.

一
四 **禱** TŌ. *Ino(ru)* to pray.

禰 NE; NEI; DEI; NAI ancestor's shrine.

一二
四

内

一
五　　**禾**

When at the left it is called *Nogi-hen.*

禾 KA grain; rice.

二
T　**利** RI profit; advantage; interest. *Ki(ku)* to be efficacious: *toshi* (lit. st.) sharp; clever. *(Kaga)*【刀】

口 *Rikō* clever.

子 *Rishi* interest (on money).

己 *Riko* self-interest.

己主義 *Riko-shugi* egoism.

目 *Kikime* efficacy; effect.

用 *Riyō* use; utilization.

札 *Risatsu; rifuda* a coupon (of interest).

便 *Riben* convenience.

益 *Rieki* advantage; interest.

害 *Rigai* advantage and disadvantage; concern.

根川 *Tone-gawa* p. n.

息 *Risoku* interest (on money).

率 *Riritsu* rate of interest.

得 *Ritoku* profit.

發 *Rihatsu* intelligent; clever.

腕 *Kikiude* the right arm.

殖 *Rishoku* making money.

源 *Rigen* natural resources.

潤 *Rijun* pro t; gain.

慾 *Riyoku* avidity; covetousness.

器 *Riki* effective instrument.

権 *Riken* rights and interests,

ㄇ　**私** SHI. *Watakushi; watashi* I; private (not public or official); selfish: *hisoka ni* secretly; privately.

人 *Shijin* private person; individual.

方 *Watakushi-kata; watashi-ho* my household; my house.

心 *Shishin* selfish motive.

立 *Shiritsu* private establishment.

用 *Shiyō* private business or use.

有 *Shiyū* private ownership.

交 *Shikō* private intercourse.

宅 *Shitaku* private house.

利 *Shiri* self-interest; personal gain.

見 *Shiken* one's humble opinion.

事 *Shiji* private affairs.

信 *Shishin* private communication.

財 *Shizai* private funds.

書函 *Shishobako* P. O. box.

情 *Shijō* personal regard.

淑 *Shishuku* to take as one's model.

設 *Shisetsu* private i. e. not official.

通 *Shitsū* illicit intercourse.

(二)

腹　*Shifuku* one's owo belly; personal interest.

語　*Shigo; sasayaki* whispering.

慾　*Shiyoku* self-interest.

T秀　SHŪ beautiful. *Hii(deru)* to excel; to be luxuriant. *(Hide),*

才　*Shūsai* talented person.

逸　*Shūitsu* super-excellence.

麗　*Shūrei* beautiful.

禿　TOKU. *Ha(geru)* to be bald: *kamuro* prostitute's maid.

山　*Hageyama* barren mountain.

三 T和　WA to be reconciled with. *Yawara(geru)* to temper: *na(gu)* to subside; calm: *Yamato* Japan. 【口】

文　*Wabun* written in Japanese.

平　*Wahei* peace.

合　*Wagō* harmony; concord.

尙　*Oshō* a Buddhist priest; bonze.

服　*Wafuku* Japanese clothes.

洋　*Wayō* Japanese and European.

泉　*Izumi* p. n.

氣　*Waki* harmony; concord: *Wake* p. n.

睦　*Waboku* reconciliation.

解　*Wakai* reconciliation.

譯　*Wayaku* translate into Japanese.

歌　*Waka* Japanese poem.

歌山　*Wakayama* p. n.

製　*Wasei* Japanese make.

樂　*Waraku* happiness.

戰　*Wasen* war and peace.

議　*Wagi* a treaty of peace.

蘭　*Oranda* Holland.

T季　KI seasor. *Sue* the end. 【子】

候　*Kikō* season.

節　*Kisetsu* season.

T委　I. *Yuda(neru); maka(seru)* to entrust; commit; delegate: *kuwashii* detailed; minute. 【女】

任　*Inin* charge; commission.

任狀　*Ininjō* power-of-attorney.

曲　*kyoku* particulars; details.

託　*Itaku* charge; commission.

員　*I-in* committee; delegate; deputy.

細　*Isai* particulars; details.

囑　*Ishoku* request.

T科　KA branch of study; kind; 四 section. *Toga* offence; fault: *shina* affected pose.

目　*Kamoku* item; branch.

學　*Kagaku* science.

料　*Karyō* a fine.

T秒　BYŌ second (of time); a little.

T秋　SHŪ. *Aki* autumn: *toki* time; period.

刀魚　*Samma* mackerel pike.

(三)

秋

田 *Akita* p. n.

冷 *Shūrei* cool autumn weather.

波 *Shūha* amorous glance.

季 *Shūki* autumn.

風 *Shūfū; akikaze* autumn wind; get tired of.

毫 *Shūgō* little; in the least.

秕 HI to be defiled. *Shiina* imperfect ear of rice.

政 *Hisei* misgovernment.

^T香 See 186,0.

^T租 SO tax; tribute; duty.

界 *Sokai* a foreign settlement.

借 *Soshaku* lease.

税 *Sozei* taxes.

秤 BIN; SHŌ; HYŌ. *Hakari* scales; a balance.

量 *Hyōryō* measure.

^T秩 CHITSU order; fixed.

父 *Chichibu* p. n.

序 *Chitsujo* order; method; harmony.

秣 MATSU; BATSU. *Magusa* fodder.

^T称 See 稱 115 9.

^T秘 HI. *Hi(meru); kaku(su)* to conceal: *hisoka* private; secret. →113,5(=4)

書 *Hisho* secret book; private secretary.

密 *Himitsu* secret.

術 *Hijutsu* secret art or method.

訣 *Hiketsu* secret; mystery.

傳 *Hiden* traditional secret.

藏 *Hizō* to treasure.

露 *Perū* Peru.

^T移 I. *Utsu(ru)* to change: *utsu(su)* to transfer; remove.

入 *Inyū* introduce.

民 *Imin* emigration; immigration.

住 *Ijū* emigration; immigration; migration (animals).

氣 *Utsurigi* changeable.

動 *Idō* transition; motion.

牒 *Ichō* to transmit.

轉 *Iten* transfer; removal.

^T程 TEI distance. *Hodo* extent; limit; about: *nori* law; rule.

近 *Hodochikai* not far from; near.

度 *Teido* standard; degree; extent.

程 KAN. *Wara* straw.

稍 SHŌ. *Yaya* rather; a little; gradually.

々 *Yaya* rather; little.

(七) 稀 KI; KE. *Mare* rare; unusual; seldom; scarce.

代 *Kitai; kidai* rare; extraordinary.

有 *Keu* rare; unusual.

薄 *Kihaku* thin; rare.

税 ZEI tax; duties; tariff. *Mitsugi* tribute. (*Chikara*).

↓金→ *Zeikin* money paid as taxes, duties, etc. →税 T

關 *Zeikan* custom-house.

率 *Zeiritsu* tariff; tax rates.

黍 See 202,0.

八 T 稚 CHI. *Osanai; wakai* childish; young. →115,12

氣 *Chiki* childishness.

稗 HAI humble. *Hie* kind of grain, panicum frumentaceum.

稠 CHŪ. *Shigeshi* (lit. st.) thick; dense.

密 *Chūmitsu* thick; dense.

稜 RYŌ. *Kado* corner: *itsu* majesty; power.

威 *Ryōi; miitsu* influence of the Emperor.

稔 NEN; JIN year. *Mino(ru)* to ripen.

九 T 種 SHU. *Tane* seed: *tagui* sort; kind: *kusa-gusa* various: *u(eru)* to sow.

々 *Shuju* various; several kinds; in various ways.

(九) 子 *Shushi* seed.

目 *Shumoku* item.

本 *Tanehon* a source.

別 *Shubetsu* classification.

油 *Tane-abura* rape-seed oil.

物 *Tanemono* seeds.

族 *Shuzoku* race; tribe.

痘 *Shutō* vaccination.

類 *Shurui* sort; kind.

稱 SHŌ to call. *Tona(h)eru* to name; call; recite: *tata(h)eru* to praise. →115,5 T

呼 *Shōko* name; appellation.

號 *Shōgō* title; designation.

揚 *Shōyō* praise.

*1 讚 *Shōsan* praise.

稻 TŌ. *Ine* rice-plant. →115,9 T *1

作 *Inasaku* rice-crop.

妻 *Inazuma* lightning.

荷 *Inari* god of harvest.

稽 KEI to study. *Kanga(h)eru* to consider; to calculate.

古 *Keiko* practice; exercise.

T 稿 KŌ straw; draft (of a letter).

本 *Kōhon* manuscript.

稼 KA. *Kase(gu)* to work; labour.

稷 SHOKU kind of millet, sorghum.

黎 See 85,10. 【黍】

(一〇)

穆 BOKU respectful; to be harmonious.

T 積 SEKI product; area; volume: SHAKU. *Tsu(mu)* to load· *tsumo(ru)* to be piled up; accumulate; estimate: *tsumori* intention.

立 *Tsumita(teru)* to lay aside (as money).

出 *Tsumidashi* shipment.

年 *Sekinen* many years.

金 *Tsumikin* a fund.

卸 *Tsumioroshi* loading and discharging.

雪 *Sekisetsu* snow piled up.

荷 *Tsumini* cargo.

極 *Sekkyoku* the positive pole.

極的 *Sekkyokuteki* positive; progressive.

惡 *Sekiaku* accumulated wickedness.

換 *Tsumikae* trans-shipment.

載 *Sekisai* carrying; loading.

弊 *Sekihei* deep-rooted evil.

*

二 穉 See T 稚 115,8.

穗 SUI. *Ho* ear of rice or corn. →115,10 *² T

三 穡 SHOKU to harvest grain.

穢 WAI; E; AI. *Kega(reru)*; *kega(su)* to be defiled; soiled; to dirty; soil: *kegarawashii* defiled; unclean.

多 *Eta* pariahs; outcastes.

* T 穩 →115,14

T 穫 KAKU. *Ka(ru)* to reap.

穩 ON. *Odayaka* quiet; calm. →115,11 * T

便 *Ombin* peacefully; privately.

當 *Onto* proper; reasonable.

健 *Onken* quiet; calm.

一
四

穰 JO abundant; prosperous; fertile.

一
七

穴

一
六

Always at the top and is called *Ana-k·mmuri.*

穴 KETSU. *Ana* hole; cave.

居 *K·kkyo* living in a cave.

T 究 KYU. *Kiwa(meru)* to investigate; examine carefully.

竟 *Kyukyo* in the end; finally.

極 *Kyukyoku* ultimate; final.

二

空 KU. *Sora* sky: *kara; utsuro; munashii* empty: *a(ku); su(ku)* to be empty: *munashiku* in vain. →空 T

々 *Sorazorashii* feigned.

々寂々 *Kuku-jakujaku* null and void; listlessness.

文 *Kubun* a dead letter.

中 *Kuchu* in the air.

手 *Karate; kushu* empty-handed.

三

（三）

地 *Akichi*; *kūchi* vacant ground; unoccupied land.

名 *Kūmei* an empty name

位 *Kūi* vacant position.

似 *Sorani* accidental resemblance.

洞 *Kūdō* a cave; a hollow.

室 *Kūshitsu* vacant room.

前 *Kūzen* unprecedented.

氣 *Kūki* air; atmosphere.

恐 *Sora-osoroshii* alarmed.

席 *Kūseki* a vacant seat.

砲 *Kūhō* a blank cartridge.

理 *Kūri* an empty theory.

涙 *Sora-namida* false tears.

虛 *Kūkyo* emptiness.

間 *Kūkan* space.

腹 *Kūfuku* empty stomach.

想 *Kūsō* fancy; imagination; castles in the air.

費 *Kūhi* to waste.

漠 *Kūbaku* extensive; vague.

隙 *Kūgeki* crevice; aperture.

論 *Kūron* useless discussion.

模樣 *Sora-moyō* appearance of the weather.

談 *Kūdan* idle talk.

賴 *Sora-danomi* a vain hope.

窂 See 122,3.

*

四 窐 SEI. *Otoshi-ana* pitfall; trap.

* T 突 →116,4

（四）

穿 SEN. *Uga(tsu)* to penetrate: *ha(ku)* to put on (boots, etc.): *ho(ru)* to dig; to pry into.

鑿 *Sensaku* search; inquiry.

T 窃 See 竊 116,17.

突 TOTSU sudden. *Tsu(ku)* to strike against. →116,3 * T

入 *Totsunyū* inrush; penetration.

兀 *Tokkotsu* loftily.

出 *Tosshutsu suru*; *tsuki-deru* to project out.

如 *Totsujo* suddenly.

風 *Toppū* sudden wind.

飛 *Toppi* extravagant; queer.

起 *Tokki* projection; protuberance.

破 *Toppa* break through.

通 *Tsuki-tō(su)* to pierce; stab.

貫 *Tokkan* charge (as on enemy).

進 *Tosshin* charge; rush.

然 *Totsuzen* suddenly.

發 *Toppatsu* burst out.

當 *Tsukiatari* running against; end.

擊 *Totsugeki* to charge; attack.

T 容 See 40,7. 五

窄 SAKU. *Semai* narrow: *subo(meru)*; *subo(maru)* to narrow; shrink: *sema(ru)* to press upon.

窈 *Yō* beautiful; deep; profound.

窕 *Yōchō* beautiful; graceful.

六 窒　CHITSU to stop up; ob-
T 窒　struct.

扶斯　Chibusu typhus.

息　Chissoku suffocation.

素　Chisso nitrogen.

T 窓　Sō.　Mado window.
　　→116,7 : 116,11
掛　Madokake curtain.

七 窗　See preced.

窘　KIN.　Tashina(meru) to
blame; reprimand: kuru-
shi(meru) to cause pain.

八 窟　KUTSU.　Iwaya mountain
shelter; cave.

九 窪　AI; WA.　Kubo hollow;
cavity.

〇 T 窮　KYŪ.　Kiwama(ru) to be
in extremities; be poor;
be exhausted; to be de-
pressed; to be hard up:
kiwa(meru) to investigate.

乏　Kyūbō poverty.　→116,14

地　Kyūchi predicament.

困　Kyūkon poverty and
misery.

屈　Kyūkutsu strict; narrow;
discomfort.

狀　Kyūjō wretched condition.

策　Kyūsaku the last shift.

極　Kyūkyoku ultimateness.

境　Kyūkyō poverty; predicament.

T 窯　Yō furnace.

業　Yōgyō pottery.

窺　KI.　Ukaga(u) to inquire; —
to spy out.　　　　　一

知　Kīchi to know; perceive.

覯　Kīyu to pry into.

窻　See T 窓 116,6.

窶　Rō; KU.　Yatsu(reru) to be
emaciated: yatsu(su) to disguise oneself.

竄　ZAN; SAN to hide; to run —
away; let go.　　　　　三

入　Zannyū take refuge; mix
into.

窮　See T 窮 116,10.　　　一
　　　　　　　　　　　　四

竈　Sō.　Kamado: kama; —
hettsui kitchen-range; 六
kitchener; furnace.

竊　SETSU.　Nusu(mu) to steal: —
hisoka ni secretly; private- 七
ly.　→116,4 T

取　Sesshu theft.

盜　Settō theft.

立　　一
　　　七

T 立　RITSU built by, e. g. 市立
shi-ritsu built by the t〕wn:
RYŪ.　Ta(tsu) to stand;
start: ta(teru) to stand;
build: when read — tate,
as 2nd component after
another verb it gives the
meaning of an action just
accomplished, e. g. umitate
no tamago new-laid egg:
rittoru litre (metric).

7

白皮皿目矛矢石示禾【穴立】 **5 Str. Rad.**

上 *Tachi-aga(ru); tachinobo-(ru)* to stand up; rise.

方 *Rippō* cube.

去 *Tachisa(ru)* to depart.

石 *Ta eishi* stone sign-post.

札 *Tatefuda* sign.

地 *Tachidokoro ni* on the spot.

身 *Risshin* rise in the world.

志 *Risshi* fixing one's aim in life.

所 *Tachidokoro* at once.

並 *Tachi-nara(bu)* to be in a row.

往生 *Tachi-ōjō* remaining on one's feet.

直 *Tate-nao(su)* to recover; rally.

法 *Rippō* legislation.

春 *Risshun* the beginning of spring.

秋 *Risshū* the beginning of autumn.

派 *Rippa* fine; brilliant; splendid; skilful.

退 *Tachi-no(ku)* to leave.

消 *Tachi-gie* go out (of fire not thoroughly alight).

候補 *Rikkōho* candidature.

案 *Ritsuan* a plan; design.

脚地 *Rikkyakuchi* a stand-point.

寄 *Tachi-yo(ru)* to visit or call in passing.

處 *Tachidokoro ni* on the spot.

場 *Tachiba* standpoint; situation.

竦 *Tachi-suku(mu)* to be petrified with fear.

會人 *Tachiai-nin* witness

腹 *Rippuku* anger.

聞 *Tachigiki* eavesdropping.

論 *Ritsuron* argument.

錐 *Rissui* standing-room.

憲 *Rikken* constitutional.

憲國 *Rikken-koku* constitutional country.

證 *Risshō* proof.

體 *Rittai* solid body.

二

卅 *Dekarittoru* decalitre.

T辛 See 160,0.

三

竏 *Kirorittoru* kilolitre.

妾 SHŌ. *Mekake* concubine: *warawa* I (by women).【女】

腹 *Shōfuku* born of a concubine.

四

竕 *Deshirittoru* decilitre.

音 See 180,0.

奇 See T奇 37,5.

彦 See 彦 8,7.【彡】

五

竝 See T並 140,5.【一】

站 TAN to stop; to halt.

339

（五）_T 竜 See 龍 212,0.

六 竡 *Hekutorittoru* hectolitre.

_T 産 See 産 8,9.【生】

_T 章 SHŌ chapter; section; ornament; sign. *Akiraka* clear.

魚 *Tako* octopus.

竟 KYŌ; KEI. *Owa(ru)* to finish: *kiwa(meru)* to exhaust: *tsui ni* finally.

七 竢 See 俟 9,7.

竦 SHŌ to revere. *Suku(mu)* to crouch from fear; to fear.

然 *Shōzen* shuddering with fear.

竣 SHUN. *Owa(ru)* to finish; to stop.

功 *Shunkō* completion.

成 *Shunsei* completion.

_T 童 DŌ. *Warabe*; *warawa* child.

子 *Dōshi* child.

話 *Dōwa* fairy tale.

謡 *Dōyō* children's songs.

顔 *Dōgan* childish face.

八 靖 SEI; SHŌ. *Yasui* peaceful; quiet.【青】

國神社 *Yasukuni-jinja* p. n.

_T 意 I. *Kokoro* mind; idea; will; meaning; feelings.【心】

中 *Ichū* in one's mind.

（八）

外 *Igai* unexpected.

向 *Ikō* idea; inclination.

地 *Iji* temper.

地汚 *Ijigitanai* greedy.

匠 *Ishō* a design.

見 *Iken* opinion; view.

志 *Ishi* will; volition.

味 *Imi* meaning.

表 *Ihyō* unexpected.

氣 *Iki* spirit; mind.

氣地 *Ikiji; ikuji* spirit; courage.

義 *Igi* meaning.

圖 *Ito* plan; intention.

趣 *Ishu* malice; intention.

識 *Ishiki* consciousness.

譯 *Iyaku* free translation.

竪 JU. *Tate* height; lengthwise.

坑 *Tatekō* shaft.

_T 端 TAN sign; correct; just. 九 *Hashi; hana; ha* extremity; end; edge; margin; beginning; origin: *hata* close by.

正 *Tansei* correct; upright.

坐 *Tanza* sit straight.

書 *Hagaki* a postcard.

然 *Tanzen* solemnly; way of behaving or bearing oneself strictly in accord with formal rules of etiquette.

艇 *Tantei; bōto* a boat.

（九）

緒 *Tansho; tancho* beginning; the first step.

麗 *Tanrei* beautiful.

竭 KETSU. *Tsu(kiru); tsuku-(su)* to end; exhaust.

颯 SATSU; sō the sound of the wind; storm. 【風】

々 *Sassatsu* murmuring; rustling: *soyo-soyo* softly.

一二 龍 See 212,0.

一五T 競 KYō; KEI. *Kiso(u)* to vie; compete; race; contend: *kura(beru)* to compare: *seri* auction.

技 *Kyōgi* game; sport.

走 *Kyōsō* race.

爭 *Kyōsō* competition.

爭者 *Kyōsōsha* competitor; rival.

馬 *Keiba; kurabe-uma* horse-race.

漕 *Kyōsō* boat-race.

賣 *Kyōbai; seriuri* auction.

一二
八 竹

Always at the top and is called *Take-kammuri.*

T 竹 CHIKU. *Take* bamboo.

刀 *Shinai* bamboo sword used in fencing.

帛 *Chikuhaku* history.

馬 *Take-uma* stilts.

馬の友 *Chikuba-no-tomo* friend from childhood.

紙 *Chikushi* India paper.

箆返 *Shippei-gaeshi* retort; measure for measure.

竹
二 JIKU used for its sound.   二

竿 KAN. *Sao* bamboo pole.   三

頭 *Kantō* end of a pole.

笄 KEI. *Kōgai* a hair ornament.   四

筲 Sō. *Zaru* a basket.

T 笑 SHō. *Emi; emai* smile: *wara(u); e(mu)* to laugh; smile; rejoice.

止 *Shōshi* pitiful; absurd; laughable.

柄 *Shōhei* a laughing-stock.

納 *Shōnō* kindly receive.

草 *Waraigusa* a laughing-stock.

話 *Shōwa* funny story.

聲 *Shōsei; waraigoe* laughter.

顏 *Egao* smiling face.

笈 KYŪ a box for books (carried on the back). *Oi* a portable altar carried around by priest.

笠 RYŪ; RITSU. *Kasa* basket-shaped hat.   五

笹 *Sasa* bamboo grass.

（五）

笞 CHI. *Muchi* a whip: *shimoto* rod: *muchiu(tsu)* to whip.

T **笛** TEKI. *Fue* flute; whistle.

T **符** FU to correspond with; tally; sign; token.

合 *Fugō* coincidence; correspondence.

牒 *Fuchō* a sign; a mark.

號 *Fugō* sign; symbol.

節 *Fusetsu* the halves of a seal; to tally exactly.

T **第** DAI (prefix to numerals), number: TEI mansion. *Tsuide* order; degree. →6, 3

一 *Dai-ichi* number one; superlative meaning, the biggest, the longest, etc., according to co.text; in the first place.

一義 *Dai-ichigi* first principle.

三者 *Dai-sansha* a third person or party.

六 **筌** SEN weir; a large bamboo basket.

T **答** TŌ. *Kotae; irae* answer: *kota(h)eru)* to answer; reply.

案 *Tōan* an answer; an examination paper.

禮 *Tōrei* returning a salute.

辯 *Tōben* reply; answer.

筈 KATSU. *Hazu* ought to; obligation; fituess; reasonable expectation.

T **筆** HITSU written by; painted by. *Fude* brush (for writing or artistic painting); pen.

（六）

法 *Hippō* style of penmanship; method; manner.

者 *Hissha* a writer.

記 *Hikki* note; memorandum.

紙 *Hisshi* paper and pen.

致 *Hitchi* stroke of the pen; style.

無精 *Fudebushō* a poor correspondent.

勢 *Hissei* stroke of the pen; style of penmanship.

誅 *Hitchū* denouncing one in writing.

禍 *Hikka* incurrence of punishment on account of one's writing.

算 *Hissan* calculation with figures.

戰 *Hissen* a paper battle; literary warfare.

頭 *Hittō* the first (in a roll or list.)

蹟 *Hisseki* handwriting.

T **等** TŌ quality; sort; class. *Hitoshii* equal: *nado* and so forth: *ra* plural suffix. As bottom component when read *tō* it means class, e. g.: *it.ō, jotō, kōtō;* when read *ra* it has the force of plurality. →6, 3

分 *Tōbun* division into equal parts; same quantity; equal proportions.

外 *Tōgai* no account.

級 *Tōkyū* class; degree; rank.

閑 *Tōkan; naozari* neglect.

T **筒** TŌ funnel. *Tsutsu* cylinder; tube; pipe.

(六〇)	七

先 *Tsutsusaki* the tip; the muzzle.

袖 *Tsutsusode* a tight sleeve.

筍 *Takenoko* bamboo sprout.

T 筋 KIN. *Suji* sinew; vein; line; course; the authorities concerned.

目 *Sujime* lineage; line; reason.

肉 *Kinniku* muscles.

向 *Sujimukai* obliquely opposite.

骨 *Kinkotsu* bones and sinews.

書 *Sujigaki* a synopsis; a program.

違 *Sujichigai* unreasonableness; a sprain.

道 *Sujimichi* reason.

T 策 SAKU plan; whip.

士 *Sakushi* a man of resource.

畧 *Sakuryaku* scheme; artifice.

源地 *Sakugenchi* the base of operations.

應 *Sakuō* execute a program.

筏 BATSU. *Ikada* raft.

筑 TSUKU; CHIKU a certain musical instrument.

波 *Tsukuba* name of a mountain.

前 *Chikuzen* name of a province.

紫 *Chikushi* old name of Kyūshū.

T 節 See 節 118,9.

筭 See T 算 118,8.

筧 KEN. *Kakehi* a bamboo water-pipe.

箝 KAN; KEN to close the mouth; gag; to shut. *Ha(meru)* to fit into; to insert between: *kubikase* cangue.　八

口 *Kankō　kenkō* prohibit talking.

T 管 KAN to control; oversee. *Kuda* pipe.

々しい *Kudakudashii* tedious; lengthy.

下 *Kanka* under the jurisdiction.

内 *Kannai* within the jurisdiction.

見 *Kanken* narrow view.

理 *Kanri* management; control.

絃樂 *Kangen-gaku* orchestra.

轄 *Kankatsu* jurisdiction.

箔 HAKU metal foil; blinds made of bamboo strips.

箇 KO; KA aux. num. for counting several kinds of things that have no special aux. num.; number.

々 *Koko* one by one; separately.

所 *Kasho* place; part; passage; point.

條 *Kajō* article; clause.

處 *Kasho* place; part; passage; point.

筭　See 筞 118,4.

T 算　SAN calculation; number. *Kazo(h)eru)* to calculate; count. →118,7

入　*Sann ū* inclusion.

用　*Sanyō* calculation.

定　*Santei* calculation.

段　*Sandan* means; contrivance.

術　*Sanjutsu* arithmetic.

盤　*Soro'an* abacus.

數　*Sansū* arithmetic; calculation.

箒　SŌ; SHŪ. *Hōki* a broom.

筵　EN assemblage. *Mushiro* straw mat.

綿　*Mushirowata* layer of cotton wound on roller; lap.

箋　SEN ticket; tablet; document.

筐　See 筐 118, 0.

箕　KI. *Mi* a basket for winnowing rice; dust-pan.

九 箸　CHO. *Hashi* chopsticks.

T 箱　SŌ. *Hako* box.

入　*Hakoiri* cased; in a box.

入娘　*Hakoirimusume* a pet daughter.

庭　*Hakoniwa* a miniature garden in a box.

根　*Hakone* p. n.

詰　*Hakozume* enclosed in a box

節　SETSU chapter; paragraph; clause; part; virtue; chastity; rule: SECHI season; time; occasion. *Fushi* joint: *notto* knot (nautical). →118,7T

分　*Setsubun* change of season; special feast-day when winter changes to spring, about 4th of Feb.

用　*Setsuyō* frugality; a digest.

制　*Sessei* temperance.

季　*Sekki* the end of the year.

約　*Setsuyaku* economy; saving.

酒　*Sesshu* temperance.

減　*Setsugen* reduction; curtailment.

義　*Setsugi* fidelity to one's principles.

儉　*Sekken* economy; frugality.

操　*Sessō* integrity; chastity.

篇　HEN a document; aux. num. for counting Chinese poems, etc.

篏　See 箝 118,8.

T 範　HAN. *Nori* rule; law; example; model: *notto(ru)* to model after.

例　*Hanrei* example.

圍　*Han-i* limit; scope; sphere.

篩　SHI. *Furui* sieve: *furu(u)* to sift.

（一
〇）

篝　KŌ basket. *Kagaribi; kagari* bonfire.

T 篤　TOKU. *Atsui* kind; liberal; deep; sincere; warm.

志　*Tokushi* benevolence.

（一〇）

實 *Tokujitsu* uprightness; honesty.

學 *Tokugaku* studiousness.

T 築 CHIKU a building. *Kizu(ku); tsu(ku)* to construct; build.

山 *Tsukiyama* an artificial hill.

地 *Tsukiji* p. n.

造 *Chikuzō* construction.

港 *Chikkō* construction of harbour.

簔 See 蓑 140,10.

篦 HEI; HI. *Hera* a broad spatula used in kitchen, etc.

簒 SAN deprive; take away.

立 *Sanritsu* usurpation of the throne.

奪 *Sandatsu* usurp a throne.

二 簇 生 *Zokusei* grow together; crop up.

篠 SHŌ. *Shino; sasa* a small kind of bamboo.

三 簪 *Kanzashi* ornamental hairpin.

簞 TAN a box.

笥 *Tansu* chest of drawers.

T 簡 KAN simple; frugal; to select; a check; bamboo ticket; letter; to economize (work).

易 *Kan-i* simple; easy.

明 *Kammei* conciseness; brevity.

（一二）

便 *Kamben* convenient; handy.

略 *Kanryaku* simplicity; brevity.

捷 *Kanshō* simplicity.

單 *Kantan* brevity; simplicity.

潔 *Kanketsu* conciseness.

T 簿 BO account-book; register.　一三

記 *Boki* book-keeping.

簾 REN. *Sudare; su; misu* a blind made of strips of bamboo.

籃 RAN. *Kago* a large basket.　一四

T 籍 SEKI; SHAKU book; register; to borrow.

口 *Shakkō* under pretext of.

籌 CHŪ scheme; plan; to count.

纂 SAN to gather; compile. 【糸】

籐 TŌ rattan.　一五

籔 See 藪 140,15.

籤 See 籤 118,17.

籠 RŌ. *Kago* a basket; cage: *ko(meru)* to put in: *komo(ru)* to be in seclusion.　一六

居 *Rōkyo* seclusion.

城 *Rōjō* besieged in a castle; being shut up (as in one's room).

鳥 *Kago no tori; rochō* a bird in a cage.

345

（一六）籠
絡 *Rōraku* inveiglement; cajolement.

一七 籤 SEN. *Kuji* lot; chance.

一八 籬 RI. *Magaki; kaki* a fence.

一九 米

When at the left it is called *Kome-hen*.

T 米 BEI America: MAI; ME. *Kome; yone* rice (polished but not cooked): *mētoru* metre.

人 *Beijin* an American.

化 *Beika* to Americanize.

作 *Beisaku* rice-culture; rice-crop.

食 *Beishoku* feed on rice.

突 *Mētoru* metre.

國 *Beikoku* America.

貨 *Beika* American currency.

塩 *Beien* food; bread and butter.

壽 *Beiju* 83th anniversary of one's birth.

價 *Beika* the price of rice.

穀 *Beikoku* rice; cereals.

三 粁 *Kiro-mētoru* kilometre.

籾 *Momi* unhulled rice.

粂 (*Kume*).

（三）

T 料 RYŌ material; to estimate; consider; money; price; fee. 【斗】 四

金 *Ryōkin* rate; charge; fee

理 *Ryōri* cooking.

T 粉 FUN. *Kona; ko* powder; flour.

々 *Kona-gona* break into pieces.

末 *Fummatsu* powder.

骨碎身 *Funkotsusaishin* to do one's utmost.

微塵 *Konamijin* smash into atoms.

碎 *Funsai* to crush; shatter.

粍 *Miri-mētoru* millimetre.
*

T 粒 RYŪ. *Tsubu* grain; drop; pill. 五

T 粗 SO. *Arai* coarse; rough: *hobo* roughly.
→198,2

大 *Sodai* gross; coarse; rough.

末 *Somatsu* coarse.

朴 *Soboku* coarseness.

服 *Sofuku* coarse clothing.

忽 *Sokotsu* imprudence; care-lessness.

品 *Sohin* coarse article.

食 *Soshoku* coarse food.

略 *Soryaku* careless; heedless.

* T 粋 →119,8

（五）

野 *Soya* rustic; coarse.

密 *Somitsu* density.

飯 *Sohan* coarse food; a poor meal.

惡 *Soaku* crude; inferior.

製 *Sosei* coarse manufacture.

暴 *Sobō* roughness; violence.

雜 *Sozatsu* coarse; rough.

T **粘** NEN. *Neba(ru)* to be sticky: *neba* starch: *neba(su)* to stick.

土 *Nendo* clay; slime.

着 *Nenchaku* to stick to; adhere to.

粕 HAKU. *Kasu* vegetable or animal refuse; residue; dregs; part of vegetables or animals not used for principal object (alimentation or industry), but thrown away or used for secondary purpose (e. g. manure).

六 T **粧** SHŌ; SŌ. *Yosō(u)* to adorn; to adorn oneself.

七 **粮** See T **糧** 119,12.

粲 SAN bright.

八 **粹** SUI essence; pure.　*Iki* elegance; stylishness.
→119,4 T *

精 SEI; SHŌ refined; sure; good; ghost; spirit; mind; idea; soul. *Kuwashii* minute; detailed.
→**精** T

々 *Seizei* as far as possible.

（八）

力 *Seiryoku* energy; strength; vigour.

巧 *Seikō* fine; delicate; artistic; elaborate; ingenuity.

米 *Seimai* cleaned rice.

兵 *Seihei* picked men (troops).

妙 *Seimyō* exquisiteness; ingenuity.

美 *Seibi* refined; exquisite.

神 *Seishin* will; mind; spirit.

氣 *Seiki* soul; spirit; energy; essence.

紡機 *Seibōki* ring frame (spinners).

悍 *Seikan* dauntless.

粗 *Seiso* fineness or coarseness.

密 *Seimitsu* thorough; minute; accurate.

細 *Seisai* minute; e aborate.

華 *Seika* essence; flower.

通 *Seitsū* complete knowledge.

進 *Shōjin* devotion; assiduity; abstinence from animal food.

勤 *Seikin* diligence.

製 *Seisei* refining.

銳 *Seiei* efficiency; picked.

算 *Seisan* exact calculation.

選 *Seisen* careful selection.

確 *Seikaku* accuracy; precision.

緻 *Seichi* minute; delicate.

錬 *Seiren* refining; training.

勵 *Seirei* diligence.

讀 *Seidoku* careful perusal.

九	粳	*Senchi-mētoru* centimetre.
	糊	KO. *Nori* paste; starch.
	口	*Kokō* living.
	塗	*Koto* to gloss over; patch up.

一〇	T糖	TŌ sweetmeats; sugar.
	分	*Tōbun* percentage of sugar.

二一	糟	SŌ. *Kasu* dregs; lees.
	粕	*Sōhaku* dregs.
	糠の妻	*Sokō no tsuma* wife married in poverty.
	糠	KŌ. *Nuka* rice-bran.
	糞	FUN. *Kuso* dung.

一二	T糧	RYŌ; RŌ. *Kate* provisions; rations. →119,7
	食	*Ryōshoku* provisions; food.

一四	糯	*Mochi* glutinous; glutinous rice.

一九	糴	See 124,29. 【米】

二〇 糸

When at the left, it is called
Ito-hen.

T	糸	See 絲 120,6.
T	糺	KYŪ. *Tada(su)* to inquire into; examine; judge: *azana(u)* to twist. →120,2
	合	*Kyūgō* convocation.
	明	*Kyūmei* searching examination.
	問	*Kyūmon* judicial inquiry; minute examination.
	彈	*Kyūdan* impeachment.
T	系	See 4,6. 【糸】

糾	See T糺 120,1.	二

T	紅	KŌ; KU. *Kurenai: akai* scarlet: *beni* rouge. 三
	白	*Kōhaku* red and white.
	茶	*Kōcha* black tea.
	葉	*Momiji* maple; red leaves: *kōyō* red leaves; to turn red (of leaves).
	塵	*Kōjin* dusty wind.
	顔	*Kōgan* ruddy face.
T	約	YAKU promise. *Tsuzu-(meru)* to shorten; abridge; to economize: *tsuzumayaka* frugal; simple: *ōyoso* about; roughly; generally.
	手	*Yakute* abb. of 約束手形
	束	*Yakusoku* promise.
	束手形	*Yakusoku-tegata* a promissory note.
	言	*Yakugen* summary.

(三) 定 *Yakujō* agreement; contract.

款 *Yakkan* a stipulation.

T 紀 KI history; chronicle; to write down. *Nori* rule; law.

元 *Kigen* an era.

元節 *Kigensetsu* anniversary of the coronation of the Emperor Jimmu, Feb. 11.

州 *Kishū* another name for the province of Kii.

行 *Kikō* account of travels.

伊 *Kii* p. n.

* 念 *Kinen* commemoration.

(四) 紐 JŪ; CHŪ to tie. *Himo* cord; braid; ribbon.

育 *Nyūyōku* New York.

T 納 NŌ; TŌ; DŌ; NA; NATSU. *Osa(meru)* to pay: *i(reru)* to place in; put into; grant; consent to.

入 *Nōnyū* pay; deliver.

戸 *Nando* dressing-room; closet.

豆 *Nattō* a kind of food made of beans.

附 *Nōfu* payment.

屋 *Naya* an outhouse; a shed; a barn.

凉 *Nōryō* to cool oneself.

得 *Nattoku* to assent; understand.

税 *Nozei* payment of tax.

會 *Nōkai* last meeting of the year.

*級 →120,4

紗 SHA; SA gauze; thin silk.

T 紛 FUN be in disorder. *Magira(su); magi(reru)* to obscure; divert; beguile: *magirawashii* confusing; obscure; perplexing; **ambiguous**.

々 *Fumpun* confusedly.

失 *Funshitsu* to mislay; lose.

込 *Magire-ko(mu)* to get mixed.

糾 *Funkyū* disorder; complication.

紜 *Funnun* dissensions.

雜 *Fukuzatsu* complexity.

亂 *Funran* confusion; disturbance.

議 *Fungi* disagreement; trouble.

擾 *Funjō* confusion; disturbance.

T 紡 BŌ. *Tsumu(gu)* to spin (thread).

續 *Bōseki* spinning.

級 KYŪ class; grade; order; step; rank. →120,3 * T

T 紋 MON family crest; figure; design.

附 *Montsuki* a garment with the family crest.

章 *Monshō* a crest; badge.

T 紙 SHI. *Kami* paper.

入 *Kami-ire* pocket-book; wallet.

上 *Shijō* in the newspaper; in a letter.

（四）

紙

包 *Kamizutsumi* a paper parcel.

面 *Shimen* paper; sheet.

屑 *Kamikuzu* waste-paper.

幣 *Shihei* paper money; bank-notes.

T **純** JUN pure; good; entirely.

一 *Jun-itsu* pure; genuine.

正 *Junsei* purity.

金 *Junkin* pure gold.

良 *Junryō* pure; genuine.

益 *Jun-eki* net profit.

理論 *Junriron* rationalism.

然 *Junzen* pure; perfect; absolute.

粹 *Junsui* pure; unadulterated.

潔 *Junketsu* purity.

紜 UN. *Mo(meru): mida(reru)* to be in confusion.

T **素** So; SU simple; white. *Moto* origin; original thing.

人 *Shiroto* an amateur.

因 *Soin* a predominant cause; predisposition.

朴 *Soboku* simplicity.

早 *Subayai* quick; nimble.

行 *Sokō* conduct.

志 *Soshi* a cherished desire.

足 *Suashi* barefoot.

性 *Sujō* character; lineage.

直 *Sunao* meek.

（四）

封家 *Sohōka* a wealthy man.

破扱 *Suppanuku* to expose suddenly.

氣無い *Sokkenai* unkind; blunt.

振 *Soburi* behaviour.

通 *Sudōri* passing by without calling.

寒貧 *Sukampin* an empty purse.

晴 *Subarashii* grand; tremendous.

敵 *Suteki* great; remarkable.

質 *Soshitsu* nature; natural quality.

養 *Soyō* knowledge; acquirement.

顏 *Sugao* unpainted face.

T **索** See 24,8.【糸】

五

T **経** See **經** 120,7.

T **組** So. *Kumi* set; company; guild: *ku(mu)* to fit together; grapple.

立 *Kumita(teru)* to fit together; set up; erect.

打 *Kumiuchi* a grapple.

合 *Kumi-ai* association; guild; trade union: *kumi-a(u)* to grapple: *kumi-awa(seru)* to join together.

成 *Sosei* to be formed; be organized.

織 *Soshiki* system; constitution; to organize.

(五)

T 紺 KON dark blue.

屋 *Kōya; kon-ya* dyer.

T 紹 SHŌ to introduce; to assist. *Tsu(gu)* to connect; continue.

介 *Shōkai* to introduce; present a person to.

T 細 SAI. *Hosoi* thin; slender; narrow: *komakai* minute; fine.

々 *Koma-goma* minutely.

工 *Saiku* fine work; small manufactured objects.

大 *Saidai* everything; anything (with neg.).

心 *Saishin* prudence; scruples.

目 *Saimoku* details; particulars.

民 *Saimin* a pauper.

末 *Saimatsu* powder.

君 *Saikun* wife.

谷川 *Hosotani-gawa* small mountain stream.

長 *Hosonagai* long and slender.

胞 *Saihō; saibō* cell; cellule.

密 *Saimitsu* minute; exact.

菌 *Saikin* a bacillus.

微 *Saibi* minute; details.

説 *Saisetsu* minute explanation.

紬 CHŪ. *Tsumugi* pongee: *tsumu(gu)* to spin.

絆 HAN. *Kizuna; hodashi* bonds; fetters; encumbrance; embarrassment.

(五)

T 紳 SHIN gentleman.

士 *Shinshi* gentleman.

商 *Shinshō* wealthy merchant.

絃 GEN. *Ito* string; cord.

歌 *Genka* music and song.

T 終 SHŪ. *Owari* end: *owa(ru); o(h)eru)* to end; finish: *tsui ni* at last; finally.

了 *Shūryō* to end; finish; complete.

日 *Shūjitsu* the whole day.

止 *Shūshi* end; stop.

末 *Shūmatsu* the termination.

生 *Shūsei* lifelong; until death.

局 *Shūkyoku* end; conclusion.

身 *Shūshin* for life; the whole life.

夜 *Shūya* all night.

始 *Shūshi* the beginning and the end; constantly.

焉 *Shūen* the end of life.

極 *Shūkyoku* finality; end.

結 *Shūketsu* conclusion; end.

業 *Shūgyō* the end of a work.

熄 *Shūsoku* to come to an end.

點 *Shūten* the terminus.

T 給 KYŪ to supply. *Tama(u)* verbal honorific suffix; to deign; to give (to an inferior).

仕 *Kyūji* waiting at table; waiter; servant.

金 *Kyūkin* salary; wages.

(六)

（六）

給
炭船 *Kyūtansen* coaling vessel.

料 *Kyūryō* salary.

與 *Kyūyo* supply; allowance.

費 *Kyūhi* support.

T 結 KETSU. *Musu(bu); iwa-(h)eru); yuwa(h)eru)* to tie; bind: *yu(u)* to tie; bind; dress the hair.

了 *Ketsuryō* to complete; conclude.

句 *Kekku* after all.

末 *Ketsumatsu* end; conclusion.

氷 *Keppyō* freeze over.

合 *Ketsugō* union; combination.

托 *Kettaku* to conspire with.

局 *Kekkyoku* the final result; the end; after all; in the end.

束 *Kessoku* union; combination; binding up.

尾 *Ketsubi* end; conclusion.

社 *Kessha* association; society.

果 *Kekka* result.

納 *Yuinō* a betrothal present.

核 *Kekkaku* a tubercle.

着 *Ketchaku* settlement; end.

晶 *Kesshō* crystallization; crystals.

婚 *Kekkon* matrimony.

構 *Kekkō* construction; structure; splendour.

論 *Ketsuron* conclusion.

T 絡 RAKU to be connected; to bind; thread. *Karama(ru)* to twine round.

絣 HEI. *Kasuri* spotted pattern.

絢 KEN. *Aya* resplendent.

爛 *Kenran* brilliancy.

T 絞 KŌ. *Shibo(ru)* to wring: *shi(meru)* to squeeze.

殺 *Kōsatsu* strangle.

絨 JŪ woolen cloth; fine cloth.

毯 *Jūtan* carpet.

T 絶 ZETSU to excel. *Ta(y)eru)* to become extinct; be cut off; end; fail: *ta(tsu)* to cut.

々 *Taedae* with intervals; barely.

大 *Zetsudai* enormous; gigantic.

世 *Zessei* peerless; incomparable.

代 *Zetsudai* the greatest that ever lived.

好 *Zekkō* capital (opportunity); the best.

叫 *Zekkyō* to exclaim; cry out.

交 *Zekkō* breaking off friendship.

妙 *Zetsumyō* miraculous; exquisite.

佳 *Zekka* picturesque.

命 *Zetsumei* to die.

版 *Zeppan* out of print.

美 *Zetsubi* extraordinary beauty.

（六）

食 *Zesshoku* fasting.

倫 *Zetsurin* unique.

倒 *Zettō* be convulsed.

息 *Zessoku* ceasing to breathe.

望 *Zetsubō* despair; hopelessness.

頂 *Zetchō* apex; climax.

間 *Taema* intermission.

景 *Zekkei* indescribably fine view.

筆 *Zeppitsu* the last thing written or painted by a person.

無 *Zetsumu* an impossibility.

滅 *Zetsumetsu* extermination.

對 *Zettai* absolute.

對的 *Zettai'eki* absolutely.

對絕命 *Zettai-zetsumei* driven to the utmost desperation.

緣 *Zetsuen* insulation; severing of connections.

壁 *Zeppeki* precipice; cliff.

T 統 TŌ lineage. *Su(beru)* to unite in one; govern.

一 *Tōitsu* unity; consistency.

合 *Tōgō* combination; unification.

治 *Tōji; tōchi* to govern; rule.

計 *Tōkei* statistics.

括 *Tōkatsu* generalization.

率 *Tōsotsu* to command; lead.

御 *Tōgyo* to govern; rule.

領 *Tōryō* foreman; chief.

轄 *Tōkatsu* superintendence; control.

絲 SHI. *Ito* thread; string. →42, 3 T

口 *Itoguchi* the end of a thread; a clue.

車 *Itoguruma* spinning wheel.

絮 JO cotton.

說 *Josetsu* explanation in detail.

T 紫 * SHI. *Murasaki* purple; violet.

經 KEI circles of longitude: KYŌ rule; law; to govern; warp; line; reason; way; the ordinary course of things; usual. *Heru* (irreg.) to pass; pass through: *ta(tsu)* to pass: *tate* lengthwise. (*Tsune*). →120, 5 T 七

木 *Kyōgi* wood-shavings.

由 *Keiyu* via; by way of.

世 *Keisei* administration.

典 *Keiten* Scripture; Bible.

度 *Keido* longitude.

書 *Keisho* the Chinese classics.

理 *Keiri* dealing; management.

常費 *Keijōhi* ordinary expenditure.

路 *Keiro* a path; a channel.

費 *Keihi* expenditure.

過 *Keika* transit; lapse; progress.

綸 *Keirin* administration.

緯 *Keii* the particulars.

歷 *Keireki* career; personal experiences.

經
營 *Keiei* plan; design; management; administration.

濟 *Keizai* economy; finance.

驗 *Keiken* experience.

T継 See 繼 120,14.

綹 Ro silk gauze.

T絹 KEN. *Kinu* silk.

布 *Kempu* silk fabric.

T続 See 續 120,15.

綏 SUI. *Yasui* easy; being at
* ease.

八
T維 I to keep. *Kore* this.

也納 *Uiin; Uina* Vienna.

持 *Iji* support; maintenance.

新 *Ishin* the Restoration (A.
D. 1868).

綽 SHAKU abundant; lenient.
Ada nickname.

々 *Shaku-shaku* easy and free.

名 *Ada-na* nickname.

緋 HI vermilion; red.

綺 KI lustre; figured cloth.

羅 *Kira* fine clothes.

麗 *Kirei* fine; beautiful.

綸 RIN Imperial. *Ito* string.

子 *Rinsu* figured satin.

*T緑 →120, 8

旨 *Rinshi* Emperor's words.

言 *Ringen* Emperor's words.

網 See foll.

T綱 MŌ. *Ami* net.

羅 *Mōra* to comprise; bring
together.

T綱 KŌ. *Tsuna* rope; hawser.

目 *Kōmoku* classification;
main points; a heading;
an item.

紀 *Kōki* administrative order.

要 *Kōyō* a summary; an outline.

常 *Kōjō* moral principles.

領 *Kōryō* general principles;
essential points.

T綿 MEN uninterrupted. *Wata*
cotton (as taken from
plant); cotton-wool.

々 *Memmen* continuously.

入 *Wataire* padded kimono.

布 *Mempu* cotton cloth.

花 *Menka* raw cotton.

密 *Memmitsu* minute; detailed.

綯 TŌ. *Nawa* rope: *na(u)* to
twist rope; to twist.

綠 RYOKU; ROKU. *Midori*
green. →120 '7 * T

青 *Rokushō* green rust on
copper.

威 *Gurinitchi* Greenwich.

蔭 *Ryokuin* shade of a tree.

髮 *Ryokuhatsu* black hair.

綻 TAN. *Hokoro(biru); hokoroba(su)* to open (as a bud); to rip open.

綴 TETSU; SETSU; TEI. *Tsuzu(ru)* to compose; spell; join together; patch: *tsuzure* rags: *to(jiru)* to bind.

方 *Tsuzurikata* composition.

字 *Tsuzuriji* spelling.

込 *Tojikomi* a file.

綬 JU ribbon; braid; cord.

綾 RYŌ. *Aya* silk-damask; twill.

織 *Ayaori* twill.

綜 SŌ. *Su(beru)* to control; superintend: *osa* reed of a loom.

合 *Sōgō* collecting or gathering together.

括 *Sōkatsu* generalization.

T 総 See 總 120,11.

T 緊 KI N strict; reliable; solid. *Shima(ru)* to be tight; be in state of tension: *shi(meru)* to tighten.

急 *Kinkyū* urgent; pressing.

要 *Kin-yō* important; urgent.

張 *Kinchō* strain; tension.

*1 縮 *Kinshuku* retrenchment. *2

九 緒 SHO; CHO lineage. *Itoguchi* the end of a thread; the beginning; a clue: *o* thong. →120,8 *1 T

言 *Shogen; chogen* introductory remark.

論 *Shoron; choron* an introduction.

*1 T 緒 →120,9　*2 T 練 →120,9

355

*3 T 緣 →120,9

緬 MEN. *Hosoito* fine thread.

甸 *Biruma* Burma.

T 緯 I parallels of latitude. *Nuki; yoko-ito* woof; cross-threads: *yoko* crosswise.

度 *Ido* latitude (geog.).

緝 SHŪ to spin; to assemble; collect.

編 HEN to compile; make up; compose. *A(mu)* to plait; weave; braid: knit; crochet. →編 T

入 *Hennyū* to enrol; enter; transfer.

成 *Hensei* composition; compilation; organization.

制 *Hensei* formation.

物 *Amimono* knitting.

者 *Hensha* an editor.

輯 *Henshū* compilation; editing.

纂 *Hensan* compilation. T →締

締 TEI. *Shi(meru)* to make tight; shut; tie: *shima(ru)* to be closed; be tightened.

切 *Shimekiri* closed; private.

括 *Shimekukuri* superintendence.

約 *Teiyaku* to make an agreement.

結 *Teiketsu* conclusion (as of a treaty, etc.).

盟 *Teimei* conclusion of a treaty.

練 REN. *Ne(ru)* to drill; train; practise; reconsider. →120,8 *2 T

兵塲 *Rempeijō* parade ground.

（九）

棟

習 *Renshū* training; practice.

達 *Rentatsu* skill; dexterity.

磨 *Remma* training; practice.

篠機 *Renjōki* drawing frame (spinner's).

T 線 SEN. *Suji* line; string; thread.

香 *Senkō* incense sticks.

路 *Senro* railway or tramway line.

緣 EN marriage; veranda. *Enishi; yukari* affinity; relation: *fuchi; heri* border. →120,8 ＊³T

日 *Ennichi* a festival.

者 *Enja* relation; connection.

故 *Enko* relation; connection.

起 *Engi* history; omen; luck.

側 *Engawa* a verandah.

組 *Engumi* a marriage.

談 *Endan* proposal of marriage.

縱 See 縱 120,11.

緩 KAN. *Yuruyaka; yurui* loose; easy; remiss; slow: *yuru(mu)* to be loose: *yukkuri* without hurry; loosely. →緩 T

和 *Kanwa* mollify; mitigate.

急 *Kankyū* emergency; urgency.

慢 *Kamman; madarui* tardy.

緞子 *Donsu* damask silk.

緘 KAN to close; to bind together.

口 *Kankō* closing of one's mouth.

默 *Kammoku* be silent.

繩 See 繩 120,13.

縊 I; EI; AI. *Kubi(ru)* to strangle: *kuku(ru)* to bind; tighten.

死 *I-shi* death by hanging.

縉紳 *Shinshin* a gentleman.

T 縛 BAKU rope. *Shiba(ru)* to tie; to arrest.

縟 JOKU to ornament; luxuriant.

縞 KŌ. *Shima* striped pattern.

物 *Shimamono* cloth with striped pattern.

緻 CHI fine; minute.

巧 *Chikō* delicate.

密 *Chimitsu* minute; elaborate.

縋 TSUI. *Suga(ru)* to lean upon; cling to; hang on.

縣 See 109,11. 【糸】
＊¹ ＊³→p.308 ＊²

T 縮 SHUKU. *Chiji(mu); chijima(ru)* to shrink; shorten; crouch: *chijimi* cotton crêpe.

小 *Shukushō* reduction; diminution.

刷 *Shukusatsu* small type edition.

356 ＊¹T 縱→120,11 ＊²T 縫→120,11

（一一）

圖 *Shukuzu* drawing on a reduced scale.

寫 *Shukusha* drawing on a reduced scale.

緬 *Chirimen* silk crêpe.

繃帶 *Hōtai* bandage.

繆 BYŪ. *Ayamar* error: *mato(u)* to wrap around.

見 *Byūken* mistaken idea.

論 *Byūron* wrong argument.

縱 JŪ; SHŌ. *Tate* vertical; standing; lengthwise: *hoshiimama* arbitrariness; self-will: *tatoi; yoshi; yoshimba* although; even if. →120, 10 T * 1

令 *Tatoi; tatoe* supposing that; even if; although.

貫 *Jūkan* running lengthwise.

橫 *Jūō* lengthwise and crosswise; in all directions.

覽 *Jūran* inspection.

縫 HŌ. *Nu(u)* to sew. →120, 10 * 2 T

目 *Nuime* a seam.

物 *Nuimono* sewing; needlework.

針 *Nuibari* a needle.

纏 REN. *Motsu(reru)* to be tangled.

T 績 SEKI. *Tsumu(gu)* to spin: *isao* merit; achievement.

總 SŌ. *Subete* all; generally; altogether; entirely; without exception; total; sometimes meaning vague like the 'now' at the beginning of an English sentence; in general; about; approximately: *su(bcru)* to control; govern: *fusa* cluster; bunch; tassel. →120, 8 T

（二一）

代 *Sōdai* a representative.

代理店 *Sō-dairi-ten* sole agency.

身 *Sōmi; sōshin* the whole body.

長 *Sōchō* president.

括 *Sōkatsu* to summarize.

計 *Sōkei* grand total.

高 *Sōdaka* total amount.

員 *Sōin* all the party; whole number of persons.

崩 *Sōkuzure* collapse; total defeat.

理大臣 *Sōri Daijin* the Prime Minister.

務 *Sōmu* general business; manager.

裁 *Sōsai* president.

會 *Sōkai* general meeting.

督 *Sōtoku* Governor-general (of a colony; as Formosa).

督府 *Sōtokufu* government (of a colony; as Formosa).

管 *Sōkan* general control.

領 *Sōryō* eldest child.

領事 *Sōryōji* consul-general.

監 *Sōkan* inspector-general.

稱 *Sōshō* a generic name.

數 *Sōsū* total number.

論 *Sōron* general remarks.

選舉 *Sōsenkyo* a general election.

轄 *Sōkatsu* general control.

額 *Sōgaku* total amount.

（二一）

總

辭職 *Sōjishoku* general resignation.

體 *Sōtai* the whole.

攬 *Sōran* superintend.

縷 RU; RŌ thread; minute;
detailed.

々 *Ruru* in detail; minutely.

述 *Rujutsu* to state in detail.

繁 HAN. *Shige(ru)* to be luxuriant, dense, prosperous.
→120, 10 * ³ T

々 *Shigeshige* very often.

文縟禮 *Hambunjokurei* red
tapism.

忙 *Hambō* pressure of business.

多 *Hanta* busy.

昌 *Hanjō* prosperity; flourishing condition.

茂 *Hammo* luxuriant growth.

華 *Hanka* flourishing condition; bustle.

盛 *Hansei* prosperity.

殖 *Hanshoku* breeding; increase.

閑 *Hankan* busy or not.

榮 *Han-ei* prosperity.

劇 *Hangeki* excess of business.

簡 *Hankan* complexity and
simplicity.

雜 *Hanzatsu* complexity.

三 **繕** ZEN. *Tsukuro(u)* to repair;
mend. T

繙 HAN. *Himoto(ku)* to unfasten; untie; read.

＊ T繊 →120, 17

（二二）

織 SHOKU; SHIKI. *O(ru)* to
weave: *hata* loom. →織 T

出 *Orida(su)* (coll.); *ori-ida-
(su)* (lit. st.) to weave so
as to show design.

物 *Orimono* cloth.

繞 NYŌ; JŌ. *Megu(ru)* to surround; encompass. →162, 12

繚 RYŌ to wrap around; to
encompass; to be entan-
gled, entwined.

繪 KAI; E picture.
→120, 6 T ＊

本 *Ehon* a picture book.

具 *Enogu* pigment; paint.

草紙 *Ezōshi* children's pic-
ture-book.

畫 *Kaiga* picture.

端書 *Ehagaki* a picture post-
card.

圖 *Ezu* a drawing; a plan.

繡 SHŪ needle-work; embroidery.

繹 EKI to relate; to inquire;
to place in a row.

T**繰** SŌ. *Ku(ru)* to reel thread;
ayatsu(ru) to move a puppet; manage.

入 *Kuriire* transfer.

合 *Kuriawa(seru)* arrange;
adjust.

延 *Kurinobe* postponement.

返 *Kurikaeshi* repetition.

越 *Kurikoshi* transfer.

繩 JŌ to adjust. *Nawa* rope.

目 *Nawame* bonds; chains.

＊ T繁 →120, 11

一三

（一三）

張 *Nawabari* sphere of influence.

繋 KEI. *Tsuna(gu)* to tie; hang: *tsunaga(ru)*; *kaka-(ru)* to be tied; be related to; be connected with; to hang: *kizuna* bond; tie.

留 *Keiryū* to moor.

累 *Keirui* complicity; dependents.

（一四）

繼 KEI. *Tsu(gu)* to receive; inherit: *mama* step-(relation); foster. →120, 7 T

子 *Keishi*; *mamako* a step-child.

母 *Keibo*; *mama-haha* step-mother.

承 *Keishō* succession; inheritance.

續 *Keizoku* continuance; succession.

繻 SHU fine silk.

子 *Shusu* satin.

珍 *Shutchin* figured satin.

（一五）

纏 TEN. *Mato(u)* to wrap around; to bind; to be bound; entangled: *matsuwa(ru)* to cling about; encompass: *matoma(ru)*; *mato(meru)* to settle.

綿 *Temmen* entangled; involved.

纖 See 纖 120,17.

續 ZOKU; SHOKU. *Tsuzu(ku)* to continue *tsu(gu)* to join; connect; follow. →120, 7 T

（一五）

々 *Zokuzoku* in rapid succession.

出 *Zokushutsu* to occur in succession; come out one after another.

物 *Tsuzuki-mono* serial story.

發 *Zokuhatsu* series; succession.

篇 *Zokuhen* sequel.

一七

纏 See 纏 120,15.

纖 SEN fibre; thread; delicate; fine; slender. →120, 11 T * : 120, 15

弱 *S njaku*; *kayowai* delicate.

細 *Sensai* delicate; fine; minute.

維 *Sen-i* a fibre.

纔 ZAN. *Wazuka* a little; barely.

二一

纜 RAN. *Tomozuna* hawser.

三三

缶

二

卸 T SHA. *Oro(su)* to sell at wholesale; let down; unload: *oroshi* wholesale. 〔卩〕

四

欽 See foll.

缺 T KETSU. *Ka(ku)* to lack; be defective; be incomplete.

乏 *Ketsubō* lack; want.

席 *Kesseki* absence.

359

缺 (四)
　員 *Ketsuin* a vacancy.

　陥 *Kekkan* shortage; defect.

　損 *Kesson* damage; loss.

　勤 *Kekkin* absence from duty.

　點 *Ketten* flaw; defect; weak point.

　禮 *Ketsurei* omission to offer one's greetings.

二　**罅** KA. *Hibi* crack; hole.

一六　**罎** DON; TAN. *Bin* bottle.

一八　**罐** KAN a can; jar; bucket.

　詰 *Kanzume* tinned food.

一三　**网**

Always at the top: it generally takes the modified form 罒, sometimes 罕 or 罔.

三　**罕** KAN. *Mare* seldom: *ami* a net.

四　**眾** FŪ; FU used for its sound.

五　**罝** See foll.

　罠 BIN; MIN. *Wana* a trap; a net.

詈 RI. *Nonoshi(ru)* to rail at; speak loudly to another. 七 【言】

T**買** BAI. *Ka(u)* to buy. 【貝】

　入 *Kaiire* purchase.

　上 *Kaiage* purchase.

　手 *Kaite* buyer.

　占 *Kaishime* corner; buying up.

　出 *Kaidashi* wholesale purchase.

　言葉 *Kai-kotoba* retort.

　收 *Baishū* purchasing; bribing.

　物 *Kaimono* shopping.

　被 *Kaikaburu* buying dear; over-estimate.

T**置** CHI. *O(ku)* to put; place. 八 (KI).

　土産 *Okimiyage* a keepsake; a souvenir; something left behind.

　去 *Okizari* desertion; abandonment.

　物 *Okimono* an ornament for the alcove.

　所 *Okidokoro* a place for putting something.

　換 *Okikae* substitution.

　塲處 *Okibasho* a thing's place.

　罩 *Ko(meru)* to put into; be full; concentrate upon.

　罫 KEI; KE; KAI. *Suji* line.

　紙 *Keishi* ruled paper.

(八) **罪** ZAI. *Tsumi* offence; fault; guilt; crime.

人 *Zainin* criminal.

名 *Zaimei* (criminal) charge.

狀 *Zaijō* nature of a crime.

科 *Zaika* an offence; a crime.

惡 *Zaiaku* sin; iniquity; vice; crime.

跡 *Zaiseki* traces of a crime.

業 *Zaigō* an offence; a sin.

蜀 SHOKU old name for part of China. 【虫】

署 SHO a government office; to sign; put down in writing. Sometimes used as abb. for 警察署 *keisatsusho.* →122,8 * T

九

名 *Shomei* signature.

T **罰** BATSU punishment: BACHI punishment (inflicted by Heaven).

金 *Bakkin* fine; penalty.

(一〇) **詈** See preceding.

罵 BA. *Nonoshi(ru)* to abuse; revile.

倒 *Batō* to abuse.

冒 *Bari* abuse; insult.

罷 HI. *Ya(meru): ya(mu)* to cease: *maka(ru)* to go; come: *tsuka(reru)* to be tired out; be exhausted.

工 *Hikō* a strike.

免 *Himen* dismissal; discharge.

(一〇) 在候 *Makariarisōrō* I am; he is (epist. st.).

居 *Makariori* I am; he is (epist. st.).

業 *Higyō* a strike.

罹 RI to meet with. *Kaka(ru)* to be concerned in. 一一

災民 *Risaimin* the victims; sufferers.

病 *Ribyō* falling ill.

羅 RA gauze; thin silk stuff; to enumerate; arrange in a row. 一四

列 *Raretsu* enumeration.

甸 *Raten* Latin.

針盤 *Rashimban* a compass.

紗 *Rasha* woollen cloth.

馬 *Rōma* Rome.

馬尼 *Rūmaniya* Rumania.

羇 旅 *Kiryo* journey; travel. 一七

羈 KI bridle; to tether; fasten; to lead. *Kizuna* bond; fetter. 一九

絆 *Kihan* shackles; fetters.

羊

T **羊** YŌ. *Hitsuji* sheep.

毛 *Yōmō* wool.

羊
腸 *Yōchō* winding; zigzag.

羹 *Yōkan* sweet bean jelly.

頭狗肉 *Yōtō-kuniku* to cry up wine and sell vinegar.

三
T 美 **BI; MI.** *Utsukushii; uruwashii* pretty; beautiful; good: *yoi* good.

々しい *Bibishii* beautiful.

文 *Bibun* elegant prose.

名 *Bimei* good name.

作 *Mimasaka* p. n.

妙 *Bimyō* exquisite; delicate.

果 *Bika* good results.

味 *Bimi* a delicacy.

風 *Bifū* a fine custom.

容 *Biyō* a beautiful face.

術 *Bijutsu* fine arts.

談 *Bidan* edifying episode.

質 *Bishitsu* good quality.

德 *Bitoku* virtue; good trait.

貌 *Bibō* a beautiful face.

濃 *Mino* p. n.

擧 *Bikyo* fine action.

點 *Biten* a merit; a virtue; excellence.

麗 *Birei* beautiful.

觀 *Bikan* a fine sight.

四
T 差 **SA** difference. *Sa(su)* to thrust.【工】

入 *Sashiire* insertion.

上 *Sashi-a(geru)* to give (to a superior).

止 *Sashito(meru)* to stop.

引 *Sashihiki* balance; deduction; the net result.

支 *Sashitsukae* engagement; obstruction; opposition.

立 *Sashita(teru)* to dispatch.

出 *Sashida(su)* to send; remit.

別 *Sabetsu* distinction.

押 *Sashi-osae* attachment; seizure.

金 *Sashigane* instigation.

値 *Sashine* bid (in price).

配 *Sahai* superintendence; agency.

添 *Sashizoe* an assistant.

異 *Sai* difference.

當 *Sashi-atari* at present.

置 *Sashi-o(ku)* to set aside.

詰 *Sashizume* at present.

遣 *Saken* dispatch.

障 *Sashisawari* obstacle.

額 *Sagaku* difference.

恙 **YŌ.** *Tsutsuga* harm; grief; illness.【心】

羞 **SHŪ.** *Ha(jiru); hajira(u); hanika(mu)* to be ashamed; be shy. 五

恥 *Shūchi* shame; shyness.

蓋 See 蓋 140,10.

翔 **SHŌ.** *Kake(ru)* to soar; fly.【羽】 六

四〇

（六）
T **着** CHAKU aux. num. for counting clothes. *Tsu(ku)* to arrive: *ki(-ru)* to put on; wear: *ki(seru)* to dress (somebody else). Sometimes used for **著** 140,9.

々 *Chaku-chaku* steadily; step by step.

手 *Chakushu* commencing; setting to work.

目 *Chakumoku* fixing one's eyes upon.

用 *Chakuyō* wearing.

京 *Chakkyō* arrive in Tōkyō.

物 *Kimono* clothes; especially a certain Japanese garment.

服 *Chakufuku* embezzlement.

眼 *Chakugan* aiming at.

想 *Chakusō* turn of thought.

實 *Chakujitsu* steadiness and honesty.

七 **羨** SEN. *Uraya(mu)* to envy; covet: *urayamashii* envious.

望 *Sembō* envy.

T **義** GI right; justice. *Yoshi* good; correct; proper.

人 *Gijin* loyal man; righteous man.

子 *Gishi* adopted son; foster-child.

士 *Gishi* chivalrous warrior; righteous person.

父 *Gifu* step-father.

心 *Gishin* philanthropy.

兄 *Gikei* elder sister's husband.

（七）
兄弟 *Gikyōdai* a brother-in-law.

足 *Gisoku* artificial leg.

兵 *Gihei* loyal soldiers.

勇 *Giyū* loyalty; heroism.

勇兵 *Giyūhei* a volunteer soldier or sailor.

勇奉公 *Giyū-hōkō* patriotic and civic duties.

妹 *Gimai* younger brother's wife.

俠 *Gikyō* chivalry.

軍 *Gigun* a righteous army.

烈 *Giretsu* nobility of soul.

氣 *Giki* chivalry.

捐 *Gien* donation; contribution.

理 *Giri* duty; obligation; justice.

務 *Gimu* obligation; duty.

絶 *Gizetsu* break off friendly relations.

賊 *Gizoku* a chivalrous robber.

憤 *Gifun* righteous indignation.

舉 *Gikyo* heroic deed.

齒 *Gishi* an artificial tooth.

T **群** GUN. *Mure* group; flock; crowd: *muraga(ru)* to group together; flock together; congregate.

小 *Gunshō* insignificant.

生 *Gunsei* gregariousness.

臣 *Gunshin* the whole body of officials.

居 *Gunkyo* to reside or exist in large numbers.

（七）群

馬 *Gumma* p. n.

島 *Guntō* an archipelago.

雄 *Gun-yū* a number of rivals.

衆 *Gunshū* a crowd; mob.

集 *Gunshū* crowd; multitude.

羣 See prec.

九 T 養 YŌ. *Yashina(u)* to nourish; bring up; rear. (*Ya*).【食】

子 *Yōshi* adopted son.

分 *Yōbun* nourishment.

父 *Yōfu* foster-father.

女 *Yōjo* adopted daughter.

生 *Yōjō* care of one's health.

母 *Yōbo* foster-mother.

成 *Yōsei* fostering; cultivation; training.

育 *Yōiku* bringing up.

育院 *Yōikuin* a poor-house.

家 *Yōka* adopted family.

殖 *Yōshoku* rear; raise.

嗣子 *Yōshishi* adopted son.

蠶 *Yōsan* sericulture.

羹 KAN; KŌ. *Atsumono* soup.

一四 ·As Tōyō only:

羽 羽

T 羽 U. *Hane*; *ha* feather; wing: *wa* aux. num. for counting birds.

二重 *Habutae* very fine kind of silk fabric.

子 *Hane* shuttlecock.

子板 *Hagoita* battledore.

毛 *Umō* plumage; plume.

目 *Hame* state; condition.

振 *Haburi* social position; influence.

翼 *Uyoku* wings and feathers.

織 *Haori* Japanese coat.

T 翁 Ō. *Okina* an old man. 四

翌 T YOKU. *Akuru* next; following. 五

日 *Yokujitsu*; *akuruhi* the next day.

年 *Yokunen*; *akurutoshi* the following year.

朝 *Yokuasa*; *yokuchō*; *akuruasa* the next morning.

T 習 SHŪ; JŪ. *Nara(u)* to learn; study: *narawashi* custom; practice; fashion.

字 *Shūji* penmanship.

性 *Shūsei* acquired habit.

俗 *Shūzoku* manners and customs.

得 *Shūtoku* learning.

慣 *Shūkan* habit.

熟 *Shūjuku* accustomed; become skilful.

翠 SUI. *Midori* deep green. 八

綠 *Suiryoku* deep green.

九 翫 GAN. *Moteaso(bu)* to play with.

翩 HEN. *Hirugae(ru)*; *hirugae(su)* to wave; turn: *kake(ru)* to fly fast; soar.

々 *Hemp n* fluttering.

翩 *Hempon* fluttering.

一〇 翰 See 24,14. 【羽】

一一 T 翼 YOKU to assist. *Tsubasa* wing.

贊 *Yokusan* endorsement; support.

翳 EI shade; protection; (eyes) to become dim. *Kaza(su)* to stick in the hair; protect from the sun.

二一 T 翻 See 翻 183,12.

一四 耀 See 42,17. 【羽】

一九 糶 CHŌ rice for selling. *Seri* auction. 【米】

賣 *Seriuri* auction sale.

一三五 老

Always at the top and generally in a mutilated form.

T 老 RŌ. *Oi* old: *o(y)iru)* to grow old: *fu(keru)* to grow old; look old.

人 *Rōjin* old man.

少 *Rōshō* young and old.

巧 *Rōkō* mature skill.

功 *Rōkō* veteran.

幼 *Rōyō* young and old.

朽 *Rōkyū* superannuation.

年 *Rōnen* old age.

成 *Rōsei* maturity; skill.

後 *Rōgo* old age.

弱 *Rōjaku* young and old.

若 *Rōjaku*; *rōnyaku* young and old.

病 *Rōbyō* senile decay.

耄 *Rōmō*; *oibore* dotage; senility.

衰 *Rōsui* decrepitude.

眼 *Rōgan* aged eyes.

婆 *Rōba* old woman.

婆心 *Rōbashin* excessive kindness.

爺 *Rōya*; *ojiisan* old man.

境 *Rōkyō* declining years.

舖 *Shinise*; *rōho* old-established shop.

練 *Rōren* skilled; old; experienced.

熟 *Rōjuku* mature experience.

獪 *Rōkai* old and crafty.

軀 *Rōku* aged body.

體 *Rōtai* aged person.

T 考 KŌ one's deceased father. 二 *Kangae* opinion: *kanga-(h)eru)* to consider; think; reflect; investigate.

究 *Kōkyū* investigation.

事 *Kangaegoto* something to think over.

(二)考

物 *Kangaemono* a puzzle.

査 *Kōsa* scrutiny; examination.

案 *Kōan* idea; plan.

違 *Kangaechigai* misapprehension.

察 *Kōsatsu* consideration; reflection.

慮 *Kōryo* consideration.

三 孝 Kō filial piety. (*Taka*).
T 【子】

子 *Kōshi* dutiful child.

女 *Kōjo* dutiful daughter.

心 *Kōshin* filial affection.

行 *Kōkō* filial piety.

道 *Kōdō* filial piety.

經 *Kōkyō* lectures of Confucius on filial piety written by one of his disciples.

養 *Kōyō* discharge of filial duties.

四 者 SHA. *Mono* person. Often used as bottom component. In this case, if read *mono* it has an impolite meaning; e. g.: *inaka-mono* a rustic, *namake-mono* a lazy fellow; but if read *sha* it refers to a person with some special knowledge, accomplishment or quality, and it is not impolite; e. g.: *isha* doctor, *bengakusha* a man of letters, *shinja* a believer. Also used in epist. st. for particle *wa* or *ba*; e. g.: 右者＝右は，陳者＝陳ぶれば

→125, 3 * T

*1 者 →125,4
T

耆 KI old person; to grow **(四)** old.

宿 *Kishuku* a veteran.

耄 MŌ; BŌ. *Oibo(reru)* to be in one's dotage.

*2 碌 *Mōroku* second childhood.

煮 SHA. *Ni(-ru); ni(y)eru)* to **八** boil; cook. 【火】
→125,7 *² T

沸 *Shafutsu* to boil.

而 二六

而 JI. *Shikōshite; shikashite* yet; still; and. Used for termination *te* in letter writing e. g. 依而＝依つて，追而＝追つて．

已 *Nomi* only.

T 耐 TAI. *Ta(h)eru); kora(h)eru)* **三** to bear; endure.

久力 *Taikyūryoku* durability.

火 *Taika* fire-proof.

水 *Taisui* water-proof.

忍 *Tainin* patience; perseverance.

震 *Taishin* earthquake-proof.

耒 二七

耕 KŌ. *Tagaya(su)* to till; **四** cultivate.

366 ***² 煮 →125,8**
T

作 *Kōsaku* cultivation; farming.

地 *Kōchi* arable land.

種 *Kōshu* to cultivate; hoe up and sow seeds.

稼 *Kōka* farming.

T 耗 MŌ; KŌ. *Hc(ru)* to decrease; to become exhausted.

耘 UN to weed.

耳

When at the left, it is called *Mimi-hen*.

T 耳 JI. *Mimi* ear: *nomi* only; a final particle.

目 *Jimoku* public attention.

朵 *Jida; mimitabo* lobe of the ear; ear.

順 *Jijun* 60 years old.

障 *Mimizawari* discordant.

鳴 *Miminari* ringing in the ears.

語 *Jigo; sasayaku* whispering.

二 T 取 SHU. *To(ru)* to take: *ni totte wa* for; as regards. 【又】 Forms the first component of various compounds with a meaning of "to take" "to handle" or without a special meaning except emphasis.

入 *Tori-i(reru)* to take in; harvest: *tori-i(ru)* to work oneself into another's favour.

上 *Tori-a(geru)* to take in one's hand; accept; adopt.

下 *Tori-sa(geru)* to withdraw.

引 *Torihiki* transaction.

引所 *Torihikijo* a mercantile exchange.

分 *Toriwake* especially.

立 *Torita(teru)* to collect; promote.

外 *Torihazu(su)* to take apart.

去 *Torisaru* to take away.

次 *Toritsugi* agency; usher; transmitting.

交 *Tori-ma(zeru); tori-maji-(h)eru)* to mix up all together.

込 *Torikomi* confusion; trouble.

沙汰 *Torizata* current rumour.

扱 *Tori-atsuka(u)* to treat; manage; handle: *tori-a.sukai* treatment.

附 *Toritsu(keru)* to fit up; install: *toritsuke* run on a bank: *toritsu(ku)* to cling to; hold fast.

直 *Tori-nao(su)* to change one's grasp or way of holding; reconsider; change one's mind.

返 *Torikae(su)* to recover; take back.

卷 *Torima(ku)* to surround.

計 *Torihakarai* management.

持 *Torimo(tsu)* to entertain; treat; mediate.

急 *Tori-iso(gu)* to be in a hurry.

取 (二)

柄 *Torie* worth; value; strong point.

消 *Torikeshi* cancellation; withdrawal.

得 *Shutoku* acquisition.

捌 *Torisabaki* management; judgment.

高 *Toridaka* income.

除 *Torinoke* exception; exclusion.

組 *Torikumi* pair; match.

組合 *Tokkumiai* gripping each other.

捨 *Shusha* selection.

掛 *Torikaka(ru)* to begin; set to work.

寄 *Toriyo(seru)* to obtain; import; send for.

替 *Torikae* change; exchange.

極 *Toriki(meru)* to agree; settle.

圍 *Torikako(mu)* to surround.

揃 *Torisoroe* putting together.

換 *Torika(h)eru* to exchange.

亂 *Torimida(su)* to derange; confuse.

違 *Torichiga(h)eru* mistake.

締 *Torishimari* control; direction; management.

調 *Torishirabe* investigation.

離 *Torihana(su)* to take apart.

三 耶 YA interrogative particle.

蘇 *Yaso* Jesus.

耻 See ᵀ恥 128,4. 【心】 四

耽 TAN. *Fuke(ru)* to be addicted to.

溺 *Tandeki* indulgence; dissipation.

讀 *Tandoku* absorbed in reading.

ᵀ恥 CHI. *Haji* shame; disgrace: *ha(jiru)* to be ashamed: *hazukashii* ashamed; shameful. 【心】 →128,4

辱 *Chijoku* shame; disgrace.

聊 RYŌ. *Isasaka* trifling; a little. 五

聘 HEI to summon. 七

用 *Heiyō* to engage.

碇 *Shika to; tashika ni* surely; certainly. 八

聚 SHŪ; SHU; JU. *Atsuma(ru)* to assemble together; collect.

智 SEI. *Muko* man married into woman's family; husband.

聯 See 128,11 nr.1. 九

*聯 REN. *Tsurana(ru); tsura-(neru)* to unite; associate; arrange in a row. 一 一

立内閣 *Renritsunaikaku* a coalition Cabinet.

合 *Rengō* combination; union.

邦 *Rempō* federation of States.

併 *Rempei* jointly; in a body.

*ᵀ聴 →128,16

隊 *Rentai* regiment.

盟 *Remmei* league.

想 *Rensō* association (of ideas).

絡 *Renraku* connection.

聽 See 聽 128,16.

聰 Sō. *Satoi* intelligent.

明 *Sōmei* sagacious; intelligent.

聳 Shō lofty; high. *Sobi-(y)eru)* to tower up: *sobiyaka(su)* to raise the shoulders (an offensive gesture of pride, generally preparatory to a fight).

動 *Shōdō* to startle.

聲 Sei sound. *Koe* voice: *homare* good reputation; fame. →32, 4 T

名 *Seimei* reputation; fame.

色 *Seishoku* voice and expression of the face: *kowa.ro* the tone of the voice.

明 *Seimei* declaration.

望 *Seibō* popularity; fame.

援 *Seien* encouragement; support.

樂 *Seigaku* vocal music.

價 *Seika* reputation; fame.

譽 *Seiyo* honour; reputation.

二 職 Shoku occupation; office; duty; trade; business; to take charge of; direct; official in charge of. T 職
→ 職

人 *Shokunin* workman; mechanic.

工 *Shokkō* a workman.

工組合 *Shokkō-kumiai* trade-union.

分 *Shokubun* one's duty.

制 *Shokusei* organization of an office.

員 *Shokuin* the staff; personnel.

能 *Shokunō* function.

務 *Shokumu* duty.

責 *Shokuseki* duty; function.

掌 *Shokushō* official duties.

業 *Shokugyō* occupation; employment.

權 *Shokken* official powers.

叢 Sō. *Kusamura* grass plat; thicket: *mura* cluster: *muraga(ru)* to be crowded together; be collected. 【又】

書 *Sōsho* library; series.

雲 *Murakumo* cluster of clouds.

聽 Chō. *Ki(ku)* to listen; hear; to allow; grant; permit. →128, 10 T ＊ 一六

取 *Chōshu* listen to.

許 *Chōkyo* permission; grant.

衆 *Chōshū* the audience.

聞 *Chōmon* to listen to; hear.

講 *Chōkō* attend (lectures).

覺 *Chōkaku* auditory sense.

聾 See 212,6. 【耳】

一二九

聿

四 書 SHO. *Fumi* letter; docu-
T ment; literary composition;
book: *ka(ku)* to write. 【日】

入 *Kakiire* entry.

生 *Shosei* student; dependent.

式 *Shoshiki* the customary
form of writing.

附 *Kakitsuke* a note; a document; a bill; a memoran-
dum.

取 *Kakitoru* to copy: *kakitori*
dictation.

物 *Shomotsu* book.

状 *Shojō* letter; epistle.

面 *Shomen* letter; epistle.

留 *Kakitome* registration (of
a letter).

家 *Shoka* calligraphist.

記 *Shoki* clerk; secretary.

連 *Kaki-tsura(neru)* to write
down.

添 *Kaki-so(h)eru* to add in
writing or painting.

畫 *Shoga* writings and pictures.

替 *Kakikae* rewriting; renewal.

置 *Kakioki* a written will.

肆 *Shoshi* a bookshop.

翰 *Shokan* letter; epistle.

齋 *Shosai* a study.

簡 *Shokan* a letter.

類 *Shorui* documents. （四）

籍 *Shoseki* books.

畫 CHŪ. *Hiru* daytime; noon. 五
【日】 →44, 6 T : 1, 8 T

休 *Hiruyasumi* recess after
lunch.

夜 *Chūya* day and night, i. e.
24 hours; the whole day.

食 *Chūjiki; chūshoku; hiruge*
noon meal.

前 *Hirumae* forenoon.

間 *Chūkan* daytime.

飯 *Hirumeshi* lunch.

過 *Hirusugi* afternoon.

寝 *Hirune* a midday nap.

畫 GA; E picture: KAKU 六
to limit; to plan; mark off.
Ega(ku) to paint. 【田】

工 *Gakō* artist; painter. →1, 7 T

伯 *Gahaku* a master-painter.

師 *Eshi* artist; painter.

家 *Gaka* artist; painter.

報 *Gahō* pictorial newspaper.

圖 *Ezu* picture.

餅 *Gahei* naught.

畫 See prec. 【田】 七

肄 I to labour. *Nara(u)* to
study: *wakaeda* young
shoot.

肆 SHI shop. *Hoshiimama*
arbitrariness; self-will.

肇 CHŌ. *Hajime* the begin- 八
ning.

370

一三〇 肉

In composition it takes the form 月 and is called *Nikuzuki*. When 月 does not come from 肉 it is not called *Nikuzuki*.

ᵀ**肉** NIKU. *Shishi* flesh; meat.

汁 *Nikujū; soppu* meat soup.

色 *Nikuiro* flesh colour.

附 *Nikutsuki* flesh.

食 *Nikushoku; nikujiki* flesh-eating.

眼 *Nikugan* the naked eye.

筆 *Nikuhitsu* an autograph.

感的 *Nikkanteki* sensual.

慾 *Nikuyoku* animal passions; sexual desire.

薄 *Nikuhaku* to press hard (an opponent).

親 *Nikushin* real parent; blood relation.

體 *Nikutai* flesh; body.

ᵀ**月** See 74,0.

二 **肋** ROKU. *Abarabone; abara* rib.

材 *Rokuzai* rib (of a ship).

骨 *Rokkotsu* rib.

肌 KI. *Hada; hadae* the skin; naked body.

合 *Hadaai* disposition.

身 *Hadami* a body.

著 *Hadagi* underwear.

三

肛 KŌ anus.

肚 TO. *Hara* mind; stomach.

裏 *Tori* in one's mind.

ᵀ**肝** KAN. *Kimo* liver.

心 *Kanjin* important; essential.

要 *Kan-yō* important; essential.

煎 *Kimoiri* assistant; manager; mediation.

膽 *Kantan* innermost heart.

肘 CHŪ. *Hiji* elbow; arm.

鐵砲 *Hijideppō* rejection.

四

朋 HŌ. *Tomo* friend; companion. 【月】

友 *Hōyū* friend.

輩 *Hōbai* friend; comrade.

黨 *Hōtō* friendly party.

ᵀ**肪** BŌ; HŌ to be fleshy. *Abura* fat.

服 FUKU dress; clothing; aux. num. for counting whiffs of tobacco, also doses of medicine; to submit; to obey; to put on (dress). 【月】→服 ᵀ

用 *Fukuyō* to take (medicine); to administer.

役 *Fukueki* servitude.

部 *Hattori* p. n.

從 *Fukujū* to submit; obey.

務 *Fukumu* public service.

(四) 服
装 *Fukusō* dress.
罪 *Fukuzai* confession of guilt.
膺 *Fukuyō* to keep in mind; lay to heart.
薬 *Fukuyaku* taking medicine.

肢 SHI arms and legs; limbs.

股 KO. *Momo* the thigh: *mata* crotch of the legs.
引 *Momohiki* drawers.
肱 *Kokō* right-hand man; chief assistant.

T 肥 HI. *Ko(y)eru* to be fertile; fat: *futo(ru)* to grow fat: *koe; koyashi* fertilizer; manure: *koya(su)* to fatten (animals); manure (field).
大 *Hidai* fleshiness.
立 *Hidachi* convalescence.
沃 *Hiyoku* (of land) rich; fertile.
前 *Hizen* p. n.
後 *Higo* p. n.
料 *Hiryō* fertilizer.
満 *Himan* corpulence.

肱 KŌ. *Hiji* elbow.

肴 KŌ. *Sakana* fish; meat and vegetables eaten with rice or *sake*.

T 青 See 青 174,0.

冒 See 冒 13,7.

(五) T 胆 See 膽 130,13.

胚 HAI to be pregnant.
胎 *Haitai* to originate.
T 胎 TAI to be pregnant; beginning; symptom.
兒 *Taiji* an embryo.
T 肺 HAI lungs.
肝 *Haikan* innermost mind.
炎 *Haien* pneumonia.
病 *Haibyō* consumption.
腑 *Haifu* bottom of one's heart.
結核 *Haikekkaku* tuberculosis.
臓 *Haizō* lungs.

胞 HŌ. *Ena* placenta.
衣 *Ena* placenta. →胞 T

胡 GO; KO barbarian; foreign.
瓜 *Kiuri* cucumber.
坐 *Agura* to sit in tailor's fashion.
桃 *Kurumi* walnut.
椒 *Koshō* pepper.
麻化 *Gomaka(su)* to deceive; cheat.
蝶 *Kochō* butterfly.
散 *Usan* doubtful; suspicious.
亂 *Uron* suspicious.

胄 CHŪ lineage. *Kabuto* helmet.

T 背 HAI. *Se; senaka; sena; ushiro* the back; behind:

（五）

sei stature: *somu(ku)* to disobey.

戸 *Sedo* a back-gate.

反 *Haihan* contrariety.

中 *Senaka* the back.

水の陣 *Haisui no jin* to burn one's boats.

任 *Hainin* breach of trust.

面 *Haimen* the rear; the back.

理 *Hairi* unreasonable.

後 *Haigo* the rear; the back.

景 *Haikei* background.

馳 *Haichi* to run counter to.

六 脳 See 脳 130,9.

T 脂 SHI rouge. *Abura* fat; grease: *yani* resin; gum; exudation.

肪 *Shibō* fat; grease.

粉 *Shifun* rouge and powder.

T 胴 DŌ trunk; body.

卷 *Dōmaki* an abdominal belt.

着 *Dōgi* vest-shaped underwear.

慾 *Dōyoku* avarice.

T 胸 KYŌ. *Mune* breast; chest; heart.

中 *Kyōchū* bosom; heart; mind.

部 *Kyōbu* the breast.

倉 *Munagura* breast of a coat.

像 *Kyōzō* a bust.

（六）

算用 *Munazan-yō* mental calculation; scheme.

襟 *Kyōkin* the heart.

騒 *Munasawagi* agitation; uneasiness.

胯 KO. *Mata* crotch.

脇 KYŌ. *Waki* side; armpit.

目 *Wakime* looking aside.

路 *Wakimichi* a side road.

腹 *Wakibara* the side of the chest.

朕 CHIN We (used by the Emperor). 【月】

脈 MYAKU pulse; range (of mountains). →脈 T

搏 *Myakuhaku* pulse (beats).

脆 ZEI. *Moroi; yowai* brittle; weak.

弱 *Zeijaku* frailty.

朔 SAKU. *Tsuitachi* the 1st day of the month. 【月】

日 *Tsuitachi* the 1st day of the month.

風 *Sakufū* north wind.

T 骨 See 188,0.

T 脅 See 19,8. 【肉】

脊 SEKI. *Se; senaka* the back (of the body).

骨 *Sebone* backbone; spine; vertebrae.

七 脛 KEI. *Sune* shin: *hagi* leg.

T 脚 KYAKU; KAKU. *Ashi* leg; foot.

本 *Kyakuhon* book of words.

色 *Kyakushoku* the plot of a play.

氣 *Kakke* beri-beri.

註 *Kyakuchū* foot-note.

T 豚 TON. *Buta* pig; hog. 【豕】

兒 *Tonji* my child (humble).

脫 DATSU to dislocate; omit (generally by oversight). *Nu(gu)* to take off (as clothes); cast off (as a skin): *nu(ku)* to extract (as an essence): *noga(reru)* to escape. →脫 T

出 *Dasshutsu* escape.

臼 *Dakkyū* dislocation.

兎 *Datto* a running hare.

却 *Dakkyaku* to cast off; shake off.

走 *Dassō* desertion; escape.

俗 *Datsuzoku* being above the world.

脂綿 *Dasshimen* absorbent cotton.

稅 *Datsuzei* evasion of taxes.

帽 *Datsubō* taking off one's hat.

落 *Datsuraku* fall off.

獄 *Datsugoku* jail-breaking.

會 *Dakkai* leave a society.

漏 *Datsurō* omission.

稿 *Dakkō* completing manuscript.

線 *Dassen* derailment; digression.

營 *Datsuei* desertion (from barracks).

離 *Datsuri* disconnect.

黨 *Dattō* to desert from one's party.

朗 RŌ. *Hogaraka* bright; spacious; clear. 【月】→朗 T

々 *Rōrō* clearly (voice).

詠 *Rōei* reciting verses aloud.

讀 *Rōdoku* reading aloud.
*

脾 HI the spleen.　八

肉の嘆 *Hiniku no tan* to fret from forced idleness.

腑 FU understanding; intestines.

甲斐無 *Fuɟainai* spiritless.

抜 *Funuke* a dunce; a fool.

勝 SHŌ victory. *Ka(tsu)* to conquer: *masa(ru)*; *sugu-(reru)* to excel; surpass: *gachi* as 2nd component, frequently; e. g. *fuzai-gachi* frequently absent: *ta(h)e-ru)* to endure. 【力】→勝 T

手 *Katte* convenience; selfishness; following one's idea · manner; kitchen: *katte gamashii* selfish.

地 *Shōchi* beauty spot.

利 *Shōri* victory.

負 *Shōbu* contest; match.

374 *
T 腦 →130,9

（八）

勝敗 *Shōhai* victory or defeat; issue.

氣 *Kachiki* ardent; eager; filled with the spirit of rivalry.

訴 *Shōso* winning a case.

算 *Shōsan* hope of success.

脹 CHŌ. *Fuku(reru)* : *ha(reru)* to swell; be inflated; be puffed up.

腋 EKI. *Waki* side; armpit.

T **腕** WAN. *Ude; kaina* arm.

力 *Wanryoku* physical force; strength.

白 *Wampaku* naughtiness.

車 *Wansha* jinrikisha.

前 *Udemae* ability.

輪 *Udewa* a bracelet.

朝 CHŌ Imperial court; reign; dynasty; one's own country. *Asa; ashita* morning. (*Tomo*). 【月】→朝 T

夕 *Chōseki; asayū* morning and evening.

日 *Asahi* rising sun.

臣 *Chōshin; ason* courtier.

廷 *Chōtei* the Imperial court.

政 *Chōsei* the Imperial government.

起 *Asaoki* early rising.

野 *Chōya* government and people; the whole nation.

飯 *Asahan; asameshi* breakfast.

寢 *Asane* late rising.

敵 *Chōteki* rebel; traitor.

憲 *Chōken* constitution; laws.

鮮 *Chōsen* Korea.

顏 *Asagao* morning-glory; convolvulus.

T **期** KI; GO fixed time; period of time; occasion; to expect; be confident. 【月】

日 *Kijitsu* fixed day.

成 *Kisei* resolving to carry out.

米 *Kimai* future rice (speculation).

待 *Kitai* expectation.

限 *Kigen* term; period of time.

間 *Kikan* a period.

節 *Kisetsu* season.

腎 JIN kidneys.

腥 SEI. *Namagusai* disagreeable smell or taste of raw fish or meat.

腫 SHU; SHŌ. *Dekimono* tumour: *ha(reru)* to swell.

物 *Shumotsu; haremono* an ulcer.

腦 NŌ brain; intellect. →130, 7 T *

天 *Nōten* the scalp; the top of the head.

裡 *Nōri* brain; mind.

髓 *Nōzui* the brain.

T **腸** CHŌ. *Harawata* internal organs; intestines.

（八）　（九）

375

（九） 腺 *Sen* gland.

T 腹 FUKU. *Hara* abdomen; feelings.

心 *Fukushin* devoted; confidential.

立 *Haradachi* anger; wrath.

背 *Fukuhai* back and front.

案 *Fukuan* a plan; a scheme.

痛 *Fukutsū* a stomach-ache.

黒 *Haraguroi* black-hearted fellow.

藏 *Fukuzō naku* without reservation.

T 腰 YŌ. *Koshi* the loins.

抜 *Koshinuke* cowardice.

部 *Yobu* the waist.

掛 *Koshikake* a bench: *koshika(keru)* to sit down.

辧 *Koshiben* a petty official.

一〇 腽肭獸 *Ottosei* seal (animal).

膀胱 *Bōkō* bladder.

腿 TAI. *Momo* thigh; leg.

一一 膠 KŌ; KYŌ. *Nikawa* glue: *neba(ru)* to be sticky; stick fast.

州 *Kōshū* Kiaochow.

柱 *Kōchū* unadaptability.

着 *Kōchaku* sticking fast.

腸 See 腸 130.9.

（一一）

T 膜 MAKU membrane.

膝 SHITSU. *Hiza* knee; lap.

下 *Shikka* by the side of one's parents.

元 *Hizamoto* near.

栗毛 *Hizakurige* travel on foot.

膳 ZEN small dinner-table; meal set on a table; suffix for counting chopsticks and bowlfuls of rice. 一二

立 *Zendate* preparations.

部 *Zembu* the table; dishes.

T 膨 BŌ; HŌ. *Fuku(reru)* to swell.

大 *Bōdai* big; bulky.

脹 *Bōchō* expansion; swelling.

膽 TŌ to copy.【言】→謄 T 一三

本 *Tōhon* (certified) copy.

寫 *Tōsha* to copy.

膽 TAN feelings; affections. *Kimo; i* liver; gall. →130,5 T

力 *Tanryoku* boldness; courage.

氣 *Tanki* boldness; courage.

略 *Tanryaku* courage and resourcefulness.

膾 KAI. *Namasu* a kind of salad.

炙 *Kaisha* to be well known.

（一三）

膿 NŌ. *Umi* pus.

髓 See 髓 188,13.

臉 See 瞼 109,13.

臆 OKU timidity; breast; heart; mind.

面 *Okumen* (usually with negative) brazen-faced; bold.

病 *Okubyō* cowardice.

測 *Okusoku* guess; conjecture.

説 *Okusetsu* arbitrary opinion; supposition; conjecture.

断 *Okudan* arbitrary judgment.

臂 HI. *Hiji* elbow

臀 DEN. *Shiri* buttocks.

一四

臍 SAI; SEI. *Heso; hozo* navel.

繰 *Hesokuri* pin-money.

朦 MŌ dim; obscure.【月】

々 *Mōmō* dim; obscure.

朧 *Mōrō* dim; obscure. *

一五

鵬 HŌ. *Ōtori* a fabulous bird.【鳥】

臘 RŌ the end of the year; last month of the year.

一六

騰 TŌ. *Aga(ru); nobo(ru)* to rise; ascend.【馬】

（一六）

貴 *Tōki* rise (as of price).

朧 RŌ. *Oboro* dim; obscure.【月】

氣 *Oboroge* obscure.

一八

臟 ZŌ organ; after the specific name of a part of the body it need not be translated, e. g. 心臟 *shinzō* heart; however 内臟 *naizō* internal organs. *Harawata* viscera.
→130,14 T *

腑 *Zōfu* viscera.

臣

三一

T 臣 SHIN I. *Omi* Emperor's servant; subject; retainer. (*Tomi*).

下 *Shinka* subject; retainer.

民 *Shimmin* subject; retainer.

二

臥 See foll.

臥 GA. *Fu(su); fu(seru)* to lie down.

床 *Gashō* lying in bed; bed.

薪嘗膽 *Gash'nshōtan* suffer great hardships.

九

頤 See 181,6.

一一

T 臨 RIN extraordinary. *Noz-(mu)* to face; be present; be at the point of.

↓ →騰 T　*臟 T →130,18　377

（一一） 臨

月 *Ringetsu* month of parturition.

床 *Rinshō* clinical.

幸 *Rinkō* Imperial visit; Emperor's going to a place.

時 *Rinji* extraordinary; special; sudden; temporary.

席 *Rinseki* attendance; presence.

終 *Rinjū* point of death.

御 *Ringyo* Imperial visit.

場 *Rinjō* attendance.

機 *Rinki* according to circumstances.

機應變 *Rinki-ōhen* acting according to circumstances.

檢 *Rinken* visit of inspection.

一三三 自

T 自 JI self; one elf: SHI. *Onozukara; mizukara; onozuto* spontaneously; naturally; of its own accord: *yori* (inverted order) from.

及 *Jijin* suicide.

己 *Jiko* self; oneself.

今 *Jikon* henceforth.

分 *Jibun* oneself; yourself; himself.

白 *Jihaku* confession.

由 *Jiyū* liberty; freedom.

由自在 *Jiyū-jizai* free and unrestricted; without effort.

失 *Jishitsu* self-stupefaction.

他 *Jita* self and others.

主 *Jishu* independence.

任 *Jinin* self-charge; set oneself a task.

在 *Jizai* free.

宅 *Jitaku* one's own dwelling.

明 *Jimei* self-evident.

身 *Jishin* oneself.

我 *Jiga* self; ego.

決 *Jiketsu* resign; suicide.

制 *Jisei* self-control.

治 *Jichi* self-government.

治制 *Jichisei* system of self-government.

重 *Jichō* self-respect.

活 *Jikatsu* self-support.

若 *Jijaku to shite* composedly; calmly; steadfastly.

省 *Jisei* self-examination.

首 *Jishu* self-surrender.

負 *Jifu* arrogance; conceit.

炊 *Jisui* cook one's own meals.

信 *Jishin* self-confidence.

叙傳 *Jijoden* autobiography.

修 *Jishū* self-culture.

害 *Jigai* suicide.

乘 *Jijō* square (number).

家 *Jika* one's own house; oneself; personal.

家撞着 *Jika-dōchaku* self-contradiction.

殺 *Jisatsu* suicide.

動 *Jidō* self-moving; auto-matic.

動車 *Jidōsha* motor-car.

筆 *Jihitsu* one's own writing.

尊 *Jison* self-importance.

然 *Shizen* nature; naturally; spontaneously.

給 *Jikyū* self-supporting.

費 *Jihi* private expenses.

署 *Jisho* one's own signature.

業自得 *Jigōjitoku* troubles of one's own making.

愛 *Jiai* self-love.

滅 *Jimetsu* self-destruction.

慢 *Jiman* pride; self-praise.

認 *Jinin* to acknowledge; admit.

說 *Jisetsu* one's own opinion.

稱 *Jishō* self-appointed.

衞 *Jiei* self-defence.

墮落 *Jidaraku* slovenliness.

暴 *Yabe* desperation.

暴自棄 *Jibō-jiki* desperation.

辨 *Jiben* paying one's own expenses.

營 *Jiei* self-support.

轉車 *Jitensha* bicycle.

覺 *Jikaku* self-consciousness.

* 讚 *Jisan* self-praise.

四　臭 SHŪ. *Nioi* offensive smell: *kusai* stinking: *nio(u)* to smell offensively.
→132,3 * T

氣 *Shūki* offensive smell.

臭 →132,4
T

息 SOKU to leave off; cease. *Iki* breath: *iko(u)* to rest: *musuko* son. 【心】（四）

子 *Musuko* son.

女 *Sokujo* daughter.

災 *Sokusai* good health.

T 鼻 See 209,0. 八

至　一三三

T 至 SHI. *Ita(ru)* to arrive; come to; go to; as far as; as to: *itatte* very: *itari* extremity; most; very great: *made* (inverted order) until.

大 *Shidai* very great.

仁 *Shijin* most benevolent.

言 *Shigen* an apt word.

急 *Shikyū* urgency.

情 *Shijō* deep feeling; affection.

尊 *Shison* the Emperor.

極 *Shigoku* very; exceedingly.

當 *Shitō* right and proper.

誠 *Shisei* extreme conscientiousness; extreme sincerity.

T 到 TŌ. *Ita(ru)* to arrive; reach. 【刀】 二

來 *Tōrai* to come; arrive; receive (as a present).

底 *Tōtei* after all; by no means.

(二一)

到
着 *Tōchaku* arrival.
達 *Tōtatsu* arrival.
頭 *Tōtō* at last.

四
T **致** CHI. *Ita(su)* to do: *omomuki* taste (artistic).
方 *Itashikata* help; way.
死 *Chishi* killing; causing death.
居候 *Itashiori sōrō* am doing.
命 *Chimei* fatal; vital.
度候 *Itashitaku sōrō* should like to do.
候 *Itashi sōrō* I do; I did.

一
〇 **臻** SHIN. *Ita(ru)* to come; reach.

一
四 **白**

臼 KYŪ. *Usu* mortar.

二 **兒** JI; NI. *Ko* baby; infant; child. 【儿】 →10,5 T
女 *Jijo* a young girl.
童 *Jidō* children.
戲 *Jigi* child's play.

三 **舁** YO. *Ka(ku); kaki-a(geru)* to carry on the shoulder.

七 **舅** KYŪ. *Shūto* father-in-law.

(七〇)

鼠
與 See 208,0.

YO. *Ata(h)eru* to give: *azuka(ru)* to participate; take part in: *tomo ni together*: *kumisu* together with; and. →1,2 T

力 *Yoryoku* rendering aid.
太 *Yota* silly things.
國 *Yokoku* allied Power.
奪 *Yodatsu* giving or taking away; power to dispose of something.
黨 *Yotō* the Government party.

九
T **與** KŌ; KYŌ interest; entertainment; pleasure. *Oko(ru)* to rise: *oko(su)* to raise.

亡 *Kōbō* rise and fall.
行 *Kōgyō* performance.
起 *Kōki* to raise.
味 *Kyōmi* pleasure; interest.
信所 *Kōshinjo* enquiry agency.
復 *Kōfuku* to restore that which has fallen into decay.
業銀行 *Kōgyō-ginkō* Industrial Bank.
福寺 *Kōfukuji* celebrated Buddhist temple.
銀 *Kōgin* abb. of Industrial Bank.
趣 *Kyōshu* interest; pleasure.
廢 *Kōhai* rise and (or) fall; fate.
奮 *Kōfun* to be stimulated; to be excited.

二 擧　See foll.

擧　KYO.　*A(geru)* to raise:
aga(ru) to rise : *kozo(ru)* to
assemble or gather to-
gether. →37, 7 T *

止　*Kyoshi* behaviour.

手　*Kyoshu* military salute.

句　*Ageku* the end; the conclusion.

行　*Kyokō* to perform; take
place.

措　*Kyoso* behaviour.

國　*Kyokoku* the whole country.

動　*Kyodō* action; behaviour.

一四 譽　YO.　*Homare* reputation;
renown: *ho(meru)* to praise.
【言】　→149, 6 T

望　*Yobō* fame and popularity.

一三五 舌

T 舌　ZETSU.　*Shita* tongue.

代　*Zetsudai* note; message.

端　*Zettan* the tip of the tongue.

鼓　*Shitatsuzumi* sign of joy;
tasteful.

鋒　*Zeppō* the tongue.

戰　*Zessen* a wordy dispute; a
war of words.

一 T 乱　See 亂 5,12.

刮　KATSU.　*Kezu(ru)* to scrape :　二
kosu(ru) to rub the eyes.
【刀】

目　*Katsumoku* to watch eagerly.

舍　See 9,6. 【舌】

舐　SHI.　*Na(meru); nebu(ru)*　四
to lick.

甜　TEN sweet; pleasant to the　五
senses. 【甘】

菜　*Tensai* sugar-beet.

舒　JO slack.　*No(beru)* to　六
relate.

T 辭　See 辭 160,12.　七

舖　HO.　*Mise* a shop. 舖　九
→舗 T

舘　See 館 184,8.　一〇

一三六 舛

舛　SEN to be in confusion.
Somu(ku) to oppose: *taga-
(u)* to differ. Sometimes
used instead of 升 24,2.

舜　SHUN used for its sound.　六
Name of a clever Chinese
Emperor in olden times.

T 舞　BU.　*Ma(u)* to dance.　八

（八）

舞

臺 *Butai* stage ; boards.

踊 *Buyō* dancing.

踏 *Butō* dancing.

妓 *Bugi ; maiko* dancer (girl).

姫 *Maihime* dancer (girl).

鶴 *Maizuru* p.n.; flying crane.

一三七

舟

When at the left, it is called *Fune-hen.*

T 舟 SHŪ. *Fune* boat ; ship.

行 *Shūkō* sailing.

揖 *Shūshū* navigation.

遊 *Shūyū* boating.

四 舻 See 爐 137,16.

T 般 HAN time ; to transport ; to return.

T 航 KŌ navigation ; to cross over.

行 *Kōkō* sailing.

空機 *Kōkūki* aircraft.

海 *Kōkai* sea-voyage ; navigation.

海業 *Kōkaigyō* work on board a ship ; seaman's work.

路 *Kōro* navigation route ; line.

舩 See foll.

「船 SEN. *Fune* ship ; boat.　五

長 *Senchō* captain (of merchant vessel).

室 *Senshitsu* cabin (of a vessel).

客 *Senkyaku* (ship-) passenger.

便 *Funabin* sailing of a ship.

首 *Senshu* the bow.

員 *Sen-in* crew.

舶 *Sempaku* ships ; vessels.

脚 *Senkyaku ; funaashi* draught of a ship.

渠 *Dokku* dock.

荷 *Funani* freight ; load.

暈 *Sen-un* seasickness.

路 *Funaji* a ship-route.

臺 *Sendai* platform or surface on which ship is built.

賃 *Funachin* passage fare ; freight.

頭 *Sendō* boatman.

腹 *Sempuku* freight space.

體 *Sentai* hull.

T 舶 HAKU ship.

來 *Hakurai* coming from abroad ; foreign-made.

舳 JIKU. *Hesaki ; he* bow ; prow.

舵 DA. *Kaji* rudder.

手 *Dashu* a coxswain.

舷 GEN. *Funabata ; funaberi* gunwale of a boat.

七 艀 Fu. *Hashike* small boat; lighter.

船 *Hashike* small boat; lighter.

T 艇 Tei small ship; boat.

身 *Teishin* the length of a boat.

長 *Teichō* the coxswain.

庫 *Teiko* a boat-house.

一〇 艙 Sō. *Funagura* hold of a vessel.

艘 Sō aux. num. for counting ships; boat.

一二 艚 Sō small boat.

一三 艢 See 檣 75,13.

艤裝 *Gisō* equipment of a ship.

一四 艦 Kan warship; armed ship.

↓隊 *Kantai* squadron; fleet.

↓體 *Kantai* hull of a warship.

艨艫 *Mōdō* warship. →艦 T

一五 艪 Ro oar.

一六 艫 Ro. *Tomo* stern of a vessel.

一三八 艮

艮 Kon. *Ushitora* north-east.

T 良 Ryō. *Yo*... *yoshi* good; → excellent: *yaya* a little; in some degree. (*Ra*); (*Naga*). →1, 6

人 *Ryōjin; otto* husband.

心 *Ryōshin* conscience.

民 *Ryōmin* law-abiding citizens.

好 *Ryōkō* good; excellent.

否 *Ryōhi* the good and the bad; quality.

妻賢母 *Ryōsaikembo* good wife and wise mother.

家 *Ryōka* well-to-do family.

策 *Ryōsaku* good plan.

緣 *Ryōen* happy marriage.

艱 Kan hard. *Naya(mu)* to → be distressed. 一

苦 *Kanku* hardship.

難 *Kannan* distress.

色 一三九

T 色 Shoku; Shiki. *Iro* colour; kind; sort; appearance; lewdness.

々 *Iro-iro* various kinds.

分 *Irowake* classification.

合 *Iroai* colour; hue.

香 *Iroka* beauty; charms.

氣 *Iroke* colour; sexual love.

情 *Shikijō* sexual passion.

色
彩 *Shikisai* colouring.
慾 *Shikiyoku* lust.
澤 *Shikitaku* lustre.
魔 *Shikima* a libertine.

一三 艶　EN. *Tsuya* lustre: *adeyaka;*
ade; namamekashii beautiful; lovely; charming:
namame(ku) to be charming; be bewitching.

書 *Ensho* a love-letter.
福 *Empuku* fortune in love.
聞 *Embun* love affair.
麗 *Enrei* beautiful; charming.

一八 艷　See prec.

一四〇
艸

It usually takes the form **⁺⁺**
or **⁺⁺** at the top of a character;
it is then called *Kusa-kammuri*
or *Sō-kō.*

艸　SŌ. *Kusa* grass.

三 芒　BŌ; MŌ. *Nogi* the beard
of grain: *susuki* Chinese
miscanthus, something like
rush.

ᵀ羊　See 123,0.

并　See 弁 51,5.

ᵀ芋　U. *Imo; sato-imo* potato;
taro; tuber.

（二）
ᵀ芝　SHI. *Shiba* turf; also
p. n.

生 *Shibafu* lawn.
居 *Shibai* play; theatre.
罘 *Chiifū* Chefoo.

ᵀ共　KYŌ all. *Tomo ni* together:
domo sign of the plural.【八】

犯 *Kyōhan* joint offence.
有 *Kyōyū* co-ownership.
同 *Kyōdō* common; joint;
union.
同一致 *Kyōdō-itchi* co-operation.
存 *Kyōson* coexistence.
和國 *Kyōwakoku* a republic.
倒 *Tomodaore* fall together.
益 *Kyōeki* common benefit.
產主義 *Kyōsan-shugi* communism.
通 *Kyōtsū* common.
進會 *Kyōshinkai* competitive
exhibition.
鳴 *Kyōmei* resonance; sympathy; echo.
謀 *Kyōbō* conspiracy; collusion.

四
芹　*Seri* parsley.
芥　KAI; KE. *Karashi* mustard:
akuta rubbish.
塵 *Kaijin* dirt; rubbish.
苅　See ᵀ刈 18,2.
ᵀ芽　GA. *Me* bud: *megu(mu)*
to put forth buds; sprout.

（四）出度 *Medetaku* glad to say; happily.

芦 See 蘆 140,16.

芬蘭 *Fuinrando* Finland.

T芳 Hō (sweet) smell; perfume; give forth fragrance. *Kambashii; kaguwashii* fragrant; aromatic. (*Yoshi*).

名 *Hōmei* good name.

名録 *Hōmeiroku* visitors' book.

志 *Hōshi* kind thought.

紀 *Hōki* the age of a young lady.

香 *Hōkō* fragrance; sweet odour.

野 *Yoshino* p. n.

墨 *Hōboku* your honorable letter.

翰 *Hōkan* your honorable letter.

芙蓉 *Fuyō* a certain large pink and white flower.

T花 KA; KE. *Hana* flower; blossom.

々 *Hana-banashii* brilliant; valiant.

火 *Hanabi* fireworks.

見 *Hanami* flower-viewing.

束 *Hanataba* bouquet.

形 *Hanagata* a star (actor).

客 *Kakaku* customer.

柳 *Karyū* demi-monde.

柳病 *Karyūbyō* sexual disease.

粉 *Kafun* pollen.

瓶 *Kabin* flower-vase.

盛 *Hanazakari* in full bloom.

崗岩 *Kakōgan*;　*mik gei shi* granite.

婿 *Hanamuko* a bridegroom.

嫁 *Hanayome* bride.

筵 *Hanamushiro* straw matting with a design of flowers or other figures.

壇 *Kadan* a flower-bed.

環 *Hanawa* a wreath.

*芭蕉 *Bashō* banana-tree.

T莖 See 莖 140,7.　　五

T並 HEI. *Nara(beru); nara(bu)* to place in a row; to arrange in a row: *nami* med um quality: *narabi ni* together with. 【一】

木 *Namiki* avenue.　→117,5

立 *Heiritsu* to stand side by side.

列 *Heiretsu* row.

行 *Heikō* to go abreast.

製 *Namisei* medium (quality).

茄 KA *Nasu; nasubi* eggplant.

子 *Nasu; nasubi* egg-plant.

T若 JAKU; NYAKU; NYA. *Wakai* young: *moshi* if; supposing that: *shi(ku)* to be no better than; be equal to: *gotoshi* like; similar: *nanji* you.

干 *Jakkan* some.

手 *Wakate* a young man.

（五）

若

旦那 *Waka-danna* young master ; eldest son of the master.

年 *Jakunen* youth.

死 *Wakajini* early death.

者 *Wakamono* a young man.

宮 *Wakamiya* a young prince.

狹 *Wakasa* p. n.

氣 *Wakagi* youthful spirit.

樣 *Wakasama* a young lord.

輩 *Jakuhai* young people ; a youngster.

苦 SEN. *Toma* rush-mat for protecting things from rain.

T **苦** KU pain ; trouble. *Kurushii* painful : *nigai* bitter ; disagreeable : *kurushi(mu)* to feel pain ; be troubled.

々 *Niga-nigashii* bitter ; disgusting.

力 *Kūrii* a coolie.

手 *Nigate* person hard to beat.

心 *Kushin* trouble ; hard toil.

心慘憺 *Kushin-santan* hard toil and application.

行 *Kugyō* asceticism.

肉 *Kuniku* deceiving the enemy by false pretences.

役 *Kueki* hard toil.

言 *Kugen* bitter counsel.

辛 *Kushin* affliction.

衷 *Kuchū* whole-hearted devotion.

笑 *Kushō* bitter smile.

（五）

情 *Kujō* complaint.

惱 *Kunō* agony.

悶 *Kumon* agony.

痛 *Kutsū* pain ; suffering.

勞 *Kurō* trouble ; labour. Often preceded by the honorific 御, see 御苦勞 60,8.

境 *Kukyō* adverse circumstances.

節 *Kusetsu* loyalty amidst adverse circumstances.

樂 *Kuraku* pleasure and pain.

學 *Kugaku* severe study; supporting oneself while studying.

戰 *Kusen* desperate fight.

難 *Kunan* hardship.

苔 TAI. *Koke* moss.

T **昔** SEKI ; SHAKU. *Mukashi* ancient times ; a long time ago. 【日】

日 *Sekijitsu* former times.

風 *Mukashi-fū* old-fashioned.

氣質 *Mukashi-katagi* old-time spirit.

T **苗** BYŌ ; MYŌ. *Nae* young shoot.

代 *Nawashiro* rice-nursery.

字 *Myōji* family name.

苛 KA harsh. *Toga(meru)* to blame : *irada(tsu)* to lose one's temper : *ijime(-ru)* to tease.

々 *Ira-ira* impatient ; irritation.

立 *Irada(tsu)* to irritate.

（五）　責　*Kashaku* punishment.

酷　*Kakoku* cruel; harsh.

茅　Bō.　*Kaya; chi* reed used as thatch.

屋　*Bōoku* shabby house; my house (humble).

莽　ZEN to be luxuriant; dense; thick.

苟　KŌ.　*Iyashikumo* at all; if; supposing that; temporary.

且　*Karisome* temporary; slight.

T英　EI excellent; England. *Hanabusa* sepal; flower. (*Hide*).

人　*Eijin* Englishman.

文學　*Eibungaku* English literature.

領　*Eiryō* a British dominion.

吉利　*Igirisu* England.

米　*Eibei* England and America.

字　*Eiji* English letter or word.

名　*Eimei* fame; glory.

和　*Eiwa* English-Japanese.

明　*Eimei* wise; sagacious.

姿　*Eishi* an imposing figure.

書　*Eisho* an English book.

國　*Eikoku* England.

貨　*Eika* English currency.

雄　*Eiyū* hero; great man.

傑　*Eiketsu* hero; great man.

語　*Eigo* the English language.

邁　*Eimai* talented; distinguished.

斷　*Eidan* decisive judgment.

譯　*Eiyaku* an English translation.　（五）

蘭　*Ingurando* England.

蘭銀行　*Eiran-ginkō* Bank of England.

T茂　MO.　*Shige(ru)* to be luxuriant; dense.

苑　See foll.

苑　EN garden.

范　HAN kind of grass; swamp.

荏　JIN.　*Egoma; e* kind of plant.　（六）

苒　*Jinzen* putting off from day to day.

竝　See T並 140,5.　【一】

茫　BŌ wide; vast; far; absentminded; dim.

々　*Bōbō* extensive.

然　*Bōzen* at a loss what to do; aghast.

茹　JO; NYO.　*Yu(deru)* to boil.

茗　MEI; MYŌ tea.

荷　*Myōga* a kind of ginger.

T首　See 185,0.

茵　IN.　*Shitone* mattress; straw-mat.

酉　See 酋 12,7.　【酉】

T草　SŌ.　*Kusa* grass.

草

々 *Sōsō* originally, in haste; now, merely a final salutation in a letter (not very polite).

子 *Sōshi* story-book.

花 *Kusa-bana; sōka* wild field flowers; any flowering plant not a tree nor a bush.

取 *Kusatori* weeding.

臥 *Kutabire* fatigue.

紙 *Sōshi* story-book; copy-book.

案 *Sōan* draft; rough copy.

根 *Sōkon* root of a plant.

鞋 *Waraji* straw-sandals.

稿 *Sōkō* draft; rough copy.

薙劍 *Kusanagi-no-Tsurugi* one of the three sacred treasures of the Emperor; see 三種の神器 1,2.

T 革 See 177,0.

茸 Jō to be luxuriant. *Take* mushroom.

T 前 ZEN. *Mae; saki* before; in front of; former; portion, e. g. *futari-mae* portions for two persons.【刀】

日 *Zenjitsu* the previous day.

方 *Zempō* the front.

文 *Zembun* foregoing sentence; preamble.

古 *Zenko* olden times.

兆 *Zenchō* omen.

任 *Zennin* previous appointment.

言 *Zengen* previous words.

身 *Zenshin* one's past (career)

拂 *Maebarai* payment in advance.

非 *Zembi* former misdeeds.

例 *Zenrei* precedent.

夜 *Zen-ya* previous night.

者 *Zensha* the former.

面 *Zemmen* front; face.

科者 *Zenka-mono* old offender.

約 *Zen-yaku* pre-engagement

後 *Zengo* before and after; first and last; about t e time of; about; more or less.

述 *Zenjutsu* aforesaid.

借 *Zenshaku; maegari* receiving in advance.

記 *Zenki* the said; before-mentioned.

略 *Zenryaku* omission of first part (as, beginning of letter); excuse the omission of preliminary compliments.

途 *Zento* future career.

掛 *Maekake* apron.

渡 *Maewatashi* an advance pay.

項 *Zenkō* the foregoing clause.

期 *Zenki* the former period.

提 *Zentei* premise.

進 *Zenshin* advance; progress.

週 *Zenshū* previous week.

置 *Maeoki* introduction; preface.

（六）

觸 *Maebure* preliminary announcement.

驅 *Zenku* an outrider.

荊 KEI whip. *Ibara* thorny plant.

妻 *Keisai* my wife.

棘 *Keikyoku* thorn; difficulty.

荐 SEN grass. *Shikiri ni* constantly.

茨 SHI. *Ibara* thorny plant.

木 *Ibaraki* p. n.

城 *Ibaraki* p. n.

T 茶 CHA; SA tea.

代 *Chadai* a tip; gratuity.

目 *Chame* a waggish boy.

色 *Cha-iro* light brown.

屋 *Chaya* tea-house; tea-shop.

氣 *Chaki* whimsical.

間 *Cha-no-ma* a sitting-room.

菓 *Saka; chaka* tea and cake.

碗 *Chawan* a bowl; a cup.

漬 *Chazuke* simple lunch.

話會 *Sawakai; chawakai* social tea-party.

褐色 *Chakasshoku* brown.

巷 KŌ. *Chimata* street; road.

【己】

T 荒 KŌ to acquire skill; proceed further. *A(reru)* to become rough; be laid waste: *ara(su)* to damage: *arai* rough: *susa(mu)* to increase in violence; grow wild: *aba(reru); ara(biru)* to act violently; rage.

（六）

々 *Ara-arashii* violent; turbulent.

々敷 *Ara-arashiki* violent; turbulent.

立 *Arada(teru)* to excite; aggravate.

仕事 *Ara-shigoto* rough work.

地 *Arechi* uncultivated land.

物 *Aramono* general name for coarse wares and kitchen utensils.

果 *Are-ha(teru)* to be desolate.

唐無稽 *Kōtōmukei* absurdity.

浪 *Aranami* stormy waves.

野 *Koya; areno* wilderness.

涼 *Koryō* deserted and lonely; desolate.

廢 *Kōhai* desolation; devastation.

增 *Aramashi* gist; approximately.

蕪 *Kōbu* wild; barren.

膽 *Aragimo* broken spirit; terror.

療治 *Araryōji* drastic remedy.

荒 See prec.

茲 See 茲 95,5.

*

莖 KEI; KYŌ. *Kuki* stem; stalk. →140,5 T 七

莊 SŌ; SHŌ stern; majestic. →140,6 T *

子 *Sōshi* name of a Chinese philosopher.

重 *Sōchō* solemnity; gravity.

園 *Shōen* private land.

嚴 *Sōgon* magnificent; solemn.

（七）
T 益 See 益 12,8. 【皿】

苔 GAN; GON; KAN. *Tsubomi* bud: *shibe* stamens and pistils of a flower.

T 華 KA Fahrenheit; your (epist. style): KE. *Hana* flower: *hanayaka* gaudy; elegant.

々 *Hanabanashii* brilliant.

府 *Kafu* Washington.

客 *Kakaku* customer.

胄 *Kachū* the nobility.

美 *Kabi; hade* gay; gaudy.

盛頓 *Washinton* Washington.

族 *Kazoku* the nobility.

燭 *Kashoku* marriage ceremony.

麗 *Karei* brilliant; elegant.

嚴瀧 *Kegon-no-taki* p. n.

莽 BŌ; MŌ grass; thicket; large.

T 荷 KA lotus. *Ni* baggage; packed goods; cargo: *nina(u)* to carry.

厄介 *Niyakkai* an encumbrance.

主 *Ninushi* owner of goods; shipper.

印 *Nijirushi* a mark; a brand.

札 *Nifuda* a label; a tag.

車 *Niguruma* cart for goods whether pulled by animal or man.

足 *Nitari* lighter; barge.

物 *Nimotsu* baggage; packed goods; load.

造 *Nizukuri* packing.

為替 *Nigawase* a documentary draft. （七）

莫 BAKU large. *Nashi; nakare* a negative; do not; have not; must not.

大 *Bakudai* very great.

大小 *Meriyasu* knitted articles; hosiery.

逆 *Bakugyaku no* very intimate.

連 *Bakuren* impudent.

斯科 *Mosukō* Moscow.

T 兼 See 兼 12,8.

荻 TEKI. *Ogi* common reed.

莨 RŌ. *Tabako* tobacco.

莞 KAN to smile. *I* kind of rush.

爾 *Kanji to* with a smile.

茶毘 *Dabi* cremation.

T 恭 KYŌ to respect; reverence. *Uyauyashii* respectful. 【心】

悦 *Kyōetsu* delight.

賀 *Kyōga* congratulation.

順 *Kyōjun* submission; obedience.

敬 *Kyōkei* respect; reverence.

倹 *Kyōken* moderation; modesty.

虔 *Kyōken* respect; reverence.

菫 KIN. *Sumire* violet. 八

菩 BO a kind of grass.

（八）

提 *Bodai* salvation.

薩 *Bosatsu* a saint (Buddhism).

菅 KAN. *Suge; kaya* a kind of rush. (*Suga*).

公 *Kankō* p. n.

菖 SHŌ. *Ayame* iris.

蒲 *Shōbu* iris; sweet flag.

曹 See 72,7.【曰】

ᵀ菌 KIN germs. *Kinoko; take* mushroom.

萃 SUI to assemble; collect.

萍 HYŌ; HEI. *Ukigusa* floating plants.

菲 HI thin; inferior.

才 *Hisai* inability; I (humble).

萌 HŌ. *Mo(y)eru. kiza(su)* to sprout.

芽 *Hōga* germination.

黄 *Moegi* light green.

菁 SEI; SHŌ. *Kabura* turnip: *shige(ru)* to be luxuriant.

剪 SEN. *Ki(ru) hasa(mu); tsu(mu)* to cut【刀】

刀 *Hasami* a pair of scissors.

葛 See 葛 140,9.

萄 DŌ; TŌ used for its sound.

ᵀ菊 KIKU chrysanthemum.

菜 SAI food ate with rice. *Na* vegetables whose green leaves are used as food.

→菜ᵀ　　391

色 *Saishoku* pale.

食 *Saishoku* vegetable food.

種 *Natane* rape-seed.

ᵀ菓 KA fruit.

子 *Kashi* sweetmeats; cake.

實 *Kajitsu* fruit.

菱 RYŌ. *Hishi* water-chestnut; rhomb.

形 *Hishigata* rhomb.

菰 KO. *Komo* a kind of rush.

莚 See 筵 118,8.

菴 See 庵 53,8.

ᵀ黄 See 黄 201,0.

萎 I. *Na(h)eru; na(y)eru; shio(reru); shibo(mu); shina(biru)* to wither; droop.

縮 *Ishuku* to wither; flinch.

靡 *Ibi* to droop; decay.

萱 KEN. *Kaya* thatching rush. 九

菫 TŌ. *Tada(su)* to correct.

蓋 See 蓋 140,10.

ᵀ落 RAKU village. *O(chiru)* to fall; degenerate: *oto(su)* to let drop; lose; as 2nd component, to omit; e. g. *kaki-otosu* to omit to write.

丁 *Rakuchō* missing page.

口 *Ochi-guchi* outlet; overflow.

（九）

落

日 *Rakujitsu* setting sun.

手 *Rakushu* to receive; come to hand.

付 *Ochitsu(ku)* to settle.

伍 *Rakugo* drop out of the ranks.

成 *Rakusei* finishing; completion.

物 *Otoshimono* a lost article.

命 *Rakumei* to die.

度 *Ochido* fault.

馬 *Rakuba* falling from a horse.

胤 *Rakuin* secret child of a nobleman.

書 *Rakugaki* scribbling.

第 *Rakudai* to fail in an examination.

涙 *Rakurui* to shed tears.

着 *Rakuchaku* settlement.

掌 *Rakushō* receive.

雷 *Rakurai* a thunderbolt.

葉松 *Karamatsu; rakuyō-shō* the larch.

語 *Rakugo* comic story.

魄 *Rakuhaku* to be ruined.

選 *Rakusen* defeat in an election.

膽 *Rakutan* despondency.

著 CHO; CHAKU. *Ichijirushii* marked; conspicuous: *arawa(reru)* to be known: *arawa(su)* to compose; publish; make known: *ki(·ru); tsu(keru)* to put on: *tsu(ku)* to arrive.

（九）

名 *Chomei* celebrated; famous.

作 *Chosaku* literary work.

者 *Chosha* an author.

述 *Chojutsu* writing a book; literary work.

書 *Chosho* work; book.

實 *Chakujitsu* steadiness and honesty.

普 ᵀ See 72,8.

葦 I. *Ashi; yoshi* reed.

葎 RITSU to be luxuriant. *Mugura* Japanese hop.

葺 SHŪ. *Fu(ku)* to roof; thatch.

葬 ᵀ SŌ. *Hōmu(ru)* to bury.

式 *Sōshiki* funeral rites; burial.

送 *Sōsō* funeral service.

儀 *Sōgi* funeral service.

尊 ᵀ See 尊 12,10. 【寸】

萬 MAN ten thousand: BAN. *Yorozu* a large number; great many; all. →1,2T

々 *Bamban* certainly.

一 *Man-ichi* a ten thousand to one chance against; if unexpectedly.

人 *Bannin* all people.

引 *Mambiki* shop-lifting.

世 *Bansei; yorozuyo* all ages.

世橋 *Mansei-bashi* p. n.

古 *Banko* perpetuity.

（九）

民 *Bammin* the whole nation; all the people.

全 *Banzen* absolutely secure.

年筆 *Mannenhitsu* a fountain-pen.

有 *Ban-yū* nature; universe.

事 *Banji* everything.

物 *Bambutsu* all things.

能 *Bannō* almighty.

國 *Bankoku* all nations.

感 *Bankan* a thousand emotions.

障 *Banshō* all obstacles.

歲 *Banzai* long live; hurrah: *manzai* a strolling clown.

端 *Bantan* everything.

機 *Banki* all state affairs.

難 *Bannan* many obstacles.

葛 KATSU. *Kuzu* starch: *kazura* a kind of vine: *tsuzura* a bamboo trunk.

藤 *Kattō* complication.

籠 *Tsuzura* a bamboo trunk.

葡 BU; HO; FU used for its sound.

萄 *Budō* grape.

萄牙 *Porutogaru* Portugal.

萼 GAKU sepal; calyx.

T 募 BO. *Tsuno(ru)* to raise; levy; collect; obtain. 【力】

集 *Boshū* collection; floatation.

債 *Bosai* raising of a loan.

奠 See 奠 12,10. 【大】

（九）

葵 KI. *Aoi* hollyhock.

T 葉 YŌ period. *Ha* lea

卷 *Hamaki* cigar.

書 *Hagaki* post-card.

萩 SHŪ. *Hagi* a certain plant; lespedeza bicolor.

葭 KA. *Yoshi* reed.

葩 HA. *Hana* flower.

惹 JAKU. *Hi(ku)* to provoke; bring on; attract. 【心】

起 *Jakki; hikioko(su)* to give rise to; cause.

葱 SŌ. *Negi* onion.

一〇

T 墓 BO. *Haka; okutsuki* tomb; grave. 【土】

地 *Bochi* a graveyard.

所 *Bosho* a graveyard.

前 *Bozen* in front of a tomb.

場 *Hakaba* a graveyard.

碑 *Bohi* tombstone.

參 *Bosan; hakamairi* visiting a grave.

蓙 *Goza* matting.

蓋 GAI. *Futa* covering; lid: *ō(u* to cover: *kedashi* probably; for: *nanzo* how. →123,5

世 *Gaisei* unrivaled.

然 *Gaizen* probability.

蒼 SŌ luxuriant; flurried. *Aoi* gieen; blue.

393

蒼

白 *Sōhaku; aojiroi* pale.

生 *Sōsei* the people.

皇 *Sōkō* hurriedly.

空 *Sōkū* the blue sky.

海 *Sōkai* the blue sea.

蠅 *Urusai* annoying.

蓉 Yō lotus.

蓄 CHIKU. *Takuⁿa(h)eru)* to store up; save; hoard.

↓音器 *Chikuonki* a phonograph. →蓄
→

財 *Chikuzai* to lay by money.

電池 *Chikudenchi* storage battery.

電器 *Chikudenki* electric condenser.

積 *Chikuseki* to accumulate; store.

蒔 SHI. *Ma(ku)* to sow; plant.

繪 *Makie* high-class, raised gold or silver lacquer.

蓊 Ō to be luxuriant; to be prosperous.

蒲 BU; FU; HO. *Gama kama; kaba* bulrush.

公英 *Tampopo* dandelion.

柳 *Horyū* delicate; fragile.

團 *Futon* bedding.

燒 *Kabayaki* broiled eels.

蓆 SEK'. *Mushiro* straw-mat.

T 幕 MAKU; BAKU tent. *Tobari* curtain.【巾】

下 *Bakka* officials and men.

末 *Bakumatsu* end of the Shogunate.

府 *Bakufu* the Shogun's government.

僚 *Bakuryō* the staff.

T 夢 MU. *Yume* dream.【夕】

中 *Muchū* absorption; absent-mindedness.

幻 *Muɤen* dreams and phantasms.

現 *Yume-utsutsu* the dream and the reality; trance.

想 *Musō* dream; imagine.

蒟蒻 *Konnyaku* a certain plant, devil's tongue; food made from same.

蒙 MŌ dark; foolish. *K'ōmu-(ru)* to receive; incur.

古 *Mōko* Mongolia.

昧 *Mōmai* stupid; foolish.

蓑 SA to cover. *Mino* raincoat of straw.

兢 See 24,12.【儿】

蒐 SHŪ to hide. *Atsu(meru)* to gather together.

集 *Shūshū* to collect; gather.

T 慈 JI love; kindness; charity; pity; compassion. *Itsuku-shi(mu)* to love; care for. 【心】 →61,10 *1

善 *Jizen* charity.

悲 *Jihi* compassion; humanity.

愛 *Jiai* affectionate love.

(一〇)

T 蒸 Jō steam. *Mu(su); fuka-(su): mura(su)* to steam; be damp or hot : *mure(-ru)* to be cooked by steam; grow musty; ferment.

氣 *Jōki* steam; steamboat.

發 *Jōhatsu* evaporation.

暑 *Mushiatsui* sultry.

溜 *Jōryū* to distil.

煎 SEN. *I(ru)* to roast; parch. 【火】 →86, 9

茶 *Sencha* boiled tea.

餅 *Sembei* rice-cracker.

→T 暮 BO. *Ku(reru)* to grow dark; set; draw to a close : *kure* evening; end of the year: *kura(su)* to live; pass time: *kurashi* life. 【日】

方 *Kuregata* evening.

色 *Boshoku* evening tints.

向 *Kurashimuki* housekeeping.

春 *Boshun.* end of spring.

蔚 UTSU to be luxuriant, prosperous. *(Uru).*

然 *Utsuzen* luxuriant; dense.

摹 See 摸 64, 11.

蔔 FUKU giant radish

蔦 CHŌ. *Tsuta* ivy.

蔓 MAN. *Tsuru* vine: *habiko-(ru)* to creep; spread over.

延 *Man-en* diffusion; extension.

(一一)

蓬 HŌ to be in disorder. *Yomogi* mugwort.

萊 *Hōrai* island of perpetual youth.

蓮 REN. *Hasu; hachisu* lotus.

華 *Renge* lotus flower.

葉 *Hasuha* wanton; loose.

蔑 BETSU. *Anado(ru); sage-su(mu): namisuru* (irreg.) to slight; despise: *naiga-shiro* insult.

視 *Besshi* to slight; despise.

蔗 SHO sugar-cane.

T 慕 BO. *Shita(u)* to long for; love: *shitawashii* beloved. 【心】

蔭 IN. *Kage* shade; shady place; behind.

*

蕃 BAN; HAN barbarian; to be luxuriant. *Oi* numerous.   一二

人 *Banjin* a native; savage.

蕈 JN. *Kinoko; take* mushroom.

蕎麥 *Soba* buckwheat; vermicelli made from same.

蕩 TŌ wide; arbitrariness; self-will. *Toro(keru)* to melt.

兒 *Tōji* dissipated person.

盡 *Tōjin* to squander.

蕚 See 萼 140, 9.

蕨 KETSU. *Warabi* fern.

蔽 HEI. *Ō(u)* to cover: to hide.   •

395   * T 蔵 →140, 14

（二一）

蔬　So; SHO greens; vegetables.

菜　*Sosai* vegetables.

甍　BŌ. *Iraka* tiles. 【瓦】

蔭　See 蔭 140,11.

蕪　BU to be laid waste. *Kabura; kabu* turnip.

雜　*Buzatsu* crude.

辭　*Buji* humble words.

一三

薀　See 蘊 140,16.

薙　TEI. *Na(gu)* to mow; cut down.

刀　*Nagina'a* a long spear.

拂　*Nagihara(u)* to clear away by mowing.

髪　*Teihatsu* tonsure.

蕾　RAI. *Tsubomi* bud.

薔　SHŌ rose; thorny plant; lake-weed.

薇　*Bara; shōbi* rose.

薪　SHIN. *Takigi* firewood.
　→　　　→

蕭　SHŌ lonely; silent; calm; mugwort.
　　　　　　　　　　　　　↓
　　　　　　　　　　　　薪 T

ダ　*Shōshō* lonesomely.

條　*Shōjō* solitarily.

然　*Shōzen* lonesome.

T 薄　HAKU. *Usui* thin: *susuki* the shear grass.

（二二）

ダ　*Usu-usu* slightly.

化粧　*Usugeshō* to powder one's face lightly.

志　*Hakushi* wavering will.

利　*Hakuri* small profit.

命　*Hakumei* unhappy.

明　*Usuakari; hakumei* twilght.

弱　*Hakujaku* weak; feeble.

氣味惡　*Usukimiwarui* weird.

荷　*Hakka* peppermint.

情　*Hakujō* heartless; unkind.

給　*Hakkyū* low salary.

運　*Hakuun* ill-luck; misfortune.

暗　*Usugurai* gloomy; dim.

墨　*Usuzumi* thin Indian ink; grey.

暮　*Hakubo* dusk.

謝　*Hakusha* small token of one's gratitude.

T 薦　SEN straw-mat. *Susu-(meru)* to present (to a superior).

T 藥　See 薬 140,15.

薇　BI. *Zemmai* osmund, a kind of fern.

獲　See T 獲 94,14.

薨　KŌ; GŌ. *Mimaka'ru)* (said of persons of rank) to die.

去　*Kōkyo* demise.

燕　See 86,12.

396

蟇　MA; MAKU. *Gama; hiki-gaeru; hiki* toad. 【虫】

一四　薩　SATSU Buddha.

州　*Sasshū* another name for the province of *Satsuma*.

哈連　*Sagaren* Saghalien.

張　*Sappari* (not) at all.

摩　*Satsuma* p. n.

藍　RAN. *Ai* indigo.

舊　KYŪ. *Furui; moto* old; ancient; formerly; olden times. 【白】 → 2,4 T· 72,1 T,

友　*Kyūyū* old friend.

式　*Kyūshiki* old-fashioned.

交　*Kyūkō* old friendship.

知　*Kyūchi* old friend.

來　*Kyūrai* old; ancient.

套　*Kyūtō* conventionality.

約　*Kyūyaku* Old Testament.

敎　*Kyūkyō* Catholic.

習　*Kyūshū* old customs.

惡　*Kyūaku* a past misdeed.

聞　*Kyūbun* old news.

幕　*Kyūbaku* old feudal government.

慣　*Kyūkan* old customs.

弊　*Kyūhei* long-standing evil; conservatism.

曆　*Kyūreki* the old calendar.

臘　*Kyūrō* end of last year; last December.

蹟　*Kyūseki* historical spots.

薯　SHO. *Imo* potato; tuber.

藉　SEKI; SHA; JAKU. *Shi(ku)* to spread out: *ka(ru)* (lit st.); *ka(riru)* (coll.) to borrow.

口　*Shakō* to use (a matter) as an excuse for.

甚　*Sek'jin* loudly; highly.

藁　KŌ. *Wara* straw.

藏　ZŌ. *Kura* godown; warehouse: *osa(meru)* to keep; store away. →140,11 T *

相　*Zōshō* the Finance Minister.

書　*Zōsho* a library.

薰　KUN merit. *Ka (ru)* to be fragrant. →140,13 * T

風　*Kumpū* soft breeze; south wind.

陶　*Kuntō* training; education.

T藩　HAN clan; enclosure; to protect.　一五

士　*Hanshi* a clansman.

主　*Hanshu* a feudal chief.

屏　*Hampei* a bulwark.

閥　*Hambatsu* clanship.

T繭　KEN. *Mayu* silk-worm cocoon. 【糸】

藥　YAKU. *Kusuri; kusu* medicine; drugs. →140,13 T

石　*Yakuseki* medicines; medical treatment; all remedies.

*T薰 →140,14

（一五）

藥局 *Yakkyoku* a pharmacy.

品 *Yakuhin* medicines; drugs; chemicals.

師如來 *Yakushi-nyorai* God of Medicine.

餌 *Yakuji* medicine.

舖 *Yakuho* a drug store.

劑 *Yakuzai* medicine.

籠 *Yakurō* a medicine chest; under one's control.

罐 *Yakan* tea-kettle.

藤 Tō. *Fuˌi* wistaria.

藪 Sō; SU. *Yabu* grove; thicket.

入 *Yabuiri* servants' holiday.

蛇 *Yabuhebi* to wake a sleeping dog.

醫者 *Yabuisha* quack doctor.

蒦 See 穫 115,14.

藝 GEI arts; accomplishments. (Aī). →140, 4 T *

人 *Geinin* a public performer.

州 *Geishū* another name for the province of *Aki*.

妓 *Geigi* a geisha.

者 *Geisha* a geisha.

術 *Geijutsu* art.

（一六）

蘆 RO. *Ashi* reed; rush.

湖 *Ashi-no-ko* lake, often called by foreigners Lake Hakone,

（一六）

蘊 UN; ON to store up; numerous.

奧 *Un-ō* mysteries; deepest point.

蓄 *Unchiku* greaˌ learning.

藷 SHO. *Imo* potato; tuber.

藺 RIN. *I* a kind of rush.

藹 AI flourishing; to be luxuriant; to harmonize.

々 *Aiai* harmoniously.

然 *Aizen* harmonious.

藻 Sō. *Mo* seaweed; duckweed: *aya* literary composition.

屑 *Mokuzu* seaweed; die in water.

蘇 So name of a plant. *Yomigae(ru)* to rise from the dead.

士 *Suezu* Suez.

生 *Sosei* to revive.

格蘭 *Sukottorando* Scotland.

（一七）

蘚 SEN. *Koke* moss.

蘭 RAN orchid; Dutch.

貢 *Rangūn* Rangoon.

書 *Ransho* a Dutch book.

學 *Rangaku* study of the Dutch language.

驀 BAKU to ascend; to ride; to cross over. *Masshigura* impetuously. 【馬】

地 *Masshigura* impetuously.

進 *Bakushin* to rush; dash.

然 *Bakuzen* suddenly; precipitately.

一九 蘿 RA ivy; vine; giant radish.

蔔 *Daikon* giant radish.

一四一　虎

二 虎 KO. *Tora* tiger.

口 *Kokō* tiger's mouth; very dangerous situation.

穴 *Koketsu* tiger's den; very dangerous place.

列剌 *Korera* cholera.

疫 *Koeki* cholera.

狼 *Korō* a wild beast.

三 T 虐 GYAKU. *Shiita(geru)* to oppress; tyrannize over; treat with cruelty: *sokona(u)* to injure.

待 *Gyakutai* cruelty; bad treatment.

殺 *Gyakusatsu* kill in a cruel manner.

四 虔 See foll.

虔 KEN. *Tsutsushi(mu)* to be respectful; just.

五 T 虗 See 虛 141,6.

處 SHO to manage; condemn. *Tokoro* place; when; as. →35,2 T

々 *Shosho; tokorodokoro* at several places; here and there.

女 *Shojo* virgin.

方 *Shohō* prescription (medical).

分 *Shobun* settling; disposal; punishment.

世 *Shosei* living with one's fellow creatures.

刑 *Shokei* punishment.

決 *Shoketsu* resolution.

理 *Shori* to manage; transact.

置 *Shochi* management; measures.

罰 *Shobatsu* punishment.

虜 See prec.

六 虛 KYO; KO. *Munashii* in vain; empty: *sora* space; sky; lie. →141,5 T

心平氣 *Kyoshin-heiki* composure.

名 *Kyomei* an empty name.

妄 *Kyomō* falsehood.

言 *Kyogen* a lie.

病 *Kebyō* feigned sickness.

弱 *Kyojaku* weakness.

報 *Kyohō* a false report.

無 *Kyomu* nothingness.

飾 *Kyoshoku* ostentation.

勢 *Kyosei* false show of power.

榮 *Kyoei* vanity.

僞 *Kyogi* falsehood.

實 *Kyojitsu* truth or falsity.

構 *Kyokō* fabrication.

禮 *Kyorei* empty forms.

（六〇）T 虜　RYO. *Toriko* captive; prisoner of war.

七 虞　GU to consider; be anxious about. *Osore* fear.

號　See 30,10. 【唬】

九 膚　FU. *Hada; hadae* skin; naked body. 【肉】

T 慮　RYO plan. *Omompaka(ru); omo(u)* to consider; think; be anxious. 【心】

外　*Ryogai* unexpectedness; rudeness; discourtesy.

二 虧　KI to miss; fail. *Ka(keru)* to lack; wane.

一四二　**虫**

When at the left, it is called *Mushi-hen.*

T 虫　See 蟲 142,12.

二 虱　SHITSU. *Shirami* a louse.

三 虹　KŌ. *Niji* rainbow.

虻　BŌ. *Abu* horse-fly.

四 T 蚊　BUN. *Ka* mosquito.

帳　*Kaya* mosquito-net.

T 蚤　See 蠶 142,18.

蚤　SŌ. *Nomi* flea: *hayai* quick. （四）

蚯蚓　*Mimizu* worm; earth-worm. 五

蛆　So. *Uji* maggot.

蛇　DA; JA. *Hebi* snake.

目　*Janome* umbrella with rings like target.

足　*Dasoku* superfluity; needless.

蝎　*Dakatsu* viper; an abhorrent thing.

蛙　A; WA. *Kaeru; kawazu* frog. 六

蛭　TETSU; SHITSU. *Hiru* leech.

蛤　*Hamaguri* clam.

T 蛮　See 蠻 142,19.

蜂　HŌ. *Hachi* bee; wasp. 七

起　*Hōki* uprising.

蜜　*Hachimitsu* honey.

蛸　*Tako* octopus.

蛹　YŌ. *Sanagi* pupa; chrysalis.

蛾　GA moth.

蜆　*Shijimi* a kind of small shell-fish.

蜘蛛　*Kumo; sasagani* spider. 八

(八) 蜻蛉 *Tombo; seirei* dragon-fly.

蜿 EN to crawl; earth-worm. *Une(ru)* to wind; meander.

々 *En-en* winding; meandering.

九 蝟 I. *Harinezumi* hedgehog.

集 *Ishū* to throng; swarm.

蝙蝠 *Kōmori* a bat; umbrella.

蝎 KATSU. *Sasori* scorpion.

蝶 CHŌ butterfly.

々 *Chōchō* butterfly.

形 *Chōgata* a bow-tie.

番 *Chōtsugai* a hinge.

蝦 KA. *Gama* toad: *ebi* prawn.

夷 *Ezo; Emishi* p. n.

蟇 *Gama* toad.

蟇口 *Gamaguchi* purse.

蝮 FUKU. *Mamushi* viper.

一〇 螟虫 *Meichū* a certain noxious insect of the rice-plant.

螢 KEI. *Hotaru* fire-fly.

雪 *Keisetsu* diligence in study.

二 螺 RA. *Nishi* conch-shell.

旋 *Rasen* screw.

(一一) 蟋蟀 *Kōrogi; kirigirisu* cricket.

螫 SEKI. *Sa(su)* to sting; to bite.

蟄 CHITSU to be confined; hide; hibernate.

伏 *Chippuku* hibernation; concealment.

居 *Chikkyo* to keep indoors.

一二 蟠 BAN; HAN. *Wadakama(ru)* to be coiled up; tortuous; convoluted.

蟬 SEN; ZEN. *Semi* cicada.

蟲 CHŪ. *Mushi* insect; worm. →30,3T : 142,1T

干 *Mushiboshi* airing.

害 *Chūgai* damage by insects.

氣 *Mushike* nervous irritation.

の息 *Mushi no iki* faint breathing.

一三 蟷螂 *Tōrō; kamakiri* mantis.

蟻 GI. *Ari* ant.

蠅 YŌ. *Hae; hai* fly.

蟹 KAI. *Kani* crab.

一五 蠣 REI. *Kaki* oyster.

蠟 RŌ wax.

燭 *Rōsoku* candle.

蠢 （一五） SHUN foolish. *Ugome(ku); ugo(ku)* to crawl; wriggle.

動 *Shundō* to wriggle.

蠡 See 58,18. 【虫】

蠶 一八 SAN. *Kaiko; ko* (as 2nd component) silkworm.
→142,4 T : 1,9 T

兒 *Sanji* silkworm.

豆 *Soramame* broad beans.

食 *Sanshoku* encroachment.

絲 *Sanshi* raw silk; silk yarn.

蠻 一九 BAN barbarian.
→8,10 T : 142,6 T

風 *Bampū* barbarous customs.

勇 *Ban-yū* reckless courage; rashness

襟 *Bankara* unfashionable.

一四三 血

T 血 KETSU. *Chi* blood.

汐 *Chishio* blood.

色 *Kesshoku* colour of the face; complexion.

走 *Chibashi(ru)* to be bloodshot.

相 *Kessō* countenance.

書 *Kessho* writing in blood.

脈 *Ketsu.yaku; chisuji* vein; blood-vessel; blood-relation.

祭 *Chimatsuri* blood-offering

迷 *Chimayo(u)* to be mad; run amuck.

氣 *Kekki* animal spirits; physical vigour.

族 *Ketsuzoku* blood-relation.

眼 *Chimanako* bloodshot eye.

液 *Ketsueki* blood.

涙 *Ketsurui* bitter tears.

痕 *Kekkon* blood stain.

筋 *Chisuji* vein; lineage; stock.

統 *Kettō; chisuji* lineage.

塗 *Chimamire* being smeared with blood.

路 *Ketsuro* way of escape cut through the enemy's ranks.

塊 *Kekkai* clot of blood.

煙 *Chikemuri* vapour of blood.

管 *Kekkan* a blood-vessel.

縁 *Ketsuen* blood-relation.

衄 三 JIKU blood from the nose. *Yabu(ru)* to defeat; crush.

T 衆 六 SHŪ; SHU people; many; all.

人 *Shūjin* everybody; all the people.

口 *Shūkō* people's opinion.

目 *Shūmoku* public attention.

生 *Shujō* living beings.

望 *Shūbō* confidence of the people.

評 *Shūhyō* general opinion.

愚 *Shūgu* the vulgar crowd.

寡 *Shūka* number; odds.

（一六）議 *Shūgi* general consultation; discussion.

議院 *Shūgi-in* House of Representatives.

一四四　行

T行 KŌ; GYŌ row; column: AN. *Yu(ku); i(ku)* to go; walk: *okonai* act; conduct: *okona(u)* to act; do. (*Tsura*).

々 *Yuku-yuku* on the way; in the future.

々子 *Gyōgyōshi; yoshikiri* the eastern reed-thrush.

手 *Yukute* the direction in which one is going; destination.

方 *Yukue* destination; whereabouts: *yukikata* manner; whereabouts.

火 *Anka* foot-warmer.

水 *Gyōzui* tub-bathing.

末 *Yukusue* the future.

在所 *Anzaisho* Emperor's place of sojourn while away from capital.

先 *Yukusaki* destination.

列 *Gyōretsu* procession.

李 *Kōri* basket-trunk.

年 *Gyōnen* lifetime; age at which a person died.

届 *Yukitodo(ku)* to be complete; perfect.

所 *Yukidokoro* the place where one is going or has gone.

幸 *Gyōkō* going out (of the Emperor).

幸啓 *Gyōkōkei* joint going out of the Emperor and Empress.

事 *Gyōji* customary rites and ceremonies.

状 *Gyōjō* conduct; behaviour.

使 *Kōshi* use; exercise.

政 *Gyōsei* administration.

宮 *Angū* temporary palace.

書 *Gyōsho* intermediate style of writing Chinese characters between the square and the cursive styles.

倒 *Yukidaore* dying on the road.

啓 *Gyōkei* going out (of the Empress or the Crown Prince).

脚 *Angya* travelling on foot.

商 *Gyōshō* hawking.

動 *Kōdō* movement; action.

爲 *Kōi* act; conduct.

進 *Kōshin* march.

程 *Kōtei* distance; journey.

儀 *Gyōgi* behaviour.

燈 *Andō; andon* a paper-framed night-light.

一四五　衣

When at the left it takes a special form 衤 and is then called *Koromo-hen*. This Radical is sometimes divided, the top part being separated from the bottom.

衣 T I; E. *Koromo; kinu; ki* clothes; garment: *ki(-ru)* to put on.

服 *Ifuku* clothes.

食住 *Ishokujū* food, clothing and habitation; necessaries of life.

裳 *Ishō* garments.

類 *Irui* clothing.

二 **初**
→ **初** T SHO. *Hajime* beginning; origin: *hatsu; ui* first: *hajimete* at first; for the first time: *so(meru)* to begin: *ubu* inexperience. 【刀】

々 *Uiuishii* childish; green.

子 *Uigo; hatsugo* first-born child.

心 *Shoshin* beginner: *ubu* simplicity; inexperience.

日 *Shonichi* first day; first night: *hatsuhi* the sun on the New Year's morning.

耳 *Hatsumimi* new; strange.

旬 *Shojun* first ten days of the month.

老 *Shorō* age of forty years.

步 *Shoho* first steps.

志 *Shoshi* one's original intention.

物 *Hatsumono* first fruit of the season.

陣 *Uijin* one's first battle.

孫 *Uimago; hatsumago* first **grand**child.

（二）

夏 *Shoka; hatsunatsu* early summer.

產 *Uizan; hatsuzan* bearing child for the first time.

婚 *Shokon* first marriage.

雪 *Hatsuyuki* first snow.

等 *Shotō* elementary.

期 *Shoki* first stage.

對面 *Shotaimen* meeting for the first time.

學者 *Shogakusha* a beginner.

三 **表** HYŌ a table; list; memorial. *Omote* surface; the front; outside: *arawa(su)* to show; disclose. →8, 6 T

文 *Hyōbun* document presented to the Emperor.

札 *Hyōsatsu* a door-plate.

示 *Hyōji; hyōshi* designation; indication.

面 *Hyōmen* surface. *Omotemuki* public; formal.

記 *Hyōki* inscription on the face or outside.

情 *Hyōjō* expression; look.

紙 *Hyōshi* binding; cover.

現 *Hyōgen* expression.

象 *Hyōshō* symbol.

裏 *Hyōri* the face and back; outside and inside; double-dealing; false-hearted.

彰 *Hyōshō* public recognition (of merit).

題 *Hyōdai* the title or name of a book, etc.; heading.

四 衿 KIN sash; to tie. *Eri* collar.

袂 BEI; KETSU. *Tamoto* large sleeves of a Japanese garment; foot (of a bridge, etc.).

T 衷 CHŪ. *Uchi* the inside. →8,7 T *²

心 *Chūshin* in one's heart; one's inmost heart.

情 *Chūjō* the heart; mind; one's inmost feelings.

衾 See 9,8. 【衣】

五 袒 TAN to uncover the shoulder; strip to the waist.

袖 SHŪ. *Sode* sleeve.

手 *Shūshu* folded arms.

珍 *Shūchin* convenient for carrying in the pocket; pocket-book.

袢 HAN; BAN short clothing; clothing without figures.

纏 *Hanten* short coat.

袗 SHIN black clothing; hem; border; unlined garment.

T 被 H. *Kōmu(ru)* to wear; receive; incur: *ō(u); ka-(keru)* to put on; to cover: *kabu(ru)* to put on the head: *ra(reru)* (inverted order) passive verb termination, generally used in a polite sense.

下 *Kudasa(ru)* (inverted order) to give (said of a superior); to condescend; please.

告 *Hikoku* defendant; accused.

成 *Nasare* do (inverted order).

成下 *Nashikudasare* do (inverted order).

服 *Hifuku* clothing.

害 *Higai* injury; damage.

爲 *Serare* do (inverted order).

遊 *Asobasare* do (inverted order).

選擧權 *Hisenkyoken* right to be elected.

袪 KYO sleeve; edge of sleeve.

袈裟 *Kesa* scarf worn across the shoulder by Buddhist priests.

T 袋 TAI. *Fukuro* bag; sack.

叩 *Fukurotataki* drubbing.

六 袷 KŌ. *Awase* lined garment.

衣 *Awase* lined garment.

裃 *Kamishimo* old ceremonial dress.

袴 KO. *Hakama* loose skirt or trousers.

T 裂 RETSU. *Sa(ku)* to tear.

目 *Sakeme* a rent; a rip.

* 傷 *Resshō* a lacerated wound.

七 裡 RI. *Uchi* within; inner; inside.

裙 KUN skirt.

405　*T 裝 →145,7

T 裕 YŪ. *Yutaka* abundant; fertile. (*Hiro*).

福 *Yūfuku* rich; wealthy.

T 補 HO. *Ogina(u)* to supplement; restore; assist.

充 *Hojū* to supplement.

助 *Hojo* to assist; support.

足 *Hosoku* a supplement.

佐 *Hosa* aid; a guardian; a counsellor.

缺 *Hoketsu* to supplement.

給利子 *Hokyūrishi* subsidy.

償 *Hoshō* compensation.

裔 EI the skirt of a robe; a border. *Sue* descendants.

孫 *Eison* a descendant.

裝 SŌ; SHŌ. *Yosō(u); yoso(u)* to dress; adorn oneself; ornament; equip.

甲 *Sōkō* ironclad. →145, 6 * T

束 *Shōzoku* clothes; to dress.

釘 *Sōtei* binding.

塡 *Sōten* charge (of a gun).

備 *Sōbi* equipment.

飾 *Sōshoku* decoration; ornament.

置 *Sōchi* arrangement; gear.

裘 KYŪ. *Kawa-goromo* leather clothing.

裾 KYO. *Suso* skirt of a garment.

野 *Susono* base; foot (of a mountain).

裨 HI to assist; to supplement; small.

益 *Hieki* to be advantageous for; benefit.

T 裸 RA. *Hadaka* naked. →158, 8

足 *Hadashi; rasoku* barefooted.

麥 *Hadaka-mugi* rye.

體 *Ratai* nakedness.

褄 *Tsuma* skirt of a garment.

裳 SHŌ. *Mo; mosuso* clothing; underwear; skirt.

T 製 SEI to make; manufacture.

出 *Seishutsu* to manufacture.

作 *Seisaku* manufacture; fabrication; work.

法 *Seihō* method of manufacture.

品 *Seihin* manufactured goods.

造 *Seizō* to manufacture; construct.

產 *Seisan* manufacture.

造高 *Seizō-daka* output (as of goods).

煉場 *Seirenjō* smelting works; refinery.

圖 *Seizu* to draw.

艦 *Seikan* naval construction.

T 喪 See 30,9.

褌 KON drawers; trousers. *Fundoshi; shitaobi* loincloth.

褊 HEN narrow; small.

狹 *Henkyō* narrow; narrow-minded.

（九）褐 KATSU coarse cloth; brown. *Kegoromo* fur-clothing.

T 複 FUKU compound; double; sign of plurality. *Kasa-(neru)* to repeat.

本 *Fukuhon* a duplicate.

製 *Fukusei* reproduction.

寫 *Fukusha* reproduction.

數 *Fukusū* the plural number.

雜 *Fukuzatsu* complication; complexity.

一〇 縕 ON; UN coat.

袍 *Dotera* a wadded gown.

褥 JOKU. *Shitone* bed; bedding; mattress.

褪 TAI. *A(seru); sa(meru)* to fade (of colour).

褫奪 *Chidatsu* deprivation; degradation.

一二 褓褓 *Kyōho, mutsuki* infant's diaper.

一三 襖 Ō an over-garment. *Fusuma* sliding paper-door.

襟 KIN. *Eri* collar or neck of a garment.

卷 *Erimaki* a scarf.

度 *Kindo* magnanimity.

飾 *Erikazari; nekutai* a necktie.

懷 *Kinkai* mind.

一四 襤 RAN. *Boro* rags.

褸 *Ranru; boro* rags.

（一四）襦 JU. *Shitagi* shirt.

袢 *Juban* underwear; shirt.

襯 SHIN. *Shitagi; hadagi* shirt. 一六

衣 *Shatsu* shirt.

襲 See 212,6.【衣】

囊 NŌ. *Fukuro* bag; sack; purse.【口】 一七

中 *Nōchū* in one's purse.

襷 *Tasuki* a cord used for tying back the sleeves. 一九

襾 一四六

T 西 SEI; SAI. *Nishi* west.

方 *Seihō; saihō* the West.

瓜 *Suika* water-melon.

比利亞 *Shiberiya* Siberia.

印度 *Sei-Indo* West Indies.

洋 *Seiyō* Western or foreign countries.

班牙 *Supein; Isupania* Spain.

曆 *Seireki* the Christian Era.

藏 *Chibetto* Tibet.

T 要 YŌ essential; important. *Moto(meru)* to require; demand; desire: *kaname* rivet of a fan; essential, important point. 三

目 *Yōmoku* essential points.

（三）

要

用　*Yōyō* important business; useful.

件　*Yōken* requisite.

求　*Yōkyū* requirement; demand.

旨　*Yōshi* gist; essentials.

所　*Yōsho* important point.

害　*Yōgai* fortress; strong.

素　*Yōso* essential element.

部　*Yōbu* principal part.

港　*Yōkō* secondary naval port.

塞　*Yōsai* fortress; fortification.

路　*Yōro* important road; influential post.

領　*Yōryō* the point; gist.

點　*Yōten* the point; gist.

償　*Yōshō* demand for restitution; claim.

擊　*Yōgeki* a surprise-attack.

職　*Yōshoku* important position.

四　栗　RITSU.　*Kuri* chestnut.【木】

鼠　*Risu* squirrel.

五 T　票　HYŌ ticket; sign.【示】

六　粟　ZOKU.　*Awa* millet.【米】

七　賈　KO to buy; to sell; to trade; merchant.【貝】

T 覆　FUKU.　*Ō(u)* to cover : *kutsugae(su)* to upset; overthrow.

水　*Fukusui* water that is poured out; things done (cannot be undone); spilt milk.

面　*Fukumen* a mask; a veil.

轍　*Fukutetsu* other's failure or blunder.

一二

覇　HA leader; head.

府　*Hafu* the Shogunate.

者　*Hasha* a chief; hegemony.

氣　*Haki* vigour.

業　*Hagyō* achievement of a conqueror.

道　*Hadō* the rule of might.

叡　KAKU to examine; strict.

一三

覊　KI reins; fetters; to tie up. Sometimes used instead of 羈 122,19.

絆　*Kihan* fetters; restraint

一九

見

一四七

T 見　KEN.　*Mi(-ru)*; *mi(y)eru)* to see : *mi(seru)* to show : *mami(y)eru)* to have an audience with.

上　*Mia(geru)* to look up: *miageta* admirable.

下　*Misa(geru)* to look down; despise : *misageta* contemptible : *mioro(su)* to look down.

408

分 *Miwake* discrimination; judgment.

立 *Mitate* selection; choice; diagnosis.

本 *Mihon* sample; pattern; model.

比 *Mikura(beru)* to compare.

出 *Midashi* an index: *miida-(su)* to find out.

合 *Mi-awa(su)* to look at each other; put off; postpone: *miai* interview (with a view to marriage).

向 *Mi-muki* turning round to see.

込 *Mikomi* opinion; judgment; expectation.

地 *Kenchi* standpoint.

附 *Mitsu(keru)* to find: *mitsuke* a castle-gate.

事 *Migoto* beautiful; admirable.

物 *Kembutsu* sight-seeing: *mimono* sight worth seeing.

定 *Mi-sada(meru)* to see and decide; determine by seeing.

受 *Mi-u(keru)* to observe; see.

所 *Midokoro* promising; place worth seeing.

放 *Mihana(su)* to forsake.

苦 *Mi-gurushii* offensive to the sight; unsightly; ugly.

窄 *Misuborashii* poor and dirty.

送 *Mi-oku(ru)* to see off.

殺 *Mi-goroshi* leave (person) to his fate; look on powerless to prevent.

逃 *Mi-noga(su)* overlook.

捨 *Mi-su(teru)* to forsake.

做 *Mina(su)* regard; consider.

掛 *Mikake* outward appearance.

頃 *Migoro* at its best.

習 *Minarai* apprenticeship.

参 *Genzan* meeting or seeing a superior.

張 *Miharu)* to open one's eyes wide; look out to see what is passing; keep watch.

張人 *Miharinin* the lookout; watchman.

渡 *Miwata(su)* to look round; to see far.

場 *Miba* look; appearance.

晴 *Miharashi* a view; a prospect.

惡 *Mi-ku.* ugly; indistinct.

落 *Mi-otoshi* oversight.

當 *Kentō* aim; mark; expectation: *miata(ru)* come across; find.

當違 *Kentō-chigai* beside the mark.

解 *Kenkai* opinion; view.

舞 *Mima(u)* to inquire after health; pay visit (especially for above purpose).

聞 *Kembun* seeing and hearing; experience; knowledge.

榮 *Mibae* good appearance.

境 *Misakai* distinction.

積 *Mitsumori* estimate.

見

學 *Kengaku* acquire information.

識 *Kenshiki* opinion; learning.

覺 *Mi-oboe* recognition; recollection.

四
T 規 KI compasses. *Nori* rule; law: *tada(su)* to correct.

定 *Kitei* rules; regulations.

律 *Kiritsu* order; discipline; rules; regulations.

則 *Kisoku* rule; regulation.

則正 *Kisokutadashii* in a regular manner.

約 *Kiyaku* an agreement.

程 *Kitei* regulations; rules.

準 *Kijun* standard.

模 *Kibo* plan; scale.

一
五 覘 TEN. *Nera(u)* to watch for; peep into.

覘 SHI. *Nozo(ku)* to watch for; peep into.

T 覚 See 覺 147,13.

覧 See 覽 147,14.

九 親 TO. *Mi(-ru)* to see; look at.

親 SHIN. *Oya* parents: *shitashii* intimate; friendly: *shitashi(mu)* to be friendly:
→親 T *shitashiku: mizukara* in person; personally. *(Mi).* *(Chika).*

子 *Oyako* parents and children.

王 *Shinnō; Miko* Prince of the Blood.

切 *Shinsetsu* kindness.

分 *Oyabun* the head; master; chief.

友 *Shin-yū* intimate friend.

父 *Shimpu; oyaji* father.

不孝 *Oyafukō* unfilial.

日 *Shinnichi* pro-Japanese.

任 *Shinnin* direct Imperial appointment.

玉 *Oyadama* head; chief.

米 *Shimbei* pro-American.

任官 *Shinninkan* official appointed directly by His Majesty.

交 *Shinkō* friendship; intimacy.

身 *Shimmi* a relative; cordial; kind.

指 *Oyayubi* thumb.

政 *Shinsei* direct Imperial rule.

英 *Shin-ei* pro-British.

密 *Shimmitsu* intimacy.

族 *Shinzoku* relation; relative.

展 *Shinten* "private" (on envelopes).

戚 *Shinseki* relation; relative.

裁 *Shinsai* Imperial decision.

善 *Shinzen* friendly relationship.

睦 *Shimboku* friendliness.

愛 *Shin-ai* affection; love; friendship.

潮 *Oyashio* cold current.

（九）　類　*Shinrui* relation; relative.

＊　讓　*Oyayuzuri* inheritance.

一〇　覬覦　*Kiyu* to desire; request; watch secretly.

觀　*Kō* to meet; to see.

二　觀 T　See 觀 147,18.

一三　覺　KAKU. *Oboe* memory; understanding: *obo(y)eru*; *sato(ru)* to learn; consider; feel; know: *oboshii* look like; seeming: *sa(meru)* to awake. →147,5 T

束無　*Obotsukanai* doubtful.

悟　*Kakugo* resolution; preparation.

書　*Oboegaki* memorandum.

帳　*Oboechō* memorandum book.

違　*Oboechigai* misunderstanding.

醒　*Kakusei* awaking.

一四　覽　RAN. *Mi(-ru)* to see; look at. →147,9 T ＊

一五　覿　TEKI. *M(-ru)* to see; to have an audience with.

面　*Tekimen* on the spot.

一八　觀　KAN appearance; to show. *Mi(-ru)* to see; look at a sight. →147,11 T

光　*Kankō* sightseeing.

光團　*Kankōdan* tourist party.

兵式　*Kampeishiki* military review.

＊ 覽 T　→147,14

念　*Kannen* idea; sense; resignation. 　（一八）

客　*Kankaku* spectator.

音　*Kannon* goddess of mercy (Buddhism).

望　*Kambō* observation.

測　*Kansoku* observation; survey.

察　*Kansatsu* observation.

賞　*Kanshō* admiration.

艦式　*Kankan-shiki* naval review.

覽　*Kanran* looking at; inspection.

角 　一四八

When at the left, it is called *Tsuno-hen*.

角 T　KAKU to compete; compare. *Tsuno* horn: *sumi*; *kado* corner; angle.

度　*Kakudo* an angle.

袖　*Kakusode* policeman in plain clothes.

逐　*Kakuchiku* competition.

帽　*Kakubō* a square-topped cap; university student.

觝　*Sumō*; *kakutei* wrestling.

斛　KOKU a measure of ten *to*. See Introduction 44. 【斗】　四

觧　See foll.　六

411

（六）
T 解 KAI to analyse; disperse: GE. *To(ku); hodo(ku)* to undo; untie; explain: *to(keru); hodo(keru)* to melt; come loose; undone: *waka(ru)* to understand.

決 *Kaiketsu* settlement.

易 *Wakariyasui* intelligible.

放 *Kaihō* emancipation.

約 *Kaiyaku* cancellation.

除 *Kaijo* cancellation; release; disarmament.

剖 *Kaibō* dissection; analysis.

雇 *Kaiko* to be dismissed from employment.

惡 *Wakarinikui* unintelligible.

答 *Kaitō* an answer.

傭 *Kaiyō* discharge.

散 *Kaisan* dissolution; break-up.

禁 *Kaikin* removal of a prohibition.

說 *Kaisetsu* explanation.

釋 *Kaishaku* explanation; interpretation.

體 *Kaitai* dismemberment.

纜 *Kairan* departure; to sail.

T 觸 See 觸 148,13.

二 觴 SHŌ. *Sakazuki* wine-cup.

三 觸 SHOKU. *Fu(reru); sawa(ru)* to touch; infringe: *fure* a notice. →148,6 T

込 *Furekomi* a herald.

一四九

言

When at the left, it is called *Gom-ben.*

T 言 GEN; GON. *Kotoba; koto* word; expression; speech: *i(u); mō(su)* to say.

々 *Gengen* every word; word by word.

上 *Gonjō* to report (to a superior).

下 *Genka* at once; without hesitation.

及 *Genkyū* refer to.

分 *Iibun* a plea; an objection.

外 *Gengai* unexpressed.

立 *Iita(teru)* to insist in saying; report; assert.

付 *Iitsu(keru)* to command; order; tell.

合 *Iai* dispute.

行 *Genkō* words and deeds.

伏 *Iifu(seru)* to silence; refute.

交 *Iikawa(su)* to exchange vows.

拔 *Iinu(keru)* to excuse oneself; talk oneself out of a difficulty.

附 *Iitsuke* order; tell tales: *kotozuke* a verbal message.

明 *Gemmei* declaration.

洩 *Iimora(su)* to omit to say.

紛 *Ii-magira(su)* to explain away.

振 *Iiburi* way of speaking.

412

掛 *Iigakari* false charge; pretext; a thing resulting from something said.	量器 *Keiryōki* a scale.
動 *Gendō* movement; behaviour.	畫 *Keikaku* plan; project.
張 *Iiha(ru)* to persist in.	畫 *Keikaku* plan; project.
責 *Genseki* pledge; promise.	算 *Keisan* calculation; reckoning.
渡 *Iiwatashi* a sentence; an order.	T訂 TEI to examine into; judge; correct.
葉 *Kotoba* word; language.	正 *Teisei* correction; revision.
葉遣 *Kotobazukai* speech; wording.	訌 KŌ to be disorganized.
募 *Iitsuno(ru)* to insist upon.	訐 KETSU; KAN. *Aba(ku)* to expose; divulge.
過 *Iisugi* speaking too much.	T訓 KUN Japanese reading of Chinese characters: KIN. *Oshi(h)eru)* to teach: *yo(mu)* to read: *sato(su)* to admonish; advise. (*Kuni*).
質 *Genshitsu; genchi* pledge.	
語道斷 *Gongodōdan* unspeakable.	
種 *Iigusa* remark; excuse; complaint.	令 *Kunrei* instructions; orders.
語 *Gergo; gengyo* words; language.	示 *Kunji* instructions; orders.
論 *Genron* speech.	戒 *Kunkai* warning; admonition.
樣 *Iiyō* the way of speaking.	言 *Kungen* instruction.
譯 *Iiwake* excuse.	育 *Kun-iku* education; upbringing.
籠 *Iiko(meru)* to confute.	電 *Kunden* telegraphic instructions.
	話 *Kunwa* a moral tale.
訃 FU death announcement.	練 *Kunren* training.
音 *Fuin* death announcement.	導 *Kundō* teaching; teacher of an elementary school.
報 *Fuhō* death announcement.	諭 *Kun-yu* admonition.
T計 KEI total sum. *Hakarigoto* plan; stratagem: *haka(ru); kazo(h)eru)* to consider; think about; reckon; calculate: *hakara(u)* to arrange; manage; negotiate.	辭 *Kunji* instruction.
	T討 TŌ. *U(tsu)* to strike; chastise; attack.
	手 *Utte* an attacking party.
略 *Keiryaku* scheme; plan; stratagem.	伐 *Tōbatsu* to subjugate.

(三)

討
死 *Uchijini* dying in battle.
取 *Uchito(ru)* to slay.
論 *Tōron* discussion; debate.
議 *Tōgi* discussion; debate.

T 記 KI document; history; chronicle. *Shiru(su)* to write down; record: *shirushi* mark; sign.
入 *Ki-nyū* entry.
名 *Kimei* signature.
事 *Kiji* description; article or paragraph (as in a newspaper).
念 *Kinen* commemoration.
者 *Kisha* writer; editor.
述 *Kijutsu* description; an account.
載 *Kisai* to write; record.
號 *Kigō* mark; sign.
憶 *Kioku* memory.
錄 *Kiroku* records; archives.

T 託 TAKU to entrust to; charge with. *Kakotsu(keru)* to make an excuse: *kako(tsu)* to complain.

訊 JIN to investigate. *Tazu-(neru)* to ask.
問 *Jimmon* examination; inquiry.

訖 KITSU; KOTSU to stop; at last. *Owari* the end.

四九

T 許 KYO; KO. *Yuru(su)* to allow; permit; approve; pardon: *bakari* only; about: *moto* place.

(四)

可 *Kyoka* permission; approval.
多 *Kyota* a great number.
容 *Kyoyō* permission; assent.
婚 *Iinazuke* the betrothed.
嫁 *Iinazuke* the betrothed.
諾 *Kyodaku* permission; assent.

訝 GA; GE. *Ibuka(ru)* to doubt; suspect: *ibukashii* suspicious.

訥 TOTSU. *Domo(ru)* to stammer.
辯 *Totsuben* slow of speech.

T 訪 HŌ. *Otozu(reru)*; *tazu-(neru)*; *to(u)* to visit; call; inquire.
日 *Hōnichi* visiting Japan.
客 *Hōkyaku* a visitor.
問 *Hōmon* call; visit.
歐 *Hōō* visiting Europe.

T 訳 See 譯 149,13.

訣 KETSU. *Waka(reru)* to separate: *wake* reason.
別 *Ketsubetsu* parting.

T 設 SETSU. *Mō(keru)* to establish; furnish; provide: *moshi* if.
令 *Tatoi* even if.
立 *Setsuritsu* establishment; foundation.
定 *Settei* establish.
計 *Sekkei* plan; design.
計圖 *Sekkeizu* plan on paper; drawing.

（四）

備 *Setsubi* equipment; accommodation.

置 *Setchi* to establish.

訛 KA mistake; lie. *Namari* dialect: *nama(ru)* to speak with a provincial accent.

傳 *Kaden* false rumour.

T **訟** SHŌ to accuse; bring a complaint or suit against; to strive.

五 **註** CHŪ explanatory notes; commentary; to make a note of; to explain.

文 *Chūmon* order (for goods or work).

釋 *Chūshaku* commentary.

T **証** See **證** 149,12.

詛 SO. *Noro(u)* to curse.

T **詔** SHŌ to say (used of Emperor). *Mikotonori* Imperial edict.

勅 *Shōchoku* Imperial edict.

書 *Shōsho* Imperial edict.

詒 I to deceive. *Noko(su)* to leave.

T **訴** SO. *Utta(h)eru* to sue; bring a complaint or suit against; report; inform. →61,10

人 *Sonin* informer; suitor.

出 *Uttae-deru* to report; inform.

狀 *Sojō* written complaint.

訟 *Soshō* suit; action.

訟手續 *Soshō-tetsuzuki* judicial procedure.

（五）

願 *Sogan* appeal; petition.

權 *Soken* right of appeal.

T **詐** SA. *Itsuwa(ru)* to lie; deceive.

取 *Sashu* fraud.

欺 *Sagi* fraud.

稱 *Sashō* false personation.

評 HYŌ criticism; to weigh; discuss the merit of. →**評** T

判 *Hyōban* fame; reputation.

定 *Hyōjō* conference; deliberation: *hyōtei* criticize and decide.

論 *Hyōron* criticism; review.

價 *Hyōka* valuation.

議 *Hyōgi* conference; deliberation.

T **詞** SHI. *Kotoba* word; speech.

T **診** SHIN. *Mi(·ru)* to examine; diagnose.

察 *Shinsatsu* consultation (medical); diagnosis.

斷 *Shindan* diagnosis.

T **詠** EI poem. *Yo(mu)* to compose poetry.

歎 *Eitan* to sigh; admire.

詫 Often used erroneously for 詫 149,6 which see.

六 **詮** SEN to estimate; deliberate; to choose.

方 *Senkata* means; expedient.

索 *Sensaku* search; inquiry.

術 *Sensube* resources.

衡 *Senkō* choice; selection.

詮
議 *Sengi* conference; inquiry; investigation.

詬 Kō shame; to put to shame. *Nonoshi(ru)* to revile.

T 詰 Kitsu. *Naji(ru)* to find fault with: *tsu(meru); tsuma(ru)* to pack; fill; be put into: *tsumari* after all.

切 *Tsumeki(ru)* attend constantly.

込 *Tsumekomi* cramming; stuffing.

掛 *Tsumeka(keru)* to crowd into; come in great numbers.

問 *Kitsumon* cross-examination; rigid inquiry.

責 *Kisseki* to rebuke.

T 話 Wa. *Hanashi* tale; story; conversation: *hana(su)* to speak.

柄 *Wahei* topic of conversation.

頭 *Watō* topic of conversation.

題 *Wadai* topic; the subject.

詣 Kei. *Mō(deru); mai(ru)* go to a temple or a shrine; worship.

T 詳 Shō. *Tsumabiraka; kuwashii* clear; detailed; minute.

言 *Shōgen* detailed statement.

述 *Shōjutsu* a minute statement.

密 *Shōmitsu* detailed.

記 *Shōki* careful description.

細 *Shōsai* details.

報 *Shōhō* detailed report.

解 *Shōkai* detailed explanation; exposition.

說 *Shōsetsu* detailed explanation.

論 *Shoron* full discussion.

T 詩 Shi poem; Chinese poem.

人 *Shijin* poet.

句 *Shiku* verse.

的 *Shiteki* poetical.

集 *Shishū* poetical works.

歌 *Shika; shiika* poetical composition.

趣 *Shishu* poetical interest.

詢 Jun to inquire; to consult with. *Makoto* truth.

T 誇 Ko large. *Hoko(ru)* to boast; be proud.

大 *Kodai* exaggerated; inflated.

示 *Koji* to make a display of.

張 *Kochō* exaggeration; magnification.

誂 See T 該 149,6.

誅 Chū to kill; execute; to attack; make war upon.

伐 *Chūbatsu* to punish with military force.

求 *Chūkyū* exact; squeeze.

罰 *Chūbatsu* punishment with death.

誄 Rui an eulogy.

詞 *Ruishi* eulogy.

(六)
T試 SHI. *Kokoromi(-ru)* to put to the test; try; examine: *kokoromi ni* for trial.

用 *Shiyō* to use as a trial.

合 *Shiai* match.

問 *Shimon* test; question.

金石 *Shikinseki* a touchstone.

補 *Shiho* probationer.

運轉 *Shiunten* trial trip.

練 *Shiren* a trial.

驗 *Shiken* examination.

詭 KI to deceive; lie.

言 *Kigen* lie; falsehood.

辯 *Kiben* sophistry; fallacious elocution.

詫 TA. *Wa(biru); kako(tsu)* to apologize; be sad; complain.

言 *Wabigoto* apology.

狀 *Wabijō* letter of apology.

誂 CHŌ. *Atsura(h)eru* to order.

向 *Atsuraemuki* just the thing.

T該 GAI that; the said. →149,6

件 *Gaiken* the matter in question.

博 *Gaihaku* erudite; profound.

當 *Gaitō* to correspond with; answer to.

諩 See T談 149,8.

誉 See 譽 134,14. 【言】
→譽 T

七
誣 FU. *Shi(h)iru)* to accuse wrongfully; to slander; to deceive.

言 *Fugen* to accuse wrongfully.

告 *Fukoku* to accuse wrongfully.

妄 *Fumō* groundless talk.

誑 KYŌ. *Taburaka(su)* to hoodwink; deceive.

誥 KŌ. *Tsu(geru)* to tell; inform.

T語 GO language; word; saying; tales. *Kata(ru)* to speak; talk; tell; relate.

句 *Goku* words and phrases.

尾 *Gobi* a suffix; termination.

呂 *Goro* euphony; sound.

氣 *Goki* way of speaking.

調 *Gochō* accent; a tone.

弊 *Gohei* misuse.

誦 SHŌ to read: JU; ZU. *Soranjiru* (irreg.) to recite from memory.

T誘 YŪ. *Izana(u); saso(u); obi(ku)* to invite; decoy; entice; seduce; tempt.

引 *Yūin* invitation.

因 *Yūin* immediate occasion.

拐 *Yūkai* abduction.

致 *Yūchi* inducement.

掖 *Yūeki* to direct; lead.

惑 *Yūwaku* temptation.

導 *Yūdō* inducement.

誨 KAI. *Oshi(h)eru); sato(su)* to teach; instruct.

417　*T誠 →149,7

誤 GO. *Ayamari* mistake: *ayama(ru)* to make a mistake.
→誤 T

用 *Goyō* misuse.

信 *Goshin* misbelief.

脱 *Godatsu* mistakes and omissions.

植 *Goshoku* misprint.

報 *Gohō* incorrect report.

傳 *Goden* erroneous report.

解 *Gokai* misunderstanding.

聞 *Gobun* unfounded report.

認 *Gonin* misconception.

謬 *Gobyū* mistake.

譯 *Goyaku* mistranslation.

誡 KA. *Imashi(meru)* to warn; admonish.
→149, 6 * T

飭 *Kaichoku* admonish.

誠 SEI. *Makoto* sincerity; truth; indeed.

心 *Seishin* sincerity.

忠 *Seichū* true loyalty.

意 *Seii* sincerity.

實 *Seijitsu* sincerity; faithfulness.

説 SETSU opinion: ZEI. *To(ku)* to explain; preach; relate.

↓伏 *Seppuku suru; tokifu(seru)*
→ to silence; to reason. 説
附 *Tokitsu(keru)* persuade. → T

明 *Setsumei* explanation.

法 *Seppō* preaching.

述 *Setsujutsu* to mention: state.

破 *Seppa* to confute.

得 *Settoku* to persuade.

敎 *Sekkyō* sermon.

話 *Setsuwa* narration; recital.

諭 *Setsuyu* admonition.

T読 See 讀 149,15.

T誌 SHI. *Shiru(su)* to write down; record.

認 NIN. *Mito(meru)* to recognize; acknowledge: *shitata(meru)* to write.
→認 T

可 *Ninka* authorization; approval.

知 *Ninchi* acknowledgment of fact.

定 *Ni tei* conclusion; recognition; authorization.

許 *Ninkyo* authorization; approval.

諾 *Nindaku* approval.

識 *Ninshiki* cognition.

證 *Ninshō* confirmation; authentication.

T誓 SEI. *Chika(u)* to swear; promise; vow.

文 *Seimon* written oath.

言 *Seigon* oath.

約 *Seiyaku* to swear; an oath.

紙 *Seishi* written oath.

願 *Seigan* vow.

誼 GI good. *Yoshimi* friendship. 八

誰 SUI. *Tare; dare; ta* who.

方	*Donata* who.
何	*Suika* to challenge.
彼	*Tare-kare; dare-kare* this or that person.
諂	TEN. *Iletsura(u)* to flatter.
諛	*Ten-yu* flattery.
誹	HI. *Soshi(ru)* to slander; revile.
毀	*Hiki* slander.
謗	*Hibō* slander.
譏	*Hiki* slander.
諄	JUN; SHUN polite; cordial; patient.
々	*Junjun* carefully; politely.
諍	SŌ. *Isa(meru)* to remonstrate with: *isaka(u)* to strive; quarrel.
請	SE.; SHŌ. *Ko(u)* to ask; request: *u(keru)* to receive.
↓人	*Ukenin* surety (perso).
合	*Ukea(u)* to guarantee.
取	*Uketori* receipt.
求	*Seikyū* to claim; demand.
受	*Ukeuri* retail; s c. ndhand.
負人	*Ukeoi-nin* contra tor.
書	*Ukesho* written acknowledgment.
暇	*Seika* furlough.
願	*Seigan* petition.
論	RON argument; discourse; opinion. *Agetsura(u)* to discuss; dispute.
文	*Rombun* essay; treatise.
及	*Ronkyū* touch on; refer to.

功行賞	*Ronkō-kōshō* grant of rewards after examination of services.
外	*Rongai* beside the question.
旨	*Ronshi* point of argument.
告	*Ronkoku* prosecution.
決	*Ronketsu* to discuss and decide.
爭	*Ronsō* dispute; argument.
法	*Rompō* logic; reasoning.
客	*Ronkaku* controversialist; publicist.
者	*Ronsha* disputant.
破	*Rompa* refutation.
理	*Ronri* logic.
評	*Rompyō* a criticism.
駁	*R. mbaku* confutation.
語	*Rongo* the analects of Confucius.
說	*Ronsetsu* essay; treatise.
據	*Ronkyo* grou d of argument.
戰	*Ronsen* wordy warfare.
壇	*Rondan* platform.
點	*Ronten* point at issue.
斷	*Rondan* conclusion.
題	*Rondai* subject; theme.
證	*Ronshō* proof; demonstration.
難	*Ronnan* confutation.
議	*Rongi* discussion.

調 T CHŌ. *Shirabe* playing on a musical instrument; note; tone; tune: *totono(h)eru)*; *totono(u)* to adjust; regulate; arrange; make ready; be ready; procure: *shira-(beru)* to investigate; examine: *mitsugi* tribute. (*Tsuk:*).

子 *Chōshi* tune; pitch.

合 *Chōgō* mixture.

印 *Chōin* to affix a seal.

和 *Chōwa* harmony.

物 *Shirabemono* matter for inquiry.

味 *Chōmi* flavouring.

度 *Chōdo* supply; requisites.

査 *Chōsa* investigation; examination.

書 *Chōsho* a protocol.

理 *Chōri* arrangement; cooking.

停 *Chōtei* intervention; arbitration.

進 *Chōshin* purveyance; supply.

節 *Chōsetsu* regulation; modulation.

達 *Chōdatsu; chōtatsu* to supply; raise.

製 *Chōsei* concoction; preparation.

練 *Chōren* drill; parade.

剤 *Chōzai* preparation; concoction.

課 T KA lesson; task; tax; bureau; to allot.

目 *Kamoku* a subject; course.

長 *Kachō* head of a section.

程 *Katei* a curriculum.

税 *Kazei* taxation.

業 *Kagyō* lesson; occupation; task.

題 *Kadai* a subject; a theme.

談 T DAN. *Hana(su)* to talk; tell; relate. →149,6

合 *Dangō* consultation; deliberation.

判 *Dampan* discussion; deliberation.

笑 *Danshō* chatting.

話 *Danwa* conversation.

義 *Dangi* lecture; sermon.

誂 JŌ the words of a superior.

諏訪 *Suwa* p. n.

誕 TAN to be born; to deceive; arbitrariness; selfwill. *Uso* lie. →誕 T

生 *Tanjō* birth; nativity.

辰 *Tanshin* birthday.

諒 RYŌ to sympathize with; clear; to understand. (*Akira*).

察 *Ryōsatsu* to take into consideration.

闇 *Ryōan* national mourning on the death of the Emperor.

*

謚 SHI. *Okurina* posthumous name or title.

号 *Shigō* posthumous title.

420 *T 諸 →149,9

諸 DAKU. *Ukega(u)*; *ubena(u)* to consent; agree with.

々 *Dakudaku* without the least dissent.

威 *Noruei* Norway.

T 諮 SHI. *Haka(ru)* to consult with; inquire.

問 *Shimon* to question; inquire of.

詢 *Shijun* inquiry.

諸 SHO. *Moro-moro* all; various. →149, 8 T *

子 *Shoshi* all of you.

方 *Shohō* all directions.

君 *Shokun* gentlemen! (when addressing a gathering of men).

共 *Morotomo* together.

星 *Shosei* leaders.

島 *Shotō* group of islands.

般 *Shohan* various.

掛 *Shokakari* charges.

種 *Shoshu* various kinds.

説 *Shosetsu* various views.

諳 AN. *Soranjiru* (irreg.) to recite from memory: *sora* memory.

記 *Anki* to know by heart; retain in the memory.

誦 *Anshō* learning by heart; recitation.

諧 KAI to put in order; to suit; be fitting; to be in harmony.

謔 *Kaigyaku* jest; humour.

諱 KI. *Imina* posthumous name: *i(mu)* to dislike.

謂 I reason; history. *I(u)*; *ieraku* to say: *omo(u)* to think.

諦 TEI; TAI. *Akira(meru)* to be resigned.

視 *Teishi* to gaze at.

諺 GEN. *Kotowaza* proverb.

謁 ETSU to have an audience with.

見 *Ekken* Imperial audience.

諤 GAKU outspoken; righteous.

々 *Gakugaku* outspoken.

諛 YU. *Hetsura(u)* to flatter.

諜 CHŌ spy; to spy out; search. *Shime(su)* to signal.

兵 *Chōhei* military spy.

報 *Chōhō* report of a spy.

T 謀 BŌ; MU. *Hakarigoto* plan; scheme; plot: *haka(ru)* to consult; plot.

反 *Muhon* rebellion.

判 *Bōhan* false seal.

計 *Bōkei* stratagem.

叛 *Muhon* rebellion.

殺 *Bōsatsu* murder.

略 *Bōryaku* stratagem.

將 *Bōshō* a strategist.

議 *Bōgi* consultation.

421

（九）

諫 KAN. *Isa(meru)* to admonish; remonstrate with.

止 *Kanshi* dissuasion.

言 *Kangen* remonstrance; admonition.

諷 FŪ to hint; allude to.

示 *Fūshi* a hint; a suggestion.

刺 *Fūshi* sarcasm; satire.

諭 YU example; comparison. *Sato(su)* to admonish; instruct; advise. →諭 T

示 *Yushi* admonition.

旨 *Yushi* official suggestion.

告 *Yukoku* advice; instructions.

*1

一〇 謚 See 諡 149,9.

謐 HITSU peaceful; quiet.

謔 GYAKU to sport with; trifle; joke.

謠 YŌ. *Uta(u)* to sing: *uta; utai* song. →149,9 * T

曲 *Yōkyoku* a "No" song.

言 *Yōgen* wild stories.

謝 T SHA; JA to thank; to refuse. *Ayama(ru)* to apologize.

恩 *Shaon* returning thanks for a favour.

絶 *Shazetsu* refusal.

罪 *Shazai* apology; acknowledging one's fault.

意 *Shai* sense of gratitude or apology.

*1 謡 T →149,10

禮 *Sharei* thanks; fee.

辭 *Shaji* address of thanks.

講 T KŌ investigation; lecture; to think out; explain; study; practise; devise.

究 *Kōkyū* study; investigation.

和 *Kōwa* restoration of peace.

座 *Kōza* professorial chair.

師 *Kōshi* lecturer.

堂 *Kōdō* lecture hall.

習 *Kōshū* study; practice.

評 *Kōhyō* criticism.

話 *Kōwa* lecture.

義 *Kōgi* lecture; explanation.

演 *Kōen* lecture.

談 *Kōdan* relating historical incidents and anecdotes.

壇 *Kōdan* lecture platform.

釋 *Kōshaku* lecture; explanation.

謗 BŌ; HŌ. *Soshi(ru)* to slander; revile.

謙 KEN. *Herikuda(ru)* to be humble. →謙 T

遜 *Kenson* modest; humble.

讓 *Kenjō* modesty; humility.

謎 MEI. *Nazo* riddle.

謹 KIN. *Tsutsushi(mu)* to be reverential. →149,10 *2 T

言 *Kingen* polite way of finishing letter; yours respectfully.

告 *Kinkoku* to beg to inform.

（一〇）

直 *Kinchoku* scrupulousness.

啓 *Kinkei* Dear Sir (epist. st., opening of a letter.)

賀 *Kinga* congratulation.

慎 *Kinshin* prudence; circumspection.

嚴 *Kingen* restraint; seriousness.

聽 *Kinchō* to listen attentively.

謳 Ō. *Uta(u)* to sing.

歌 *Ōka* to admire.

謫 TAKU to banish; to condemn; blame.

居 *Takkyo* confinement.

所 *Takusho* confinement.

謬 BYŪ. *Ayamari* error; mistake.

見 *Byūken* fallacy.

説 *Byūse'su* mistaken opinion.

論 *Byūron* mistaken argument.

謨 BO; MU to deliberate; plan.

謾 MAN to despise; to deceive.

謦 KEI. *Shiwabuki* clearing the throat.

咳 *Keigai* cough.

咳に接す *Keigai ni sessu* to meet one's superior.

謷 GŌ foolish; very; large; to jest; noisy.

證 SHŌ. *Shirushi; akashi* proof; evidence. →149,5 T

人 *Shōnin* a witness.

文 *Shōmon* bond; written contract.

左 *Shōsʒ* proof; evidence

印 *Shōin* seal affixed to a document.

言 *Shōgen* testimony.

明 *Shōmei* proof; verification.

劵 *Shōken* bill; bond; policy.

書 *Shōsho* bond; certificate.

跡 *Shōseki* evidence; trace.

據 *Shōko* proof; evidence.

譖 SHIN to accuse. *Soshi(ru)* to revile.

譚 TAN. *Hanashi* story.

譎 KITSU; KETSU to lie; deceive.

計 *Kikei* trickery; trick.

詐 *Kissa* trickery.

譌 KA to lie; deceive.

識 SHIKI; SHI. *Shi(ru)* to know well; discriminate: *shiru(su)* to write. →識 T

別 *Shikibetsu* to discriminate.

見 *Shikiken* knowledge and judgment.

者 *Shikisha* learned man.

得 *Shikitoku* to understand.

譏 KI. *Soshi(ru)* to slander.

一
三 譖 SEN. *Tawagoto* delirious or silly words.

妄 *Sembō* delirium.

語 *Uwagoto* talk in delirium.

T 譜 FU record; chronicle; tune; note; to jot down.

代 *Fudai* hereditary; successive generations.

譯 YAKU to translate; to explain. *Wake* meaning; reason.

文 *Yakubun* a translation.

者 *Yakusha* a translator.

解 *Yakkai* to translate and explain.

語 *Yakugo* words used in a translation.

讀 *Yakudoku* translation.

譟 SŌ. *Sawa*(*gu*) to make a noise; be clamorous; to be confused.

T 議 GI proposal; discussion; to consult with; discuss; debate.

了 *Giryō* finish discussion.

決 *Giketsu* decision (of a meeting).

長 *Gichō* president; chairman.

事 *Giji* proceedings.

事堂 *Gijidō* assembly hall; Congress; Diet.

定 *Gitei; gijō* to agree upon.

政 *Gisei* legislature.

席 *Giseki* seat in an assembly hall.

院 *Giin* the Diet (the building).

案 *Gian* bill (Parliamentary).

員 *Giin* member (of an assembly).

場 *Gijō* assembly hall.

會 *Gikai* Diet; Parliament; Congress.

論 *Giron* discussion.

題 *Gidai* subject for discussion.

譬 HI. *Tatoe* example: *tato*-(*h*)*eru*) to illustrate.

喻 *Hiyu* comparison; parable.

T 警 KEI. *Imashi*(*meru*) to warn; admonish.

句 *Keiku* witty remark.

戒 *Keikai* warning; caution.

告 *Keikoku* warning; advice.

官 *Keikan* a policeman.

固 *Keigo* guard; escort.

視廳 *Keishichō* Metropolitan Police Board.

報 *Keihō* warning; alarm.

視 *Keishi* police superintendent.

備 *Keibi* defence; guard.

語 *Keigo* a witty remark.

察 *Keisatsu* police.

察署 *Keisatsusho* police station.

醒 *Keisei* to awake.

衛 *Keiei* watch; guard.

鐘 *Keishō* alarm bell.

護 *Keigo* guard; escort.

一四T 護 GO. *Mamo(ru)* to protect; defend.

送 *Gosō* to escort; send under guard.

衛 *Goei* to guard; protect.

謨 *Gomu* gum; rubber.

譴 KEN. *Shika(ru)* to scold; to reprimand.

責 *Kanseki* censure.

一五 讀 DOKU; TOKU; TŌ punctuation. *Yo(mu)* to read. →149, 7 T

方 *Yomikata* the way of reading; reading.

本 *Tokuhon* reader book).

合 *Yomiawa(seru)* to read and compare or verify.

者 *Dokusha* reader (person).

書 *Tokusho* reading.

破 *Dokuha* read through.

書三味 *Dokusho-sammai* constant reading.

會 *Dokukai* reading (of a bill).

誦 *Dokushō* recitation.

難 *Yominikui* hard to read.

讃 See 讃 149,19.

一六 讐 SHŪ to avenge. *Ada; kataki* enemy.

討 *Katakiuchi* revenge.

一七 讓 JŌ. *Yuzu(ru)* to defer; be inferior; transfer. →149, 13 T *

合 *Yuzuriai* compromise mutual concessions.

歩 *Jōho* concession.

受 *Yuzuriuke* transfer; receive.

渡 *Yuzuriwata(su)* to transfer; hand over.

與 *Jōyo* concession; transfer.

讒 ZAN to slander; to accuse.

言 *Zangen* slander; calumny.

誣 *Zambu* a false charge.

謗 *Zambō* slander; calumny.

讃 SAN eulogy. *Ho(meru)* to praise: *tasu(keru)* to assist. 一九

岐 *Sanuki* p. n.

美 *Sambi* praise; commendation.

美歌 *Sambika* a hymn.

嘆 *Santan* admiration.

辭 *Sanji* a eulogy.

谷 一五〇

T谷 KOKU. *Tani* valley: *kiwama(ru)* to be in a fix. (*Ya*). (*Yatsu*).

川 *Tanigawa* mountain stream.

間 *Tanima* a ravine.

卻 See T却 26,5. 二

郤 GEKI. *Sukima* crevice: *hima* leisure. 【邑】 三

425

欲 T YOKU. *Hossuru* (irreg.) to wish; desire: *hoshii* desirable; desirous. 【欠】

望 *Yokubō* desire.

一五〇 豁 KATSU empty; wide.

然 *Katsuzen* in a flash; suddenly; clearly.

達 *Kattatsu* broad-minded.

谿 KEI rivulet. *Tani* valley with water.

谷 *Keikoku* a valley.

流 *Keiryū* mountain torrent.

一五一 **豆**

When at the left, it is called *Mame-hen.*

豆 T TŌ; ZU. *Mame* beans; peas.

州 *Zushū* another name for the province of *Izu.*

腐 *Tōfu* bean-curd.

六 T 豊 See 豐 151,11.

八 豌 豆 *Endō* peas.

九 T 頭 TŌ aux. num. for counting animals: ZU. *Atama; kōbe; kashira* head; top; chief. (*Kami*). 【頁】

巾 *Zukin* a hood.

目 *Tōmoku* a chief; a leader.

字 *Kashiraji* initial letter.

角を現す *Tōkaku wo arawa-(su)* to raise one's head; make oneself prominent.

取 *Tōdori* president (of a bank, etc.).

首 *Tōshu* head; chief.

書 *Tōsho; kashiragaki* footnote (in Japanese written at the top of the page).

骨 *Zukotsu* cranium; skull.

株 *Atamakabu* a chief.

割 *Atamawari* dividing by the number of persons.

痛 *Zutsū* headache.

腦 *Zunō* the head.

領 *Tōryō* a chief.

數 *Atamakazu* number of individuals.

髪 *Tōhatsu* hair of the head.

豐 HŌ; BU. *Yutaka* abundant; plentiful; fertile. (*Toyo*). →151, 6 T

凶 *Hōkyō* good or bad harvest.

年 *Hōnen* fruitful year.

作 *Hōsaku* a good harvest.

富 *Hōfu* abundant; rich.

葦原瑞穂國 *Toyoashihara no mizuho no kuni* old name for Japan.

頬 *Hōkyō* a round cheek.

饒 *Hōjō* fertility.

一五二

豕

豕 SHI. *Inoko* pig; hog.

五 象 Zō elephant: SHŌ. *Katachi*
T form; shape; image; ap-
pearance.

牙 *Zōge* ivory.

眼 *Zōgan* inlaying.

徵 *Shōchō* symbol.

九 豫 YO. *Kanete* previously;
beforehand: *arakajime*
previously; roughly.
→6, 3② T

々 *Kanegane* already; previously.

防 *Yobō* precautionary action;
to provide against.

告 *Yokoku* a previous notice.

言 *Yogen* a prediction.

知 *Yochi* foreknow; forecast.

定 *Yotei* pre-arrangement;
expectation.

約 *Yoyaku* subscription; previous contract.

後 *Yogo* prognosis.

習 *Yoshū* preparation (as of
lessons); rehearsal.

測 *Yosoku* forecast; estimate.

期 *Yoki* expectation.

備 *Yobi* reserve.

報 *Yohō* forecast.

(九〇)

想 *Yosō* presumption; expectation; anticipation.

算 *Yosan* an estimate; budget.

審 *Yoshin* preliminary examination (as of a criminal).

選 *Yosen* provisional selection.

斷 *Yodan* presuppose.

一五三

豸

三 豺 SAI; ZAI. *Yamainu* wild
dog.

狼 *Sairō* ruffian.

豹 HYŌ leopard.

變 *Hyōhen* sudden change.

五 貂 CHŌ. *Ten* marten; sable.

七 貍 See 狸 94,7.

貌 BŌ. *Katachi* shape; form:
kao face; appearance.

一五四

貝

When at the left, it is called
Kai-hen; in other positions it is
called *Ko-gai.*

T 貝 BAI. *Kai* shell.

殼 *Kaigara* shell.

427

二
T 則　SOKU. *Nori* rule: *notto(ru)* to model after: *sunawachi* and then; that is to say. 【刀】

T 負　FU. *O(u)* to carry on the back: *ma(keru)* to be defeated; lose: *oime* debt.

惜　*Makeoshimi* excuse (for failure).

傷　*Fushō* wound.

債　*Fusai* a debt.

擔　*Futan* burden; charge; responsibility.

三
T 財　ZAI; SAI. *Takara* possessions; property; wealth.

力　*Zairyoku* financial power.

布　*Saifu* purse.

政　*Zaisei* finance.

界　*Zaikai* moneyed interests; economic world.

產　*Zaisan* property; possessions.

產差押　*Zaisan-sashiosae* attachment of property.

貨　*Zaika* wealth.

源　*Zaigen* source of revenue.

團　*Zaidan* a foundation.

閥　*Zaibatsu* plutocracy.

寶　*Zaihō* a treasure; wealth.

四
T 販　HAN to sell; trade.

路　*Hanro* market for goods.

賣　*Hambai* sale.

T 敗　HAI to go bad; decompose. *Yabu(reru)*; *ma(keru)* to be defeated. 【攴】

北　*Haiboku* be defeated.

走　*Haisō* be routed.

軍　*Haigun* defeated army.

尾　*Haioku* dilapidated house.

報　*Haihō* news of a reverse.

殘　*Haizan* a ruin; scattered.

訴　*Haiso* losing a suit.

頽　*Haitai* corrupt; decadence.

貶　HEN to disapprove. *Oto(su)* to degrade: *kena(su)* to abuse.

黜　*Henchutsu* to degrade from office or rank.

T 責　SEKI to condemn. *Seme* responsibility; duty: *se(meru)* to blame; torture; bring to task.

任　*Sekinin* responsibility.

苦　*Semeku* torture.

務　*Sekimu* obligation; duty.

貪　See 9,9. 【貝】

T 貧　HIN. *Mazushii* poor.

乏　*Bimbō* poverty.

民　*Himmin* the poor.

血　*Hinketsu* anaemia.

困　*Hinkon* distress caused by poverty; privation; want.

苦　*Hinku* hardship of poverty.

相　*Hinsō* indigent appearance.

弱　*Hinjaku* poor; scanty.

富　*Himpu* poverty and wealth; means.

428

窮 *Hinkyū* poverty; poor.

賤 *Hinsen* poverty and humbleness.

T 貫 See 80,7.【貝】

賢 See T 賢 154,8.

T 貨 KA wealth; goods; property; coin.

物 *Kamotsu; kabutsu* goods.

財 *Kazai* wealth; riches.

殖 *Kashoku* money-making.

幣 *Kahei* coin.

五 貼 TEN; CHŌ dose of medicine. *Ha(ru)* to stick on.

付 *Chōfu; tempu; haritsu(keru)* to affix to; stick on.

用 *Chōyō* application.

札 *Harifuda* placard.

紙 *Harigami* paper patching.

貽 I give. *Noko(su)* leave behind.

T 貯 CHO. *Takuwa(h)eru)* to save ..store up; lay up.

金 *Chokin* savings (money).

蓄 *Chochiku* storing up; hoarding.

蓄銀行 *Chochiku-ginkō* Savings Bank.

藏 *Chozō* storing up; preserving.

T 貴 KI your. *Tattoi; tōtoi* valuable; noble; high; dear: *tatto(bu); tōto(bu)* to value highly; esteem. (*Taka*).

人 *Kijin* nobleman.

下 *Kīka* you (polite).

女 *Kijo; anata* you (woman).

方 *Anata* you (man or woman).

公子 *Kikōshi* young noble.

兄 *Kīkei* you (used in letter writing).

君 *Kīkun; anata* you (man).

金屬 *Kikinzoku* the precious metal.

重 *Kichō* precious; valuable.

郞 *Anata* you (man).

院 *Kiin* abb. of 貴族院·

族 *Kizoku* peer.

族政治 *Kizoku-seiji* aristocracy.

族院 *Kizokuin* House of Peers.

紳 *Kishin* men of rank.

婦人 *Kifujin* a lady.

酬 *Kishū* a reply to your letter.

意 *Kii* your will.

賓 *Kihin* a noble guest.

殿 *Kiden* you (man).

賤 *Kisen* high and low; rank.

樣 *Kisama* you.

翰 *Kikan* your esteemed letter.

顯 *Kiken* dignitaries.

貰 SEI. *Mora(u)* to receive.

子 *Moraigo* adopted child.

【五】貰

手 *Moraite* a receiver; a suitor.

物 *Moraimono* anything received.

泣 *Morainaki* cry for company.

T 賀 GA; KA to congratulate; be glad; rejoice.

正 *Gasei* New Year conglatulations.

表 *Gahyō* a congratulatory address.

状 *Gajō* congratulatory letter.

貢 See 24,10. 【貝】

T 貿 Bō to exchange; trade.

易 *Bōeki* trade; commerce; business.

T 費 HI. *Tsuie* expense: *tsuiya(su)* to spend.

用 *Hiyō* expenses.

目 *Himoku* item of expenses.

府 *Hifu* Philadelphia.

消 *Hishō* consumption.

途 *Hito* way money is spent.

T 貸 TAI. *Ka(su)* to lend.

手 *Kashite* lender.

切 *Kashikiri* reserved.

主 *Kashinushi* the creditor.

金 *Kashikin* loan; money lent.

附 *Kashitsuke* loaning.

倒 *Kashidaore* bad debts.

【五】座敷 *Kashizashiki* house of ill fame.

家 *Kashiya* house to let.

借 *Taishaku; kashi-kari* loan; lending and borrowing.

費 *Taihi* money lent for expenses.

間 *Kashima* a room to let.

与 *Taiyo* lending.

賣 *Kashiuri* sa'e on credit.

脏 See 贜 154,18.　　六

賂 RO. *Mainai* present; bribe: *maina(u)* to bribe.

T 賄 WA'. *Ma'nai* bribe: *makana u)* to cater for.

賂 *Wairo; mainai* bribe; bribery.

T 賊 ZOKU rebel; robber. *Soko na(u)* to injure; harm.

子 *Zokushi* rebel; insurgent

軍 *Zokugun* army of rebels.

徒 *Zokuto* band of rebels.

賤 See 賎 154,8.

T 賃 CHIN fare; wages; rent; to hire.

仕事 *Chin-shigoto* job-work.

金 *Chinkin* wages; fare.

借 *Chinshaku; chin-gari* to hire; lease.

貸 *Chintai; chingashi* lett'ng out on hire; lease.

銀 *Chingin* wages; fare.

錢　*Chinsen* charge; wages; cost of labour; fare.

資　SHI riches. *Motode* capital (money): *tasu(keru)* to assist.
→資 T

力　*Shiryoku* funds; resources.

本　*Shihon* capital (money); fund.

本家　*Shihonka* capitalist.

金　*Shikin* capital (money); fund.

性　*Shisei* nature; disposition.

格　*Shikaku* qualification.

料　*Shiryō* materials.

財　*Shizai* property.

産　*Shisan* property.

質　*Shishitsu* nature; quality.

贄　SHI to redeem; wealth.

賑　七　SHIN. *Nigiwa(u)* to be bustling; crowded: *nigiyaka* flourishing; bustling; cheerful: *nigiwa(su)* to enliven; to help with alms.

恤　*Shinjutsu* give alms.

賠　八 T　BAI. *Tsuguna(u)* to indemnify.

償　*Baishō* indemnity.

賜　T　SHI. *Tamawa(ru)* to bestow (used of the Emperor, etc.); to give: *tamamono* gift.

金　*Shikin* government grant.

物　*Tamamono* gift.

宴　*Shien* Imperial dinner.

暇　*Shika* leave of absence.

賦　T　FU taxes.

役　*Fueki* forced labour.

税　*Fuzei* taxation.

與　*Fuyo* endowment.

課　*Fuka* to levy; impose.

賤　SEN. *Iyashi(mu)* (lit. st.); *iyashi(meru)* (coll.) to detest: *iyashii; shizu* humble; lowly; low-born.

民　*Semmin* the lowly.

劣　*Senretsu* mean; base.

業　*Sengyō* mean occupation.

賞　T　SHŌ prize; reward. *Ho(meru)* to praise; approve.

状　*Shōjō* a certificate of merit.

玩　*Shōgan* appreciate; take pleasure.

味　*Shōmi* to taste and admire; relish.

品　*Shōhin* a prize.

美　*Shōbi* praise; esteem; admiration.

牌　*Shōhai* medal.

與　*Shōyo* a reward; bonus.

罰　*Shōbatsu* reward and penalties.

嘆　*Shōtan* admiration.

讃　*Shōsan* praise; commendation.

質　T　SHITSU quality; nature; material; natural disposition; matter, (e. g. *mokushitsu* tree matter, i. e.

（八）質
wood）: SHICHI pawn; pledge. *Tada(su)* to question; examine; inquire.

入 *Shichiire* pawning.

朴 *Shitsuboku* plain; homely; simple-minded.

屋 *Shichi-ya* pawnbroker.

素 *Shisso* simplicity; plainness

問 *Shitsumon* question; interpellation.

量 *Shitsuryō* mass.

實 *Shitsujitsu* sincerity.

疑 *Shitsugi* question; inquiry.

T 贊 SAN to help; assist; agree; praise. →154, 12

同 *Sandō* approval; support

成 *Sansei* seconding; support.

助 *Sanjo* support; help.

否 *Sampi* yes or no.

辭 *Sanji* eulogy.

T 賢 KEN. *Kashikoi* wise; clever; you (epist. st., honorific). (*Kata*). →154, 4

人 *Kenjin* wise man; sage.

才 *Kensai* man of ability.

所 *Kashikodokoro* ancestral shrine in the Imperial Palace.

明 *Kemmei* wise; intelligent.

哲 *Kentetsu* a sage.

愚 *Kengu* wise or foolish.

（八）
察 *Kensatsu* your discernment; sympathy.

賭 TO. *Ka(keru)* to bet; gamble. 九

博 *Tobaku* gambling.

賴 RAI. *Tano(mu)* to order (as in a shop); to request: *tayo(ru); yo(ru)* to rely on; depend on: *tanomoshii* reliable; promising. (*Yori*). →頼 T

母 *Tanomoshii* promising; reliable; trustworthy.

信紙 *Raishinshi* telegram form.

購 KŌ. *Agana(u)* to ransom; atone; to purchase. 一〇

入 *Kōnyū* purchase.

求 *Kōkyū* purchase.

買 *Kōbai* purchase.

讀 *Kōdoku* reading.

賺 TAN. REN. *Suka(su)* to hoax; to deceive.

贅 ZEI wen; knob. *Muda* superfluous; excessive. 一一

言 *Zeigen* a pleonasm; lengthy remark.

澤 *Zeitaku* luxury; extravagance.

贄 SHI. *Nie* religious offering; present made when calling.

*贈 T →154, 12

一五四

三 贈 ZŌ; SŌ. *Oku(ru)* to send; to present. →154, 11 * T

位 *Zōi* conferment of a post-humous rank.

呈 *Zōtei* present.

物 *Okurimono* present; gift.

答 *Zōtō* exchange; correspondence.

賄 *Zōwai* to give a bribe.

與 *Zōyo* donation.

贗 See 27,17. 【貝】

贊 See T贄 154,8.

一三 贍 SEN to supplement; to help; to cause to flourish.

富 *Senpu* abundant.

一四 贐 JIN. *Hanamuke* present to one departing.

贓 See 贓 154,18.

贔 HI strength.

負 *Hiiki* favour; a favourite.

負客 *Hiiki-kyaku* patron; customer.

屓 *Hiiki* favour; a favourite.

一五 贖 SHOKU. *Agana(u)* atone for; indemnify.

一八 贓 ZŌ to bribe; stolen goods.

物 *Zōbutsu* stolen goods.

品 *Zōhin* stolen goods.

一五五

赤

赤 SEKI; SHAKU. *Akai* red; brown.

十字 *Sekijūji* the Red Cross.

子 *Akago; sekishi* baby; subject; the people.

手 *Sekishu* empty-handed.

心 *Sekishin* sincerity.

毛布 *Akagetto* red blanket; a rustic.

化 *Sekika* to Bolshevize.

坊 *Akambō* baby.

坂 *Akasaka* p. n.

門 *Akamon* a red gate: Tōkyō Imperial University.

門出 *Akamonde* graduate of Tōkyō Imperial University.

面 *Sekimen* to blush; be ashamed of.

恥 *Akahaji* public disgrace.

貧 *Sekihin* great poverty.

帽 *Akabō* baggage porter.

痢 *Sekiri* dysentery.

飯 *Sekihan* rice boiled with red beans.

道 *Sekidō* equator.

誠 *Sekisei* sincerity.

赤

銅 *Shakudō* alloy of copper (100), antimony (30) and gold (7).

裸々 *Sekirara* nakedness; out-spoken.

四
T 赦 SHA. *Yuru(su)* to forgive; pardon.

免 *Shamen* to pardon; release.

罪 *Shazai* to pardon.

五 赧 TAN. *Akara(meru)* to become red; to feel ashamed.

然 *Tanzen* blushingly.

顔 *Tangan* to feel ashamed.

七 赫 KAKU to shine; anger; red.

々 *Kakkaku* splendid; glorious; majestic.

灼 *Kakushaku* splendid; brilliant.

怒 *Kakudo* rage; wrath.

耀 *Kakuyō* splendid; brilliant.

九 赭 SHA. *Akai* red: *akatsuchi* red earth.

一五六　　　走

Always at the left and bottom; it is called *Sōnyū.*

T 走 SŌ. *Hashi(ru)* to run.
→32, 3

卒 *Sosotsu* errand boy; one of the lower class.

狗 *Sōku* hound; a tool.

書 *Hashirigaki* running handwriting.

馬燈 *Sōmatō* revolving lantern.

二
T 赴 FU to announce. *Omomu-(ku)* to go.

任 *Funin* repairing to a post to which one has been nominated.

三 起 KI. *O(k ru)* to get up: *oko(ru)* to come about; happen; appear; originate: *oko(su)* to raise: *ta tsu)* to rise; stand up: *okori* origin.　→起 T

工 *Kikō* set to work.

立 *Kiritsu* stand up.

出 *Oki-i(zuru)* (lit. st.) to get up.

因 *Kiin* origin; source.

伏 *Kifuku* ups and downs.

床 *Kishō* getting up; rising.

居 *Kikyo* getting along.

居振舞 *Tachi-furumai* behaviour.

臥 *Kiga; oki-fushi* getting up and lying down.

重機 *Kijūki* crane (machine).

（三二）

草 *Kisō* to draft; draw up.

原 *Kigen* the origin.

訴 *Kiso* prosecution.

算 *Kisan* count from.

點 *Kiten* starting point.

五
T 超 CHŌ. *Ko(y)eru)* to pass over; surpass.

人 *Chōjin* superman.

自然 *Chō-shizen* supernatural.

弩級 *Chō-dokyū* Super-Dreadnought.

俗 *Chōzoku* unconventional.

脱 *Chōdatsu* to stand aloof from.

越 *Chōetsu* to be superior; to transcend.

然 *Chōzen* surpassing; to transcend.

絶 *Chōzetsu* standing aloof.

過 *Chōka* to exceed.

趁 SHIN; CHIN to run. *O(u)* to chase.

r 越 ETSU old name for part of China: ECHI; OTSU; OCHI. *Ko(y)eru); ko(su)* to cross; go over; exceed; move (change house).

中 *Etchū* p. n.

年 *Otsunen* passing from the old year to the new.

前 *Echizen* p. n.

度 *Ochido* a fault.

後 *Echigo* p. n.

權 *Ekken* go beyond one's powers.

趙 CHŌ old name for part of China. 七

T 趣 SHU. *Omomuki* taste (artistic); purport. 八

旨 *Shushi* intention; purport.

向 *Shukō* design.

味 *Shumi* taste; interest.

意 *Shui* sense; purport.

趨 SŪ quick; to tend towards. *Hashi(ru)* to run. 一〇

向 *Sūkō* tendency; current.

勢 *Sūsei* tendency; current.

足

一五七

When at the left, it takes a slightly modified form and is called *Ashi-hen*.

T 足 SOKU aux. num. for counting pairs of boots, etc. *Ashi* foot; leg: *ta(riru); ta(ru)* to be sufficient: *ta(su)* to add; make up a lack. →30, 3

足
下 *Sokka* you (respectful).

止 *Ashidome* confining in-doors.

手纒 *Ashitematoi* encumbrance.

尾 *Ashio* p. n.

拍子 *Ashibyōshi* beating time with the feet.

並 *Ashinami* a pace; a step.

音 *Ashioto* sound of a foot-step.

掛 *Ashikake* a foot-stool; not more than: *ashigakari* footing.

袋 *Tabi* socks.

塲 *Ashiba* a footing.

勞 *Sokurō* trouble to walk (polite).

跡 *Sokuseki; ashiato* footprint.

搔 *Aga(ku)* to paw.

摺 *Ashizuri* scraping one's feet.

輕 *Ashigaru* footman; low ranking samurai.

馱 *Ashida* high clogs.

踏 *Ashibumi* a tread; step.

纒 *Ashimatoi* obstacle.

四 趾 SHI footprint; feet. *Ato* remains.

跂 KI to creep; stand on tiptoe.

五 距 T KYO. *Sa(ru); hedata(ru); heda(teru)* to be distant from.

離 *Kyori* distance.

跗 FU instep.

跌 TETSU. *Tsumazu(ku)* to stumble.

跋 BATSU epilogue (of a book); to tread.

文 *Batsubun* epilogue (of a book).

涉 *Basshō* to travel about.

扈 *Bakko* to be arrogant; presumptuous.

跛 HA; HI. *Bikko; chimba; ashinae* cripple; lame person.

T 路 RO. *Michi; ji* road; 六 path.

上 *Rojō* on the road.

地 *Roji* lane; road.

傍 *Robō* roadside.

銀 *Rogin* travelling expenses.

頭 *Rotō* roadside.

跨 KO. *Mata(gu); mataga(ru)* to straddle; extend a-cross; bestride.

跪 KI. *Hizamazu(ku)* to kneel.

伏 *Kifuku* kneeling down.

坐 *Kiza* kneeling down.

跣 SEN. *Hadashi* barefooted.

足 *Sensoku; hadashi* bare-footed.

T 跳 CHŌ. *Odo(ru). ha(neru); to(bu)* to jump; leap; dance.

（六）

反 *Hane-kae(ru)* to rebound.

泥 *Hane* splashes (of mud).

梁 *Chōryō* to frolic; gambol.

躍 *Chōyaku* a skip; a jump.

T 跡 SEKI. *Ato* footmarks; trace; clue.

片附 *Atokatazuke* putting in order.

目 *Atome* succession; inheritance.

形 *Atokata* trace; mark; evidence.

取 *Atotori* a successor.

繼 *Atotsugi* a successor.

跫 KYŌ sound of steps.

七 踊 YŌ. *Odo(ru)* to dance; leap. →157,9
T

跼 KYOKU. *Kaga(mu)*; *kogo-(mu)*; *segukuma(ru)* to be bent over in the back.

蹐 *Kyokuseki* to crouch down.

踈 See T 疎 103,7.

踉 RŌ. *Yorome(ku)* stagger; totter.

八 踟 CHI to roam about; to hesitate.

蹰 *Chichū* to hesitate.

踞 KYO to sit down. *Uzukuma(ru)* to crouch; squat down.

T 踏 TŌ. *Fu(mu)* to step on; tread on.

* T 踐 →157,8

（八）

切 *Fumikiri* a crossing.

外 *Fumihazu(su)* to miss one's footing.

附 *Fumitsu(keru)* to trample down.

查 *Tōsa* exploration; prospecting.

倒 *Fumi.ao(su)* to kick down; evade payment.

迷 *Fumimayo(u)* to lose one's way; go astray.

破 *Tōha* travel about.

張 *Fumba(ru)* to stretch the legs; to hold fast to the end.

臺 *Fumidai* a step; footstool.

襲 *Tōshū* imitation; follow the footsteps of.

踐 SEN. *Fu(mu)* to tread on; fulfil; ascend. →157,6 * T

祚 *Senso* accession to the Throne.

踠 EN. *Moga(ku)* to struggle; to wriggle.

踪 SŌ clue; footprint.

跡 *Sōseki* trace; whereabouts.

踵 SHŌ; SHU. *Kibisu; kakato* the heel. 九

蹄 TEI. *Hizume* hoof.

鐵 *Teitetsu* a horseshoe.

踴 See T 踊 157,7.

蹂 JŪ. *Fuminiji(ru)* to crush under foot.

躪 *Jūrin* to trample under foot; oppress.

（九） 蹂　YU. *Ko(y)eru)*; *ko(su)* to cross over.

（一一一） 蹴　SHŪ. *Ke(-ru)* (lit. st.); *ke(ru)* (coll.) to kick.

立　*Keta(teru)* kick up.

飛　*Ketoba(su)* kick.

球　*Shūkyū; futto-bōru* football.

鞠　*Kemari* foot-ball (old-fashioned).

（一〇） 蹉　SA. *Tsumazu ku)* to misstep; stumble.

跌　*Satetsu* stumbling; failure.

躓　*Sachi* stumbling.

蹈　TŌ. *Fu(mu)* to tread; trample.

襲　*Tōshū* imitation.

蹌　SŌ to move; to run. *Yorome(ku)* to stagger.

踉　*Sōrō* staggering.

蹰　CHO. *Tamera(u)* to hesitate.　一三

躄　HEKI. *Ashinae; izari* cripple; lame.

躍　YAKU to ascend. *Odo(ru)* to leap; dance. →躍 T　一四

如　*Yakujo* vividly.

起　*Yakki* zeal; to be excited.

進　*Yakushin* rush on.

躊蹰　*Chūcho* hesitation.

（一一） 蹣跚　*Mansan* staggering.

蹤　SHŌ. *Ato* clue: *ashiato* footprint.

蹟　SEKI. *Ato* remains; ruins; trace; footprint.

蹠　SHŌ sole (of the foot).

蹙　SHUKU; SEKI to draw near; press close. *Shika(meru)* to make a wry face: *chijima(ru)* to shrink.

躑躅　*Tsutsuji* azalea.　一五

躓　CHI; SHITSU. *Tsumazu(ku)* to stumble.

躙　RIN to tread; to crush with the foot.　一六

（一三） 蹰　CHŪ; CHU to hesitate.

蹲　SON. *Uzukuma(ru); shaga-(mu)* to crouch; squat down.

踞　*Sonkyo* to crouch.

躓　KETSU to be overturned. *Tsumazu(ku)* to stumble: *ke(-ru)* (lit.st.); *ke(ru)* (coll.) to kick.

起　*Kekki* to spring up.

躋　JŌ to ascend. *Fu(mu)* to tread.　一八

躪　See 躙 157,16.　二〇

身　一五八

438

Always at the left; it is called *Mi-hen*.

T 身 SHIN. *Mi* body; flesh; self.

上 *Minoue* one's fortunes; one's personal history.

内 *Miuchi* one's relations.

分 *Mibun* social position.

支度 *Mijitaku* getting oneself ready.

元 *Mimoto* one's social position; one's antecedents; parentage.

代 *Shindai* possession; property.

仕度 *Mijitaku* equip oneself for.

投 *Minage* to drown oneself.

命 *Shimmei* life.

受 *Miuke* to redeem (person); ransom.

長 *Shincho mitake* stature.

持 *Mimochi* conduct; behaviour; pregnancy.

振 *Miburi* attitude; gesture.

寄 *Miyori* a relation.

動 *Miugoki* moving.

許 *Mimoto* parentage.

勝手 *Migatte* one's own convenience.

輕 *Migaru* light; sprightly.

構 *Migamae* attitude.

邊 *Shimpen* person; the body.

體 *Shintai karada* body.

T 射 SHA. *I*(-*ru*) to shoot (arrow): *sa*(*su*) to dart. 【寸】 三

利 *Shari* love of gain.

倖心 *Shakōshin* a speculative spirit.

貫 *Inu*(*ku*) to shoot through.

程 *Shatei* rifle-range.

撃 *Shageki* firing; shooting.

躬 KYŪ. *Mi* the body: *mizukara* oneself; self.

行 *Kyūkō* doing personally.

躰 See 體 188,13. 五

躶 See T 裸 145,8. 八

躾 *Shitsuke* instruction in politeness; culture. 九

方 *Shitsukekata* training in manners.

軀 KU. *Mi; karada* the body. 一一

幹 *Kukan* the body.

軈 *Yagate* directly; by and by; soon; presently; shortly. 一七

車 一五九

When at the left, it is called *Kuruma-hen*.

439

車 SHA. *Kuruma* carriage; cart; vehicle; wheel.

力 *Shariki* cart-coolie.

夫 *Shafu* rikisha-man.

止 *Kurumadome* no thorough-fare.

馬 *Shaba* vehicles and horses.

庫 *Shako* a car-shed.

寄 *Kurumayose* entrance (of a palace).

軸 *Shajiku* axle.

掌 *Shashō* conductor (as of tram-car).

道 *Shadō* roadway.

輪 *Sharin* wheel.

輛 *Sharyō* vehicle.

一 **軋** ATSU. *Kishi(ru)* to grate; scrape.

轢 *Atsureki* friction.

二 **軌** KI rut; track; line.

條 *Kijō; reiru* rail.

道 *Kidō* track; orbit.

範 *Kihan* example; model; rule; law.

三 **軒** KEN house; aux. num. for counting houses. *Noki* eaves of a house.

別 *Kembetsu* house by house.

昂 *Kenkō* high-spirited.

輕 *Kenchi* difference.

端 *Nokiba* near the eaves.

斬 ZAN. *Ki(ru)* to cut. 【斤】 四

新 *Zanshin* original; new.

軟 NAN. *Yawarakai* soft; weak.

化 *Nanka* softening.

派 *Nampa* moderate party.

風 *Nampū* breeze.

弱 *Nanjaku* weak; feeble.

*

軽 See 輕 159,7. 五

軸 JIKU stem; stalk; holder; axis; scroll.

軫 SHIN to revolve; to move; to worry.

念 *Shinnen* Emperor's anxiety.

較 KAKU; KŌ. *Kura(beru)* 六 to compare; examine: T *yaya* in a certain degree. →較

輕 KEI. *Karui* light (not 七 heavy): *karonzuru* (irreg.) to despise; belittle; make light of. →159,5 T

々 *Karu-garu; karo-garo; keikei* lightly; easily.

井澤 *Karuizawa* p. n.

少 *Keishō* little; slight.

妙 *Keimyō* light and easy.

快 *Keikai* light-hearted.

卒 *Keisotsu* rash; careless.

佻 *Keichō* fickle.

重 *Keijū; keichō* relative importance.

*T 転 →159,11

（七）

侮 *Keibu* contempt; insult.

便 *Keiben* simple and convenient; handy.

便鐵道 *Keiben-tetsudō* light railway.

信 *Keishin* ready credence.

症 *Keishō* a slight touch.

氣球 *Keikikyū* a balloon.

浮 *Keifu* superficiality; shallowness.

率 *Keisotsu* rash; careless.

視 *Keishi* disregard; to trifle.

減 *Keigen* mitigation; reduction.

微 *Keibi* trifling.

業 *Karuwaza* acrobatic feats.

裝 *Keisō* a light dress.

傷 *Keishō* a slight wound.

蔑 *Keibetsu* contempt; scorn.

薄 *Keihaku* perfidious; insincere.

擧 *Keikyo* a rash attempt.

輔 HO; FU. *Tasu(keru)* to aid; help; assist; rescue; support. (*Suke*).

佐 *Hosa* to assist.

弼 *Hohitsu* assistance.

導 *Hodō* lead; guide.

輒 CHŌ. *Sunawachi* thereupon: *tayasui* easy.

輓 BAN. *Hi(ku)* to pull.

近 *Bankin* recent times.

八

輜 SHI wagon.

重車 *Shichō-sha* provision wagon.

重兵 *Shichō-hei* commissariat.

T輪 RIN to revolve. *Wa* wheel; ring.

廻 *Rinne* transmigration of soul.

奐 *Rinkan* magnificence.

番 *Rimban* alternately.

廓 *Rinkaku* outline.

講 *Rinkō* explanation by turns.

輛 RYŌ aux. num. for counting carriages.

輀 See 輀 159,7.

T輝 See 42,12. 【車】

輦 REN an Imperial carriage.

轂の下 *Renkoku no moto* in the capital.

九

輻 FUKU to gather together.

湊 *Fukusō* assembling.

輳 *Fukusō* assembling; congestion.

輯 SHŪ to pay in. *Atsu(meru)* to collect; compile; edit.

錄 *Shūroku* collect; compile.

輸 YU; SHU to transport; send.　→輸 T

入 *Yunyū* importation.

（九）

輸
出 *Yu-hutsu* exportation.

出入 *Yushutsu-nyū* exporting and importing.

出品 *Yushutsu-hin* exports.

卒 *Yusotsu* transport soldier.

送 *Yusō* to transport.

贏 *Yuei* victory or defeat.

一〇 轄 KATSU to rule; have jurisdiction over.

轉 See 轉 159,11. →轄 T

輾 TEN. *Kishi(ru)* to grate; creak: *megu(ru)* to revolve.

轉反側 *Tenten-hansoku* rolling and tumbling.

轅 EN. *Nagae* shaft of a carriage.

一一 轉 TEN to change. *Koroga-(ru)*; *koro(geru)*; *koro(bu)*; *maro(bu)* to stumble; fall: *megu(ru)* to revolve: *utata* more and more; increasingly; somehow; in some way.→159,4 T ＊ : →159,10

々 *Tenten* change hands; wander; roam.

化 *Tenka* change.

任 *Tennin* change of post.

地 *Tenchi* change of air.

宅 *Tentaku* removal.

居 *Tenkyo* to change one's residence.

居先 *Tenkyo-saki* place to which one has removed.

借 *Tenshaku: matagari* borrowing a thing from one

（一一）

who has borrowed it from another.

送 *Tensō* transmission.

換 *Tenkan* to change; convert.

婆 *Otemba* tomboy.

貸 *Tentai; matagashi* underlease.

業 *Tengyō* change of occupation or trade.

載 *Tensai* reproduction.

嫁 *Tenka* imputation; shifting of responsibility.

勤 *Tenkin* change one's office.

機 *Tenki* a turning point.

覆 *Tempuku* overturn; upset.

變 *Tempen* vicissitudes.

轆 ROKU pulley.

轤 *Rokuro* winch.

轍 TETSU. *Wadachi* rut; wheel-track.

一二

轗軻 *Kanka* neglect by the world.

一三

轟 GŌ. *Todoro(ku)* to rumble.

一四

々 *Gōgō* rumbling sound.

然 *Gōzen* thunderously.

轢 REKI to grate; creak. *Hi(ku)* to run over.

一五

死 *Rekishi* to be run over and killed.

442

（一五）殺 *Rekisatsu* kill by running over.

（一六）轢 REKI wagon-rut.

一六〇

辛

T 辛 SHIN. *Karai* pungent; hard: *tsurai* painful; try-ing: *karōji'e* barely; with difficulty; at last: *kanoto* 8th calendar sign. See Introduction 42, 43.

抱 *Shimbō* patience; endur-ance.

苦 *Shinku* toil; labour; hard-ship.

棒 *Shimbō* patience.

勞 *Shinrō* hardship.

辣 *Shinratsu* harshness; severity.

酸 *Shinsan* bitterness; hard-ship.

六 辟 HEKI to call; lord.

易 *Hekieki* to shrink back; flinch.

七 辣 RATSU bitter; awful.

腕 *Ratsuwan* shrewdness.

九 辨 BEN to discriminate. *Wa-kima(h)eru*) to understand; know. →28, 3 T

（九）別 *Bembetsu* discrimination.

理士 *Benrishi* attorney.

理公使 *Benri-kōshi* a min-ister resident.

當 *Bentō* luncheon, generally put up in a box.

濟 *Bensai* repayment.

償 *Benshō* compensation.

辨 BEN to labour; to offer; prepare.

一二 瓣 BEN valve. *Hanabira* petal.【瓜】→28, 3 T

辭 JI. *Kotoba* word; lan-guage; speech: *ina(mu)* to refuse; resign; decline.

世 *Jisei* death-song. →135, 7 T

令 *Jirei* written order; com-mission; diction.

去 *Jikyo* leave.

任 *Jinin* resignation.

典 *Jiten* dictionary.

柄 *Jihei* a pretext.

表 *Jihyō* letter of resignation.

書 *Jisho* dictionary.

退 *Jitai* to refuse; decline.

職 *Jishoku* resignation.

一四 辯 BEN to discriminate; to argue; to correct; to ex-plain; to make an ex-cuse. →28, 3 T

士 *Benshi* a speaker.

才 *Bensai* eloquence.

舌 *Benzetsu* speech; elo-quence.

443

(一四) 辯

明 *Bemmei* explanation; vindication.

疏 *Benso* to plead.

解 *Benkai* explanation; excuse; vindication.

駁 *Bembaku* refutation.

論 *Benron* argument; discussion.

護 *Bengo* to advocate; vindicate.

護士 *Bengoshi* an advocate; lawyer.

(六) 林省 *Nōrinshō* Department of Agriculture and Forestry.

林大臣 *Nōrindaijin* Minister of Agriculture and Forestry.

相 *Nōshō* Minister of Agriculture and Forestry.

家 *Nōka* farmer's house; farmer.

産物 *Nōsambutsu* agricultural products.

場 *Nōjō* a plantation.

業 *Nōgyō* agriculture.

一六一　辰

辰 SHIN. *Tatsu* 5th zodiacal sign; the dragon. See Introduction 42, 43.

三 唇 SHIN. *Kuchibiru* lips. 【口】

T 辱 JOKU; NIKU. *Hazukashi-(meru)* to put to shame; disgrace: *katajikenai* thankful.

知 *Jokuchi* acquaintance.

六T 農 NŌ agriculture.

夫 *Nōfu* farmer; husbandman.

民 *Nōmin* a peasant.

村 *Nōson* agricultural district.

事 *Nōji* agriculture.

一六二　辵

In composition it always takes a modified form at the left and bottom 辶 and is called *Shinnyū*.
In Tōyō always : ⎯ 辶

一 辷 *Sube(ru)* to slip.

二 辻 *Tsuji* cross-roads.

褄 *Tsujitsuma* connection; coherence.

T 辺 See 邊 162,15.

T 込 *Ko(mu); ko(meru)* to crowd into; be crowded; put into.

合 *Komia(u)* to be crowded together.

三 迚 TEN. *Tado(ru)* to grope one's way.

444

(三)

迂 U far; round about; to turn.

迴 *Ukai* detour.

迂生 *Usei* I (humble).

迂愚 *Ugu* silly; stupid.

迂遠 *Uen* roundabout; circuitous; stupid.

迂闊 *Ukatsu* inattentive; stupid.

迅 JIN quick; fast.

迅速 *Jinsoku* swift.

迅雷 *Jinrai* severe thunderstorm.

迄 KITSU; KOCHI to reach; extend to. *Made* to; as far as; till; by.

T 巡 JUN. *Megu(ru)* to go round; patrol.【巛】

巡回 *Junkai* going round; tour of inspection.

巡幸 *Junkō* Imperial tour.

巡査 *Junsa* policeman.

巡洋艦 *Jun-yō-kan* cruiser.

巡洋戰艦 *Jun-yō-senkan* battle cruiser.

巡視 *Junshi* tour of inspection.

巡遊 *Jun-yū* travelling about.

巡察 *Junsatsu* a round of inspection.

巡禮 *Junrei* pilgrim.

巡覽 *Junran* inspection; going round seeing (a building).

四 T 近 KIN; KON. *Chikai* near; *chikazu(ku)* to approach.

(四)

近日 *Kinjitsu* soon; in a few days.

近火 *Kinka* a fire nearby.

近代 *Kindai* modern times.

近世 *Kinsei* modern times.

近刊 *Kinkan* recent publication.

近付 *Chikazuki* an acquaintance.

近江 *Ōmi* p. n.

近在 *Kinzai* neighbouring villages.

近年 *Kinnen* of late years.

近所 *Kinjo* neighbourhood.

近狀 *Kinjō* present conditions.

近來 *Kinrai* of late.

近況 *Kinkyō* present state; recent condition.

近郊 *Kinkō* neighbouring fields; suburbs.

近時 *Kinji* recently.

近海 *Kinkai* adjacent seas.

近寄 *Chikayo(ru)* to approach.

近眼 *Kingan; chikame* near-sightedness.

近處 *Kinjo* neighbourhood.

近視眼 *Kinshigan* near-sighedness.

近頃 *Chikagoro* lately.

近傍 *Kimbō* neighbourhood.

近道 *Chikamichi* a short-cut.

近畿 *Kinki* provinces near Kyōto.

近隣 *Kinrin* neighbourhood.

近衞 *Konoe* Imperial guards; also, p. n.

（四）

近 *Kimpen* neighbourhood.

親 *Kinshin* near relations.

藤 *Kondō* p. n.

T迎 GEI ; GYŌ. *Muka(h)eru* to go to meet ; to welcome.

合 *Geigō* adulation.

春 *Geishun* welcome in the New Year.

賓 *Geihin* reception of guests.

迚 *Tote mo* by no means : *tomo* although : *tote* because.

T返 HEN. *Kae(ru)* : *kae(su)* to return ; restore.

々 *Kaesu-gaesu mo* repeatedly

上 *Henjō* returning or sending back (polite).

却 *Henkyaku* return ; repayment.

附 *Hempu* to return.

事 *Henji* answer ; reply.

金 *Henkin* repayment.

信 *Henshin* an answer.

咲 *Kaerizaki* blooming a second time.

送 *Hensō* return ; send back.

答 *Hentō* answer ; reply.

報 *Hempō* answer ; paying back (favour or injury).

歌 *Henka* poem composed in reply to another.

濟 *Hensai* repayment.

還 *Henkan* return.

禮 *Henrei* a return present.

迦 KA used for its sound. 五

迕 See 迄 162,3.

T迫 HAKU. *Sema(ru)* to press upon ; urge.

害 *Hakugai* persecution.

迯 See 逃 162,6.

T迭 TETSU. *Kawa(ru)* to transfer ; change : *t gai ni* mutually.

述 JUTSU. *No b ru)* to state ; relate. →述T

懷 *Jukkai* recollections.

逅 KŌ to meet unexpectedly. 六

T追 TSUI a supplement. *O(u)* to pursue ; follow : *otte* postscript.

々 *Oi-oi* gradually ; by and by.

手 *Oite; otte* pursuer ; a fair wind.

及 *Tsuikyū* overtake.

弔 *Tsuichō* condolence.

出 *Oida(su)* to drive out ; send away.

加 *Tsuika* appendix ; addition.

申 *Tsuishin* postscript.

付 *Ottsuke* soon.

尾 *Tsuibi* to pursue.

求 *Tsuikyū* pursuit ; chase.

究 *Tsuikyū* chase ; close inquiry.

伸 *Tsuishin* a postscript.

（六）

附 *Oitsu ku*) to overtake.

拂 *Oihara(u); oppara(u)* to drive away.

放 *Tsuihō* expulsion.

風 *Oite; oikaze* driving or favourable wind.

剝 *Oihagi* highwayman.

啓 *Tsuikei* postscript.

悼 *Tsuitō* mourn for.

悼會 *Tsuitōe; tsuitōkai* memorial service.

從 *Tsuishō* flattery.

捲 *Oimaku(ru)* to rout; chase.

善 *Tsuizen* praying for the happiness of the dead; mass for the dead.

詰 *Oitsu(meru)* to drive into a corner.

越 *Oiko(su)* to outstrip.

跡 *Tsuiseki* pursuit.

想 *Tsuisō* recollection; retrospection.

認 *Tsuinin* ratification.

徵 *Tsuichō* collect the balance.

慕 *Tsuibo* to hold in reverence.

駈 *Okka(keru)* to run after.

憶 *Tsuioku* recollection.

隨 *Tsuizui* to follow.

擊 *Tsuigeki* pursuit; attack.

懷 *Tsuikai* reflecting upon the past.

迴 See 廻 54,6.

迺 NAI; DAI. *No* of: *sunawachi* thereupon: *nanji* you.

進 Hō; HEI. *Hodobashi(ru)* to splash; scatter.

逆 GYAKU; GEKI to be contrary to. *Sakasama* upside down: *sakara(u)* to oppose; resist; disobey.

上 *Gyakujō; nobose* dizziness; rush of blood to the head.

手 *Sakate* with the point downwards.

行 *Gyakkō* retrogressive motion.

戾 *Gyakumodori* go back.

流 *Gyakuryū* adverse tide.

捩 *Sakaneji* retaliation.

賊 *Gyakuzoku* a rebel.

意 *Gyakui* rebellious mind.

睹 *Gyakuto* foresee.

境 *Gyakkyō* adverse situation.

襲 *Gyakushū* a counter-attack.

鱗 *Gekirin* Imperial wrath.

送 SŌ. *Oku(ru)* to send; escort.　→送 T

別 *Sōbetsu* farewell.

金 *Sōkin* remittance; to send money.

附 *Sōfu* sending.

狀 *Okurijō* invoice.

迎 *Sōgei* speeding and welcoming.

料 *Sōryō* postage; cost of conveying.

達 *Sōtatsu* to convey; deliver.

還 *Sōkan* send back.

籍 *Sōseki* transfer of domicile.

（六）

迷 **T** MEI. *Mayo(u)* to go astray; err; be bewildered; be in doubt.

信 *Meishin* superstition.

宮 *Meikyū* a maze.

想 *Meisō* illusion; fancy.

惑 *Meiwaku* perplexity; trouble; inconvenience.

夢 *Meimu* delusion.

霧 *Meimu* delusion; fallacy.

退 **T** TAI. *Shirizo(ku)*; *no(ku)*; *saga(ru)*; *hi(ku)*: *do(ku)* to retire; retreat; leave; withdraw; get out of the way.

化 *Taika* degeneration.

出 *Taishutsu* to leave; withdraw; retire: *hike* closing.

去 *Taikyo* to leave; depart.

廷 *Taitei* leaving the court.

却 *Taikyaku* to retreat.

步 *Taiho* retrogression.

京 *Taikyō* leave the capital.

役 *Taieki* retirement (from the army).

社 *Taisha* retirement (from a company).

屈 *Taikutsu* tedium.

治 *Taiji* to subdue.

官 *Taikan* resignation.

軍 *Taigun* retreating army.

校 *Taikō* dismissal from school; leaving school.

院 *Taiin* leaving hospital.

席 *Taiseki* leave one's seat.

場 *Taijō* exit; leaving.

散 *Taisan* dispersion.

學 *Taigaku* leaving school.

會 *Taikai* withdrawal from a party.

隱 *Taiin* retirement; seclusion.

職 *Taishoku* retirement (from one's post).

嬰 *Taiei* retrogression; shrink.

逃 **T** TŌ. *Noga(reru)*; *ni(geru)* to escape; run away.

口上 *Nige-kōjō* an excuse.

亡 *Tōbō* flight; desertion; escape.

支度 *Nigejitaku* preparation for flight.

足 *Nigeashi* feet placed as if to flee away.

走 *Tōsō* flight.

場 *Nigeba* place of refuge.

迹 SEKI; SHAKU. *Ato* remains; footprints.

—

七

逕 KEI. *Komichi* path.

庭 *Keitei* gap; difference.

逞 TEI. *Takumashii* powerful: *takumashū suru* to practise freely; draw on one's imagination.

逗 TŌ; ZU. *Todoma(ru)* to stop.

子 *Zushi* p. n.

留 *Tōryū* sojourn.

這 SHA. *Ha(u)* to crawl; creep: *kono* this.

入 *Hai(ru)* to go in.

448

々の體 *Hoho-no-tei* precipitately.

般 *Shahan* such; of such kind; like this.

T 造 Zō. *Tsuku(ru)* to make; build; construct; create.

化 *Zōka* creation; nature; the Creator.

次 *Zōji* always.

付 *Tsukuritsuke* fixture.

作 *Zōsaku* fixtures: *zōsa nai* without trouble.

花 *Zōka* artificial flowers.

物主 *Zōbutsushu* the Creator.

林 *Zōrin* afforestation.

船 *Zōsen* shipbuilding.

詣 *Zōkei* attainment.

幣 *Zōhei* to coin money.

營 *Zōei* constructing; building.

逝 SEI. *Yu(ku)* to go; die.

去 *Seikyo* to die.

逢 HŌ. *A(u)* to meet.

着 *Hōchaku* to meet with.

T 連 REN sign of the plural. *Tsura(neru)*; *tsurana(ru)* to connect; be connected with; stand in a row; attend: *tsu(reru)* to go along with: *tsure* companion: *shikiri ni* continually; continuously.

子 *Tsureko* child brought into a family by its parent's marriage.

日 *Renjitsu* day after day; several days in succession.

中 *Renchū*; *renjū* party; company.

立 *Tsureda(tsu)* go along with.

名 *Remmei* joint signature.

合 *Tsureai* consort; a married couple: *rengō* joint; combination.

判 *Rempan* joint signature.

坐 *Renza* implication.

夜 *Ren-ya* every night; night after night.

借 *Renshaku* joint debt.

帶 *Rentai* jointly responsible.

袂 *Rembei* hand in hand; together.

敗 *Rempai* successive defeats.

累 *Renrui* being involved in.

累者 *Renruisha* accomplice.

接 *Rensetsu* connection.

結 *Renketsu* joining.

絡 *Renraku* combination; connection.

勝 *Renshō* victory after victory.

發 *Rempatsu* running fire; repeated action.

署 *Rensho* joint signature.

載 *Rensai* publish serially.

綿 *Remmen* continuously.

戰 *Rensen* succession of battles.

銷 *Rensa* chain; connection.

類 *Renrui* an accomplice.

續 *Renzoku* continuity.

（七）

逍 SHŌ to saunter; ramble; loaf.

遙 *Shōyō* stroll.

T 通 TSŪ aux. num. for counting letters and documents; to be well versed in. *Kayo(u)* to go or pass to and fro: *kayoi* pass-book: *tō(ru)*; *tō(su)* to pass through: *tōri* way; road; street; kind; as 2nd component, in accordance with; e. g. *yakusoku-dōri* in accordance with (my) promise: *michi* way; road.

人 *Tsūjin* man of the world.

用 *Tsūyō* common use; current.

行 *Tsūkō* passage; transit; passing.

有 *Tsūyū* common.

告 *Tsūkoku* announcement; notice.

知 *Tsūchi* to inform; communicate.

例 *Tsūrei* usually.

拔 *Tōrinuke* passing through.

夜 *Tsuya* wake; death-watch.

信 *Tsūshin* correspondence; communication.

俗 *Tsūzoku* popular.

風 *Tsūfu* ventilation.

則 *Tsūsoku* general rules.

航 *Tsūkō* navigation.

常 *Tsūjō* common; ordinary; usually.

帳 *Tsūchō; kayoi-chō* pass-book.

（七）

商 *Tsūshō* commerce.

貨 *Tsūka* currency.

勤 *Tsūkin* attending office.

牒 *Tsūchō* a note; a report; notification.

路 *Tsūro* roadway; passage.

運 *Tsūun* forwarding.

過 *Tsūka* passage; to pass through.

稱 *Tsūshō* common name.

弊 *Tsūhei* a common evil.

論 *Tsūron* general rules; outline.

曉 *Tsūgyō* full knowledge.

譯 *Tsūyaku* interpretation; interpreter.

辯 *Tsūben* interpreter.

覽 *Tsūran* survey; glance over.

讀 *Tsūdoku* to read to the end.

遞 See 遞 162,10.

T 透 TŌ. *Tō(ru); su(ku)* to be transparent; pass through: *suka(su)* to hold to the light; look through; thin out.

明 *Tōmei* transparency.

T 速 SOKU. *Sumiyaka; hayai* rapidity; quick; fast: *haya(meru)* to hasten. (*Mi*).

力 *Sokuryoku* speed; velocity.

成 *Sokusei* rapid completion.

決 *Sokketsu* immediate decision.

（七）

度 *Sokudo* velocity; speed.

記 *Sokki* stenography.

射砲 *Sokushahō* quick-firing gun.

達 *Sokutatsu* express delivery (of letters).

斷 *Sokudan* immediate conclusion.

T 逐 CHIKU. *O(u)* to chase; follow.

一 *Chikuichi* minutely.

次 *Chikuji* in succession.

年 *Chikunen* year after year.

條 *Chikujō* article by article.

鹿 *Chikuroku* competition; stand as a candidate.

電 *Chikuten* absconding.

逵 See 逹 162,9.

逡 SHUN. *Shiza(ru)* to withdraw; go backwards.

巡 *Shunjun* hesitation.

T 途 TO; ZU. *Michi* road; way.

上 *Tojō* on the way.

中 *Tochū* on the way.

方 *Tohō* the way; direction.

切 *Togire* a pause; a break.

次 *Toji* on the way.

絕 *Toda(y)eru)* cease entirely.

端 *Totan* just as; at the moment.

轍 *Totetsu mo nai* extravagant; unreasonable.

*T 逸 →162,8

T 進 SHIN serve; give. *Susu(mu)* to advance; march: *susu(meru)* promote; offer; advance.

入 *Shinnyū* penetration; entrance.

上 *Shinjō* giving as a present.

化 *Shinka* evolution.

水 *Shinsui* launching.

行 *Shinkō* advance; progress.

呈 *Shintei* giving as a present.

步 *Shimpo* progress.

物 *Shimmotsu* a present.

取 *Shinshu* eagerness to progress.

軍 *Shingun* march; advance (of army).

退 *Shintai* advancing or retreating; m.vement.

退伺 *Shintai-ukagai* an inquiry as to whether one should hand in a resignation.

級 *Shinkyū* promotion.

捗 *Shinchoku* progress; advance.

路 *Shinro* course; access.

境 *Shinkyō* advanced state.

擊 *Shingeki* to charge; assault.

T 週 SHŪ week; all; everywhere; circumference. *Megu(ru)* to turn; revolve; go round.

末 *Shūmatsu* a week-end.

刊 *Shūkan* weekly publication.

八

451

週
期 *Shūki* periodic time.

報 *Shūhō* a weekly report.

間 *Shūkan* week.

T 逮 TAI to chase.

捕 *aiho* to arrest.

逸 ITSU; ICHI excellent. *Hayai* fast: *haya ru*) to be impetuous: *so(reru)* to escape; go astray; miss; lose. →162,7 * T

才 *Issai; itsuzai* excellent ability.

早 *Ichihayaku* quickly.

走 *Issō* to run away; escape.

事 *Itsuji* anecdote.

品 *Ippin* a rarity.

散 *Issan ni* at full speed.

話 *Itsuwa* anecdote.

樂 *Itsuraku* pleasure; enjoyment.

九 遑 KŌ. *Itoma* leisure.

遁 TON. *Ni(geru); noga(reru)* to run away; escape.

世 *Tonsei* to retire from the world.

走 *Tonsō* flight.

辭 *Tonji* excuse.

T 道 DŌ each province in Korea. *Michi* road; street; branch of knowledge; doctrine.

中 *Dōchū* travelling; journey.

行 *Michi-yuki* walking along the road; process.

具 *Dōgu* utensil; tool.

破 *Dōha* refute; express fully.

案内 *Michi-annai* guide.

理 *Dōri* reason; justice; right.

連 *Michizure* travelling companion.

程 *Dōtei; michinori* distance.

筋 *Michisuji* course; path; track.

路 *Dōro* road.

義 *Dōgi* moral principles.

樂 *Dōraku* dissipation; eccentricity; hobby.

德 *Dōtoku* morality.

逼 HIKI; FUKU. *Sema(ru)* to press; urge.

迫 *Hippaku* to be hard up; destitute.

T 遅 See 遅 162,11.

T 達 TATSU. *Tas(suru)* (irreg.) to arrive; reach forward; be well versed in: *tachi* sign of plural: *tasshi* public notification.

人 *Tatsujin* expert.

成 *Tassei* to accomplish.

見 *Takken* clear-sightedness.

者 *Tassha* healthy; robust.

筆 *Tappitsu* ready pen.

意 *Tatsui* intelligibility.

識 *Tasshiki* great insight.

(九) 覲 *Takkan* clear discernment; wide view.

T 違 I. *Chiga(u)* to be different: *chigai* difference: *taga(h)eru)* to alter: ...... *ni chigai nai* there is no doubt.

反 *Ihan* to act contrary to.

犯 *Ihan* to violate laws.

法 *Ihō* infringement of the law; illegality.

約 *Iyaku* breach of agreement or contract.

背 *Ihai* violation; breach.

算 *Isan* miscalculation

憲 *Iken* illegality.

T 運 UN fortune (good or bad); chance. *Hak (bu)* to transport: *megura(su)* to revolve; ponder over.

用 *Un-yō* employing or using anything.

行 *Unkō* revolution.

否天賦 *Umpu-tempu* hazard; chance

命 *Ummei* fate; destiny.

河 *Unga* canal.

送 *Unsō* transportation.

送屋 *Unsōya* forwarding agency.

動 *Undō* exercise; movement; walk.

勢 *Unsei* luck; fortune; nativity.

搬 *Umpan* transport; conveyance.

賃 *Unchin* freightage.

漕 *Unsō* marine transportation.

賦天賦 *Umpu-tempu* hazard; chance.

輸 *Un-yu* traffic; transport.

轉 *Unten* motion of, or produced by, revolving wheels; employ.

轉手 *Untenshu* mate (of a ship); driver (tram-car; motor-car).

T 遊 YŪ; YU pleasure. *Aso(bu)* to play; amuse oneself; go anywhere for pleasure: *asoba(seru)* a polite verbal suffix.

弋 *Yūyoku* cruise.

山 *Yusan* picnic.

女 *Yūjo* prostitute.

民 *Yūmin* idle people.

步 *Yūho* saunter.

牧 *Yūboku* nomadism.

金 *Yūkin* idle money.

惰 *Yūda* indolence.

廓 *Yūkaku; kuruwa* prostitute quarters.

說 *Yūzei* electioneering tour.

樂 *Yūraku* pleasure; amusement.

學 *Yūgaku* travelling for study.

蕩 *Yūtō* dissipation.

興 *Yūkyō* pleasure; amusement.

歷 *Yūreki* a pleasure-trip.

戲 *Yūgi* amusement; play.

離 *Yūri* isolation; separation.

(九)

（九）

遊藝 *Yūgei* a light accomplishment.

覽 *Yūran* going about seeing celebrated places.

T 遍 HEN. *Am neku* the whole; everywhere.

在 *Henzai* omnipresence.

歷 *Henreki* to travel about.

T 過 KA. *Su(giru)* (often used as 2nd component with meaning of to exceed, be in excess, e. g. *shi-sugiru* to overdo); *sugo(su)* to exceed; pass; go through: *ayamachi* mistake; error; fault: *ayama(tsu)* to make a mistake: *yogi(ru)* to pass; go through.

大 *Kadai* excessive.

日 *Kajitsu; itsuzoya* the other day; once.

分 *Ka'un* excessive; more than one deserves.

不及 *Kafukyū* excess and deficiency.

半 *Kahan* more than half.

失 *Kashitsu: ayamachi* error.

去 *Kako* the past.

行 *Sugiyu(ku)* to pass by.

多 *Kata* excessive.

言 *Kagen; kagon* saying too much; slip of the tongue.

度 *Kado* excessive; undue.

信 *Kashin* be credulous.

般 *Kahan* some time ago; the other day.

敏 *Kabin* sensibility.

（九）

渡 *Kato* transition.

勞 *Karō* excessive labour.

剩 *Kajō* excess; surplus.

激 *Kageki* excess; violent.

激派 *Kagekiha* Bolshevik.

適 *Appare* splendid; well done; bravo!

T 遇 GŪ unexpectedly; occasionally. *A(u)* to meet: *ashira(u)* to entertain.

遏 ATSU to suppress *Todo-(meru)* to stop; cease.

遂 SUI. *To(geru)* to accomplish; finish: *tsui ni* at last; finally. →遂 T

行 *Suikō* to execute; carry out.

退 KA. *Haruka* far; distant.

遉 TEI to seek. *Sasuga* even such; as one might have expected.

遙 YŌ. *Haruka* far; distant. 一〇

々 *Haru-baru* from afar.

拜 *Yōhai* worshipping from a distance.

T 遣 KEN. *Ya(ru); tsukawa(su)* to give; send; transmit.

口 *Yarikuchi* the way of doing.

手 *Yarite* man of ability; doer; giver.

物 *Tsukaimono* a present.

放 *Yarippanashi; yaribanashi* leaving work in disorder.

（一〇）

塲 *Yariba* disposal.

繰 *Yarikuri* shifting; to tide over.

瀬 *Yaruse nai* inconsolable; unbearable.

遡 SO. *Sakanobo(ru)* to go against; trace up to its source.

T **遠** EN; ON. *Tōi* far: *tōzaka-(ru)* to go far from; get away from: *tōza(keru)* to keep away.

大 *Endai* far-reaching; great.

方 *Empō* distant place.

江 *Tōtōmi* p. n.

州 *Enshū* another name for the province of *Tōtōmi*.

因 *En-in* remote cause.

足 *Ensoku* long walk; walking tour.

征 *Ensei* expedition.

近 *Enkin* distance; far and near.

來 *Enrai* coming from afar.

洋 *En-yō* a deep sea.

島 *Entō* banishing criminals to distant island.

淺 *Tōasa* shallow water close in shore.

隔 *Enkaku* remote; distant.

路 *Enro; tōmichi* long way.

慮 *Enryo* reserve; forethought.

緣 *Tōen* remote; distant.

遞 TEI post-town; to change.

次 *Teiji* successively.

（一〇）

相 *Teishō* Minister of Communications.

信大臣 *Teishin-daijin* Minister of Communications.

信省 *Teishinshō* the Department of Communications.

送 *Teisō* sending by post.

減 *Teigen* successive diminution.

遜 SON. *Herikuda(ru)* to humble oneself.

色 *Sonshoku* humiliation; inferiority.

二一

T **遭** SŌ. *A(u)* to meet.

遇 *Sōgū* encounter.

難 *Sōnan* casualty; disaster.

遲 CHI. *Osoi* late; slow: *oku(reru)* to be late. →162,9 T : 162,9 T

々 *Chichi* slow.

延 *Chien* delay.

刻 *Chikoku* to be behind time.

參 *Chisan* come late.

速 *Chisoku* speed.

鈍 *Chidon* stupid; dull.

滯 *Chitai* delay.

疑 *Chigi* hesitation.

緩 *Chikan* slow; tardy.

蓮 See 蓮 140,11.

T **適** TEKI. *Kana(u); a(u)* to suit; fit: *yu(ku)* to go: *tama-tama* occasionally.

切 *Tekisetsu* pertinent; fit.

（一一）

適
用 *Tekiyō* application; adaptation.

任 *Tekinin* competent; well-qualified.

合 *Tekigō* conformity.

否 *Tekihi* suitable or not; suitability.

材 *Tekizai* a man fit for a post.

例 *Tekirei* a good example.

所 *Tekisho* the right position.

宜 *Tekigi* according to circumstances.

法 *Tekihō* proper method; legitimate.

度 *Tekido* moderation.

評 *Tekihyō* just criticism.

當 *Tekitō* fit; suitable.

應 *Tekiō* to fit; be appropriate.

齢 *Tekirei* suitable age; conscription age.

遯 TON. *Noga(reru); ni(geru)* to escape; abscond.

世 *Tonsei* secluding oneself.

遮 SHA. *Saegi(ru)* to intercept; to put a stop to.

莫 *Samo-araba are* be it as it may.

蔽 *Shahei* to cover; conceal.

斷 *Shadan* interception.

二二 **暹** SEN. *Susu(mu)* to advance. 【日】

羅 *Shamu* Siam.

（一一）

遵 JUN to learn. *Shitaga(u)* to follow; obey.

守 *Junshu* to observe; obey.

遷 SEN. *Utsu(su); utsu(ru)* to remove; move (change residence). →

化 *Senge* death (of a priest).

延 *Sen-en* delay. 遷 T ←

幸 *Senkō* changing residence (of the Emperor).

都 *Sento* removal of the capital (seat of government).

遶 NYŌ; JŌ. *Megu(ru)* to revolve: *megura(su)* to surround. Alternative form of 繞 120, 12.

選 SEN. *Era(bu); yo(ru)* to choose; select. →選 T

手 *Senshu* a picked team.

出 *Senshutsu* election.

任 *Sennin* election.

外 *Sengai* failure to be selected; rejected piece.

好 *Eri-kono(mu)* to have one's choice; be fastidious.

定 *Sentei* selection.

拔 *Sembatsu* selection.

擇 *Sentaku* selection.

舉 *Senkyo* election.

T **遺** I; YUI. *Noko(su); noko(ru)* to leave behind; bequeath: *wasu(reru)* to leave behind; forget; lose.

失 *Ishitsu* losing (as by dropping).

志 *Ishi* desire of a deceased person.

(一二)

言 *Yuigon* a will; death-bed injunction.

物 *Ibutsu* a relic.

恨 *Ikon* malice; grievances.

風 *Ifū* customs and spirit left by preceding generations.

留 *Iryū* to leave behind; bequeath.

書 *Isho* a will; a posthumous work.

骨 *Ikotsu* remains; ashes.

産 *Isan* an inheritance.

族 *Izoku* the family of a deceased person.

傳 *Iden* heredity.

棄 *Iki* desertion.

業 *Igyō* work left by someone.

漏 *Irō* omission; oversight.

跡 *Iseki* remains.

稿 *Ikō* posthumous work.

骸 *Igai* dead body.

憾 *Ikan* regret; grief; remorse.

遼 RYŌ. *Haruka* far; distant.

東 *Ryōtō* Liaotong.

遠 *Ryōen* far; distant.

三 T避 HI. *Sa(keru)* to avoid; escape.

忌 *Hiki* evasion.

病院 *Hibyōin* isolation hospital.

寒 *Hikan* avoiding the cold of winter.

(一三)

暑 *Hisho* avoiding the heat of summer; going to a summer resort.

雷針 *Hiraishin* lightning conductor.

難 *Hinan* to take refuge.

邂 KAI. *Meguria(u)* to meet unexpectedly.

逅 *Kaikō* chance meeting.

邁 MAI great; to excel; to go.

進 *Maishin* to dash forward.

遽 KYO to fear. *Niwaka; awatadashii* quick; flurried: *awa(teru)* to be agitated.

T還 KAN: GEN. *Kae(ru)*: *kae(su)* to return: *megu(ru)* to go round.

附 *Kampu* return; retrocession.

幸 *Kankō* return of the Emperor to the capital from a journey.

御 *Kangyo* return of His Majesty.

啓 *Kankei* return of the Empress or the Crown Prince.

曆 *Kanreki* 60 years of age.

邀 YŌ invite. *Mika(h)eru* to go to meet; to welcome.

擊 *Yōgeki* to ambush.

邃 SUI profound; deep.　一四

邊 HEN. *Hot/ri; atari; he* side; besid; close to; region, place. (*Nabe*); (*Nobe*). →162, 2 T　一五

（一五）

邊

幅　*Hempuku* personal appearance.

鄙　*Hempi* out-of-the-way.

境　*Henkyō* frontier.

一九　邏　RA. *Megu(ru)* to go around: *shino(bu)* to conceal; keep secret.

一六三　邑

In composition it always takes a modified form ß; it is placed at the right and is called *Ōzato*.

邑　YŪ. *Mura* village; city.

四　邦　HŌ. *Kuni* country; Japan.

人　*Hōjin* Japanese.　→邦 T

文　*Hōbun* Japanese sentence.

字新聞　*Hōji-shimbun* Japanese newspaper.

家　*Hōka* our country.

語　*Hōgo* our language; Japanese.

譯　*Hōyaku* translated into Japanese.

那　NA. *Ano* that: *nani*; *nanzo* how; why.

覇　*Nawa* p. n.

邊　*Nahen* where; whereabouts.

邨　See ᵀ村 75,3.

邸　TEI residence; mansion.　五

宅　*Teitaku* mansion.

郁　IKU fragrant; flourishing.　六

郊　KŌ the country; suburbs.

外　*Kōgai* suburbs; outskirts.

＊野　*Kōya* the country; a field.

郡　GUN. *Kōri* rural district.　七

部　*Gumbu* within country limits (as opposed to city limits).

郎　RŌ generally used as last syllable of men's names. O man (male).
→163,6 ＊ T

黨　*Rōdō* a retainer.

郵　YŪ mail; post-station.　八

券　*Yūken* postage-stamp.

便　*Yūbin* post; mail.

便切手　*Yūbin-kitte* postage-stamp.

便局　*Yūbin-kyoku* post-office.

便爲替　*Yūbin-kawase* postal money order.

便函　*Yūbin-bako* post-box; pillar-box.

送　*Yūsō* to send by post.

船　*Yūsen* a mail-steamer; abb. of N.Y.K.

税　*Yūzei* postage.

部　BU part; section; copy of a book; bureau. (*Be*).

＊ᵀ郎→163,7

（八〇）

下 *Buka* a subordinate (soldiers; officials, etc.).

分 *Bubun* part; section.

内 *Bunai* military (or naval) circles, services.

門 *Bumon* a class; department.

屋 *Heya* room.

員 *Buin* the staff.

隊 *Butai* detachment; troops.

署 *Busho* allotment of service.

落 *Buraku* tribe; village.

類 *Burui* class; kind; order.

T郭 KAKU. *Kuruwa* an enclosure; fortification.

*1 公 *Hototogisu; kakkō* cuckoo.

九 都 TO; TSU. *Miyako* capital: *subete* all; generally. (*Kuni*). →163,8 *1T

下 *Toka* in the capital.

市 *Toshi* city.

合 *Tsugō* arrangement; convenience; opportunity.

度 *Tsudo* every time.

會 *Tokai* city.

鄙 *Tohi* city and country; metropolitan and provincial.

*2 督 *Totoku* a governor-general.

一〇 鄉 KYŌ; GŌ. *Sato* country place; village; one's native place. 163,9 *2T

土 *Kyōdo* one's native place.

里 *Kyōri* home; one's native place.

鄙 HI. *Hina* the country: *iyashii* mean; low; rustic.　一　一

鄰 See T隣 170,12.　三

鄭 TEI kind; polite.

重 *Teichō* courteous; polite.

酉

一六四

Called *Hiyomi-no-tori*.

酉 YŪ. *Tori* 10th zodiacal sign, the bird. See Introduction 42, 43.

酎 CHŪ strong liquor; alcohol.　三

T酌 SHAKU to weigh; consider. *Ku(mu)* to dip out or ladle *sake*.

婦 *Shakufu* waitress.

量 *Shakuryō* to weigh; consider.

T配 HAI. *Kuba(ru)* to distribute: *meawa(su)* to marry.

下 *Haika* under the command.

付 *Haifu* distribution.

布 *Haifu* distribute.

合 *Haigō* distribution; disposition; combination; match.

列 *Hairetsu* arrangement.

偶 *Haigū* a couple; spouse.

偶者 *Haigūsha* spouse.

（三）配

達 *Haitatsu* delivery; to distribute.

置 *Haichi* to arrange; set in order.

當 *Haitō* apportionment; distribution, dividend.

慮 *Hairyo* trouble; anxiety.

劑 *Haizai* dispensation.

屬 *Haizoku* attachment. *

五 酣 KAN. *Takenawa* at its height; the acme.

T 酢 SAKU; SO sour. *Su* vinegar.

六 酩酊 *Meitei* drunkenness.

T 酪 RAKU cream; cheese.

T 酬 SHŪ. *Muku(y)iru)* to repay; give back.

七 酷 KOKU. *Hidoi* excessive; very; painful: *mugoi* cruel.

T

似 *Kokuji* close resemblance.

使 *Kokushi* work one's servants hard.

烈 *Kokuretsu* severe.

評 *Kokuhyō* severe criticism.

暑 *Kokusho* severe summer.

遇 *Kokugū* maltreatment.

T 酵 KŌ. *Moto* materials of *sake*.

母 *Kōbo* yeast; ferment.

T 酸 SAN acid; vinegar. *Sui* sour.

* T 酔 →164,8

化 *Sanka* oxidation.

味 *Sammi; sumi* acid taste.

性 *Sansei* acidity.

素 *Sanso* oxygen.

鼻 *Sambi* disastrous.

醋 SAKU. *Su* vinegar.

醉 SUI. *Yo(u)* (lit. st. ェフ; coll. ヨフ; see Introduction 40 to be intoxicated, sea-sick. →164,4 T *

生夢死 *Suiseimushi* dream one's life away.

狂 *Suikyō* becoming violent by intoxication; freak.

拂 *Yoppara(u)* to get tipsy.

眼 *Suigan* intoxicated eyes.

態 *Suitai* drunkenness.

漢 *Suikan* drunken fellow.

醇 JUN strong *sake*; completely.

化 *Junka* idealization.

乎 *Junko* pure.

醒 SEI. *Sa(meru)* to awake; become sober.

T 醜 SHŪ to hate. *Minikui; shiko* ugly.

名 *Shūmei* infamy.

行 *Shūkō* ignominious conduct.

婦 *Shūfu* ugly woman.

惡 *Shūaku* ugliness.

業 *Shūgyō* shameful calling.

（七）

八

九

一〇

(一〇)

業婦 *Shūgyōfu* woman of ill fame.

聞 *Shūbun* scandal; infamy.

態 *Shūtai* disagreeable behaviour; unseemly sight.

類 *Shūrui* corrupt elements.

二　醬油 *Shōyu* soy.

醫 I. *Iya(su)* to cure. →23, 5 T

者 *Isha* doctor; physician.

師 *Ishi* physician.

院 *Iin* doctor's office.

術 *Ijutsu* medical science.

療 *Iryō* medical treatment.

藥 *Iyaku* medicine.

二　醱 HATSU to brew.

酵 *Hakkō* fermentation.

二三　醵 KYO to contribute.

出 *Kyoshutsu* contribution.

金 *Kyokin* contribution.

一七　釀 JŌ. *Kamo(su)* to brew. →164, 13 T *

造 *Jōzō* brewing.

一六五　　釆

When at the left it is called *Nogome-hen.*

* 釀 →164, 17
T

釆 HAN; BEN. *Waka(tsu)* to divide; distinguish. Often used mistakenly for 采 87,4.

彩 See 彩 59,8.　三

T釈 See 釋 165,13.　四

悉 SHITSU. *Kotogotoku* all: *tsuku(su)* to exhaust. 【心】

皆 *Shikkai* all.

釉藥 *Yūyaku; uwa-gusuri* glaze.　五

T番 BAN number; guard; watch; turn: BA. *Tsuga-(h)eru): tsu ̄a(u)* to pair; copulate: *tsugai* a pair (male and female). 【田】

人 *Bannin* caretaker; watchman.

外 *Bangai* extra.

地 *Banchi* house number.

組 *Bangumi* programme.

號 *Bangō* number.

頭 *Bantō* clerk.

釋 SHAKU to understand; Buddha: SEKI. *To(ku); yuru(su)* to unfasten; set free; let go. →165, 4 T　一三

放 *Shakuhō* to discharge; set at liberty.

明 *Shakumei* explanation.

迦 *Shaka* Gautama (founder of Buddhism).

尊 *Shakuson* founder of Buddhism.

然 *Shakuzen* clearly understand.

一六六 里

When at the left it is called
Sato-hen.

T 里 RI unit of length: see
Introduction 44. *Sato*
village.

子 *Satogo* child sent out to
nurse.

昂 *Riyon* Lyons.

程 *Ritei* mileage.

歸 *Satogaeri* bride's first visit
to her parents after wed-
ding.

四 T 野 YA. *No* moor; wild plain;
field; the country.

人 *Yajin* a rustic.

牛 *Yagyū* wild ox; buffalo.

分 *Nowaki* autumn (or winter)
storm.

心 *Yashin* ambition.

生 *Yasei* wild.

外 *Yagai* fields; the country.

合 *Yagō* illicit intercourse.

州 *Yashū* another name for the
province of Shimotsuke.

性 *Yasei* unpolished nature.

卑 *Yahi* vulgar.

良 *Nora* field; moor.

郎 *Yarō* low fellow; rustic;
you rascal!

原 *Nohara* a plain; moor.

砲 *Yahō* field-gun.

（四〇）

宿 *Nojuku* camping out.

球 *Yakyū* baseball.

菜 *Yasai* vegetables.

暮 *Yabo* boorish.

趣 *Yashu* rural beauty.

戰 *Yasen* field operations.

營 *Yaei* encampment.

邊 *Nobe* field; moor.

獸 *Yajū* wild animal.

黨 *Yatō* party out of power.

蠻 *Yaban* savage.

一六七 金

When at the left it is called
Kane-hen.

T 金 KIN; KON gold. *Kane*
metal; money.

力 *Kinryoku* power of money.

子 *Kinsu* money; cash:
Kaneko p. n.

巾 *Kanakin* shirting.

切聲 *Kanakirigoe* shrill
voice.

主 *Kinshu* patron; capitalist.

目 *Kaneme* value.

色 *Konjiki* golden colour.

言 *Kingen* golden saying;
maxim.

利 *Kinri* interest (on money).

物 *Kanamono* hardware.

枝玉葉 *Kinshi-gyokuyō* the
Imperial family.

462

星 *Kinsei* Venus (astron).

持 *Kanemochi* a rich man.

科玉條 *Kinka-gyokujō* most precious rule.

廻 *Kanemawari* pecuniary condition.

庫 *Kinko* safe; treasury.

高 *Kindaka* amount of money.

員 *Kin-in* money; cash.

魚 *Kingyo* goldfish.

婚式 *Kinkon-shiki* golden wedding.

貨 *Kinka* gold coin.

剛石 *Kongōseki; daiamondo* diamond.

貸 *Kanekashi* money-lender.

策 *Kinsaku* plan for raising money.

塊 *Kinkai* gold bullion.

蒔繪 *Kin-makie* gold lacquer.

殿玉樓 *Kinden-gyokurō* magnificent palaces.

槌 *Kanazuchi* hammer.

遣 *Kanezukai* money-spending.

髮 *Kimpatsu* golden hair.

滿家 *Kimmanka* rich man.

盥 *Kanadarai* metal basin.

錢 *Kinsen* money.

融 *Kin-yū* circulation of money; state of exchange.

鵄勳章 *Kinshi-kunshō* the Order of the Golden Kite.

儲 *Kanemōke* money-making.

鍍金 *Kim-mekki* gilding.

曜 *Kin-yō* Friday.

屬 *Kinzoku* metal.

額 *Kingaku* sum of money.

ᵀ針 SHIN. *Hari* needle; pin; sting (of insect). 二

小棒大 *Shinshō-bōdai* exaggeration.

仕事 *Hari-shigoto* needlework.

金 *Harigane* wire.

路 *Shinro* course; direction.

釘 TEI. *Kugi* nail; peg.

鈕 KŌ. *Botan* button; stud. 三

釧 SEN bracelet.

路 *Kushiro* p. n.

ᵀ釣 CHŌ. *Tsu(ru)* to fish: *tsuri* change; small coins; money returned when paying bill.

合 *Tsuriai* balance.

込 *Tsuri-ko(mu)* to entice.

錢 *Tsurisen* change; small coins; money returned when paying bill.

欽 KIN to reverence. 【欠】 四

定 *Kintei* compiled by Imperial order.

ᵀ鈍 DON. *Nibui; noroi* dull; blunt; slow; foolish: *nibu(ru)* to be blunt.

才 *Donsai* stupidity.

物 *Dombutsu* blockhead.

五
T 鉛 EN. *Namari* lead (metal).

筆 *Empitsu* pencil.

鈿 TEN; DEN. *Kanzashi* a hair ornament.

T 鈴 REI. *Suzu* spherical bell: *rin* small bell.

生 *Suzunari* to hang in clusters.

鉤 KŌ. *Kagi* hook: *maga(ru)* to be bent.

T 鉄 See 鐵 167,13.

鉢 HATSU. *Hachi* bowl; basin.

卷 *Hachimaki* towel or handkerchief tied round the head.

植 *Hachiue* potted-plant.

鉞 ETSU. *Masakari* large axe.

鉈 *Nata* hatchet.

鉋 HŌ. *Kanna* plane (carpenter's).

* 屑 *Kannakuzu* shavings.

六 鉒 SEN balance; scales; to calculate; weigh.

衡 *Senkō* to select; investigate.

銛 SEN. *Mori* harpoon.

T 銘 MEI name; epitaph; to name; record.

茶 *Meicha* superior tea.

酒 *Meishu* superior *sake*.

酒屋 *Meishuya* bawdy-house.

* T 鉱 →167,15

鉾 *Hoko* spear.

T 銅 DŌ. *Akagane; aka* copper.

版 *Dōban* copper-plate.

貨 *Dōka* copper coin.

像 *Dōzō* bronze statue.

銕 See 鐵 167,13.

T 銀 GIN. *Shirogane* silver.

世界 *Ginsekai* snow scene.

行 *Ginkō* Bank.

杏 *Ichō; ginnan* maidenhair-tree.

座 *Ginza* p. n.

貨 *Ginka* silver coin.

婚式 *Ginkon-shiki* silver wedding.

鍍金 *Gimmekki* silver plating.

T 錢 See 錢 167,8.

T 銑鐵 *Sentetsu* pig-iron.

T 銃 JŪ. *Tsutsu* rifle; gun.

砲 *Jūhō* guns.

殺 *Jūsatsu* shoot to death.

劍 *Jūken* bayonet.

獵 *Jūryō* hunting.

銚子 *Chōshi* a *sake* bottle; also p. n.

鋒 HŌ point of a weapon.
Hoko spear.

鋩 *Hōbō* sword-point.

七

464

（七）

鑄　See 鑄 167,14.

銷　Shō to erase.

沈　Shōchin to be despondent.

夏　Shōka to pass the summer.

鋪　See 舗 135,9.

鋤　Jo. *Suki* spade; hoe: *su(ku)* to dig.

鋏　Kyō. *Hasami* scissors.

銳　Ei. *Surudoi* sharp; pointed.
→銳 T

利　*Eiri* sharp; pointed.

兵　*Eihei* efficient army.

敏　*Eibin* sagacious; clever.

意　*Eii* zeal.

鋒　*Eihō* the onset.

鋲　Byō rivet; nail; tack.

（八）T錘　Sui. *Omori* weight used in weighing.

錏　A. *Shi or* armour protecting the neck.

錐　Sui cone. *Kiri* gimlet.

鋸　Kyo. *Nokogiri* saw.

T錯　Saku to be in disorder; to mix.

亂　*Sakuran* to be deranged.

誤　*Sakugo* error.

綜　*Sakusō* complication.

雜　*Sakuzatsu* complexity.

＊ T録 →167,8

覺　*Sakkaku* illusion.

錮　Ko to close up; hard.

錚　Sō a bell; sound of a bell.

々　*Sōsō* prominent; conspicuous.

錆　Shō. *Sabi* rust: *sa(biru)* to rust.

T鋼　Kō. *Hagane* steel.

鐵　*Kōtetsu* steel.

錦　Kin your (honorific). *Nishiki* embroidered silk; brocade.

旗　*Kinki* the Imperial standard.

繪　*Nishikie* colour-print.

繡　*Kinshū* brocade.

錫　Seki; shaku. *Suzu* tin.

蘭　*Seiron* Ceylon.

録　Roku. *Shiru(su)* to record; write down; copy.
→167,7 ＊ T

T錠　Jō; tei lock.

前　*Jōmae* lock.

劑　*Jōzai* a tablet; pill.

錻力　*Buriki* tin-plate.

錢　Sen monetary unit, $\frac{1}{100}$ of yen. *Zeni; oashi* coin; money. →61,2 : 167,6 T

湯　*Sentō* bath-house; public bath.

465

九 鍾 SHŌ; SHU winecup. *Atsu-(meru)* to collect; assemble.

愛 *Shōai* love very much.

錨 BYŌ. *Ikari* anchor.

地 *Byōchi* anchoring place.

鍋 KA. *Nabe* pot; pan.

鍊 REN. *Ne(ru)* to temper; forge; drill (morally).

磨 *Remma* exercise; drilling.

鍬 SHŌ. *Kuwa* hoe; spade.

鍍 TO. *Mekki* plating; gilding.

金 *Mekki; tokin* plating.

T 鍛 TAN. *Kita(heru)* to temper; forge.

冶屋 *Kajiya* blacksmith.

練 *Tanren* diligent practice.

鍊 *Tanren* diligent practice.

鍵 KEN. *Kagi* key.

盤 *Kemban* key (piano, etc.).

一〇 鎧 GAI. *Yoroi* coat of mail; armour.

袖 *Gaishū* armour-sleeve.

鎗 SŌ. *Yari* spear.

鎔 YŌ. *I(-ru)* to cast (metal): *toka(su); toroka(su)* to melt.

解 *Yōkai* melting.

鎌 REN; KEN. *Kama* sickle.

倉 *Kamakura* p. n.

鎚 TSUI. *Tsuchi* hammer.

鎮 CHIN. *Shizu(meru)* to calm; tranquilize. →鏡 T

火 *Chinka* putting out a fire.

守 *Chinju* to protect; guardian god of a place.

守府 *Chinjufu* admiralty.

定 *Chintei* pacify.

座 *Chinza* to be dedicated to.

痛 *Chintsū* alleviation of pain.

撫 *Chimbu* suppress; subdue.

壓 *Chin-atsu* suppression.

靜 *Chinsei* subside; pacify.

鎖 SA. *Kusari* chain : *toza(su)* to shut : *chein* chain (measure, 22 yards).

↓國 *Sakoku* closing of the country. →鑰 *Sayaku* key. →鎖 T

鎖 See prec.

鏡 KYŌ. *Kagami* looking-glass. →鎮 T

餅 *Kagamimochi* round and flat rice-cake.

臺 *Kyōdai* mirror-stand.

鏤 RU. *Chiriba(meru); e(ru)* to engrave; carve.

T 鐘 SHŌ. *Kane* a bell.

鐚 *Bita* iron coin of very little value.

一文 *Bita-ichimon* small coin.

三 鐸 TAKU large bell.

鐵 TETSU. *Kurogane* iron.
→167,5 T : 167,6

工場 *Tekkōjō* iron foundry.

石 *Tesseki* iron and stone; adamant; firm.

面皮 *Tetsumempi* brazen-faced.

柵 *Tessaku* iron fence.

相 *Tesshō* Minister of Railways.

骨 *Tekkotsu* iron frame.

拳 *Tekken* fist.

砲 *Teppō* gun; rifle.

瓶 *Tetsubin* iron-kettle.

窓 *Tessō* iron window; prison.

條網 *Tetsujōmō* wire-entanglements.

筋混凝土 *Tekkin-konkuriito* reinforced concrete.

葉 *Buriki* tin-plate.

道 *Tetsudō* railway.

道大臣 *Tetsudō-daijin* Minister of Railways.

道省 *Tetsudōshō* Department of Railways.

管 *Tekkan* iron pipe.

製 *Tessei* made of iron.

壁 *Teppeki* iron wall.

橋 *Tekkyō* iron bridge.

蹄 *Tettei* iron horseshoe.

鎚 *Tettsui* iron hammer; hard blow.

鎖 *Tessa* iron chain.

鑑 KAN. *Kagami* mirror; example: *kangami(-ru)* to regard as an example; discriminate. 一四
→T 鑑

札 *Kansatsu* government license.

別 *Kambetsu* to discriminate.

定 *Kantei* expert opinion; valuation.

賞 *Kanshō* appreciation.

識 *Kanshiki* judgment; discernment.

鑄 CHŪ. *I(-ru)* to cast (metal). →167,7 T

物 *Imono* casting.

造 *Chūzō* to cast.

鑛 KŌ ore; mineral; raw metal. →167,5 T ⁕ 一五

山 *Kōzan* a mine.

石 *Kōseki* ore.

坑 *Kōkō* mine; quarry.

物 *Kōbutsu* minerals; raw metal.

泉 *Kōsen* mineral spring.

脈 *Kōmyaku* vein of ore.

業 *Kōgyō* mining industry.

鑰 YAKU lock; to lock up. 一七

鑵 See 罐 121,18. 一八

鑽 SAN to cut; go deep into. 一九

鑿 SAKU to dig. *Nomi* chisel. 二〇

井 *Sakusei* digging of a well.

一六八 長

T 長 Chō chief; head; senior; to grow; increase; advance; make progress. *Nagai; tokoshie* long; for ever. (*Osa*).

上 *Chōjō* senior; superior.

大息 *Chōdaisoku* heavy sigh.

久 *Chōkyū* continuance; permanence.

女 *Chōjo* eldest daughter.

日月 *Chōjitsugetsu* long time.

月 *Nagatsuki* poetical name f r 9th month (old cal.).

方形 *Chōhōkei* oblong.

幼 *Chōyō* the old and the young.

州 *Chōshū* another name for the province of Nagato.

老 *Chōrō* superior.

谷 *Hase* p. n.

男 *Chōnan* eldest son.

足 *Chōsoku* great stride; rapid.

門 *Nagato* p. n.

所 *Chōsho* strong point.

屋 *Nagaya* tenement-house.

官 *Chōkan* a chief.

命 *Chōmei* long life.

者 *Chōsha* one's elders; a sage; virtuous man: *chōja* wealthy person.

春 *Chōshun* Chang Chung.

徑 *Chōkei* length; long diameter.

座 *Chōza* staying long (on a visit).

野 *Nagano* p. n.

崎 *Nagasaki* p. n.

逝 *Chōsei* to pass away; die.

短 *Chōtan* long and short; length; merits and defects.

圍 *Chōi* to besiege for a long time.

椅子 *Nagaisu* sofa.

閑 *Nodoka* pleasant; mild; cheerful; tranquil.

期 *Chōki* long period.

廣舌 *Chōkōzetsu* rant; a long speech.

閥 *Chōbatsu* the Chōshū exclusivism.

壽 *Chōju* long life.

談義 *Nagadangi* long-winded speech.

肆 See 129,7.　　六

髪 See 190,5.　　八

門 一六九

Generally embraces the rest of the characte ; then called *Mon-gamae* or *Kado-gamae*.

T 門 MON sect; lineage; family. *Kado; to* gate; door; outside entrance; opening.

人 *Monjin* pupil; disciple.

下 *Monka* pupil; disciple.

口 *Kadoguchi* a door.

戸 *Monko* a door; entrance; gate.

生 *Monsei* pupil; disciple.

出 *Kadode* departure.

外漢 *Mongaikan* outsider.

司 *Moji* p. n.

地 *Monchi* lineage.

先 *Kadosaki* the front of a house.

弟 *Montei* pupil; disciple.

並 *Kadonami* from door to door.

松 *Kadomatsu* New Year's pine-decoration.

限 *Mongen* closing-time.

前拂 *Monzembarai* dismissing callers.

番 *Momban* gate-keeper.

違 *Kadochigai* knock at a wrong door.

閥 *Mombatsu* good family.

鑑 *Monkan* a gate-pass.

一 閂 SAN; SEN. *Kannuki* gate-bar.

二 閃 SEN. *Hirame(ku)* to flash.

光 *Senkō* glitter.

三 閊 *Tsuka(h)eru* to be obstructed.

問 MON. *To(u)* to question; inquire; examine into; visit.【口】

合 *Toiawase* inquiry.

屋 *Toiya; ton-ya* office for wholesale transactions; commission agent.

責 *Monseki* impeachment.

答 *Mondō* questions and answers.

題 *Mondai* problems.

T閉 HEI. *To(jiru); toza(su); shi(meru)* to close; shut; stop up.

口 *Heikō* defeat; to be beaten.

店 *Heiten* closing of a shop.

廷 *Heitei* closing of a court.

塲 *Heijō* closing of a place.

會 *Heikai* close a meeting.

鎖 *Heisa* closing; locking.

閏 JUN. *Urū* leap year. 四

T間 KAN; KEN unit of length; see Introduction 44. *A da* interval; space; between; among; during; as; because (in epist. st): *ai; ma* between (of time); interval; space; room. (*Hazama*).

一髮 *Kan-ippatsu* hair's breadth.

々 *Mama* now and then.

口 *Maguchi* frontage.

合 *Ma-ai* interval; distance.

取 *Madori* arrangement of rooms (in a house).

近 *Majikai* very near.

拔 *Manuke* a fool; stupidity.

食 *Kanshoku* eat between meals.

469

（四）

間

柄　*Aidagara* terms; relations.

接　*Kansetsu* indirect.

借　*Magari* rent a room.

然　*Kanzen* find fault with.

道　*Kandō* secret path.

歇　*Kanketsu* intermittence.

違　*Machigai* mistake.

隔　*Kankaku* space; distance.

隙　*Kangeki* chink; interstice.

際　*Magiwa* the verge; eve.

諜　*Kanchō* spy.

斷　*Kandan* intermission.

開　KAI. *Hira(ku)*: *a(keru)*; *a(ku)* to open; bloom: *hira(keru)* to become civilized; be open.

化　*Kaika* civilization.

拓　*Kaitaku* bringing under cultivation; colonization.

始　*Kaishi* to begin; commence.

放　*Kaihō* to open.

店　*Kaiten* open a shop.

封　*Kaifū* to break a seal; open a letter or sealed packet.

城　*Kaijō* surrender of fortress.

院　*Kaiin* opening of the Diet, etc.

設　*Kaisetsu* open; establish.

通　*Kaitsū* opening for traffic.

閉　*Kaihei* opening and shutting.

票　*Kaihyō* opening of the ballot.

（四）

發　*Kaihatsu* enlightenment.

港塲　*Kaikōjō* open port.

陳　*Kaichin* to state; set forth.

會　*Kaikai* opening a meeting.

業　*Kaigyō* opening of a business.

演　*Kaien* raising of the curtain.

墾　*Kaikon* breaking new soil.

闢　*Kaibyaku* the creation; foundation.

閑　KAN quiet. *Hima* leisure.

日月　*Kanjitsugetsu* leisure.

地　*Kanchi* quiet region.

却　*Kankyaku* negligence.

居　*Kankyo* secluded life.

雅　*Kanga* refined; elegant.

話　*Kanwa* quiet conversation; idle talk.

散　*Kansan* leisure; quiet.

暇　*Kanka* leisure time.

靜　*Kansei* tranquillity.

職　*Kanshoku* easy post.

悶　MON. *Moda(y)eru* to be in agony; distress. 【心】

々　*Mommon* in distress.

死　*Monshi* to die in agony.

着　*Monchaku* quarrel; trouble.

絶　*Monzetsu* swoon.

閙　See 鬧 191,5.

五

六 閨 KEI room. *Neya* sleeping-room.

秀 *Keishū* eminent woman.

閥 *Keibatsu* influence of one's wife's family.

T 閣 KAKU tower; palace.

下 *Kakka* Your Honour; Your Excellency.

員 *Kakuin* Cabinet member.

臣 *Kakushin* Cabinet Ministers.

僚 *Kakuryō* Cabinet Ministers.

議 *Kakugi* Cabinet conference.

T 聞 BUN; MON news. *Ki(ku)*; *kiko(y)eru* to hear; ask; enquire. 【耳】

分 *Kikiwa(keru)* to understand.

召 *Kikoshime(su)* hear; learn; have.

合 *Kikiawa(seru)* to inquire; refer to.

糺 *Kiki-tada(su)* to ascertain by hearing.

知 *Bunchi* to learn; be informed.

咎 *Kiki-toga(meru)* to reprove.

流 *Kikinaga(su)* take no notice.

傳 *Kiki-tsutae* hearing from others.

道らく *Kikunaraku* we hear that.

說らく *Kikunaraku* we hear that.

T 関 See 關 169,11.

T 閥 BATSU clique; family station; merit. (六)

族 *Batsuzoku* noble lineage.

鬪 See 鬬 191,6.

閭 RYO entrance of a village; 七 village; gate.

閱 ETSU. *Kemisuru* (irreg.) to inspect; review; examine; read; elapse. → 閱 T

兵 *Eppei* inspection of troops.

歷 *Etsureki* past history; career.

覽 *Etsuran* to read over.

讀 *Etsudoku* perusal.

閻魔 *Emma* King of Hades. 八

閾 YOKU. *Shikii*; *shikimi* threshold.

闊 KATSU long time. *Hiroi* 九 broad; wide.

闇 AN dark. *Yami* darkness.

打 *Yamiuchi* to attack in the dark.

黑 *Ankoku* darkness.

路 *Yamiji* a dark road.

闌 RAN. *Takenawa* at its height.

闔 KŌ to close; door. 一〇

T 鬭 See 鬬 191,10.

闖 CHIN precipitately.

入 *Chinnyū* inroad.

471

關 KETSU gate; to make a mistake. *Ka(keru)*; *ka(ku)* to lack.

下 *Kekka* the throne.

關 KAN. *Seki* barrier: *kakawa(ru)* to participate; concern; be related to; be concerned in. →169,6 下

心 *Kanshin* anxiety; concern.

西 *Kansai* p. n.

所 *Sekisho* a barrier place.

東 *Kantō* p. n.

門 *Kammon* a barrier.

取 *Sekitori* champion wrestler.

係 *Kankei* relation; connection.

係者 *Kankeisha* people concerned in.

税 *Kanzei* customs duty.

節 *Kansetsu* joint.

聯 *Kanren* connection.

闡 SEN clear. *Hira(ku)* to open.

明 *Semmei* to explain.

闢 BYAKU; HEKI to open.

闥 TATSU door; gate-bar.

一七〇 阜

In composition it always takes a modified form ß: it is placed at the left and is called *Kozatohen*.

阜 FU; FŪ large. *Oka* mound.

頭 *Futō* wharf.

阡 SEN ridge; furrow. Often used in writing for 千 thousand.

防 BŌ; HŌ dike. *Fuse(gu)* to prevent; ward off; defend.

止 *Bōshi* check; prevention.

水 *Bōsui* water-proof.

火 *Bōka* fire-proof.

波堤 *Bōhatei* breakwater.

長 *Bōchō* the provinces of Suō and Nagato.

備 *Bōbi* defence.

遏 *Bōatsu* prevention.

腐 *Bōfu* prevention against putrefaction.

衛 *Bōei* defence.

禦 *Bōgyo* defence.

阪 HAN; BAN. *Saka* an incline

東 *Bandō* another name for the *Kantō* 關東.

神 *Hanshin* Ōsaka-Kōbe.

阨 YAKU; AKU; AI steep; narrow.

阻 SO to separate from; steep. *Haba(mu)* to prevent; stop.

止 *Soshi* to stop; check.

害 *Sogai* to check; hinder.

隔 *Sokaku* become distant.

阿 A corner. *Omone(ru)* to flatter.

（五）

片 *Ahen* opium.

呆 *Ahō* a fool.

諛 *Ayu* flattery.

彌陀 *Amida* the name of Buddha.

附 FU to hand over; submit to. *Tsu(keru)* to attach; affix; add to: *tsu(ku)* to adhere to: *tsuki* attached to; way.

火 *Tsukebi* arson.

加 *Fuka* supplement; addition.

合 *Tsukiai* associating with; keeping company.

近 *Fukin* neighbourhood.

和雷同 *Fuwaraidō* chime in.

則 *Fusoku* additional rule.

記 *Fuki* appendix.

託 *Futaku* commitment.

帶 *Futai* incidental.

添人 *Tsukisoi-nin* attendant; suite.

着 *Fuchaku* to adhere.

箋 *Fusen* tag; label.

錄 *Furoku* supplement; appendix.

隨 *Fuzui* to attend; follow.

属 *Fuzoku* belonging to; attached to.

属具 *Fuzokugu* accessories; fittings.

陀 DA; TA steep.

六

陋 *Rō* low; mean; narrow.

（六）

劣 *Rōretsu* low; mean.

習 *Rōshū* bad custom.

巷 *Rōkō* dirty side street.

T 降 KŌ; GŌ. *Fu(ru)* to fall (sad of rain, snow, etc.): *kuda(ru)* to surrender; yield; submit; descend: *kuda(su); oro(su); o(riru)* to send down; descend.

伏 *Kōfuku* to surrender.

雨 *Kōu* rainfall.

服 *Kōfuku* to surrender.

參 *Kōsan* to surrender.

嫁 *Kōka* marrying of a royal Princess to a subject.

誕 *Kōtan* birth.

壇 *Kōdan* leave a platform.

T 限 GEN. *Kagiri* limit; end; utmost degree: *kagi(ru)* to limit; fix or restrict: *kiri* limit; end.

定 *Gentei* limitation.

度 *Gendo* limit.

界 *Genkai* limit; boundary.

陜 Kū steep.

七

陞 SHŌ. *Nobo(ru)* to rise; advance: *nobo(seru); nobo(su)* to raise in rank.

任 *Shōnin* promotion.

敍 *Shōjo* promotion in rank.

爵 *Shōshaku* promotion in peerage.

T 陛 HEI. *Kizahashi* the steps of the throne.

下 *Heika* His (Your) Majesty.

(七〇)

陣 JIN camp.

立 *Jindate* plan of campaign.

地 *Jinchi* fortified position.

形 *Jinkei* battle formation.

取 *Jindo(ru)* to encamp.

容 *Jin-yō* camp formation.

笠 *Jingasa* rank and file of a party; a soldier's hat.

頭 *Jintō* at the head of the troops.

營 *Jin-ei* encampment.

陟 CHOKU to rise; advance.

T**院** IN building for religious uses; school; (affixed to the names of several public institutions, colleges, hospitals, etc.).

外團 *Ingaidan* a party of non-parliamentary members.

議 *Ingi* decision of the House.

T**除** JO to subtract; divide: JI. *Nozo(ku ; no(keru)* to exclude: *yo(keru)* to get out of the way.

外 *Jogai* exception; exclusion.

斥 *Joseki* exclusion.

名 *Jomei* expulsion.

却 *Jokyaku* to exclude; reject.

夜 *Joya* New Year's Eve.

*1 隊 *Jotai* disbandment.

八 T**陸** RIKU; ROKU. *Oka; kuga* land.

上 *Rikujō* land; shore.

地 *Rikuchi* land (as distinguished from water).

*1 陷 T→170,8

軍 *Rikugun* army.

前 *Rikuzen* p. n.

相 *Rikushō* Minister of War.

海軍 *Rikkaigun* army and navy.

揚 *Rikuage* disembarkment.

路 *Rikuro* land journey; by land.

戰 *Rikusen* land-battle.

離 *Rikuri* dazzling.

續 *Rikuzoku* successively.

陷 KAN. *Ochi-i(ru)* to fall; fall into: *otoshi-i(reru)* to ensnare; capture. →170, 8T * 2

沒 *Kambotsu* sinking.

穽 *Kansei* a pitfall.

落 *Kanraku* to fall in: subside; fall; surrender.

T**陪** BAI to be piled up; to accompany; attend on.

食 *Baishoku* to eat with a superior especially royalty.

席 *Baiseki* being present not on one's own business but as an assistant or attendant.

席判事 *Baiseki-hanji* associate judges.

乘 *Baijō* riding with one's superior.

從 *Baijū* to attend on; follow.

賓 *Baihin* person invited with the guest of honour.

審官 *Baishinkan* jury.

審制度 *Baishin-seido* the jury system.

觀 *Baikan* see with one's superior.

(八〇)

474

（八）T

陶 TŌ pottery; porcelain.

冶 *Tōya* education; cultivation.

器 *Tōki* porcelain; pottery.

然 *Tōzen* congenially.

T **陳** CHIN. *Tsura(neru)*; *no-(beru)* to enumerate; state: *nara(beru)* to show: *furui* old.

列 *Chinretsu* exhibition; show.

者 *Nobureba* what I have to say is.........(epist. st.)

述 *Chinjutsu* to state; declare.

套 *Chintō* antiquated.

情 *Chinjō* statement of opinion; declaration.

腐 *Chimpu* antiquated.

謝 *Chinsha* apologize.

T **陵** RYŌ hill. *Misasagi* Imperial tomb.

駕 *Ryōga* excel.

T **陰** IN negative; female principle in nature. *Kage* shade; behind; shady place; dark: *hisoka* secret.
→170, 9

氣 *Inki* gloomy.

部 *Imbu* privy parts.

雲 *In-un* dark clouds.

陽 *In-yō* shade and sunshine; night and day; male and female principles in nature; negative and positive elements; the universe.

德 *Intoku* secret act of charity.

謀 *Imbō* secret plot or intrigue.

*²隆 T→170,9

475

（八）

險 *Inken* subtle; crafty.

欝 *In-utsu* gloomy; melancholy.
*2　　　　　　*3

隆 RYŪ. *Sakan* prosperous: 九 *takai* high. →170,8 T *²

々 *Ryūryū* high; prosperous; flourishing.

昌 *Ryūshō* prosperity.

起 *Ryūki* rising.

盛 *Ryūsei* prosperity.

T **階** KAI storey; floor; grade; quality. *Kizahashi* stairs; ladder.

上 *Kaijō* upstairs.

段 *Kaidan* steps; staircase.

級 *Kaikyū* rank; degree.

梯 *Kaitei* guide; ladder.

隋 ZUI name of an old country in China.

隅 GŪ. *Sumi* corner.

々 *Sumi-zumi* every corner; everywhere.

田川 *Sumida-gawa* p. n.

T **陽** YŌ positive; male principle in nature; sun; sunshine. *Arawa* open; frank.

春 *Yōshun* spring (season).

氣 *Yōki* weather; cheerful.

隊 TAI company (of soldiers); squadron; regiment; crew; crowd. →隊 T

伍 *Taigo* ranks.

商 *Taishō* caravan.

*³T 險 →170,13

（九）隖 WAI. *Kuma* dark spot; corner.

T 隨 See 隨 170,13.

隂 See T 陰 170,8.

一〇 隘 AI narrow; to obstruct.

T 隔 KAKU distance. *Heda-(teru)* to separate; be separated from.

日 *Kakujitsu* alternate days; every other day.

世 *Kakusei* another age; another world.

絕 *Kakuzetsu* separated from.

意 *Kakui* reserve.

靴搔痒 *Kakkasōyō* irritating.

離 *Kakuri* to be separated; be distant.

隙 See 隙 170,11.

一二 障 SHŌ to defend; support. *Sawari* obstacle; objection: *sawa(ru)* to affect; hinder; bar. → 障 T

子 *Shōji* sliding-door or window-sash covered with translucent paper.

害 *Shōgai* obstacle.

碍 *Shōgai* obstacle.

壁 *Shōheki* fence; barrier.

隙 GEKI. *Suki*: *hima* crack; opening; leisure.

間 *Sukima* crack; opening; intermission.

（一一）際 SAI occasion. *Kiwa* limit; edge.

物 *Kiwamono* things of the season.

限 *Saigen* limit.

涯 *Saigai* limit.

* 會 *Saikai* meet by chance.

一二 T 隣 RIN. *Tonari* neighbouring; a neighbour: *tona(ru)* to adjoin. → 163, 12

邦 *Rimpō* adjacent countries.

家 *Rinka* neighbouring house.

國 *Ringoku* neighbouring country.

接 *Rinsetsu* contiguity.

一三 隨 ZUI. *Shitaga(u)* to obey; follow: *shitagatte* accordingly; according to; correspondingly. → 170,9 T

一 *Zuiichi* has the force of a superlative; the first; the best, etc.

分 *Zuibun* very; extremely; rather; fairly.

行 *Zuikō* attendance on a journey.

伴 *Zuihan* accompany.

時 *Zuiji* when necessary; at any time.

員 *Zuiin* suite; party; attendant.

處 *Zuisho* everywhere.

喜 *Zuiki* adoration.

筆 *Zuihitsu* jottings.

意 *Zuii* freedom; option; at will.

（一三）
隧 SUI tunnel; underground passage; to fall.

道 *Tonneru; suidō* tunnel.

險 KEN. *Kewashii* steep; precipitous. →170, 8 T * ³

山 *Kenzan* a steep mountain.

吞 *Kennon* dangerous; risky.

阻 *Kenso* steep; dangerous.

峻 *Kenshun* steepness.

路 *Kenro* a steep path.

惡 *Ken-aku* steep; dangerous; disquieting.

―――

一四
隱 IN. *Kaku(reru)* to hide; be in retirement: *kaku(su)* to hide; conceal. →170, 11 T

立 *Kakushidate* concealment (of a fact, etc.).

岐 *Oki* p. n.

忍 *Innin* patience.

見 *Inken* appearance and disappearance.

居 *Inkyo* retirement; resignation of headship of house or family; person who has thus retired; old man.

家 *Kakurega* a hiding place.

匿 *Intoku* concealment.

退 *Intai* retirement.

密 *Immitsu* secret: *ommitsu* detective.

然 *Inzen* in practice.

遁 *Inton* retirement from the world.

遯 *Inton* retirement from the world.

蔽 *Impei* to conceal.

顯 *Inken* appear and disappear.

隶 一七一

隸 REI to belong to; to obey; servant.

屬 *Reizoku* being under the jurisdiction of.

隷 See prec.

―――

隹 一七二

It is called *Furu-tori.*

隼 JUN; SHUN. *Hayabusa* peregrine falcon. 二

人 *Haya o* people from Satsuma province.

隻 SEKI aux. num. for counting ships; one of a pair; one. (T)

手 *Sekishu* one hand.

句 *Sekiku* sentence.

眼 *Sekigan* one eye.

脚 *Sekkyaku* one leg.

影 *Sekiei* (foll. by neg.) no trace; no sign.

―――

集 SHŪ. *Atsuma(ru); tsudo(u)* to assemble: *atsu(meru)* to collect. 四 (T)

中 *Shūchū* concentration.

合 *Shūgō* collection; gathering.

金 *Shūkin* to collect money.

477

（四）集

配 *Shūhai* collection and delivery.

會 *Shūkai* meeting.

散 *Shūsan* gathering and dispersion.

散地 *Shūsanchi* distributing centre.

T 焦 SHŌ. *Koga(su)*; *koge(-ru)* to char; scorch: *koga(reru)* to long for: *ase(ru)* grow impatient, hurry; struggle. 【火】

土 *Shōdo* burnt ground; ashes.

心 *Shōshin* to be anxious.

眉 *Shōbi* impending.

慮 *Shōryo* anxious thoughts.

點 *Shōten* focus.

T 雄 YŪ bold; fearless; strong; vigorous. *Osu; o* male. (*O*).

々しい *Ooshii* manful; heroic.

大 *Yūdai* grandeur; magnificence.

飛 *Yūhi* to take a great leap; soar up.

健 *Yūken* vigorous.

姿 *Yūshi* a brave figure.

偉 *Yūi* imposing; strapping.

圖 *Yūto* an ambitious enterprise.

* 辯 *Yūben* eloquence.

五 雅 GA. *Miyabi; miyabiyaka* refined; elegant. (*Masa*). →172,4 * T

言 *Gagen* elegant words.

典 *Atens; Azensu* Athens.

*T 雅 →172,5

478

俗 *Gazoku* refined and vulgar.

致 *Gachi* good taste; artistic.

量 *Garyō* generosity.

號 *Gagō* pen-name.

趣 *Gashu* elegance.

懷 *Gakai* refined mind.

麗 *Garei* refined; elegant.

T 雑 See 雜 172,10. 六

T 雌 See 77,10. 【隹】

雜 See 雜 172,10. 九

雖 SUI. *Iedomo* although.

然 *Shikaredomo* but.

雛 SŪ; SU. *Hina* chicken; 一〇 small doll.

形 *Hinagata* pattern; form.

雞 See 鷄 196,10.

雜 ZATSU; ZŌ of various kinds; miscellaneous; coarse: roughly made. *Maji(ru)* to be mixed; assemble. →172,6 T : 172,9

巾 *Zōkin* house-cloth.

木 *Zōki* various trees.

用 *Zatsuyō* used for various purposes: *zōyō* miscellaneous expenses.

多 *Zatta* sundry.

兵 *Zōhyō* private (soldier).

居 *Zakkyo* mixed residence (foreigners among natives).

（一○）

沓 *Zattō* bustle.

炊 *Zōsui* medley soup.

念 *Zatsunen* idle thoughts.

書 *Zassho* pamphlet; miscellaneous books.

草 *Zassō* weed.

記 *Zakki* miscellany.

務 *Zatsumu* miscellaneous business.

貨 *Zakka* miscellaneous goods.

費 *Zappi* miscellaneous expenses.

然 *Zatsuzen* in confusion.

話 *Zatsuwa* desultory talk.

感 *Zakkan* miscellaneous thoughts.

種 *Zasshu* hybrid.

誌 *Zasshi* magazine.

談 *Zatsudan* idle talk.

T 離 RI. *Hana(su)* to separate; divide: *hana(reru)* to be separated from.

々 *Hanare-banare* separately.

別 *Ribetsu* parting; divorce.

座敷 *Hanare-zashiki* detached room.

宮 *Rikyū* Detached Palace.

婚 *Rikon* divorce.

陸 *Ririku* taking off (of aeroplanes).

間 *Rikan* to cause discord.

散 *Risan* dispersion.

緣 *Rien* divorce.

難 NAN danger; calamity. 一 一 *Katai; muzukashii; nikui* difficult, hard.
→172,10 * T

有 *Arigatai* (inverted order) thankful.

行 *Nangyō* asceticism.

局 *Nankyoku* grave situation.

事 *Nanji* difficult thing.

易 *Nan-i* hardness and easiness.

物 *Nambutsu* awkward fellow; to deal with thing hard to dispose of.

波 *Naniwa* old name for Ōsaka: *Namba* p. n.

破 *Nampa* shipwreck.

破船 *Nampasen* wrecked ship.

致 *Itashi-gatai* (inverted order) cannot.

病 *Nambyō* fatal disease.

產 *Nanzan* difficult labour; difficult delivery.

船 *Nansen* shipwreck.

問 *Nammon* a difficult question.

解 *Nankai* hard to understand.

詰 *Nankitsu* accusation.

澁 *Nanjū* trouble; distress.

儀 *Nangi* hardship.

題 *Nandai* difficult theme or subject; unreasonable proposal.

癖 *Nankuse* bad name; fault.

關 *Nankan* a barrier; difficulty.

讎 See 讐 149,16. 一五

一七三

雨

Almost always at the top;
then called *Ame-kammuri.*

T 雨 U. *Ame; same* rain.

上 *Ameagari* after rain.

戸 *Amado* outside shutter.

天 *Uten* rainy weather.

季 *Uki* rainy season.

模樣 *Amamoyō; amemoyō* threatening rain.

曇 *Amagumori* cloudy weather.

曝 *Amazirashi* exposure to rain.

露 *Uro* rain and dew.

續 *Amatsuzuki* long rain.

三 T 雪 SETSU. *Yuki* snow: *susu-(gu)* to wash; rinse.

洞 *Bombori* hand-lantern.

辱 *Setsujoku* to wipe out a humiliation.

崩 *Nadare* avalanche.

隱 *Setsuin; setchin* privy.

雫 *Shizuku* drop.

四 T 雲 UN. *Kumo* cloud.

上 *Unjō; kumo-no-ue* above the clouds; Imperial family; court.

水 *Unsui* clouds and water; itinerant priest.

母 *Umbo; kirara* mica.

行 *Kumoyuki* appearance of the clouds; the course of events.

泥の差 *Undei-no-sa* all the difference in the world.

雀 *Hibari* skylark.

散霧消 *Unsan-mushō* disappear; vanish.

霓 *Ungei* the threatening sky.

隱 *Kumogakure* disappearance.

霞 *Unka* enormous number of.

T 雷 RAI. *Kaminari; ikazuchi* thunder. 五

名 *Raimei* far-resounding name.

同 *Raidō* to adopt the opinions of others without reflection.

雨 *Rai-u* thunder-storm.

電 *Raiden* thunder and lightning.

霆 *Raitei* thunder.

鳴 *Raimei* thunder.

T 零 REI to fall. *Zero* zero.

時 *Reiji* twelve o'clock.

細 *Reisai* very little.

落 *Reiraku* ruin.

雹 HŌ; HAKU. *Hyō* hail.

T 電 DEN electricity; often used as abb., especially for *denshin* or *dempō. Inazuma* lightning.

480

（五）

力 *Denryoku* electric power.

文 *Dembun* text of a telegram.

光 *Denkō; inabikari* flash of lightning.

車 *Densha* electric-car.

池 *Denchi* battery.

命 *Demmei* order by telegraph.

柱 *Denchū* telegraph pole.

信 *Denshin* telegraph.

氣 *Denki* electricity.

送 *Densō* sending by telegraph.

流 *Denryū* electric current.

球 *Denkyū* bulb of electric lamp.

報 *Dempō* telegram.

話 *Denwa* telephone.

鈴 *Denrei* electric bell.

線 *Densen* electric wire or cable.

燈 *Dentō* electric lamp.

六 T 需 Ju. *Moto(meru)* to demand; claim; ask for.

要 *Juyō* demand.

給 *Jukyū* supply and demand.

七 T 靈 See 靈 173,16.

霄 SHŌ the sky; heavens.

壤の差 *Shōjō-no-sa* all the difference in the world.

T 震 SHIN to fear. *Furu(h)eru)* (coll.); *furu(u)* (lit. st.) to shake; quake.

（七）

上 *Furueaga(ru)* tremble violently.

死 *Shinshi* killed by lightning or earthquake.

災 *Shinsai* earthquake disaster.

動 *Shindō* shaking; vibration.

源 *Shingen* earthquake centre.

駭 *Shingai* to be astonished, horrified, shocked.

聲 *Furuegoe* trembling voice.

八

霑 TEN. *Uruo(u); uruo(su)* to become wet; soak.

霏 HI flight of the clouds; mist.

々 *Hihi* falling heavily (snow).

霖雨 *Rin-u; naga-ame* long rain.

霓 GEI rainbow:

九

T 霜 SŌ. *Shimo* frost.

柱 *Shimo-bashira* icy columns formed in frozen ground.

枯 *Shimogare* withered by the frost.

降 *Shimofuri* frost; pepper-and-salt (colour of cloth).

害 *Sōgai* damage from frost.

霙 EI. *Mizore* sleet.

霞 KA. *Kasumi* haze; mist: *kasu(mu)* to grow hazy; to grow dim.

關 *Kasumigaseki* p. n.; also, another name for the Foreign Office.

一T 霧　MU.　*Kiri* mist; fog.

雨　*Kiriame*; *kirisame* drizzling rain.

三 霰　SAN; SEN.　*Arare* hail.

三 霛　See 靈 173,16

T 露　RO abb. of *Roshiya* (Russia). *Tsuyu* dew: *arawa(reru)*; *arawa(su)* to be exposed: *arawa* open; frank.

出　*Roshutsu* to be exposed.

西亞　*Roshiya* Russia.

見　*Roken* disclosure.

店　*Roten* street-stall.

命　*Romei* transitory life; (miserable) life.

骨　*Rokotsu* simple; blunt; outspoken.

臺　*Rodai* balcony.

營　*Roei* field encampment.

顯　*Roken* discovery.

霹靂　*Hekireki* a sudden peal of thunder.

霸　See 覇 146,13.

一四 霽　SEI.　*Ha(reru)*; *hara(su)* to clear up.

一六 靈　REI sacred: RYŌ. *Tamashii*; *tama* soul; spirit; ghost. →173,7T

妙　*Reimyō* wonderful; mysterious.

長　*Reichō* chief; lord.

的　*Reiteki* spiritual.

柩　*Reikyū* coffin.

前　*Reizen* in front of the tablet or before the spirit of the dead.

感　*Reikan* wonderful answer to prayer; inspiration.

魂　*Reikon* soul.

驗　*Reiken* wonderful answer to prayer.

靄　AI to become clouded over. *Moya* mist; fog.

々　*Ai-ai* harmonious.

一七 靉　AI to trail; become clouded over.

々　*Ai-ai* trailing; harmonious.

靆　*Aitai* trailing.

青 一七四

青　SEI; SHŌ.　*Aoi* blue; green: unripe; nexperienced. →青T

二才　*Aonisai* a stripling; beardless youth.

天　*Seiten* clear sky.

史　*Seishi* history.

年　*Seinen* youth.

物　*Aomono* vegetables.

春　*Seishun* youth.

柳　*Aoyagi* green willow.

島　*Seitō* Tsingtau.

息　*Aoiki* gasp; deep sigh.

筋 *Aosuji* blue veins.

森 *Aomori* p. n.

雲 *Seiun* blue cloud; high rank; aspiration.

磁 *Seiji* celadon porcelain.

* 銅 *Seidō; karakane* bronze.

静 SEI; JŌ. *Shizuka* quiet; peaceful: *shizuma(ru)* to be quiet; rest. →174, 6 * T

々 *Shizu-shizu* with measured steps.

止 *Seishi* stillness; repose.

岡 *Shizuoka* p. n.

思 *Seishi* meditation.

脈 *Jōmyaku* vein (as distinguished from artery).

寂 *Seijaku* silence; stillness.

肅 *Seishuku* silence; stillness.

養 *Seiyō* rest; recuperating.

謐 *Seihitsu* tranquillity; peaceful.

穩 *Seion* quietness; calmness.

一七五 非

T 非 HI neg. prefix; bad; wrong; to speak ill of; criticize. *Arazu* not; is not.

人 *Hinin* beggar.

人情 *Hininjō* inhuman; superhuman:

人道 *Hijindō* inhuman.

凡 *Hibon* uncommon; remarkable; wonderful.

公式 *Hikōshiki* informal.

立憲 *Hirikken* unconstitutional.

望 *Hibō* inordinate ambition.

常 *Hijō* unusual; very.

常識 *Hijōshiki* lack of common sense.

番 *Hiban* being off duty.

買同盟 *Hibaidōmei* boycott.

道 *Hidō; hidoi* unjust; cruel.

業 *Higō* unnatural; violent.

戰論 *Hisenron* pacific plea.

禮 *Hirei* rudeness.

難 *Hinan* criticism; denunciation; blame.

斐 HI pretty; pattern. 【文】 四

T 悲 HI. *Kanashi(mu)* to grieve: *kanashii* sorrowful. 【心】

壯 *Hisō* tragic; pathetic.

哀 *Hiai* sorrow; grief.

痛 *Hitsū* grief; distress.

運 *Hiun* ill-luck.

境 *Hikyō* pitiful condition.

鳴 *Himei* cry of distress.

慘 *Hisan* miserable.

歎 *Hitan* grief; sorrow.

劇 *Higeki* tragedy.

憤 *Hifun* indignation; anger.

觀 *Hikan* pessimism.

六 蜚 HI. *Abura-mushi* cockroach; plant louse. 【虫】

七 輩 HAI. *Tomogara; yakara* companions; comrades. 【車】

出 *Haishutsu* (of persons) to appear in large numbers.

一七六 面

面 MEN to face. *Omote; omo; tsura; kao; mo* face; front; surface: *manoatari* face to face.

々 *Memmen* each one; one and all.

白 *Omoshiroi* interesting; amusing.

白半分 *Omoshiro-hambun* half in fun.

目 *Memboku; memmoku* countenance; honour.

汚 *Tsurayogoshi* disgrace.

前 *Menzen* in the presence of.

相 *Mensō* countenance.

倒 *Mendō* trouble; bother.

接 *Mensetsu* interview.

會 *Menkai* meeting each other.

當 *Tsuraate* indirect hit.

談 *Mendan* interview; to meet and speak to.

謁 *Men-etsu* audience; interview.

積 *Menseki* area.

識 *Menshiki* acquaintance.

一七七 革

革 KAKU. *Nameshi-gawa; kawa* tanned skin; leather; hide; skin: *arata-(meru); aratama(ru)* to improve; reform; change; renew; restore.

命 *Kakumei* revolution (political, etc.).

新 *Kakushin* reform; renovation.

三 靱 JIN. *Shinayaka* soft; pliable: *utsubo; yugi* a quiver.

四 靴 KA. *Kutsu* boots; shoes.

下 *Kutsushita* stockings.

足袋 *Kutsutabi* stockings.

五 鞆 *Tomo* archer's wrist-shield.

鞅掌 *Ōshō* to be engaged in.

鞄 HŌ. *Kaban* travelling bag.

六 鞋 AI. *Waraji* straw-sandals.

鞍 AN. *Kura* saddle.

馬 *Kurama* p. n.

鞏 KYŌ. *Katai* hard; firm.

固 *Kyōko* hard; strong; firm.

七 鞘 SHŌ. *Saya* scabbard.

484

八 鞠 KIKU to bring up.   *Mari* ball.

躬如 *Kikukyūjo* politely; respectfully.

九 鞣 JŪ soft.   *Nameshi-gawa* dressed leather.

鞭 BEN.   *Muchi* whip: *muchi-u(tsu)* to whip.

撻 *Bentatsu* to encourage; urge.

一〇 鞴 HI; BI.   *Fuigo* bellows.

一三 韃 TATSU; DATSU name of a Mongolian tribe.

一七八 韋

韋 I.   *Nameshi-gawa* tanned leather: *somu(ku)* to rebel.

駄天走 *Idaten-bashiri* running at lightning speed.

韓 KAN old name of Korea.

一七九 韭

一八〇 音

In Tōyō always: 音

T 音 ON Chinese reading of the characters: IN.   *Oto; ne* sound; noise; voice; tone: *otona(u)* to visit.

*T 響 →180,13

曲 *Ongyoku* music; tune.

色 *Onshoku; neiro* tone.

吐 *Onto* voice.

沙汰 *Otosata* message; tidings.

便 *Ombin* euphonic change.

信 *Inshin; onshin* message; tidings.

樂 *Ongaku* music.

頭 *Ondo* leading (in singing).

聲 *Onsei* voice; sound.

響 *Onkyō* sound; echo.

讀 *Ondoku* reading aloud.

五 韶 SHŌ beautiful; to succeed to (*Aki*).

七 龍 See 212,0.

一〇 T 韻 IN rhyme; elegance; tone.

文 *Imbun* poetry.

* 律 *Inritsu* rhythm.

一三 響 KYŌ.   *Hibi(ku)* to resound; echo; sound. →180,11 T *

應 *Kyōō* respond promptly.

一八一 頁

Almost always at the right: it is called *Ō-gai*.

頁 *Peiji* page.

二 T 頂 CHŌ. *Itadaki* top; summit: *itada(ku)* to place on the head; receive (polite).

上 *Chōjō* the top; on the top.

門の一針 *Chōmon-no-isshin* a severe warning.

垂 *Unada(reru)* to hang down the head.

戴 *Chōdai* to receive (as a present).

三 T 順 JUN regular order; gentle. *Shitaga(u)* to obey; follow.

次 *Junji* regular order; in turn.

序 *Junjo* regular order; correct procedure.

位 *Jun-i* order.

延 *Jun-en* postponement.

風 *Jumpū* favourable wind.

逆 *Jungyaku* direct and reverse; forwards and backwards; right and wrong.

番 *Jumban* regular turn; order.

路 *Junro* usual route.

當 *Juntō* appropriateness.

境 *Junkyō* favourable condition.

調 *Junchō* normal condition.

應 *Jun-ō* adaptation; accommodation.

繰 *Junguri* in order.

四 T 預 YO previously; beforehand. *Azu(keru)* to deposit; give into the care of: *azuka(ru)* to be entrusted with; have charge of; it sometimes has a passive meaning as *o tazune ni azukaru* to be requested.

入 *Azukeire* to deposit.

金 *Yokin* deposit.

頒 HAN. *Waka(tsu)* to divide; distribute.

布 *Hampu* to issue; distribute.

頓 TON to salute; bow the head. *Tomi ni* suddenly; in due time.

才 *Tonsai* wit.

死 *Tonshi* sudden death.

狂 *Tonkyō* freakish; discordant.

首 *Tonshu* bowing the head low; (epist. st.) yours respectfully.

珍漢 *Tonchinkan* incoherent.

挫 *Tonza* check; hitch.

智 *Tonchi* wit.

着 *Tonjaku* to be concerned about.

頑 GAN foolish. *Katakuna* stubborn.

丈 *Ganjō* strong.

固 *Ganko* obstinacy.

是無 *Ganzenai* innocent.

冥 *Gammei* obstinacy.

迷 *Gammei* obstinacy.

張 *Gamba(ru)* to insist stoutly.

健 *Ganken* healthy.

強 *Gankyō* obstinacy.

頌 SHŌ eulogy; to praise; sing.

德 *Shōtoku* to commend virtue.

五 領 RYŌ possession; jurisdiction; aux. num. for counting clothes; suit; neck; to govern; rule; receive.

土 *Ryōdo* territory; dominion; domain.

分 *Ryōbun* domain; territory.

內 *Ryōnai* within a territory.

收 *Ryōshū* to receive.

地 *Ryōchi* dominion; territory.

事 *Ryōji* consul.

事館 *Ryōjikan* consulate.

海 *Ryōkai* territorial waters.

袖 *Ryōshū* leader (of political party, etc.).

域 *Ryōiki* dominion.

六 頤 I. *Ago; otogai* the chin; jaw.

使 *Ishi* to order about; treat contemptuously.

七 頸 KEI. *Kubi* the neck.

飾 *Kubikazari* necklace.

輪 *Kubiwa* necklace; dog's collar.

顧 See 頤 181,6.

頷 GAN. *Ago* chin: *unazu(ku)* to nod; assent.

頻 HIN quickly. *Shikiri ni* constantly; eagerly.

々 *Himpin* following one upon the other.

出 *Hinshutsu* occurring frequently.

發 *Himpatsu* occurring frequently.

繁 *Himpan* frequent.

頰 KYŌ. *Hō* cheek.

杖 *Hōzue* rest one's chin on one's hand.

穎 EI point of an awl; clever. *Nogi* ear of grain. 【禾】

才 *Eisai* great ability; man of high intelligence.

頹 TAI. *Kuzu(reru)* to crumble to pieces: *suta(ru)* to be abandoned.

敗 *Taihai* corruption.

勢 *Taisei* downward tendency.

廢 *Taihai* deterioration.

齡 *Tairei* declining age.

頴 See 穎 181,7.

顆 KA small, round object; 八 clod of earth.

題 DAI subject; topic; text; 九 name.

目 *Daimoku* title; subject.

辭 *Daiji* motto or verse used as heading or sub-title of a book or chapter.

顯 See 顯 181,14.

額 KAKU; GAKU amount; price; tablet; picture. *Hitai; nuka* forehead: *nukazu(ku)* to bow.

面 *Gakumen* face-value.

顏 GAN. *Kao; kambase* face.

→顏 T

487

（九）

顏

立 *Kaodachi* features ; countenance.

出 *Kaodashi* show one's face.

色 *Ganshoku ; kaoiro* complexion.

向 *Kaomuke* showing one's face.

附 *Kaotsuki* look ; expression of the face.

面 *Gammen* face.

料 *Ganryō* cosmetics.

觸 *Kaobure* list of men composing a party.

顎 GAKU. *Ago ; agito ; otogai* chin.

顋 SAI. *Era* gills : *ago* jawbone ; chin.

*

一〇

類 RUI and so forth. *Tagui* sort ; kind ; race ; family ; various kinds of ; all kinds
↓ of ; unequalled : *tagu(u)* to
181,9 * T　compare ; resemble.

似 *Ruiji* resembling.

例 *Ruirei* similar case.

別 *Ruibetsu* classification.

推 *Ruisui* analogy.

燒 *Ruishō* to be burnt down by a spreading fire.

顚 TEN upside down. *Kutsugae(ru)* to be upset.

末 *Temmatsu* account ; details.

沛 *Tempai* instant ; moment.

倒 *Tentō* overturning ; upsetting ; inversion.

落 *Tenraku* roll down.

覆 *Tempuku* overthrow ; overturn.

*
T **類** →181,10

483

（一〇）

T **願** GAN desire. *Nega(u)* to ask ; request.

上候 *Negaiagesōrō* I beg you.

下 *Negaisage* withdrawing a suit.

出 *Negaideru ; ganshutsu* to apply for.

書 *Gansho* petition ; application.

望 *Gammō* wish ; desire ; hope.

一二

T **顧** KO. *Kaerimi(-ru)* to look back : *omo(u)* to think ; reflect.

客 *Kokaku* a customer.

問 *Komon* counsellor ; adviser.

慮 *Koryo* to be anxious about ; care for ; regard.

一三

顫 SEN. *Furu(h)eru)* (coll.) ; *furu(u)* (lit. st) ; *wanana-(ku)* to shiver ; shudder.

動 *Sendō* vibration ; tremble.

一四

顯 KEN ; GEN clear. *Arawa-(reru)* to be revealed ; appear : *arawa(su)* to reveal.
　→181,9 T

位 *Ken-i* a high rank.

官 *Kenkan* high official.

要 *Ken-yō* important ; prominent.

微鏡 *Kembikyō* microscope.

著 *Kencho* conspicuous.

職 *Kenshoku* prominent post.

一五

顰 See 24,22. 【頁】

一六

顱 RO head ; skull.

(二)

渇 *Kikatsu* hunger and thirst.

餓 *Kiga* hunger; starvation.

饉 *Kikin* famine.

四 飲 IN. *No(mu)* to drink; to take (medicine). T

用水 *In-yōsui* drinking water.

食 *Inshoku* eating and drinking; diet.

食物 *Inshokubutsu* drink and food.

料水 *Inryōsui* drinking water.

酒 *Inshu* drinking.

T 飯 HAN. *Meshi; ii; mama; mamma* food, especially rice; a meal.

粒 *Meshitsubu* grain of cooked rice.

五 飴 I. *Ame* sweetish syrup or jelly made from various kinds of grains.

T 飼 SHI. *Ka(u)* to keep (an animal); nourish.

主 *Kainushi* keeper; owner.

育 *Shiiku* breeding.

養 *Shiyō* keeping (as of domestic animals); rearing.

T 飾 SHOKU. *Kazari* ornament: *kaza(ru)* to adorn.

飽 HŌ. *A(ku)* to have enough; be satiated; be tired of: *aka(su)* to satiate; satisfy.

足 *Akita(ru)* to be satiated. ↓

迄 *Akumade* to the utmost.

食 *Hōshoku* well-fed.

満 *Hōman* satiety.

餌 JI. *E; esa; eba* food of animals; bait. 六

食 *Ejiki* food; victim.

餅 HEI. *Mochi* rice-cake.

餉 SHŌ provisions. *Ge* a meal: *karei* boiled, dried rice.

蝕 SHOKU to be defective. *Mushiba(mu)* to be moth-eaten or worm-eaten. 【虫】

T 餓 GA. *Ue* hunger; starvation: *u(eru)* to be starved; famished; hungry. 七

死 *Gashi; uejini* starving to death.

鬼 *Gaki* a hungry devil; an imp; (humble term for a child).

T 餘 YO. *Amari* remainder; remains; more than; too: *ama(ru)* to exceed; be left over: *ama(su)* to leave over: *amari na* excessive. In certain cases used for 余 9,5.

力 *Yoryoku* remaining power.

分 *Yobun* excess.

生 *Yosei* the rest of one's life.

白 *Yohaku* blank; margin.

地 *Yochi* room; space left.

所 *Yoso* another place; elsewhere.

所目 *Yosome* another's eyes; point of view of an outsider.

命 *Yomei* the remainder of a life.

飽 T

事 *Yoji* other things.

（七）

僁 波 *Yoha* after-effect.

念 *Yonen* other thoughts.

念無 *Yonen-naku* eagerly; intently.

香 *Yokō* remaining odour; graciousness.

計 *Yokei* excessive; superfluous.

病 *Yobyō* secondary disease.

程 *Yohodo* very; much.

寒 *Yokan* cold at the close of winter.

裕 *Yoyū* surplus; spare room; spare time.

喘 *Yozen* lingering life.

剰 *Yojō* remainder.

罪 *Yozai* another crime.

暇 *Yoka* leisure; time.

震 *Yoshin* after-quake.

儀無 *Yoginaku* unavoidably.

談 *Yodan* follow-up story; digression.

興 *Yokyō* entertainments.

韻 *Yoin* reverberation; aftertaste.

類 *Yorui* accomplices.

蘊 *Youn* abundant store.

餐 SAN to eat; to drink; swallow.

八 餡 AN bean jam.

┌館 KAN abb. for name of building of which 館 is bottom character, as *taishikan, toshokan*. *Yakata; tachi* building; mansion; palace; lodging-place. (*Tate*). →135, 10

（八）

餅 See 餅 184, 6.

餞 SEN. *Hanamuke* present to one departing: *oku(ru)* to present; see off.

別 *Sembetsu* parting present.

餲 AI; EI putrid. *Su(y)eru* to be decayed. 九

餛 飩 *Udon* vermicelli. 一〇

餽 KI to send. *Karei* dried, boiled rice.

饉 KIN. *U(eru)* to be starved; 一一 hungry; famished.

饑 See ᵀ飢 184, 2. 一二

饒 JŌ; NYŌ abundant; liberal; to be in excess.

舌 *Nyōzetsu; jōzetsu; shabe(ru)* talkativeness; to babble.

饌 SEN food; an offering.

饗 KYŌ banquet. *Motena(su)* 一三 to entertain guests.

宴 *Kyōen* banquet.

應 *Kyōō* entertainment.

饕 See 27, 21. 【食】 一四

首 一八五

ᵀ首 SHU a chief; aux. num. for counting poems: SU. *Kubi* neck: *kōbe; kashira* head: *hajime* first; beginning.

位 *Shui* the chief seat.

尾 *Shubi* beginning and end; result.

府 *Shufu* capital (of a country).

肯 *Shukō* to consent; agree.

相 *Shushō* Premier.

席 *Shuseki* the chief seat.

班 *Shuhan* the first place.

唱 *Shushō* promotion; advocacy.

級 *Shukyū; shirushi* head.

都 *Shuto* metropolis.

途 *Kadode; shuto* departure; starting.

腦 *Shunō* chief; head; centre.

魁 *Shukai* ringleader.

領 *Shuryō* leader (as of political party).

謀者 *Shubōsha* ringleader.

馘 KAKU. *Kubiki (ru)* to behead; dismiss from service.

首 *Kakushu* to behead; dismiss from service.

香

T 香 KŌ; KYŌ. *Ka; kaori; nioi* odour; fragrance; incense: *kōbashii; kambashii* fragrant; aromatic.

川 *Kagawa* p. n.

水 *Kōsui* a perfume (fluid).

花 *Kōge* incense and flowers; religious offerings.

油 *Kōyu* hair-oil; perfumed oil.

料 *Kōryō* spices.

氣 *Kōki* fragrance.

奠 *Kōden* present made in condolence.

港 *Honkon* Hongkong.

華 *Kōge* offerings.

馥 FUKU fragrant; fragrance.

郁 *Fukuiku* sweet-smelling.

馨 KEI; KYŌ. *Kao(ru)* to be fragrant: *kōbashii; kambashii* fragrant.

馬

When at the left it is called *Uma-hen.*

T 馬 BA; ME. *Uma; ma* horse.

丁 *Batei* groom; footman.

力 *Bariki* horse-power; horse-cart.

子 *Mago* one who leads a pack-horse.

匹 *Bahitsu* horses.

加 *Marakka* Malacca.

尼剌 *Manira* Manila.

耳東風 *Baji-tōfū* utter indifference.

耳塞 *Maruseiyu* Marseilles.

馬

車 *Basha* carriage.

克 *Maruku* mark (German money).

來 *Marei* Malay.

術 *Bajutsu* horsemanship.

鹿 *Baka* fool.

塲 *Baba* race-course.

鈴薯 *Jagatara-imo; jagaimo; bareisho* potato.

達加斯加爾 *Madakasukaru* Madagascar.

賊 *Bazoku* mounted bandits; the Chunchuses.

二 馭 GYO to ride; drive; to manage; rule.

者 *Gyosha* coachman.

三 馴 JUN to obey; follow. *Na(reru)* to be accustomed to; familiar with: *nara(su)* to tame; accustom.

染 *Najimi* familiarity.

鹿 *Tonakai* reindeer.

馳 CHI. *Ha(seru)* to ride rapidly; gallop; run.

走 *Chisō* feast.

四 T 駅 See 驛 187,13.

駄 DA aux. num. for counting horse-loads: TA to load on a horse.

々 *Dada* petulance; crossness.

目 *Dame* useless; no good.

法螺 *Dabora* bluster; big talk.

洒落 *Dajare* poor joke.

賃 *Dachin* pack-horse charge; recompense.

辯 *Daben* foolish talk.

駁 HAKU; BAKU to refute; to correct.

論 *Bakuron* refutation; objection.

擊 *Bakugeki* to attack; controvert.

*

T 駐 CHŪ. *Todoma(ru)* to stop; reside. 五

屯 *Chūton* to be stationed.

在 *Chūzai* residing; resident.

紮 *Chūsatsu* residing; resident.

劄 *Chūsatsu* residing; resident.

輦 *Chūren* stopping of the Imperial carriage.

駈 KU to urge on. *Kake(-ru); ka(ru)* to run; drive.

引 *Kakehiki* tactics; tact; bargaining.

足 *Kakeashi* double-quick.

廻 *Kakemawa(ru)* run about.

落 *Kake-ochi* elopement; running away.

駒 KU. *Koma* a colt; chessman; bridge (of a musical instrument).

下駄 *Komageta* low wooden-clogs.

鳥 *Komadori* robin.

駛 SHI. *Hayai* quick; fast.

走 *Shisō* to run quickly.

494

* T 驅 →187,11

（五）駝鳥 *Dachō* ostrich.

駕 GA; KA vehicle; to ride; surpass. *Kago* palanquin; sedan-chair.

籠 *Kago* palanquin; sedan-chair.

駑 Do slow horse; stupid.

馬 *Doba* hack; jade.

六 駱駝 *Rakuda* camel.

駭 GAI. *Odoro(ku)* to be frightened.

然 *Gaizen* in astonishment.

七 駸 SHIN rapid; to run.

々 *Shinshin* rapidly.

駿 SHUN to be excellent; quick.

才 *Shunsai* a man of talent.

州 *Sunshū* another name for the province of *Suruga*.

足 *Shunsoku* a man of talent; swift horse.

河 *Suruga* p. n.

馬 *Shumba; shumme* swift horse.

八T 騎 KI aux. num. for counting horsemen. *No(ru)* to ride.

手 *Kishu* rider; jockey.

兵 *Kihei* cavalry.

者 *Kisha* rider; jockey.

馬 *Kiba* horse-riding.

騙 HEN. *Kata(ru); taburaka-(su); dama(su); damaka(su)* to cheat; deceive. 九

取 *Henshu* swindling.

騷 SŌ. *Sawa(gu)* to be noisy; excited: *sawaga(su)* to disturb. →187,8 * ²T 一〇

々 *Sōzōshii* noisy.

動 *Sōdō* confusion.

亂 *Sōran* confusion; tumult.

擾 *Sōjō* confusion; tumult.

驅 KU. *Kake(-ru): ka(ru)* to run; drive; drive away. →187,4 T * 一一

出 *Karida(su)* hunt out.

使 *Kushi* to order about.

除 *Kujo* extermination.

逐 *Kuchiku* expulsion; **dri-ving away.**

逐艇 *Kuchiku-tei* destroyer (naval).

逐艦 *Kuchiku-kan* destroyer (naval).

驒 DA used for **its sound** 一二

驕 KYŌ. *Ogo(ru)* to be stubborn; be proud; to live in luxury.

奢 *Kyōsha* luxury; extrava-gance.

慢 *Kyōman* arrogance; conceit.

驍 GYŌ good horse; fast; strong.

名 *Gyōmei* heroic name.

勇 *Gyōyū* bravery.

將 *Gyōshō* brave general; leader.

一三 驛 EKI station; post-station.
→187,4 T

長 Ekichō station-master.

驗 KEN; GEN. Tame(su) to examine; consider: shirushi sign; effect; mark; efficacy; proof. →187,8 T *[1]

T 驚 KYŌ. Odoro(ru) to be surprised; frightened.

入 Odoroki-i(ru) to be very much amazed.

怖 Kyōfu be frightened.

破 Suwa good gracious!

異 Kyōi surprise.

愕 Kyōgaku consternation.

嘆 Kyōtan admiration.

一四 驟 SHŪ run; sudden; often.

雨 Shūu shower.

一六 驥 KI an excellent steed; ability.

尾に附す Kibi ni fusu to follow at another's heels.

一八八 骨

When at the left, it is called Hone-hen.

T 骨 KOTSU. Hone bone.

子 Kosshi gist; essence.

肉 Kotsuniku flesh and bone; blood relation.

折 Hone-ori effort; exertion: kossetsu fracture (of a bone).

身 Honemi marrow; the heart; sparing oneself.

抜 Honenuki boneless; emasculated.

相 Kossō phrenology.

格 Kokkaku frame of the body; the build.

頂 Kotchō the height.

組 Honegumi constitution: frame-work.

惜 Honeoshimi laziness.

牌 Karuta playing cards.

董 Kottō curios.

髓 Kotsuzui marrow.

骰 TŌ. Sai a die. 四

子 Sai a die.

骸 GAI bone; body. Mukuro corpse. 六

骨 Gaikotsu skeleton.

炭 Gaitan coke.

軀 Gaiku body.

髓 See 髓 188,13. 九 *

髏 RO; RU; RŌ. Sarekōbe skull. 一一

體 TAI; TEI substance; state; condition; appearance. Karada body. →9,5 T →158,5 一三

力 Tairyoku physical strength.

（一三）

系　*Taikei* system.

育　*Taiiku* physical training.

面　*Taimen* honour.

格　*Taikaku* physique.

得　*Taitoku* to acquire; comprehend; realize.

量　*Tairyō* weight of a body.

裁　*Teisai* style; appearance.

温　*Tai-on* temperature of the body.

操　*Taisō* gymnastic exercises.

軀　*Taiku* body.

驗　*Taiken* experience.

髑　DOKU. *Sarekōbe* skull.

髏　*Dokuro; sarekōbe* skull.

髓　ZUI marrow.
→ 188, 9 * T : 130, 13

一八九

高

T 高　KŌ. *Takai* high; tall; dear: *taka* amount: *takama(ru)* to rise: *taka-(meru)* to raise.

下　*Kōge* dearness; degree; fluctuation (of price, quality, etc.).

工　*Kōkō* abb. for Higher Technical School.

加索　*Kōkasasu* Caucasus.

名　*Kōmei* renown.

言　*Kōgen* tall talk.

利貸　*Kōri-kashi* usurer.

弟　*Kōtei* best pupil.

低　*Kōtei* fluctuation (of price, quality, etc.); undulation (of ground, etc.).

見　*Kōken* your (august) opinion.

知　*Kōchi* p. n.

尚　*Kōshō* noble; lofty; high-class.

飛　*Takatobi* high jump; absconding.

級　*Kōkyū* high-class.

評　*Kōhyō* your criticism; famous.

商　*Kōshō* abb. for Higher Commercial School.

等　*Kōtō* high; advanced.

貴　*Kōki* noble.

慢　*Kōman* arrogant.

遠　*Kōen* lofty.

調　*Kōchō* emphasize.

價　*Kōka* a high price.

潔　*Kōketsu* noble.

潮　*Kōchō* high tide; climax.

壓　*Kōatsu* high pressure; oppression.

襟　*Haikara* stylish; dandy.

輪　*Takanawa* p. n.

覽　*Kōran* your inspection.

敲　KŌ. *Tata(ku)* to strike; knock. 【攴】

497

一九〇 髟

四 髣 髴 *Hōfutsu* resembling closely; to appear dimly.

五 髯 ZEN. *Hige* beard; whiskers.

髪 HATSU. *Kami; ogushi* hair of the head (human). →190,4 * T

結 *Kamiyui* woman's hairdresser.

飾 *Kamikazari* hair ornaments.

六 髷 KYOKU. *Mage* certain style of hair-dressing.

髭 SHI. *Hige* moustache.

一二 鬘 *Kazura; katsura* wig.

一三 鬚 SHU. *Hige* beard; whiskers.

一四 鬢 BIN; HIN hair on the sides of the head.

一五 鬣 RYŌ. *Tategami* mane.

一九一 門

鬧 DŌ; NYŌ noisy. →169,5

鬨 KŌ to fight. *Toki* warcry. →169,6

*T 髪 →190,5

鬪 TŌ. *Tataka(u)* to fight; dispute; quarrel. →169,10 T

爭 *Tōsō* a fight; a combat; a wrangle.

一九二 邑

鬱 See 欝 75,22. 【邑】

一九三 鬲

鬲 YŪ to circulate; to soften; pacify; harmonize. *To-(keru)* to melt; thaw. 【虫】

合 *Yūgō* melting down; harmony.

和 *Yūwa* melting; reconciliation.

通 *Yūzū* circulation; accommodation; versatility; elasticity.

鬻 SHUKU; IKU rice gruel. *Hisa(gu)* to sell; peddle.

一九四 鬼

T 鬼 KI. *Oni* devil; ghost; evil spirit.

才 *Kisai* excellent talent.

門 *Kimon* unlucky quarter.

神 *Kijin* gods; deities.

氣 *Kiki* ghastliness.

498

一九五

四 魁 KAI. *Sakigake* the head; leader.

偉 *Kaii* well-built (body); stately.

T 魂 KON. *Tamashii; tama* soul; spirit.

魄 *Kompaku* soul; spirit.

膽 *Kontan* thought; idea; scheme.

五 魅 T MI; BI ghost. *Mi-i(ru); misuru* (irreg.) to bewitch; charm; delude.

魃 BATSU; HATSU. *Hideri* drought.

八 魍魎 *Moryō* demons.

魏 GI high; large; old name for part of China.

一〇 魑魅 *Chimi* demons.

一九五

魚

When at the left it is called *Uo-hen.*

T 魚 GYO. *Uo, sakana* fish.

介 *Gyokai* marine animals.

肉 *Gyoniku* flesh of fish.

四 魯 Ro old name for part of China; abb. for Russia. *Oroka* foolish; dull.

西亞 *Roshiya* Russia.

（四〇）

國 *Rokoku* Russia.

鈍 *Rodon* dull.

五

鮎 *Ayu* trout.

鮒 FU. *Funa* kind of carp.

鮑 HŌ. *Awabi* sea-ear.

六

鮭 KEI. *Sake; shake* salmon.

鮨 *Sushi* rice and raw fish seasoned with vinegar.

鮮 T SEN abb. for Korea. *Azayaka* clear; bright; fresh: *sukunai* few.

少 *Senshō* little; few.

血 *Senketsu* fresh blood.

明 *Semmei* clear.

魚 *Sengyo* fresh fish.

銀 *Sengin* abb. for Chōsen Bank（朝鮮銀行）

滿 *Semman* Korea and Manchuria.

鮪 *Maguro* tunny.

鮫 KŌ. *Same* shark.

七

鯉 RI. *Koi* carp.

八

鯖 SEI. *Saba* mackerel.

鯡 HI. *Nishin* herring.

鯛 CHŌ. *Tai* sea-bream.

499

(八) 鯱 *Shachi; shachihoko* dolphin.

立 *Shachihokodachi* standing on one's head.

T鯨 GEI. *Kujira* whale.

尺 *Kujirajaku* Japanese cloth measure (=1.25 foot): see Introduction 44.

波 *Toki; geiha* battle-cry.

飲 *Geiin* drink hard.

鯰 *Namazu* cat-fish.

九 鰌 *Dojō* loach; lamprey.

鰑 YŌ. *Surume* dried cuttle-fish.

鰐 GAKU. *Wani* crocodile.

鰊 REN. *Nishin* herring.

鰕 KA. *Ebi* shrimp; prawn; lobster.

一〇 鰭 KI. *Hire* fin.

鰯 *Iwashi* sardine; pilchard.

一一 鰹 KEN. *Katsuo* bonito.

節 *Katsuobushi* dried bonito.

鱈 *Tara* cod.

鰻 *Unagi* eel.

一三 鱗 RIN. *Uroko; koke* scales of a fish or snake.

鱒 *Masu* salmon-trout. (一二)

鱶 *Fuka* shark. 一五

鱸 *Suzuki* perch. 一六

鳥　　一九六

T鳥 CHŌ. *Tori* bird.

打 *Tori-uchi* soft cap; bird-shooting.

打帽 *Toriuchibō* soft cap.

羽 *Toba* p. n.

居 *Torii* gateway in front of a Shinto shrine.

取 *Tottori* p. n.

瞰圖 *Chōkanzu* bird's-eye view.

烏 See 86,6.

二 鳧 *Keri* wild duck; an end (e. g. *keri ga tsuku* to come to an end); verbal suffix (lit. st.).

鳩 KYŪ. *Hato* pigeon: *atsu-(meru)* to collect.

首 *Kyūshu* lay heads together.

三 鳶 See 56,11. 【鳥】

五 鴨 Ō. *Kamo* wild duck.

緑江 *Ōryokkō* Yalu River.

（五）

鴉　A.　*Karasu* crow.

鳶　SHI.　*Tobi* kite (bird).

鴛鴦　*En-ō; oshidori* mandarin duck.

六　鴿　KŌ; GŌ.　*Hato* dove; pigeon.

七　鵠　KOKU.　*Kugui; kuge* swan: *kōnotori* Japanese stork.

鵜　TEI.　*U* cormorant.

吞　*Unomi* swallowing whole.

鵞　See foll.

鵞　GA goose.

鳥　*Gachō* goose.

八　鶉　JUN.　*Uzura* quail.

鵺　*Nue* kind of owl; fabulous bird.

*

九　鶩　BOKU.　*Ahiru* duck.

一〇　鶴　KAKU.　*Tsuru* crane.

首　*Kakushu* anxiously waiting.

唳　*Kakurei* crying of a crane.

龜　*Tsurukame* crane and tortoise; congratulatory expression.

齡　*Kakurei* long life.

鶵　See 雛 172,10.

*T 鶏 →196,10

鶏　KEI.　*Niwatori; tori* barn-door fowl. →196,8 T *　**（一〇）**

肋　*Keiroku* a superfluity.

卵　*Keiran* a hen's egg.

鶯　Ō.　*Uguisu* nightingale.

鷗　Ō.　*Kamome* sea-gull.　**一一**

鷲　SHŪ.　*Washi* eagle.　**一二**

鷺　RO.　*Sagi* snowy heron.　**一三**

鸚鵡　*Ōmu* parrot.　**一七**

鹵　一九七

鹵　RO shield; plunder; poor; barren.

簿　*Robo* Imperial cortege.

鹹　KAN.　*Shiokarai; karai* salty.

水　*Kansui* salty water.

鹼　KEN lye; salt.

鹿　一九八

When at the left, it is called *Shika-hen*.

鹿 ROKU. *Shika; ka* deer; stag.

爪 *Shikatsumerashii* serious.
兒島 *Kagoshima* p. n.
島 *Kashima* p. n.

麁 SO. *Arai* rough; coarse. Sometimes used for 粗 119,5 which see for compounds.

塵 JIN. *Chiri* dirt; dust; rubbish. 【土】

芥 *Jinkai* dirt.
埃 *Jin-ai; chiri-hokori* dust.
煙 *Jin-en* cloud of dust.

麗 See ᵀ麗 198,8.

麒麟 *Kirin* giraffe; fabulous animal; marvellous person.

鏖 Ō. *Minagoroshi* extermination. 【金】

殺 *Ōsatsu* slaughter; massacre.

麑 GEI. *Kago* fawn.

島 *Kagoshima* p. n.

ᵀ麗 REI. *Uruwashii* beautiful: *uraraka* bright weather. →198,5 : 1, 15
々 *Reirei* ostentatious.
人 *Reijin* beautiful woman.

麓 ROKU. *Fumoto* foot of a mountain.

麝香 *Jakō* musk.

麥 一九九

When at the left, it is called *Mugi-hen.*

麥 BAKU. *Mugi* corn (wheat, barley, etc.). →35, 4 ᵀ

酒 *Biiru* beer.
粉 *Mugiko* wheat flour.
稈 *Bakkan; mugiwara* straw.

麪 MEN wheat flour.

包 *Pan* bread.
麭 *Pan* bread.

麩 FU kind of bread.

麴 KIKU. *Kōji* yeast.

町 *Kōjimachi* p. n.

麵 MEN a kind of vermicelli; wheat flour.

包 *Pan* bread.
麭 *Pan* bread.

In Tōyō always : 麻

麻 二〇〇

ᵀ麻 MA linen. *Asa* hemp.

生 *Asō* p. n.
布 *Azabu* p. n.: *mafu* linen cloth.

T 摩 MA. *Kosu(ru); su(ru); s.isu(ru)* to polish; rub; rub off; grind. 【手】

洛加 *Morokko* Morocco.

擦 *Masatsu* friction; rubbing.

麾 KI flag. *Sashimane(ku)* to call; beckon.

下 *Kika* troops under one's command.

磨 MA. *Miga(ku); to(gu); su(ru)* to polish; sharpen; mill; grind; clean. 【石】

滅 *Mametsu* defacement.

糜 BI. *Tada(reru)* to be inflamed. 【米】

爛 *Biran* being inflamed.

麿 (*Maro*).

靡 HI; BI. *Nabi(ku); nabi-ka(su)* to bend; obey; yield to; wave. 【非】

T 魔 MA evil spirit; devil. 【鬼】

力 *Maryoku* charm; spell.

物 *Mamono* demon; devil.

法 *Mahō* sorcery; witchcraft; magic.

法瓶 *Mahōbin* thermos bottle.

術 *Majutsu* sorcery; witchcraft; magic.

道 *Madō* evil ways.

窟 *Makutsu* a disorderly house.

黄

黄 KŌ; Ō. *Ki* yellow. →140, 8 T

口 *Kōkō* young; green.

白 *Kōhaku* money; bribery.

色 *Ki-iro; kōshoku* yellow.

金 *Ōgon; kogane* gold; money.

昏 *Tasogare; kōkon* dusk; evening.

河 *Kōga* Hoang-ho River.

泉 *Kōsen; yomiji* Hades.

海 *Kōkai* Yellow Sea.

塵 *Kōjin* dust.

禍 *Kōka* the Yellow Peril.

黍

黍 SHO. *Kibi* millet.

In Tōyō always 黒

黑

T 黑 KOKU. *Kuroi* black.

人 *Kokujin; kurombo* negro: *kurōto* expert; professional.

子 *Hokuro* mole (on the skin).

白 *Kokubyaku* black and white; right and wrong.

黑

奴 *Kurombō; kokudo* a negro.

表 *Kokuhyō; burakkurisuto* black list.

海 *Kokkai* Black Sea.

幕 *Kuromaku* wire-puller.

潮 *Kuroshio* name of sea current that washes the coast of Japan.

龍江 *Kokuryūkō* Amur River.

檀 *Kokutan* ebony.

三 墨 BOKU abb. for Mexico. T *Sumi* India ink; blacking. 【土】

西哥 *Mekishiko* Mexico.

守 *Bokushu* to adhere obstinately to.

染 *Sumizome* black; dark.

痕 *Bokkon* ink mark.

四 默 MOKU; BOKU. *Dama(ru)*; T *moda(su)* to be silent.

々 *Moku-moku* silently.

示 *Mokushi* revelation.

考 *Mokkō* meditation.

契 *Mokkei* tacit understanding.

思 *Mokushi* musing.

殺 *Mokusatsu* ignore.

許 *Mokkyo* to wink at; condone.

視 *Mokushi* overlook.

然 *Mokuzen; mokunen* silently.

想 *Mokusō* contemplation.

過 *Mokka* overlook.

認 *Mokunin* toleration.

禮 *Mokurei* to bow in silence.

黜 CHUTSU. *Shirizo(keru)* to 五 send away; cause to retire.

陟 *Chutchoku* promotion and (or) degradation.

點 TEN to light; dot; point; spot; mark; aux. num. for indefinite objects. *Unazu-(ku)* to nod. →25, 7 T 86, 5 T

々 *Tenten* here and there; scattered about.

火 *Tenka* to light; ignite

在 *Tenzai* to lie scattered about.

呼 *Tenko* roll-call.

綴 *Tentetsu; tensetsu* to intersperse; stud.

線 *Tensen* dotted line.

燈 *Tentō* lighting.

頭 *Tentō* to nod.

檢 *Tenken* inspection.

黛 TAI. *Mayu-zumi* black for the eyebrows.

黨 TŌ companions; party. 八 →42, 7 T : 10, 8 T

人 *Tōjin* a partisan; partyman.

員 *Tōin* member of a party.

爭 *Tōsō* party strife.

派 *Tōha* a political party.

略 *Tōryaku* policy of a party.

與 *Tōyo* a band; association; adherents.

類 *Tōrui* partisans; confederates.

議 *Tōgi* party policy.

504

九 黯 AN dark; darkness.

然 *Anzen* gloomily.

二〇四 翁

二〇五 黽

黽 BIN to exert oneself. →72,4

勉 *Bimben* to exert oneself; industrious.

鼇 Gō. *Ō-game* sea-tortoise.

頭 *Gotō* footnote (in Japanese books, written at top of page).

鼈 BETSU. *Suppon; kame* turtle.

甲 *Bekkō* tortoise-shell.

二〇六 鼎

鼎 TEI. *Kanae* tripod utensil; cauldron. →72,8

立 *Teiritsu* triangular position.

坐 *Teiza* three people sitting together.

二〇七 鼓

T鼓 Ko to beat. *Tsuzumi* small hand-drum. →107,9

手 *Koshu* drummer.

吹 *Kosui* to inspire; infuse.

動 *Kodō* pulse; beat.

舞 *Kobu* to encourage.

瞽 KO. *Meshii; mekura* blind person. 【目】

二〇八 鼠

鼠 SO. *Nezumi* rat; mouse.

色 *Nezumi-iro; nezuiro* grey.

疫 *Pesuto* pest.

賊 *Sozoku* petty thief.

輩 *Sohai* contemptible fellow.

二〇九 鼻

T鼻 BI. *Hana* nose.

下長 *Bikachō* amorous; spoony.

先 *Hanasaki* under one's nose.

祖 *Biso* founder.

高々 *Hanataka-daka* proudly.

鼻
息　*Bisoku* a superior's pleasure: *hanaiki* self-importance; another's opinion.

紙　*Hanagami* paper handkerchief.

緒　*Hanao* clog-thong.

藥　*Hana usuri* a bribe.

鼾　KAN. *Ibiki* snoring

聲　*Kansei* snoring.

二一〇 齊

齊　SAI; SEI old name for part of China; to regulate. *Hitoshii* alike; even. (*Nari*). →67, 4 T

一
整　*Seiitsu* uniformity.
　　Seisei orderly.

劑　ZAI; SEI medicine; to compound. 【刀】→18, 8 T

齋　SAI a room for study; to restrain oneself; pure. *Itsuki* fasting and purification: *toki* dinner. →67. 7 T

戒　*Saikai* purification.

塲　*Saijō* place for funeral service.

齎　SEI. *Motara(su)* to bring; carry; present. →67, 11

二一一 In Tōyō always :
齒 歯

齒　SHI. *Ha* tooth: *yowai* age. →77, 8 T

牙　*Shiga* teeth; regard; heed.

止　*Hadome* brake.

車　*Haguruma* cog-wheel.

科醫　*Shikai* dentist.

痒　*Hagayui* to be impatient.

痛　*Shitsū* toothache.

磨　*Hamigaki* tooth-powder.

齟　SO uneven; to bite; to disagree.

齬　*Sogo* to disagree; discord.

T 齡　REI. *Yowai* age.

齣　SETSU. *Kusari* act (drama).

齦　GIN. *Haguki* the gums.

齧　KETSU; GETSU. *Kaji(ru)* to chew; gnaw.

齷齪　*Akusoku; akuseku* in a busy and bustling manner.

齲齒　*Ushi; mushiba* decayed tooth.

二一二 龍

龍　RYŪ; RYŌ Imperial. *Tatsu* dragon. →117, 5 T

虎　*Ryūko; ryoko* dragon and tiger; two contending heroes.

骨　*Ryūkotsu* keel.

腦　*Ryūnō* refined camphor.

頭　*Ryūzu* the stem of a watch.

頭蛇尾 *Ryūtō-dabi* grand beginning and miserable end.

顔 *Kyūgan* Imperial countenance.

壟 Rō. *Oka* a hill. 【土】

斷 *Rōdan* monopolization.

聾 Rō. *Tsumbo* deafness; deaf. 【耳】

襲 SHŪ. *Oso(u)* to attack: *kasa(neru)* to pile up: *tsu(gu)* to inherit: *kasane* a suit (of clothes). 【衣】
↓ ※

名 *Shūmei* succession to a name.

來 *Shūrai* an invasion.

擊 *Shūgeki* attack.
→ 　　　　→ 襲T

爵 *Shūshaku* succession to a peerage.

龜 三三三

龜 KI. *Kame* tortoise.
→72,7

甲 *Kame-no-kō; kikkō* tortoise-shell.

裂 *Kiretsu* cracking.

鑑 *Kikan* mirror; model.

龠 三三四

尸	户	虍	广	鹿	庫	匸	尢	产	羌	戈	弍	气
戶	戶	唐	疒	麻	辰	匚	疒	产		戋	弍	勺

LEFT   RIGHT

2	仇	冫	匕	力	十	又						乚	1
3	彳	氵	女	弓	士	彡	己	又	匕	几	卜		2
	犭	忄	子	巾	山	牙	斗	力	刂	卩	厶		
	扌	夕	幺	口	工	阝	干	刀	卩	阝			
4	牛	歹	彡	日	王	斤	戈	彐	刄	卩	阝		3
	戶	方	炙	彑	止	牙		双	弋	寸	彡		
	火	木	礻	片	月	文		弋	戈	帀	夂		
5	歩	禾	礻	白	矛	皮	月	戈	犬	欠		4
	矢	正	石	田	弓	瓦	少	斤	尤	攵		
	歩	而	玄	目	甘		毛	斗	死	支		
6	缶	米	糸	虫	耳	角	臣	日	匕	役	支		5
	缶	耒	至	舌	血	而	羊	生	瓜	瓦	皮		
7	車	采	貝	足	赤		艮	聿	色	羽		6
	豸	酉	身	言	麦		羊	弍	多		
	辛	里	角	豆	谷		辛	見	谷		7
8	幸	青	齐	舍	隹	金	食	隶	隹	炎		8
9	革	音	食	首	香	廉	風	韋	頁	飛		9
10/15	馬	骨	魚	齒	鹿	鬲	高	奥		鬼		10
	麥	黑	鼻	齒	齒	齊				鳥		11

CENTRE or CROSSED BY OTHER LINES

乚	乙	一	口	丨	十	丁	人	弓	大	戈	日	木

尤	風	瓦	爻	走	麥	夂	日	臣	日	凡	凡	門
毛	鬼	尺	辶	走	麦	夊	支	日	同	戌	尺	鬥

TOP

一	三	八	ナ			ノ	ヒ		八	入	1/2
卜	山	ソ	十	力	又		卜	宀	入	厶	
工	子	丷	土	小	夂	巛	口	山	八	公	3
己	亡	丄	士	屮	夕	弋	幺	彐	大	廾	
止	去	父	屮	业	戈	爪	比	囚	木	廿	4
斤	文	毌	生	少	氏	凸	目	曰	水	屮	
矛	立	田	四	癶	足	禾	白	目	夫	甘	5
而							自	白	聿	其	6
西	衣	羊	肥	羽	竹	叩	血	耳	共	曲	
雷		羔	共	非	玨	釆	雀	廉	辰	齒	其	7/9
	麻	鳥	髟	鼓	黑	龍	魚	鹿	麻	與	興	10/16

BOTTOM

二	乙	八	力	刀	十	儿	又	口	ノ	ミ	1/2
土	弓	小	山	口	子	凡	夂	大	寸	女	夕	
				廾	巾	方	攵	犬				3/4
壬	巛	小	心	月	日	手	彐	木	氏	水	火	
玉	正	兩	甘	石	目	兒		矢		氷		5
立	皿	示	白	同	田	母		廷				
聿	羊	糸	耳	向	回	羽	虫	米	衣	豕	舛	6
金	豆	貝	西	言	余	見	車	足	辰	食	廉	7/15
黑	鳥	馬	革	香	音	黽	風	蜀	高	齒	鹿	

A CATALOG OF SELECTED
DOVER BOOKS
IN ALL FIELDS OF INTEREST

A CATALOG OF SELECTED DOVER
BOOKS IN ALL FIELDS OF INTEREST

THE ART NOUVEAU STYLE, edited by Roberta Waddell. 579 rare photographs of works in jewelry, metalwork, glass, ceramics, textiles, architecture and furniture by 175 artists—Mucha, Seguy, Lalique, Tiffany, many others. 288pp. 8⅜ × 11¼.
23515-7 Pa. $9.95

AMERICAN COUNTRY HOUSES OF THE GILDED AGE (Sheldon's "Artistic Country-Seats"), A. Lewis. All of Sheldon's fascinating and historically important photographs and plans. New text by Arnold Lewis. Approx. 200 illustrations. 128pp. 9⅜ × 12¼.
24301-X Pa. $7.95

THE WAY WE LIVE NOW, Anthony Trollope. Trollope's late masterpiece, marks shift to bitter satire. Character Melmotte "his greatest villain." Reproduced from original edition with 40 illustrations. 416pp. 6⅛ × 9¼.
24360-5 Pa. $7.95

BENCHLEY LOST AND FOUND, Robert Benchley. Finest humor from early 30's, about pet peeves, child psychologists, post office and others. Mostly unavailable elsewhere. 73 illustrations by Peter Arno and others. 183pp. 5⅜ × 8½.
22410-4 Pa. $3.50

ISOMETRIC PERSPECTIVE DESIGNS AND HOW TO CREATE THEM, John Locke. Isometric perspective is the picture of an object adrift in imaginary space. 75 mindboggling designs. 52pp. 8¼ × 11.
24123-8 Pa. $2.75

PERSPECTIVE FOR ARTISTS, Rex Vicat Cole. Depth, perspective of sky and sea, shadows, much more, not usually covered. 391 diagrams, 81 reproductions of drawings and paintings. 279pp. 5⅜ × 8½.
22487-2 Pa. $4.00

MOVIE-STAR PORTRAITS OF THE FORTIES, edited by John Kobal. 163 glamor, studio photos of 106 stars of the 1940s: Rita Hayworth, Ava Gardner, Marlon Brando, Clark Gable, many more. 176pp. 8⅜ × 11¼.
23546-7 Pa. $6.95

STARS OF THE BROADWAY STAGE, 1940-1967, Fred Fehl. Marlon Brando, Uta Hagen, John Kerr, John Gielgud, Jessica Tandy in great shows—*South Pacific, Galileo, West Side Story*, more. 240 black-and-white photos. 144pp. 8⅜ × 11¼.
24398-2 Pa. $8.95

ILLUSTRATED DICTIONARY OF HISTORIC ARCHITECTURE, edited by Cyril M. Harris. Extraordinary compendium of clear, concise definitions for over 5000 important architectural terms complemented by over 2000 line drawings. 592pp. 7½ × 9⅜.
24444-X Pa. $14.95

THE EARLY WORK OF FRANK LLOYD WRIGHT, F.L. Wright. 207 rare photos of Oak Park period, first great buildings: Unity Temple, Dana house, Larkin factory. Complete photos of Wasmuth edition. New Introduction. 160pp. 8⅜ × 11¼.
24381-8 Pa. $7.95

LIVING MY LIFE, Emma Goldman. Candid, no holds barred account by foremost American anarchist: her own life, anarchist movement, famous contemporaries, ideas and their impact. 944pp. 5⅜ × 8½. 22543-7, 22544-5 Pa., Two-vol. set $13.00

UNDERSTANDING THERMODYNAMICS, H.C. Van Ness. Clear, lucid treatment of first and second laws of thermodynamics. Excellent supplement to basic textbook in undergraduate science or engineering class. 103pp. 5⅜ × 8.
63277-6 Pa. $5.50

SURREAL STICKERS AND UNREAL STAMPS, William Rowe. 224 haunting, hilarious stamps on gummed, perforated stock, with images of elephants, geisha girls, George Washington, etc. 16pp. one side. 8¼ × 11. 24371-0 Pa. $3.50

GOURMET KITCHEN LABELS, Ed Sibbett, Jr. 112 full-color labels (4 copies each of 28 designs). Fruit, bread, other culinary motifs. Gummed and perforated. 16pp. 8¼ × 11. 24087-8 Pa. $2.95

PATTERNS AND INSTRUCTIONS FOR CARVING AUTHENTIC BIRDS, H.D. Green. Detailed instructions, 27 diagrams, 85 photographs for carving 15 species of birds so life-like, they'll seem ready to fly! 8¼ × 11. 24222-6 Pa. $2.75

FLATLAND, E.A. Abbott. Science-fiction classic explores life of 2-D being in 3-D world. 16 illustrations. 103pp. 5⅜ × 8. 20001-9 Pa. $2.00

DRIED FLOWERS, Sarah Whitlock and Martha Rankin. Concise, clear, practical guide to dehydration, glycerinizing, pressing plant material, and more. Covers use of silica gel. 12 drawings. 32pp. 5⅜ × 8½. 21802-3 Pa. $1.00

EASY-TO-MAKE CANDLES, Gary V. Guy. Learn how easy it is to make all kinds of decorative candles. Step-by-step instructions. 82 illustrations. 48pp. 8¼ × 11. 23881-4 Pa. $2.50

SUPER STICKERS FOR KIDS, Carolyn Bracken. 128 gummed and perforated full-color stickers: GIRL WANTED, KEEP OUT, BORED OF EDUCATION, X-RATED, COMBAT ZONE, many others. 16pp. 8¼ × 11. 24092-4 Pa. $2.50

CUT AND COLOR PAPER MASKS, Michael Grater. Clowns, animals, funny faces...simply color them in, cut them out, and put them together, and you have 9 paper masks to play with and enjoy. 32pp. 8¼ × 11. 23171-2 Pa. $2.25

A CHRISTMAS CAROL: THE ORIGINAL MANUSCRIPT, Charles Dickens. Clear facsimile of Dickens manuscript, on facing pages with final printed text. 8 illustrations by John Leech, 4 in color on covers. 144pp. 8⅜ × 11¼. 20980-6 Pa. $5.95

CARVING SHOREBIRDS, Harry V. Shourds & Anthony Hillman. 16 full-size patterns (all double-page spreads) for 19 North American shorebirds with step-by-step instructions. 72pp. 9¼ × 12¼. 24287-0 Pa. $4.95

THE GENTLE ART OF MATHEMATICS, Dan Pedoe. Mathematical games, probability, the question of infinity, topology, how the laws of algebra work, problems of irrational numbers, and more. 42 figures. 143pp. 5⅜ × 8½. (EBE) 22949-1 Pa. $3.50

READY-TO-USE DOLLHOUSE WALLPAPER, Katzenbach & Warren, Inc. Stripe, 2 floral stripes, 2 allover florals, polka dot; all in full color. 4 sheets (350 sq. in.) of each, enough for average room. 48pp. 8¼ × 11. 23495-9 Pa. $2.95

MINIATURE IRON-ON TRANSFER PATTERNS FOR DOLLHOUSES, DOLLS, AND SMALL PROJECTS, Rita Weiss and Frank Fontana. Over 100 miniature patterns: rugs, bedspreads, quilts, chair seats, etc. In standard dollhouse size. 48pp. 8¼ × 11. 23741-9 Pa. $1.95

THE DINOSAUR COLORING BOOK, Anthony Rao. 45 renderings of dinosaurs, fossil birds, turtles, other creatures of Mesozoic Era. Scientifically accurate. Captions. 48pp. 8¼ × 11. 24022-3 Pa. $2.50

CHANCERY CURSIVE STROKE BY STROKE, Arthur Baker. Instructions and illustrations for each stroke of each letter (upper and lower case) and numerals. 54 full-page plates. 64pp. 8¼ × 11. 24278-1 Pa. $2.50

THE ENJOYMENT AND USE OF COLOR, Walter Sargent. Color relationships, values, intensities; complementary colors, illumination, similar topics. Color in nature and art. 7 color plates, 29 illustrations. 274pp. 5⅜ × 8½. 20944-X Pa. $4.95

SCULPTURE PRINCIPLES AND PRACTICE, Louis Slobodkin. Step-by-step approach to clay, plaster, metals, stone; classical and modern. 253 drawings, photos. 255pp. 8⅛ × 11. 22960-2 Pa. $7.50

VICTORIAN FASHION PAPER DOLLS FROM HARPER'S BAZAR, 1867-1898, Theodore Menten. Four female dolls with 28 elegant high fashion costumes, printed in full color. 32pp. 9¼ × 12¼. 23453-3 Pa. $3.50

FLOPSY, MOPSY AND COTTONTAIL: A Little Book of Paper Dolls in Full Color, Susan LaBelle. Three dolls and 21 costumes (7 for each doll) show Peter Rabbit's siblings dressed for holidays, gardening, hiking, etc. Charming borders, captions. 48pp. 4¼ × 5½. 24376-1 Pa. $2.25

NATIONAL LEAGUE BASEBALL CARD CLASSICS, Bert Randolph Sugar. 83 big-leaguers from 1909-69 on facsimile cards. Hubbell, Dean, Spahn, Brock plus advertising, info, no duplications. Perforated, detachable. 16pp. 8¼ × 11.
24308-7 Pa. $2.95

THE LOGICAL APPROACH TO CHESS, Dr. Max Euwe, et al. First-rate text of comprehensive strategy, tactics, theory for the amateur. No gambits to memorize, just a clear, logical approach. 224pp. 5⅜ × 8½. 24353-2 Pa. $4.50

MAGICK IN THEORY AND PRACTICE, Aleister Crowley. The summation of the thought and practice of the century's most famous necromancer, long hard to find. Crowley's best book. 436pp. 5⅜ × 8½. (Available in U.S. only)
23295-6 Pa. $6.50

THE HAUNTED HOTEL, Wilkie Collins. Collins' last great tale; doom and destiny in a Venetian palace. Praised by T.S. Eliot. 127pp. 5⅜ × 8½.
24333-8 Pa. $3.00

ART DECO DISPLAY ALPHABETS, Dan X. Solo. Wide variety of bold yet elegant lettering in handsome Art Deco styles. 100 complete fonts, with numerals, punctuation, more. 104pp. 8⅛ × 11. 24372-9 Pa. $4.50

CALLIGRAPHIC ALPHABETS, Arthur Baker. Nearly 150 complete alphabets by outstanding contemporary. Stimulating ideas; useful source for unique effects. 154 plates. 157pp. 8⅜ × 11¼. 21045-6 Pa. $5.95

ARTHUR BAKER'S HISTORIC CALLIGRAPHIC ALPHABETS, Arthur Baker. From monumental capitals of first-century Rome to humanistic cursive of 16th century, 33 alphabets in fresh interpretations. 88 plates. 96pp. 9 × 12.
24054-1 Pa. $4.50

LETTIE LANE PAPER DOLLS, Sheila Young. Genteel turn-of-the-century family very popular then and now. 24 paper dolls. 16 plates in full color. 32pp. 9¼ × 12¼. 24089-4 Pa. $3.50

CHILDREN'S BOOKPLATES AND LABELS, Ed Sibbett, Jr. 6 each of 12 types based on *Wizard of Oz, Alice,* nursery rhymes, fairy tales. Perforated; full color. 24pp. 8¼ × 11. 23538-6 Pa. $3.50

READY-TO-USE VICTORIAN COLOR STICKERS: 96 Pressure-Sensitive Seals, Carol Belanger Grafton. Drawn from authentic period sources. Motifs include heads of men, women, children, plus florals, animals, birds, more. Will adhere to any clean surface. 8pp. 8½ × 11. 24551-9 Pa. $2.95

CUT AND FOLD PAPER SPACESHIPS THAT FLY, Michael Grater. 16 colorful, easy-to-build spaceships that really fly. Star Shuttle, Lunar Freighter, Star Probe, 13 others. 32pp. 8¼ × 11. 23978-0 Pa. $2.50

CUT AND ASSEMBLE PAPER AIRPLANES THAT FLY, Arthur Baker. 8 aerodynamically sound, ready-to-build paper airplanes, designed with latest techniques. Fly *Pegasus, Daedalus, Songbird,* 5 other aircraft. Instructions. 32pp. 9¼ × 11¼. 24302-8 Pa. $3.95

SIDELIGHTS ON RELATIVITY, Albert Einstein. Two lectures delivered in 1920-21: *Ether and Relativity* and *Geometry and Experience.* Elegant ideas in non-mathematical form. 56pp. 5⅜ × 8½. 24511-X Pa. $2.25

FADS AND FALLACIES IN THE NAME OF SCIENCE, Martin Gardner. Fair, witty appraisal of cranks and quacks of science: Velikovsky, orgone energy, Bridey Murphy, medical fads, etc. 373pp. 5⅜ × 8½. 20394-8 Pa. $5.95

VACATION HOMES AND CABINS, U.S. Dept. of Agriculture. Complete plans for 16 cabins, vacation homes and other shelters. 105pp. 9 × 12. 23631-5 Pa. $4.95

HOW TO BUILD A WOOD-FRAME HOUSE, L.O. Anderson. Placement, foundations, framing, sheathing, roof, insulation, plaster, finishing—almost everything else. 179 illustrations. 223pp. 7⅞ × 10¾. 22954-8 Pa. $5.50

THE MYSTERY OF A HANSOM CAB, Fergus W. Hume. Bizarre murder in a hansom cab leads to engrossing investigation. Memorable characters, rich atmosphere. 19th-century bestseller, still enjoyable, exciting. 256pp. 5⅜ × 8. 21956-9 Pa. $4.00

MANUAL OF TRADITIONAL WOOD CARVING, edited by Paul N. Hasluck. Possibly the best book in English on the craft of wood carving. Practical instructions, along with 1,146 working drawings and photographic illustrations. 576pp. 6½ × 9¼. 23489-4 Pa. $8.95

WHITTLING AND WOODCARVING, E.J Tangerman. Best book on market; clear, full. If you can cut a potato, you can carve toys, puzzles, chains, etc. Over 464 illustrations. 293pp. 5⅜ × 8½. 20965-2 Pa. $4.95

AMERICAN TRADEMARK DESIGNS, Barbara Baer Capitman. 732 marks, logos and corporate-identity symbols. Categories include entertainment, heavy industry, food and beverage. All black-and-white in standard forms. 160pp. 8⅛ × 11. 23259-X Pa. $6.95

DECORATIVE FRAMES AND BORDERS, edited by Edmund V. Gillon, Jr. Largest collection of borders and frames ever compiled for use of artists and designers. Renaissance, neo-Greek, Art Nouveau, Art Deco, to mention only a few styles. 396 illustrations. 192pp. 8⅜ × 11¼. 22928-9 Pa. $6.00

JAPANESE DESIGN MOTIFS, Matsuya Co. Mon, or heraldic designs. Over 4000 typical, beautiful designs: birds, animals, flowers, swords, fans, geometrics; all beautifully stylized. 213pp. 11⅜ × 8¼. 22874-6 Pa. $7.95

THE TALE OF BENJAMIN BUNNY, Beatrix Potter. Peter Rabbit's cousin coaxes him back into Mr. McGregor's garden for a whole new set of adventures. All 27 full-color illustrations. 59pp. 4¼ × 5½. (Available in U.S. only) 21102-9 Pa. $1.75

THE TALE OF PETER RABBIT AND OTHER FAVORITE STORIES BOXED SET, Beatrix Potter. Seven of Beatrix Potter's best-loved tales including Peter Rabbit in a specially designed, durable boxed set. 4¼ × 5½. Total of 447pp. 158 color illustrations. (Available in U.S. only) 23903-9 Pa. $10.80

PRACTICAL MENTAL MAGIC, Theodore Annemann. Nearly 200 astonishing feats of mental magic revealed in step-by-step detail. Complete advice on staging, patter, etc. Illustrated. 320pp. 5⅜ × 8½. 24426-1 Pa. $5.95

CELEBRATED CASES OF JUDGE DEE (DEE GOONG AN), translated by Robert Van Gulik. Authentic 18th-century Chinese detective novel; Dee and associates solve three interlocked cases. Led to van Gulik's own stories with same characters. Extensive introduction. 9 illustrations. 237pp. 5⅜ × 8½. 23337-5 Pa. $4.50

CUT & FOLD EXTRATERRESTRIAL INVADERS THAT FLY, M. Grater. Stage your own lilliputian space battles.By following the step-by-step instructions and explanatory diagrams you can launch 22 full-color fliers into space. 36pp. 8¼ × 11. 24478-4 Pa. $2.95

CUT & ASSEMBLE VICTORIAN HOUSES, Edmund V. Gillon, Jr. Printed in full color on heavy cardboard stock, 4 authentic Victorian houses in H-O scale: Italian-style Villa, Octagon, Second Empire, Stick Style. 48pp. 9¼ × 12¼. 23849-0 Pa. $3.95

BEST SCIENCE FICTION STORIES OF H.G. WELLS, H.G. Wells. Full novel *The Invisible Man,* plus 17 short stories: "The Crystal Egg," "Aepyornis Island," "The Strange Orchid," etc. 303pp. 5⅜ × 8½. (Available in U.S. only) 21531-8 Pa. $4.95

TRADEMARK DESIGNS OF THE WORLD, Yusaku Kamekura. A lavish collection of nearly 700 trademarks, the work of Wright, Loewy, Klee, Binder, hundreds of others. 160pp. 8¾ × 8. (Available in U.S. only) 24191-2 Pa. $5.95

THE ARTIST'S AND CRAFTSMAN'S GUIDE TO REDUCING, ENLARGING AND TRANSFERRING DESIGNS, Rita Weiss. Discover, reduce, enlarge, transfer designs from any objects to any craft project. 12pp. plus 16 sheets special graph paper. 8¼ × 11. 24142-4 Pa. $3.50

TREASURY OF JAPANESE DESIGNS AND MOTIFS FOR ARTISTS AND CRAFTSMEN, edited by Carol Belanger Grafton. Indispensable collection of 360 traditional Japanese designs and motifs redrawn in clean, crisp black-and-white, copyright-free illustrations. 96pp. 8¼ × 11. 24435-0 Pa. $3.95

THE BOOK OF WOOD CARVING, Charles Marshall Sayers. Still finest book for beginning student. Fundamentals, technique; gives 34 designs, over 34 projects for panels, bookends, mirrors, etc. 33 photos. 118pp. 7¾ × 10⅝. 23654-4 Pa. $3.95

CARVING COUNTRY CHARACTERS, Bill Higginbotham. Expert advice for beginning, advanced carvers on materials, techniques for creating 18 projects— mirthful panorama of American characters. 105 illustrations. 80pp. 8⅜ × 11. 24135-1 Pa. $2.50

300 ART NOUVEAU DESIGNS AND MOTIFS IN FULL COLOR, C.B. Grafton. 44 full-page plates display swirling lines and muted colors typical of Art Nouveau. Borders, frames, panels, cartouches, dingbats, etc. 48pp. 9⅜ × 12¼. 24354-0 Pa. $6.95

SELF-WORKING CARD TRICKS, Karl Fulves. Editor of *Pallbearer* offers 72 tricks that work automatically through nature of card deck. No sleight of hand needed. Often spectacular. 42 illustrations. 113pp. 5⅜ × 8½. 23334-0 Pa. $3.50

CUT AND ASSEMBLE A WESTERN FRONTIER TOWN, Edmund V. Gillon, Jr. Ten authentic full-color buildings on heavy cardboard stock in H-O scale. Sheriff's Office and Jail, Saloon, Wells Fargo, Opera House, others. 48pp. 9¼ × 12¼. 23736-2 Pa. $3.95

CUT AND ASSEMBLE AN EARLY NEW ENGLAND VILLAGE, Edmund V. Gillon, Jr. Printed in full color on heavy cardboard stock. 12 authentic buildings in H-O scale: Adams home in Quincy, Mass., Oliver Wight house in Sturbridge, smithy, store, church, others. 48pp. 9¼ × 12¼. 23536-X Pa. $4.95

THE TALE OF TWO BAD MICE, Beatrix Potter. Tom Thumb and Hunca Munca squeeze out of their hole and go exploring. 27 full-color Potter illustrations. 59pp. 4¼ × 5½. (Available in U.S. only) 23065-1 Pa. $1.75

CARVING FIGURE CARICATURES IN THE OZARK STYLE, Harold L. Enlow. Instructions and illustrations for ten delightful projects, plus general carving instructions. 22 drawings and 47 photographs altogether. 39pp. 8⅜ × 11. 23151-8 Pa. $2.50

A TREASURY OF FLOWER DESIGNS FOR ARTISTS, EMBROIDERERS AND CRAFTSMEN, Susan Gaber. 100 garden favorites lushly rendered by artist for artists, craftsmen, needleworkers. Many form frames, borders. 80pp. 8¼ × 11. 24096-7 Pa. $3.50

CUT & ASSEMBLE A TOY THEATER/THE NUTCRACKER BALLET, Tom Tierney. Model of a complete, full-color production of Tchaikovsky's classic. 6 backdrops, dozens of characters, familiar dance sequences. 32pp. 9⅜ × 12¼. 24194-7 Pa. $4.50

ANIMALS: 1,419 COPYRIGHT-FREE ILLUSTRATIONS OF MAMMALS, BIRDS, FISH, INSECTS, ETC., edited by Jim Harter. Clear wood engravings present, in extremely lifelike poses, over 1,000 species of animals. 284pp. 9 × 12. 23766-4 Pa. $9.95

MORE HAND SHADOWS, Henry Bursill. For those at their 'finger ends," 16 more effects—Shakespeare, a hare, a squirrel, Mr. Punch, and twelve more—each explained by a full-page illustration. Considerable period charm. 30pp. 6½ × 9¼. 21384-6 Pa. $1.95

SMOCKING: TECHNIQUE, PROJECTS, AND DESIGNS, Dianne Durand. Foremost smocking designer provides complete instructions on how to smock. Over 10 projects, over 100 illustrations. 56pp. 8¼ × 11. 23788-5 Pa. $2.00

AUDUBON'S BIRDS IN COLOR FOR DECOUPAGE, edited by Eleanor H. Rawlings. 24 sheets, 37 most decorative birds, full color, on one side of paper. Instructions, including work under glass. 56pp. 8¼ × 11. 23492-4 Pa. $3.95

THE COMPLETE BOOK OF SILK SCREEN PRINTING PRODUCTION, J.I. Biegeleisen. For commercial user, teacher in advanced classes, serious hobbyist. Most modern techniques, materials, equipment for optimal results. 124 illustrations. 253pp. 5⅜ × 8½. 21100-2 Pa. $4.50

A TREASURY OF ART NOUVEAU DESIGN AND ORNAMENT, edited by Carol Belanger Grafton. 577 designs for the practicing artist. Full-page, spots, borders, bookplates by Klimt, Bradley, others. 144pp. 8⅜ × 11¼. 24001-0 Pa. $5.95

ART NOUVEAU TYPOGRAPHIC ORNAMENTS, Dan X. Solo. Over 800 Art Nouveau florals, swirls, women, animals, borders, scrolls, wreaths, spots and dingbats, copyright-free. 100pp. 8⅛ × 11. 24366-4 Pa. $4.00

HAND SHADOWS TO BE THROWN UPON THE WALL, Henry Bursill. Wonderful Victorian novelty tells how to make flying birds, dog, goose, deer, and 14 others, each explained by a full-page illustration. 32pp. 6½ × 9¼. 21779-5 Pa. $1.50

AUDUBON'S BIRDS OF AMERICA COLORING BOOK, John James Audubon. Rendered for coloring by Paul Kennedy. 46 of Audubon's noted illustrations: red-winged black-bird, cardinal, etc. Original plates reproduced in full-color on the covers. Captions. 48pp. 8¼ × 11. 23049-X Pa. $2.25

SILK SCREEN TECHNIQUES, J.I. Biegeleisen, M.A. Cohn. Clear, practical, modern, economical. Minimal equipment (self-built), materials, easy methods. For amateur, hobbyist, 1st book. 141 illustrations. 185pp. 6⅛ × 9¼. 20433-2 Pa. $3.95

101 PATCHWORK PATTERNS, Ruby S. McKim. 101 beautiful, immediately useable patterns, full-size, modern and traditional. Also general information, estimating, quilt lore. 140 illustrations. 124pp. 7⅞ × 10¾. 20773-0 Pa. $3.50

READY-TO-USE FLORAL DESIGNS, Ed Sibbett, Jr. Over 100 floral designs (most in three sizes) of popular individual blossoms as well as bouquets, sprays, garlands. 64pp. 8¼ × 11. 23976-4 Pa. $2.95

AMERICAN WILD FLOWERS COLORING BOOK, Paul Kennedy. Planned coverage of 46 most important wildflowers, from Rickett's collection; instructive as well as entertaining. Color versions on covers. Captions. 48pp. 8¼ × 11. 20095-7 Pa. $2.50

CARVING DUCK DECOYS, Harry V. Shourds and Anthony Hillman. Detailed instructions and full-size templates for constructing 16 beautiful, marvelously practical decoys according to time-honored South Jersey method. 70pp. 9¼ × 12¼. 24083-5 Pa. $4.95

TRADITIONAL PATCHWORK PATTERNS, Carol Belanger Grafton. Cardboard cut-out pieces for use as templates to make 12 quilts: Buttercup, Ribbon Border, Tree of Paradise, nine more. Full instructions. 57pp. 8¼ × 11. 23015-5 Pa. $3.50

SOURCE BOOK OF MEDICAL HISTORY, edited by Logan Clendening, M.D. Original accounts ranging from Ancient Egypt and Greece to discovery of X-rays: Galen, Pasteur, Lavoisier, Harvey, Parkinson, others. 685pp. 5⅜ × 8½.

20621-1 Pa. $10.95

THE ROSE AND THE KEY, J.S. Lefanu. Superb mystery novel from Irish master. Dark doings among an ancient and aristocratic English family. Well-drawn characters; capital suspense. Introduction by N. Donaldson. 448pp. 5⅜ × 8½.

24377-X Pa. $6.95

SOUTH WIND, Norman Douglas. Witty, elegant novel of ideas set on languorous Mediterranean island of Nepenthe. Elegant prose, glittering epigrams, mordant satire. 1917 masterpiece. 416pp. 5⅜ × 8½. (Available in U.S. only)

24361-3 Pa. $5.95

RUSSELL'S CIVIL WAR PHOTOGRAPHS, Capt. A.J. Russell. 116 rare Civil War Photos: Bull Run, Virginia campaigns, bridges, railroads, Richmond, Lincoln's funeral car. Many never seen before. Captions. 128pp. 9⅜ × 12¼.

24283-8 Pa. $6.95

PHOTOGRAPHS BY MAN RAY: 105 Works, 1920-1934. Nudes, still lifes, landscapes, women's faces, celebrity portraits (Dali, Matisse, Picasso, others), rayographs. Reprinted from rare gravure edition. 128pp. 9⅜ × 12¼. (Available in U.S. only)

23842-3 Pa. $7.95

STAR NAMES: THEIR LORE AND MEANING, Richard H. Allen. Star names, the zodiac, constellations: folklore and literature associated with heavens. The basic book of its field, fascinating reading. 563pp. 5⅜ × 8½.

21079-0 Pa. $7.95

BURNHAM'S CELESTIAL HANDBOOK, Robert Burnham, Jr. Thorough guide to the stars beyond our solar system. Exhaustive treatment. Alphabetical by constellation: Andromeda to Cetus in Vol. 1; Chamaeleon to Orion in Vol. 2; and Pavo to Vulpecula in Vol. 3. Hundreds of illustrations. Index in Vol. 3. 2000pp. 6⅛ × 9¼.

23567-X, 23568-8, 23673-0 Pa. Three-vol. set $36.85

THE ART NOUVEAU STYLE BOOK OF ALPHONSE MUCHA, Alphonse Mucha. All 72 plates from *Documents Decoratifs* in original color. Stunning, essential work of Art Nouveau. 80pp. 9⅜ × 12¼.

24044-4 Pa. $7.95

DESIGNS BY ERTE; FASHION DRAWINGS AND ILLUSTRATIONS FROM "HARPER'S BAZAR," Erte. 310 fabulous line drawings and 14 *Harper's Bazar* covers, 8 in full color. Erte's exotic temptresses with tassels, fur muffs, long trains, coifs, more. 129pp. 9⅜ × 12¼.

23397-9 Pa. $6.95

HISTORY OF STRENGTH OF MATERIALS, Stephen P. Timoshenko. Excellent historical survey of the strength of materials with many references to the theories of elasticity and structure. 245 figures. 452pp. 5⅜ × 8½.

61187-6 Pa. $8.95

Prices subject to change without notice.

Available at your book dealer or write for free catalog to Dept. GI, Dover Publications, Inc., 31 East 2nd St. Mineola, N.Y. 11501. Dover publishes more than 175 books each year on science, elementary and advanced mathematics, biology, music, art, literary history, social sciences and other areas.